This book offers a distinctive and accessible approach to the earliest encounters of the Germanic tribes of Northern Europe with classical antiquity and with early Christianity. It brings together linguistic evidence ranging in date from before Caesar to about AD 900, and in geographical scope from Ireland to the Crimea and Visigothic Spain to the Eastern Baltic, to shed light on important aspects of Germanic culture and to show how they were affected by contact with the (mainly but not exclusively Latin) outside world.

It shows how semantics and loanword studies, often regarded with trepidation by non-specialists, can form part of a fascinating jigsaw puzzle and provide important clues for historians and archaeologists of the period. Likewise, it demonstrates that philologists and linguists ignore historical evidence at their peril.

LANGUAGE AND HISTORY IN THE EARLY GERMANIC WORLD

The York Helmet: an Anglo-Saxon artefact of the eighth century. Decorated with a Christian prayer in Latin, but also incorporating Germanic decorative elements and based on a Roman parade helmet, it embodies the cultural fusion which can also be traced in the linguistic evidence of the period. By courtesy of York Castle Museum.

LANGUAGE AND HISTORY IN THE EARLY GERMANIC WORLD

D. H. GREEN

Schröder Professor Emeritus, University of Cambridge
Fellow of Trinity College, Cambridge

CAMBRIDGE
UNIVERSITY PRESS

PUBLISHED BY THE PRESS SYNDICATE OF THE UNIVERSITY OF CAMBRIDGE
The Pitt Building, Trumpington Street, Cambridge CB2 1RP, United Kingdom

CAMBRIDGE UNIVERSITY PRESS
The Edinburgh Building, Cambridge CB2 2RU, United Kingdom
40 West 20th Street, New York, NY 10011-4211, USA
10 Stamford Road, Oakleigh, Melbourne 3166, Australia

First published 1998

Transferred to digital printing 2000

Printed in Great Britain by Biddles Short Run Books

Typeset in Baskerville MT 11/12.5 [SE]

A catalogue record for this book is available from the British Library

Library of Congress Cataloguing in Publication Data

Green, Dennis Howard, 1922–
Language and history in the early Germanic world / D. H. Green.
p.   cm.
Includes bibliographical references and index.
ISBN 0 521 47134 6 hardback
1. Germanic languages – History.   2. Germanic tribes – History.
3. Europe – History – 392–814.   4. Languages in contact – Europe –
History.   1. Title.
PD75.G74   1998
430'9–dc21   97-9527 CIP

ISBN 0 521 47134 6 hardback

Contents

Preface

This book derives from a three-year cycle of lectures given to Cambridge undergraduates, revised and adapted over many years. It makes no claim to advance the frontiers of knowledge, but is meant instead to provide students with a broad survey which they could not be expected to map out for themselves. What originality the book does possess lies in its arrangement of the linguistic material, correlating it with historical findings and seeing it as illustrating the encounter of the early Germanic tribes with Rome and Christianity. Compressing a three-year cycle into a book has led to a drastic reduction of the material originally presented. My wish to give as broad a survey as possible, however, means that each of the words discussed has had to be treated briefly: difficulties are pointed out, conclusions are suggested, but in many cases the detailed argument is to be retrieved from the secondary literature cited. Even so, I am painfully aware of many themes and examples which have had to be sacrificed.

I owe a debt of gratitude to former students who attended the lectures and who, now colleagues, have encouraged me to convert the material into a book. Foremost amongst these are Kate Brett of the Cambridge University Press and David Dumville. To the latter, as well as to Peter Johnson, I am further grateful for critical comments on individual chapters in draft form. Financial support, making research stays in Germany possible, from my University, my College and the British Academy is gratefully acknowledged. I am especially grateful to Catherine Walters for her skill in transferring my handwriting to the computer and for her willingness to cope with the range of linguistic difficulties which this involved.

Stimulus and the opportunity to discuss shared problems across disciplinary boundaries have also come from meetings of the Center for Interdisciplinary Research on Social Stress in San Marino. The Introduction is an abridgment of a paper in *After Empire. Towards an ethnology of Europe's barbarians*, Woodbridge 1995. Chapter 9 is an adaptation of a paper given at a CIROSS conference in 1995, the proceedings of which are to appear in a volume, *Franks and Alamans in the Merovingian period. An ethnographic perspective*, in preparation. Chapter 18 is related to a paper given at a CIROSS conference in 1996, the proceedings of which will appear in *The Visigoths from the migration period to the seventh century. An ethnographic perspective*, in preparation.

My last book I dedicated to my wife Margaret. This one I dedicate to her memory.

Abbreviations

ABäG	*Amsterdamer Beiträge zur älteren Germanistik*
AfdA	*Anzeiger für deutsches Altertum*
AfK	*Archiv für Kulturgeschichte*
AfR	*Archiv für Religionswissenschaft*
Al.	Alemannic
ANF	*Arkiv för nordisk Filologi*
ASE	*Anglo-Saxon England*
BAR	British Archaeological Reports
BzN	*Beiträge zur Namenforschung*
CG	Common Germanic
Du.	Dutch
EFr.	East Franconian
EFri.	East Frisian
EG	East Germanic
Engl.	English
FEW	*Französisches Etymologisches Wörterbuch*, ed. W. von Wartburg, Bonn 1928ff.
FMS	*Frühmittelalterliche Studien*
Fr.	French
Fri.	Frisian
Frk.	Frankish
FS	Festschrift
FuF	*Forschungen und Fortschritte*
Gmc.	Germanic
Go.	Gothic
Gr.	Greek
GR	*Germania Romana*, second edition, vol. i, T. Frings, Halle 1966; vol. ii, T. Frings and G. Müller, Halle 1968.
GRev.	*Germanic Review*
GRBS	*Greek, Roman and Byzantine Studies*
GRM	*Germanisch-Romanische Monatsschrift*
HJLg	*Hessisches Jahrbuch für Landesgeschichte*

Hung.	Hungarian
HZ	*Historische Zeitschrift*
IE	Indo-European
IF	*Indogermanische Forschungen*
Ir.	Irish
It.	Italian
JIES	*Journal of Indo-European Studies*
JRGZM	*Jahrbuch des Römisch-Germanischen Zentralmuseums Mainz*
Lat.	Latin
LFr.	Low Franconian
LG	Low German
Lith.	Lithuanian
MDu.	Middle Dutch
MFr.	Middle Franconian
MGH AA	Monumenta Germaniae Historica, Auctores Antiquissimi
MGH SS	Monumenta Germaniae Historica, Scriptores
MHG	Middle High German
MIÖG	*Mitteilungen des Instituts für österreichische Geschichtsforschung*
MIr.	Middle Irish
MLat.	Medieval Latin
MLG	Middle Low German
MLR	*Modern Language Review*
MWe.	Middle Welsh
NdJb	*Niederdeutsches Jahrbuch*
NG	North Germanic
NoB	*Namn och Bygd*
Norw.	Norwegian
NOWELE	*North-Western European Language Evolution*
NWG	North West Germanic
OC	Old Catalan
OE	Old English
OFr.	Old French
OFri.	Old Frisian
OHG	Old High German
OIr.	Old Irish
OLFr.	Old Low Franconian
OLith.	Old Lithuanian
ON	Old Norse
OPort.	Old Portuguese
OPr.	Old Provençal

OPru.	Old Prussian
OS	Old Saxon
OSl.	Old Slavonic
OSp.	Old Spanish
PBA	*Proceedings of the British Academy*
PBB	*Paul und Braunes Beiträge*
PG	Primitive Germanic
Pol.	Polish
Port.	Portuguese
RhM	*Rheinisches Museum*
RhV	*Rheinische Vierteljahrsblätter*
RLAC	*Reallexikon für Antike und Christentum*, ed. T. Klauser, Stuttgart 1950ff.
RLGA	*Reallexikon der germanischen Altertumskunde*, first edition ed. J. Hoops, Strassburg, 1911ff.; second edition ed. H. Jankuhn *et al.*, Berlin, 1968ff.
Rum.	Rumanian
Sl.	Slavonic
Sp.	Spanish
SRhFr.	South Rhenish Franconian
Sw.	Swedish
UG	Upper German
VG	Vulgar Greek
VL	Vulgar Latin
We.	Welsh
WFrk.	West Frankish
WG	West Germanic
WuS	*Wörter und Sachen*
ZfbLg	*Zeitschrift für bayerische Landesgeschichte*
ZfdA	*Zeitschrift für deutsches Altertum*
ZfdPh	*Zeitschrift für deutsche Philologie*
ZfdS	*Zeitschrift für die deutsche Sprache*
ZfdW	*Zeitschrift für deutsche Wortforschung*
ZfMf	*Zeitschrift für Mundartforschung*
ZfMR	*Zeitschrift für Missionswissenschaft und Religionswissenschaft*
ZfrPh	*Zeitschrift für romanische Philologie*
ZKG	*Zeitschrift für Kirchengeschichte*
ZNF	*Zeitschrift für Namenforschung*
ZRG(GA)	*Zeitschrift für Rechtsgeschichte (Germanistische Abteilung)*
ZSlPh	*Zeitschrift für slavische Philologie*
ZVS	*Zeitschrift für vergleichende Sprachforschung*

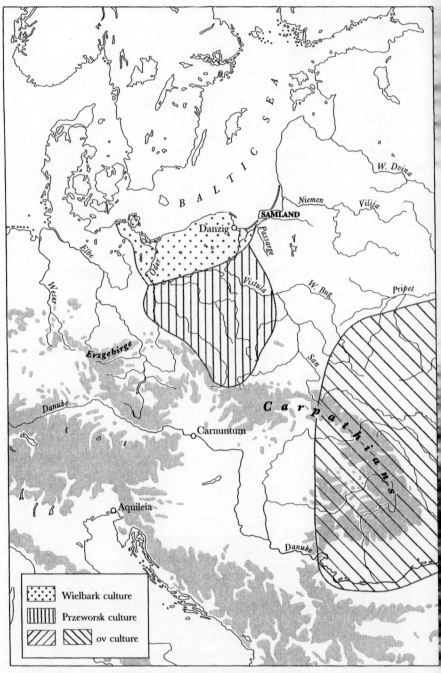

Map of the area covered by the migrations of Goths from northern Poland to the Black Sea
(Chapter 9).

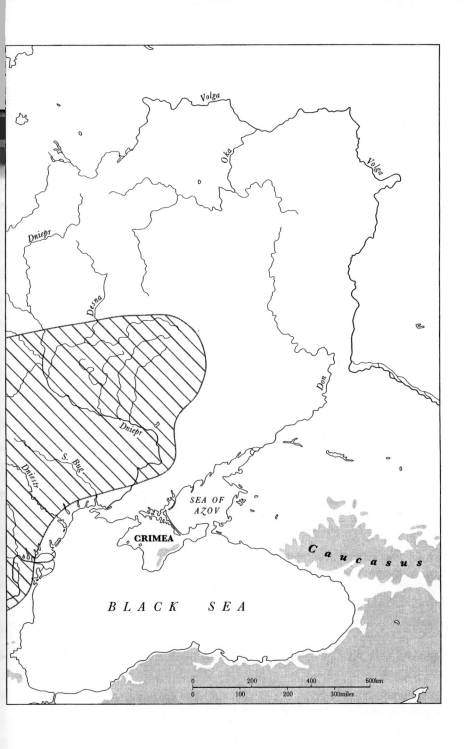

Volga

Oka

Volga

Dniepr

Desna

Don

Dniepr

S. Bug

Dniestr

SEA OF
AZOV

CRIMEA

C a u c a s u s

B L A C K   S E A

0   200   400   600km
0   100   200   300miles

General introduction

The disciplines concerned with the encounter between the early Germanic world and the Roman Empire as well as Christianity are archaeology, history and philology. Although they have not always been ready to make use of each other's findings recent work has been markedly more interdisciplinary,[1] which in turn has accentuated the problems which arise when one discipline, in the case of this book philology, seeks assistance from the others.

Archaeology finds it notoriously difficult to connect the finds which for it constitute a distinct culture or group with a particular tribe to which a name can be given, thereby associating them with written historical sources or linguistic evidence.[2] Ethnic groups which may share a similar material culture cannot always be distinguished from one another (e.g. Goths and Heruli).[3] Where a particular class of find is missing altogether (as with the absence of military gear from Gothic grave goods) we are left even more in the lurch by archaeology and have no choice but to fall back on the evidence of language, where even the restricted vocabulary of Wulfila's Gothic bible offers examples such as *brunjo* 'breastplate', *mēki* 'sword' and *wēpna* 'weapons'.[4] This illustrates drastically the main disadvantage of archaeological evidence for philology: it opens the door on a past which is silent, because wordless, it records aspects of the material basis of an early society, but permits only inferences about the social, institutional and religious thought-world of a society which left no written records.[5]

On the other hand, archaeology disposes of a finely calibrated and reliable dating scheme, covering a number of distinct periods, with further subdivisions, which far surpasses the known inability of philology

<hr />

[1] E.g. Wenskus (1961) or the indispensable volumes of *RLGA*, many of whose entries are divided into sections labelled archaeological, historical or linguistic.   [2] Green (1995), 143.
[3] Heather (1991), 4, 87.   [4] Wolfram (1988), 99f.
[5] Jankuhn (1967), 118; Murray (1983), 221; Roberts (1994), 185.

to establish more than a broadly based relative chronology.[6] How helpful archaeology can be in resolving linguistic problems has been shown in the case of the Goths' migration from the Baltic coastline to the Black Sea, in the course of which they made contacts, including linguistic exchanges, with a number of other peoples.[7] Thanks to archaeological dating methods it has been possible to reconstruct this migration chronologically and geographically, to relate these findings to contemporary historical records and thus to provide a background against which to set the question of linguistic exchange.[8] Even on a much smaller scale archaeology can also throw light on linguistic problems, either in the case of Go. *wein* as an early loan from Lat. *vinum* or, on the basis of the Sutton Hoo helmet, in explaining details of the description of helmets in *Beowulf*.[9] The gaps in our evidence on this early period, both linguistic and archaeological, are so frequent that neither discipline can afford to ignore what it might learn from the other.[10]

The same is true, both negatively and positively, when we attempt to correlate historical with linguistic evidence. For many of the debates amongst historians the evidence is so sparse or ambiguous that it would be unwise to neglect the possible relevance of information from a neighbouring discipline – and the same applies equally to debates amongst philologists. Moreover, although historical sources have the advantage over archaeological evidence in speaking to us in words, the language of these sources is overwhelmingly Latin (or Greek), not the barbarians' vernacular. This raises the question how far a classical language was able to render the details of a more primitive society at all accurately, how far these may have been distorted, linguistically or conceptually, by being subjected to an *interpretatio Romana*.[11] If early barbarian laws, codified in Latin, found it necessary to employ vernacular terms for want of a reliable Latin equivalent,[12] this suggests that historical sources in Latin, whatever their nature, risk distorting the thought-world of the barbarians on whom they report. Less distortion, but still difficulties of interpretation, are involved when we approach the world of the Germani from the language which they themselves used.

How necessary it is for a linguistic discussion of early Germania to take the historical dimension into account is shown by the occasional

---

[6] Birkhan (1970), 97. For an example see Heather (1996), 19.   [7] See below, p. 168.
[8] Bierbrauer (1994), 51ff.; Heather (1996), 18ff., 35ff. (both with maps).
[9] *Wein*: see below, pp. 227ff; *Beowulf*: Cramp (1957), 6off.; Newton (1994), 33ff.
[10] Cramp (1957), 57.   [11] Richter (1994), 99f. On *interpretatio Romana* see below, pp. 11f., 246ff.
[12] Schmidt-Wiegand (1979), 56ff.

oversimplified view of the Germanic world at large.[13] The Germani
described by Tacitus need not be the same as those described over a
century earlier by Caesar, so that differences between these two sources,
far from needing to be explained away, may reflect the result of the
encounter of the Germani with the world of Rome.[14] Similarly, to
compare Arminius of the Cherusci with the Goth Athanaric means
ignoring the three and a half centuries separating them and the different acculturation processes undergone by WG and EG tribes.[15] Too
often linguistic conclusions have been reached on the basis of what can
be termed a linguistic absolutism, ignoring the question of their intrin-
sic historical possibility, as when a Gothic mission to Germany (even
purportedly affecting Scandinavia) has been put forward without any
trace of historical backing.[16]

Historical factors can at times account for a linguistic feature, as with
the different employment of the Gmc. stem *rîk- in WG and EG. This
word, denoting 'powerful', 'authority' or the area in which authority is
exercised, was also used in the names of rulers (especially in the east: e.g.
Ermanaric, Theoderic), decking themselves out with the trappings of
extended authority by adopting this outlandish mode of Celtic origin.[17]
Concentration of power could run into opposition and be regarded as
tyranny, in western Germania (Maroboduus, Arminius), but also, in view
of what Tacitus says of the more centralised authority of EG kingship,
in the east.[18] This is reflected in the negative use of this word by
Wulfila,[19] whose objection to the despotic authority it denoted was not
aimed at a Roman Empire by now Christian, but at Ermanaric's
concentration of power. (This Ostrogothic ruler is similarly criticised in
other sources.)[20] If, by contrast, WG uses the word positively (of the
Frankish empire, but also of Christ's kingdom)[21] the explanation may be
sought in the adoption of Roman imperial ideology by the Franks and
the Anglo-Saxons, which supplied them with a justification unavailable
to the Goths in the fourth century.[22]

However profitable it may therefore be to correlate the findings of

---

[13] Green (1995), 143f.   [14] Wallace-Hadrill (1971), 4.   [15] Wolfram (1975), 23.
[16] Schäferdiek (1978a), 521f. Cf. also Rotsaert (1977), 182f.
[17] Herold (1941), 274f.; Ris (1971), 15ff.
[18] Maroboduus and Arminius: Thompson (1965), 66ff., 83f.; Tacitus: *Germania* 43.
[19] See below, p. 139.
[20] Jordanes, *Getica* 129; *Widsith* 8f. (cf. Chambers (1912), 190); *Deor* 21ff. Cf. also Schneider (1928),
    246f.; Dronke (1969), 217, 220; Gillespie (1973), 37, 39.   [21] See below, pp. 139f.
[22] Franks: Levison (1946), 122f.; Erdmann (1951), 3ff.; Anglo-Saxons: Erdmann (1951), 10, 14;
    Drögereit (1952), 32; Yorke (1981), 175; Fanning (1991), 15, 17, 19. On the argument of this
    Introduction see also Green (1997), xxixff.

General introduction

these three disciplines, this must be done in full awareness of a methodological danger. Archaeological findings, for example, are often based on conclusions which have been reached by historians, whilst the latter can also seek support from archaeological theories which can then be re-imported into archaeological discourse as if they were an independent historical confirmation.[23] The danger of a vicious circle is manifest, unless each discipline argues towards its conclusion only from its own material, looking across its boundaries only at the end.

The argument of this book concerns the encounter of Germania with classical antiquity and Christianity. The three parts into which it falls represent the three factors commonly regarded as accounting for the rise of medieval Europe (in a context wider than this book we should need to extend Germania to embrace tribal Europe at large in order to include the Celts and the Slavs).[24] Each of these factors existed alongside the others, sometimes in opposition and sometimes as a complement, but all gradually fusing together in the transition from late antiquity to the early Middle Ages.[25] Against this wider historical background our linguistic evidence will have to be placed.

Late antiquity is the period in which two of these factors, the classical tradition and Christianity, enter upon a culturally fertile symbiosis.[26] Even though this symbiosis found its institutional expression in the conversion of a Roman emperor, Constantine, and the Christianisation of the Roman state in the fourth century, this decisive change was preceded and made possible by the gradual readiness of Christian leaders to identify with the classical world in a number of respects, to work in and through Roman society, rather than in opposition to it. The conversion of the Roman world to Christianity was therefore accompanied by a conversion of Christianity to the Roman world.[27] Where, for example, the emperor Domitian, the object of a pre-Christian cult of emperor-worship, was given the double title *Dominus et Deus*, the gospel of St John gave a polemical twist to this by having the apostle Thomas address the risen Christ as 'my Lord and my God' (Joh. 20.29).[28]

Antiquity and Germania came together not merely along the imper-

[23] Hachmann (1971), 11; Bierbrauer (1994), 52, 76. For an example see Wagner (1967), 109, fn. 17.
[24] E.g. Hübinger (1969), 203f.; Goetz and Welwei (1995), 2; Allen Brown (1996), 3, 15; Davies (1996), 15.
[25] Examples of cultural fusion in written texts, but also in objects and buildings, have been discussed by Wood (1997), 111ff. Whereas the former are for him Latin texts, our concern will be with vernacular words.   [26] Lane Fox (1988); Brown (1993) (1996).   [27] Brown (1993), 82.
[28] Heiler (1959), 548ff.

ial frontier which, in addition to its function as a barrier, acted as a zone in which the two worlds converged,[29] but also by the readiness of Germanic leaders to heighten their standing by appropriating Roman models of authority for themselves. Many of these leaders sought official approval of their occupation of Roman territory from the eastern capital, Constantinople. Odoaker deposed Romulus Augustulus, but asked the emperor Zeno for the title of patrician and expected to govern in Zeno's name.[30] After his victory over the Goths the Frankish ruler Chlodwig received from the emperor Anastasius I a diploma conferring the title of consul. Clad in purple, chlamys and a diadem Chlodwig rode through Tours, scattering gold and silver like a Roman ruler, but the crowd's shouts of *Augustus* suggest, if not officially, that for some the political claims may have gone further.[31] The burial of Chlodwig's father, Childeric, shows a conjunction of Germanic features with the trappings of Roman authority in a different way.[32] As in other wealthy Germanic graves the burial goods include equipment fittings, gold buckles and arm-rings, but also typically Frankish weapons (*francisca* and *scramasax*), gold-and-garnet jewellery and, possibly connected with Childeric's own funeral, the remains of (sacrificed?) horses. Also included, however, is Childeric's seal-ring, a feature of Roman, not Germanic, civilisation (and inscribed with his name in Roman letters). It portrays the Frankish king in Roman military dress and holding a lance. It is a typically composite picture of sub-Roman power in an emergent Germanic state.[33]

For all the contradictions between them Christianity and the Germanic world could occasionally find common ground on which, in some regions of Germania, the Church could concentrate to ease the task of Christianisation. On the other hand a Germanic king could accept a new God whose usefulness was demonstrated to him, especially on the battlefield, as was already the case with Constantine at the Milvian Bridge. In the Germanic world this precedent was repeated by (or attributed to) Chlodwig, who staked his chance of victory at Tolbiac on the new God because, in the face of what looked like certain defeat, his native gods apparently had let him down.[34] Although from a Christian point of view this cannot be called an inner conversion (for the Christian God is seen in the same light as the pagan ones), this conjunction of the

---

[29] Brown (1996), 15, 16.   [30] Herrin (1989), 19.
[31] Wallace-Hadrill (1962), 65f., 175f.; Herrin (1989), 35f.; McCormick (1990), 335ff.
[32] James (1991), 61ff.; Richter (1994), 19f.; Brown (1996), 85f.
[33] For a Langobardic example, the visor of king Agilulf, see McCormick (1990), 289ff.; Brown (1993), 128f.   [34] Wallace-Hadrill (1962), 169.

old with the new characterises the slow fusion of cultural worlds in the period with which we are concerned. It is also true of the Anglo-Saxon helmet from Benty Grange, where the image of the boar (a pagan symbol of ferocious fighting qualities, providing miraculous protection to the wearer)[35] was not felt to be inconsistent with the new religion, for this helmet also has a silver cross (another protective symbol) on its nose-guard.[36] The double insurance policy, pagan and Christian, which the owner of this helmet appears to have taken out is of a piece with what Bede reports of king Redwald, setting up a heathen as well as a Christian altar in the same building, and with the similar evidence from Gregory of Tours (paying respects to heathen as well as Christian altars if one passes them).[37]

The richness of this process of cultural fusion over the centuries is demonstrated best, however, when not merely two, but all three cultural traditions, Roman, Christian and Germanic, come together on particular occasions. Three examples from Anglo-Saxon England, whose representative significance goes far beyond this country, may illustrate this.[38]

With the Ruthwell Cross the Germanic past is adapted to Christian ends in the use of runes to inscribe part of the poem *Dream of the Rood*.[39] Christianity is also present in the cross itself, a poem dealing with the crucifixion, the inclusion of passages from the Vulgate, and the themes of some sculptural panels (e.g. Christ in Judgment, the Annunciation). The sculptures themselves are examples of realistic work in the classical tradition, their programme is of Byzantine origin, and the inhabited vine-scroll ornament is likewise inspired by classical models. These same three traditions also come together in the Franks Casket in what has been described as a 'heady mix', even though the meaning of their conjunction may still escape us.[40] Germanic tradition is present again in the runes recording vernacular (and occasionally Latin) words, but also in scenes depicting Weland the Smith and Egil. Christianity is represented by the scene of the Adoration of the Magi, but also by the conquest of Jerusalem by Titus. Roman tradition could also be summed up in this last scene, but is present in any case in the theme of Romulus and Remus. Even if no unifying theme suggests itself, the three traditions which converge in the Middle Ages are all at least present here.

---

[35] Beck (1965), 14f.

[36] Campbell (1991), 55; Webster and Backhouse (1991), 50f.; Newton (1994), 42.

[37] Bede: *Historia ecclesiastica* II 15; Gregory of Tours: *Historiarum libri decem* V 43. Cf. Wallace-Hadrill (1962), 172.   [38] Green (1995), 152f.

[39] Swanton (1970), 9ff.; Wormald (1991), 91; Howlett (1992), 71ff.

[40] Webster and Backhouse (1991), 101ff.

A magnificent example is provided by the Anglo-Saxon helmet found in the Coppergate at York.[41] Its Germanic background is clear, since its type is known only in England (Benty Grange, Sutton Hoo) and Sweden (Vendel, Valsgärde) and a protective animal is carved between the eyebrows. A late Roman parade helmet of a general (attested from Holland and from Burgh Castle)[42] was the prototype for this Germanic adaptation, but convergence of two traditions does not exclude Christianity which is even more obviously present here than in the cross on the Benty Grange helmet, for a metal strip on the York find, running from the back of the helmet over the crown to the nose-guard, has a Christian Latin prayer inscribed upon it.

These last three examples illustrate in visible, physical terms (in stone, whalebone, metal) what will emerge from the following pages with regard to the Germanic languages in these early centuries: their vocabulary, preserved in fossilised form in writing centuries later, likewise reflects aspects of Germanic society in contact with the Roman world and Christianity. In language, too, we must avoid seeing these three constituent traditions in isolation from one another. Even though, for clarity of exposition, these traditions are treated in three separate parts of this book, cross-connections enough remain to underline the forces which drew these traditions together to constitute a new whole. For Romans as for Christians in the Empire the arrival of Germanic barbarians on the horizon must have signified chaos and destruction, which is how the history of these centuries, written by Roman or Christian authors, was presented by contemporaries. Such a view may be justified, but only insofar as we recognise that it is only one point of view. To it should be added, if only we could reconstruct it, the experience of the barbarians themselves, shaken by their encounter with a vastly superior civilisation, but also enriched by it and attracted by the promises it held out to them.[43] No written historical sources convey their point of view to us, however, so that an analysis of the linguistic evidence, however difficult, may allow us a 'barbarocentric' approach to these centuries, supplementing the traditional ones based on Roman and Christian perceptions only.

The linguistic evidence discussed in this book comes from all the Germanic languages with the exception of Frisian, whose written tradition

---

[41] Campbell (1991), 66f.; Webster and Backhouse (1991), 6ff.
[42] The Dutch example is reproduced in Webster and Brown (1997), plate 48.
[43] Davies (1996), 214.

is too late for the chosen timespan. The term 'Common Germanic' is therefore to be understood with this reservation, but even so the geographical span covered extends from Ireland to the Crimea, from Visigothic Spain to the eastern Baltic. The timespan which is taken into account ranges from about 300 BC through to about AD 900, occasionally later in order to take account of so important a German source as Notker.

Although English possesses the adjective 'Germanic' (as distinct from 'German') and although the geographical term 'Germania' (as distinct from 'Germany') causes no difficulty, it lacks a noun, corresponding to German 'Germanen', for those who speak the languages or inhabit the area. To call them 'Germans', however, invites confusion[44] and it is quite unhistorical to use the term of a period before the tribes involved regarded themselves as Germans and had evolved a word for this (*deutsch*)[45]. I have therefore used the Latin word 'Germani' to fill this gap. On the other side of the linguistic frontier the word 'Romania' is used of the area in which the Romance languages are spoken, as distinct from one specific example in eastern Europe, 'Rumania'.

[44] E.g. the title of Todd (1992), by contrast with his use of 'Germani' in the text, or Allen Brown (1996), 34, where 'East German tribes' clearly means 'East Germanic'.
[45] Weisgerber (1949), 105ff., 117ff.

PART I

The Germanic world

Introduction to Part *I*

Our earliest written evidence about the Germanic tribes comes to us from outside, from their civilised neighbours of the Mediterranean world, the Greeks and the Romans, as they gradually came into contact with northern Europe. This dependence on what Greek and Roman geographers and historians tell us about Germania is not without its dangers, for it forces upon us a view which, because it is from outside, follows the conventions and the conceptual patterns of classical ethnography and historiography (going back to Herodotus), whether or not they do justice to the particular barbarians with whom contact was made.[1] Seeing Germania in this way through classical eyes in foreign categories amounts to an *interpretatio Romana*, a term used by Tacitus (*Germania* 43) when he equates two named Germanic gods (*Alci*) with the Roman pair Castor and Pollux.[2] This equation, like others which we may assume were made, rests on a feature shared by the Germanic and Roman deities, but ignores the differences, so that any interpretation of the unknown (*Alci*) by the better known is fraught with danger.

The danger of relying on an *interpretatio Romana* goes much further than this. The information available to classical authors writing about Germania may have been incomplete, since they depended on chance reports from military and trading sources, isolated contacts with a still largely unexplored world.[3] This information may also have been distorted, first by the difficulty of conveying the strangeness of a barbarian world in a classical language with quite different concepts, but also by the tendency of classical ethnography to shape its descriptions according to its established conventions. Greek ethnography, for example, knew at first nothing of the Germani, but did know that northern Europe was inhabited in the west by Celts and in the east by Scythians.[4] Accordingly, earliest contacts with the Germani confuse them with Celts if the

---

[1] Geary (1988), 39f.   [2] Wissowa (1918), 1ff.   [3] Timpe (1989), 307ff.
[4] Hachmann (1971), 33ff.

encounter is made in the west and with Scythians if in the east, but in either case the barbarian newcomers are understood and presented in terms of what they are not.[5]

Another factor affecting our view of Germania when classical sources first report on it is the fact that at this time the Germanic tribes were already heavily influenced by the Mediterranean world, especially Rome, so that we are deprived of any picture of the Germanic world in its 'purity'. Indeed, those parts of this world about which we are best informed are precisely those most exposed to the influence of Rome (and later of Christianity). In Parts II and III we shall be preoccupied with detailed aspects of this influence, but at this point we need to stress more the disturbing effects of this encounter between a barbarian society and a higher civilisation, accentuating divisions between Germanic tribes and within them.[6] It was part of Roman policy to encourage such divisions for its own ends: to promote pro-Roman factions, which often led also to anti-Roman parties and thus to a fragmentation of tribal society from which Rome could only profit. Moreover, the progressive encounter with Rome led to a militarisation of Germanic society and to the formation of military and ethnic confederations to deal with the challenge. What our earliest written sources present us is therefore a picture of Germanic society at one particular, highly critical point in time.[7] They rarely allow us to penetrate to a time earlier than this when traditional Germanic society may have been dominated more by agricultural than by military concerns.[8]

Only in part can this deficiency be made good by archaeology which, in analysing the material remains of an early society, can only venture hypotheses about its social, political and religious superstructure. For the rest, we are dependent on what conclusions may be drawn from later (early medieval) sources about what preceded them. For us the most important of those sources is language, whose conservative ability to retain something of the past in fossilised form in vocabulary recorded later provides a hope of undoing the limitations imposed by our sources upon our attempt to reconstruct a picture of early Germanic society at the time of its encounter with Rome and in its transformation to the early Middle Ages.

---

[5] *Ibid.*, p. 33; Wagner (1967), 92.   [6] Geary (1988), 59.   [7] Wenskus (1961), 426f.
[8] Wallace-Hadrill (1975), 21.

CHAPTER I

Religion

Reports by classical historians on the Germanic tribes containing evidence about the barbarians' religious practices range from the second century BC (dealing with the Cimbri) to the collapse of the Roman Empire in the west in the fifth century AD, but are then continued in what the Church had to say about their paganism in homiletic literature and in decisions taken by its councils. From this wide chronological span of historical evidence, largely from a time when the Germanic tribes, living in a preliterate culture, left no written evidence themselves, we can expect to be reasonably well informed about the Germanic religion. Despite the considerable difficulties in interpreting this evidence, which also recur in both the other disciplines (archaeology and philology) from which information can be extracted, it is possible to sketch an outline of Germanic religious practice.

We start with a feature central to any religion, namely the word for the divine powers worshipped.[1] To judge by ON evidence (apposite here because Christianity came so much later and because of the rich evidence of mythological poetry) the Germanic languages disposed of a variety of terms for the pagan gods, only one of which survived by proving adaptable to Christian ends. In their ON forms these terms are: *týr* (sing.) and *tívar* (plur.), *rögn* and *regin* (two variants), *bönd*, *höpt* and *goþ*. These terms are also attested elsewhere in Germanic, some in a recognisably religious function. Thus *týr*, which in its singular form in ON is more commonly used as the name of the god *Týr*, is attested in WG in the same function in the name of a day of the week (OE *tiwesdæg*, OHG *ziestag*)[2] and has a further parallel in Lat. *deus*. The second ON pair of words corresponds to Go. *ragin* 'decision reached by a council' and OS *reganogiskapu* 'divine decision, decree of fate', which suggests, as

---

[1] Cahen (1921); Kuhn (1978), 258ff.; Marold (1992), 705.   [2] See below, pp. 249f.

with Lat. *numen*, a semantic development 'decision' > 'divine decision' > 'the gods who decide'. Both *bönd* and *höpt* meant originally 'bonds, fetters' and are attested only in this general sense elsewhere in Germanic.[3] *Goþ* has parallels in every Germanic language, all with a religious function only. It is on this word that we shall concentrate, asking why it was the only term to be used throughout Germania for the Christian God. Etymologically, its IE origin **ghu-tó-m* was a neuter past participle, designating an abstract power and therefore neuter, like all the other ON terms apart from *Týr/tívar*. IE evidence for the verbal stem to which this word belongs suggests either the meaning 'to call, appeal' or 'to pour (a sacrificial libation)', where the latter is less likely since what is poured is the libation, not the god.[4]

All the ON terms listed above were commonly used in the plural, denoting the gods collectively. When *týr* occurred in the singular it was commonly not as an appellative meaning 'god', but as the name of one particular god. Apart from this their collective function is clear: *regin* denoted a legislative body or an assembly of those wielding power, whilst the general meaning of *bönd* and *höpt* 'bonds, fetters' suggests that the gods could only be conceived as such by their combination, forming a joint network. (Their rare occurrence in the singular as a poetic term for a goddess arose exceptionally from the need for a stylistic variation.) *Goþ* agrees with these other terms in being employed in a collective sense, especially when in mythological literature the gods are seen in joint battle against the equally combined forces of the giants and monsters. It differs from the others, however, in that it was also used in the singular without any forcing of the language. Moreover, as a neuter noun it could be used of a god (Oðin as *hanga-goþ*) and of a goddess (Skaði as *öndur-goþ*).[5] *Goþ* therefore resembles the other terms (apart from *Týr/tívar*) in being a neuter and in being used as a collective plural. It differs from them in also being employed in the singular (*Týr* is not comparable, being a name, not an appellative). Gender and number are therefore key factors in determining the word's further history in the context of Christianity.

Whereas ON *goþ* was neuter as a pagan term, the Church in adopting this word converted it into a masculine.[6] Traces of the original neuter are still detectable, however, throughout Germania. In Gothic the nom. sing. *a*-stem *guþ* agrees with the neuter *a*-stem *waúrd* and differs from a masculine *a*-stem such as *dags* in having no final *s*, characteristic of mas-

---

[3] Dronke (1992), 657ff.   [4] Meid (1992), 494.   [5] Cahen (1921), 28.   [6] *Ibid.*, pp. 29ff.

culines. The position is comparable in ON: *goþ* agrees in its lack of ending with *orþ*, as opposed to *dagr*. Masculine and neuter *a*-stems in Germanic also differed in their nom. plur. endings: here, too, Go. *guda* agrees with *waúrda*, but differs from *dagái*. In OHG, even though the plural form *gota* with its masculine ending is used of the pagan gods, the plural form *helligot* (where the lack of an ending is characteristic of neuters) occurs twice as a rendering for the pagan *manes* 'souls of the dead'.[7] Moreover, where the pagan implications cannot be missed, as with *abgot* 'idol', the neuter is clear beyond doubt: *daz abgot* (never the masculine *der* in OHG) and plural forms such as *abgot* (with no ending, as with neuters) or *abgotir/abgutir* (cf. the neuter *lembir* or *wihtir*).[8] Although OE can sometimes inflect the word as a masculine plur. (*godas*) it also uses the neuter form *godu* for *dei, daemonia*. In ON, although the traces are restricted, the neuter is still to be found in *afgoþ* (loaned from Germany) and in certain oath-formulas where the pre-Christian form has been conservatively retained.[9]

The change of this word's gender to masculine is true of all the Germanic languages after the conversion as a means of distinguishing the personal God of the Christians from the impersonal divine powers acknowledged by the pagans.[10] Although the morphology of the word can remain characteristic of a neuter noun, its syntactical context often reveals its change of gender. For example, in Wulfila's phrase *guþ meins* the noun inflects like a neuter (no final -*s*), whereas the possessive adjective shows the -*s* of a masculine. Similarly, in ON *almáttigr guþ* the noun is inflectionally neuter, but syntactically masculine. Other examples reveal the same change. In OHG the *Isidor* translators' wording *ih bim eino got* shows that the noun is conceived as a masculine since the numeral *eino* is a weak masculine, and the same is true in OE: *god āna*. In OS the phrase *alomahtigna god (loƀôn)* applies the masculine acc. sing. adjective to the noun. Throughout Germania Christianity therefore personalised the earlier conception of divine power by this change of gender. This process is taken one step further in OHG when this word for what is now seen as a personal God is used almost as if it were a name for Him. Where in this language masculine *a*-stems had the same form for nom. and acc. (*tag*), with names the acc. case added -*an* (*Hartmuat*, but *Hartmuatan*). This ending was also used of 'Christ', seen as a name (*Kristan*), but also of epithets applied to Him (*truhtinan, gotan*). With that

---

[7] Karg-Gasterstädt (1945), 422.   [8] *Ibid.*, pp. 426f.
[9] Cahen (1921), 33ff.; Baetke (1948), 351ff.; Kuhn (1971a), 325.   [10] Cahen (1921), 35ff.

the OHG word for God has become as much a name as was the case with the ON god *Týr*, but whereas this name is attested alongside the plural *tívar* and other plural terms for the gods, the OHG Christian term remains in singular isolation (the plural form *gota* occurs in learned translations of Lat. *dii* and refers to what no Christian could regard as divine).

The other factor in the history of the word *got* was its number (singular or plural). The pre-Christian use of this word was generally in the plural, to be expected in a polytheistic religion, but the singular, if not common in ON, was possible, especially in mythological poetry of the late pagan period.[11] The plural quality of this pagan word (and of the other terms for divine powers) was not strictly plural, but rather collective in function. The collective use of *tívar* was imposed on it by its singular form having become the name for one particular god. The collective idea of the gods in legal assembly called up by *regin* meant that it could not be readily used of one god. The general usage of *bönd* and *höpt* as bonds and fetters, conceived as ties or shackles, hindered their easy adaptation to singular usage. Only *goþ*, if we can generalise from ON usage, was free for use in the singular without linguistic forcing.

Our next step is to proceed from the Germanic gods to the good fortune (*heil*) which they were held to bestow on their worshippers or withhold from them, but also to the adjective *heilag*, applied to this supernatural gift of good fortune, to those intermediaries who transmitted it and to places, objects or persons which embodied it. These two words have been dealt with in detail in their Germanic ramifications by Baetke, whose argument I largely follow.[12]

Heilag is attested in every Germanic language, for even if the Gothic form was not used by Wulfila, it is found in the runic inscription on the ring from Pietroassa. Although the problem which for long preoccupied scholarship (did this adjective derive from another adjective or from a noun?) has been shown to be ultimately irrelevant, it would be as well to proceed from these two possibilities. The adjective from which *heilag* could derive is attested in Go., OHG, OS and OE and meant 'hale, healthy', 'whole, intact' (and in a Christian context 'saved'), whilst the noun is found in OHG, OE and ON and meant 'good luck, good fortune' (and 'salvation' as a Christian term).[13]

The Germanic adjective represented by OHG *heil* is cognate with OSl. *cělŭ*, likewise meaning both 'healthy' and 'whole'. If we accept this

---

[11] Baetke (1948), 367.   [12] Baetke (1942), 57ff.   [13] *Ibid.*, pp. 57f.

as the original meaning in Germanic this still tells us nothing about the origin of the religious implications of the substantive *heil* or of the derived adjective *heilag*. Attempts to bridge this gap have been criticised for jumping from a profane category ('whole') to a religious one ('holy') and for illicitly smuggling in an unwarranted intermediate step.[14] Difficulties of this kind disappear if instead we derive *heilag* from the noun *heil*: since the noun possesses a religious and magical meaning this would account for the religious function of the adjective. The OHG neuter noun *heil* (together with its cognates in OE and ON) translates such terms as *omen*, *augurium* and *auspicium*, whilst in OHG it also renders the idea of salvation (*salus, salutare*).[15] The noun also occurs in ON as a feminine meaning 'good fortune', which prompts the question as to the relationship of these two meanings of ON *heill*.

This can be answered by recalling that not merely the ON feminine, but also the OHG neuter noun could signify 'good fortune, blessing', as when it glosses 'salvation' or when Otfrid describes his religious undertaking (I 1,113: *nu wil ih scrîban unser heil*).[16] The change of meaning from the abstract 'good fortune' to the concrete 'omen' is quite plausible, for in ON the feminine *heill* also occurs in the sense of 'amulet'. By this shift from abstract to concrete (cf. 'he is the pride of his family') an omen (e.g. a bird or animal) could therefore be regarded as incorporating good fortune. The original shift produced the meaning 'good omen', but later 'any kind of omen'. If the meaning 'good fortune' suggests an originally religious function, so too does the meaning 'omen'. Tacitus makes it clear that the consultation of oracles was closely connected with Germanic religion: it was performed by someone with a priestly function who prayed to the gods and looked up into the sky.[17] An ON term for consulting the oracle (*fella blótspán*) suggests by the first element *blót-* that the action was accompanied by a sacrifice. In consulting the oracle it was therefore hoped that a sign bringing good fortune would be received from the gods. Sacrifice to them at the oracle was a means of gaining such fortune.

All this implies that *heil* came from the gods, but could be withheld by them. *Heil* was 'good fortune' not in a profane or simply magical sense, but rather a blessing won by correct observance of religious ritual. It could attach itself to certain people (e.g. a particular king, leader or priest) or to certain objects (e.g. an amulet or weapon), but its origin was still supernatural. As in other archaic religions, the good or bad fortune

---

[14] *Ibid.*, pp. 58ff. [15] *Ibid.*, pp. 60f. [16] *Ibid.*, pp. 63f. [17] Tacitus, *Germania* 10.

of men was felt to depend on the favour or anger of the gods. The ON feminine *heill* designated this abstract quality of good fortune, while the neuter noun denoted the concrete sign in which it was made manifest.

So far we have seen a clear semantic connection between the noun *heil* and the adjective *heilag*: both had a religious function. This still leaves the link between the noun *heil* and the adjective *heil* unaccounted for.

The fact that the meaning 'whole', 'healthy' is attested for this adjective throughout Germania does not necessarily suggest that it was therefore the original one. In the first place, the abstract noun derived from this adjective (OHG *heilî*, OS *hêli*, OE *hǣl*) may well be used in the sense of 'health' (*sanitas*), but is primarily used to render *salus, salutare* 'salvation' (e.g. *Weißenburger Katechismus* 32,88: *ad aeternam salutem ci euuigeru heili*).[18] Secondly, a religious function is also implied for the adjective itself in various formulas of greeting, as in *Beowulf* (407: *wæs þū Hrōðgār hāl*) or in Gabriel's annunciation to Mary in *Tatian* (3,2: *heil wis thu gebono follu*).[19] To derive this usage from a meaning 'healthy' might explain some of these examples, but not all: Gabriel is certainly wishing Mary much more than a pregnancy free from gynaecological complications. Similarly, if Wulfila (who uses *háils* in the context of health) also employs it in a formula of greeting for Gr. *chaíre*, this is because the meaning 'good fortune', hence 'joy', was still associated with his vernacular word. Thirdly, other usages show that this adjective could be used in the sense 'salutary', meaning not 'health-giving' in any profane function, but rather bringing, conveying, assuring nothing less than salvation, good fortune in the Christian sense.[20] Wulfila therefore used *in láiseinái háilái* in the sense of 'teaching which brings salvation', OE *hāl dōn*, like *heil tuon* in *Tatian*, conveys the religious sense of *salvare*, whilst Otfrid employed the same adjective to express the state of salvation achieved by baptism.

These functions of the adjective ('conveying or granted good fortune') can be derived easily from the meaning of the noun ('good fortune'), but not so easily from the other meaning of the adjective ('whole, healthy'). Instead, the position is likely to be the converse: if someone is blessed with *heil*, this will show itself in his good fortune, in his returning uninjured from battle or in his good health.[21] This raises the possible objection that the verb *heilen* was used frequently in the sense of *sanare, curare*, i.e. with reference to the apparently profane idea of health, not to any religious concept of *heil*. Alongside this, however, *heilen* is also attested in the (older?) meaning of *salvare*, and the WG term for Christ as saviour

---

[18] Baetke (1942), 69.   [19] *Ibid.*, pp. 69ff.   [20] *Ibid.*, p. 72.   [21] *Ibid.*, pp. 74ff.

(OHG *heilant*) is best understood against the background of *salvare*. In OHG *heilant* therefore rendered *salvator* or *salutaris*, whilst in OS *hêliand* varied *nerigend*, which likewise implied *salvare*, not *sanare*. The development of *heilen* from 'to save' (metaphysically) to 'to cure' is explicable by the religious and magical associations of primitive medicine, resting on the driving out of demons and evil spirits. To 'heal' someone meant rescuing him from their power by giving him back his *heil*. The semantic development of the verb *heilen* (from *salvare* to *sanare*) therefore corresponds to that of the noun *heilî* (from *salus* to *sanitas*).

In view of this close semantic connection between the adjective *heil* and the noun *heil* the initial question whether *heilag* derived from the adjective or from the noun loses its relevance. If *heilag* derived from the noun *heil*, it denoted a person or object standing in some sort of relationship with *heil*, therefore 'conveying *heil*' or 'imbued with *heil*'. Equally, if it derived from the adjective, it had the same function, since we have seen that the adjective *heil* is attested with the same meanings. (The suffix *-ig/-ag* acted as an intensifier, as with OHG *ein: einac* or *reht: rihtig*.) *Heil* therefore came from the gods, directly or through an intermediary, whilst *heilag* could be applied to the originator, the transmitter or the recipient of this gift from above.

As regards the nature of this *heil* (what kind of person or object was involved?) Baetke has discussed a wide range of contexts in which it was used in Germania, but the Christian slant of our written evidence is such that we need to concentrate on pagan ON examples, even here only on early ones so as to avoid the risk of contamination with Christian ideas.[22] In the ON *Battle of the Goths and Huns* we learn of a 'holy border district' (1,8: *á mörk enni helgu*), where the force of the adjective can best be understood from the parallel in the *Landnámabók*: a settler dedicates his land to the god Thor and therefore calls it *Þórsmörk*. The territory in the lay may have been similarly entrusted to the care of the gods or it may have been regarded as hallowed by the presence of a king imbued with special *heil*. How someone of royal birth could be so regarded, especially in the context of victory in battle, is suggested by the description of Erpr in the *Hamðismál* as 'hallowed, blessed in battle' (28,8: *gumi inn gunnhelgi*). As the son of a king, he is expected to have his share of *heil* in battle, to be victorious (as in the OHG *Ludwigslied* v. 57, where the ruler is designated as *wîgsâlig*). *Heil* as a special royal prerogative is also suggested by the ON name *Helgi* (together with its feminine counterpart reflected in Russian

---

[22] *Ibid.*, pp. 130f., 136ff. (but also Dronke (1969), 175).

Oleg and Olga), occurring earliest as a royal name in Scandinavia, long before the earliest contact with Christianity. The welfare of a land (its prosperity and military success) depended on the gods, on the *heil* they transmitted through the person of the king.

To sum up. Like the Christian *sanctus* the Germanic term *heilag* denoted a quality of divine origin, but unlike *sanctus* the gift it represented was not to be enjoyed in the afterlife, but in the here and now. This only partial agreement was later to create difficulties in establishing a Christian vocabulary in Germanic.

We pass now from the gods and the gifts they bestowed to the way in which their favours were won, by the act of ritual worship, above all by sacrifices. Worship of the gods is to be understood not as subjective religious experience, but as participation in an act of publicly performed ritual. Accordingly, ritual rather than belief was the focus of Germanic religion: whereas OHG vocabulary possessed numerous terms for *offerre* inherited from the past, the position was quite different for *credere*, even if we do not accept the theory of Gothic origin for *gilouben*.[23] As far as the lexical evidence permits a conclusion, there was no general term for ritual worship as such, but instead separate terms for different aspects of religious practice.[24]

One such term, attested in OHG and OE, is *bigang* (together with the verb *bigangan*).[25] Its original meaning was 'to go round, to process' but since OHG *bigang* glosses *ritus* and *cultus* it must have been applied to acts of religious worship involving a procession, such as are attested for the worship of the goddess Nerthus and elsewhere in Germania. Such practices were at first anathema to the Church, but were also at times adapted to Christian use (*Echternacher Springprozession*), so that in modern German one can still say *die Felder begehen* for going round the fields on Rogation days and *das Fest begehen* is to celebrate any festival. In OHG the term was similarly used of any festival (Christian, Jewish or pagan), but the pre-Christian evidence for processional rites in Germania combines with their comparative infrequency in Christian worship to suggest a pagan origin. Rhythmic movement as part of religious ritual may also be suggested by OE *lāc*, a word attested throughout Germania meaning, among other things, 'dance'.[26] Religious implications are suggested by the further meaning of the OE form 'sacrifice', so that a sacrificial cer-

---

[23] Lange (1958), 282.   [24] Wesche (1937), 26.
[25] Jente (1921), 35f.; Philippson (1929), 194; Wesche (1937), 26f.; Helm (1937), 59; (1953), 190, 210.
[26] Jente (1921), 44ff.; Helm (1953), 192; Beck (1968a), 1ff.; Düwel (1970), 235f.

emony involving a dance would seem to lie behind OE usage. Since the meaning 'sacrifice' is attested only in OE, it might seem rash to postulate a Germanic origin for this practice, were it not for the evidence of the personal names ON *Ásleikr*, Latinised OHG *Ansleicus* and OE *Ōslāc*, suggesting someone who sacrificed to, or worshipped, the group of Germanic gods known to Jordanes as the *Anses* and in ON as the *Æsir*.

The centre of Germanic ritual worship was the act of sacrifice itself, including blood-sacrifices and bloodless ones, the former embracing animals and human beings, the latter, for example, the weapons and other gear of the defeated enemy.[27] Although historical testimony and archaeological finds can be confirmed by linguistic evidence, the terms to be adduced under this heading, both in OHG and OE, were slowly driven back and replaced by words like OHG *opfarôn* and OE *offrian*.[28]

The most important sacrifice was of an animal some parts of which after slaughter were offered up to the gods and others consumed ritually by the worshippers who thereby enjoyed communion with their gods.[29] Although the historical evidence for this is slight (e.g. Tacitus, the martyrdom of Saba amongst the Goths, Christian reports on the WG pagans),[30] the archaeological evidence occurs more frequently (bones of sacrificed animals, particularly horses), as long as we feel enough confidence in the archaeologists' ability to distinguish natural death from sacrificial death and to maintain in the latter case that the flesh was consumed ritually. If we can accept this it provides valuable support for the linguistic testimony.

Human sacrifice, like animal sacrifice, can be assumed archaeologically when skeletons are found on what other evidence suggests were religious or sacrificial sites. Historical evidence supports this assumption, not merely in the context of warfare (sacrifice of prisoners of war).[31] Already from Tacitus we learn not merely that Mercury (=Wodan) was worshipped above all, but that human sacrifices were made to win his favour. The account of the processional worship of the goddess Nerthus also concludes with the ritual killing of slaves who took part in the ceremony.[32] Scandinavian examples mention human sacrifices to Oðin outside the context of warfare.[33] Since danger was to be averted by

---

[27] Düwel (1970), 238f. [28] Philippson (1929), 195; Wesche (1937), 62, 71.

[29] Helm (1937), 55f.; (1953), 197, 198f.; de Vries (1956a), 406f.; Jankuhn (1967), 119, 129, 143, 145; Much (1967), 176ff.; Polomé (1986), 276.

[30] Tacitus, *Germania* 9; Saba: Helm (1937), 55f.; Thompson (1966), 64f.; WG pagans: Helm (1953), 197ff.

[31] Mogk (1909), 601ff.; Helm (1937), 56; (1953), 199f.; de Vries (1956a), 408ff.; Jankuhn (1967), 120, 132; Beck (1970), 240ff. [32] Tacitus, *Germania* 9 and 40. [33] Mogk (1909), 614.

sacrificing someone else this practice may have come particularly to the fore in time of battle, but need not have been confined to it.

The OHG word *bluozan* 'to sacrifice' (noun: *bluostar*) has cognates throughout Germania except in OS.[34] It occurs in all OHG dialects, but must have died out in all of them at about the same time (probably because of the victorious advance of *opfarôn*), since it is not attested after about 800. Although the word is probably cognate with Lat. *fla(d)men* 'priest' the etymology is too uncertain to help us with the original function of the Germanic word, although its loan into Finno-Lappish terms for 'to sing' could suggest a sacrificial rite accompanied by sung recital.[35] In OHG the verb rendered Latin terms like *sacrificare, immolare, libare* and *victimare*, suggesting various forms of sacrifice (libation, burnt offering, animal), but this wide range may result more from the variety of Latin words which the vernacular term translated only approximately. Less questionable is the pagan flavour of the term, for it glosses *idolatriae* and occurs in the Franconian baptismal formula with regard to the pagan practices to be abjured. In OHG and OE some traces of (pagan) sacrifices are still preserved, but in Gothic the word *blōtan* has been safely christianised by a change of construction: it no longer governs the dative ('to sacrifice to a god'), but the accusative with a different meaning ('to worship God'), so that *guþblostreis* renders *theosebḗs* 'worshipping God, devout'.[36] Wulfila therefore retained no trace of worship by means of sacrifice and has extracted the word from its pagan origins.

A unique sacrificial term was christianised in the form of OE *blētsian* 'to bless'.[37] Its dialectal variants *blēdsian* and *bloedsia* suggest derivation from *blōdisōn*, a verb formed from *blōd* 'blood', which implies blood sacrifice (animal or human) and possibly consecration of a pagan altar by sprinkling it with the blood of the victim.

The archaeological evidence for animal sacrifice suggests a division between those animals which could not be consumed in a ritual meal and those which could be, as part of the communion between gods and worshippers. Some of our linguistic terms support this idea of sacrificial food.

The OHG *zebar* is attested in all dialects and its cognates are found in most Germanic languages.[38] In OHG the word glosses *sacrificium*, but also *hostia, victima, holocaustoma*, where the latter terms imply the sacrifice

---

[34] Wesche (1937), 39ff.; Helm (1953), 194; Düwel (1970), 226f.; Polomé (1986), 287.
[35] Wesche (1937), 44.   [36] *Ibid.*, p. 43.   [37] Jente (1921), 41; de Vries (1956a), 415.
[38] Jente (1921), 42ff.; Philippson (1929), 195; Wesche (1937), 45ff.; Helm (1937), 58; (1953), 196; de Vries (1956a), 423; Düwel (1976), 227.

of animals. Again, this could be more a reflection of various Latin terms imperfectly translated by one German term, but other factors speak against this. The Germanic word is cognate with Latin *daps* 'sacrificial meal', but also with Armenian *tvar* 'herd of cattle' or 'ram'. The word was also loaned into Finnish: *teuras* 'animal for slaughter'. Furthermore, the idea of an animal fit for communion consumption is emphatically suggested by the negative of the OHG form, preserved in MHG *unzifer*, *ungezibere*, modern German *Ungeziefer* 'vermin'. Only what could be sacrificed for a ritual meal was regarded as *zebar*, everything else (unclean and inedible) was *ungezibere*.

Another term with similar implications, Gothic *hunsl*, is also found in ON (the runic inscription of Rök) and in OE, but not in OS or OHG.[39] Wulfila employed the term in the general sense 'sacrificial offering', but also in a context where the New Testament meant specifically 'sacrificial food', so that the idea of animal sacrifice was presumably still present in Gothic. This possibility is confirmed by the OE counterpart *hūsel*, originally conveying the sense 'sacrifice', as in Gothic, but by its Christianisation to 'communion' implying that this had been combined with a ritual meal. If the ON term later also acquires this Christian meaning, this is likely to be under OE influence, but by means of loan-meaning, not as a loanword, since the example from Rök shows that the word was known in Scandinavia from early on.

A last example of animals sacrificed for religious purposes is provided by Gothic *sáups* 'sacrifice'.[40] Its conjunction with *hunsl*, but especially with *alabrunsts* 'burnt offering' suggests an animal sacrifice, while the parallel of ON *sauðr* 'sheep' could mean that this was the animal in question. However, the equation of *sauðr* with *blótnaut* 'sacrificial cattle' could imply a more general usage, but still the sacrifice of an animal. Other Germanic languages retain no trace of this word as a religious term. Instead, they use the related verb **seuðan* as a general term for 'to seethe, boil', suggesting the manner in which the beast may have been prepared for a ritual meal.

From worship of the gods and sacrifice to them we move to the location where this was performed, to the place of worship. Tacitus reported of the Germani that their holy places were in the open, in woods or groves, since they did not regard it as consistent with the majesty of the gods

---

[39] Philippson (1929), 195; Helm (1937), 57; (1953), 195; Düwel (1970), 228f.
[40] De Vries (1956a), 370; Düwel (1976), 227, 232f.

either to represent them in human form or to imprison them within the walls of a building.[41] Although it has been suggested that Tacitus made use here of a topos of Stoic philosophy (the superiority of religious worship not tied to concrete forms in any way), this is a case where an *interpretatio Romana* need not simply have been imposed upon Germania, but could have been used to understand a given feature of Germanic religion. In other passages where he was not concerned to make this general point about their worship, but was reporting on specific aspects of a variety of Germanic tribes as learned from different informants, Tacitus made numerous allusions to the religious awe in which the Germani held woods and groves.[42] There was a sacred grove for the worshippers of Nerthus, the Suebi gathered for their sacrifices in a hallowed wood, the figures and emblems which they took into battle were kept in their sacred groves, Civilis summoned tribal chieftains for consultation in a hallowed grove, and near the Weser there was a forest consecrated to the god whom Tacitus equated with Hercules. Only on the improbable assumption that on all these scattered occasions Tacitus was imposing a topos of classical thought on his Germanic material can we ignore this variegated evidence, the more so since it is confirmed from quite a different angle by later Christian references to pagan worship at similar sites.[43] Some of these references may admittedly be conventional (applying to all pagans at any time or place what had been observed only in one case), but their frequent mention of the religious importance of trees and woods to Germanic pagans, agreeing with Tacitus, is borne out by some of our linguistic evidence.

Confirmation is also provided by the finds of archaeology, as far as these go.[44] They support Tacitus to the extent that temples (buildings for religious purposes) do not appear to have existed, whilst the focus of worship on woods and groves is borne out by excavations of sacrificial sites, fenced off against profane use, in moorland (and presumably also in woodland).

Richer information on pagan places of worship is forthcoming from early place-names which survived the coming of Christianity. Place-names which can assist us are of two types, each composed of two elements: the first type contains the name of a god as its first element (theophoric place-names), the second has a term for a place of worship as its second element.[45] (We may deal now with the first type only, since

[41] Tacitus, *Germania* 9; Timpe (1992), 452, 483.
[42] Tacitus, *Germania* 7, 39 and 40; *Historiae* IV 14; *Annales* II 12; de Vries (1956a), 351f.
[43] Helm (1953), 167ff.   [44] Jankuhn (1966), 421.   [45] Helm (1953), 174.

the second presupposes words for a place of worship which we have yet to consider.) Most of the evidence, but by no means all, comes from Scandinavia, which raises the often unanswerable question as to how far these NG examples can be generalised for Germania at large.

Theophoric place-names may contain a general term for the gods at large or the name of an individual god.[46] Scandinavian place-names of the type *Gudhjem, Gudme, Gudum* (< *Gudhem*) derive from an appellative meaning 'home of the gods', extended to mean the place where the gods dwell and are the object of a special rite, then designating places where such worship took place. In addition to this collective word for the gods, the term *ansu-* (one group of gods within the Germanic pantheon) can also be used, as in Sw. *Åsum* (< *-hem*), Norw. *Oslo* and German *Aßlar*. Much more common are place-names which specify an individual god, throughout Scandinavia and especially with reference to the gods *Freyr, Óðinn, Þórr* (but also *Ullr, Freyja* and *Týr*). This category is also represented in WG evidence: *Wodan* in Germany (*Godesberg* < *Wudinisberg*) and in England (*Wednesbury, Wenslow*), *Donar* in Germany (*Donnersberg*, whilst in England *Thursley* shows Viking influence), *Tiu* in Germany (*Ciesburg* for Augsburg) and in England (*Tuesley*).[47] For all such place-names of theophoric nature (generic or individual deities) we may assume the presence of a religious site in or near the places in question.

The problems of interpretation raised by such place-names concern both the second element (how far is a place of worship really involved instead of a term with no religious function?) and the first element (is a deity necessarily referred to?). As an example of the latter difficulty we may take what have been regarded as non-Scandinavian parallels to such a theophoric place-name as Norw. *Frøysaker*, where similar names such as *Óðinsakr, Ullinsakr, Njarðarakr* suggest the presence of an individual god.[48] The position is by no means so clearcut outside Scandinavia, however, with such place-names as Fri. *Franeker* and Du. *Vroonloo*. Not merely would regarding these latter names as theophoric involve assuming the existence of a WG god *Frô* for whom we have no other reliable evidence, it would also ignore the persistence of the non-religious meaning of the word *frô* ('lord, ruler') which in Scandinavia came to be used as the name of a god. In view of these reservations the WG examples probably refer not to a pagan god, but to the property of a Germanic or even feudal lord. Apart from the qualifications which are called for, onomastic evidence of this kind can enlighten us on the location of

[46] Andersson (1992), 524ff., 527ff.   [47] Helm (1953), 175ff.   [48] Green (1965), 19f.

places of religious practice and on the worship of particular gods, even though most of the conclusions are confined to Scandinavia.

In addition to place-names the linguistic evidence includes a number of appellatives denoting a place of worship. Some of these occur as the second element of one of the place-name types just considered and most of them imply that the site was an open-air one or in woodland. Without being dependent on Tacitus the argument can confirm him.

The OHG word *harug* has cognates in OE and ON.[49] In OHG it occurs in the earliest sources and persists until the tenth century, translating such Latin terms as *ara, delubrum, fanum, lucus* and *nemus*, i.e. ranging from 'altar' through 'sanctuary, chapel' to 'holy grove'. None of the examples suggests a large place of worship, but rather a small grove, particularly when *harug* renders *lucus* or *nemus* or when in one gloss it occurs as a translation variant of *forst*. No German example shows *harug* as a translation of *silva* (with a non-religious function), but the position is different in OE, where *hearg* can denote 'wood' as well as 'holy grove', but in addition a pagan 'sanctuary' or 'idol'. In ON *hörgr* is attested as 'heap of stones', but also 'place of worship' (with stones as a primitive altar?) and 'mountain'. If we accept the etymological connection with OIr. *carn* 'heap of stones' and Lat. *carcer* '(stone) enclosure, prison', the semantic starting-point would seem to have been 'altar', then, as with the Latin terms above rendered into OHG, moving to 'sanctuary, chapel' and finally 'holy grove'. The word can also occur as (or in) a place-name (e.g. *Harrow* or *Harrowden* in England), but the double function of the appellative, religious or non-religious, means that we cannot be certain whether the place-name refers to an original place of worship.

The position is largely comparable with OHG *lôh*, OE *lēah*.[50] These words are cognate with Lat. *lucus* 'open clearing, holy grove' and in agreement with Latin the German form means 'clearing, holy grove', whilst English proceeds from 'open ground' to 'meadow'. Although infrequently, the religious function is still attested in OHG, but with the evidence from place-names it is again difficult to tell whether they refer to an earlier religious site (perhaps most probably in the case of *Heiligenloh*).

The word *nimid* is attested only once, in the *Indiculus superstitionum* where it refers to religious rites performed in the woods (*De sacris silvarum,*

[49] Jente (1921), 9ff.; Philippson (1929), 186f.; Wesche (1932), 17ff.; de Vries (1956a), 376f., 380; Andersson (1992), 528f.; Holmberg (1992), 541f.

[50] Wesche (1932), 25f.; Helm (1953), 169; de Vries (1956a), 352.

quae nimidas vocant).[51] Although the *Indiculus* has been suspected of simply transferring features of late antique paganism to northern Europe it is now considered more probable that it was geared specifically to the conversion of the Saxons and that *nimidas* is in fact an OS word.[52] There are no other Germanic cognates, but in Celtic *nemetos* meant 'holy' and *nemeton* 'sanctuary', so that we are possibly dealing with a Celtic loan-word into OS.[53] The word's ultimate relationship with Lat. *nemus* confirms the placing of these religious rites in a wood.

The OHG word *baro* translates Latin *ara* in a sacrificial context, while its OE counterpart *bearo*, although normally used for 'wood' in a non-religious context, occurs once with the meaning 'sanctuary'.[54] Moreover, this religious meaning is suggested for the OE word when Christian buildings are said to be erected *æt Bearwe* 'at the site of a (pagan) sanctuary' in view of the Anglo-Saxon practice of converting pagan places of worship into Christian ones where possible. The use of the cognate ON *börr* to mean 'tree' (or the parallel of Sl. *boru* 'pine forest') suggests 'wood' as a semantic starting-point, so that this word's development *via* 'place of worship' to 'altar' in OHG would be the converse of what we saw with *harug*. Both words, however, testify the close connection between ritual ceremonies and a woodland setting.

This is no longer explicitly the case with two remaining terms. The first (OS *alah* '(Jewish) temple') has cognates in Gothic and OE as appellatives, but in ON and OHG only traces as an element in name-formation.[55] It is cognate with OE *ealgian* 'to protect', so that as a term for a hallowed place it may have implied an area fenced off and guarded against intrusion. If more remote cognates suggest a woodland setting (OLith. *alkas/elkas* 'holy grove', Gr. *álsos* 'grove, temple') there is no indication that the same setting was also true of Germania. The occurrence of this word as the second element in place-names is not enough to establish them as religious places. In a Scandinavian place-name like *Fröjel* (< *Freyja*) it is the goddess's name, not the word **al*, which establishes its sacral function, whilst in OHG place-names we have no means of clearly distinguishing a religious meaning from the use of *alach* to denote a settlement, fenced off for the practical reason of defence. The other term with no explicit location in a wood is OHG

---

[51] Wesche (1932), 27; Helm (1953), 169.
[52] Boudriot (1964), 18; Wesche (1932), 27; Homann (1965), 12ff.   [53] Cf. Powell (1987), 166ff.
[54] Jente (1921), 8f.; Philippson (1929), 186f.; Wesche (1932), 27f.; Helm (1953), 170.
[55] Jente (1921), 7f.; Philippson (1929), 185; Wesche (1932), 28ff.; Helm (1937), 46; de Vries (1956a), 373; Schmidt-Wiegand (1967), 21ff.; Andersson (1992), 530.

wîh, the substantival form of a Germanic adjective for 'holy' which existed alongside *heilag*.[56] It occurs once in OHG with the meaning 'sanctuary', more frequently in OS, where it denotes the Jewish temple, and in ON ('sanctuary' or 'temple'). In OE the meaning of the word has been restricted to 'idol'. The pre-Christian origin of the adjective, together with some usages of the substantive, suggests that the latter could have denoted a pagan sanctuary. However, we cannot claim on the basis of the OHG example (where *wîh*, *forst* and *haruc* are alternative translations of *nemus*) that *wîh* must have been a woodland sanctuary: what brought these words together was their hallowed nature, not necessarily any woodland setting. Where the word is used as the second element of a place-name (as in Danish *Odense* < *Óðins vé*) there can be no doubt about its theophoric nature: by contrast with *Fröjel* both elements of the compound indicate this.

From the pagan place of worship we move on to the person who was the focus of the ritual performed there, the priest. With him we touch on Caesar's contrast between Celts and Germani in their religious practice and the different view of the Germani shown by Tacitus.[57] As part of his contrast Caesar maintained that, unlike the Celts with their druids, the Germani had no priests in charge of religious matters, whereas Tacitus was more precise (or better informed), distinguishing religious ritual performed *publice* and *privatim*. For the former a *sacerdos civitatis* was responsible, for the latter the *pater familias*. Although Tacitus makes it clear that certain people performed certain functions at religious ceremonies, he nowhere suggests the existence of a priestly caste, so that in this respect his opinions may be reconciled with Caesar's, who viewed the position in Germania from what he knew of the Celts. About these priests, however, about their precise functions and position or about any possible differentiation between tribes we are singularly ill-informed and are dependent on linguistic testimony for further enlightenment.

Apart from terms (*goting, esago/ewart*) which had a legal as well as religious function, OHG had three words which could designate the pagan priest: *harugari, parawari* and *bluostrari*.[58] Each occurs only once, so that theoretically they could be *ad hoc* gloss translations, never really alive in

---

[56] Wesche (1932), 30ff.; Baetke (1942), 90ff., 172, 176, 188, 196f.; Helm (1953), 170; Ilkow (1968), 410, 413f.; Andersson (1992), 527f.

[57] Caesar, *De bello Gallico* VI 21; Tacitus, *Germania* 7, 10, 11, 40 and 43; Helm (1937), 50f.; Kuhn (1978), 231ff.; Timpe (1992), 439f., 484.

[58] On the first group of terms see below, p. 33. On the second group cf. Wesche (1937), 2f.

the spoken language and in any case suspiciously late in showing the *nomen agentis* suffix *-ari*, borrowed from Lat. *-arius*. Against the suggestion that these words may have had no pre-Christian existence, however, there speaks OE *heargweard* (attesting the tendency to derive a word for 'priest' from *harug*), but also the presence of other terms derived from *bluostar* to denote a priest in other Germanic languages (Go. *guþblostreis*, OE *blōteras*). Although *parawari* is attested in three manuscripts, only one also attests the base-word *paro*, so that the derivative may have been more widely known. These three OHG words were therefore probably pagan in origin, even if late pagan.

Harugari was used to render *aruspices*, which suggests an original connection between the priest and the interpreter of the oracle and reinforces what Tacitus said about auspices and the casting of lots by the *sacerdos civitatis*.[59] *Parawari* likewise translates *aruspes*, which is further specified as the person who sacrifices at the altar (*qui ad aras sacrificat = de ce demo parawe ploazzit*).[60] *Parawari* was therefore the person responsible for the rites performed in a holy grove. The word may be suspected of relatively late formation: not merely because of its suffix, but also because other Germanic languages, although they may possess the equivalent of *baro*, have no trace of this derivative. The same may be true of *harugari*, for its solitary counterpart, OE *heargweard*, was formed by different means. *Bluostrari* renders *sacrificatores* and denotes the priest in his function of performing sacrifices, which is confirmed by the testimony of OE *blōteras*, applied to the hangman who tortured the martyrs and therefore registering a decline in meaning from the pagan priest in his role as sacrificer.[61] Wulfila rescued the word from this fate and rendered it fit for Christianisation by means of the compound *guþblostreis*, meaning no longer one who sacrifices to the gods, but one who worships God. Revealing about the Gothic word-formation is the fact that the *nomen agentis* is created by a suffix older in Germanic than the loan from Lat. *-arius*, which process suggests the presence of a word in Germanic for the priest in this function earlier than those attested in the three OHG examples. With that we reach possibly a little further back into Germanic antiquity, but hardly as far back as is likely with *goting* and its cognates.[62]

[59] Wesche (1937), 3f.; Helm (1953), 186.   [60] Wesche (1937), 4.
[61] *Ibid.*, pp. 4ff.; Helm (1937), 48; (1953), 187f.   [62] Wesche (1937), 7.

CHAPTER 2

Law

The earliest historical information on Germanic law, focused on the tribal assembly as a legislative authority, comes to us from Tacitus.[1] In *Germania* 11 we are told that the assembly came together on fixed days, but could also be specially convoked. Those attending came armed and the procedure for approving or rejecting proposals is described. Chapter 12 is concerned with accusation and punishment, as well as the dispensation of justice outside the assembly. Only part of Chapter 13, dealing with the legal, political status of the warrior, is relevant here, because Tacitus passes on to consider the war-band. In order to obtain further insight on the basis of language we have to wait until it was felt necessary, with the codification of barbarian laws in the early Middle Ages, to introduce vernacular legal terms, even in a partly Latinised form, into Latin versions of these law-codes, for only the vernacular term was legally precise enough to convey what barbarian practice meant.[2]

Another source for vernacular legal terms is to be found in vernacular texts with a legal context in which legal developments are reflected. Otfrid's biblical epic as well as the OS *Heliand* had ample opportunity, not least in their depiction of Christ's trial before Pilate, to accentuate these legal implications, showing them in terms understandable to an audience acquainted with Frankish law practice, either directly (as with Otfrid) or under its influence (as with the OS work).[3]

The scene of the Last Judgment is treated in the OHG *Muspilli* where its implications in terms of contemporary legal practice are brought out.[4] On the lexical level the Last Judgment is depicted with reference to

---

[1] Much (1967), 201ff.

[2] The *Lex Salica*, for example, falls back on Frankish key-terms when dealing with a summons to attend at a court of law: *mannitus* 'summoned' and *sunnis* 'legitimate excuse', retained in the vernacular version (*gimenit, sunne*), but also *mallum* 'court of law', the equivalent of *mahal* in OHG and OS. Cf. Steinmeyer (1916), 55ff. (under I); Weisweiler and Betz (1974), 72f.

[3] E.g. Otfrid, *Evangelienbuch* v 19, 61f. Cf. Kolb (1971), 299f.   [4] Kolb (1962), 88ff.; (1971), 284ff.

well-known legal concepts: the king summons a legal assembly (*daz mahal kipannit*) at which no one dare not appear (*den pan furisizzan*).[5] Categories like these called up a picture of the Last Judgment resembling contemporary secular practice, but the author was concerned to bring out the antithesis beyond the obvious point that a legal excuse for non-appearance would no longer be valid at the end of time. He does this by referring to the contemporary belief in the *iudicium Dei*, pointing out its inapplicability on this occasion and imputing this belief to those knowledgeable in secular law (*weroltrehtwîson*) as opposed to theologians (*gotman*).[6] This contrast presupposes an encounter between traditional legal practice and Christianity, but even in the demotion of the former it is possible to detect aspects of contemporary practice. When those laymen skilled in law are termed *wîson* 'wise' this is in agreement with the *viri sapientes* consulted in the codification of WG barbarian law and with the legal functions of the *witan* in OE sources. Even when Christianity displaces or devalues previous customs something of their nature can be revealed to us.

The most common OHG term for 'law', *êwa*, is paralleled by OE *ǣ* and OS *êo*. Although the attempt to establish a counterpart in Gothic is too hypothetical, the onomastic evidence for early reflections in NG (and elsewhere in Germania) is more convincing.[7] *Êwa* and its cognates appear frequently in conjunction with words suggesting 'custom, habitual practice'.[8] In OS *êo* is linked with *aldsido* 'time-honoured practice' and *landwîsa* 'custom of the country', in OE *ǣ* with words of similar meaning (*þêaw, wîs, gewuna*), in OHG *êwa* with *situ*. From OS *landwîsa* it is only a short step to *liudo landreht* 'law of the land', with which *êo* is also associated twice in *Heliand* (3859f., 5320f.). In each case (crucifying a blasphemer or stoning an adulteress) what is at stake is not simply any time-honoured practice, but a particular legal practice, belonging to the *landreht*. That *êwa* had this technical legal function alongside the more general meaning 'custom' is made clear by its adoption into the Latin vocabulary of the *Leges Barbarorum* to denote the unwritten customary law of different Germanic tribes as distinct from laws established by capitularies (even though, following the transition from oral to written law, the term *ewa Saxonum* came to signify tribal law in written form).[9]

---

[5] *Muspilli* 31ff.; Kolb (1971), 294f.   [6] Kolb (1962), 88ff.
[7] Mezger (1965a), 38ff.; Beck (1974), 54f. On *êwa* at large see Weisweiler (1929), 419ff.; von See (1964), 105ff.; Ilkow (1968), 104ff.; Beck (1974), 52ff.; Schmidt-Wiegand (1994), 35ff.
[8] Weisweiler (1929), 422ff.   [9] *Ibid.*, pp. 426f.; Schmidt-Wiegand (1994), 35.

Onomastic evidence suggests that the word was not confined to WG in this sense, for it occurs as the first element in such names as OHG *Ewald* and *Eward*, originally 'someone administering or in charge of the law', with parallels in the ON names *Ávaldr* and *Ávarðr*, not to mention the further correspondence with the Visigothic name *Evarix* (fifth century) = *Aiwareiks*.[10]

This is only one aspect of the word *êwa*, for it was also used to denote a religious ceremony or religion at large. One occasion when OS *êo* is associated with *aldsido* and *landwîsa* (*Heliand* 4553) refers to the Jews' religious celebration of the Passover, whilst the link between *êo* and *landwîsa* (v. 795) concerns the tribute paid in the temple (*alah*). In OE and in OHG the related words can render *ceremoniae* in the religious context, and in these languages *religio* is translated as *æfæstnes* and *êhaltida*.[11] The agreement in this usage between OHG, OS and OE suggests the possibility of a WG origin at the least, just as its spread to denote the ceremonies and religious practices of pagans alongside Jews and Christians points to a pre-Christian origin. The semantic development from 'religious practice' to 'religion' may not be entirely due to Christian influence, even though it was assisted by it.

The same question is raised by the much more frequent use of *êwa* in WG with a specifically Christian meaning.[12] In this context OE generally makes this meaning clear by a preceding genitive (e.g. *godes ǣ, Cristes ǣ*), a construction which also occurs in German, admittedly after Notker (*gotes ê, Cristes ê*), but also earlier in OS (*godes êo*). In combination with one or other adjective the same word can be used to translate *vetus* or *novum testamentum*, where the religious employment of the legal term *testamentum* suggests a combination of religious with legal in the case of *êwa*, too. The use of this vernacular word in such a context or when rendering Christian phrases like *lex Dei* or *divina lex* prompts the question once more whether this religious function of *êwa* derives from such Christian usage or goes back to a pre-Christian unity of law with religion. The consensus of scholarly opinion seems to be in favour of a pre-Christian origin for such twofold usage, but with Schmidt-Wiegand firmly opposed to the view that *êwa* denoted 'religious cult' before it was used to translate Christian concepts. In doing so she bases herself explicitly on von See whose views on this point, however, are much more qualified.[13] Although he denies that the *sacerdos* who opened the legal assembly in

[10] Beck (1974), 54f.   [11] Weisweiler (1929), 429f.; Wesche (1937), 20ff.; von See (1964), 106f.
[12] Weisweiler (1929), 431ff.   [13] Schmidt-Wiegand (1994), 36; von See (1964), 106f.

Tacitus's account was a fully fledged judge or lawspeaker, he concedes that it was at least a priest who performed this function at a law-giving assembly. In the specific case of the word *êwa* he is ready to concede it a religious function in WG, especially in Germany, in the *late* pagan period, even though he still denies the PG origins of this function or the NG evidence for it. In other words, the religious implications of this word seem not to be entirely due to extraneous influences, but to have native roots in Germania alongside its legal usage. In late OHG the meaning of the word is restricted to being the legal equivalent of *matrimonium*, as in modern German *Ehe*.[14]

The combined religious and legal function of *êwa* can be buttressed by the evidence of two compounds: OHG *êwart* and *êosago*.[15] The first of these, the appellative equivalent of the personal names *Ewart* and *Ávarðr*, is the most frequent term in OHG for 'priest' ('guardian of the (religious) law'), but occurs once in OE *æweweard*, whose isolated and late attestation might suggest loan-traffic or at the most a restriction to WG, were it not for the ON name. *Êosago*, on the other hand, is only legal in function (literally 'lawspeaker'): in OHG it stands for terms like *iuridicus*, *legislator* and in OS it designates the scribe skilled in Jewish law. As might be the case with *êwart*, it is restricted to WG. These words belong closely together, deriving from *êwa* implying law in its fullest sense (secular and religious), with a later differentiation in either direction producing compounds for the priest and the lawspeaker. Both words were still employed on German soil in mental association with the legal assembly which was the focus of law practices in Germania. In OS the *Heliand* uses *êosago* in combination with *hwarf* 'legal assembly', *râdan* 'to deliberate', but also with *wîs*, corresponding to the legal *viri sapientes*, whilst Otfrid employs the other term *êwart* in association with *girâti* 'deliberation', *thing* and *githingi*, corresponding to *concilium*.[16] Even *êwart* in its priestly function has not been entirely divorced from the legal context which in its widest sense, involving religion as well as law, was the original home of *êwa*.

A connection between these two spheres is also suggested by OHG *goting*, used to gloss *tribunus* as a man of public, legal authority.[17] It is relevant to our argument because of its formation from a word attested in Go. *gudja* and ON *goði* (for this type of word-formation cf. ON *konr* and

[14] Weisweiler (1929), 443; Schmidt-Wiegand (1987), 956.
[15] Weisweiler (1929), 444ff.; Waag (1932), 31ff.; Wesche (1937), 8ff.; von See (1964), 106f.; Ilkow (1968), 104ff.; Kuhn (1978), 235f.
[16] *Heliand* 4466ff., 5058ff.; Otfrid, *Evangelienbuch* III 25, 5; IV 1, 1 and 8, 3.
[17] Wesche (1937), 6ff.; von See (1964), 107ff.; Kuhn (1978), 232ff.

konungr),[18] terms derived from the word for 'god' and denoting literally
someone who has to deal with the gods. Whereas the Gothic word
retains this function in meaning 'priest', the ON term, which because of
its derivation and also in view of the theophoric epithet *Freys-goði* must
have started from the same point, came to acquire a legal and administrative function. The agreement between Gothic, ON and (despite the
suffix) OHG suggests a CG antiquity and not a creation, as suggested for
Gothic, to meet a Christian need.[19] Likewise, the agreement in legal
meaning between ON and OHG *goting* (reinforced by OHG *gotten* = *ius-
tificare*)[20] implies an early combination of priestly with legal obligations.
This word is probably the earliest we have for the priest, but its exclusive
restriction to religious duties in Gothic need not tell against its wider
application before the coming of Christianity.

Central to the argument that there was a religious background to
Germanic law is the question whether there is any evidence actually
involving the gods, or one of them, in legal practices focused on the
Germanic assembly as described by Tacitus, who mentions priests, but
no deities. Here the most telling evidence comes from England, from
Latin votive inscriptions (second century AD) by a Germanic military
unit (specified as *Tuihanti*) in the Roman army, found at Housesteads on
Hadrian's Wall and reading: *Deo Marti Thingso et duabus Alaesiagis Bede et
Fimmilene*.[21] The legal associations of this inscription are suggested by the
term *Thingsus*, the Latinised form of a Germanic masculine **þingsa-*,
derived from a neuter *s*-stem **þingsa-*, a variant (also attested in
Langobardic *thinx*) of the more common **þinga-* 'legal assembly'. This
legal background is reinforced by the mention of two female deities
whose names are associated with two Frisian terms for different types of
legal assembly, *bodthing* (to which those attending had to be summoned)
and *fimelthing* (called for a special purpose).[22] These legal parallels from
Frisian are particularly significant given the Germanic unit stationed in
north Britain, for the *Tuihanti* came from Twente in Holland and are
specified on one of the inscriptions as Frisians.[23]

The religious implications are equally clear. *Thingsus* is an epithet
applied to the god Mars, standing for the Germanic god Tiu by *interpretatio Romana*, who is accompanied by two feminine deities of a type
found in many inscriptions (often by Germani) to twin goddesses in the
Roman-occupied Rhineland. Justification for regarding *Thingsus* in a

---

[18] See below, pp. 130f, 132.   [19] Kuhn (1978), 232.   [20] Wesche (1937), 7.
[21] Gutenbrunner (1936), 24ff.; von See (1964), 117ff.; Beck (1984), 443; Innocente (1990), 48f.
[22] Gutenbrunner (1936), 30.   [23] *Ibid.*, pp. 25 (second inscription), 48.

religious as well as a legal light is further provided by the word's survival
in the place-name *Dinslaken* (= *lacus Martis*) and in the name of the day
of the week *dingsdag* (later *Dienstag*) as a variant of *tîsdag* and, like other
names of days, containing the name of a pagan god.[24] There is little
objection to postulating a double naming of this day of the week in the
lower Rhine area (as *Tiu* and as **Thingsa-*), nor to the designation of Tiu,
the early Germanic god of war before the rise of Wodan, as a god of law
as well in view of the fact that the Germanic legal assembly was also a
military assembly. Even though the passing of laws and judgments
remained in human hands, the meeting at which deliberations took
place was under the protection of a god.

From this we pass to the Germanic term for the legal assembly itself,
OHG *thing*.[25] Despite recent questioning there is no call to doubt the
connection between this word and Go. *þeihs* (like the neuter **þingsa-* a
neuter *s*-stem), denoting not simply 'time', but a time appointed for a
particular purpose (Gr. *kairós*). This suggestion that the Germanic *þing*
was an assembly recurring at an appointed time agrees with Tacitus's
remark about *certis diebus* and with the distinction between assemblies
convoked for a special purpose and those where a summons was not
called for (because of their regular recurrence at a fixed time). Between
Tacitus and the start of a written tradition in OHG there took place
many political and legal changes affecting the nature of this assembly.[26]
Where the migrations resulted in settlement on geographically extensive
colonial soil such meetings were no longer so feasible or frequent as in
the past, while the rise of large-scale kingship led to a concentration of
legal power. What had once been the legal rights of freemen of the tribe
was now invested more in the king or his representatives. The word *thing*
may still at times conservatively reflect earlier conditions, as when it
glosses *conventus populi* or when the Israelites are assembled for legislation
at Mount Sinai: *ding kisamanot uuard*.[27] Apart from such survivals,
however, political and legal changes amount to a gradual dissolution of
the Germanic idea of the *thing*, subjecting it to pressure from two directions.

In the first place, the word was restricted to a partial meaning of the
original concept.[28] That one of these restrictions should be 'time when

[24] *Ibid.*, p. 27; Beck (1984), 443.
[25] Karg-Gasterstädt (1958); Wenskus (1984), 444ff.; Innocente (1990), 39ff.
[26] Karg-Gasterstädt (1958), 4f.; Wenskus (1984), 445ff., 452. [27] Karg-Gasterstädt (1958), 5.
[28] *Ibid.*, pp. 4ff. (examples are taken from here).

an assembly is held' or 'time' at large (e.g. to render the idea of a 'reprieve in time, delay', in temporal constructions for 'until', in OE *þinggemearc* 'measurement of time') need not surprise us in view of the word's etymological link with Go. *þeihs*. In addition, *thing* could narrow its meaning to the 'place where an assembly was held' (it therefore translates *forum* or *synagoga* as a meeting-place), but also to the legal discussion or deliberation which took place there (when in the *Georgslied* the saint is taken to trial, *ze malo*, it is also *ze heuigemo dinge. daz thinc uuas marista*, vv.1 and 3f., where the adjectives point to the weightiness and importance of what was at issue there). In addition *thing* can also denote the result of such legal deliberation, either in the sense of 'judgment' (Otfrid says II 6,45f. that God's verdict would have been more favourable, *iz irgiange thanne zi beziremo thinge*, if Adam had not put the blame on Eve) or to mean 'treaty, agreement', as in the *Straßburger Eide*: 82,22. *Thing* can also denote the matter which comes up for legal decision, so that Pilate, sitting in judgment, can say to Christ that he has complete authority over the case (Otfrid IV 23,37: *giweltig ubar ellu thinu thing*). At this point the word *thing*, originally denoting a collective assembly dealing with matters affecting the whole tribe, has been narrowed down to a matter of personal concern.

Once this stage was reached *thing* could begin to render Latin terms such as *causa*, *res* or *negotium*, as was the case first with Otfrid and then frequently with Notker.[29] The result was to extract the word from the context of the tribal assembly and to generalise it to the point of denoting a matter, affair or process at large. In this extended usage *thing* could be the object of verbs like *phlegan* or *sih flîzan* and therefore denote 'matter, concern, task', it could vary with *werk* or *tât* (therefore meaning 'deed, action') or it could simply mean 'everything' (*alliu thing*) or any natural thing (God as the creator *allero dero dingo*). Although the word could still retain its legal force, particularly in verbal forms such as *thingon* 'to hold a trial, give judgment', *anathingon* 'to summon to a trial' or *firthingon* 'to appeal', with Otfrid *thingen* has been generalised to mean 'to hope, strive'.[30] Similarly, although nominal compounds still point to the legal origins of *thing* (e.g. *githingi* 'assembly' or *tagathing* 'trial'), Otfrid again broke away from the legal sphere in *woroltthing* 'sinful deeds of the world' and Notker in *lugithing* 'delusion', *uuehsaltthing* 'inconstancy' and *thingolîh* 'everything'.

This tug-of-war in two opposite semantic directions reflects how the

29 *Ibid.*, pp. 8ff.   30 *Ibid.*, pp. 12ff.

word *thing* lost its connection with the law as the tribal assembly ceased to be an institution of the tribe at large. (In Scandinavia, where this development did not take place, the dissolution of the legal meaning of the word did not occur, as is shown by Danish *Folketing* or Norwegian *Storting*.) Difficulties in maintaining the tribal assembly in its traditional form arose as a result of the migrations (the occupation of geographically more extensive areas, the rise of a more powerful kingship, the acquisition of greater authority by the *principes*), but these were increased by the growth of Frankish power, especially under the Carolingians (an incomparably greater geographical spread, the coexistence of different law-codes in one kingdom, a buttressing of royal power by theocratic concepts of Christian origin, the transition of oral law in the vernacular to written law in Latin, the institution of legally trained lay assessors, *Schöffen*, in place of justice administered at tribal assemblies).

If light can be thrown on Tacitus's description of the Germanic *concilium* by the word *thing*, similar information is provided by another term on what he says about how proposals were accepted or rejected. The OHG verb *phlegan* has cognates in OS and OE (*plegan*), but with a differentiation between the OE form (to indicate rapid or violent movement) and the employment of the continental ones as legal terms. The problem is to account for this disparity.[31]

In OE the verb *plegan* and the noun *plega* (modern English 'play') were used to indicate (violent) movement: of the body (*plegan* 'to dance', *hand-plega* 'fighting'), of the mind or feelings (*hyhtplega* 'joy', cf. Lat. *emotio*), but especially with weapons (*sweordplega* 'sword-play', *æscplega* 'spear-play') and in fighting (*wīgplega*, *gūþplega* 'combat'). The equivalent semantic function was normally performed in continental WG not by the cognate verb *phlegan*, but by *spilôn* 'to play': of the body (OS *spilôn* 'to dance'), of the mind or feelings (MHG *spilndiu vröide*) and of weapons (OS *wâpno spil*).[32]

By contrast, OHG and OS use the forms cognate with OE in a legal sense: the OHG noun *phlec*, alongside *karatan*, glosses *synodale in synodo consultum*, the verb *phligit* translates *consultat*, whilst OS *plegan* means 'to accept responsibility for something'.[33] The scene of Christ's trial provides most enlightenment on the legal function of these words.[34] In the *Heliand* Pilate wishes to play safe legally and therefore absolves himself of responsibility (5478: '*ne uuilliu ik thes uuihtes plegan*', *quathie*, / '*umbi thesan hêlagan mann*'), whilst the Jews twice affirm their readiness to take this

[31] Kauffmann (1918), 155ff.   [32] *Ibid.*, pp. 157ff.   [33] *Ibid.*, p. 162.   [34] *Ibid.*, pp. 160ff.

responsibility upon themselves (5482, 5485: '*uui uuilliat is alles plegan*'). In both these cases the verb *plegan* is used, denoting the collective assent of the Jews, gathered together as a legal assembly (5461: *hwarf*). The same word is used by Otfrid: again Pilate refuses to accept responsibility (IV 24,27: '*Ni will ih . . . therero dato plegan*') and again the Jews, constituting a legal assembly (IV 19,22: *biskofo thing*) take it upon themselves. In his description of the Last Judgment (likewise presented as a *thing* or *daga-thing*: V 19,1 and 4) Otfrid stresses that even the most fleeting thought will be judged there, by contrast with the way in which man is not held immediately accountable in this life for the deeds he manages to conceal (V 19,39: *Giborganero dato ni pligit man hiar nu thrato*). This legal usage in continental WG presupposes, applied to the perpetrator, a meaning 'to accept accountability for an offence' and, when said of those sitting in judgment, 'to accept responsibility and give (collective) assent to the execution of a verdict'. In either case the legal assembly (*thing, hwarf*) is gathered before the accused.

In order to tie up this legal meaning of continental WG with the variant meaning of OE (violent movement, especially of weapons) we need to turn back to Tacitus, who says of the barbarians' practice at the assembly that if a proposal did not please them they roared out their disagreement, but if they approved they clashed their spears. In other words, the beating of weapons by those who constituted the *thing* was a form of voting, granting approval (*armis laudare*) and accepting legal responsibility for any decision reached.[35] The shaking and beating of weapons in this context provides a common starting point for the legal usage of *phlegan/plegan* in OHG and OS and also for the rapid movement, especially with weapons, conveyed by the OE word. The confirmation by Tacitus suggests that this was early legal practice in Germania, yet the word we have been concerned with is only WG. However, apart from phonological evidence suggesting that the word was of considerable antiquity ON uses another term, *vápnatak* 'consent expressed by brandishing weapons', for the same purpose, as when the verdict of outlawing was reached by weapons being beaten together.[36] This ON word was borrowed into OE in Danelaw as *wæpengetæc*, explained (in agreement with *armis laudare* with Tacitus) as *armorum confirmatio*.

In late OHG Notker's linguistic usage shows that *phlegan* has extracted

---

[35] Cf. Tacitus, *Historiae* v 17; Kauffmann (1918), 163.
[36] Kauffmann (1918), 165f. (and p. 165, fn. 4).

itself from the strictly legal sphere by designating not simply administration of justice, but administration at large.[37] As such it was used to render words like *curare* and *ministrare*, but at least retained a connection with the Germanic function of the word by the feature of responsibility. That this responsibility could be seen as a possible risk is clear from the word's occasional association with the idea of danger: OHG *phligida* therefore glosses *periculum*, OE *pliht* means 'danger' (cf. modern English 'plight').

The gradual widening of this word's usage beyond the legal sphere resembles the position with the term *thing* and it is probable that similar legal changes underlie the semantic development of both words.[38] The earliest function of *phlegan* passed into desuetude once the Germanic custom of *armorum confirmatio* by the whole assembly was replaced by a new practice in reaching a decision, no longer by the primitive and undifferentiated clashing of weapons, but by a vocal means of expressing agreement or disagreement (cf. OS *ênwordi* 'unanimous'). Here, too, legal innovations of the Carolingian period were of decisive importance, for the introduction of lay assessors (*Schöffen*) responsible to the emperor for the administration of justice imposed limitations on the legislative rights of the old assembly. Whereas every freeman of the tribe had earlier had the right to take an active part at the *thing* and express his approval in the time-honoured way, now this right was confined to the assessors, whilst the freeman was entitled only to attend. These law-reforms, characteristic of a far-flung Empire with a more centralised authority, constituted as much of a semantic crisis for *phlegan* as they did for *thing*.[39]

The right to bear arms and to play a part in the tribal assembly was also a duty: both were the prerogative of freemen in Germanic society as distinct from the semi-free and the unfree. With that distinction we touch upon the concept of legal freedom in Germania, as expressed in OHG by the adjective *frî*, attested in all the Germanic languages (in ON in the compound *frjáls* < **fríhals*).[40] To understand the legal force of this word we shall have to consider it in connection with the related words *frijōn* 'to be fond of, to love' and *fridu* 'peace', bearing in mind that the IE cognates of the adjective had the semantic force of 'own', especially in connection with kinsmen and parts of the body. From this function of denoting one's own kinsmen and members of one's own tribe the

---

[37] *Ibid.*, pp. 169f.   [38] *Ibid.*, pp. 168f.   [39] Thompson (1965), 44; Much (1967), 209.
[40] Scheller (1950), 23ff.; Mezger (1956), 12ff.

concept of legitimate, fully fledged membership of the kindred or tribe (as opposed to unfree slaves from other tribes) evolved, leading to the idea 'free' (by birth). The evidence for this semantic development from 'own' to 'free' can be found for each step in OE, which in this respect can be regarded as typical of Germanic at large.

A starting-point, where the meaning 'own' occurs in the context of blood-kinship, is provided by OE *frēobrōðor* 'one's own brother', *frēodohtor*, *frēomǣg* 'blood-kinsman', *consanguineus*.[41] It would be wrong to argue from the emotional force of the verb *frijōn* that the first element of these compounds meant 'dear, beloved', if only because *frēomǣg* occurs in the context of Cain killing Abel, who is therefore seen as his own brother, not as one dear to him. Parallel with these compounds is *frēobearn* 'one's own (therefore legitimate) child', so that when Christ is described as *frēobearn godes* this is the equivalent of the formula *godes āgen bearn* 'God's own son'.[42] The legal implications of this compound (only a child of one's own is legally qualified as one's heir and successor) are relevant only to the situation of those for whom legitimacy of birth had practical consequences, i.e. in Germanic society the nobles and freemen, not the unfree. This amounts to a semantic restriction whereby an original concept 'one's own children' now meant 'the legitimate offspring of the free members of society', a restriction underlined when the ancestor to whom these *frēobearn* trace back their descent is also mentioned. This limitation of the word to a particular class in society also applies to the variant *frēoman* or to the adjective *frēo/frig* used as a noun, especially when they are contrasted in legal texts with *þeow* 'slave'.[43] At this point the semantic development of the OE adjective from 'own' (in the context of kinship) to 'free' (in the context of social birth) is completed and we have reached the stage illustrated by other Germanic languages which, lacking testimony for the word's prehistory which OE still shows, use the adjective only in the sphere of social birth, 'free' as opposed to 'unfree' (Go. *jaþþe skalkos jaþþe frijái*, OHG *edo scalch edo frier*).[44] When in an OHG legal text Franks are described as *frî* this is not meant as a contrast between a tribe boasting of its independence and others which are subjugated, but as an internal distinction between Franks of free birth and those who are unfree.[45] This social distinction, conferring or withholding certain legal rights, stands at the beginning of the written history of OHG *frî*.

[41] Scheller (1950), 25ff.; Mezger (1956), 13f.   [42] Scheller (1950), 27ff., 45ff.
[43] *Ibid.*, pp. 33f.   [44] Wulfila I Cor. 12, 13; OHG *Benediktinerregel* 199, 35 (p. 17).
[45] *Würzburger Markbeschreibung* 116, 64. Cf. Scheller (1950), 46 and 48, fn. 1.

The cognate word in IE, meaning 'own', was applied not only to one's kinsmen, however, but to parts of one's body. Traces of this latter usage survive in different Germanic languages (*auf freiem Fuß sein*, 'to have a free hand'), but most important is the conjunction of the adjective with another part of the body, the neck, to convey the status of freedom. Forms corresponding to OHG *frîhals* occur in all the Germanic languages, both as an adjective meaning 'free, not in bondage' and as a noun 'freedom'.[46] The function of this word was more precise than this, for in origin the first element still stood close to meaning 'own', so that the compound denoted someone who, by contrast to the bondsman, was still 'master of his own neck' and whose body was therefore legally inviolable (unless he forfeited this right by a criminal offence which made an outlaw of him).[47] The employment of the word for 'neck' in the second part of this compound is best explained by the variation between 'head' and 'neck' in legal terminology (*decollare* alongside *decapitare*) and by the use of *hals* in prescribing punishments for different offences.[48] Both parts of the compound place it firmly within legal vocabulary.

Of greater interest than the use of *frîhals* as a noun ('freedom') is the occurrence of another compound: OE *frēodōm*, OHG *frîtuam*, where again both parts have legal force.[49] The second element exists as an independent word which has survived its adaptation to forming abstract suffixes. This independent word had a wide range of meanings whose nucleus was clearly legal: 'doom, judgment, sentence', but also 'power, dominion, authority', which suggests a more precise original meaning for some of the compounds than if it were no more than a suffix for forming an abstract noun. If OE *cyninges dōm* denotes the king's power of decision (judicial or otherwise), the compound *cyningdōm* stands for the ruler's power or authority (and then the region over which it is exercised).[50] Various degrees of legal-political power are expressed by OHG parallels (*kuningdôm, keisartuom, herizogtuom*) as well as in OS *kuningdôm, kêsurdôm*, with meanings such as the authority of a king, an emperor, a duke. These terms could also express the rank or status of such an officeholder, which explains the formation of an OS compound like *jungardôm* 'discipleship' and the eventual function of this suffix to form an abstract noun.

It is possible to relate OE *frēodōm* to this group of compounds, regarding the first element as an adjective used as a noun, so that the word

---

[46] Scheller (1950), 58ff.   [47] *Ibid.*, p. 59.   [48] Mezger (1956), 16.
[49] Scheller (1950), 63ff.; Mezger (1956), 17ff.   [50] Scheller (1950), 66f.

denoted the status of a freeman, by contrast with that of a bondsman (*þeowdōm*). On the other hand, *-dōm* can occasionally be linked with an adjective, even in a legal context. In OE *wīsdōm* more commonly means 'wisdom' (but also, in agreement with the use of *wīs* as a technical legal term, with legal implications).[51] More informative is OHG *wîstuom* 'verdict, legal decision', where the original meaning 'decision reached by one knowledgeable in the law, by a *legis peritus*' is more readily tangible. If we interpret *frîtuam* similarly it would denote the active aspect of a freeman's status, his right to act on his own judgment and to take the legal initiative, so that it translates *suo arbitrio viventes* 'living by their own will' (in MHG *vrîtuom* denotes 'privilege'). *Arbitrium* was also glossed by *selptoom* 'one's own judgment', a term which corresponds to the legal practice of self-judgment, known in ON as *sjálfdæmi* 'right to judge in one's own case'.[52] According to this explanation *frîtuam* originally designated the legal privilege of self-judgment enjoyed by a freeman, hence the status of a freeman. Whether we take the first element as an adjective used as a noun or not, the compound originally denoted the legal status of those of free birth.

The word *frî* is also attested in a verbal form where we have to distinguish two formative periods (and two usages).[53] The later one, represented by OE *frēogan* 'to make free, liberate', derives from the adjective 'free', could only be formed once the word's meaning had developed from 'own' to 'free', and presents no new problems. The earlier usage, represented by OS *friehan* or Go. *frijōn* 'to treat as a friend, to love', stands closer to the earlier meaning of the adjective (and has parallels in Slavonic). In addition to meaning 'to love' (clear in Gothic by employment in contrast to *fijan* 'to hate') the verb also occurs in England and in Germany in the context of courtship (cf. German *freien*) as a step leading to a legally contracted marriage, so that it belonged as much to legal vocabulary as did *êwa* when in late OHG it was confined to the meaning *matrimonium*. The formation of this verb implies an original meaning 'to treat as *frî*, to make *frî*', where *frî* still had the sense of 'one's own (kinsmen)', since marriage is the means by which a kindred based on blood ties is enlarged by the admission of an outsider who by that legal act comes to enjoy the rights and protection of that kindred.

The idea of protection is also conveyed by another word belonging to this productive and socially important Germanic stem, the CG term represented by OHG *fridu*, the most widespread word in Germania for

[51] *Ibid.*, p. 67.   [52] *Ibid.*, pp. 67f.; Mezger (1956), 17f.   [53] Scheller (1950), 88ff.

'peace', formed from **fri-* and denoting the state or condition prevailing amongst those who regard each other as their own kindred.[54] Whereas in modern eyes the antithesis of peace is war, in Germania (and through much of the Middle Ages) the contrast was rather with feuding and violence within a community.[55] Instead of a modern contradiction between violence and non-violence the early history of the word *fridu* is concerned with the destabilisation or the maintenance of the rule of law within society. It was this rule of law by upholding internal peace which provided Germanic society with what security and protection it enjoyed. Attesting the earlier meaning from our written vernacular sources is rendered particularly difficult because of the influence, inevitable in sources written by clerics, of the Christian idea of peace (especially the New Testament) and even Roman ideas (*pax Romana*). Although, corresponding to its formation with a stem denoting one's own kindred, the legal concept of *fridu* was originally confined to the kindred, it later expanded its scope (as did *frî*) to embrace the community at large, the king's peace in the sense of protection and security which he was to provide.[56]

Accordingly, a common meaning of *fridu* is 'protection, help' rather than 'peace'. In the *Heliand friðu* is thus varied by *helpa* and by *mundburd* (just as OE combines *friþ* with *mundbyrde* in a legal context) and the verb (OS *friðôn*, OE *friðian*, OHG *gefridôn*) denotes 'protect, provide security'.[57] In the *Heliand* Christ as *friðubarn godes* is seen as a protector of men (*liudio uuard*) and governs verbs like *uuardon* and *nerien* 'rescue'.[58] A condition of peace may be the result of this, but the primary meaning was the protection (legal and military) at first provided by the kindred community (any offender expelled from it was deprived of such protection and assistance, was outlawed, *friedlos*), then by the ruler, whether secular or Christ as *adiutor* and *protector*.

How far *fridu* 'protection' was distant from the modern concept 'peace' should be clear from the fact that a kindred or ruler provided security against external and internal foes and that Christ brought protection by victoriously struggling against the Devil. It is in this sense, rather than as a peace-bringer, that the author of the *Heliand* presented Him to his Saxon audience. A similar idea was also implicit in some usages of Latin *pax*, whether deriving from classical Roman ideas

---

[54] Scheller (1950), 113ff.; Mezger (1956), 21ff.; Ilkow (1968), 135ff.; Hagenlocher (1992), 19ff.; Tiefenbach (1995), 594ff.   [55] Scheller (1950), 113; Hagenlocher (1992), 316.

[56] Mezger (1956), 21, 22f.; Ilkow (1968), 136.

[57] Mezger (1956), 23f.; Ilkow (1968), 137; Hagenlocher (1992), 26; Tiefenbach (1995), 595.

[58] Vv. 983f., 2099ff., 3836f.

(meaning 'rule' as in *pax Romana* or 'assistance of the gods') or from Christian reinterpretation (Christ as *princeps pacis*, bringing assistance under His rule). The possibility of equating *pax* in this sense with Germanic *fridu* provided an obvious linguistic bridge, making it possible for *fridu* to become the conventional equivalent of *pax*. At this point the possibility of a loan-meaning comes into play, for Latin *pax* also meant 'peace' in something more like our sense of the word (it could be contrasted with *bellum* and used in the sense of 'peace-treaty' or 'armistice'). With the establishment of *fridu* as the ready equivalent of *pax* it was now possible for the vernacular word to expand its semantic force by taking over the further meaning of *pax*, as when Simeon's departure *in pace* is translated by OS *friðuuuâra*, literally a 'peace-treaty or pact'.[59] What had been implicit in Germanic *fridu* (or a secondary result) has now come to the fore under the influence of Christian usage.

In conclusion we come to the vernacular terms used for 'judge' (verb and noun) and 'judgment', where Latin made use of related words: *iudicare*, *iudex*, *iudicium*.[60] In meeting this lexical need OHG at first made use of three words.

The first is *dôm*, which we now treat not as the second element in a compound, but as a legal term in its own right. The nucleus of this word's wide spread of meanings was legal, from which we must now isolate its ability to render 'judge' and 'judgment'. It was enabled to do this because of its use (probably CG) to mean 'to have or express an opinion' (cf. elevated English 'to deem') and the application of this usage to the legal context.[61] We have no indication that the Germanic legal assembly, in reaching a decision or verdict, made use of anyone whose function could be called that of a judge; instead, a proposal based on an individual opinion was made (who expressed this opinion we are not told) and then accepted or rejected in the manner we have seen with *phlegan*. The proposed verdict and the agreed verdict were expressed by the same word, meaning both 'opinion' and 'judgment' (cf. modern English 'in my judgment' or German *nach meinem Urteil*).

In this legal sense the word is employed in all the Germanic languages (although legal use is attested in Gothic for the verb, but not the noun).[62] Alongside this legal function *dōmjan* in Gothic also shows the meaning 'to hold or express an opinion' from which its technical legal function may

---

[59] Ilkow (1968), 137f.   [60] Freudenthal (1949), 54ff.; Köbler (1970), 57ff.
[61] Freudenthal (1949), 95f.   [62] *Ibid.*, pp. 54ff.

have arisen. This more general meaning of the verb is attested for the Gothic noun *dōms* 'renown' (other people's opinion of a person), but also in OE for the noun *dōm* 'honour, praise' and the verb *dēman* 'to think', in ON for the noun *dómr* 'opinion' and the verb *dœma* 'to talk, express opinions' and in OS for the noun *dōm* 'honour, praise'. Within OHG the word and its variants need to be looked at for their legal usage according to dialects if we are to assess the interplay with the two other legal terms.[63] In its verbal form *tuomen* the word is not attested in Bavarian or Alemannic, but occurs frequently enough in the Franconian dialects (including *Tatian*) and in OS (including *Heliand*). As a noun (*tuomo* 'judge') the word is again absent from Bavarian and Alemannic, but present in Franconian (*Tatian*), yet this time not attested in OS. The other nominal form (*tuom* 'judgment') is found on a restricted number of occasions in Bavarian, but also in Franconian (*Tatian*) and OS. From this geographical distribution it emerges that the word is only rarely attested in Bavarian and not at all in Alemannic, whilst even in so early a Franconian text as *Isidor* it is missing, having given ground to the third of the words we are considering, *irteilen*. One reason for this incipient eclipse of a CG legal term in Germany may have to do with the fact that the word shared a legal with a more general, non-legal function, a fact attested as much in OHG as in the other Germanic languages.[64] Although this spread of semantic functions may account for the genesis of the word's legal use it meant that it lacked the precision of expressly legal terminology. Already in Gothic an explicitly technical purpose was better served by another word (*stojan*),[65] just as in Germany *tuomen* succumbed to the word which replaced it in *Isidor*: *arteilen*. Even OE *dōm*, in the sense of 'judgment, decree', safeguarded for longer by the conservatism of OE legal vocabulary, eventually lost ground to a NG loanword from Danelaw, *lög* 'law'.

The second word, represented by OHG *suona* 'judgment', is narrower in scope: as a legal term it is only German, and within OHG it is really attested only in Bavarian and Alemannic, the dialects largely or completely untouched by the first word.[66] (The handful of attestations in Franconian and OS, by contrast with the far greater number from Bavarian and Alemannic, have been regarded as reflections of the latter.) The word survives in modern German *sühnen* 'to expiate a crime' and *versöhnen* 'to conciliate', suggesting that the variants attested in the UG

---

[63] *Ibid.*, pp. 58ff.; Köbler (1970), 74ff.   [64] Freudenthal (1949), 92ff.
[65] On the isolated occurrence of this word in OHG see below, pp. 318f.
[66] Freudenthal (1949), 58ff.; Köbler (1970), 77f.

dialects of OHG derived their legal force from attempts at conciliation between two parties in conflict and at imposing punishment on an offender.[67] In the sense of conflicts which were settled at court the aim was to effect a conciliation between the parties, to bring about a settlement (whose terms were decided by the court) in place of open physical conflict. The court's decision, imposing this settlement, was therefore a *suona*, the judge who was responsible was a *suoneo* (or *suonari*) and his activity was expressed by the verb *suonen*. In this case, too, the evidence of *Muspilli* is particularly valuable for explaining the range of a legal term: from 'settlement' the word *suona* could develop the meaning 'court' (where this settlement was brought about), whilst the verb implies both 'to adjudicate' and 'to pronounce a verdict'.[68]

The spread of these three variants in the two UG dialects is as follows. The verb *suonen* appears in Bavarian above all in the glossaries of the *Abrogans* group, as well as in Alemannic, e.g. in the *Benediktinerregel* (with only scattered traces beyond this UG area). *Suoneo/suonari* 'judge' (a *nomen agentis*) is found in the earliest Bavarian glossaries and in the Alemannic *Benediktinerregel* and *Murbacher Hymnen* (again with an isolated outrider in Franconian). The other noun, *suona*, is likewise confined to Bavarian and Alemannic, apart from two late glosses (Mainz and Essen). Whatever the degree of restriction of these legal terms to south Germany may be, it is difficult to find an explanation for this. It has been argued that the ability to impose a legal settlement on parties in conflict presupposes the development of a strong central authority, but no convincing reason has been advanced why we should accept this more readily for the Bavarian and Alemannic areas than for the Franks.[69] Indeed, we might rather expect the opposite. It is clear that by their use of *suona*, etc. Bavarian and Alemannic stand apart from the rest of Germany before the third word, *irteilen*, begins to expand and introduce a dialectal regrouping.

This third word differs from the others: like *suona*, it is confined to Germany, but differs from it in being well represented in all dialects.[70] It might seem unsafe to claim the word for OHG alone when it is also attested for OE and OS, but in these languages the word must be regarded as a loan from outside. OE *ordāl* betrays its Frankish origin by the prefix *or-* and by its restriction to the *iudicium Dei*, a legal practice borrowed from the continent,[71] while a similar influence of OHG may be

---

[67] Freudenthal (1949), 77ff.   [68] *Ibid.*, pp. 8of.   [69] *Ibid.*, pp. 85f.
[70] *Ibid.*, pp. 58ff.; Köbler (1970), 78ff. Cf. also Mezger (1957), 62ff.
[71] Freudenthal (1949), 124.

suspected with OS *urdêli* (in the general sense of 'judgment'), occurring but once and with a prefix different from what might be expected (as in OS *adêlian*). However derivative OS *urdêli* may therefore be, the use of alliteration in the *Heliand* (and also in the legal language of Germanic) helps us to reconstruct how this word may have acquired its legal force (even though the restricted range of alliterative verse in OHG means that we lack parallels for the area of origin). Given the general, non-legal meaning of OHG *irteilen* and OS *adêlian* 'to grant, hand out', a phrase like OS *dômos adêlian*, with the personal object in the dative, meant 'to grant judgment to', 'to pass judgment on'.[72] From this construction it was a short step to dropping the direct object (*dômos*) while retaining the dative object so that the verb now expressed a legal meaning by itself. Finally, after the sense of the original construction had been lost, the personal object could be expressed in the accusative (e.g. *Predigtsammlung A* 156,6f: *die irteilo ih selbo = iudicabo*).

The verb *irteilen* in a legal sense is attested in Bavarian: not in the earliest sources, but in later glossaries and in the sermon just quoted (eleventh century). The same chronological distinction is true of Alemannic (where Notker uses it frequently for *iudicare*). In Franconian the position is markedly different: not merely is the word attested frequently, it also occurs in early sources such as *Isidor* and the *Monseer Fragmente*. In OS the *Heliand* author uses *adêlian* seven times. *Irteilare*, the *nomen agentis*, occurs relatively frequently and only in late sources (both Bavarian and Alemannic). The other noun, *urteili*, is better attested. In Bavarian and Alemannic its equation with *iudicium* as a legal term is established, but only in later texts (again, especially with Notker), whereas in Franconian it is attested much earlier (*Isidor* and the *Monseer Fragmente*). In OS the word occurs only once.

From a combined geographical and chronological survey of this legal terminology it is clear that *irteilen* was the latest to establish itself: in the Franconian dialects (as well as in OS) it replaced *tuomen*, whilst in Bavarian and Alemannic it spread after *suonen* (which itself seems to have come after an earlier *tuomen*). The geographical implications of this chronological grouping are equally informative. *Irteilen* (the word on which we must concentrate because of its ultimate victory in the whole of the German language-area) cannot have begun its expansion either in the Bavarian or Alemannic area (where it is attested too late) or in north Germany (in the *Heliand* it has only just begun to establish itself

---

[72] *Ibid.*, pp. 75f.

alongside the older *dômian*, whilst the East Franconian *Tatian* knows only *tuomen*). In other words, the origin of this word's spread must be sought south of the OS area, west of East Franconian and north of Alemannic and Bavarian, i.e. in the western-lying Franconian area.[73] This is an area from which other legal terms, for example *urkundo* 'witness',[74] expanded into other areas of Germany, accompanying the extension of Frankish political power, reaching Bavaria and Alemannia as early as the Merovingians and Saxony under the Carolingians. It was possibly in connection with particular forms of Frankish legal administration (district courts of justice, royal courts of justice and the employment of *missi dominici* in judicial affairs) that Frankish legal terminology was carried throughout Germany.[75]

[73] *Ibid.*, pp. 74f.   [74] *Ibid.*, pp. 27ff.

[75] *Ibid.*, pp. 184ff. Only in late OHG are the three Latin terms *iudicare, iudex, iudicium* expressed by terms likewise formed from the same stem: *rihten, rihtare, gerihte.* Cf. Köbler (1970), 82f., 102ff.

CHAPTER 3

Kinship

The earliest detailed information about the Germanic kindred and its importance in society to reach us in written form comes from Tacitus, but even he discusses it somewhat unsystematically. In *Germania* 7 he discusses the grouping of battle formations by kindreds. Chapter 12 treats of punishments, with redress being made to the injured man's kindred in the case of a capital offence. Chapter 20 emphasises the importance of the avunculate (sons are closely tied to their uncles, which establishes a link between two kindreds brought together by marriage). Chapter 21 is concerned with feuds between kindreds and their settlement (the *satisfactio* was received by the whole kindred, so that the offence was not just to the individual, but to his kindred).

Already by Caesar's time Germanic society consisted of kindreds, constituting (instead of the family) the basic units of society and grouped together to form larger units or tribes.[1] In a pre-state tribal society kinship relations were the main source of protection for the individual, promising him legal and military assistance and, on the basis of wergeld, providing him with a badge of status.[2] The kindred also made claims on the individual, involving him in any feud or legal obligation in which it might be engaged. Other bonds came to reinforce, or cut across, this network of kindreds, but as long as they offered the main promise of protection which could not be held out by any central authority they remain the hallmark of a tribal society which has not yet made the transition to a state society.

In Germanic society the individual counted for nothing alone; his legal status depended on his kinsmen to the extent that a man without kinsmen was the equivalent of an unfree man, unable to take part in legal or political decisions and deprived of rights.[3] How the kindred

---

[1] Thompson (1965), 15, 17.   [2] Campbell (1991), 168.
[3] Kroeschell (1960), 3f.; Schlesinger (1963a), 292 and fn. 11 (quoting Stenton and Whitelock).

provided legal support in particular is still apparent in the *Lex Salica* in connection with such questions as oath-helpers, the payment and receipt of the wergeld by kinsmen, the relative role of kinship degrees in the process of compensation.[4] By oath-helping is meant the recognised procedure of a plaintiff or defendant supporting his case with the assistance of a number of co-swearers, known in the early codifications of Germanic law by such terms as *consacramentales, sacramentales* or *iuratores*.[5] Characteristic of this legal practice in Germania is the fact that these legal helpers were chiefly found amongst a man's kinsmen. Although it is attested in the *Lex Salica*, the practice of calling on kinsmen to swear on one's behalf was progressively called into question as social conditions changed. Provisions in some of the Anglo-Saxon laws suggest that the king, the representative of a state form of society which can now dispense with the kindred as a source of legal protection or even see it in competition with the king's authority as the guarantee of this protection, could mistrust the validity of an oath taken by a group in support of one of its own kind.[6] In quite a different context a similar questioning of this practice comes to the fore in the OHG *Muspilli* when the difference between what awaits men at the Last Judgment and contemporary legal practice is brought home by the contrast between standing alone before God as judge and appearing at a secular court with the assistance of kinsmen (v. 57: *dar ni mac denne mak andremo helfan vora demo muspille*).[7] What is criticised as suspicious in a king's eyes in Anglo-Saxon laws or as irrelevant to the author of an OHG religious text was a practice from the Germanic past, now under pressure from different directions.

The other form of protection provided by the kindred concerns blood-vengeance and the prosecution of a feud, for these act as a disincentive to violence and therefore offer protection in advance. It is not enough to define a feud as a state of hostility between kindreds; we must extend it to the threat of such hostility, but also, if the mere threat fails to prevent the outbreak of actual hostility, to a settlement on terms acceptable to both parties by means of an established procedure.[8] In other words, the feud is a means of settling disputes between kindreds through violence or negotiation or both. The feud, or more precisely the obligation to take part in it against another kindred together with the knowledge that one is similarly protected by one's own kinsmen, defined how far a kindred extended and provided a powerful force working for

---

[4] Schlesinger (1963a), 294; Murray (1983), 135ff.   [5] Schwab (1972), 107, n. 193.
[6] Schlesinger (1963a), 292, fn. 11 (quoting Stenton).   [7] Kolb (1964), 6ff.
[8] Wallace-Hadrill (1962), 122.

its unity.[9] For this unity to be achieved, however, the external obligation (to take up arms against another kindred) had to be reinforced by a matching internal duty not to enter into violent conflict with one's own kinsmen, to observe the peace within the kindred which alone enabled it to inflict (or threaten) violence on its external foes. In this sense peace, when applied to the internal condition of the kindred, embraced not merely the state of non-violence amongst kinsmen, but also the protection of the kindred's members by their readiness to act collectively against any external threat.

Central to feuding is the idea of vengeance, the willingness of all members of a kindred to defend one of their number and to obtain redress for him.[10] The importance of this idea at a time when no central state authority existed is clear, for it constituted the best available protection for the individual; the knowledge that an attack on one person would be regarded by his kinsmen as an attack on all acted as a restraining force. If a conflict nonetheless broke out it was waged not between individuals, but collectively between kindreds, as is best revealed by the way in which satisfaction could be obtained by vengeance on any member of the culprit's kindred, not necessarily on the perpetrator himself. An offence to one was therefore an offence to all, as is most pithily expressed by Gregory of Tours in the case of a feud involving a woman with the words: *ad ulciscendam humilitatem generis sui.*[11] In this case the kindred exacts vengeance from one of its members who is felt to have disgraced it; a refusal to act thus would have brought even greater shame upon the kindred. An example like this shows, even in the language used, just what difficulties the Church had to face in dealing with such a mentality, for the word *humilitas,* in Germanic eyes the 'humiliation' or 'shame' done to the kindred, was for the Christian the virtue of humility. This virtue, including even a readiness to forgive an insult, was the undoing of Sigbert of Essex who, so Bede reports, was killed by his kinsmen who complained that he had been too ready to forgive his enemies and had thereby brought dishonour on his kindred.[12] Such forgiveness and willingness to abandon the duty of feuding dealt a shocking blow to the kindred as a central support of Germanic society.

Despite these two examples, which for all the light they shed on the mentality of the feud must be regarded as exceptions where the theory breaks down, the requirement was that peace should obtain within the

[9] Geary (1988), 52.   [10] Genzmer (1951), 130f.
[11] *Historiae* vi 36 (vol. ii, p. 62); Wallace-Hadrill (1962), 138.   [12] *Historia ecclesiastica* iii 22.

kindred and that the need for self-protection against other kindreds demanded a state of non-violence within. The Germanic word corresponding to OHG *sippa* thus develops two meanings: both 'kindred, kinship' and 'peace'. Similarly, the OHG word *friunt*, meaning 'kinsman' (but also 'friend'), is cognate with *fridu* 'peace'. However much Gregory's Franks and Bede's East Saxons may have felt it incumbent on them to punish a kinsman who had disgraced them, they are exceptions that prove the rule: within the kindred peace was meant to hold sway.

Peace was also theoretically the state which should obtain between kindreds, so that if a feud broke out an established procedure was called for to reach a settlement. No tribal society could afford to be permanently weakened (against other tribes or Rome) by an unending series of internal feuds and in a conflict between ill-matched kindreds the weaker would have an obvious interest in seeking a peaceful settlement.[13] The payment of a *satisfactio* served this purpose, even in the case of a killing, and its widespread acceptance shows that in a tribal society an alternative to central authority had to be found to restore peace. Just as the kindred as a whole was obliged to take part in the feud, so were all members involved in the payment of a wergeld: both the deed and its settlement concerned not simply the individual perpetrator, but all his kinsmen. Even if the perpetrator and his victim were more closely concerned (in finding the means of a *satisfactio* and in receiving it) this did not exclude the other members of each kindred. The result was that when, for example, composition was agreed upon for a case of homicide this frequently involved not merely the guilty man and the heirs of the deceased, but also a larger or smaller number of kinsmen on either side, so that the wergeld was collected from a variety of kinsmen on the perpetrator's side, but also divided up amongst the members of the receiving kindred. Whilst later, with the rise of state societies, it was the king who maintained or restored peace, this task earlier fell to those who were directly involved, not as individuals, but as kindreds.

That peace was as much tied up with the practice of offering a *satisfactio* or wergeld as it was with terms for the kindred or kinsman (OHG *sippa, friunt*) has been shown from a Gothic word.[14] Wulfila translated Gr. *eirḗne* 'peace' by *gawaírþi*, a neuter *ja*-stem formed with the collective prefix *ga-* on the same pattern as *gawaúrdi* 'conversation' (cf. *waúrd*

[13]　Genzmer (1951), 130f.; Schlesinger (1963a), 290f.; Murray (1983), 137.
[14]　Kauffmann (1913), 321f.

'word'). Derivatives in this group are formed from a noun so that it is likely that *gawaírþi* was formed not from the adjective *waírþs* 'worth, valuable', but from the noun *waírþ* 'worth, price'. Since this noun is used by Wulfila as the equivalent of *pretium* to denote an object of value which could be used in payment or exchange, it follows that *gawaírþi* originally denoted a number of such objects, the equivalent of what we should term 'money' (even though actual coins need not be involved). Wulfila's use of this word for 'peace' implies that it was also used in the legal sense of a composition payment made in settlement of a conflict. The Gothic verb *gagawaírþjan* therefore originally meant 'to reach an agreement about the composition to be paid to settle a dispute' and could mean 'to be reconciled'. Here at least Germanic feuding, or rather the procedure developed for putting an end to it, could be harmonised with the Christian view of peace.

Already with Tacitus it was clear that the larger and more ramified a kindred was the greater its chances were of surviving the vicissitudes of a violence-prone society without the overarching protection of a state. To increase the strength of a kindred various artificial methods could be employed to pass beyond the immediate ties of blood.[15]

Marriage is the most frequent way in which a kindred was renewed and enlarged and we have already seen in the case of German *freien* 'to court' that this institution was the means of enlarging a kindred based on blood by admitting an outsider who now enjoyed the protection of her new kindred as well as the old. For a kindred to conduct a prudent marriage policy with other kindreds meant enlarging the scope of the protection it could enjoy, provided that the wife's kindred was prepared to assist the husband in any emergency as much as if he were a kinsman of theirs.[16] In this way a protective peace could be established between two kindreds in much the same way as, on a higher political level, a queen is married in *Beowulf* in order to strengthen peace between two peoples and is accordingly described as *friðusibb folca* (v. 2017). Whether the compound means 'protective peace' or combines two different terms for 'peace' or suggests that peace or protection (*friðu*) was established by an artificial kinship (*sibb*) is open to discussion, but beyond doubt here is the function of marriage to bring about peace.

If there were doubts about the precise semantic function of *sibb* in

---

[15] *Germania* 20; Pappenheim (1908), 304ff.; Genzmer (1951), 133; Nolte (1990), 130.
[16] Wenskus (1961), 26f.

Beowulf, there is testimony from elsewhere to show that this word denoting kinship by birth was also used to suggest kinship by marriage. In OHG glosses the noun *sibba* renders kinship by blood (*propinquitas*), but also by marriage (*affinitas*), just as the adjective *sibbi* renders both *consanguineus* and *affinis,* where the latter term in each case in Latin is confined to a relationship established by marriage.[17] How constant this usage could remain throughout OHG is shown by Notker, who uses the noun *sippa* both for *propinquitas* and for *affinitas,* and the verb *gesippôn* for 'to join in marriage'.[18] This extension of kinship is not confined to OHG, for in ON the cognate word, generally in the plural form *sifjar,* designates kinship by marriage, whilst *sifjungr* and *sifkona* refer to relatives by affinity, and *sifjaslit* has been so much restricted to the marriage relationship that it stands for 'adultery'.[19]

Another term which illustrates the union of two kindreds by marriage and which also strikingly confirms Tacitus is OHG *ôheim* (cf. OE *ēam*), rendering *avunculus* specifically with reference to the mother's brother.[20] As such, the word provides a link between two kindreds which goes beyond the woman who was adopted into the new kindred. The reconstructed PG form **awahaima-* consists of two elements, the first of which is cognate with Lat. *avus* 'grandfather, ancestor on the mother's side' and Go. *awo* 'grandmother'. A contracted form **auhaima-* would have led regularly to the OHG form, whilst loss of the intervocalic -*h*- would have led to OE *ēam* and MDu. *ôm.* The second element has occasioned more dissent, but rather than postulate otherwise unattested Celtic parallels it is safer to see in it the standard Germanic term for 'homestead', so that the word is to be understood as a *bahuvrihi* compound meaning 'he who has the home of the maternal grandfather' (as his own home). This presupposes that the uncle as the heir and owner of the maternal grandfather's homestead takes over the duty of protecting his sister and also her son. Protection was owed to this son not as the nephew of his mother's brother, but rather because of his descent from his grandfather (OHG *eninchil,* modern German *Enkel* 'grandson' is a diminutive of OHG *ano* 'grandfather', meaning therefore originally 'little grandfather').[21] The mother's brother who had inherited the homestead of their father thereby took over responsibility for maintaining the earlier protective link between grandfather and grandson. If one of the primary functions of the kindred was to provide protection in a troubled society the role of

---

[17] Herold (1941), 130, 280.   [18] Sehrt (1962), 177.
[19] Kuhn (1971a), 416 (but see also p. 418 on *sifjaslit*).   [20] Much (1932), 46ff.; Mezger (1960), 296ff.
[21] Hermann (1918), 215f.

the avunculate demonstrates how this could be extended from one kindred to another as a result of marriage. It was already clear to Tacitus that a man's influence rested not merely with the size of his kindred (*propinqui*), but also with the number of his kinsmen by marriage (*affines*).[22]

Another association which could be assimilated to the kindred was the Germanic war-band whose members could be seen as tied to each other by the same kind of bonds making for unity as between kinsmen.[23] Although according to Tacitus kindreds could be drawn up in battle-groups in tribal warfare, the war-band, another type of formation, cut across this grouping by kinsmen in drawing its recruits from far and wide without regard to kindred. To some extent the kindred could still play a part: the uncle's responsibility for his sister's son could go so far that he accepted him into his war-band, whilst in *Beowulf* the relationship between Hröðgār and the hero goes beyond that of leader and follower and takes on the tone of father and son. For the rest, however, the ties between followers are strengthened by being seen as (artificial) kinship ties.[24] A term for kinsman, OHG *friunt*, is used of them when they are termed *nôtfriunt* 'battle-friend', *Beowulf* uses another word for kinsman of the members of a war-band (*māgas*) and in employing the word *sibbegedriht* of the war-band itself it implies either that the cohesion of the retinue was comparable to that of the kindred or that an internal peace held amongst them as it did amongst kinsmen. In either case, the ethos of the kindred informs that of the war-band.

We come now to three words which in OHG had their home in the kindred in the strict sense of blood-relationship. The words are *friunt* 'kinsman', *sibba* and *kunni*, both meaning 'kindred'.

On the formation of *friunt* no agreement has been reached between two rival explanations.[25] On the one hand, as is most clear in the Gothic form *frijōnds*, the word can be seen as the present participle of the verb *frijōn* 'to love', employed as an independent noun. The meaning would therefore have been 'someone who loves', which is reconcilable with the use of the verb in the context of courtship and marriage, but also with the meaning 'friend' (in Gothic *frijōnds* is the equivalent of Gr. *phílos*

---

[22] *Germania* 20. Another extension of kinship beyond the ties of birth was 'sworn friendship', a Frankish institution which placed two parties under the same obligation of mutual loyalty as between kinsmen. See Fritze (1954), 74ff.; Schlesinger (1963a), 295; Nolte (1990), 129f.; Althoff (1995), 577ff.   [23] Fritze (1954), 8of.; Wenskus (1961), 363; Schlesinger (1963a), 19f.

[24] Fritze (1954), 83, fn. 30; Schlesinger (1963a), 19f.

[25] Scheller (1950), 105 (cf. also Nolte (1990), 126f; Meineke (1995c), 576f.); Mezger (1965b), 32ff.

'friend'), as is also attested in Sl. *prijatel* 'friend'.[26] This explanation does not exclude, however, the possibility of kinship, since the verb *frijōn* originally meant 'to treat as one's own kinsman', 'to admit into one's kindred', above all in the context of marriage.

Frijōnds has also been explained as an IE *-nt-* formation (above all with Hittite parallels) from a noun attested in Germanic as **frijo* 'wife'. Our word accordingly denoted 'those who belong to a married woman', presumably in the plural because kinsmen were normally referred to in the plural. Both explanations depend on the rôle of marriage and wife-taking, thus accounting for the meanings love or friendship as well as kinship (by marriage). Nor is the formation of the word postulated by each explanation all that different. The second theory derives *frijōnds* directly from a noun 'wife', whilst the first does the same indirectly, deriving it from a verb which in turn was formed from an adjective employed as a noun meaning 'wife, someone incorporated into one's kindred'.

Both explanations also agree in seeing the word *frijōnds* as formed from the same stem as two other words already considered as legal terms: *fridu* and *frî*.[27] *Fridu* denoted not peace (and the protection required to guarantee it) as opposed to war with an external foe, but rather the maintenance of order within a tribal society by controlling and putting an end to internal feuding, so that there is a conceptual as well as linguistic connection between *fridu* and *frijōnds* in the sense of kinsman.[28] For peace in this sense to reign between kindreds it must also be in force within a kindred, peace and protection denote the condition obtaining amongst kinsmen as a collective unity. How self-evident this connection between peace and kinship was in Germanic society is shown not merely by the linguistic link between *fridu* and *frijōnds*, but also by the double usage of *sippa* to denote both 'peace' and 'kinship'.[29]

The conceptual link between *frî* and *frijōnds* is just as clear if we recall that the semantic starting-point of the adjective was 'own', especially with regard to one's own kinsman by birth, *consanguineus*, even though the later development of *frî* may have passed beyond this. Freedom in this sense, just as much as peace, depends on the protection, military and legal, granted by the kindred and on being part of one's own kindred, unlike the slave or unfree man.[30] Some of the legal examples for *frîhals* are therefore connected with vengeance and feuding, the area in which the protective unity of the kindred was most obvious.[31]

[26] Scheller (1950), 108ff.　　[27] See above, pp. 39ff.　　[28] Scheller (1950), 113; Mezger (1956), 22f.
[29] See below, pp. 59ff.　　[30] Scheller (1950), 123; Mezger (1956), 12.　　[31] Mezger (1956), 16.

If, as we shall see, *frijōnds* is attested throughout Germania in the two
contexts of kinship and friendship this raises the difficult question
whether one of these may have been earlier than the other. Or indeed
whether both functions may have belonged together from the beginning:
love and friendship may be implied by the context of courtship and marriage (*frijōn, freien*), but equally kinship by the admission of the woman
into the kindred of her husband. How much reliance we may place on
the distribution of these two meanings in the Germanic languages is
quite uncertain. Whereas the meaning 'kinsman' is attested in every language (except Gothic), the meaning 'friend' is not found in the markedly
more conservative ON, which could indicate that the latter meaning was
a later innovation. Significantly, the two scholars each of whom has
argued most recently for a different one of the formations of *frijōnds*
(from the verb or the noun) both agree in regarding kinship as providing
the point of departure.[32] On the one hand Scheller is attracted by the
possibility of linking up the rich spectrum of semantic variations in all
the Germanic languages by regarding *frijōnds* as originally indicating
kinsmen gained by marriage – if accepted, this would strengthen the
case for marriage as an example of extended kinship. Mezger reaches
the conclusion that the original function of the word was to denote the
kinsman, although he refrains from opting for kinship by marriage as
opposed to kinship by blood.

We may now consider examples of these two usages in the various
Germanic languages. In OE the meaning 'kinsman' is clear when *frēond*
is employed in a legal context.[33] If a man illegally takes up arms and is
killed, his kinsmen (*eallen his freondon*) have no claim to wergeld. If a
widow remarries within a year of her husband's death his estate passes
to the nearest kinsmen (*þa nehstan frynd*, translated by *proximi parentes* or
agnati). The man who has no kinsmen to support him legally is *frēondlēas*.
Even outside the legal context the same meaning is clearly attested:
friōndum ond mēgum corresponds to *cognatis et amicis* (Medieval Latin *amicus*
took over the meaning 'kinsman' from Germanic),[34] *wið frēondum* translates *in parentes*, and *nēahfrēond* denotes a near kinsman. Alongside this,
OE *frēond* also stands for 'friend', above all when contrasted with *fēond*
'enemy' in a double formula or when someone is termed *Godes frēond*
'God's friend' (with parallels in the Vulgate, but presupposing *amicus*
'friend', not a kinsman).[35]

---

[32] Scheller (1950), 107f.; Mezger (1965b), 38.   [33] Scheller (1950), 106; Mezger (1965b), 35f.
[34] Nolte (1990), 127.   [35] Bosworth and Toller (1954), 335.

In ON only the meaning 'kinsman' is found.[36] The word *frændi* is applied to blood-kinship, where it can be used of a brother, son, ancestor or the family at large, so that *frændlauss*, like OE *frēondlēas*, refers to someone whose position is endangered through having no kinsmen. This meaning survives intact in the modern Scandinavian languages (e.g. Sw. *frände* 'a relative'), where the concept 'friend' is conveyed by a totally different word (Sw. *vän*, cf. OHG *wini*). This concept was accordingly never expressed at any stage in Scandinavia by a word corresponding to *frijōnds*.

In OS both meanings are found. In the *Heliand* the kinsman meaning of *friund* is made clear by a series of variations accompanying *friund*, all pointing in this direction (1492ff.): *swâs man, an sibbiun bilang* and *mâgskepi*. This meaning also persisted into MLG: *vrünt* 'kinsman', *vrunde rât* 'family decision' (especially in the context of marriage), *vrunde unde mage* (cf. the OE double formula quoted above) 'distant and close kinsmen'.[37] In addition, the *Heliand* also employs *friund* to suggest a friendly, loyal disposition towards someone, as in 2725ff. or 5358f. (in apposition with *hold*).

In OHG both meanings are also attested.[38] Indirect testimony for the meaning 'kinsman', at least for Franconian, is perhaps suggested by the way in which Medieval Latin *amicus*, unlike Classical Latin, can point to kinship by birth or marriage as well as to friendship, for which, as also with OFr. *ami* with a comparable double function, Germanic influence provides a likely explanation.[39] More direct evidence is provided by the gloss rendering of *parentes* 'kinsmen' by *friunt* or by Otfrid's conjunction of *filu manag friunt* and *ther lantliut* as his counterpart to Lc. 1.58 *vicini et cognati*. This meaning has also been retained in a wide range of modern German dialects.[40] Alongside it, however, the application of the word to friendship is found in German from the beginning of the written tradition. Admittedly, we cannot safely turn to glossaries where *friunt* corresponds to *amicus*, for we cannot be sure that the Latin meaning must be 'friend' and therefore throws light on the German word, since *amicus* may instead have taken over the meaning 'kinsman' from Germanic. The position is less open to doubt, however, where *friunt* is equated with a word whose meaning 'friend, dear one' is well established, such as *wini* and *trût*.

Finally, in Gothic the word *frijōnds* translates Gr. *phílos* 'friend' and denotes only friendship. The kinsman (Gr. *syngenḗs*) is instead expressed by *(ga)niþjis*.

---

[36] Scheller (1950), 107; Mezger (1956), 20; (1965b), 35.   [37] Mezger (1965b), 36f.
[38] Nolte (1990), 127f.   [39] See above, fn. 34.   [40] Nolte (1990), 135.

The usage of the German word *friunt* shows a number of points of contact with what we have seen of the kindred at large. In the first place, whether in the stricter terms of kinship or as an extension of the kindred to sworn friendship, the word denotes someone whose duties include the assistance of another *friunt* in the feud, as brought out by the term *nôt-friunt* or *amicus necessarius*.[41] The protection afforded by the kindred covered military assistance in the feud, it also embraced legal assistance in oath-helping, so that the man who lacked kinsmen to perform this service was in a precarious position, exposed to harsher punishments.[42] This danger, at once military and legal, hanging over the man with no kindred or separated from his kinsmen by exile was expressed by the technical adjective OE *frēondlēas*, ON *frændlauss*, but is also attested in the OHG *Hildebrandslied*, applied to Hildebrand (v. 23: *dat uuas so friuntlaos man*). As an exile Hildebrand was separated from his kinsmen and from any assistance which they could provide, including the legal protection without which men were reduced to helplessness as isolated individuals. Lastly, corresponding to the application of kinship terms to the warband, *friunt* can also render *cliens* 'follower, protégé', parallel to Beowulf being regarded as the son of Hrōðgār.[43] Other terms suggesting friendship, such as *wini* and *trût*, can be used of such a relationship, but only with *friunt* do kinship associations also inform a relationship which, because of the vertical difference between lord and follower, was of quite a different origin.

The second word, represented by OHG *sibba* 'kindred', is attested in all the Germanic languages. Etymologically it goes back to a reflexive root **s(w)e-*, present also in such tribal names as ON *Svíar* 'Swedes' and Lat. *Suēbi* and indicating that the idea of 'self' or 'own' could be productive of names to denote an association based on birth, setting itself apart on the level of either the kindred or the tribe.[44] *Sibba*, formed from this root by the same stem-forming suffix (**-bh-*) as with *Suēbi*, probably meant originally 'those of one's own kind'. As such it was well fitted to denote, on the smaller level of association by blood, a grouping of kinsmen. It resembles *frijōnds* in one respect: whereas this word for the kinsman was cognate with *fridu*, denoting the peace which should obtain amongst kinsmen, *sibba* shows two meanings throughout the spread of Germanic languages: 'kinship', but also 'peace'. This concept, expressed by *fridu* or

---

[41] Fritze (1954), 82f., 84; Nolte (1990), 140, fn. 84.
[42] Kroeschell (1960), 19; Nolte (1990), 128f. On the *Hildebrandslied* cf. Lühr (1982), 522f.
[43] Fritze (1954), 8of. [44] Herold (1941), 278; Mezger (1956), 20.

by *sibba*, governed the relationship between members of a kindred as a social necessity, rather than as a virtue (it could only be regarded as such with the coming of Christianity and even then there are grounds for suspecting that this view was slow in impressing itself upon Germanic converts). Peace in the pre-Christian sense was not simply a passive state (the absence of hostilities), but an active one (a readiness to help and defend one another). When looking through the examples for *friunt* in the various Germanic languages we had to distinguish between kinship and friendship, but with *sibba* we have to determine where it designates the kindred and where peace.

This word occurs in Gothic as a noun (*sibja*), a verb (*gasibjōn*) and a negative adjective (*unsibjis*).[45] Since the verb has the force 'to reconcile', therefore to bring about a state of peace between two people, it has been proposed that this was the original meaning (leaving the etymology unaccounted for) from which the other functions were derived. This need not be so: the reconciliation is between brothers, so that the peace could be specifically that which should obtain between kinsmen. This is strengthened by the context in which the noun is used, for both *suniwē sibja* 'adoption of sons' and *frastisibja* 'adoption' imply incorporation into a kindred, an artificial extension of the kindred comparable to others. With the verb a relationship with a brother is made explicit and with the noun one with a child (*frasts*) or son (*sunus*), so that we are justified in considering first the fact of kinship, then the need for peace. Although the negative adjective appears to stand apart in meaning 'unlawful' or 'impious' it can be connected with the kindred if we recall that the man without a kindred was deprived of the legal protection due to a freeman and was not far removed from the status of an outlaw.[46]

In ON the cognate word is almost always used in the plural, denoting kinship by marriage.[47] Although blood-kinship has also been proposed for *sifjar*, this still leaves untouched the fact of kinship in a wider sense, especially since there is no explicit evidence for the word's employment with regard to peace: where Go. *gasibjōn* meant 'to reconcile', the ON past participle *sifjaðr* meant 'related by marriage'. In agreement with ON the OS equivalent *sibbia* refers only to kinship, although in the context of birth, not marriage.[48] Herod is therefore described as no Israelite by birth (*Heliand* 64: *mid sibbeon bilang*; cf. *eðiligiburdi, cnuosle*), the brotherhood of men is expressed in terms of their kinship (1439ff.:

[45] Herold (1941), 279; Mezger (1956), 22; Kuhn (1971a), 414f.   [46] Kroeschell (1960), 3f.
[47] Herold (1941), 279; Mezger (1956), 20, 21f.; Kuhn (1971a), 418.   [48] Herold (1941), 67, 279.

gebrôðar, sibbeon bitengea, mâgskepi) and the evil temptations of even a kinsman are to be resisted (1492ff.: *friund, suâs man, an sibbiun bilang, mâgskepi, mâg*). Thanks to the use of variation there can be little doubt that *sibbia* here means kinship, not peace.

In OE, as in Gothic, both meanings of the word are attested: kinship is therefore seen in its function of enforcing or guaranteeing peace.[49] Kinship is implied in *Beowulf*, for example, when a king, mindful of his kinship with the recipient (2431: *sibbe gemunde*), gave him a gift, by *sibling* 'kinsman' or by compounds such as *brōðorsibb* 'kinship between brothers', *nēahsibb* 'close relationship through marriage' or *sibbgebyrd* 'blood-kinship'. On the other hand, peace is implied by the same word when two kings maintain peace for a long time between themselves (*Widsith* 45: *heoldon lengest / sibbe ǣtsomne*): even though they are kinsmen, it can only be peace which they maintain over time. Elsewhere, *sibbecoss* denotes the kiss of peace, *sibsum* stands for *pacificus* (especially in the beatitudes) and *gesibsumian* 'to bring about a reconciliation' corresponds closely to Go. *gasibjōn*.

The position in OHG resembles that in OE in that both meanings can be attested.[50] Kinship is implied when *propinquitas* or *progenies* is glossed by *sippa* or *consanguineus* by *gisibbo*. Sometimes the bond can be extended to suggest a relationship brought about by marriage (as when *affinis, affinitas* are glossed by *sibbi, sippa*), but the context is still one of kinship. The same is true outside the realm of gloss translations when Otfrid boasts of the Franks' descent from Alexander (*Evangelienbuch* 1 1,88: *in sibbu*) or when the tragedy of the *Hildebrandslied* is enhanced by the son's failure to realise the close kinship of his opponent (v. 31: *mit sus sippan man*). The range of these examples does not preclude the meaning 'peace'. In gloss translations the word can be closely associated with Lat. *foedus* 'treaty' as the legal basis of a peace relationship: *sibba* thus renders *foedus*, *gisippo* stands for *foederatus*, while *sippôn* translates *foederare*. As in OE, the meaning 'peace' can even become primary at times in OHG: in the *Tatian* translation *sibbisam* corresponds to *pacificus* in the beatitudes, as in OE, while *sibba* is the standing equivalent of Lat. *pax*. How far this equation could go is best revealed by a gloss translation where *seditio* is rendered by two alternatives: *unsibba* and *unfridu*.

Sibba differs from other kindred terms in OHG in being the only term not merely to designate blood-kinship, but also to imply peace as the basis of that bond. Perhaps because of this welcome adaptability to

[49] *Ibid.*, p. 279; Mezger (1956), 22.　　[50] Herold (1941), 130, 157, 280f.; Nolte (1990), 128.

Christian ends, suggesting that all men make up one *sibba* so that peace should reign amongst them (as in the *Heliand* passage 1439ff. referred to above), *sibba* was enabled to retain its original kindred function intact.[51]

The last word, OHG *kunni*, is attested in all the Germanic languages and is cognate with Gr. *génos* 'descent, nation', Lat. *genus* 'descent, kinship, tribe' and *gigno* 'procreate'.[52] The ending of PG **kunja-* was used to form neuter substantives, so that the word meant 'what is procreated', hence 'progeny, kindred', a meaning attested throughout Germania.

Wulfila uses *kuni* primarily to translate a variety of Greek kinship terms such as *génos*, *geneá* 'generation', *syngéneia* 'kindred', *phylé* 'tribe, clan'.[53] In OE the association of *cyn* with the kindred is just as close.[54] In *Beowulf* a young warrior can be described as 'the last of our kindred' (2813: *endeláf ūsses cynnes*) because all other kinsmen (*māgas*) have been swept away by fate, a man can be of a famous kindred or descent (1729: *mǣres cynnes*) and the deeds of individuals can so far reflect on their kindred that Wīglāf prophesies to the disloyal followers of Beowulf that gifts of treasure and swords will cease for their kindred as a whole (2884ff.: *ēowrum cynne*). In ON the same function is present with *kyn* when descent can be traced back within a kindred.[55] The extensive use of variation in the *Heliand* makes it easier to establish the kinship function of OS *kunni* when the royal descent of Christ from the house of David is emphasised with regard to the linear descent of Mary and Joseph from that king (365ff.: *hiuuiscas, cnôsla, cunneas gôdes, bi giburdiun*).[56] The choice of a name for John the Baptist is an occasion to present it, as with name-giving in Germanic society, as a decision concerning the kindred as a whole, with names being passed down or undergoing recognised variations from one generation to another. The suggestion of 'John' is therefore at first rejected because it is foreign to his kindred (221ff.: *gaduling, ûses cunnies, cnôsles*). In OHG glosses *kunni* is regularly used in translating Latin terms with kinship associations such as *genus, cognatio, sanguis, progenies* or *genimina*.[57] The author of *Muspilli*, stressing that no one can avoid the Last Judgment, brings this home by presenting this not in terms of individual persons, but of the kindreds to which they belong (v. 32: *dara scal queman chunno kilihaz*). We may see in this verbal detail a reflection of the legal practice of the kindred appearing as a body at court to support one of its kind, a practice with which the clerical author takes issue.[58]

---

[51] Herold (1941), 281.   [52] *Ibid.*, pp. 245f.   [53] *Ibid.*, p. 246.   [54] *Ibid.*, p. 248.   [55] *Ibid.*
[56] *Ibid.*, p. 247.   [57] *Ibid.*, pp. 129, 156, 246.   [58] *Ibid.*, pp. 35, 247.

In addition to this kinship function *kunni* extended its meaning in various Germanic languages to embrace wider entities such as 'tribe' or even 'people'. On the level of 'tribe' *kunni* can be used as the equivalent of Lat. *tribus* and can often be applied to the twelve tribes of Israel.[59] Thus, in the *Heliand* Zachariah is *Levias cunnes* (v. 74), in Gothic Anna is of the tribe of Aser (Lc. 2.36: *us kunja Aseris*) and in OE *omnes tribus terrae* can be rendered by *ealle cyn eorðan*. On the level of 'people' the same word can be used not merely of one of the tribes of Israel, but of the Jewish people as a whole, a wider sense which also occurs in a non-biblical context (*gens* can therefore be glossed by OHG *chunni*).[60] Even wider is the use of this word to designate the sum of all men living at any one time, standing therefore for 'mankind' at large (in the *Heliand* therefore *manno cunni*, *heliðo cunni* or *gumono cunni*, with Notker *menniscon chunne*).[61] Just as far removed from the kindred is the use of *kunni* of other categories of living beings or even things. This word is therefore applied to the 'kind' of evil spirit to be cast out by prayer and fasting both in Gothic (Mc. 9.29) and in OHG (*Tatian* 92,8) and to all 'kinds' of sin by the *Isidor* translators (538).[62]

Whereas these last two semantic extensions ('mankind' and 'kind') result from nothing more than loan-meanings acquired from Lat. *genus* (or Gr. *génos*), wider considerations probably come into play with the first two ('tribe' and 'people'): the vicissitudes undergone by the kindred in the period of the migrations and after, together with the attitude towards it taken up by early Germanic kingship and the Church. To these wider problems we now turn.

The kindred and the rôle it played can be judged in two ways, positive and negative, dependent on whether the society of which it forms part is still of a tribal nature or has developed a central state authority.[63] Where no strong kingship could impose order and guarantee protection the individual found this best in the support of his kinsmen. Before the establishment of royal power justice was an affair of the kindred and resided in the last resort in the feud; without any developed state-apparatus a man's protection against strangers rested with his immediate fellows.[64] Paradoxically the threat of violence could act as a disincentive to violence for as long as the coherence of the kindred was maintained and settlement by compensation acknowledged by both parties. In a

[59] *Ibid.*, pp. 64, 249.   [60] *Ibid.*, pp. 156, 250f.   [61] *Ibid.*, p. 252.   [62] *Ibid.*, pp. 157, 252f.
[63] Cf. Kroeschell (1960), 11; Kuhn (1971b), 125 (on the feud).
[64] Scheller (1950), 105; Wallace-Hadrill (1962), 187; Campbell (1991), 98f.

tribal society the feud was not regarded as the expression of a personal grudge or an outlet for uncontrolled violence, but rather as an obligation owed to society, as a means of maintaining law and order. The feud is far from being wanton violence, for when we first meet it it is already linked to an elaborate procedure for avoiding or putting an end to violence by legal composition, in which the threat of bloodshed is the ultimate sanction.[65]

With the establishment of state power, however, in which royal authority took over the responsibility for maintaining order which had earlier lain with the interplay between kindreds feuding was seen in a very different light: in competition with and undermining the ruler's authority and making for the disintegration of society. This danger was already apparent in Tacitus's day when he notes that settlement of feuds was advantageous to the community (*utiliter in publicum*) where feuds are accompanied by no central authority.[66] Already at this time the feud was a fault-line running through the tribal community, providing the only available, but still unpredictable answer to endemic disorder.[67] With the close of the migrations and with social conditions of a wholly new kind the kindred and the feud revealed their incapacity to evolve means of providing administrative and legal authority over tribal areas of incomparably greater extent and ethnic complexity. Even though the evidence of Gregory of Tours shows that feuds could still be settled in his day, the dominant impression is of a society disintegrating through the uninhibited civil wars against which he warns the Merovingians.[68]

Where central authority was jeopardised by feuding, opposition to the kindred, as the bedrock of such feuding, was expressed from a number of sources. One of these, especially important in Francia, was Roman law, which rejected the feud on the grounds that the offender alone was responsible for his crime and that his kindred should not suffer with him.[69] A parallel to this legal attitude is found in Britain in the petition of the men of Kerry in Montgomeryshire to live under English law because it had suppressed the blood-feud and did not punish the innocent along with the guilty.

Much more important was the Church, which could base its rejection on a far wider range of arguments. Despite equivocations brought about by political circumstances, it was opposed to bloodshed and, itself dependent on protection by central authority, disposed to support the ruler's

---

[65] Wallace-Hadrill (1962), 146.   [66] Much (1967), 301.   [67] Todd (1992), 33.
[68] *Historiae* v, *praefatio*: *Cavete discordiam, cavete bella civilia*.
[69] Wallace-Hadrill (1962), 128; Loyn (1974), 208.

maintenance of order. It therefore seized the opportunity already provided by Germanic practice and threw the weight of its authority behind the settlement of feuds by composition and wergeld instead of vengeance.[70] This does not mean that the Church's equivocations about bloodshed did not affect its attitude to the blood-feud, but in such a way that it sought to remove the prosecution of the feud from the kindred. When St Paul said of God that vengeance was His (Rom. 12.19) the blood-feud was the last thing he had in mind, but this was not how Germanic converts would necessarily see it, for the *ultio divina* frequently illustrated by Gregory of Tours takes the form of a superior, more powerfully executed vengeance, but essentially of the same nature as that sought by a Germanic kindred.[71] What is significantly different about God's intervention in human affairs in this way is the fact that vengeance is obtained by God Himself (striking down the offender by miraculous means) or by a human agent (often the king), but in neither case by kindred pitted against kindred or leading to the disintegration of a Christian society.

Another argument used by the Church, more in keeping with what St Paul had meant by God's vengeance, was to see it in connection with the Last Judgment. Although evil may therefore be unavenged in this life the tables will be turned on the offender in the world to come, a Christian argument against the kindred mentality which informs the OHG *Muspilli*.[72] In Otfrid's depiction of the Last Judgment the arguments used by the Church and by Roman law occupy common ground, for both stress the individual's responsibility for his own deeds, an attitude foreign to the kindred mentality, where punishment and composition concern the whole kindred to which the individual belongs.[73] Writing for a Frankish audience, Otfrid points out the novelty of this legal procedure by expressly contrasting it with the practice to which they were accustomed. At the Last Judgment no settlement by payment in kind will be acceptable, the lord can expect no legal assistance from his dependants or family, for they will be too preoccupied with themselves (v 19,48: *sie sorgent iro thare*), just as every man will be concerned only with himself on that occasion (v 19,51: *thar sorget mánnilih bi sih, / bi sines sélbes sela; nist wíht in thanne méra*). The entry of the Germanic tribes into the world of Rome, their adoption of Roman legal ideas and exposure to the ethical individualism of Christianity thus combined to constitute a crisis for Germanic ideas on the feud and the function of the kindred.

---

[70] Wallace-Hadrill (1962), 146; Green (1965), 309f. [71] Wallace-Hadrill (1962), 127f.
[72] Kolb (1971), 284ff. [73] *Ibid.*, pp. 289, 301; Vollmann-Profe (1987), 241f.

Lordship and kingship, two forces operating to bring about a more highly organised society, also work at the expense of the kindred. As regards lordship, the accumulation of wealth in the hands of *principes* who could afford to maintain a war-band and undertake their own military raids cut across the ties of kinship in decisive ways.[74] The differences of wealth which this presupposes undermined the unity of the kindred. Whereas larger battle formations had been made up of kinsmen, this was not the case with the war-band for which artificial kinship ties were created; some members of a kindred might choose to take part in an expedition, but this imposed no obligation on others, whilst a successful warrior-leader could attract followers from a number of different kindreds. The military effectiveness of these war-bands could therefore be bought at the price of the disruption of the kindred structure of their society. This was especially the case where loyalty to a warrior-leader came into conflict with loyalty to a follower's own kindred, as is strikingly illustrated in the *Anglo-Saxon Chronicle* in the words of the main body of Cynewulf's army to Cyneheard (in whose following some of their kinsmen served): 'They replied that no kinsman was dearer to them than their lord and they would never serve his slayer.'[75] In a case like this the bond between lord and follower proved stronger than the ties of kinship when the two came into conflict.[76]

Kingship, too, had an interest in subordinating feuds and the conflicting claims of kindreds to its own authority, not merely because these claims called into question the ruler's responsibility for public order, but also in view of the profit coming from fines due to the king rather than the kindred.[77] The development was therefore from settlement between kindreds to royal arbitration where, as with the Church's encouragement of composition in place of vengeance, the king did not force a new, unwelcome practice on his subjects, but lent his authority to an alternative already familiar to them.[78] When king Edmund, attempting to curb feuding, ordered that a slayer's kindred were to have the right to abandon him and that they were to be legally exempt from the feud this indicates the presence of a more powerful authority, capable of giving the protection formerly coming from the kindred.[79] Kingship, like lordship, eventually curtailed the power of the kindred.[80]

---

[74] Thompson (1965), 18, 28, 49; Campbell (1991), 169.   [75] Whitelock (1979), 175f.
[76] Magoun (1933), 373, fn. 2; Loyn (1962), 298; Hunter Blair (1963), 252; Mitchell and Robinson (1987), 192. However, cf. the alternative view of White (1989), 1ff.
[77] Wallace-Hadrill (1962), 129; Jacoby (1974), 38.   [78] Wallace-Hadrill (1962), 121, 188.
[79] Loyn (1974), 203.   [80] Cf. also Rexrodt (1995), 454f.

CHAPTER 4

Warfare

The subject of this chapter was central to life in Germania for many centuries, both within a tribal community (feuding between kindreds) and in its relations with others (competing tribes, original inhabitants of territory to be seized, Rome). Under such conditions an adult male, as long as his strength permitted it, was a warrior. It is not therefore because of their Roman perspective that most of our classical sources are largely preoccupied with warfare with the Germanic tribes; from the latters' point of view things would have looked no different.

The shifting power-relationships which such fluctuating conditions of life brought about encouraged, alongside the kindred as a fighting group and the tribal army as the people in arms, the rise of numerous war-bands. Without such followers in their personal retinue no Germanic leaders could lay a claim to power, so that they were driven to outbid one another if they were to keep their warriors with them, for these were not necessarily of the same kindred or even the same tribe. In this competition they had to offer, and keep on offering, sufficient inducement to their followers to remain with them, which amounted to their being exposed to the pressure of expectations from below.[1] How this pressure could stimulate warfare is expressed pithily in an OE gnomic saying: 'Good companions are to encourage the young prince to battle (*byldan to beaduwe*) and to ring-giving.'[2] These two goals belong closely together: the loyalty of followers had to be sustained by generous rewards, whilst the leader's generosity, based on plunder and tributes, had to have war to feed it. Peace was no way in which to keep a war-band together or for the leader to maintain his power, as was already clear to Tacitus (*Germania* 14: 'you cannot maintain a large war-band except by violence and war'), who also saw the pressure coming from below ('The followers are prodigal in their demands on the leader's generosity'). Power,

---

[1] Heather (1991), 314. [2] Quoted by Much (1967), 232.

generosity and warfare therefore all belong together. It is not just poetic diction, but describes a central feature of this institution, when the leader or ruler is described as the ring-giver (OE *bēahgifa*, OS *bôggeƀo*) and the follower as a ring-friend or ring-receiver (OS *bôgwini*). (The gift in question need not be confined to rings or precious metals: Tacitus also refers to a war-horse or a spear.) The parallel between OE and OS suggests a common WG vocabulary and even practice, as is borne out for OHG, too, in the *Hildebrandslied* (vv. 32ff., 46f.), where the father's possession of rings (*bauga*) and weapons is attributed to the lord from whom they come.

Gift-giving within the war-band both feeds on warfare and leads to warfare, constituting what has been called a warrior ideology.[3] To retain his power a leader had to tie his followers to himself through a bond of loyalty, which he earned through his generosity, but to keep this flow of gifts going plundering and tributes, the fruits of war, were constantly necessary. The whole system therefore rested on warfare and the enrichment of the local economy which raiding brought with it. A period of peace, by interrupting the flow of wealth from outside, would mean a crisis for gift-giving whose needs could not be met by a primitive domestic economy, but also a crisis for the power structure of a tribal society in which the war-band occupied an important position from the first century AD. Without battle this institution would have lost its function and fallen apart, occasioning considerable difficulties for the leaders whose hold on power depended on their armed followers.

Under such circumstances, where warfare was endemic to Germania as a whole (feuds waged between kindreds, conflict between tribes), but also resulted from its collision with other expansionary powers (e.g. Romans, Huns) it is not surprising that our sources should have much to say about Germanic warfare. However, in what follows two aspects of the problem will be excluded: vernacular terms for the army or military formation (OHG *heri, folk*) because these also have a political function and are therefore better treated under the political organisation of Germanic society, but also a term for the élite war-band (OHG *truht*) which we shall look at instead in the context of lordship.

To start with the Romans' stress on the lack of military discipline and tactical control of their Germanic adversaries might seem to fall victim to an *interpretatio Romana* ('all barbarians lack Roman order'), were it not

---

[3] Hedeager (1994), 28of.

for other evidence that the Germani in particular lacked any sense of obedience, military or otherwise, including even a word for this concept so foreign to them.[4] It need not be inaccurate when Tacitus (*Germania* 7) says of Germanic leaders that they achieve more in combat by their example (military prowess, presence in the van of the fight) than by any exercise of authority. If any word sums up the relationship between Germanic leader and follower it is the concept of loyalty rather than obedience, two concepts which sum up the difference in military control between the Romans and their opponents.[5] Even outside the war-band the same lack of overall control may be assumed, for if the tribal army went into battle in formations made up of kindreds each tended to act on its own without regard to any overall tactical plan.[6] Discipline in the sense of a central control of fighting was lacking, a shortcoming which placed the Germanic leaders at a disadvantage vis-à-vis the Romans.

Another disadvantage for the Germani lay in the paucity of iron in their equipment.[7] Its use in Germania was fairly restricted, a fact which Tacitus explicitly ties up with the mode of warfare by inferring paucity of iron in Germania from the nature of the weapons used (only a few possess a sword).[8] This cannot mean a total absence of iron (the manufacture of which the Germani had learnt in many respects from the Celts several centuries before),[9] but only that it was used much more sparingly than in the Roman army. This is particularly true if we take into account the most common equipment of the Germanic warrior, the shield and the spear, for these were largely made of wood with only a small amount of metal. As such, these two weapons go back to an age before metal (bronze or iron) and remained in use, with the addition of a minimal amount of metal, after the introduction of iron. Alongside this standard equipment the sword, made entirely of metal, was a prestige object used only by leaders who could afford it.

The offensive weapons used by the Germanic warrior were mainly the spear and the sword. Both are known to Tacitus (*Germania* 6), who uses a native word (*framea*) for the former[10] and says of the latter that only a few are equipped with it. These weapons placed the Germanic warriors under a further disadvantage: although their spears might be the equals of the Romans' *pilum* the same could not be said of the quality of their swords, quite apart from their rarity.[11] The spear, used for thrusting as well as throwing, consisted of a shaft, normally of ash-wood

---

[4] See below, pp. 230f. and 377f.   [5] See below, pp. 375ff.   [6] Thompson (1965), 63ff.
[7] *Ibid.*, p. 111; Much (1967), 128; Beck and Buchholz (1976), 474.   [8] *Germania* 6.
[9] See below, pp. 148, 153ff.   [10] See below, pp. 185f.   [11] Thompson (1965), 112.

(which could provide the name for the weapon itself, as in OE *æsc*, OHG *asck* 'spear'), equipped with an iron point or blade (earlier types had been fire-hardened before the use of metal).[12] Other terms for the spear are OHG *gêr* (frequently used in the formation of personal names, e.g. *Geisericus* < PG **gaiza-*), *spioz*, but also *sper*. Onomastic evidence is relevant, for several NG and EG spear blades have a runic inscription carved on them, giving the name of the weapon with what could be a magical function, e.g. *raunijaR* 'tester', *ranja* 'charger', *tilarids* 'attacker'. The rarity of the sword, as observed by Tacitus, may be due also to the infrequency of defensive equipment (apart from the shield), for this made it advisable to keep the well-armoured Roman at bay for as long as possible and to avoid close combat with the sword.[13] During the course of the migrations the sword became a more frequent and valued weapon, it was manufactured in different types for hacking and thrusting and called forth a variety of designations. To these belong OHG *brant* 'sword' and 'sword blade' (perhaps a metaphor for the blade gleaming like fire), Go. *haírus* and *mēki*, OHG *sahs* 'sword, dagger, knife', therefore presumably a short-bladed sword.

The Germani were at an even greater disadvantage with their defensive equipment.[14] The description by Tacitus (*Germania* 6) of the barbarians' weapons makes it clear that they attached much greater importance to those for attack than to those for protection, largely restricted to the shield alone. Tacitus even claims that the Germani went into battle naked or lightly clad, certainly without protective gear, a practice which he also describes (*Historiae* II 22) as their traditional custom (*more patrio*) and which is confirmed by the depiction of Germanic warriors, naked to the waist, on Roman monuments.[15]

The main protection was provided by the shield, generally made of wood, covered with leather and strengthened round the rim with iron.[16] It could be used by the individual warrior to parry blows, but also by a group drawn up with overlapping shields, as is suggested by OE terms for such a 'shield-wall': *scildweall*, *scyldburh*, *bordhaga*. The wood from which the shield was made is suggested by the word itself (e.g. Go. *skildus*), etymologically connected with a root 'to split' and suggesting a piece of wood split off, and the type of wood used is clear from OE *lind* 'shield', but also 'lime-tree'. Another word for the shield (OE *bord*) could

---

[12] Much (1967), 135f.; Beck and Buchholz (1976), 477f.
[13] Much (1967), 133ff.; Beck and Buchholz (1976), 476f.   [14] Thompson (1965), 112f.
[15] Much (1937), plate III, illustration 6 (Germanic captive, Adamklissi).
[16] Much (1967), 141f.; Beck and Buchholz (1976), 475, 479f.

imply the same, since it also means 'board, plank', but this explanation is complicated by a further meaning of the word, 'border, rim', possibly applied to the rim of the shield, important because of its metal strengthening. In this case the word would be paralleled by OHG *rant* 'shield', but also 'rim, edge', with a similar *pars pro toto* development.

Protection by breastplate and helmet was much more rare, confined to leaders.[17] The rarity of these two forms of protection was already apparent to Tacitus, who comments that few Germani had breastplates and that only here and there was a helmet of metal (or hide) to be seen. Although the Germanic word for breastplate (OHG *brunna*) is of Celtic origin, so that the Germani probably adopted this form of iron body-armour from their more advanced neighbours,[18] the rarity of its use was such that some classical sources deny them its employment altogether or imply that they could have acquired it as booty. Something similar is true of the Germanic helmet. Even though archaeological finds have recovered some magnificent examples (Sutton Hoo, York, Vendel) these are prestige objects of great value, hence rare in the extreme, so that the word *helm* was fit to be applied to someone of uniquely high status, the king (cf. OE *cynehelm*, OHG *chuninchelm* 'crown'). Its rarity was such that classical authors can simply claim that the Germani went into battle without any head-covering. This distinction between leaders and rank-and-file must have persisted for some time if we can attach significance to the illustrations of the *Utrecht Psalter*, where groups of armed warriors are depicted carrying shield and spear, whereas their leaders are generally equipped with a helmet.[19]

Passing from equipment to methods of combat we may note that there is no general evidence suggesting a systematic ranking of formations of different sizes as in the Roman army. The only formation of which we learn (Tacitus, *Germania* 6: *acies per cuneos componitur*) is the wedge-formation (*cuneus*).[20] In this formation the leader and his handpicked followers, better equipped than the others, stood at the point of the wedge, whilst the flanks gradually widened to the rear and were protected by overlapping shields. Arranged in this way the wedge charged the better-protected Roman soldiers in the hope of breaking their ranks by the sheer weight of the onslaught, avoiding piecemeal hand-to-hand fighting in which Roman equipment could establish its superiority. A

[17] Much (1967), 142ff.; Beck and Buchholz (1976), 480f.; Hüpper-Dröge (1981), 107ff.; Hüpper (1986a), 288, 296, fn. 48.   [18] See below, pp. 155f.   [19] Hüpper-Dröge (1981), 113.
[20] Thompson (1965), 114; Much (1967), 150f.; Beck (1965), 41ff.

vernacular name for this formation is ON *svínfylking* (literally 'wildboar formation'), together with *rani* 'snout' to designate the point of the wedge. These terms correspond closely to ones used by Latin authors, *caput porci* and *caput porcinum*, attested first in the fourth century in place of the earlier *cuneus* and possibly a loan from Germanic, transmitted through Germanic mercenaries in the imperial army. This would imply that the vernacular term, or something resembling it, was more wide-spread in Germania than the attestation in ON alone might suggest.

The Germanic armies were made up of foot-soldiers, assisted on occasions by mounted troops whose qualities even the Romans (including Caesar himself) respected, at times making use of them in their own army.[21] Because of the expense few Germani could afford to keep a horse, so that their use of cavalry was somewhat restricted, with few tribes relying on this arm mainly. A geographical distinction must be made, however, between the EG tribes and the rest of Germania, for in the east contact was made with the nomadic peoples of the steppes. From their acculturation in the steppes and their sharing of the same living conditions as these horse peoples the Germanic tribes that migrated eastwards found a military use for the horse largely unknown to the western tribes whose natural environment had not impelled them in this direction.[22]

We have had occasion to remark upon Roman superiority in various aspects of warfare: in discipline and overall tactical control, in the greater use of metal in equipment and in protection by helmet and breastplate. The fact that Germanic warriors occasionally stripped the Roman dead of their equipment after a battle points to their recognition of at least the Romans' technical advantages.[23] And yet the Roman Empire finally succumbed to the barbarian invaders. Various explanations for their victory are possible, including sheer numbers, the wide front along which their migrations brought them into conflict with the Empire, land-hunger and the pressure from other tribes behind them. In addition, if these tribes successfully occupied large tracts of the Empire despite their technical inferiority this suggests that non-pragmatic considerations may have played a part, that the Germanic warrior may have been driven on by irrational features of his fighting mentality.

There remains one other feature of Germanic warfare, single combat, where vernacular evidence can assist us. Our first example con-

---

[21] Kuhn (1951c), 109; Thompson (1965), 116ff.; Much (1967), 146ff.
[22] See below, pp. 177, 178f.   [23] Thompson (1965), 119f.

cerns a common WG feature (shared by Germany and England), whilst the second is centred on the transition from Germanic paganism to a Christianity syncretistically affected by it.

The noun *urhêtto* occurs once only in OHG, at the opening of the *Hildebrandslied* where father and son encounter one another in single combat.[24] They confront one another (*sih . . . muotin*) alone (*ænon*) between the two armies to which they belong (*untar heriun tuem*), so that our problem is to determine whether *urhêttun* (as both father and son are termed) conveys anything of their role in a single combat fought in full view of both their armies (and as a substitute for pitched battle between these armies?). Because the word occurs only once in OHG we have to content ourselves with what closely related parallels may tell us, as when the *Isidor* translation (108) uses *biheizssen* in the sense 'to be so bold (as to claim something)'. This verb has the same stem as the noun *urhêttun* and they also belong together when Otfrid twice uses the verb ('to make a bold claim') in immediate conjunction with a noun *urheiz* (IV 13,49f.; 23,28), on one occasion in a 'military' context, as in the *Hildebrandslied* (Peter and others boasting that they will stand by Christ in the hour of need). In Gothic Wulfila uses the verb *usháitan* (Gal. 5.26) in the sense 'to provoke (challengingly, boastfully)'; in ON the verb *heita* can have the force of 'to threaten'.

It is however from OE, which has nominal cognates with the OHG noun (*ōret* 'struggle', *ōretta* 'warrior, champion'), that most light can be shed on the military usage of the OHG word. Beowulf is twice designated an *ōretta* (1532, 2538), on each occasion in single combat with a monstrous foe, but also after he has expressly committed himself to the exploit. On the first occasion he makes a solemn promise to Hrōðgār, using the same verbal stem (1392: *Ic hit þē gehāte*), on the second he undertakes with boastful words (2510: *bēotwordum*) to fight the dragon, where the derivation of OE *bēot* from *bī-hāt points yet again to the same stem. The context in which we may best place a *nomen agentis* meaning 'warrior, champion' and a stem suggesting a boastful promise is shown by a third passage in *Beowulf*, using the compound *ōretmecg* 'warrior'. This word is employed of warriors in the lord's beer hall, drunkenly boasting in their cups that they are willing to face the monster Grendel (vv. 48off.). In OE religious literature *ōretta* can also be used in David's single combat (where it can be varied by *(Cristes) cempa* 'champion'). Elsewhere, however, a Christian rejection of warrior boastfulness can be surmised: in Gothic

---

[24] Erben (1979), 4ff.; Haubrichs (1988), 150f.

by the parallel between *usháitan* 'to provoke' and *biháitja* 'boaster', with Otfrid's use of *urheiz* and *biheizan* in criticising Peter's vain promise to die for Christ, and even in the *Hildebrandslied* if we accept it as intended to be a Christian negative *exemplum* for Germanic converts.[25]

A particular form of single combat, at home in the legal sphere, is the judicial combat or *iudicium Dei* attested in the early codifications of Germanic law and practised on the continent in Francia and other areas under its influence, but not in Scandinavia or Britain.[26] It was used as a means of establishing the truth in secular law wherever witnesses were not forthcoming and rested on the assumption that God would proclaim the truth by intervening to grant victory to the party in the right. Or to his representative, because both the plaintiff and the accused had the right to make use of someone else, almost to be regarded as a professional for this particular purpose, to fight on his behalf. Amongst the terms used for this judicial fighter we find Lat. *campio* and its loanword equivalent (e.g. OHG *kempho*), whilst the judicial combat itself was termed *campus* and *kamph* respectively.[27] Another vernacular term used for this combat (OHG *wehadinc* as the equivalent of *pugna duorum*) throws more light on this practice if we relate the first part to an OHG verb *wehan* 'to fight' (cf. *ubarwehan* 'to defeat, resist'), for this implies for the compound a meaning 'trial by combat'.[28] Although this practice could be described as a traditional tribal custom (*consuitutinem gentis nostrae, mos antiquus Francorum*) this is not enough to establish a CG pagan origin for it: it is attested only on the continent and within the sphere of influence of Frankish law. The most that can be claimed for a pagan ancestry of this practice is the suggestion that it betrays the same mentality as the Germanic worshipper's conviction that his gods were powerful enough to assist him by intervening in this life when called upon. In the *iudicium Dei*, as the term indicates, this view is held of the Christian God instead, so that the practice probably arose on the continent in the confused transition between paganism and Christianity and demonstrated a sufficiently non-Christian attitude (harnessing God to man's needs) to call forth criticism by the clergy.[29]

Repeatedly in the legal texts attesting the *iudicium Dei* mention is made of oath-taking as well as combat: the truth must be established by fighting if the plaintiff refuses to accept an oath, one or other method may be regarded as acceptable (*aut per sacramentum, aut per camfionem*), a

---

[25] Otfrid: Green (1965), 332, fn. 1; *Hildebrandslied*: Erben (1979), 8f.
[26] Kolb (1971), 284; Hüpper-Dröge (1984a), 620ff.   [27] See below, p. 234.
[28] Hüpper-Dröge (1984a), 642f.   [29] Kolb (1971), 291.

kinsman accompanied by oath-helpers may take the oath or undertake combat on the accused's behalf. Legal assistance by a kinsman and by oath-helpers reminds us of the legal protection provided by the kindred discussed in the last chapter, but the frequent double references to oaths and combat reinforce the Christian attitude of the OHG *Muspilli*. Not merely does the author dismiss contemporary legal practice (the assistance of kinsmen, above all as oath-helpers) as irrelevant at the Last Judgment,[30] he also rejects on principle the possibility of a stand-in fighting on one's behalf to establish the truth. He does this by interpolating a description of the single combat between Elijah and Antichrist (both are termed *khenfun*, their fight is seen in legal terms: *diu kôsa ist so mihhil*), where the (incorrect) view that Elijah will be victorious and thereby rescue men is attributed to those skilled in secular law (*weroltrehtwîson*). By contrast, the clerical view is correct: the Last Judgment cannot be anticipated by this single combat, men must answer for themselves and not avail themselves of a stand-in, therefore Elijah is defeated.[31] Both the legal practices which characterise the *iudicium Dei*, oaths sworn by kinsmen and combat waged on the accused's behalf, are mentioned in this work only to be dismissed.

Germanic warfare was waged in three different ways: by the kindred (in feuds with other kindreds), by the war-band (in raids) and by the tribe (in large-scale wars with other tribes or an external foe).[32] Each of these is treated elsewhere: the first under kinship, the second in the context of lordship, the third in connection with people and army. By bringing them briefly together at this point we may hope to see something of the full scope of warfare in Germania.

Rather than describe the feud waged by the kindred as a private war to restore injured honour it is better to regard it as an intra-tribal war whose purpose was to maintain or re-establish the protected status of the kindred.[33] It was the Germanic equivalent of small-scale guerrilla warfare, taking the usual form of a sudden attack or ambush. The terms used in MLat. for 'feud' (*faida, faidus*) derive from Germanic, as in OE *fǽhþ*, but with a prefix in OHG *gifêhida* 'enmity, vengeance' (from the adjective *gifêh* 'hostile, inimical'). The fact that this word for 'feud' frequently translates Lat. *inimicitia* confirms in reverse that when Tacitus said that a man took on the *inimicitiae* of his father or kinsman (*Germania* 21) he specifically had the feud in mind.

---

[30] Kolb (1964), 4ff.   [31] Kolb (1971), 294ff.   [32] Kuhn (1951c), 98.
[33] *Ibid.*, pp. 98f.; Meineke (1994), 279ff.

Hostilities conducted by the war-band resemble the feud waged by a kindred in that both take place on a level well short of the tribe as a whole, yet hostilities by the war-band for the most part were raids for plunder directed at targets outside the tribal area, often far removed (as with the Vikings).[34] Nor were they concerned to safeguard a protected status at home, but instead to undermine such a status abroad by violence and the quest for booty. The leaders of Germanic society could be involved in raiding-parties: chieftains sought support for their expeditions at tribal gatherings and made use of repeated raids not merely for the sake of loot, but as a means of keeping their hold on power.

Finally, tribal wars pass beyond the small scale of the other two types and involve the whole people in arms.[35] The military force put in the field for such wars was composed of all men in the tribe who had legal rights and were qualified to bear arms. The call to arms was an automatic reaction to an invasion of tribal territory by another people, but aggressive raids by war-bands of one's own tribe against another could easily escalate into full-scale intertribal warfare. Once this happened, what had once started as a restricted undertaking, involving only the members of a war-band, developed into a tribal war in the fullest sense.

Despite a number of features which they share or the possibility of one escalating into another these three types of Germanic warfare can be clearly established in principle. Already for Caesar the last two types, where the danger of one slipping into the other most obviously existed, were distinct enough for him to label the plundering raid as little more than robbery (*latrocinium*) and to reserve the term *bellum* for tribal warfare, whether aggressive or defensive.[36] In modern scholarship some have gone further, distinguishing these same two types of warfare by the part played in them by pagan religious considerations: not by imputing these considerations to one type of warfare and denying them to the other, but by arguing that different religious practices underlie different kinds of warfare.[37] The distinctions made here are not clearcut enough, they rest on special pleading and on exceptions being ignored. It is safer to consider the possibility of a religious background to Germanic warfare at large, without attempting to attribute certain features to one type of warfare rather than another. We now have to consider warfare no longer simply as a matter of weapons, equipment and combat formations or as

---

[34] Kuhn (1951c), 99ff.   [35] *Ibid.*, pp. 101f.   [36] *De bello Gallico* VI 23.
[37] Schlesinger (1963b), 119ff.

a search for land or plunder, but rather as an undertaking with a religious or irrational dimension.

In his discussion of leadership and battle Tacitus reports that punishments (presumably for offences in the field) were not inflicted on the leader's orders, but were carried out by the priests obedient to the god whom they believed to preside over battle (*Germania* 7: *deo imperante, quem adesse bellantibus credunt*).[38] Whether we see in this divinity the god Tiu (regarded as the equivalent of the Roman Mars) or Wodan is a secondary matter at this point beside the overriding presence of a god on the battlefield. Given this belief, it is but a short step to consulting the gods before battle to determine whether a favourable outcome could be expected.[39] The divinatory method could involve the sacrifice of prisoners of war, as when priestesses of the Cimbri prophesied a tribal victory from the blood and entrails of their sacrificial victims. Caesar drew strategic profit from superstitious beliefs: on learning from Germanic captives that the prophetesses of the Suebi advised them against entering battle because of the state of the moon he delivered battle on the following day and defeated an enemy already psychologically incapacitated.

The conviction that the gods preside over battle and assist their worshippers underlies the hope that they will also lead or guide the warrior in battle.[40] Three skaldic passages attest this belief for Scandinavia by using the phrase 'the gods guide them' (*þeim stýra goð*) of warriors in battle. Whether or not a particular god such as Oðin is also implied, the use of *goð* in the plural attributes this guidance of warriors to the gods at large. Elsewhere it can be a matter only of a particular god. The iconography of the stamping dies for figure decorations from Torslunda (Sweden) includes a motif (for which there are continental parallels) showing a warrior following or being guided by a supernatural figure identified as Oðin. This provides visual confirmation of the skaldic evidence. Further justification for seeing such divine battle-guidance as not confined to Scandinavia comes from Tacitus, whose description of the tribe of the Lugii shows them as worshipping Alci, seen by the Roman as the Germanic equivalent of Castor and Pollux, interpreted likewise as divine leaders of the tribe into battle.

For the insignia taken into battle there exist a number of vernacular

---

[38] Much (1967), 159. [39] Polomé (1992), 400, 404ff.
[40] Beck (1965), 28ff.; (1968b), 240, 247ff.; Timpe (1992), 467ff.

terms, none of which throws unquestioned light on their possible religious function.[41] This lacuna is made good by Tacitus, who reports (*Germania* 7) that the Germani carry into battle figures and emblems taken from their holy groves (*lucis*). Whatever the precise nature of these figures and emblems may have been, they were taken into battle as insignia, whilst their storage in holy groves (confirmed also by Tacitus, *Historiae* IV 22) points to their being sacral objects.

If the gods were to grant their worshippers *heil* in victory in battle this was best achieved by sacrifices made to them. With this we come to a specific aspect of the religious sacrifices considered earlier. Sacrifice for victory could take various forms. It could be expressed by a solemn oath in advance of the battle to carry out the sacrifice in the event of victory.[42] Thus the Hermunduri, facing battle with the Chatti, destine their foe to Mars and Mercury (Tiu and Wodan) and carry this out after defeating them, just as Radagaisus promises to deliver all the Christians to his gods if they grant him success. Especially frequent is a second class of evidence: without a preliminary vow human sacrifices are performed after a victorious battle.[43] This was the case with the ritual slaughter of prisoners of war by the Cimbri (coupled with divination for victory in the next battle), who destroyed on another occasion everything that fell into their hands after the battle (clothing, gold and silver, armour and horse-trappings, even the horses themselves). The same type of destruction is attested after the annihilation of Varus's legions in the Teutoburger Wald (deliberately broken weapons, slaughtered horses and Roman captives). The irrationality of such destructiveness (the antithesis of any readiness to seize superior equipment from the Romans) suggests an act of ritual sacrifice in response to victory, complete with the macabre details left unmentioned when, for example, Einarr is simply said to have given his opponent to Oðin for the victory granted him (*gaf hann Óðni til sigrs sér*). Prisoners of war constitute the obvious material for such sacrifices and their ritual slaughter is attested throughout Germania. What the historical sources report as the systematic destruction of men, horses and equipment has also been confirmed from archaeological finds, particularly bog sacrifices where weapons and equipment of great value to a warrior society were committed to destruction together with their defeated owners.[44] These finds have been interpreted as evidence of a religious sacrifice comparable to what the written sources make more

---

[41] Beck (1965), 37ff.; Much (1967), 160f.; Reichert (1994), 307f., 323ff.　　[42] Mogk (1909), 607f.
[43] *Ibid.*, pp. 608f., 638f.; Polomé (1992), 401.　　[44] Ellmers (1992), 100, 115.

explicit, although it remains unexplained why sometimes such sacrificial destruction was the order of the day, whilst on other occasions victory was an opportunity for personal plunder. Wherever in the first type of evidence a god is expressly mentioned it is unsurprisingly a god of war: Wodan or, by *interpretatio Romana*, Mars or Ares.[45]

Another feature of the religious dimension of warfare concerns two details: the god Wodan to whom sacrifices could be made for victory and the war-band, for the members of some of these appear to have dedicated themselves ritually to him as the god of war. The evidence for this is most explicit in Scandinavia. One example concerns Harold Battletooth (*Hilditönn*) of whom it was said that he had received the gift of invulnerability from Oðin (so that he fought successfully without any body-armour) and that this god had taught him the secret of the wedge-formation in battle. In exchange Harold vowed himself to Oðin, promising to dedicate to him all those he killed with his sword, but just as a leader's power and success also depended pragmatically on his band of warriors so must they too have been dedicated by similar ties to this god.[46] This type of relationship is also true of the warriors known as *berserkir* in ON: they, too, fight as a select band of followers, decline to use any armour and dedicate themselves to the god Oðin.[47]

The fact that this evidence comes from Scandinavia should not lead us to conclude that the association of the war-band with Wodan is confined to this part of Germania alone. The origin of the god's name, attested in WG as well as NG, tells against this, for *Wôdan* is formed with a CG suffix *-an-* denoting someone having authority over what is expressed by the stem (cf. Go. *þiuda* 'people': *þiudans* 'king').[48] Etymologically this god's name indicates someone who is a 'leader or lord of the *wôd*', a word surviving in modern German *Wut* 'rage, fury'. The Germanic word could certainly be seen in a negative sense (in Gothic the form *wôþs* was used to render 'possessed by demons'), but also positively if we take into account such cognates as Lat. *vātēs* 'divinely inspired poet or prophet' and Gaulish *vātis*, OIr. *fáith* 'prophet, poet' (in Germania Wodan was also seen as a god of poetry). What precise force we are to give the god's name formed in this way, however, is suggested by the explanation provided by Rudolf von Fulda in the ninth century: *Wodan id est furor*,[49] but this still leaves unexplained: of what kind of rage or fury was Wodan felt to be in command?

---

[45] Mogk (1909), 611f.; Beck (1970), 253.   [46] Mogk (1909), 613f.; Beck (1970), 254.
[47] Müller (1967), 208.   [48] Meid (1992), 501f.   [49] Helm (1953), 259.

Words formed with this suffix in Germanic are derived from a stem denoting a person or concrete thing, not an abstract, as would be suggested by 'rage, fury'. This difficulty can be overcome by recalling the double usage of some nouns in an abstract, but also in a concrete, collective function. In OE the word *dugoð* means both 'manhood' and a 'troop of warriors' collectively incorporating that abstract quality, in OHG the term *trôst* 'assistance, confidence' is paralleled by OS *gitrôst* 'band of warriors' showing their leader these qualities, whilst MHG *kraft* means both 'power, might' and a troop of fighting men. If we focus on Wodan as a god of war to whom warriors stand in a specially close relationship, even dedicating themselves to him, then *wôd* could have meant both ecstatic warrior frenzy and also a body of warriors incorporating this warlike fury or *furor*.[50] Wodan is hence the name of the god of war, but also the god of those military bands that devote themselves to his worship and are given superhuman warrior virtues by him. Since the name Wodan is widely attested in Germania and since some of the examples we have considered come from the continent this helps to confirm that the religious background to warfare was by no means restricted to Scandinavia.

Amongst theophoric personal names there are some compound names in which the first element is a term for the gods at large or for a particular god, whilst the second denotes a warrior or the warfare which he personifies or an aggressive animal (or beast of the battlefield) whose qualities he incorporates. Such compound names establish a connection between the god(s) and the name-bearer in the specific context of battle. The wide spread of this type of name throughout Germania confirms that this conception was CG. Out of the wide range of examples only one or two can be given.[51] Thus, the CG word for 'god' occurs in such warrior names as ON *Guðbrandr* (the second element denotes the sword he wields) and Ostrogothic *Gudinandus*, while the term for one of the categories of pagan gods is found in ON *Ásulfr*, OS *Osger*, OHG *Anshramn*, Visigothic *Ansemundus*. As in Germanic name-formation at large, the second element in these theophoric names can at times denote not 'warrior', but the battle for which he stands, as in OHG *Cotahilt, Gotafrid*, but this does nothing to weaken the connection between gods and warfare.

---

[50] For literature on the Wild Host or *feralis exercitus* see Timpe (1992), 469, fn. 74.
[51] Schramm (1957), 103f.; Beck (1965), 102f.; Müller (1970), 197.

The evidence of personal names can be made use of to establish an irrational aspect of Germanic warfare, not necessarily of a religious nature, but certainly close to the supernatural sphere. (The value of this onomastic evidence is that it allows us to penetrate the barrier to the prehistoric past erected by the relatively late start of a written tradition in the vernacular.) What concerns us now is not a theophoric type of name (containing a word or name for a god), but a theriophoric type (containing a word for an animal). If the first type established a connection between god and man (on the battlefield or not), what purpose was served by linking man with animal specifically in the context of the battlefield?

That these theriophoric names are closely connected with warfare and fighting there can be no doubt. This is particularly clear with the many names formed throughout Germania with *ebur* 'wild boar' (or its equivalent) as the first part, whose quality of aggressiveness is then heightened by the addition of a second element such as *hard* 'strong, brave', *wakar* 'strong' or *muot* 'anger, bravery'.[52] The wish expressed by giving such a name as *Eburhard* is that the name-bearer will grow to be a warrior endowed with qualities which resemble those of the animal. The assimilation of man to animal is even closer when the method of compounding a name is reversed and the animal name placed second, for linguistically this not merely compares the bearer (the future warrior) with the animal, it even equates them. In this case, too, the military nature of the first element leaves us in no doubt but that the basis of this identification is the common factor of fighting.[53] The first element, signifying 'battle' by one word or another, can thus combine with a word for an aggressive animal, such as OHG *Hildulf* 'battle-wolf', OS *Hildebern* 'battle-bear', OE *Heathulf* 'battle-wolf', OHG *Gundolf* 'battle-wolf', ON *Gunnbjörn* 'battle-bear', OS *Wigbern* 'battle-bear'. The first element can also be a word for 'army', producing such names as OHG *Heriulf* and OS *Heribern*, with numerous parallels in other Germanic languages. Words for a weapon or piece of defensive equipment can also occur. The sword is reflected in OE *Heoruwulf*, ON *Saxulf*, OHG *Sahsbern*, Frankish *Brandulf*. The spear comes to the fore in ON *Geirúlfr*, OS *Gerbern*, OHG *Ortolf*, OE *Æscwulf*. The shield is used in ON *Skjöldúlfr*, OHG *Randulf*; the breastplate in ON *Bryniólfr*; the helmet in OE *Helmwulf*.

The large stock of names of this type reveals a hope that the warrior will incorporate the qualities of various animals best suited to his military

---

[52] Müller (1968), 211, 214, 216; (1970), 178, 191.   [53] Müller (1970), 179ff.

tasks. That this was the attitude behind such name-giving is indicated by the unknown author of the *Opus imperfectum in Matthaeum* in the fifth or sixth century, who criticises what is most probably this practice with the Germani.[54] He says that it is the custom of barbarian peoples to name their sons in accordance with the devastation of wild beasts and birds of prey, regarding it a source of pride to have such sons, fit for war and raving for blood. What is criticised here from a Christian point of view could indeed be a source of pride in Germania: some of the OE warrior kennings employed positively in the context of heroic poetry show striking parallels with theriophoric names.[55] The warrior can therefore be designated in OE poetry as *hildewulf* 'battle-wolf', *heoruwulf* 'sword-wolf', *herewulf* 'army-wolf' or *gūðbeorn* 'battle-bear'. In addition, the OE noun *beorn* 'warrior' is cognate with ON *björn* 'bear', in ON the word *jöfurr* meant originally 'wild boar', but came to signify 'prince' (in his function as leader in battle). The practice was therefore by no means restricted to compounds.

As an explanation of these theriophoric names (and words) it has been suggested that the animals in question were regarded as the attributes of certain Germanic gods, for whom they stand as taboo substitutes: the eagle as a pointer to Wodan, the boar as an attribute of Freyr.[56] If this theory were accepted, these theriophoric names would testify as much as the directly theophoric ones to a close link between warfare and the gods. It is doubtful, however, whether we are justified in interpreting these names in this way.[57] It is an arbitrary decision to argue that because certain animals can sometimes be associated with certain gods in Scandinavian mythology (but can we safely generalise this to Germanic mythology at large?), therefore the occurrence of an animal in a personal name must necessarily point to the god in question. To interpret the name *Arnulf*, consisting of the words for 'eagle' and 'wolf', as signifying a Wodan cult because both these animals were holy to this god means, because of the frequency of names with 'wolf' as the second element, unconvincingly appropriating all these names, too, for this cult. It also ignores, as regards the element 'wolf', an important feature of compound names. Only those examples can be regarded as theophoric warrior names where the reference to a god is contained in the first element, for any reference in the second would inevitably identify the name-bearer with that god instead of merely associating them.[58]

---

[54] Müller (1968), 211; (1970), 178.   [55] Schramm (1957), 78f.; Müller (1968), 211f.; (1970), 178.
[56] Müller (1968), 202ff., discusses this suggestion.   [57] *Ibid.*, p. 205; Müller (1970), 196f.
[58] Müller (1968), 205.

Instead of interpreting theriophoric names as if they were really theo-phoric it is safer to regard them as expressing reverence and admiration for the animal in question, a wish to share its qualities, especially those called for in battle (strength, speed, pronounced aggressiveness).[59] This can take the form of simply imitating the animal and its abilities (as in a name of the type *Eburhard*), but it can also imply a magical, irrational ability to transform oneself autosuggestively into an animal, by claiming descent from an animal ancestor or by disguising oneself as an animal.[60] This belief could inform names of the type *Hildulf* where the animal, by its position in the compound, stands much closer to the name-bearer who is not merely brave like a wild boar, but is himself a wolf in battle. This belief in a man's ability to transform himself into an animal is not confined to Germanic, as can be seen in the difference between two names in Greek. Whereas *Phílippos* 'horse-lover' presents the horse as the object of the action carried out by the man, a name such as *Autólykos* 'himself a wolf' establishes an identity between man and animal. With such a name and Germanic ones like *Hildulf* the warrior is seen as iden-tical with the beast of prey because it is the beast's qualities which he shows in being magically transformed into that animal when in battle.[61]

The argument of this chapter has fallen into two distinct parts: a review of the pragmatic aspects of Germanic warfare (lack of discipline, paucity of iron in equipment) and of the disadvantages which these imposed, followed by a consideration of the religious and even irrational dimensions to fighting. There can be little doubt but that the Romans regarded both these aspects of their opponents as hallmarks of their barbarism: the first because it demonstrated how inferior the Germani were to Roman technology and sense of order, the second because the wild savagery of their foes' fighting methods may have reminded them of features of the Roman past which had now been safely left behind. With the benefit of hindsight, however, we may make a distinction between these two aspects, for technical inferiority was counterbal-anced, among other things, by the élan and wild impetus with which the Germani eventually swept aside the defences of the Empire. Both these aspects belong to any consideration of Germanic warfare.

---

[59] *Ibid.*, p. 214; Müller (1970), 199ff.   [60] Müller (1968), 215; (1970), 194.

[61] Imitation of, even identification with a beast of prey has been argued for the OHG name *Wolfhetan* (Müller (1967), 200ff.; Höfler (1976), 301; cf. also Beck (1968), 237) and for the ON common noun *berserkir* (Höfler (1976), 298ff.; Müller (1970), 222, fn. 103, against Kuhn (1971a), 521ff.; von See (1981), 121ff.).

CHAPTER 5

People and army

In this chapter we have to consider three vernacular words for 'people' (OHG *heri, folk, liuti*) each one of which also had a military function.[1] Of these three words the first (*heri*) originally denoted the army at large, the sum of all those freemen qualified to bear arms, the second (*folk*) was used of a constituent formation of the army, whilst the military function of *liuti* stems from its original designation of (male) adults, those whose coming of age equipped them for service in the army. In combining a military with a political function these three terms go beyond the preceding chapter and form a bridge to the political subject of the next two chapters (lordship, kingship).

The OHG word *heri* has cognates in every Germanic language, which together with its recurrence in personal names in the Roman period (e.g. *Chariomerus*) establishes its antiquity.[2] This can be confirmed by its cognates in other IE languages, e.g. Lith. *kãrias* 'army', Gaulish *Tricorii* and *Petrucorii* (tribal names meaning literally 'three or four armies'). The IE base for these words was derived by an adjectival suffix *-io-/-ia-* from a substantive surviving in OSl. *kara* 'conflict', Lith. *kãras* 'war', so that the original meaning of the Germanic word was 'that which has to do with war', therefore 'army'.

This military meaning is attested in all the Germanic languages.[3] In Gothic the form *harjis* once renders Gr. *stratiá* 'army' with reference to the heavenly host and once Gr. *legeón* 'legion' in the sense of a large number. Admittedly, the first example is a metaphorical extension and the second a loan-meaning from Greek (or Latin), but neither would have been possible without an original military meaning for the Gothic word. In ON the word *herr* is used of the tribal army on a military

---

[1] Treated at length by Herold (1941) on whom this chapter largely draws. [2] *Ibid.*, p. 171.
[3] *Ibid.*, pp. 172f.

expedition,[4] but even when applied to a smaller band of warriors the larger formation is present in the background, as in the *Atlamál* 93,6, where *herr manna* suggests a band of warriors as numerous as a tribal army.

The army scale implied by this word is also clear in OE. In glosses *here* normally renders Lat. *exercitus* rather than any subdivision of the army, and in the OE chronicles the word is used of the Viking army, regarded as a collective unit.[5] In *Widsith* (v. 120) the *here* of the Goths is said to have done battle with the people of Attila, a reference to a battle between the Goths and the Huns in a tribal war between full-scale armies. An army of this size is also suggested for OS *heri* in Christ's prophecy of the destruction of Jerusalem by the Roman army (*Heliand* 3693), where the army itself is expressed in the singular (*heries craftu*), but in apposition to subordinate formations which are in the plural (*mid folcun*).

In OHG glosses *heri* frequently renders Lat. *exercitus*, but also *militia* and *agmen*, i.e. terms for the army as a whole. It can also translate terms for a subordinate, but still large-scale army formation, e.g. *milites, equites, pedes* or *hostis*. The same scale of tribal warfare is suggested by continuous texts. The single combat between father and son in the *Hildebrandslied* is waged in full view of their armies (v. 3: *untar heriun tuem*), where the clash between Theoderic and Odoaker for possession of Italy implies the wider dimensions of tribal warfare. When the valkyrie-like figures of the first *Merseburger Zauberspruch* impede or bind the opposing army (v. 2: *suma heri lezidun*) their concern is with all the enemy ranks, not just one formation within it. The *Tatian* translators render *exercitus* by *heri*, while Notker uses the word with reference to the total destruction of Pharaoh's army in the Red Sea.[6] As with Gothic, OHG *heri* can sometimes be used of the heavenly host – a transferred usage, but still a military one.

The word *heri* was also used to indicate a people in the ethnic sense or as the body of those responsible for political and legal decision-making.[7] That one and the same word could be used in two senses (military and what for the sake of brevity we may term political) need not surprise us, for the Germanic legal assembly was also a military assembly and the young male admitted to the status of a warrior was now also fit to participate in political and legal deliberations. The double function of *heri* is a reflection of Germanic society as already described by Tacitus.[8]

The traditional union of two semantic functions is best demonstrated

[4] E.g. *Helgakviða Hundingsbana II* 16, 2. Cf. Neckel (1936), 77.   [5] Bosworth and Toller (1954), 532.
[6] E.g. *Tatian* 145, 11; Notker, *Canticum Moysi* 4 (1071, 3). Heavenly host: Herold (1941), 173, fn. 13.
[7] Herold (1941), 173ff.   [8] See above, p. 30.

in OS and ON, the two Germanic languages which, because least involved in the migrations and least exposed to extraneous influences, were the most conservative. In an example of the political-legal function of *heri* in OS the author of the *Heliand* (vv. 5056ff.), describing the Jews' plotting against Christ, says that the *heri* gathered together, that many lawspeakers (*êosago*) came together, forming a legal assembly (*hwarf*) where they discussed (*rûna*) and took counsel (*râdan*). The setting of a legal assembly is made evident here, but no matter whether *êosago* is used simply in apposition to *heri* or represents a class of lawspeakers distinct from the *heri*, the latter are equally involved in this legal deliberation. The *heri* comprises those taking part in the legal assembly of the people, freemen qualified to attend the *thing* and to bear arms. In ON the position is similar, for in addition to meaning 'army' *herr* could be used of 'people' in the political sense: in regard to the relationship between a ruler and his people the latter (*allr herr*) are said to love king Olaf, whilst the Icelandic people (*íslenskum her*) are commanded to keep God's laws.[9]

The position is quite different elsewhere in Germania. In Gothic, where *harjis* occurs only in the military sense, this may be due to the restricted lexis of a bible translation. This cannot be true of the richer evidence in OE, where *here* is not employed for 'people' in regard to English conditions. The *Anglo-Saxon Chronicle* used *here* in its military sense almost as a technical term for the Viking army, reserving *fyrd* for the English army. Still in this restricted sense *here* was also applied to the inhabitants of Danelaw, denoting 'people' in a political sense only in this area, never to the English or to all the inhabitants of England (English and Danes).[10] Given this restriction and the use of ON *herr* to denote 'people' in the political sense, it is likely that this use of OE *here* was in imitation of ON usage. In OHG no political or legal function is attested for this word, only the military one. Apart from this, *heri* can sometimes be used in the generalised sense of 'crowd, multitude' in OHG (as in other Germanic languages), but with no political or legal implication.[11]

The more conservative evidence of ON and OS suggests that originally the word *heri* had two meanings, 'army' and 'people' (in the political sense), and that it designated the body of freemen in Germanic society with their combined military and political obligations, as described by Tacitus (*Germania* 13). The semantic development of the word in Germany (apart from the north) and England, both 'colonial' territory occupied after migrations and exposure to change, suggests a

---

[9] Herold (1941), 174f.   [10] *Ibid.*, p. 175, fn. 22.   [11] *Ibid.*, p. 175 and fn. 21.

break-up of this original unity, an exclusive concentration of *heri* on the meaning 'army' and an abandonment of its political function ('people').[12] How far this break-up and the linguistic changes were due to internal or external causes can only be judged in the light of historical changes, but also in connection with the other terms (*folk, liuti*). At this stage we can only suggest general historical reasons for this disintegration of the earlier Germanic 'people in arms' and for a distinction between the army and the people on colonial soil.

An early factor making for the growing independence of the leadership of the army, separating it from the authority of the tribal assembly, is connected with the military lessons which the Germani learned from their Roman opponents concerning military discipline. Several Germanic leaders, e.g. Arminius and Civilis, served for a time in the Roman army, learned its military methods, especially the advantages of discipline, and on returning to Germania sought to turn what they had learned against their former masters and to wean their Germanic armies from their traditional indiscipline. This period therefore witnessed not merely the barbarisation of a Roman army increasingly dependent on Germani, sometimes even with the rank of general, but also to some extent the military education of Germanic leaders in new methods. Or in linguistic terms: alongside the replacement of Classical Lat. *bellum* in Vulgar Latin by a word of Germanic origin, *werra*, we find Latin military terms taken over into Germanic.[13] As far as military discipline is concerned, the obedience now owed on the Roman model to the military leader made of him more than a *primus inter pares* and brought about a fundamental change in the organisation of the army, removing it from the still nominal equality of rights of all who took part in the tribal assembly.

The early Germanic army had been based on a horizontal type of organisation, conferring less authority on the army leader who was chosen by his equals (and only for the duration of a campaign) and who possessed no absolute command. During the migrations military necessity dictated that the leader, for the sake of rapid decisions, should make himself independent of the tribal assembly, which contributed to the weakening of that assembly which we saw in the semantic changes undergone by the word *thing*.[14] Eastern Germania, almost entirely colonial territory and in its vast extent posing new problems of command, is where we encounter marked evidence for stricter forms of royal

---

[12] *Ibid.*, pp. 175ff.   [13] See below, pp. 202ff. and 230ff.   [14] See above, pp. 35ff.

authoritarianism, based on military leadership.[15] The more powerful such a leader became and the more directly he could exercise his authority over his warriors, the more distance he placed between his army and the tribal assembly.

The importance of the Germanic army as the people or freemen in arms was called into question by a development once the invaders had settled in Francia: a tendency to attach much less importance to the general levy, to the expectation that a man with political rights also had military obligations. Different reasons come into play here.[16] In the first place, the geographical extent of the Frankish kingdom made such a general call to arms too cumbersome a measure to deal with a local attack. The greater importance attached to agriculture once the migrations gave way to fixed settlement on the soil of Francia meant a greater reluctance to interrupt the agricultural cycle by campaigning, especially since the crucial months were precisely the summer months when military activity was generally at its height. To abandon agriculture for warfare in this season, but also to equip oneself with weapons and sustain oneself in the field meant a considerable economic burden, especially for those who enjoyed no great wealth or standing. Such difficulties are reflected in the readiness of many voluntarily to abandon their free status in order to be rid of the burden of military obligations.

Developments like these, amounting to a progressive weakening of the earlier tribal army, could be tolerated by Frankish rulers only if they could instead fall back on a military force better equipped to deal with the new problems at the close of the migrations. The traditional argument has been to suggest that in the answer found to these questions the origins of feudalism are to be sought.[17] Whereas most warriors in the Frankish armies had originally been foot-soldiers fighting because it was the duty of all freemen to bear arms, their rulers are said to have felt more and more the need for a standing force of warriors, immediately available at all times and over the wide expanse of Frankish territory. The economic foundations of this professionalisation of warfare are seen in the *beneficium*, the granting of an estate in exchange for military service, enabling the now permanent warrior to keep himself afloat economically, especially if, as has been suggested in the case of the army reforms of Charles Martel, he bore the expense of being mounted in order to cope with mounted Arab incursions into Gaul.[18] The conjunc-

---

[15] See above, p. 3.   [16] Von Frauenholz (1935), 12, 14, 22f.   [17] Brunner (1887), 1ff.
[18] Von Frauenholz (1935), 6of., 64f.; White (1962), 1ff. On the expense of keeping a horse cf. Steuer (1994), 166.

tion of vassalage (swearing personal allegiance and military service to a leader) with the *beneficium* is said to have produced feudalism. Whether we accept this or not, the relationship in question was a personal one between lord and vassal, not one based on the political and legal authority of the tribal assembly. The emergence of this new professional permanent caste of warriors further diminished the social function of the *thing* and the relevance of the form of military organisation which it had provided.

Recent questioning of this traditional view by historians means that we are far from a consensus about these military developments of the Franks, especially with regard to dating them. Philology may be notoriously incapable of solving its own problems of dating and is only too ready to accept help from historians, but in this case even the latter are too far from unanimity to provide any support. For Brunner, the classical proponent of the traditional view of the origin of feudalism, the turning-point was personified in Charles Martel, but others have suggested either an earlier (Merovingian) origin or a later one (Carolingian).[19] With the historians' field so wide open the philologist has little hope of a precise dating of his linguistic changes. He may, however, console himself with one consideration: no matter whether the political and military changes in Francia go back to the Merovingians, to Charles Martel in particular in the first half of the eighth century or to the Carolingians, they start sufficiently early to leave linguistic traces in OHG when its written tradition begins. Already at that point the language reflects what had taken place in Frankish society: the abandonment of what had been true of the Germanic past, the break-up of a form of military organisation based on the obligation of all freemen to take part in the tribal assembly and to bear arms in tribal warfare.

The social and military developments which underlie this break-up took place in Francia, affecting that WG tribe which was most crucially involved in the changes brought about by the close of the migrations. With the expansion of Frankish ascendancy to Upper Germany (in social, political, legal and religious matters)[20] their innovations were carried to the Bavarians and the Alemanni (features of vassalage can be initially referred to in these areas as *iuxta morem Francorum* or *more francico*).[21] The fact that by about the middle of the eighth century OHG *heri*

---

[19] Charles Martel: White (1962), 1ff.; Critchley (1978), 33. Merovingian: Dopsch (1961) II 308 (cf. Bachrach (1970), 58, 60, 71f.). Carolingian: von Olberg (1991), 117.

[20] On legal and religious examples cf. above, pp. 44ff. and below, pp. 331ff..

[21] Kauffmann (1923a) II 338, fn. 4.

must have completely lost the meaning 'people' is a measure of the extent to which the Frankish military changes had been carried to Middle and Upper Germany. By contrast, OS retained its conservative position (using *heri* both as a political and as a military term) because it was exposed to Frankish expansionism only later, whilst Scandinavia was even further removed from such influence.

Not merely *heri*, but also *folk* originally designated 'people' as well as 'army'. If *heri* later abandoned the first of these meanings and concentrated on the second, this raises a question about *folk*: did its semantic development proceed in the same way or conversely to what we have seen with *heri*?

About the etymology of *folk*, attested in every Germanic language except Gothic, few difficulties present themselves.[22] It derives from the same root as the OHG adjective *fol* 'full', just as the cognate Greek noun *plēthos* 'people, crowd' is connected with *pímplēmi* 'to fill' and the Lat. *populus* or *plebs* with *plenus* 'full'. These IE parallels suggest an original meaning 'plenty, plenitude' for the Germanic noun, developing to 'crowd, group, people'. They also imply some antiquity for the formation of this word with this meaning, alongside which the military meaning may also have arisen fairly early, as is suggested by the loan of the Germanic word into OSl. *plŭkŭ* 'band of warriors' and by the further loan into Lith. *pulkas* 'band'. This etymological information already presents us with the two spheres of meaning which can be attested for the Germanic word.

The application to 'army' is attested for every Germanic language (with the exception of Gothic), even though, unlike *heri*, *folk* cannot simply be equated with 'army'.[23] In OHG this is clear from the glosses, for they nowhere translate Lat. *exercitus*, whereas precisely this equivalent was registered for *heri*. Instead, *folk* occurs as a gloss for terms indicating a smaller military unit such as *cohors, manipulus* and *cuneus* (all of which can also be translated by *scara* 'band, troop').[24] Apart from these glosses (and *Isidor* 362, where the Christian *celestis exercitus* is admittedly translated as *himilisc folc*) this word occurs in a military sense only in the *Hildebrandslied*. When it is said of Hildebrand that he was always in the van of the fight (v. 27: *eo folches at ente*) it is dubious what kind of formation is conveyed by *folk*, for he could have been fighting at the point of a wedge-formation (*svínfylking*) or at an exposed part of a larger fighting formation such as an army (the single combat after all takes place *untar*

---

[22] Herold (1941), 184.   [23] *Ibid.*, pp. 184ff.   [24] *Ibid.*, pp. 184f.

heriun tuem). A decision in favour of a smaller formation is suggested when Hildebrand says that he was always allocated a place in the troop of those who shot (v. 51: *dar man mih eo scerita in folc sceotantero*). Whatever the precise force of *sceotantero*,[25] this points to a specially armed subdivision of the whole army, which is confirmed by the use of the verb *scerita*, formed from the noun *scara* with its smaller dimension 'troop'.

The OHG evidence that the military usage of *folk* pointed to a fighting formation smaller than the army and therefore only a part of the *heri* is confirmed by OS. This is shown by the passage in the *Heliand* (vv. 3693ff.) in which Christ prophesies the destruction of Jerusalem. The attacking Roman army is termed a *heri* and this is varied by *folc*, but whereas the first word is used in the singular the second occurs in the plural. The whole body of the army was therefore composed of a number of subordinate smaller formations. Accordingly, when *folc* is used in the singular it denotes no more than a band of warriors, as when Christ addresses Judas at the moment of being seized (v. 4835: *behuî kumis thu sô mid thius folcu te mi*). The soldiers who accompany Judas are also termed a *werod* 'troop' (4832), corresponding to the biblical use of *turba* (Mt. 26.27) and *cohors* (Joh. 18.3).

A similar picture is presented in ON not merely by the corresponding word *fólk*, but also by a derivative form *fylki*. The first noun denotes a troop of warriors, as in the *Helgakviða Hundingsbana I* where a number of troops, making up the total force, are specifically referred to (v. 50,1: *ganga fimtán fólk upp á land*). The second noun, probably formed as a collective with *gi-* (regularly lost in ON), is paralleled by OE *gefylce* 'troop, division' and denotes a constituent formation within a larger military force.[26] This can be seen from the derivative verb *fylkia* 'to group warriors in their correct formation for battle' and by the compound *svínfylking* which we saw denoted an individual wedge-formation, but not the whole army (too large to be manageable in such a grouping). That the position was not different in OE is shown by *gefylce* which in the glosses renders such Latin words as *manipulus*, *caterva* and *legio* – again, smaller fighting units beneath the level of an army.[27]

The fact that *folk* is attested in a military sense in every Germanic language (except Gothic), but also that it signified a fighting unit forming only a part of the whole army, suggests some antiquity for this. How we are to consider the nature of such smaller fighting units is best seen in the organisation of the Germanic army,[28] based not on numerical

---

[25] Haug and Vollmann (1991), 1034f.   [26] Herold (1941), 187.   [27] *Ibid.*   [28] *Ibid.*, pp. 188ff.

subdivisions of varying size (this was a practice which the Germani acquired from the Romans, but also from the Iranian peoples),[29] but on a grouping by kindreds, as was already clear to Tacitus (*Germania* 7). Tacitus uses the word *cuneus* for such a smaller fighting unit, but also in the comment that the battle-line of the Germani is made up of wedge formations (*Germania* 6: *acies per cuneos componitur*).

What is described here is occasionally illustrated in practice in reports of specific encounters between the Roman and Germanic armies. It need not always be the case that a *cuneus* was made up of warriors from a kindred, since in large-scale encounters the grouping can sometimes betray a tribal basis, as when Caesar reports how Ariovistus drew up his line in tribal contingents which are then named (Harudes, Marcomanni, etc.).[30] Whether the grouping was based on the kindred or sometimes on the tribe, the common factor is the organisation of the army for battle into a number of smaller fighting units. In his *Historiae* Tacitus gives a number of examples of this practice with the Germani, where the constituent formation is generally referred to as a *cuneus*, but occasionally as a *caterva* 'troop, band'.[31]

The linguistic employment of *cuneus* by Tacitus is not always as unambiguous as we should wish, for sometimes it denotes no more than a group or contingent within a larger formation (as with *cuneus Frisiorum* on Roman inscriptions), but sometimes it has the specific force of a wedge-shaped formation (as in *Germania* 6). Despite this lack of clarity, the fact of smaller battle-groups within the army as a whole remains unaffected. In this respect Germanic terminology is more clear. *Folk* denoted this battle-group and the same is true of the second element in the ON compound *svínfylking*, whose first element has the function of indicating the wedge shape of that formation.[32] The two functions of the Latin word *cuneus* are expressed here by the different words making up this compound.

To sum up the military function of *folk*: whereas *heri* corresponded to *exercitus* and denoted the whole army (the people or tribe in arms), *folk* was the equivalent of *cohors* or *cuneus* and signified a subdivision within the army, based sometimes on the kindred.

Alongside this military function *folk* also denoted 'people' in a political or legal sense.[33] *Heri* also combined two functions (a military one, however different in scope, and a political-legal one) because it denoted

---

[29] See below, pp. 180f. [30] *De bello Gallico* I 51. [31] Herold (1941), 188f. [32] See above, pp. 77f.
[33] Herold (1941), 191ff.

the totality of those entitled to bear arms and to take part in the tribal assembly. In the case of *folk* we face the difficulty that the political-legal meaning of the word is 'the whole people' and not just a subdivision of them, as we might expect from the distinction in military use between *folk* and *heri*.[34] This expansion of scope for *folk* in its political sense may have taken place only in this sphere (but for what reason?), but it could also have begun in the military sphere. In favour of this would speak the historical cases reporting that a Germanic army formation in a large-scale encounter was made up of a whole tribe (as with Caesar's words on the battle-line of Ariovistus). This would explain the anomaly of the *Isidor* translation in using *folk* to render *exercitus*.

The political-legal function of *folk* is clear when it is used of those participating in the tribal assembly. In the trial-scene in the OS *Heliand* the Jews, presented as if they were involved in a native *thing* and asked whether Christ or the thief is to be put to death, are termed the *folc* (vv. 5409ff.). From this particular sense of all those entitled to take part in such legal proceedings the word *folk* could extend its scope to the whole people in their political-legal function. This function of the word can be demonstrated whenever employed in association with a ruler or king to indicate his authority over tribe or people or whenever linked with a named tribe or the land which they occupy. OS *folc* has thus acquired the meaning 'people' in the widest political sense in the *Heliand* when Herod is described as chosen as a king at Jerusalem over the Jewish people (v. 61: *that Iudeono folc*), when Pilate rules over them (5335: *thie thes folkes giweld*) or when Herod, as part of what is presented as his royal authority (*kuningdôm*), is responsible for laws and peace amongst the Jewish people (5254: *undar themu folke*). Whereas in its military sense *folk* denoted only a single formation within the army there is no suggestion in these OS examples that its political usage signified anything less than the whole people.

Something similar can be shown for ON and OE. In the former a prince can be described as *fólks iaðar* 'ruler of a people' (*Helgakviða Hundingsbana II* 42,3), a compressed equivalent of Herod's royal authority exercised amongst the Jewish people in the *Heliand*, whilst four kings ruling over their people (*Sigurðarkviða in skamma* 18,4: *fólki ráðom*) correspond to the phrase in the *Heliand* 5335. The same kind of evidence leads to the same conclusion in OE. When Beowulf visits the *Suðdena folc* (v. 463) he is seeking out the people (or territory) of the south Danes, not a

---

[34] *Ibid.*, p. 191 and fn. 104.

military formation composed of south Danes, whilst the double formula *folc ond rīce* (1179) implies an equally wide scope for *folc*. In *Deor* the far-flung empire of Ermanaric, polyethnic if any Germanic kingdom was,[35] is summed up by his 'possessing widely the peoples of the Goths' kingdom' (22: *ahte wide folc / Gotena rices*).

Since the meanings 'people' as well as 'army formation' are attested for ON and OS, the two most conservative Germanic languages, and also for OE this double semantic function of *folk* is likely to be of considerable antiquity. We find it also in OHG, where the need for *folk* to denote 'people' in the political sense was all the greater once *heri* concentrated its meaning on the military sphere alone. The distinction between army and people made by the Franks and then in Germany at large brought about a differentiation of *heri* and *folk* in two different directions. Whereas *heri* acquired an exclusively military function in OHG and shows no sign of the meaning 'people', *folk* does manage to preserve some trace of the former function alongside the latter meaning.

In OHG glosses the legal meaning of *folk* is made clear when, in apposition to *dinc*, it renders Lat. *contio* 'assembly of the people', whilst the ethnic (and political?) function comes more to the fore when Lat. *tribus*, explained as a division of the people, is translated as *khunni, folkes ziteilitha*.[36] In the *Hildebrandslied* the son is asked who his father might be amongst 'the men in the people' (10: *fireo in folche*). That we are justified in seeing *folk* in this sense (and not meaning 'in the army formation') is suggested by the variation of this phrase in v. 13 (*in chunincriche*), an association of people in the widest sense with kingdom such as we found also in OS and OE. A similar combination of a ruler with the people over whom he ruled is found in *Isidor* (529: *Dher selbo infenc haerduom dhes israhelischin folches*), whilst in *Tatian* the elders of the people who exercise legal authority (*seniores populi*) are translated by *thie altôston thes folkes* (153,3). What does not emerge from these examples is the significance of a negative fact. No example of *folk* in this political-legal sense is to be found in so lengthy a text as Otfrid's *Evangelienbuch* (instead, he uses the word in a general, non-political sense 'crowd, group of people') or after Otfrid.[37]

Equally remarkable is the fact that the frequency of the word *folk* (irrespective of its political sense or not) underwent a noticeable decline in late OHG. Herold has analysed the material statistically, dividing it into texts dated before and after *Tatian*.[38] In early OHG continuous texts (i.e.

---

[35] See below, pp. 170ff.   [36] Herold (1941), 194.   [37] *Ibid.*, pp. 194f.   [38] *Ibid.*, p. 195.

up to and including *Tatian*) the word occurs in all 66 times, spread over six works, but with the lion's share (51 cases) going to *Tatian*. After this the word is attested only 21 times, again spread over six works. This contrast in frequency is even more marked if we take into account the shortness of the earlier period (less than a hundred years) and the length of the later period (more than two hundred years) as well as the consideration that the earlier period contains only relatively small-scale works (e.g. the *Hildebrandslied* with sixty-eight lines) by contrast with the size of the works by Otfrid and Notker in the later period. It is probable that this decline in the use of *folk* over the whole of the OHG period is connected with its loss of a former political-legal connotation (from Otfrid on) and the marked rise in frequency of our third term, *liut(i)*.

This statistical evidence suggests that *folk* was on the retreat in OHG: first, as a military term since the earliest texts, but then also as a political-legal term since about 830. Its recurrent use in a Christian context (Israel or Christendom as 'God's people'), whilst throwing light on its ability to render *populus*, further removed it from the military and political spheres in which it was originally at home.[39] Historical reasons for this linguistic development are provided by the two words with which *folk* was in competition. First, by *heri*, since both *heri* and *folk* originally had a double function, but then differentiated in opposite directions. Secondly, by *liut(i)* whose statistical ascendancy in the period when *folk* declines makes it highly likely that the fate of both words was determined by the same historical factors. Before considering these we must look at the linguistic evidence for this last word for people.

The OHG singular noun *liut* (with its plural variant *liuti*) agrees with *heri* and *folk* in possessing two meanings, one of which is 'people' in the political-legal sense, but differs from them in its other meaning, which is not military, but rather denotes a status of subordination ('subjects, vassals'). Any military function this word may once have had is suggested by the not always reliable testimony of etymology.

This word is attested throughout Germania, with the exception of Gothic, but also in OSl. *ljudŭ* 'people' and Lith. *liáudis* 'people'.[40] Whether these cognates derive from a joint IE vocabulary or are loanwords from Germanic, the spread of all these forms suggests the antiquity of this word with the meaning 'people'. Etymologically, the word derives from an IE verbal root meaning 'to grow', with traces in Go.

[39] *Ibid.*, pp. 202f.   [40] *Ibid.*, pp. 205f.

liudan 'to grow' (with corresponding forms in OHG, OS, OE, cf. also ON *loðinn* 'grown over with hair, shaggy'). Gothic also has the words *juggaláups* 'a youth' (someone of young growth) and *hwēláups* 'how big' ('grown to what size'). An original meaning may be surmised: the generation of those who have grown up to maturity, i.e. 'people' in the political-legal sense (since the young man acquired the right to attend the tribal assembly only at maturity), but also conceivably 'army' (at a stage too early to have left any written trace), since the young man acquired this military obligation at the same time.

The range of cognates for this word also includes Burgundo-Latin *leudis* 'freeman' and OSl. *ljudinu* (same meaning).[41] The meaning of these two cognates developed from the concept 'member of one's own people' in contrast to those subjected or enslaved by them, which is paralleled by the cognate Gr. *eleútheros* and Lat. *liber* (< *loufero*-), both of which developed the meaning 'free' from 'member of one's own people'. (A similar semantic change underlay Germanic *frî*.)[42] The idea of political or social freedom was therefore inherent in the meaning 'people' in a number of different IE languages.

The political-legal meaning 'people', involving also an ethnic sense distinguishing one tribe from another, can be established, if not at all frequently for Germany.[43] An early example comes from the *Hildebrandslied*, where the son claims that his exiled father's fate was recounted to him by members of his tribe (v. 15: *dat sagetun mi usere liuti*), those best equipped to know this. Even if the words could instead have a quite general, non-ethnic meaning here ('our people') an ethnic meaning for *liuti* can still be rescued for this poem by the later reference (v. 58) to *ostarliuto* 'people from the east' to designate the Huns.[44] A tribal dimension is also present in Otfrid's use of the word: in his praise of the Franks he twice claims for their military strength the fact that no other people dares take up arms against them, using *liut* for these other tribes (I 1,37 and 81).

As with *folk*, the political or ethnic meaning of *liuti* can often be established when reference is made to a named tribe with whom *liuti* is associated (behind *ostarliuto* in the *Hildebrandslied* there stands the more explicit *Hun*, v. 39) or to the territory occupied by the tribe. In *Beowulf* *lēode* shows the ethnic meaning 'people' when it is linked with a specific tribe, e.g. *Sige-Scyldinga* (596) or Danes (599: *lēode Deninga*). Elsewhere this

---

[41] *Ibid.*, p. 206 and fn. 160.   [42] See above, pp. 39ff. and Scheller (1950), 35, 42.
[43] Herold (1941), 207.   [44] Lühr (1982), 464.

word for 'people' can be linked alliteratively with *land* for the tribal territory, as in *Edward's Death* 10 in OE or in the *Oddrúnargrátr* 17,3 in ON. In OS the same double formula is transferred to the religious sphere to describe the universality of Christ's sway (*Heliand* 2287f.).

The number of examples for this usage in OHG is remarkably small. The same is true of OS, by comparison with the frequency both of other terms for 'people' in the *Heliand* and of *liudi* in a non-political function. Over the whole of Germany the most commonly used political term for 'people' was not *liuti*, but *folk*, at least until about 830.[45] According to Herold's calculations: up to and including *Tatian folk* is used in a political sense 66 times, but *liuti* only 22 times, whilst in the period after 830 *folk* occurs only 21 times, but *liuti* as often as 530 times. These overall proportions are not contradicted by the figures for individual works: in *Tatian folk* is used 51 times, but *liut* only once. By contrast, Otfrid has *folk* 7 times and *liut(i)* nearly 200 times, while with Notker the matching figures are 7 and 242.

From all this it is clear that *liut(i)* took over the political function which was abandoned by *folk* in OHG. For a time these two words were in competition before *liut(i)* eventually won the day, but since the competition concerns the political usage of these words it is tempting to assume political changes behind the linguistic one, as with *heri* and *folk*.[46] Yet *liuti* in the political sense as we have so far understood it is attested rarely in OHG (twice in the *Hildebrandslied*, twice with Otfrid). This raises a further question. What new meaning does this word show on all the other occasions? The answer to this was anticipated above: *liut(i)* came to denote a status of subordination, of subjects towards a king, of followers (or vassals) towards a lord, of subordinates towards those in authority. Whereas with *folk* the final political and legal authority had lain with the people assembled at the *thing*, with *liut(i)* this authority lies elsewhere, above and beyond them.[47]

The word can gloss *subditi* 'subjects' in OHG, but also describe the relationship between a ruler and his subjects in literary texts. Secular usage is transferred to a religious context when it is a question of Christ's kingship, as at the Annunciation in Otfrid's text (I 5,29: *Er richisot githiuto kuning therero liuto*). Here *liuto* is not simply 'these people' (*diese Menschen*),[48] but rather 'this people' or 'these subjects', as is implied by the presence of *richisot* 'rules' and *kuning* 'king', corresponding to the biblical source

---

[45] Herold (1941), 195, 207.   [46] *Ibid.*, p. 196.   [47] *Ibid.*, pp. 207ff.
[48] As suggested by Vollmann-Profe (1987), 59.

(Lc. 1.32f.: *regnare, regnum*; Mt. 1.21: *populus suus*). Christ's kingship over His people is also highlighted in the entry into Jerusalem, in His royal descent from king David and rule over His people (IV 4,43: *Thu weltis liutes manages Davides sun thes kuninges, / bist kuning ouh githiuto therero lantliuto*). This subjection of *liuti* to someone in authority is not confined to Christ's transcendental kingship, it can also recur in the secular sphere, as when Otfrid refers to Nicodemus's position as the 'first or prince of the people' (II 12,2: *furisto thero liuto*). Whereas the biblical source (Joh. 3.1: *princeps Judaeorum*) has an ethnic construction, Otfrid has replaced this by one which places more weight on the people seen as subordinates.

How far this loss of authority by the people who had exercised it collectively as freemen at the tribal assembly could go can be seen in Otfrid's presentation of Christ's trial. The author uses *liut(i)* here several times in the sense of those assembled at a trial, but generally in contrast to a named authority in whom alone the right to pass legal judgment is now invested.[49] (This usage reflects one of the legal changes, especially amongst the Franks, which contributed to the gradual dissolution of the tribal assembly of the past.)[50] One example may demonstrate this, concerning the readiness of the high priests of the Jews to speak on behalf of the people and to reject Pilate's offer of clemency in not putting Christ to death (IV 24,19: *Thie biskofa zi noti firsprachun tho thie liuti / firsuahun sino guati joh selb thaz heroti*). Two legal terms present this biblical situation in a form intelligible to a contemporary audience.[51] *Firsahhan* means to reject a legal offer (of clemency, *guati*), whilst *firsprehhan* denotes the right to speak on someone else's behalf. Those who exercise this legal right are the *biskofa* or high priests, whilst those whom they represent are simply the *liuti*. In other examples from Otfrid describing the same situation those who speak up are also referred to as *ewarton, furiston* and *heroti*,[52] in each case a special authority with active responsibilities at a court of law, whereas the *liuti*, although still present, have no active legal rights. This situation has been compared with the legal reforms introduced by Charles the Great, by which professional lay assessors at courts (*Schöffen*) represented the emperor at the cost of the people, present but inactive.[53] Whereas *folk* is used in connection with this trial scene in the *Heliand* this word is not employed by Otfrid in this context, whilst conversely the *Heliand* makes no use of *liudi*.[54] This was probably because the relative remoteness of Saxony from the legal reforms of the Franks, imposed

[49] Herold (1941), 209f.   [50] See above, pp. 35ff.   [51] Kelle (1881), 130f., 132.
[52] Herold (1941), 105, 209f.   [53] *Ibid.*, p. 199.   [54] *Ibid.*, p. 209, fn. 168.

upon them only by Charles the Great, also meant a time-lag in introducing the corresponding vocabulary.

If the semantic evidence for *liut(i)* implies a political-legal development from freemen who, like the *folk*, have the right to attend and deliberate at a court of law to subjects of a higher authority who have lost this right, we must ask what changes in Frankish society account for this linguistic transformation.[55] Whereas our earlier sketch of the historical background concerned the break-up of military and political responsibility (*heri* and *folk*) we are now dealing with a development within the political realm alone (the freeman's loss of legal rights at the *thing*).

One factor making for this demotion of the freeman was the increasing centralisation of Frankish kingship. The large number of *reguli* or petty kings in the period when the Franks first occupied northern France gave way to a unified monarchy under Chlodwig after his eradication of these competing *reguli* and defeat of the Visigoths in 507.[56] The extension of Chlodwig's rule to include Roman subjects and hence the influence of Roman political ideas with their inbuilt tendency towards a greater authoritarianism than had ever been known in Germania reinforced this growth in royal power. By making use of former Roman structures of political control, even Roman personnel, military and civilian, lay and ecclesiastical, Chlodwig was enabled to buttress his authority as a Frankish king by means of administrative methods taken over from imperial Rome. A king wielding such power was no longer subjected to the checks and balances imposed on a Germanic ruler and would be less ready to acknowledge the right of the freeman to have a say in political and legal deliberations.

What had once, in simpler days, been the legal assembly at which the *folk* directly exercised collective power gave way to an assembly of nobles representing the king. As a result, the appointment of authorised officials was made by the ruler, no longer by the popular assembly. Just as the general obligation of all freemen to bear arms disappeared in the face of a growing professionalisation of a permanent army, so too was the complementary obligation to appear at the *thing* abolished in favour of a similarly professional body of legislators, standing royal nominees (*scabini*), chosen by the king from among his highranking vassals.

The Church's growing dependence on royal power and the extent to which it succeeded in imposing its own ideas of Christian kingship on

---

[55] *Ibid.*, pp. 196ff.   [56] See below, pp. 137f.

society also had a part to play in this process of extracting the Christian ruler from any control by those who had elected him.[57] Once the Church set the king as God's representative (*vicarius Dei*) above the people the latter lost more of their right to share in decision-taking. In the past the tribal assembly had elected the king from amongst those of noble birth, so that this assembly was the original source of royal power which, by that derivation from below, could not be regarded in absolute terms. From the Merovingian period this gave ground to a new conception of the origin of royal authority, summed up most succinctly in the newly introduced royal title: *rex Dei gratia* 'king by the grace of God'. With this formula the king broke with his earlier dependence on the people and freed himself from the checks which they imposed on his freedom of movement, but at the same time he established a close connection between himself and God, partaking of the latter's absolute power insofar as an offence against one could be seen as an offence against the other. Earlier folk-law consequently was replaced by royal law for which the consent of the people was no longer required. Since, in this Christian view of theocratic kingship, royal power derived from God and not from the people, the position was reached where the people was subjected to royal power (and to the divine authority now held to stand behind it). The people could now therefore be referred to as the king's subjects, his *subiecti* or his *subditi*.

As a result of these changes, above all in the relatively advanced state of Francia, the 'people' (freemen equipped with their own political and legal rights) were now regarded as 'subjects', enjoying only the right of attendance, not of active participation in decision-making at the assembly. With the establishment of Frankish political ascendancy these legal reforms, together with the semantic changes which gave them expression, were carried to Germany itself, first to Central and Upper Germany, but only later to Saxony as well.[58]

None of the three words discussed can be treated in isolation. *Heri* and *folk* must be seen in their interplay because of their complementary developments (both originally denoted 'army' as well as 'people' but, moving in opposite directions, came to signify only one of these). Nor can *folk* and *liuti* be regarded separately because the decline of the first as a political-legal term is matched by the rise of the second. Behind the close tie-up of these three words there stands the whole complex of mil-

---

[57] Ullmann (1961), 22f., 117ff.   [58] Herold (1941), 199, 213.

itary, political and legal changes in continental western Germania, especially in Francia.

From about 830 *folk* ceased to be in regular use as a political-legal word. It could still be used as a general term, suggesting 'crowd, group', with neither military nor political implications, but its decline from its former status made it free to render such a word as Latin *vulgus* 'common people' in a derogatory sense, deprived of any political rights.[59] Characteristic of the linguistic changes from 830 on is not simply the fact that *liut(i)* largely replaced *folk* as a political term, but also the idea of subjection and subordination to a higher authority which it expressed, acting as the equivalent of *subditi, fideles* and *homines*, but also giving rise to the loanword MLat. *leudes*.[60] This change of meaning in OHG is most clearly visible in Rhenish Franconian (Herold's most telling examples come from Otfrid), the dialect of the boundary area between Germany proper and northern France where the Frankish legal reforms were first carried through.[61] The history of these three words for 'people' is largely coterminous with the transition from Germanic antiquity to the early Middle Ages on Frankish territory.

[59] *Ibid.*, pp. 204 ('crowd, group'), 150, 201, fn. 150 (*vulgus*).   [60] *Ibid.*, pp. 212f.   [61] *Ibid.*, p. 213.

CHAPTER 6

Lordship

In this chapter we turn to the first of the two forces which worked against the survival of the kindred.[1] We shall be concerned with three terms for the 'lord' (OHG *frô, truhtin* and *hêrro*, together with their cognates), with their chronological sequence and with the historical changes which underlie it.

The word *frô* is attested in all the Germanic languages (even if in ON only in the form of names for the gods Freyr and Freyja about whose existence in the rest of Germania there is no reliable evidence).[2] Its meaning 'lord' arises straightforwardly from the etymological connection with IE **pro-* 'forward, ahead' and parallels from the same root, such as terms for 'first' and 'early' in other IE languages.[3] That a word with this semantic force could designate a lord is made clear by some of the Merovingian Latin terms for noblemen (*primi, priores, principes* and *primates*) and by OHG *furisto* 'prince, ruler' (literally 'first, foremost').

Three secular functions can be determined for OHG *frô*, of which the first (and possibly earliest) is to denote the 'lord of a household' whose legal responsibility covered wife, children, dependants, slaves and property.[4] Go. *fráuja* is therefore used in apposition with *gardawaldands* 'master of the household' or in the same context as *gards* 'house, family'. OE *frēa* refers to the relationship of the master of a household to his wife or children, just as in OS the *frôho* has dependants within the household (*Heliand* 2119: *at mînumu hûs*). In such cases the household embraces the dwelling and outhouses not merely of the lord himself, but also of his dependants.[5] This is suggested by Go. *heiwafráuja* as a rendering of *oikodespótēs* 'lord of the house', where the first element of the Gothic compound is cognate with other Germanic words for 'family' (e.g. OHG

---

[1] See above, p. 66. [2] Green (1965), 19f. [3] Feist (1923), 123; Lehmann (1986), 126.
[4] Ehrismann (1906), 189; Green (1965), 21ff. [5] Cf. Schlesinger (1963a), 13f.

hîwun 'married couple', *hîwiski* 'family'), but also with Go. *háims* 'village', OE *hām* 'villa, estate' and OE *hīd* 'hide of land (enough to support a family)'. This suggests a semi-independent economic unit of the size of a small settlement or even village. (The objection that if *fráuja* in fact had this meaning there would have been no need for Wulfila to make use of the specifying compound *heiwafráuja* can be met by the suggestion that he is here rendering, somewhat slavishly as elsewhere, the Greek compound *oikodespótēs*.)[6] In interpreting *frô* as 'lord of a household' we have to understand 'household' as more than a modern nuclear family, as larger even than an extended family, since it also included slaves, serfs and other dependants. That authority of this kind could pass well beyond the confines of the house is suggested by IE parallels such as Gr. *despótēs* (< **dem-s-póti*) and Lat. *dominus* (from *domus*).[7] The Latin term extended in classical antiquity from the household context (the master of a slave) to the emperor and in Frankish legal texts from the owner of cattle, slaves, landed property to the secular or heavenly king.[8]

Frô could also denote something more like 'chieftain' and was probably the vernacular equivalent of the *principes* to whom Tacitus refers.[9] The possibility of associating these *principes* with OHG *frô* is suggested by the regular use of the Latin term in the plural and by the OHG adjective *frôno*, a stereotyped genitive plural of *frô*. The Germanic *principes* deliberate as a body, together they play a leading rôle in the assembly, they are seen as collectively responsible for administering justice and for receiving tributes (in all these cases only the plural is used).[10] The public authority which the *principes* represent means that *frôno*, referring to these chieftains, can be used as a rendering for *publicus* or *communis*. It also occurs in connection with public tribute rendered to the authorities (*frônagelt* translates *fiscus*, so that the tribute is seen as a tax), paralleling what Tacitus says of tributes to the *principes*. The deliberations in which they collectively took part are also echoed in phrases like *frôno dinc* and *frôno einunga*. Whether *frô* in this function also designated a 'nobleman' is uncertain, but probable in view of its feminine counterpart *frouwa* 'noblewoman'.

Thirdly, our word could also be applied to the king or ruler.[11] In OE the compound *folcfrēa* 'ruler' points in this direction, just as do phrases like *frēa Scyldinga* and *Deniga frēa* to denote Hrōðgār's royal status in *Beowulf* (the tribal name, like *folc-* in the compound, implies that the *frēa*

---

[6] Cf. Kroeschell (1968), 25, fn. 60.   [7] Wenskus (1961), 365.   [8] Kroeschell (1968), 24.
[9] *Germania* 11, 12 and 15; Ehrismann (1906), 189; Green (1965), 23f.
[10] Ehrismann (1906), 200; Kristensen (1983), 58f.   [11] Ehrismann (1906), 189; Green (1965), 25f.

is lord over the tribe, i.e. its king). *Frēa* can also be used in close association with other epithets for a ruler (*þēoden, þēodcyning, ríce, folcāgend*).
Apparent parallels in OHG must be used with caution. When Lat.
respublica is glossed by *kunicriche* as well as *frônereht* it is much more likely
that the first vernacular term is used because, with the later rise of
Frankish kingship, the king now exercised an authority formerly wielded
by the *principes*. The same historical development from Germanic to
Frankish social conditions underlies the suggested translation of *fridu
frôno* in the *Lorscher Bienensegen* (v. 2) as implying the king's peace alongside
God's peace.[12] Even if this were accepted, the same reservations as with
frônereht make it unlikely that this phrase constitutes evidence that *frô* had
once been synonymous with 'king'. Such evidence as we have seems to
be confined to OE. Even here, though, the lack of any adjective equivalent to OHG *frôno*, together with the rise of royal power as on the continent, means that the concept 'public' can be rendered by *frôno* in OHG,
but by a royal term in OE, e.g. Lat. *fiscus*, OHG *frôno scaz*, OE *kyninga
seod*.[13]

The antiquity of the word in these three functions is suggested by the
fact that it appears to be on the retreat by the time when our written
sources first start.[14] The position is most drastic in ON where the word
occurs in the names of two divinities, but nowhere as an appellative. In
OHG the word survives only as a fixed term of vocative address (*frô mîn*)
and as an equally fixed adjectival form (*frôno*, together with *frônisg*). OS
usage shows more elasticity: alongside the vocative phrase *frô mîn* the
appellative *frôho* is also used as an independent noun (although always in
alliteration in the *Heliand*, hence perhaps dictated by formal needs).
Much greater vigour is shown by OE *frēa*: it is used frequently as an
appellative of a secular lord (and of God), but also in compounds where
it has the force of an intensifying prefix (*frēamicel* 'very great', *frēamǣre*
'very famous'). In Gothic Wulfila uses *fráuja* as a religious and secular
appellative: in the former function it is the equivalent of Gr. *kýrios*, under
no competition, as is the case in WG, from other terms (cf. *truhtin, hêrro*).
Apart from Gothic (perhaps protected by the early date of our testimony) we therefore register a progressive atrophy of this word. This suggests that it was of some antiquity and may have been in process of being
supplanted by a more up-to-date term, above all by *hêrro* as an originally
Frankish term for the new social institution of vassalage.

A second point concerns the simultaneous threat to *frô* in the religious

---

[12] Ehrismann (1906), 196f.   [13] *Ibid.*, p. 198.   [14] Green (1965), 30f.

sphere by the rise of OHG *truhtin* as a standing term for the Christian *dominus*.[15] This suggests that before this threat arose *frô* may have been used not merely as a secular term with the functions so far established, but also as a religious one. To establish this for pre-Christian Germania we need to look at the stereotyped OHG adjective *frôno*.[16] Although it functions as an adjective it is the genitive plural form of the appellative *frô*, hence uninflected as an adjective and normally following its noun (although already with Otfrid it can precede it, like an ordinary adjective). The conversion of a genitive plural noun into an adjective, although not common, is certainly not without parallels, as with OFr. *francor* 'Frankish' (< *Francorum* 'of the Franks'). Difficulties arise, however, in accounting for the three meanings of the adjectival use of *frôno*.

Its first meaning lies closest to *frô* 'chieftain', namely 'belonging to a lord or to the lords' or 'to do with a lord or lords', an adjectival usage protected from the threat which *hêrro* otherwise meant for *frô* by the fact that *hêrro* was late in producing an adjective. *Frôno* in this sense is illustrated in the second *Würzburger Markbeschreibung*, where ecclesiastical property is distinguished from lay property specified as *frono ioh friero Franchono erbi*.[17] This twofold expression covers the inherited property of two classes of people: of all those known by the title *frô* (*frôno erbi* thus stands for *hereditas dominica*) and of free-born Frankish peasants (*friero Franchono erbi*). Other examples of this usage are attested from MHG, but must be earlier in origin: *vrôndienest* 'service rendered to the (feudal) lord', *vrôngerihte* 'baronial court of justice', *vrônwalt* 'wood belonging to a lord'. What had earlier been seen in connection with the *principes* as a collective authority within the tribe (hence *frôno* as a genitive *plural*) is now, after the rise of centralised kingship and feudalism, the property of one lord.[18] The word *frôno*, stereotyped and undeclinable, survived this change from plural to singular insofar as its origin can no longer have been recognisable.

The second function of *frôno* we have already had occasion to look at: it conveys the meaning 'public, communal', since the collective body of all those called *frô* represented public authority.[19] Funds owned by or due to tribal authority are in the hands of the *principes*, of those called *frô*, as in the translation of *fiscus* by *frônagelt* or *frôno scaz*, and of *respublica* by *frônereht*. MHG still testifies, for example, *vrônreht* 'public law' and *vrônveste* 'public prison'.

---

[15] *Ibid.*, pp. 31f.   [16] *Ibid.*, pp. 38ff.   [17] Ehrismann (1906), 194f.   [18] Möller (1903), 122.
[19] *Ibid.*, p. 119; Ehrismann (1906), 197.

With the third meaning of *frôno*, however, we enter a semantic field quite different from what we have so far seen: 'holy'.[20] Otfrid, in addition to applying *frôno* to Christ, also uses it of Mary, the scriptures and the good deeds of a Christian. These cases indicate that *frôno* did not acquire the meaning 'holy' simply from its use to render *dominicus*. Instead, this meaning antedates the contact with the Christian adjective, as is best indicated by the German adjective's derivation from a genitive *plural* suitable for the needs of a polytheistic religion (which commonly employed its terms for the gods in the plural), not for Christianity.

Of these three meanings of *frôno* the first ('to do with the lords') and the second ('public') are closely connected, so much so that the first could have led quite easily to the second. The problem lies with the meaning 'holy'. Two suggestions are diametrically opposed,[21] but neither successfully explains the relationship between all three functions of *frôno*. They can be resolved, however, if we regard *frô* as an appellative meaning 'lord, chieftain' (from which *frôno* 'public, communal' was derived), but also as applicable to the gods (accounting for *frôno* 'belonging to the gods, holy').[22]

The second term for 'lord' is represented by OHG *truhtin*, derived from the noun *truht*, widely accepted as the original vernacular equivalent of the war-band described by Tacitus as a central institution in Germanic society and warfare. *Truhtin* therefore originally denoted the leader of such a war-band. This leader can be associated with the *principes* as chieftains if we realise that, although any freeman was theoretically entitled to maintain a war-band, in practice only those who had the means to reward followers came into question, i.e. the *principes* (although not every *princeps* necessarily had a war-band).[23] In view of the two functions of the *princeps* (legal and military) our question must be: if the *princeps* in one realm of activity was probably denoted by the term *frô* could he in the more explicitly military context be referred to as a *truhtin*? That this was possible has been shown in the case of *Beowulf*, where *dryhten* is employed as a secular term in a heroic or warlike context, but *frēa* with no such implications.[24]

In seeking information about the Germanic war-band from classical sources we must distinguish between Caesar and Tacitus. The former

---

[20] Green (1965), 40f.   [21] Ehrismann (1906), 195ff; Möller (1903), 97, 108ff.
[22] Green (1965), 45ff.
[23] Schlesinger (1963a), 20; Much (1967), 223; Kristensen (1983), 22f., 25, 28f.
[24] Ehrismann (1906), 189f.; Green (1965), 276ff.

describes what may be termed a raiding-party, a military grouping which may have belonged to the prehistory of the *comitatus*, but was not identical with it.[25] A leading man would propose in the assembly to undertake a raid and call for voluntary followers. The implication is that the relationship between a leader of this type and his followers was temporary. The *comitatus*, as presented by Tacitus in the first century AD, is different, transformed into a more permanent relationship.[26] Leader and followers now formed a unity not merely in wartime, but also in peacetime for, although the leader did not reward his men with land, he kept them about him by providing food and shelter and gained prestige by their number (*Germania* 13: *in pace decus, in bello praesidium*). These followers also assisted their leader off the battlefield, accompanying him on his judicial duties where their presence lent obvious force to his authority. They kept with him after any campaign not merely to receive the gifts of swords or horses, but also to enjoy the feasting (*Germania* 14: *epulae et . . . apparatus*).

The difference between Caesar's temporary raiding-party and Tacitus's more permanent war-band illustrates that this variety must be taken into account in attempting any definition of the war-band and its leader. Kuhn defines it as a voluntary association of freemen in the regular (but not necessarily lifelong) service of a more powerful man, to whose household they belong and to whom they owe military service and representation duties, and with whom they stand in a relationship of reciprocal loyalty.[27] (A lengthy list of characteristic features of the *comitatus*, as described by Tacitus, has been offered by Kristensen, grouped under the headings of the leader, *princeps*, followers, *comites*, and association, *comitatus*.)[28] Working with such a detailed characterisation enabled Kuhn to distinguish the war-band from earlier types of military unit which contributed to its formation, not merely the raiding-party of Caesar's day, but also the *Gesinde* 'household servants or followers' (probably with a military obligation).

Another social feature of the war-band was its intertribal nature.[29] Tacitus describes how in times of peace youths seek out tribes where war is afoot to offer their services to the leader of a war-band which, unlike the kindred formation or tribal army, was therefore not confined to the

[25] Caesar, *De bello Gallico* VI 23; Kuhn (1956), 4 ('Heerhaufen'); Thompson (1965), 48f.
[26] Kuhn (1956), 4; Thompson (1965), 50; Kristensen (1983), 42f., 54f.
[27] Kuhn (1956), 12, refining the definition given by Schlesinger (1963a), 18.
[28] Kristensen (1983), 53ff.
[29] Kuhn (1956), 9; Thompson (1965), 58; Wenskus (1961), 368, 369, 371.

members of one tribe only. Equally, a leader who had proved successful could attract warriors from outside his own tribe, lured by the prospect of further success. The presence of outsiders in the war-band could explain the presence of the element *gast* 'stranger' in the formation of warrior names (e.g. *Harigasti*, already on the Negau helmet) or the use of a noun such as OHG *wreckeo*, originally 'outcast', also in the sense 'warrior (in exile)'. However, in thus cutting across the boundaries between tribes the war-band was also a disruptive force in Germanic society.[30] In creating his own power base where his followers were immediately beholden only to him the leader of a war-band acquired a measure of independence (of his kindred as well as the tribal assembly). If the assembly had no direct control over a powerful leader whose followers ensured him freedom of action his military activity could certainly have an effect on his tribe when it invited retaliatory raids in turn. The victory for which the leader and his followers fought profited the war-band alone and might even jeopardise the wider interests of the tribe. In ways such as these the war-band worked to undermine the strength and cohesion of the tribe in which it was established.

It is clear that the *comitatus* required certain conditions, economic, social, political and military, in which it could arise and flourish, as is indicated by the fact that it apparently did not exist in Caesar's day, but was flourishing by the time of Tacitus. To maintain a retinue was an expensive affair and demanded, as Tacitus emphasises, a state of almost continuous warfare to provide the wherewithal. That was possible only in times of extreme turmoil, such as the military encounters with Rome and the migrations at large (and later the Viking expeditions), which would account for the rise of this institution in the years between Caesar and Tacitus.[31] By contrast, more settled conditions following on the colonisation of new territory created difficulties in sustaining the war-band economically. The obvious answer (for the leader to reward with the gift of land which had now become available, the beginning of the feudal *beneficium*) undermined the essence of the war-band, for now leader and followers, separated geographically, ceased to constitute a permanent association in peace as well as in war.[32] Kuhn has gone much further, however, in arguing that with the close of the migrations the relationship between lord and followers changed so fundamentally and so quickly that continuity into the Merovingian period and therewith a

---

[30] Thompson (1965), 55, 56, 59f. Cf. Todd (1992), 33 ('a faultline').   [31] Kuhn (1956), 12ff.
[32] *Ibid.*, pp. 4f.

contribution of the war-band relationship to emergent feudalism was out of the question. He adduces no evidence why this change must have been so quick and ignores the possibility that continuity in terminology (from the war-band to the feudal relationship) could underline the gradual nature of this change. Terms used later in written texts (e.g. *gisîði* and *gitrôst* in the *Heliand*) are no longer applied to a war-band, but still could descend from that earlier institution and throw light on the past.

This implies that it is possible to detect some degree of continuity in the war-band. Kuhn himself is ready to concede continuity between earlier institutions and the *comitatus* in that, however distinct it may be from the raiding-party described by Caesar or from the *Gesinde* 'household servants/followers', these may have contributed to the rise of the new institution.[33] He suggests that after the conclusion of a successful raiding-party its leader could have seen the point of using the plunder to keep his followers around him for a longer period, thereby strengthening his position and guarding against a counter-blow from his defeated victims. Continuity may also be suspected, however, into the following period. Precisely the point where Kuhn sees the end of a war-band relationship (permanent settlement on new territory, the gift of land to followers) has been regarded as a point of contact between war-band and feudalism, a tendency within the former to develop into the latter.[34]

As yet we have barely looked at the linguistic implications of the war-band. What was the Germanic equivalent for the *comitatus* as a grouping, for its individual members and for its leader? It is important to pay attention to this range of three terms, duly recorded in Latin in Tacitus's account (*comitatus, comites, princeps*) and used as organising features in Kristensen's detailed characterisation of the war-band. Kuhn has stressed that these are the three features most richly represented by synonyms in heroic poetry celebrating the exploits of the war-band and that terms for the first two must exist side by side (suggesting the individual follower as a member of a permanent group) if we are to talk of a war-band.[35]

Particularly important in Kuhn's eyes is the juxtaposition of such terms as OHG neuter *gisindi* 'a following, retinue' and masculine *gisindo* 'follower' (both Otfrid) or OS *gitrôst* 'a following' and *(helm)gitrôsteo* 'warrior'. Although these terms are not used in the sense of a Germanic war-band by either Otfrid or the author of the *Heliand*, Kuhn accepts a war-band origin for them on the grounds that they denote the follower

---

[33] *Ibid.*, pp. 6, 23.　　[34] Sprandel (1978), 66.　　[35] Kuhn (1956), 21, 22.

as belonging to a group whose cohesion lasts beyond any exploit on the battlefield. If we agree with this on the basis of these lexical pairs, we must also acknowledge it in connection with another pair whose origin in the war-band Kuhn questions throughout: Go. *draúhti(witoþ)* 'campaign' and *gadraúhts* 'soldier' or OHG *truht* and *truhting/truhtigomo*. These lexical pairs suggest that *truht* designated the war-band in the past as much as *gisindi* and *gitrôst*. Although Kuhn takes account of Frankish Latin *trustis* and *antrustiones* in considering one of the above pairs, von Olberg's survey of Germanic loanwords in the Latin vocabulary of the Merovingian and Carolingian periods bridges the gap between the close of the migrations and the beginning of vernacular written tradition and establishes continuity in terminology between the war-band relationship and vassalage.[36]

Lastly, although it is correct to attach importance to lexical pairs denoting the war-band as a group and its individual members, the same must hold of pairs which include the third feature, the leader himself, as with OHG *truht* and *truhtin*, indicating the close relationship between the group and its leader. This stem is the only one of those belonging to this context to provide terms corresponding to the three Latin words used by Tacitus (*comitatus* = *truht*, *comites* or *comes* = *truhting/truhtigomo*, *princeps* = *truhtin*) and the only one to supply a term for the lord himself. This lexical range suggests that *truht* and its derivatives have a claim to be seen in connection with the war-band.

OHG *truhtin* has cognates in every Germanic language except Gothic, although even here the presence of related words suggests that it existed (but was not used by Wulfila).[37] The word is formed with a CG suffix *-in* (cf. Go. *kindins* 'governor of a province', but also Lat. *dominus*), a variant of the suffix *-an* (cf. Go. *þiuda* 'people': *þiudans* 'ruler'). The force of these suffixes is to indicate authority over what is expressed by the stem, so that *truhtin* meant 'leader/lord of a *truht*'.

Truht is also CG.[38] It is attested in Gothic in such compounds and derivatives as *draúhtiwitoþ* 'campaign', *gadraúhts* 'soldier', *draúhtinôn* 'to wage war' and *drauhtinassus* 'campaign'. In OE and ON the meanings 'band of warriors' and 'people' are conveyed by *dryht* and *drótt*. In Frankish-Latin legal texts *dructis*, by itself or in compounds, means a 'band of warriors' in various contexts.[39] Elsewhere the word does not occur as a simplex, but in compounds or derivatives. OS *druhtfolk* means

---

[36] Cf. von Olberg (1983), 202ff., 244ff.; (1991), 112ff.   [37] Green (1965), 265, fn. 1.
[38] *Ibid.*, pp. 270f.
[39] Schmidt-Wiegand (1974), 524ff.; Wenskus (1986a), 202f.; von Olberg (1991), 129ff.

'multitude', whilst OHG *truhtigomo, truhting* (cf. OS *druhting*) and OE *dryht-guma, dryhtealdor(man)* all stand for *architriclinus* 'steward, master of ceremonies' or *paranymphus* 'bride's male attendant'.[40] This wide semantic spread constitutes a problem, but the meanings can be divided into two groups: 'a band of warriors' or a non-military function, denoting an 'assembly of people', whether in the general sense of 'people' or in the particular sense of 'festive gathering' (at a wedding or not).

Truht itself is formed with the suffix *-ti*, used to produce abstracts, although disagreement arises over the root to which it is added. Kuhn, who rejects this word as a term for the war-band and plays down its military function, postulates a PG form **drûht-* < **drunk-* (the phonological changes involved are all quite regular) and sees the original meaning of *truht* as 'festive gathering'.[41] This is theoretically possible for all the Germanic forms except Gothic where this derivation should regularly have produced **drūhti-* instead of *draúhti-*. Unless we assume two distinct stems (meaning 'festive gathering' and 'band of warriors', still unexplained) we are driven to reject this explanation. We may ask whether there is any need to suggest two separate stems: both semantic groups share a collective meaning and the spheres of warfare and festivity are complementary aspects of the *comitatus* as described by Tacitus in war and in peace and central to Kuhn's own definition.

Moreover, the military function of **druht-* which Kuhn avoided with his alternative derivation is likely to go back one stage further if we consider the stem **drug-* from which it is derived (the addition of *-ti* to *-g* would regularly produce *-h-*).[42] This stem stands in ablaut relationship with Go. *driugan* 'to wage war', but also with OE *drēogan* and ON *drýgja*, both meaning 'to perform, to carry out', generally used in a military context. This military function of **drug-* may also be supported by OSl. *drugъ* 'friend' and ablaut variants in Lith. *draũgas* 'companion' and ON *draugr* 'warrior'. Theoretically, the Balto-Slavonic examples ('friend') could have developed from a festive context (cf. OHG *gisello* 'hall-companion'), but it is difficult to see how a festive meaning which Kuhn postulates only for the stage **drûht-* '(drinking) festivity' could already be present in the stage **drug-*. All this suggests a primarily military function for **druht-*, but also for **drug-/driug-*.[43]

There remains one final function of this word-family to be accounted

---

[40] Green (1965), 270, fn. 3.   [41] Kuhn (1956), 24.   [42] Green (1965), 272.

[43] The priority of this military over any festive meaning is also suggested by the formation of OE *drēam*, OS *drôm* 'rejoicing (in the lord's hall)' from **draug-* + *-ma*, where the stem had a military meaning, as in ON *draugr*, Go. *driugan*. Cf. Green (1965), 273, fn. 4.

for: the use of *truht* in compounds and derivatives in OE, OS and OHG to render Lat. *architriclinus* 'master of a feast' and *paranymphus* 'bride's male attendant'.[44] It is not difficult to account for the first context, given the possibility that members of the war-band had duties also in their lord's household and that ranks in the medieval royal and aristocratic household derive from this latter context, including the term for the chamberlain, OHG *truhtsâzo*. The second usage (*paranymphus*) can be explained with reference to Germanic marriage customs, including the practice of conducting the bride in a procession to her new kindred, but often with specific reference to the procession taking the form of an armed band, which accounts for the use of *truht*. It is in this context that Frankish-Latin *dructis* is employed in the *Lex Salica* (*puella sponsata ducte ducente ad maritum*).[45]

We may conclude that OHG *truht* originally designated a war-band and *truhtin* its leader, although the employment of these terms in written texts by no means implies that they must still refer to the same institution. Since the *truht* had a festive, household dimension as well as a military one the word could also be applied to this non-military context. Although in *Tatian*, for example, *truhtin* (because of this non-military, 'domestic' usage) is used primarily of the lord of a household in his relationship to his subordinates,[46] its normal usage was to denote a leader on the battlefield. That this meaning occurs so rarely in OHG, by contrast with OE and ON, is because of the almost complete Christianisation of the word (12 secular cases as opposed to over 1,500 applications to God or Christ), extracting it from the military sphere in which it had originated.

The third word for 'lord' is much less widespread within Germania, for OHG *hêrro* is also attested in OS, but has only faint echoes in OE and ON. From the juxtaposition in OHG of the contracted form *hêrro* and the fuller forms *hêrôro/hêriro*, together with the superlative parallels *hêrôsto/hêristo*, it is clear that *hêrro* originated as a comparative of the adjective *hêr* and was then used as a noun.[47]

The cognates of this German adjective (OE *hār*, ON *hárr*) mean 'grey' and 'old'. OHG, by contrast, has no cases where *hêr* means 'grey' and only a few where it denotes 'old'.[48] Amongst these is the *Hildebrandslied*

---

[44] Roeder (1899), 25, 83f., 110, 116; Schultze (1941), 58f.; (1943), 51f.; Green (1965), 274; Schmidt-Wiegand (1974), 525ff.; von Olberg (1991), 129f.   [45] Wenskus (1986a), 202.
[46] Green (1965), 495; Schmidt-Wiegand (1974), 528ff.   [47] Green (1965), 405.
[48] *Ibid.*, pp. 406f.

with its parallel between vv. 56 (*sus hêremo man*) and 41 (*alsô gialtêt man*) or the *Benediktinerregel*, which uses *heriro/heroro* to render *senior* in the sense 'older'. These examples show that the sense of age still persisted in the comparative form of the adjective for some time, but must have been weakened when it was felt necessary, in translating *presbyter* 'elder' or *senex* 'old man' by *althêrro*, to add the adjective *alt* and lost altogether in the eleventh-century compound *juncherre*. In place of the meaning 'old' OHG and OS *hêr* means 'elevated, distinguished, commanding respect'. If only these two languages testify this meaning and are also unique in developing the comparative to denote 'lord' this suggests a causal link. If so, the existence of the comparative with that meaning and the super-lative *hêrôsto* to render *monarchus* and *princeps* could have imbued the adjective *hêr* with a degree of authority far surpassing the respect due to age.[49] This semantic influence of *hêrro*, in particular, on *hêr* is revealed when the verb *hêrisôn* 'to rule' sometimes occurs as *hêrrisôn* or the adjec-tive *hêrlîch* as *herrenlîch*. The rise of *hêrôro* and *hêrôsto* to denote authority imparted this same meaning to the adjective *hêr*, so that it came to lose its former meaning 'old'. That the main impetus came from the compar-ative form is suggested by the way in which in OS it attracts the adjec-tive to itself (*Heliand* 980, MSS C and P: *herran hebencuning*), but also at times the superlative (3441, 5887: *hêrrosto*).[50] Only on German soil did an adjective implying age come to suggest authority and power and this extension of meaning was connected with the substantive *hêrro* 'lord'.

In asking how *hêrro* acquired this meaning, we must stress that it was in origin a comparative adjective used as a noun and that when *hêrro* was first created the adjective had the meaning 'old'. This suggests a possi-ble connection with Merovingian Lat. *senior*, likewise the comparative of an adjective for 'old', used as a noun meaning 'lord'. One consideration above all suggests that the German word was fashioned on the Latin model: its origin is to be sought in Germany and its sporadic presence in other Germanic languages is the result of loanword traffic from Germany. A unique position for Germany, distinguishing it from the rest of Germania, and close agreement, morphological and semantic, between *hêrro* and Lat. *senior* suggest a loan-meaning coined in Germany and imitated in ON and OE.

ON had its own adjective *hárr* 'grey, old', but also the noun which con-cerns us, in two forms: *herra* and *harri*.[51] The first of these is obviously a loanword. The presence of *-e-* is irregular in ON and presupposes a loan

<hr />

[49] *Ibid.*, pp. 408f. (on *hêrôsto* see pp. 445ff.).   [50] *Ibid.*, p. 411.   [51] *Ibid.*, pp. 415ff.

from a language where -*e*- is regular (i.e. Germany, where *hêrro* was often shortened to *herro*). It is also anomalous in having a strong plural *herrar*, instead of a weak form (German may not show a strong plural, but it is the common fate of a loanword to be subject to anomalous changes). *Herra* also occurs late in ON, either in court literature or to denote the Christian God. Everything suggests a late loan into ON from Germany. The other form, *harri*, is also suspect. The presence of short -*a*- is irregular, and could be attributed not to Germany, like *herra*, but to OE *hearra*. Here it is significant that this form first occurs in ON with Egill, who lived in Danelaw, in a poem praising an English ruler. It can be regarded as a loanword from OE.

Like ON, OE possessed the adjective *hār* 'grey, old', with a number of variants of the noun: *hearra, heorra, herra, hierra*.[52] It is equally unlikely to be of native origin. The multiplicity of variants, none of which could be a regular comparative of the OE adjective, is in itself suspicious, whilst one of them, *herra*, suggests German origin. All but four of the attestations of this word are found in the OE *Genesis*, translated from OS, whilst the remaining four come from works later than the *Genesis*, which has the appearance of being the point of transmission for this word from Germany to England.

Within Germany it is difficult to tell whether the point of origin was in OS or in OHG, for there are no phonological irregularities to guide us. Despite this, a general consideration makes it likely that the word originated in OHG.[53] If it represents a continental innovation it is *a priori* probable that it was introduced in the south and west, with their more extensive contacts with Rome leading to changes in social structure, rather than in the more conservative north. Moreover, the political ascendancy of the Franks (already with the Merovingians, then more pronouncedly with the Carolingian subjugation of Saxony) led to a spread of Frankish political terms northwards, as we have seen in the case of *heri, folk* and *liuti*.

Our search for the origin of *hêrro* can be pushed back to the position within OHG itself where the choice, given the passive rôle played by Alemannic in early linguistic history, is between Bavarian and Franconian.[54] The former might seem to be suggested by the two earliest attestations of *hêrro* (*Hildebrandslied* and *Abrogans*). Yet if *hêrro* is in fact a loan-translation dependent on *senior* we need not attach too much importance to isolated attempts at translating foreign concepts in a glos-

---

[52] *Ibid.*, pp. 417f.   [53] *Ibid.*, pp. 419ff.   [54] *Ibid.*, pp. 425ff.

sary such as *Abrogans*, but must also look for the social context in which the new term could express a social innovation such as the rise of vassalage in Francia. Here the dialectal distribution of *hêrro* in OHG up to Otfrid is revealing: three cases in Bavarian, eleven in Alemannic (all from the *Benediktinerregel*) and sixty-five in Franconian, so that the centre of gravity for this term in the first century of its recorded existence is markedly Franconian. In one respect the early attestation of the word in Bavarian is significant. If *hêrro* was used as a gloss translation in *Abrogans* it must have been transmitted to Bavaria and become established there some considerable time before 770. If we reckon with transmission from Franconian it seems likely that *hêrro* was a coinage of the Franks in the seventh century (or earlier?).[55]

On what grounds can it be said that the impetus to this coinage came from Lat. *senior*? It has been argued that, in contrast to Germania, age in the Mediterranean world commanded respect, but was also closely connected with rank and authority, as with the elders of the Jews (in the Septuagint *gerousía*, in the Vulgate *seniores*), the *gérontes* and *présbeis* of the Greeks, the *seniores* and *senatus* of the Romans.[56] All these words employ a term designating age to denote rank or authority. Where the Germanic languages show examples of a similar equation they are confined to only one language (therefore not CG) and are loan-translations from Greek or Latin.[57] (Examples include Go. *sinista* as a rendering of Gr. *presbýteros*, literally 'elder'; OHG *mêro* as an equivalent of Lat. *maior* 'elder', but also 'superior'; OE *yldra*, possibly a calque on Merovingian Latin *senior*.) Each of these terms stands isolated within Germanic in using age to express authority, but they also reflect Greek or Latin usage in using a comparative (or superlative) form of an adjective as a noun. Both these features are shared by OHG *hêrro*, which therefore probably belongs to this group as an imitation of Lat. *senior*.

This is confirmed by the evidence for *senior* in Gallo-Roman society under Frankish occupation.[58] The word occurs in sources from the sixth century on, designating those who exercise secular (or spiritual) authority over *cives* or *iuniores*, the authority of a lord over his dependant or *vassallus*. Moreover, just as OHG *hêrro* replaced *frô* as the more modern term for the secular, feudal lord, so too in northern France did the term *dominus* lose ground to *senior* from the sixth century. Both languages also agree in showing this change of terminology for the lord, whilst leaving

---

[55] *Ibid.*, pp. 428f.   [56] Schirokauer (1946), 55ff.   [57] Kuhn (1956), 28f.
[58] Hollyman (1957), 98ff.; Green (1965), 435.

his lady unaffected by this change in power-structure, so that the OHG pair *hêrro* and *frouwa* is matched by OFr. *seignor* and *dame*.[59] This suggests a common starting-point for the replacement of the older term by a more recent one only in the masculine. The ascendancy of *senior* at the expense of *dominus* seems to have taken place in northern France (the area of Frankish occupation) in particular.[60] In this area *dominus* was more rarely employed as a term for the secular lord and was used proclitically with a phonetic weakening to *domnus* and to *dam*. Finally, northern France stands alone within the Romance world in retaining a number of Latin comparatives used substantivally, including OFr. *geindre* (< Lat. *iunior*), the counterpart of *seignor*.

The widespread employment of *senior* is therefore an innovation of the mixed society of Francia in the sixth century as part of the genesis of the new social relationship of vassalage. Its adoption as *hêrro* into Frankish, then with the spread of Frankish dominance into other German dialects (and ultimately, in isolated traces, into OE and ON), is the counterpart to the expansion of *senior* from northern France into other Romance languages.[61]

In placing these three words in a chronological sequence we work backwards, starting with the rise in importance of *hêrro* as the latest in this group. It was probably a creation of the Merovingian Franks in the seventh century, but then took further time to extend its scope from relative superiority to absolute authority.[62] The relative position of *hêrro* is suggested by the frequency of its conjunction with a term for the inferior in the relationship (*skalk, ambaht, man, thegan*), where its origin as a comparative tied it initially to expressing only a relative position in society (that between a lord and his immediate subordinate) rather than an absolute authority. The superlative formation of *hêrôsto* equipped it better for denoting absolute authority of a wider scope, without any need to refer explicitly to the subordinate.[63] If *hêrro* extended its scope from the relative to the absolute (denoting 'lord' in a close personal relationship, but also 'sovereign' or 'ruler'), this is because the decline of *hêrôsto* (in the face of *furisto*)[64] created a semantic gap for a term of

[59] Hollyman (1957), 103f., 108f.   [60] Green (1965), 437f.
[61] The new relationship between lord and vassal also produced a new term for the latter: OHG, OS *jungiro* on the basis of Lat. *iunior*. Cf. Kuhn (1956), 28f.; Eggers (1964), 62ff.; Green (1965), 440ff. Two other terms for 'follower, vassal' also belong here: OHG *man* on the model of Lat. *homo* (Kuhn (1956), 56f.; (1971), 394, 395; Green (1965), 93f.) and *wini*, based on Lat. *amicus* (Hofmann (1955), 94f.; Green (1965), 106ff.).   [62] Green (1965), 449ff.   [63] *Ibid.*, p. 453.
[64] Schröder (1924a), 9ff.

absolute authority and because the contracted form *hêrro/herro* was no longer always felt as a comparative.[65] As a result *hêrro* could designate either supreme authority (in the *Exhortatio ad plebem Christianam* it refers to the emperor and elsewhere it glosses *tyrannus*) or extensive authority (in glossing *omnibus gentibus imperantes*).[66] This extension of scope by *hêrro* reaches its climax with Notker, who uses it to denote the ruler of a people (he translates *principes* 'rulers of this world' by *lantherren* and *werltherren*), but also the supreme authority of God (*dominus regum* is rendered by *hêrro allero chuningo*).[67] With this the authority expressed by *hêrro* reaches its furthest point, but only towards the close of the OHG period.

By comparison with *hêrro* both *frô* and *truhtin* declined earlier as terms of secular lordship. Although *frô* is attested for the Germanic languages with reference to secular lords it was possible to register the word's progressive atrophy (from Gothic to OE, then to OS and OHG) and its exposure to rivalry from competing terms (*dryhten* and *hláford* in OE, *drohtin* and *hêrro* in OS). In OS and OHG it is no longer active enough to form compounds (as it does in OE and Gothic), whilst in OHG it survives weakly as an independent noun with a social function only in the conventional formula of address *frô mîn* (so stereotyped that it is used even when the grammatical subject is plural).[68] Even though OHG *truhtin* also has cognates in all the Germanic languages and despite the enormous lease of life it was granted as a Christian term for God it is possible to follow a comparable decline in this word.[69] Whereas OE employs *dryhten* in a number of secular compounds, in OS this possibility is confined to only one (*mandrohtin*; *sigidrohtin* refers to Christ or God), whilst OHG has none. Even though the stereotyped vocative use of the secular *truhtin* may not be so thoroughgoing as with *frô* it is still the case that half the examples are confined to vocative address. Were it not for the adoption and regular use of OHG *truhtin* in Christian vocabulary its overall infrequency would be little different from *frô*. Both these words are seldom used in a secular context: seven times for *frô* and twelve times for *truhtin* in OHG.[70] The position is comparable in OS (two examples only of secular *drohtin* in the *Heliand*) and in OE (despite its occurrence in poetic diction it is used in prose in this function only in the earliest laws).

Despite their shared decline it is possible to differentiate between *frô* and *truhtin*: the former declined earlier than the latter.[71] By becoming a

---

[65] Green (1965), 405.   [66] *Ibid.*, p. 457.   [67] *Ibid.*, pp. 459f.   [68] *Ibid.*, pp. 491f.
[69] *Ibid.*, pp. 492, 494.   [70] *Ibid.*, p. 493 and fn. 3.   [71] *Ibid.*, pp. 498f.

stereotyped term of formal address *frô* lost some of its earlier functions which to some extent could be taken over by *truhtin*. *Frô* had originally designated the lord of a household in his relationship to those dependent on him, including the slave, whereas the authority of the *truhtin* extended over followers who had freely entered into their relationship with him and could withdraw from it at any time. This difference means that a word such as *skalk* 'slave' was historically a correlate of *frô*, not of *truhtin*. If so, it is revealing that seven of the twelve cases where *truhtin* is employed in a secular context see this lord in his relationship with a *skalk*, whereas this is nowhere the case with *frô*.[72] From this we may conclude that *frô* declined earlier by losing something of what had originally been its central function and that *truhtin* proved more resistant. This contrast perhaps explains why *truhtin* could be adopted as a Christian term for *dominus*, whereas not one of the examples of OHG *frô* (unlike its cognates in OS and OE) is used of God. By the time of the earliest written texts in OHG both *frô* and *truhtin* were undergoing a decline as secular terms (at a time when *hêrro* had reached Germany from Francia and was beginning its victorious expansion), but with *frô* this decline had progressed further. The sequence in which we have considered these three terms corresponds therefore to their chronological sequence ('chronological' in the sense of when the first two terms underwent their semantic weakening).

In asking what lay behind the weakening of the first two words and the rise of the third we must content ourselves with general suggestions. Whereas the Germanic leader could be termed either *frô* or *truhtin*, this original balance was disturbed by the importance of his military function in the period of migrations. As a result *truhtin* came to enjoy an importance denied to *frô* and it is from the institution presided over by the *truhtin* that the new form of kingship emerged at the close of the migrations.[73] *Frô* is likely to have been further displaced by social changes of the Merovingian period, by the eclipse of the Germanic tribal *principes* before the Frankish *optimates*.[74] In linguistic terms this means that the *frô* of Germanic tribal society was subject to pressure from *hêrro* or *hêrôsto*, at first as new terms of social rank, then as technical terms of Frankish vassalage. The *frô* was also subject to pressure from another source, from the increasing concentration of power in the hands of the Frankish ruler.[75] What we saw earlier (that this increase in royal power took place

---

[72] *Ibid.*, p. 495.   [73] *Ibid.*, p. 501.   [74] Ehrismann (1906), 199; Green (1965), 500.
[75] Green (1965), 501f.

at the expense of the *folk* in their political-legal function)[76] is also relevant to the position of the Germanic *principes*. To the extent that the
political authority of these *principes* is replaced by the power of the
Frankish king *frô* as a political term is forced to give ground. This is
reflected in the translation of *respublica* by *frônereht*, but also by *kunicriche*,
where the earlier authority of the *principes* has been replaced by that of
the king.

The decline of *truhtin* in its turn is to some extent a parallel development and therefore perhaps due to the same general reasons. As a term
designating the leader of a war-band it must have been of central importance in the warlike conditions of the migrations, but equally, once they
had given way to the reorganisation of society on colonial soil, the rôle
of the war-band and hence the semantic function of *truhtin* could no
longer be the same.[77] We have had occasion to doubt the rapidity with
which, according to Kuhn, the war-band disappeared and we have also
seen the term *truht* applied to institutions similar to, but not identical
with, the earlier Germanic one, but may agree that once followers were
rewarded with land of their own the *comitatus* was a thing of the past. Its
disappearance did not mean that its vocabulary was also destined to
vanish, for it lived on in other contexts: *truht* in connection with marriage
customs, for example, and *truhtin* in Christian vocabulary. Although
truhtin could also occasionally acquire the meaning 'king' it was eventually made obsolete in this function and was displaced by *kuning*.[78] Here,
too, its initial resilience, greater than with *frô*, did not prevent this fate.
Finally, the striking discrepancy between only 12 instances of *truhtin* as a
secular term and more than 1,500 examples of religious usage means
that in the former function it has become archaic. This amounted to a
lack of agreement between the vocabulary of social authority and that
of religious authority, disturbing in an age which stressed the divine
origin of royal authority. Here Notker presents a contrast for, although
truhtin continues with him only as a religious term, he uses *hêrro* in both
its secular and its religious sense.[79]

The expansive force of *hêrro*, first in its spread from the Franks to the
rest of Germany, but also in its semantic extension (from relative to
absolute authority, from the secular to a religious context), is a reflection
of the expansive force of Frankish vassalage. By so thoroughly becoming the secular term for 'lord' by the start of our written tradition *hêrro*
ousted *truhtin* from its former secular function, but also *frô* insofar as this

---

[76] See above, p. 99.   [77] Green (1965), 504f.   [78] *Ibid.*, p. 507.   [79] *Ibid.*, pp. 511f.

word still survived at all. Just as *truhtin* had taken over some of the functions of *frô* as lord of a household, so does *hêrro* do the same (*paterfamilias*
can therefore be glossed as *husherre*).[80] In this the semantic rôles earlier
played by *frô* and *truhtin* come together in the many-sided flexibility of
the word which replaced them, *hêrro*.

[80] *Ibid.*, p. 515.

CHAPTER 7

Kingship

Germanic kingship, about whose origins there are institutional as well as linguistic problems, was already well established enough to be known to Tacitus, although this does not mean that it was to be found everywhere in Germania. When Tacitus refers in his general section to 'the king or the chieftain' (*Germania* 10 and 11: *rex vel princeps/principes*) this could imply that both offices were present and that either office-holder is meant, but equally that a particular tribe knew only one or the other. That this could sometimes mean that a tribe was governed by chieftains, not by a king, is clear when the Roman author specifies those Germanic peoples which are ruled by kings (*Germania* 25: *iis gentibus quae regnantur*).[1] Something similar is true when a group of tribes are said to be distinguished from others by various features, their round shields, their short swords and their submission to the authority of kings (*Germania* 43: *regnantur . . . erga reges obsequium*).[2] From this it follows that some could do without kings, as is known to have been the case with the Saxons, the Gepids and for a time at least the Heruli.[3] On the continental Saxons, for example, Bede comments that they knew no kings, but only satraps who still in the eighth century were active as a body at the tribal assembly at Markloh.[4]

Those tribes which have a king are said by Tacitus to choose him in accordance with his degree of nobility (*Germania* 7: *reges ex nobilitate . . . sumunt*), which implies the closest possible descent from earlier kings or at least from the family to which they had belonged, but also the combination of a hereditary with an elective principle.[5] This means that, however much the criterion of *nobilitas* restricted the choice, a possible candidate became a king only by being chosen. It follows from this dependence on election (as distinct from any God-given authority in theocratic kingship) that the Germanic kings exercised no absolute

---

[1] Much (1967), 330; Picard (1991), 46f., 92f.   [2] Much (1967), 492.   [3] Wallace-Hadrill (1971), 8.
[4] Ilkow (1968), 246; Wood (1995), 262.   [5] Höfler (1963), 97; Much (1967), 154.

authority.[6] Immediately after describing their election Tacitus claims that these kings had no free power of command (*nec regibus infinita aut libera potestas*). If even the *duces* or military leaders in this same passage are denied any power of command (*imperium*) on the battlefield other than the example they set we can be sure that the kings' authority was no greater in the civilian context. How far this may be regarded as the norm is clear from the exceptional position which Tacitus attributes to certain tribes on the Baltic coastline (Gutones, Rugii, Lemovii and Suiones) with whom the authority wielded by their kings goes much further than elsewhere in Germania.

These passages raise the question as to how the relationship between the king and two other office-holders in Germanic society is to be seen. In a tribe which was ruled by a king how are we to imagine his position vis-à-vis the chieftains (*principes*)?[7] Presumably in the sense that they governed local regions and were subordinate to him, comparable perhaps to the position occupied by a *kindins* 'provincial ruler' in Gothic. How the authority of the king was distinguished from that of the chieftains, understood in this sense, still remains unclear. The same is true of the relationship between the king and the war-leader (*dux*), although in some cases the answer is made easier if we can assume an identity of office-holders.[8] Wherever a tribe was ruled by a king he was their natural war-leader insofar as age and strength still made this possible. When Tacitus says that kings were chosen with regard to nobility, but adds that war-leaders were chosen with an eye to their *virtus* or prowess in battle this does not mean that kings could not be war-leaders, but merely that they owed their position to different qualities. (A war-leader who led a confederation to victory, but also occupied new territory during the migrations, may already have been of a royal family, but could also find it advantageous to claim such descent for himself and point to his success to establish the claim.) The rôle of the king as a war-leader is clear when Vibilius, the king of the Hermunduri, is referred to as their war-leader (*dux*) in battle with the Marcomanni, but on the other hand Arminius, despite the king-like power he had gained for himself, was not the sole leader of the Cherusci in the campaign of Germanicus. (Where the supreme authority of a tribe lies with the *principes* rather than a king it is they collectively who can be in military command, as with the invasion of Gaul by the Usipi and Tencteri.)

[6] Much (1967), 157, 500f.; Picard (1991), 98f.　　[7] Much (1967), 155.
[8] *Ibid.*, p. 156; Wallace-Hadrill (1971), 3; Naumann (1986), 297; Wenskus (1986b), 302.

There can be little doubt that the institution of kingship could be strengthened during the migrations which provided many *principes* with the opportunity of shining as war-leaders and opened the path to kingship for them or, if they were already kings, strengthened their royal status.[9] Leaders such as Arminius and Maroboduus amassed such power for themselves in the clash with the Empire that the Romans referred to them with the title of 'king'.[10] The opportunities for kingship offered by successful campaigning and the seizure of new territory explain why EG kingship was noticeably more authoritarian, even to the point of endangering the traditional *libertas* of Germanic society, which Tacitus regarded more favourably than other Romans.[11] Not merely was the territory into which the EG tribes moved largely colonial soil, its vast geographical extent encouraged the development of a more centralised power to exercise control. Against this view it has been argued that the greater power exercised by kings in eastern Germania or even the presence of kings in the eastern tribes is characteristic of primeval Germania (according to their tribal legend the Goths landed on the Polish coastline already under the leadership of a king, Berig). However, an early kingship of this kind, especially if crowned with military success and confronted with the novel geographical problems of the south Russian steppes, need not argue against the development of a more powerful institution than ever before. We see this also in western Germania in the case of Arminius and other successful leaders who aim at royal power for themselves.[12] The fact that these leaders, in the west as in the east, should encounter opposition amongst their own tribesmen is a pointer to the new developments in kingship which the migrations made possible.

A much wider problem, whether a sacral kingship was known to Germania, has exercised scholars and divided their ranks without, perhaps fortunately, being relevant to our linguistic concerns. None of the three words for 'king' discussed in this chapter (Go. *þiudans*, OHG *truhtin* and *kuning*, together with cognates) can safely be associated with sacral kingship. Although it has been claimed that *þiudans* is an old term for sacral kingship, this is based on little more than an equation between the (correct) view that this is an old term for 'king' and the by no means generally accepted assumption that sacral kingship was an early feature of Germanic society.[13] Similarly, the proposal that there was a priestly,

---

[9] Much (1967), 154, 492, but against this cf. Picard (1991), 50, 53, fn. 17.   [10] See below, pp. 136f.
[11] *Germania* 43; Much (1967), 154, 330, 488.   [12] Thompson (1965), 66ff., 83f.
[13] Wenskus (1961), 419.

therefore religious background to OHG *kuning* rests on an uncertain etymology which has not been generally accepted and on the propriety of regarding the particular evidence of the ON *Rígspula* as applicable not merely to Scandinavia at large, but also to the PG formation of this word a good thousand years earlier.[14]

In view of such reservations the concept of sacral kingship will play no part in the following pages. Instead, we shall be concerned with the usage of the three vernacular terms for 'king' just listed, where the greatest difficulties occur in explaining the last of these, *kuning*, the term which established itself as ultimately successful down to the present. We shall also be occupied with the chronological sequence of these terms and with possible reasons why the first two ultimately give way to the third. Finally, we shall pass beyond the strict limits of kingship to consider a term from the sphere of overlordship, OHG *rîhhi*.

Our first example, Go. *þiudans* (used by Wulfila to render Gr. *basileús* 'king'), is CG.[15] Although OHG is commonly omitted from the languages which attest it, Salic Franconian appears to have had it, even if it occurs only once. There is every reason for thinking that this must be one of the earliest Germanic words for 'king', above all because of the antiquity of its formation.[16] The suffix, used to express authority or leadership over what is expressed in the stem, occurs in other Germanic terms for political authority: OHG *truhtin*, Burgundian *hendinos* 'king', Go. *kindins* 'provincial ruler', ON *herjann* 'army-leader' and the god's name *Wuotan*. The ablaut relationship between the two vowels of the suffix (present also in OHG *Wuotan*: ON *Óðinn*) suggests the antiquity of its origin, also borne out by IE parallels: Lat. *dominus, tribunus*, Gr. *koíranos* 'ruler'.

The Germanic word formed with this suffix is derived from *þiuda* (as in Gothic) 'people', so that the word for 'king' originally denoted the lord of a people. The word *þiuda* is again attested in every Germanic language, but also with several IE cognates, such as Oscan *touto* 'people, city', OPru. *tauto* 'land', Latvian *tauta* 'people', Gaulish *Teuto-* and Gr. *Teuta-* (both in proper names).[17] Here, too, the presence of ablaut suggests the antiquity of this word. We can go one step further, however, for the Germanic word for 'king', formed from this word for 'people'

---

[14] Kahl (1960), 198ff., especially 201ff. (etymology), 204ff. (*Rígspula*).
[15] Herold (1941), 231f.; Much (1967), 155. For OHG cf. Kahl (1960), 196, fn. 91; Wenskus (1961), 308.
[16] Wenskus (1961), 308; Schlesinger (1963b), 107; Lehmann (1986), 361f.
[17] Herold (1941), 230; Meid (1966), 184f.

together with this suffix, has parallels elsewhere in IE, as with Illyrian *teutana* 'queen' and the Gaulish personal name *Toutonos*. Taken together, these parallels for *þiudans*, throughout Germanic and in IE, suggest the antiquity of its formation meaning 'ruler of a people'. In agreement with this is the fact that the suffix was no longer productive in the historical period.

To determine the function of this word for 'ruler of a people' we have to proceed from *þiuda*, asking in what sense it designates a people.[18] Here the clearcut usage of Wulfila (also confirmed by our OHG evidence) helps us best, for despite the restrictions of his lexis (for the concept 'people' he makes use only of *þiuda* and has no terms cognate with OHG *heri*, *folk* or *liut*) he employs this one word strictly to render only Gr. *éthnos*. Nowhere does he use *þiuda* to translate Greek words like *laós* (= *populus*) or *óchlos* (= *plebs*), for which he uses an obvious makeshift like *managei* 'crowd' or *kuni* 'kindred' in an extended meaning. Wulfila's systematic regularity implies a close semantic equation between *þiuda* and *éthnos*, suggesting that *þiuda* designated the whole people, bound together by ties of blood and constituting an ethnological and political whole. In denoting the whole people *þiuda* is clearly different in function from *heri* and *folk*, each of which was originally more restricted in scope, denoting only those members of the tribe who were qualified to bear arms and to attend the tribal assembly.

This meaning reconstructed from Wulfila's translation practice can be supported by the usage of the various Germanic languages. As far as Gothic is concerned we can escape the vicious circle of using Wulfila to prove Wulfila by turning instead to the Gothic Calendar where *Gutþiuda* designates the Gothic people at large (and their territory) and is confirmed by ethnic parallels like OE *Engelþēod* and ON *Svíþjóð* 'Sweden'.[19] These parallels show that the meaning of this word ('people, tribe', but also the territory occupied by them) was not confined to Gothic, but both OE and ON show further examples.[20] Thus, in OE the prologue to Ine's laws refers to his kingdom of Wessex by the word *þēod* (the people organised as what is now a Christian state); Lat. *gentes* in the sense of 'peoples' is rendered by the same word, as is also the case with *genus Hebraeorum* 'Hebrew people'. In ON, too, the undifferentiated sense of the whole people is conveyed in much the same kind of construction. Like Ine, king of his people, Sigurd can be seen as the ruler of his (*Grípisspá* 41,7: *þjóðar*

---

[18] Herold (1941), 230ff. [19] Streitberg (1919), 472; Wenskus (1961), 49.
[20] Herold (1941), 233f.

þengill) and as a counterpart to OE *þēod* for the Hebrew people we find its ON equivalent used of the Huns (*Guðrúnarkviða I* 26,2: *húnskrar þjóðar*). In OS the Jewish people as an ethnic entity is referred to by the same word (*Heliand* 3035: *thiodu Iudeono*), the flight into Egypt is seen in terms of Joseph seeking another *thiod* 'people, land' (713), and Rome's imperial power is expressed as authority over all *thioda* (56). In OHG the word *deota* is frequently employed as a translation of Latin *gens, natio* and *plebs*, but this usage is not confined to the needs of translation.[21] The most telling evidence is provided by Otfrid who, like the author of the *Ludwigslied* (v. 12), refers to the Frankish people as *Frankono thiete* (*Evangelienbuch*, Lud. 90), but also uses the same word to designate other peoples whose rulers have no hope of ruling over the Franks (1 1,96). Whether the word designates the western Franks, as in the *Ludwigslied*, or the German tribes ruled by Ludwig the German, as with Otfrid, the ethnic-political function of the word is as clear as in the other Germanic languages.

If *þiuda* had this meaning, then *þiudans* must have designated a ruler over a people in this sense. However, the unity established for *þiuda* (every language attests the same ethnic meaning) should not lead us to assume a similar unity for the derivative *þiudans* since there are indications that this word was on the retreat in some Germanic languages. The position is most acute in OHG (where the word occurs only once, as a gloss translation), but even in OE, where *þēoden* is employed in the conservative usage of poetic diction, it significantly does not occur in the rich corpus of prose literature. The comparative paucity of OS prose excludes a similar argument in this case, but in the *Heliand thiodan* is used not only frequently of Christ's kingship, but also of Roman imperial authority and of the native authority of the Jews,[22] which suggests that the word may have been more alive in the Saxon society of the ninth century than in the rest of Germany. In Scandinavia *þjóðann* occurs, but infrequently and only in poetic texts.[23] It is in Gothic, however, that the word shows its greatest vigour, both producing derivatives like *þiudanōn* 'to rule' and *þiudinassus* 'kingdom, rule' and forming a compound *þiudangardi* 'kingdom'. Semantically, too, this Gothic word was still very much alive. It may be applied most frequently to Christ in such phrases as 'king of the Jews' and 'king of kings', but is also active enough to be used in a secular context. As such it can designate named rulers such as Herod and Artaxerxes, but can also be employed outside the context of the

---

[21] *Ibid.*, pp. 232, 236f.   [22] Sehrt (1966), 604f.   [23] Meid (1966), 185.

bible, as in the Gothic Calendar (*Kustanteinus þiudanis*, where the name is a scribal error for the emperor Constantius II).[24]

Normally, when confronted with a situation where a word is in obvious decline in OHG and in OE, but rather more active in OS, the suggestion is made that we are dealing with the result of social changes brought about by the migrations, where those tribes which wandered furthest and came under greatest external influence were forced to adapt their old institutions to new exigencies. Where this need was felt less strongly, as in Saxony, a traditional word for a traditional institution had a greater chance of survival. This might seem to be contradicted in this case by ON, where *þjóðann* is not as obviously active as we might expect, but this may be because, as we shall see, *dróttinn* was in early use for 'king' in Scandinavia, driving the even earlier *þjóðann* more into the background. However, explaining the decline of our word in OHG and OE by reference to settlement on colonial soil confronts us with the further difficulty of the Goths, likewise now on colonial soil, but still actively using the traditional term *þiudans*. This Gothic word may have been given a new lease of life by the early strength of Germanic kingship in the east (as reported by Tacitus) and by the leadership of Gothic kings in their early wanderings (as suggested by Jordanes).[25] In addition, the written testimony of Wulfila's Gothic is so early that *þiudans* may not have declined so far by then. In Gothic it certainly faced no competition from elsewhere: Wulfila nowhere uses the term **draúhtins* and there is no evidence at all that **kuniggs* ever existed in Gothic (which could imply that the use of this latter word in the sense 'king' postdated the Goths' trek from northern Poland which removed them from the main orbit of Germania).

The second word which could designate a Germanic ruler is represented by OHG *truhtin*. We have already discussed the formation of this word, its spread throughout Germania (including Gothic?) and its use to refer to the leader of a war-band. In this use the word could easily be applied to a Germanic king (amongst many other people), since it was one of his functions to act as a war-leader and to maintain a war-band. Such a body of warriors, kept together in peacetime and not merely in times of war, was only feasible for those who performed a public function in Germanic society, for *reges* or *principes*, who were the war-band leaders *par excellence*.[26] This still does not mean that any *truhtin* was a king

---

[24] Streitberg (1919), 472.   [25] *Getica* 25 and 94.   [26] Meid (1966), 188.

(although the converse was much more likely), nor does it mean that we are justified in automatically translating this word as denoting a king.

In looking for evidence that *truhtin* can sometimes be understood in this way we have no choice but to impose a self-denying ordinance on ourselves: we have to exclude all the examples of specifically religious usage in the Germanic languages, in other words the vast bulk of our earliest written testimony, from our survey.[27] The reason for this is clear. Once *truhtin* had become the standing equivalent of Christian *dominus* in WG and NG the fact that Christian Latin literature frequently termed Christ *rex* as well as *dominus* brought about a conjunction of *truhtin* with kingship in vernacular literature which gives us no safe guarantee that this juxtaposition had ever been true of Germanic before contact with Christianity. Only by ignoring all Christian religious usage in the Germanic vernaculars can we hope to come across reliable indications that *truhtin* could mean 'king', a restriction which at least has the fortunate result of making our survey more easily manageable. (Gothic is excluded in any case because of the absence of **draúhtins* from Wulfila's text.)

We find one example only in OHG, but a telling one. In the *Hildebrandslied* (vv. 34f.) the word *chuning* in one line is varied in the next by *Huneo truhtin*, so that this leader of the Huns is seen expressly as their king. Here there is no suggestion that the words *chuning* and *truhtin* express different aspects of the same office, for they are simply used synonymously. *Huneo truhtin* therefore does not mean 'leader of a war-band made up of Hunnic warriors' but rather, as the association with *chuning* implies, 'lord or ruler of the Huns'. Nor can the semantic equation of the two terms be weakened by an appeal to the formal needs of poetic diction since, although *chuning* stands in the alliterative position, the same is not true of the word which concerns us, *truhtin*. For OS the *Heliand*, despite its biblical subject-matter, provides two examples which, unlike all the other cases of *drohtin*, do not refer to God or Christ, but to a secular context. One of these examples is the compound *mandrohtin* (cf. OE *mandryhten* 'lord of men'), used to personify the Roman state served by Matthew as a tax-gatherer before his discipleship. This *mandrohtin* in whose service (v. 1200) Matthew stood is a variation on *cuning* (1199), so that the two words are as interchangeable as in the *Hildebrandslied*. Nor do formal needs explain this equation in the *Heliand* either, since although *mandrohtin* stands in the alliterative position this only explains

----
[27] Green (1965), 346f.

the choice of *man-*, not of the word which concerns us. (Not *drohtin* itself, but the related *druhtskepi*, v. 363, is used in close association with *aðalcuning* 'ancestral king' of David's rule as a king.)

In OE examples can be found in *Beowulf*. In vv. 862f. the word *winedrihten* is varied in the next line by *gōd cyning*, and in v. 2186 the term *drihten Wedera* is followed five lines later by *heaðorōf cyning* in apposition.[28] Taken together these two variations correspond closely to the juxtaposition of *chuning* and *Huneo truhtin* in OHG, including the naming of the people over whom royal authority is exercised and the fact that alliteration does not come into question. Where, as in all these cases, the two variants occur in the same context, separated only by a line or two, the position is quite different from what we find elsewhere in *Beowulf*. The fact that Hygelāc is termed *Gēata dryhten* in v. 1484 and much later *Gēata cyning* (2356) could mean that in one context he is seen in his function as *rex* and in the other as *dux*, without this establishing that *dryhten* has acquired the meaning 'king'.[29] This likelihood is present only when the variation is confined to the same context. In NG, as in WG, the combination of the cognate *dróttinn* with a tribal name (e.g. *dróttinn yfir Svíum*)[30] denotes rulership over a people rather than command of a band made up of Swedes. Similarly, when Níðuðr in the *Völundarkviða* is called *Níára dróttinn* the force of the second word is made clear in the prose introduction (1: *Níðuðr hét konungr í Svíþjóð*).[31] Further, just as OE *cwēn* (meaning both 'queen' and 'woman') could be made unmistakably regal by the compound *dryhtcwēn* (once *dryhten* had acquired the force of royalty), so too did ON *dróttning*, the feminine of *dróttinn*, come to mean 'queen' (cf. modern Swedish *drottning*).[32] Fully in agreement with our linguistic evidence and not to be dismissed out of hand as an etymological game is Snorri's remark in the *Heimskringla* that in the north kings were formerly called *dróttnar*, their wives *dróttningar* and their royal troop the *drótt*.[33] We have recently seen that this linguistic development could also account for the infrequency of *þjóðann* in ON.

Amongst the three terms listed by Snorri only *drótt* remained close to the original meaning 'war-band', whilst the others expanded their scope to rulership of a people. Elsewhere *drótt* and its cognates can denote 'people, nation' in OE and ON (e.g. *drótt írskrar þjóðar = populus Hibernicus*), but in Germany the semantic extension of the word seems to have gone no further than 'crowd, multitude',[34] a weakening of the original military

[28] *Ibid.*, p. 348.   [29] *Ibid.*, pp. 348, 349, fn. 1.   [30] Cf. Kahl (1960), 235, fn. 198.
[31] Meid (1966), 188.   [32] Green (1965), 349.   [33] *Ibid.* and fn. 2; Meid (1966), 188.
[34] Green (1965), 350; Ilkow (1968), 90.

function comparable to what we saw with *folk* (a military formation, but also meaning 'people' and 'crowd'). Whatever other forces may have lain behind these semantic changes the shift of *truhtin* from 'leader of a warband' to 'ruler of a people' can only have assisted the word from which it was derived in the direction of 'people'.

We come now to OHG *kuning*, historically the most important (because ultimately successful) word for 'king', but linguistically the most difficult one. The word is present in every Germanic language except Gothic, even though the bible gave Wulfila every opportunity to use the word. This means either that the word did not exist in the Gothic of his day or that he chose not to make use of it (as was the case with **drauhtins* and *háilags*). Without the kind of supplementary evidence which we possess for these other two words we cannot argue positively that **kuniggs* must have existed in Gothic,[35] still less that it was from this Germanic language that the Slavs and Finns took their loanword.

With *kuning* difficulties are presented both by the suffix and by the stem to which it is added. The various functions of the Germanic suffix *-ing* can for convenience be grouped under three headings. First, it is used as a patronymic, denoting a descendant, as with *Scyld*, a mythical Danish king in *Beowulf*, and *Scyldingas*, his descendants or members of the Danish dynasty, or with *Carolus* 'Charles (the Great)' and *Carolingi*.[36] Secondly, this suffix conveys the idea of belonging to or being connected with whatever is expressed by the stem, as with Go. *gards* 'royal house, court' and Gothic Latin *gardingus* 'palace official' or OHG *hûs* 'house' and *hûsinga*, rendering *penates* 'household gods'.[37] Thirdly, *-ing* or *-ung* can be used simply as an extended form with no detectable nuance of meaning, although it has been suggested that it could have conveyed the idea of close emotional attachment.[38] Examples are ON *niðr* and *niðjungr* (both meaning 'descendant'), ON *sifr* and *sifjungr* 'kinsman' and Go. *gudja* 'priest' and OHG *goting* (to gloss *tribunus*). One of the tasks in any explanation of *kuning* must therefore be to determine in which of these three functions the suffix is added to whatever meaning the stem conveys.

For the stem in its turn three possibilities have been entertained which we may consider more conveniently under two headings. The first is the suggestion that the stem is PG **kunjam* 'kindred', which would have pro-

---

[35] This against Ritter (1993), 167.   [36] Ekblom (1945), 6.
[37] Sehrt (1962), 97; Wolfram (1988), 242.   [38] Ekblom (1945), 4f.

duced for *kuning* a meaning either 'descending from a kindred' or 'belonging to a kindred'.[39] To this the objection has been made that this reconstructed meaning could apply to any kinsman and therefore not designate only the king. This objection rests on the conviction that **kunjam* denoted any kindred, not specifically an aristocratic family or a *stirps regia* from which the king may have descended, but this in turn can be undercut by examples from other languages where a term for 'family, kindred' at large refers to a noble family in particular (Lat. *gens*, but OFr. *gentil* 'noble'; OHG *slahta*, but Czech *šlehtic* 'nobleman').[40] The family in question would therefore be a prominent one, of noble birth. That the Germanic king descended from such a family was suggested by Tacitus (*Germania* 7: *reges ex nobilitate . . . sumunt*) and is borne out centuries later by the Heruli who in the course of their migrations sent a party back to Scandinavia for a king from amongst the members of their royal family who had remained behind.[41] In this connection it is significant that any member of such a *stirps regia*, not just the reigning king, could be called a *kuning*, since all belonged to the same family or kindred.[42] In ON Sigurd, not reigning as king himself, is called *konungr* for this reason and Högni, the brother of king Gunnar, can also be termed thus. That this practice was not confined to Scandinavia is confirmed by non-reigning members of Merovingian royal families bearing the title *rex* and later by the *Nibelungenlied* (Stanza 4), where three brothers are all designated *künege*, whilst the office is held by only one of them, Gunther.

However much such considerations suggest a link between *kuning* and this word for kindred there are phonological difficulties which stand in the way. In ON the *j* of **kunjam* should normally have been preserved (as with *niðjungr* and *sifjungr*) and it should also have produced umlaut, leading to a form **kynjungr*, which is nowhere attested, in contrast to the forms actually used, *kunungr* (probably the older form) or *konungr*.[43] The other difficulty lies with WG. Although the umlaut is attested here (OE *cyning*, whereas the orthography of OHG does not indicate the umlaut of *u*), none of the WG examples shows the gemination of *n* which *j* should also have produced. In other words, both for NG and WG, for that area of Germania which attests *kuning* at all, the derivation of the word from **kunjam*, whilst acceptable semantically, creates considerable difficulties phonologically. These difficulties are just the same if we

[39] Kahl (1960), 200.   [40] Ekblom (1945), 7; Kern (1954), 15; Ilkow (1968), 247; Meid (1966), 186.
[41] De Vries (1956b), 293; Schlesinger (1963b), 136.
[42] ON: Meid (1966), 186. Merovingians: Kern (1954), 16, fn. 32. *Nibelungenlied*: Meid (1966), 186; Ilkow (1968), 247.   [43] Kahl (1960), 163, fn. 21.

derive our word, as has been suggested, from **kunjaz* instead, a masculine form of **kunjam*, therefore denoting someone who represents or incorporates the royal kindred (cf. OE *lēod* feminine 'people, country', masculine 'prince').[44] Unlike **kunjam* (and the other possibility still to be looked at) the form **kunjaz* is purely a reconstruction, nowhere attested.

The other possibility is to derive *kuning* from the same stem, but to postulate, in addition to the more common forms with *-ing*, an original masculine **kuniz*, again implying someone who incorporates the royal kindred.[45] This has the double advantage of retaining the semantic parallels between *kuning* and the (royal) kindred discussed above, whilst avoiding the phonological difficulties caused by the *j* in **kunjam*. Nor is it strictly true to say that this explanation depends on postulating the form **kuniz* because, however few they may be by contrast with *kuning*, there are traces of it surviving in both WG and NG. In OE we find, for example, alongside *cyningdōm* 'royal power' and *cyningrīce* 'kingdom' variants such as *cynedōm* and *cynerīce*, but also further examples like *cynehelm* 'diadem' (cf. OHG *chuninghelm*), *cynebearn* 'royal offspring' and *cynelīc* 'royal'.[46] Although OHG may have *chuninghelm* in place of the shorter form in OE, this does not mean that traces of **kuniz* are lacking on the continent. We find them, for example, in OHG *kunirîhhi* alongside *kuningrîhhi* and in a gloss to Notker's translation of Psalm 104.15, where *regali unguento* is rendered by *chunio salbe* (with the genitive plural of 'king' doing duty for the adjective 'royal').[47] In addition, there is the word *cuoniowidi* of the first *Merseburger Zauberspruch* (v. 3), with parallels elsewhere in OHG *kunawid* and Go. *kunawida* meaning 'chain, fetter', but also in OE *cynewiððe* with a different meaning, 'royal diadem'.[48] The meaning of this OE form clearly associates it with the other royal compounds with *cyne-*, but the same has been suggested for the *Merseburger Zauberspruch*, where the binding of prisoners of war (preparatory to their ritual sacrifice?) is interpreted as a task falling to the chieftain. (This is a rare example of a word for chieftain, later king, with a possibly sacral function, but even this rests on the assumption that a ritual sacrifice was involved and that the chieftain played a priestly rôle.) In ON the cognate word survives as *konr*, meaning 'descendant, son' (and even 'man' in poetic diction), but also 'king' (originally?) when in the *Helgakviða Hundingsbana I* 23,8 it is in apposition with *konungr* in the next line.[49]

44 Von Kienle (1939), 268f.   45 Meissner (1921), 136; Ekblom (1945), 1; Kahl (1960), 198f.
46 Meissner (1921), 134.   47 Sieg (1960), 367f.; Sehrt (1962), 111; Starck and Wells (1990), 352.
48 Meissner (1921), 126ff.; Sieg (1960), 365ff.
49 Meissner (1921), 135; Ekblom (1945), 1; Kahl (1960), 199.

Throughout Germania, therefore, there is scattered evidence for the form **kuniz*, standing for someone who represents a (royal) kindred, but whose range of authority probably corresponded more to that of a chieftain than a king. To this word the suffix *-ing* was added (possibly in the third function listed above) very much as with Go. *gudja* and OHG *goting*. That ON should have *-ungr* as a suffix rather than *-ingr* should not surprise us in view of the vocalic variations of the suffix in Germanic (even within the same language). The stem-vowel of the ON form was probably originally *-u-*, as in WG, but later *-o-* (under the influence of *konr?*).[50]

The suggestion that the word **kuniz* and then *kuning* denoted someone more like a chieftain than a king means that with the rise of kingship in a tribal society we are dealing at first essentially with a petty kingship (*Kleinkönigtum*). Unsurprisingly, given its distance from the changes taking place above all in the colonial south, much of our evidence for this is forthcoming from Scandinavia. The inscription on the rune-stone from Rök refers to twenty sea-kings banded together for warlike undertakings, so that the territory over which each exercised authority must have been restricted in size.[51] Two compounds in which ON *konungr* appears point in the same direction of small-scale kingship.[52] The word *fylkiskonungr*, compounded with *fylki* 'district' (as well as a 'military formation') and the equivalent of the possibly older term *fylkir* 'chieftain', denotes a petty king, ruling over no more than a district. The same is true of *heraðskonungr*: compounded with *herað*, likewise meaning 'district', and the equivalent of *hersir* 'local chieftain', it also denoted a petty king. This restricted scope is also clear from the wording of the prose introduction to the *Völundarkviða* which we have already mentioned. Here Níðuðr is described as a king *in* Sweden (1: *konungr í Svíþjóð*), not as the king *of* or *over* Sweden, which suggests that his status was that of a regional prince or ruler before the unification of Sweden.[53] The position cannot have been very different initially amongst the WG tribes, for our historical sources refer to numbers of petty kings amongst the Alemanni, the Franks and the Anglo-Saxons.[54] (For five kings of Wessex to have been killed in 626 and for two others still to have been alive two years later there must have been a multiplicity of kings in Wessex.) Such petty kings are the equivalent of what the Roman historians called *reguli* or *regales*

---

[50] Suffix: Ekblom (1945), 22f.; de Vries (1956b), 292; Meid (1966), 187. Stem-vowel: Ekblom (1945), 10; Kahl (1960), 229.   [51] Schlesinger (1963b), 106.

[52] *Ibid.* Schlesinger also mentions *þjóðkonungr*, but on this see below, p. 138.

[53] Neckel (1936), 95.   [54] Wenskus (1961), 322; Wood (1977), 19.

and it was in this very small-scale sense that the word *kuning* was first applied to them as distinct from *þiudans*, which was now moribund but whose scope had been much larger.

After considering these three terms for 'king' we must now attempt to place them in their chronological sequence. The word *þiudans* may be regarded as the earliest because it is the only one with clear parallels in other IE languages (the other two terms are Germanic formations), but also because of the evidence that it was already on the retreat in Germania by the time of our earliest written sources. It must however have still been in active use in Gothic towards the end of the fourth century for Wulfila to use it in a secular as well as religious context and for the emperor Constantius II (who died in 361) to be commemorated with this title in the Gothic Calendar.[55] Nor is there any reason to think that this word was not still in use at this time in other parts of Germania, since its occurrence as a standing term for the ruler in heroic poetry suggests that it was in active use in the age of migrations which saw the rise of heroic poetry. With the close of the migrations the word must have declined as a designation for 'king' if we are to account for its weakness at the start of the written tradition in western Germania.

There is every reason to think that *truhtin* is another old formation although, for want of IE parallels, probably not so old as *þiudans*. We saw that its original function was a military one, to designate the leader of a war-band, so that its application to the ruler may well have been secondary. Its original military function (by contrast with *þiudans*) suggests that it rose in importance as a royal term at a time when warfare was the essential basis of Germanic kingship. The fact that the ruler (whatever the extent of his authority) was also a military leader and kept his own war-band around him meant that, above all in the constant warfare of the migrations, *truhtin* came to be seen more and more as a term for the king's overriding function, displacing *þiudans* in the process.[56]

The latest in this group is *kuning*. This is not simply because it is the only one to have survived as the standard term for 'king' into the early Middle Ages and beyond and in every Germanic language. Although its derivation from a stem ending in *-iz* suggests an early formation in Germanic, the word at this stage had only the restricted meaning of 'petty king' or *regulus*. What is late about this word is therefore not its formation, but rather its expansion from *regulus* to becoming a term for

---

[55] Meid (1966), 186.   [56] *Ibid.*, p. 189.

large-scale kingship (an expansion which we have yet to consider). We saw that there is some evidence, mainly Scandinavian but not confined to the north, that the use of *kuning* in a much wider context was a relatively late development.[57] If that is so, it might explain the absence of this word in Wulfila's Gothic, suggesting that at the time of the Goths' departure from the north this word did not exist in Germanic or, if it did, had not acquired the ability to designate large-scale kingship which would have made it suitable to Wulfila's purposes in translating Gr. *basileús*. Beyond this it would be rash to draw any conclusions from the negative evidence of Gothic.

Placing these three words in their chronological sequence is only a preparatory step to accounting for this sequence, suggesting historical reasons why one term may have replaced another. We may attempt this in two steps, considering first the move from *piudans* to *truhtin*, then the ousting of *truhtin* by *kuning*.

Underlying the changes in the institution of kingship which these lexical movements suggest are the pressures to which confrontation with the Roman Empire exposed traditional tribal society in Germania, as elsewhere. Confrontation with an advanced state such as the Empire had effects on the social structure of the Germanic tribes involved (as in the modern contact between the developed world and the third world), not least in the sense that the access to new wealth and the prospects of seizing land encouraged the growth of predatory war-bands, out for more lasting gains than could be won from the occasional raid. All this disrupted the traditional society and ultimately led to the leadership of new peoples by kings of considerable power.[58] For their part, too, the Romans had an interest in encouraging such developments. The incipient centralisation of power in the person of a king (rather than with traditional chieftains ultimately responsible to the tribal assembly) constituted an authority with whom the Romans could deal, with some hope that his followers would accept what the king had decided.[59] From the Roman point of view this held out the prospect of stabilising the frontier region by building a buffer-zone more amenable to diplomatic arrangements. This was a policy which Rome had successfully applied elsewhere, so that what Tacitus says of its method in Britain can be said of Germania, too, for he refers to the established Roman practice of employing even kings to make others slaves (*Agricola* 14: *ut haberet instrumenta servitutis et reges*).[60]

---

[57] Kahl (1960), 234f.; Meid (1966), 187. [58] Campbell (1991), 149.
[59] Wallace-Hadrill (1971), 7, 17, 20. [60] Suerbaum (1977), 95.

In the first of the two changes which concern us (from *þiudans* to *truhtin*) two factors are of importance. The first concerns the greater role of warfare in tribes on the move, jostling with each other in the quest for land and facing the opposition of the Romans, for this conferred more importance on the military aspects of royal authority, seeing the king as a war-leader (*truhtin*) rather than as a *þiudans*, a word with no military associations.[61] If it has been said that in the age of migrations war-bands are tribes in the making[62] we may go one step further and say that war-band leaders are kings in the making (wherever they are not already kings). What Schlesinger has termed Germanic *Heerkönigtum* is not the simple fact of the leadership of an army by a king in time of war, but rather the establishment (or strengthening) of royal power by virtue of such leadership, involving not merely authority over the war-leader's followers during the campaign, but also over land won by conquest.[63] The goal of such military undertakings was not simply plunder (which had been the object of the raiding-parties mentioned by Caesar), but primarily settlement and the exercise of power in new territory. Only rarely, as in Iceland, was the territory empty of inhabitants, so that elsewhere colonisation inevitably took the form of military conquest, together with military occupation (as with the Goths or in Anglo-Saxon England).[64] Kingship established or strengthened in this way was now a primarily military institution (at least for the duration of the migrations and their immediate aftermath), so that the leader who had successfully won a new power-base for himself in this way was more aptly termed a *truhtin*, rather than a traditional *þiudans*.

There is another factor, however, which made the first of these words more relevant to new conditions than the other. Not merely is it the case that the war-band was from the beginning an intertribal association attracting warriors from other tribes to its ranks.[65] In addition, the conquest of new territory carried out by war-bands was itself an intertribal undertaking in which scattered tribal groups of disparate origins took part. The evidence for this reaches back to the first unsettling encounters between Germani and Romans.[66] Ariovistus (called *rex Germanorum* by Caesar) sought to win land by leading a force made up of a variety of tribal members (Harudes, Marcomanni, Triboci, Nemetes, Suebi, Vangiones). Similarly, Maroboduus (exercising what Velleius Paterculus described as a *vis regia*) seized new territory and strengthened his position

---

[61] Schlesinger (1963b), 107, 129.   [62] Wallace-Hadrill (1971), 11.
[63] Schlesinger (1963b), 105f., 123.   [64] Höfler (1963), 103.   [65] See above, pp. 107f.
[66] Schlesinger (1963b), 117ff.; Wallace-Hadrill (1971), 5ff.

by attracting not merely individuals, but also various tribes (*gentes*). Arminius strove for royal power and also had several *gentes* under his leadership. Civilis, a member of the Batavian *stirps regia*, also sought to gain royal authority for himself with the help of a wide range of tribal groups (Batavi, Tencteri, Mattiaci, Chauci, Chatti). Comparable armies amongst the Franks have been described as heterogeneous war-bands rather than ethnic groups.[67] Much further afield, with the Goths in southern Russia, the position was no different insofar as the Ostrogothic kingdom of Ermanaric included (not necessarily as warriors, but at least as subjects) Goths, but also Finns, Slavs, Alans, Heruli and Sarmatians.[68] The Cernjahov Gothic culture also included an ethnic mix made up of Goths, Heruli, Bastarnae, Dacians and Carpi.[69] What all such examples have in common is the quest for new land, an established kingship (or the attempt to realise it) and ethnic heterogeneity amongst the armies gaining possession and in the territories they occupy. Under such conditions of ethnic chaos a term for the ruler such as *piudans*, denoting the king of a people seen as an ethnic unity, would lose all relevance, whilst *truhtin*, the leader of an association which had always cut across tribal boundaries, would recommend itself even more strongly for kingship over new realms.

In considering the second change in the terminology of kingship (from *truhtin* to *kuning*) we have to take account of three factors. The first is the conversion of a temporary or occasional kingship (not all tribes were ruled by kings and with some kingship could lapse for a time) into a permanent institution. Of several tribes (Saxons, Franks, Langobards) it is reported that originally they were governed only by *duces*, but later acquired kings, although the converse was equally possible.[70] By the fourth century, however, in contrast to what had been the position in Tacitus's day, kingship was established in most tribes, so that the move towards kingship (as a new phenomenon or in strengthened form) could well have been brought about by the dislocation of the migrations, facilitating the emergence of royal dynasties.

Implicit in the rise of a strengthened kingship is the second factor, the development (not universal, but certainly marked) from a petty kingship to large-scale kingship (from *Kleinkönigtum* to *Großkönigtum*). With the Franks, but not only with them, this process is visible. Gregory of Tours,

---

[67] Wood (1994b), 39.   [68] See below, pp. 170ff.   [69] Heather (1991), 87, 92, fn. 24.
[70] De Vries (1956b), 297; Schlesinger (1963b), 113, 115; Wood (1977), 7f.

taking the centralised Frankish kingship of his day for granted, looked for its predecessor in the days before the Franks occupied Gaul and was disconcerted to find instead only numerous *regales* or *duces* in the earliest accounts.[71] Within the earliest confederation of the Franks there had been many tribes, each headed by its own leader with his war-band, who seemed to act as a king without actually being called a *rex* in the sources. Behind this discontinuity lies the success of one Frankish leader, Chlodwig, in eliminating rival dynasties, putting an end to other royal families in favour of his own, which was even granted imperial recognition by Anastasius when Chlodwig received the consulship at Tours.[72] What elevated status Frankish kingship, now firmly established, could claim for itself is shown by the Merovingians' monopoly of the royal title *rex* for themselves, denying it to the leaders of other tribes such as the Frisians and Bavarians (whom they demoted by calling them *duces*), even though non-Frankish sources refer to them as *reges*.[73] The authority wielded by Chlodwig and other Frankish kings after him was no longer that of a petty king over his own branch of the Franks, but also extended over other tribal groups. Of the Goths, driven to a centralised kingship by the immense size of the territory they held in southern Russia, it has been said that their leaders were able to focus the loyalties of their followers upon royal service in ways impossible for their predecessors who had led much smaller and poorer groups.[74] How this extension of authority by the Germanic king was reflected in the word *kuning* can best be seen in the ON compound *þjóðkonungr* 'powerful king, sovereign' (with cognates in OS and OE).[75] Whereas the compounds *fylkiskonungr* and *heraðskonungr* designated the ruler in the small-scale context of a district, so that he was strictly a *regulus*, *þjóðkonungr* sees him now exercising authority over a whole people (*þjóð*), as *þiudans* had once done. Snorri's *Edda* similarly maintains that only the ruler who has *reguli tributarii* under him may be called a *þjóðkonungr*.

The third development in the institution of kingship was the change from the elective kingship reported by Tacitus to a hereditary royal dynasty. However precarious the tenure of royal power, subject to election, may have been in the earlier period, by the beginning of the sixth

---

[71] Wallace-Hadrill (1971), 16f.; Wood (1994b), 36.
[72] Wood (1977), 10, 25; (1994b), 49; McCormick (1990), 335ff.
[73] Schlesinger (1963b), 127; Wood (1994a), 236.
[74] Heather (1991), 318 (cf. also p. 312: 'warband-leaders had appropriated the forms of royalty').
[75] Ilkow (1968), 378f., 380f. I differ from Schlesinger (1963b), 106, who sees *þjóðkonungr* expressing the same small-scale kingship as *fylkiskonungr* and *heraðskonungr*.

century most Germanic kingdoms had a royal dynasty and most of these dynasties were claiming a monopoly of kingship since before the migrations.[76] Once again the Franks present us with the most telling example, for the Merovingians held royal power in their hands for three centuries, until 751. Hereditary kingship of this kind was best served by a term for 'king' which, like *kuning*, stressed the *stirps regia* by the root from which it was formed.

The last stage of our argument has led us from petty to large-scale kingship, but even the scope of such authority is surpassed when we come to the subject of overlordship or supreme power, as expressed by OHG *rîhhi*. Cognates are attested in all the Germanic languages, which borrowed it at an early stage from Celtic.[77] At the moment our concern is with this word's function within Germanic, where as an adjective it meant 'powerful, exercising authority', as a noun 'power, authority', but also the geographical area in which such authority is exercised, and as a verb 'to rule'.[78] The word was applied to the larger conglomerations of political power, especially those resulting from the conquest of new territory brought about by the migrations. Since traditional kingship in Germania had been tied to the tribal assembly, the introduction of a far-reaching authority, conveyed by Go. *reiks* and *reiki*, was a revolutionary innovation, capable of suggesting at times something more like despotism.

Wulfila can use it neutrally, but also noticeably where secular authority is seen in opposition to Christ,[79] for secular authority expressly opposed to divine power (e.g. Eph. 6.12), to denote the Devil's tyranny[80] and in a passage (I Cor. 15.24) in which God's just authority is contrasted with the despotism of this world.

The linguistic position in WG is quite clear.[81] In OHG Otfrid employs the word of God's kingdom in the Lord's Prayer (II 21,29), he sees the crucifixion as a defence of Christ's kingdom (*rîchi*) against the Devil, and Christ as Messiah ruling (*rîchisôn*) over His people. In *Muspilli* (v. 35) *rîhhi* stands for God as king and judge at the Last Judgment. Otfrid also refers in laudatory terms to Ludwig the German ruling over the Frankish Empire (Lud. 67), using *rîhhi* of the eastern Frankish realm, just as in the

---

[76] De Vries (1956b), 290; Meid (1966), 189; Wood (1977), 8, 9; (1994b), 1, 322.

[77] See below, pp. 150f.　　[78] Herold (1941), 274f.; Ris (1971), 15ff.

[79] Neutral use (cf. Meid (1966), 183): Neh.7.17; Mt.9.18; Mc.10.42; Lc.18.18. Opposition to Christ (cf. Wolfram (1975), 304): Lc.20.20; Joh.7.26; *Skeireins* 8, 15. Opposition to divine power: Eph.6.12; Col.2.15.　　[80] Mc.3.22; Joh.12, 31; 14.30; 16.11 (against Meid (1966), 183); Eph.2.2.

[81] Herold (1941), 274f.; Kolb (1971), 295.

Ludwigslied (v. 19) it is applied to the western Franks. In the OS *Heliand* the corresponding word can be similarly used positively of the heavenly kingdom and of the Roman Empire.

From this range of evidence it emerges that in WG *rîchi* was capable of denoting something highly positive (in the secular as well as in the religious context) in comparison with the critical attitude still evident in Wulfila's usage. The context for *imperium*, for the Anglo-Saxons and the Franks and earlier with the Goths under Ermanaric, is the subjugation of other peoples by conquest or military intimidation, but with the Anglo-Saxons and the Franks the use made of Roman imperial ideology, coupled with Christian expansionism, supplied a justification which had not been available (or acceptable) to the Goths in the fourth century.[82]

This last word to be discussed illustrates, in different ways, the influence of the Celts and the Romans on the languages and political institutions of Germania. These are two aspects of what will preoccupy us in Part II where we consider, more explicitly and systematically than hitherto, the first contacts of the Germanic tribes with the wider world outside the confines of Germania.

[82] See above, p. 3.

PART II

Contact with the non-Germanic world

Introduction to Part II

For the remainder of this book we shall be dealing with the relationship of the Germanic tribes with the wider world beyond the north. In their gradual expansion they came into contact with a great variety of different peoples and cultures, ranging for example from the Celts in the west to the Romans in the south and the Huns in the east. By far the most important of these contacts (not merely because it also involved an encounter with Christianity) was that with the Roman world, a subject which accordingly claims most of our attention in what follows. As is to be expected with an encounter between an advanced civilisation and a barbarian society, what the Germani received from Rome far exceeds what they may have given in exchange, which explains why in our linguistic survey only one chapter will be devoted to the latter aspect.

This imbalance needs to be redressed to some extent by an important historical consideration. In one respect the encounter between Rome and Germania was more reciprocal than the last paragraph may have suggested, for the first centuries of our era witness not merely a progressive Romanisation of barbarian society, but also an undeniable barbarisation of the Roman world. The imperial frontier along which the two worlds met should be seen not so much separating them as constituting a zone in which they could interact. Military encounters there may have been, but also long periods of peaceful exchange, especially in the border-zone along the Rhine and Danube.[1] Even the military encounters provided the means, as we shall see, for the Germani to learn from their opponents and adopt some of their ways. This also worked the other way, however, for just as the Roman army had been the main agent of Romanisation in the Empire, so did it also become the main agent of barbarisation.[2] The Romans came more and more to depend on recruiting from Germanic tribes on or near the frontier, sometimes

---

[1] Geary (1988), 4f.   [2] *Ibid.*, pp. 20ff.

settling whole groups of barbarians within the confines of the Empire and even appointing Germanic leaders to posts of military commanders (*magistri militum*) within their own ranks. What contact with Germanic barbarians meant for Roman history lies beyond the scope of this book, but has to be borne in mind as the wider setting for our concern: what contact with Rome meant for Germania.

CHAPTER 8

Contact with the Celts

The gradual penetration of the Germanic tribes southwards eventually brought them into contact with the Mediterranean world, the subject of this and the following part. Before that contact was made, however, they impinged on, and were influenced by, many other barbarian tribes dwelling north of the classical oecumene. The most important of these were the Celts, associated archaeologically with the Hallstatt culture from the seventh century BC and with the La Tène culture from the fifth. At its height this Celtic civilisation held sway from the Atlantic through central and southern Germany to the Carpathians and the Balkans, even reaching Asia Minor (the Galatians to whom St Paul wrote were of Celtic origin).

Direct contact between Germani and Celts was established more by the explosive expansion of the Celts than (at this early stage) of the Germani. In their migrations the Celts are attested in the Iberian peninsula, Gaul, Germany, northern Italy, Bohemia, and through the Carpathians deep into the Balkans and Greece.[1] This expansion not merely constituted a danger to Rome (leading ultimately to Caesar's campaign in Gaul), it also brought about the geographical possibility of contact (warfare and trade) between Germani and Celts. One pronounced zone of contact and exchange was the lower Rhine in the west (exemplified by the question whether the Belgae were Celts, Germani or a fusion of both), but another was in Bohemia and Moravia, a major centre of Celtic political and cultural power since about 500 BC.[2] To this latter area we shall repeatedly have to devote our attention. The archaeological evidence for this contiguity confirms what the linguistic evidence suggests: that in prehistoric terms this contact was made in a relatively late period, but also that it lasted over a considerable period of

---

[1] De Vries (1960), 20f.; Schmidt (1984), 120; Todd (1992), 22; Scardigli (1995), 559.

[2] Belgae: de Vries (1960), 48ff.; Wenskus (1961), 216ff.; Birkhan (1970), 226f. Bohemia and Moravia: Todd (1992), 22.

time, constituting a time-depth from about the middle of the first millennium BC down to the first century AD.[3]

There is no doubt that the relationship between Germani and Celts was often one of military antagonism, but equally that, on the basis of trade and exchange, there was in large measure a shared Celto-Germanic unity in material culture and social organisation, even a recognisable linguistic similarity.[4] Although the earlier view that the Celts established a political hegemony over Germanic tribes may no longer be acceptable, the cultural flow, as revealed by archaeological finds, is clearly from the Celtic south to the Germanic north.[5] Against this the Germani had to offer only amber, furs and slaves, an imbalance which is also reflected in loanword traffic.

We may start with the less important aspect of this cultural exchange, with what the north could give the south: as with the later contact between Germanic and Latin, loanwords *from* Germanic are far fewer than *into* it from a superior civilisation.[6]

Two words which were probably loaned from Germanic into Celtic and belong to the same semantic context agree further in signifying not a Germanic innovation, but rather transmission from a third party. The first of these words is Lat. *brācae* 'breeches', for which a loan from Celtic is commonly assumed.[7] Trousers were not a traditional garment in the Mediterranean world; the Romans' attention was first drawn to this clothing of their Celtic opponents at the battle of Telamon (225 BC) and they regarded it as so typically Gaulish that the Narbonensis was known as *Gallia brācata* (even though the Goidelic Celts may have differed from them in this).[8] Despite this it is commonly held that the etymological parallel with Lat. *suffrāgines* 'posterior, buttocks' (the term for a part of the body stands for an item of clothing)[9] suggests a derivation of the Gaulish *c* from a *g*, which underlies the commonly accepted view that the Celtic word was taken over from Germanic after the First Sound Shift which in turn shows its effect in the Germanic forms: ON *brók*, OE *brōc* (plur. *brēc*), OHG *bruoh*. (The substitution of Celtic *ā* for Gmc. *ō* cannot reliably be used to date the loan before the Gmc. shift of IE *ā* to *ō*, since Gaulish, lacking *ō*, could have substituted *ā* for it.)

In agreement with this linguistic pointer there are other suggestions

[3] Evans (1980), 252f., 254, 255; Polomé (1987), 22f.   [4] Evans (1980), 239.
[5] Birkhan (1970), 244, 247; Polomé (1983), 283.   [6] Birkhan (1970), 250.
[7] Birkhan (1970), 247f.   [8] De Vries (1960), 71; Much (1967), 140.
[9] Birkhan (1970), 247, fn. 493.

that the Germani wore trousers – not so much from archaeological finds (because of the perishability of the material) as from depictions of Germanic prisoners of war on Roman monuments.[10] However, the suggestion that the Celts may have taken over this type of clothing and the word for it from the Germani for a particular reason justifies asking the same question of the Germani themselves, whose early contacts with the horse-riding nomadic peoples of the south Russian steppes may provide an answer.[11] Research on the earliest contacts of these nomads with other civilisations has shown repeatedly the military superiority of mounted warriors to the clumsier horse-drawn charioteer favoured by peoples on the borders of the steppes, how the latter were impelled by the success of their opponents to adopt their tactics and make the transition to horse-riding warfare, in every case accompanied by the adoption of trousers as the garment best suited to this purpose (again, as depicted on monuments).[12] Amongst the horse-riding nomads responsible for this development are to be found a number of Iranian tribes of the Pontic region, including above all the Scythians whose influence also reached the Thracians of the north-eastern Balkans. Since this is an area to which Germanic tribes such as the Bastarnae and the Sciri penetrated long before the Goths, it is possible that their acculturation to the needs of the steppes included not merely mounted tactics, but also the type of garment which they called for.[13] By comparison, the attempt to by-pass Germanic transmission by deriving Celtic *brācae* directly from Thracian is much less persuasive. It rests on the view that the Thracian language shows evidence of a sound shift similar to Germanic, so that Gaulish *c* could be explained from Thracian, rather than Germanic.[14] However, we know very little about Thracian, about the extent and chronology of its sound shift, or even whether it possessed the word in question, which is amply attested in Germanic. It seems safer to argue from the known than from the merely hypothetical, especially since there are other cases where the Bastarnae made similar contacts in the Pontic region at a time earlier than the First Sound Shift.[15]

Our second example of a possible loan from Germanic into Celtic takes us in the same direction, since it concerns a word for 'horse'. The word in question has to be distinguished from that represented by Lat.

[10] Much (1937), Illustration 6 (for the contrast between Germanic and Roman attire) and 7 (from the Thorsberg moor). Cf. also Much (1967), 264, 266; Birkhan (1970), 248.

[11] De Vries (1960), 71; Much (1967), 266f.; Birkhan (1970), 248, 403.

[12] Wiesner (1968), 22, 25f., 143.   [13] See below, pp. 164f.

[14] Birkhan (1970), 403; Polomé (1987), 226, fn. 9. On Thracian horsemen's attire and possible contact with the Celts in the Balkans cf. Wiesner (1963), 117, 132.   [15] See below, pp. 164f.

equus.[16] Although cognates of this word are found in Germanic and Celtic (e.g. OE *eoh*, OIr. *ech*) and although it is used in both in the formation of personal names, its presence in Latin (and in other IE languages) makes us hesitate to assume a specific connection between the Germanic and Celtic forms. The position is different with the term which concerns us, for the word which survives in its feminine form (English 'mare', German *Mähre*) is attested only in Germanic and Celtic (e.g. OHG *marahscalc* 'groom', OIr. *marc*).[17] Although cognates are unknown elsewhere in IE, the formation of animal names with a *-g* suffix suggests transmission through a language which underwent the sound-shift of *g* to *k*, which again it is safer to identify as Germanic rather than a largely unknown Thracian. What lies behind the adoption of this word (and its possible association with *brāca*) is the differentiation suggested between it and *equus*: between two different breeds of horse meant for different purposes, *equus* as a draught-animal and **markos* as a speedier one for riding, better suited for combat than breeds hitherto available in northern Europe.[18] This again suggests early contact with horse-riding peoples of the steppes, Scythians or Sarmatians whose horses are described as small, but very fast and strong enough to carry the weight of an armoured rider.[19]

We come now to the more important converse side of this two-way relationship, to the much greater number of examples where Celtic influenced Germanic. That loanwords reflect the wider relationship is made likely by Celtic influence on the material culture of Germania, involving Celtic craftsmanship (especially in metal), above all in the shape of much prized weapons, acquired by Germanic chieftains through trade, gift-exchange and successful warfare. In metalwork the archaeological evidence suggests a growing openness of the north to imports from the Celts in the course of the La Tène period, together with acquaintance with the range of techniques evolved by them for relatively large-scale ironworking.[20] That this superiority of the Celts was not confined to their technology is suggested by Caesar's observation, echoed by Tacitus, that they earlier excelled the Germani in political or military power.[21] This raises the question whether, as with the contact between the Germani and the Roman world, this superiority of the Celts left linguistic traces.

---

[16] Birkhan (1970), 391ff.; Lehmann (1986), 15.   [17] Birkhan (1970), 401ff.
[18] *Ibid.*, pp. 396, 399f. and fn. 1019; Polomé (1983), 293.   [19] Wiesner (1968), 110f.
[20] Birkhan (1970), 127f.; Todd (1992), 20ff.   [21] Caesar, *De bello Gallico* VI 24; Tacitus, *Germania* 28.

In dealing with this question the reservations which are called for have recently been amply rehearsed.[22] To meet difficulties of this kind certain criteria are required. First, an agreement between Celtic and Germanic has to be established positively (on the basis of common innovations not shared by other IE languages), and secondly the priority of Celtic over Germanic has to be shown (on phonological or semantic grounds). These were the criteria applied in the converse direction in the case of *brācae* and **markos*, but a noticeably larger number of cases survives this test when the criteria are applied to Celtic words which are thought to have been loaned into Germanic.

We shall use two approaches, linguistic and cultural, to this problem. First to be considered are three types of linguistic contact (pointers suggesting, with varying degrees of persuasiveness, an influence exercised by Celtic instead of an IE inheritance shared with Germanic), but then various categories of cultural contact (the different fields in which Celtic influence made itself felt).

The first and most convincing type of linguistic contact is when we can be reasonably certain that we are in fact dealing with a Celtic loanword into Germanic. Two examples may suffice, the first of which is OHG *ambaht*, attested in all the Germanic languages, meaning 'follower, servant' as a masculine and 'service' as a neuter.[23] A corresponding Celtic word is also attested by Caesar's use of *ambactus*, in conjunction with *clientes*, when describing the renown and authority of Gaulish chieftains as residing in the number of followers whom they can gather around them.[24] An echo of the Celtic word is found in We. *amaeth* (*servus arans*).[25] This still leaves open the origin of the word, but when Latin glossaries refer to Ennius for its origin (*lingua gallica servus appellatur*) and he defines the word (*servus ambactus, id est circumactus dicitur*), this explanation makes linguistic sense in terms of Celtic, but not Germanic.[26] Contrary to what has been suggested, the presence of *ht* in the Germanic forms instead of Gallo-Latin *ct* cannot be used as an argument for dating the loan from Celtic into Germanic before the First Sound Shift, since the change of a guttural before a dental to χ in Germanic is quite independent of the Sound Shift.[27] If that undermines the case for so early a borrowing, there is equally little case for a late dating (from Gallo-Latin),

[22] Polomé (1981), 507f.; (1983), 284f.; Schmidt (1986), 232; (1991), 141.
[23] Ilkow (1968), 52; Schmidt (1986), 238.   [24] Caesar, *De bello Gallico* VI 15.
[25] Cf. Evans (1967), 134ff.
[26] Walde (1906), 23; Schmidt (1986), 238; (1987), 267; Polomé (1987), 221, fn. 5.
[27] Against von Olberg (1991), 207.

since the word must have been borrowed early enough to reach the Goths while they were still with the main body of the Germanic tribes in northern Europe.[28] Only if *ambaht* and the next word to be considered, Go. *reiks*, together representing converse positions in a power relationship (a follower and someone in authority), were loaned together into Germanic could it be argued that *ambaht* must antedate the First Sound Shift.

Go. *reiks* and its cognates in the other Germanic languages have long been considered as loanwords from Celtic, despite cognates in other IE languages.[29] The justification for apparently ignoring our self-imposed criteria in this particular case is clear when we place the Germanic and Celtic forms of this word in their IE context. All the Germanic cognates of the Gothic form agree with it in showing a long *ī* and the same is true of their Celtic counterparts (names such as *Caturīges* 'kings of battle', *Rīgomagus* = Remagen 'field of the king', OIr. *rí*, gen. *ríg*).[30] By contrast, Lat. *rēx* (stem *rēg-*) shows a different long vowel. What is significant about this distribution is the fact that the raising of IE *ē* to *ī* is a regular development in Celtic, but not elsewhere in IE or in Germanic, where *ē* is retained in Gothic (cf. Gr. *mḗn* 'month' and Go. *mēna* 'moon'), presumably voiced low in view of its counterparts elsewhere in Germanic (ON *máni*, OS/OHG *mâno*, OE *mōna*). Since these changes undergone by IE *ē* in Germanic and Celtic are quite regular, it follows that the Celtic forms for 'king' are equally regular, whilst the Germanic forms for this word are anomalous, hence best explained as loans from Celtic.[31] (Even if we accept the suggestion that contamination may have taken place with a native variant of the IE root (as in ON *folkrekr* 'ruler') this still does not exclude Celtic influence.)[32]

Where this influence first made itself felt is perhaps seen in the frequency of Celtic personal names with *-rīx* as their second element (e.g. *Dagorīx*, *Clutorīx*), their adoption in Germanic (e.g. OHG *Tagarîh*, WFrk. *Chlodericus*) and the fact, assisted by the nature of the sources which record them, that these names, both in Celtic and Germanic, are so often the names of kings.[33] Whereas, however, the Celtic noun signified 'king', its Germanic derivative was not used in this sense (here the need was early met by the native *þiudans*), but as an adjective meaning 'pow-

---

[28] Kuhn (1956), 66.

[29] Germanic evidence: Lehmann (1986), 283; IE evidence includes Lat. *rēx*, but not Vedic *rāj* (Lehmann (1987), 79).   [30] Polomé (1954), 161.

[31] Evans (1980), 249; Lehmann (1987), 80.   [32] Polomé (1954), 161; Schmidt (1984), 124f.

[33] Scherer (1955), 199, 205; de Vries (1960), 70; Schmidt (1984), 124.

erful' and as a noun denoting 'authority' or 'conglomeration of power'.[34] As with the loan of OHG *kaisar* from Lat. *Caesar* and of OSl. *kral* from *Carolus (Magnus)*, the borrowing of *reiks* from Celtic implies contact with a politically superior culture, as exemplified by the wide range of Celtic expansion in the La Tène period by contrast with the relative weakness of the Germanic tribes at that time, still only relatively slowly emerging from the north.[35] What we can reconstruct as the probable dating of the adoption of *reiks* is in agreement with this, since the presence of Germanic *k* in place of Celtic *g* suggests a time before the First Sound Shift (for which there are parallels in the linguistic interchange between the two groups), in any case early enough for various Germanic languages to develop different verbal derivatives (Go. *reikinōn*, OE *rīcsian*, ON *ríkja*).[36]

The second type of linguistic contact concerns isoglosses restricted to Celtic and Germanic (so that we are no longer affected by the implications of the word's presence in other IE languages), but with phonological pointers to the Germanic forms' dependence on Celtic. Both our examples suggest this on the basis of a characteristically Celtic feature, the loss of an IE initial *p-*. Our first example, at home in metallurgy, is one of the two Germanic terms for 'lead': PG *lauða-* as exemplified in OE *lēad* or MHG *lôt* 'lead, metal weight', with a Celtic parallel in OIr. *luaide*.[37] The presence of an easily castable metal, used in soldering, lies behind the etymological connection of these words with the IE root **pleud-* 'to flow, run, melt (easily)'.[38] Acceptance of this etymology means that the Germanic words for 'lead' cannot derive directly from the IE root (which would have yielded initial *f-* after the First Sound Shift, as in OE *flōd* 'flowing, flood'). Since only Celtic regularly dropped the initial *p-*, the Germanic forms must be derived from this source, after the loss of *p-*. We do not have to assume, as a result of this linguistic argument, that the Germani became acquainted with lead only thanks to the Celts: the existence of a second (native) term, German *Blei*, argues against this, as does the use of this metal in the handles of Bronze Age swords to provide better hand-balance.[39] Instead, as the use of the Germanic words suggests, the word was introduced much later in conjunction with the technique of soldering, attested in Germania from the first centuries AD and thereby indicating the long duration of Celtic influence in this

[34] De Vries (1960), 70.   [35] Lehmann (1987), 80.
[36] Ross and Thomson (1976), 178; Evans (1980), 249; Schmidt (1984), 124.
[37] Polomé (1954), 154; Birkhan (1970), 147ff.   [38] Birkhan (1970), 147; Polomé (1981), 511.
[39] *Blei*: Beck (1978), 73; hand-balance: Polomé (1983), 291.

field.[40] That Celtic metallurgy had something to teach even the Romans is likely if we accept the proposal that Lat. *libra* 'weight, scales' originally denoted 'lead' or 'lead weight' and, *via* the form **loudh-rā*, was also a loan from Celtic.[41]

The last type of linguistic contact again deals with isoglosses confined to Celtic and Germanic, but sees the common innovation which sets them apart not in any phonological development, but rather less tangibly on the basis of a shared semantic change. The first example, represented by OHG *frî* 'free', we have already considered in the context of Germanic legal vocabulary, where we saw that it had IE cognates whose original meaning had been 'one's own' (of kinsmen especially) and hence 'dear, beloved'.[42] Although traces of this earlier usage are still detectable in the Germanic languages, especially in OE, they also early developed the meaning 'free', an innovation which they share with Celtic (cf. We. *rhydd* 'free'). Phonologically the Welsh form proceeds quite regularly from IE **prio*, but the same is true of the Germanic forms, so that we can no longer turn to the contrast between a regular Celtic development and an anomalous one in Germanic in order to argue for Celtic influence on Germanic.[43] Instead, we have to proceed from the unique position of these two groups within IE in developing this particular meaning. Theoretically, three possibilities exist. First, this novel meaning could have arisen in both groups independently, without any interconnection (although it is remarkable that this should have taken place in two contiguous language groups).[44] If we are suspicious of this coincidence we have to accept the possibility of a loan from one language to another or rather, since each group inherited the IE word independently of the other, the likelihood of a loan-meaning affecting the range of meaning already present in the cognate word of the recipient language.[45] This process could take place in either direction. The presence of the meaning 'free' in all the Germanic languages by contrast to its restriction within Celtic to Welsh alone might seem to tell in favour of Germanic influence on Celtic (but how did it reach British alone?).[46] Conversely, influence from Celtic might be more likely in view of other probable examples in the sphere of law and government, but above all in the light of Lehmann's argument in favour of an earlier development of this new meaning in Celtic.[47]

---

[40] Birkhan (1970), 147, 148, 151.   [41] Szemerényi (1952), 99ff.; Birkhan (1970), 151.
[42] See above, p. 39 and also Polomé (1954), 160; Evans (1980), 246; Lehmann (1987), 8of.
[43] Scheller (1950), 81, 82f.   [44] *Ibid.*, p. 84; Polomé (1954), 161.   [45] Scheller (1950), 83.
[46] *Ibid.*, p. 84.   [47] Schmidt (1991), 143, 144; Lehmann (1987), 81.

The reservations which are called for here are certainly no less in the case of a second example from the legal sphere. An IE word for 'orphan' (attested by Armenian *orb*, Gr. *orphanós*, Lat. *orbus*) has phonological counterparts in Celtic and Germanic with a shift of meaning to 'heir, inheritance': OIr. *orbbae* masc. and neut. (as well as the Gaulish name *Orbius*), Go. *arbja* masc. and *arbi* neut.[48] The agreement between these two groups in contrast to all others certainly conforms to one of the criteria earlier laid down, but can it be said that the semantic initiative came from Celtic? It is not convincing enough to appropriate this word to a general Celtic influence on Germania; to suggest that, like *frî*, it is another legal term moving in this direction is to buttress one uncertainty with another.[49]

We turn now from linguistic to cultural contact, asking what light possible loanwords from Celtic into Germanic may throw on the different spheres affected. We shall be concerned with three such spheres: metallurgy, warfare and social organisation.

Under metallurgy, where Celtic influence on the north made itself particularly felt in the Iron Age, pride of place belongs unsurprisingly to the word 'iron'. Geographical access to supplies and command of the technology of iron-making, such as the Celts enjoyed, constituted a revolution in warmaking and underlay their expansion, military and political, in the La Tène period as well as the reaction of the Germanic tribes to it. The result was that whereas the Germanic north had been largely independent in the Bronze Age it came increasingly under the sway of the south during the Iron Age, with perceptible Celtic influence in iron-making and its products.[50] Chronologically, the beginnings of iron-making in Germania cannot be earlier than the fourth/third century BC; traces of the earliest furnaces for this purpose have been found in the north-east of the area then occupied by the Celts (Bohemia, Moravia, south-western Poland).[51] Although Tacitus could still speak much later of a general paucity of iron amongst the Germani (it was in high demand for weapons largely monopolised by leaders) he explicitly refers to a Celtic tribe, the Cotini, dwelling in what was now Germanic territory (Moravia), mining iron and paying tribute with it. Ptolemy also knew that the neighbouring Germanic tribe of the Quadi were in possession of iron-works.[52]

---

[48] Polomé (1954), 159; Schmidt (1986), 238f.   [49] Schmidt (1986), 240; (1987), 268.
[50] Birkhan (1970), 244f.   [51] Pleiner (1989), 60; Capelle (1989), 61.
[52] Tacitus, *Germania* 43; Ptolemy: Capelle (1989), 63.

The view that Celtic and Germanic share a word for 'iron' which is not attested elsewhere needs to be specified in more detail.[53] On the Celtic side the starting-point must be *ĭsarno-*, attested in the name of the fortress *Isarnodori*, but also OIr. *iarn*, We. *haearn*, whilst Germanic proceeds from *ĭsarna-* and yields examples such as Go. *eisarn*, OHG *îsarn* and *(H)iranhart* (personal name) and OE *īsern, īren.*[54] The main problems in attempting to correlate these forms are two. First, amongst the Germanic examples we find forms with -*r*- alongside those with -*s*-: these point to a different accentuation of the prototype (and the operation of Verner's Law): *ĭsarna-* as opposed to *īsárna-*, which parallels the prototype of We. *haearn* < *sĭárnos* < *siárnos*, with metathesis < *isárnos.*[55] Secondly, although there is a discrepancy between Germanic forms with a long *ī* and the short *i* required by the Insular Celtic forms it is possible that shortening took place in a position before the word accent and Birkhan has concluded that there is more to be said for an original long vowel in Celtic, as in Germanic.[56] A further complication is introduced by the ON forms of this word (*éarn, járn*), which stand apart from other Germanic forms, but for which the possibility of a borrowing from Ireland or even from Wales has been entertained.[57] Finally, the secondary position of Germanic within this web of isoglosses has been stressed on purely phonological grounds by Lehmann who, in considering Go. *eisarn* within the framework of Gothic word-formation, has pointed to the extreme anomaly of a word beginning with *ei*-, the rarity of native words ending in -*rn* and the suspicious variation of forms in the different Germanic languages.[58] From all this he has concluded that the Germanic word for 'iron' is unlikely to be native, but rather borrowed from a non-Germanic language. The closeness of the Celtic isoglosses and the absence of any other counterparts suggest that this source was Celtic, a conclusion borne out by the significant fact of accent doublets in both Celtic and Germanic,[59] as well as by the non-linguistic evidence for the dominance of Celtic iron-working over Germania. As was the case with lead, however, this should not lead us to assume that before contact with advanced Celtic technology the Germani had been totally unacquainted with this mineral, since a native word is found in ON *rauði* 'bog iron ore' (loaned further into Slavonic

---

[53] Krahe (1954), 79ff.; Birkhan (1970), 121; Schmidt (1984), 115f.; Polomé (1987), 228.
[54] Evans (1980), 250; Polomé (1983), 288; Schmidt (1987), 270; Beck (1989), 59.
[55] Polomé (1983), 288. For accent differentiation in Celtic see Birkhan (1970), 141.
[56] Birkhan (1970), 128f.   [57] *Ibid.*, pp. 132, 173, fn. 256.   [58] Lehmann (1987), 76ff.
[59] Birkhan (1970), 141.

rūdà 'ore' and ultimately into Finnish *rauta* 'iron').[60] However, the etymological association of this ON word with the adjective *rauðr* 'red' makes it likely that it indicates knowledge of the mineral, not necessarily of any finished product. We are left with the probability that the Germani derived from the Celts not merely acquaintance with iron technology, but also their word for the product.[61]

Another example is represented by English 'wire' (OE *wīr* 'metal thread, ornament made of wire', OHG *wiara* 'gold or silver thread', ON *víravirki* 'filigree'). These forms reflect an IE source **ụeiros* meaning 'curved, twisted',[62] but presuppose transmission through Celtic in its varying dialectal forms. Insular Celtic monophthongised *ei* to *ē* (cf. OIr. *fíar*, We. *gŵyr* 'crooked'), whilst on the continent the same development to *ē* took place (reflected in Germanic *ē²*, hence OHG *wiara*), but also a different monophthongisation to *ī* (hence OE *wīr*).[63] To assume direct descent from IE would not account for the variants found in Germanic, which instead reflect dialectal differentiation within Celtic. When this loan is to be dated is more uncertain. Are we to see it as contemporary with the borrowing of *rīg* (which shows a similar development of *ē* to *ī*)? Or are we to see it in connection with the later rise of the war-band, whose members were rewarded by their leader with gifts of gold often worn as bracelets (*Hildebrandslied* 33)?[64] Or are we to reckon with two loans at two different times?

The Gothic word *brunjo* 'breastplate' has cognates in all the Germanic languages, but is also related to a Celtic word for 'breast' (OIr. *bruinne*; cf. MWe. *brynn* 'hill, breast').[65] The Celtic forms do not denote an item of armour, but the parallel of Gr. *thórax* ('breast(plate)') illustrates the ease with which this semantic extension could be made. However, the fact that behind these Celto-Germanic isoglosses there stands an IE **bhreus-* 'to swell' (also surviving in such a form as Go. *brusts* 'breast') makes it imperative to explain why Gmc. *brunjo* should have come *via* Celtic and not directly from IE. The answer lies in the derivation of the word for 'breastplate' from IE **bhrusn-*, for the combination *-sn-* would have yielded either **bruss-* or **bruzn-* > **brurn-* in Germanic, whilst the development to *-nn-* is regular in Celtic.[66] Even though the word may not

[60] *Ibid.*, p. 141, fn. 142; Schmidt (1987), 270 and fn. 24; Beck (1989), 59.
[61] Another example of Celtic influence in this field has been suggested in the word 'oven' in the sense of a furnace (for iron-making). Cf. Otrębski (1966), 60; Birkhan (1970), 142ff.; Polomé (1983), 288, but also Szemerényi (1960), 26, fn. 2.
[62] Birkhan (1970), 152; Polomé (1983), 291. On Pliny's use of *viriae/viriolae* 'bracelet' see Birkhan (1970), 153; Schmidt (1987), 271.   [63] Birkhan (1970), 152f.; Polomé (1983), 291.
[64] Birkhan (1970), 154.   [65] *Ibid.*, p. 155; Hüpper-Dröge (1981), 108.   [66] Birkhan (1970), 155f.

be attested in Celtic with the meaning which it has in Germanic, it therefore seems likely that the word was acquired from Celtic (after the First
Sound Shift). The OHG glossary evidence for *brunna* (by comparison
with *brustroch*) shows that *brunna* denoted a better form of body-protection (almost certainly of metal), such as was still uncommon in
Germania in Tacitus's day.[67] There is indeed archaeological and historical evidence for the use of such protection by Celtic warriors of high
rank. Evidence is also forthcoming from Germania, where it may not be
fortuitous that some of these cases reveal a Celtic connection:[68] the
Cimbri equipped themselves with armour from the Celts, the twenty-
odd sets of armour recovered from Hjortspring have been attributed to
Celtic influence in the La Tène period, whilst the degree of workman-
ship shown by EG finds has been explained by contact with the Celts,
possibly with the Cotini. Rare this form of protection may have been,
but even rare objects need to be named.[69]

If we turn now to the second sphere of contact between Celts and
Germani, warfare, it is clear that the last example placed under metallurgy (*brunjo*, but also *wēpna*) could equally well belong here. It is all the
more necessary to stress this since some of the terms which follow
(*siponeis*, *áips*) are tentatively placed here only because of the suggestion
that they may have belonged to the vocabulary of the war-band and that
the Celtic institution influenced its Germanic counterpart.[70] Even if
they do not belong here, they could still be placed under the next
heading (social organisation).

We start with two words which, within Germania, are attested only in
Gothic and therefore raise the special question how contact may have
been made between the Celts and the Goths alone. Wulfila used the first
of these words, *sipōneis*, to render 'disciple',[71] but if we accept the suggestion of a loan from Celtic its original meaning would have been 'follower' (in a war-band or simply as a term of social subordination?), with
a semantic restriction to 'disciple' in the biblical context of our Gothic
evidence. Admittedly, no Celtic *sepānios* is attested, but this weakness is
in part made good if we proceed from the IE verbal root *sekч- 'to follow'
where the labiovelar became *p* in Continental Celtic (which also retained

---

[67] Maschke (1926), 170. See also above, pp. 70f.
[68] Celts and Cimbri: Maschke (1926), 171; Birkhan (1970), 157; Hjortspring: Birkhan (1970), 161; EG armour: Much (1967), 128f.; Birkhan (1970), 158, fn. 197.
[69] Birkhan (1970), 421ff., has also discussed Go. *wēpna* 'weapons', with cognates in all Gmc. lan-guages, as possibly another loanword from Celtic in the field of metalwork.
[70] Kuhn (1956), 77f.; Wenskus (1961), 357f.
[71] Schwarz (1951), 24f.; Wenskus (1961), 359; Swiggers (1985), 109f.

the initial *s*-). Any remaining differences between the Gothic and reconstructed Celtic forms can be attributed to the former (short *e* > *i* is regular
in Gothic; for *ā* > *ō* we have the parallel *Rōmāni* > *Rūmōneis*).

Possible areas of contact between Celtic and Gothic can only be con-
jectured, but at least the possibilities need to be stated. Two chronological extremes can be excluded: first, the view that the Cimbri acquired
the word in Gaul in the second century BC and passed it back to the
Goths in the north (such a west Celtic origin would be difficult to reconcile with the development of *ku̯* and the retention of *s*-),[72] but also
the suggestion that the Goths, once in the Pontic region, acquired the
word from the Galatians[73] (but can we be certain that they still spoke
Celtic in the third century AD?). Another suggestion has been to point to
possible contacts made by the Goths towards the start of their trek from
the north (with the Celtic-dominated Lugii in southern Poland) or, a little
further on, with Celts in Bohemia, Moravia and Silesia.[74] Finally, to
meet the difficulty that this word found its way into Gothic, but into no
other Germanic language, contact with Celts in the Balkans has been
proposed (but where?).[75]

The second Gothic word, *kelikn*, translates Gr. *pýrgos*, meaning both a
'defence tower' and (as with Wulfila) an 'upper room, elevated dining-
room'.[76] A word *celicnon* is twice attested in Gaulish inscriptions and has
been connected with an IE base *kelH*- 'to tower up, raise high' (from
which also derive cognates such as Lat. *collis* 'hill' and *columna*). The
difficulties attaching to the *e* of the Gothic word (if the Celtic vowel had
been long we should have expected transition to *ī*, as in *reiks*, but if it
had been short we should have expected transition to *i*, as in *sipōneis*)
have been met by suggesting that loanwords from another language
may contain phonemes not otherwise part of the native stock. In place
of this Celtic origin a derivation from Iranian *kalaka*- 'house, fortress'
has been put forward.[77] Although we consider Iranian contacts with
Gothic in the next chapter this example seems much more dubious,
both by reason of its vocalism and the unusual addition of a nasal suffix
to a loanword.

Like *sipōneis*, this word raises the question of possible areas of contact.
Again the Cimbri have been proposed as intermediaries between Celts

[72] Schwarz (1951), 26; Swiggers (1985), 110, fn. 7.   [73] Schütte (1902), 14; Jellinek (1926), 178.
[74] Much (1893), 33. Suggested (in a different Celto-Germanic context) by Untermann (1954), 397f.
On the Lugii see Schwarz (1956), 68; Wenskus (1961), 464; Much (1967), 479; Wolfram (1988), 40,
112.   [75] Wolfram (1988), 113.   [76] Polomé (1987), 223ff.; Eska (1990), 63ff.
[77] Polomé (1987), 225, fn. 8. Against this Eska (1990), 65f.

and Goths, this time with reference to Go. *alēw* 'oil' and *lukarn* 'lamp', words which the Cimbri are also thought to have transmitted to the Goths.[78] Whatever the merit of the case for these two words, the position with them is quite different: they are trade words which accompany the objects of trade, whilst *kelikn* represents a static object which does not 'move' to the recipient, but awaits his coming. The Galatians we may doubt as before (the third century is also late for the loss of final *-on* in Gothic).[79] This leaves us again with two possibilities: the Lugii, together with Celts in Bohemia, Moravia and Silesia, or the Celts in the Balkans.[80] At least these proposals have the advantage over the Cimbri, since it is probable that the Germani, long before they came across Roman *castella*, encountered Celtic fortresses and towers (it is as a defence tower that Gr. *pýrgos*, translated by Wulfila as *kelikn*, primarily functioned).[81]

A last word which may belong to the sphere of warfare is represented by Go. *áips* 'oath', with cognates in all the Germanic languages. The Germanic word corresponds to OIr. *oeth* both phonologically and semantically, and both have been traced back to IE **oitos* 'walk, going', with the implicit idea of ceremonially going to an oathswearing (as in Sw. *edgång*).[82] This IE background suggests a Celto-Germanic innovation in the meaning of this word, but there is nothing to suggest anything more than a shared community, at the most, between the two groups. The only arguments advanced in favour of Celtic influence (cultural superiority in general terms, the presence of other cases from the same sphere) are not persuasive enough in every specific case.[83] Nor is the argument that the function of the oath in the Germanic war-band (Tacitus, *Germania* 14) was of Celtic origin a proof that the word for 'oath' was likewise of Celtic origin. If there are doubts about connecting this word with the war-band there is little case for including it under the heading of warfare at all: as a legal term it might more properly form part of our third cultural sphere, social organisation.

If we transfer *áips* to this last sphere it will join other terms which have already been considered: *ambaht, reiks, frî* and *arbja*. To these we may add simply one more example, the word for 'hostage', present in the Germanic languages as an appellative (OHG *gîsal*) or as an element in personal names (*Gislaharius*), but also with parallels in Celtic (OIr. *giall*,

---

[78] Schwarz (1951), 22ff.   [79] Proposed by Schütte (1902), 14, questioned by Schwarz (1951), 25.
[80] Much (1893), 33; Wolfram (1988), 113.
[81] Schwarz (1951), 24; Kuhn (1951c), 107; Wenskus (1961), 403f.; Kuhn (1972), 48f.
[82] Evans (1980), 245; Beck (1986a), 537f.   [83] Lehmann (1987), 80; Schmidt (1991), 143.

We. *gûystl*).[84] This phonological and semantic agreement has no counterpart in IE outside Celtic and Germanic, but there is equally nothing which could be termed characteristically Celtic about any of the forms. We may conclude that this is a case of a shared Celto-Germanic community and that here, too, the appeal to the cultural superiority of the Celts is not persuasive enough (inasmuch as the Celts had a well-developed legal tradition, the same can be said of the Germani).[85]

Up to now we have been concerned with appellatives which may have found their way from Celtic into Germanic, but Celtic linguistic influence also extended to onomastic material. Chosen examples from geographical names and the names of certain tribes can illustrate this.

Linguistic contact was made in the sphere of Celtic place-names as the initially slow expansion of the Germanic tribes brought them gradually into the Celtic sphere of political and military influence and ultimately, with the increase of Germanic pressure, into occupation of Celtic territory with its Celtic (or pre-Celtic) names.

One of the most important, but difficult examples is the name given by Caesar and Tacitus to the central German highland (*Mittelgebirge*): *Hercynia silva/Hercynius saltus*.[86] The presence of *y* in these forms (together with Caesar's explicit observation) points to a Greek source, confirmed by Greek references to a mountain-range called *Orkýnios* or *Arkýnia*.[87] The same name occurs in Germanic for parts of the *Mittelgebirge* (OHG *Fergunna*, *Virgundia*), but also as an appellative: Go. *faírguni* 'mountain (-range)', OE *firgen* 'mountain'.[88] Correlating these forms makes it likely that behind the Greek forms there was a Celtic informant, since the Germanic forms with *f-* derive from a *p-* (First Sound Shift) which would have been regularly lost only in Celtic (Lat. *H-* must be regarded as prosthetic). That we are right to assume an original initial *p-* is confirmed by a wider range of evidence from Balto-Slavonic.[89] In Slavonic *Perunъ* occurs as the name of a thunder-god and in Lithuanian *Perkúnas* as the name of a god (in close association with oak-trees). The word is also found as an appellative: in the Baltic languages it means 'thunder', but in Latin (*quercus* < **perquus*) 'oak'.[90]

The first question which this range of parallels poses is whether the Germanic examples derive directly from an IE form or whether, as has

---

[84] Schmidt (1987), 268.   [85] Schmidt (1991), 141.
[86] Caesar, *De bello Gallico* VI 24f.; Tacitus, *Germania* 28 and 30.   [87] Much (1967), 351.
[88] Wenskus (1961), 225; Friedrich (1970), 137; Lehmann (1986), 104.   [89] Friedrich (1970), 135f.
[90] *Ibid.*, p. 137.

been suggested, they were taken over from Celtic before its loss of initial *p-* (and before the First Sound Shift, with the operation of Verner's Law).[91] The answer to this hinges on the relevance of the Balto-Slavonic evidence, for its presence apparently weakens the exclusive Celto-Germanic connection required for any suggestion of Celtic influence. In the first place, the Baltic forms are not necessarily independent, for they could derive from Germanic.[92] Secondly, we need to stress a difference in the onomastic use of this word: in Balto-Slavonic it is used as the name of a god, but in Germanic, Greek and Latin (and, behind these, Celtic) only as the name of a mountain-range (confirmed by the meaning of the Germanic appellatives). Thirdly, if the Greeks acquired the name of this north European range from Celtic, it is likely that the Germani did, too, for at many other points they encountered the Celts and adopted geographical names from them (e.g. Gmc. **Rînaz* 'Rhine').[93] From this we may conclude that the Germani, whose contact with the Celts fits in chronologically with this, acquired knowledge of this geographical name from them.

The other question is where precisely we may locate the *Hercynia silva* and this particular contact. The greatest extent (and therefore for us unusable) is attributed to it by Caesar's mention of sixty days' travelling time, but apart from this the name appears to have been applied to different parts of the *Mittelgebirge* (OHG *Fergunna* refers to the *Erzgebirge*, *Virgundia* to a range between Ansbach and Ellwangen).[94] Two other points, however, may allow us to place greater stress on the *Erzgebirge*. First, in view of what we shall see in connection with the name 'Bohemia' it is significant that Velleius Paterculus, Strabo and Posidonius all located the *Hercynia silva* in this region, just as, secondly, Caesar also associated the Celtic tribe of the Volcae (who were probably settled a little to the east, in Moravia, and with whom the Germani also made contact) with this same wooded highland.[95] It is in this area, probably not before 500 BC, that we have to see one of the most important zones of contact between Celts and Germani – important perhaps because of military encounters, but certainly in view of its rich mineral resources of which the Celts made such good use.[96]

The mention of Bohemia is of linguistic interest, too, since it contains

---

[91] Lehmann (1986), 104f.   [92] Karsten (1915), 75f.

[93] Lehmann (1986), 105. On **Rînaz* cf. Schmidt (1984), 122.

[94] Much (1967), 352; Wenskus (1961), 225.

[95] Much (1967), 353f.; Wenskus (1978), 207; Timpe (1989), 360.

[96] Wenskus (1961), 227; Wolfram (1976), 242.

the name of another Celtic tribe in this region, the *Boii*.[97] True to the wide extent of the Celtic migrations the name of this particular tribe is attested from different parts of Europe and it also occurs in personal names (e.g. *Boiorix*) and place-names (e.g. *Boiodurum*, surviving in modern *Beiderwies*, opposite Passau). The settlement area of theirs which concerns us is their occupation of the basin of the upper Elbe, for the classical authors who locate the *Hercynia silva* in this area are also quite explicit in mentioning the names of the Boii or Bohemia, or both.[98] Tacitus, with an eye to the later occupations of this area by Germani says that the name *Boihaimum* still clings to the former land of the Boii, even after its change of inhabitants (*Germania* 28). The same name occurs in the form *Boiohaemum* with Velleius Paterculus, whilst in *Baias* (Geographer of Ravenna) the s-shaped sign is taken as a mark of abbreviation (**Baiahaimum*).[99] There seems little doubt that this name, composed of a Celtic tribal name combined with a Germanic word for 'homeland' (cf. Go. *háims*), was coined to designate formerly Celtic territory now occupied by Germani, as was already clear to Tacitus. As part of the assimilation of Germanic names to Celtic practice the form *Boi(o)haemum* shows a Celtic *o* (both in the stem and in the thematic vowel), whilst **Baiahaimum* suggests a fully Germanised variant.[100] It is from this latter form that MHG *Bêheim* and the modern *Böhmen* are derived, even though subsequent history means that it is now applied to yet another people. The geographical name has proved more static than the inhabitants.

The Celtic Boii have also given their name to yet another tribe: the Bavarians. The earliest attestations of this tribal name are Lat. *Baibari* (Jordanes, where the *-b-* stands for *-w-*), *Baioarii* (Venantius Fortunatus, where *o* stands for *w*) and OHG *Peigira* (where *g* acts as a glide).[101] These forms we may derive from **Bai(a)warjōz* which, apart from the fact that it shows a Germanised form of *Boii* (*o* > *a*, as in **Baiahaimum*), presents difficulties. Germanic formations with *-warjōz* to indicate inhabitants of a region generally show a geographical name as their first element, as with Anglo-Latin *Cantuarii* 'inhabitants of Kent' (cf. OE *Cantware*) or the OHG personal name *Lantweri* (literally 'he who protects the land', cf. Go. *warjan* 'to protect').[102] This explanation hardly applies to **Bai(a)warjōz*,

---

[97] Birkhan (1978), 205; Callies (1978), 207.   [98] Much (1967), 353f.; Wenskus (1978), 207.

[99] Schnetz (1938), 90, fn. 1; (1951/2), 1ff.; Neumann (1973), 600; Wenskus (1978), 205.

[100] Birkhan (1970), 175, fn. 259; (1978), 206.

[101] Schönfeld (1911), 42f.; Beck (1973b), 601. On Latin orthographic variants for Gmc. *w* see Schönfeld (1911), pp. xxiiif.

[102] Beck (1973b), 601f. *Lantweri*: Scherer (1955), 206; Starck and Wells (1990), 361.

since the only evidence for **Baija* as a possible geographical name was *Baias* with the Geographer of Ravenna, now regarded as an abbreviation of **Baiahaimum*. For this reason the reconstructed earliest form for 'Bavarians' is now regarded as a contraction of **Baiahaimwarjōz*.[103] This linguistic reconstruction might suggest that in the course of their ethnogenesis the later Bavarians entered their new homeland from the north, from Bohemia, but this need not necessarily be so. If we take *Boiohaemum* in its original literal sense it meant not what we now know as Bohemia, but the land of the Boii who, on abandoning 'Bohemian' territory under Germanic pressure, moved elsewhere, including Pannonia, where Pliny located the *deserta Boiorum*.[104] This aspect of the problem of Bavarian ethnogenesis (settlement from the north, from Bohemia, or from the east, from Pannonia?) will come up for discussion later when we consider the possibility of loanwords of Gothic origin in Bavarian.[105]

The last Celtic tribe for us to consider are the *Volcae* (*Tectosages*) mentioned by Caesar in the region of the *Hercynia silva*,[106] for there is linguistic evidence that the Germani early came into contact with them. Although the Volcae, like other Celtic tribes, were taken far and wide in the course of their migrations Caesar placed those he had in mind in Germania, east of the Rhine. What he reported of them is said in the past tense and what we know of the location of the Volcae in Caesar's day does not suggest that they were still neighbours of the Germani.[107] Caesar's statement is therefore about the past, as is borne out by his dependence on Greek sources in this passage.[108] This is confirmed by our linguistic evidence from Germanic, since this tribal name, like that of the Boii, was borrowed into Germanic, yielding the form **Walh-* (attested in OHG, OE, ON),[109] where the development of k to χ shows that the loan preceded the First Sound Shift and that contact between Germani and this Celtic tribe was probably made before the third century BC.

Locating the place of contact geographically is made difficult by two factors: by the wide extent which Caesar attributed to the *Hercynia silva* and by the far-flung movements of the Volcae whom he associated with it. Accordingly, numerous attempts have been made to do this.[110] These include the Rhineland (but do we know of Volcae in this region?), but also Hessen, the upper Main and southern Germany, all rendered unlikely by being too far to the south for contact between Germani and

---

[103] Beck (1973b), 602.   [104] Much (1967), 354.   [105] See below, pp. 320f.
[106] *De bello Gallico* VI 24.   [107] Weisgerber (1953), 164.   [108] *Ibid.*, p. 166.   [109] *Ibid.*, p. 161.
[110] Listed by Wenskus (1961), 211.

Celts at so early a date. Much more probable (even though there may be no proof) is the area to which we have had our attention drawn more than once, the eastern range of the *Mittelgebirge*, with the Volcae settled perhaps east of the Boii, in Moravia rather than Slovakia, but certainly not much further eastwards (in what later became EG territory) if we are to account for the absence of the word **Walh-* in Gothic, as opposed to WG.[111] (There may have been no occasion to use such a word in Wulfila's bible, but the word is also significantly absent from the formation of Gothic personal names, again in contrast to WG.) Locating the Volcae in this area also sheds further light on Caesar's remark on the land in which the Volcae were once settled. His reference to the wealth of this region (*fertilissima Germaniae . . . loca*) may mean not only agriculture but perhaps also the mineral deposits there, whilst the renown attributed to the Volcae in peace and in war (*summamque . . . iustitiam et bellicae laudis opinionem*) rested on their skill in metallurgy and the quality of their weapons. On both scores they attracted the attention of their northern neighbours.

In different ways and with different implications these three geographical terms (Bohemia, Bavaria and Wales)[112] are thus all fossilised survivals of the encounter between Celts and Germani which add valuable new material to the often uncertain evidence of loanwords.

---

[111] Moravia: Todd (1992), 22; Slovakia: de Vries (1960), 56; EG territory: Weisgerber (1953), 171 and fn. 28; Wenskus (1961), 227f.

[112] Weisgerber (1953), 155ff., has discussed the further development of Gmc. **Walh-*, producing the German adjective *welsch* (cf. Engl. 'Welsh') and also the noun 'Wales'.

CHAPTER 9

The migration of the Goths

The Goths were not the first EG tribe to move to the Black Sea from the Baltic. Various tribes were settled in the Lower Vistula area several centuries BC and the Bastarnae, together with others like the Sciri and the Vandals, reached as far as the Upper Vistula, from where they migrated further, so that the Bastarnae reached the Black Sea at the close of the third century BC, centuries before the Goths.[1] Their presence is attested at the mouth of the Danube about 200 BC, where they are mentioned alongside the Thracians, but a stage on their route may be reflected in the name *Alpes Bastarnicae* for the Carpathians in the *Tabula Peutingeriana*.[2] If we go by the later migration of the Goths over much the same route (archaeological evidence suggests that it took them about a hundred years to reach the Pontic area),[3] the Bastarnae may have set out from the Lower Vistula at about the beginning of the third century BC.

This dating is helpful, since amongst the words designating novel objects or places encountered by the Bastarnae which they are thought to have passed on to the rest of Germania are two which were early enough to undergo the effects of the First Sound Shift. The first is the designation for the Carpathians (Ptolemy: *Karpátēs óros*), where the Bastarnae were settled for some time.[4] In ON this mountain-range is known as the *Harfaðafjöll*, where the second element refers to mountains (English 'fell') and the first shows the triple effect of the Sound Shift ($k >$ $h, p > f, t > ð$). For these changes to occur we may assume that the Shift (spread over some length of time) had not been concluded by the third century BC, but had at least begun at the time when the Bastarnae separated geographically from the rest of Germania.[5]

---

[1] Altheim (1943), 87; Untermann (1954), 397; Schwarz (1956), 52f.; La Baume (1959), 7, 10.

[2] Vernadsky (1951), 350f.; Wenskus (1961), 206; Much (1967), 523.

[3] Wolfram (1988), 43; (1991), 139.

[4] Karsten (1928), 98; de Vries (1941), 36f.; Schwarz (1951), 33; (1956), 50.

[5] Wenskus (1961), 208f.

A similar conclusion can be drawn from the second word which, because it also undergoes the Sound Shift, must have been loaned early enough into Germanic to make an association with the Bastarnae feasible. The word is attested in several Germanic languages (e.g. OE *hænep* 'hemp') and corresponds to Gr. *kánnabis* with the same meaning, showing now two results of the Shift ($k > h$, $b > p$).[6] This agreement with Greek does not mean that we are dealing with an early loan from Greek into Germanic, but instead with a loan into both languages from a common source. Where this source may be found is suggested by the observation of Herodotus that hemp was cultivated especially in the east by Scythians and Thracians.[7] This conjunction of an early dating and the Thracians suggests the same background for 'hemp' as for the 'Carpathians' (where Thracians were also settled).[8] Although the evidence for the Thracians as a possible source for both words may be quite fortuitous, the origin of the words in the south-east and adoption into Germanic long before the arrival of the Goths in this region seem unquestioned.

The Goths, too, were drawn in this direction in the course of their migration, following the rivers Oder and Vistula which permitted penetration far inland.[9] The Baltic and the Black Sea were also linked by a prehistoric trade-route whose products may have held out the promise of wealth and agricultural gains to tribes in search of land.[10] Nor should we disregard the precedent set by the Bastarnae and others (whose links with the north must have been maintained if their loan-words were spread throughout Germania) as a stimulus for subsequent waves of migration.[11] The second and third centuries AD see therefore numerous Germanic tribes in the Pontic area (south Russian steppes and lower Danube), amongst whom the Goths appeared early in the third century in Thrace, launching attacks by land and sea (across the Black Sea and into the Aegean) against Roman territory.[12] This movement of the Goths from a northern to a south-eastern sea poses the question how far the evidence allows us to follow their tracks in the approximately hundred years which it took them.[13]

---

[6] Kluge (1913), 45; Karsten (1928), 194f.; Wenskus (1961), 206.
[7] Wiesner (1963), 32; Scardigli (1995), 557.   [8] Karsten (1928), 98; Wiesner (1963), 117.
[9] Schwarz (1953a), 15.   [10] Kmieciński (1962), 280; Wagner (1967), 225f.
[11] Ellegård (1986), 46.   [12] Rappaport (1899); Vernadsky (1951), 353; Schwarcz (1992), 47ff.
[13] In talking of the Goths we are using a blanket term, for it is often impossible to distinguish them from other EG tribes, and their settlement area in the Ukraine was markedly polyethnic.

The geographical course taken by the Gothic migration was probably largely that taken by the Bastarnae before them along an established trade-route,[14] since the terrain did not offer many alternatives between a common starting-point and a shared goal. The first penetration inland would have been from the lower to the upper Vistula as far as the junction with the western Bug, from there to the southern Bug and thence downstream to its estuary in the Black Sea. Alternatively, up the Vistula as far as the San, then to the Dniestr, thence to the Black Sea.[15]

This sketch of a possible route in the light of geographical possibilities agrees in general terms with the route given by Jordanes (*Getica* 16f., 25ff.). Although doubts about his historical reliability may raise difficulties,[16] his statement that the Goths began their trek in northern Poland agrees with what Tacitus and Pliny say of their settlement in the north and their arrival in the Pontic area is likewise reported by classical sources.[17] Our task is therefore to consider whether Jordanes's report of their movement between these two regions can also be confirmed from other sources.

We may do this by following through some of the names listed by Jordanes as points on the trek, relating them briefly to what is known from other sources. For Jordanes the *Vistula* represents the starting-point for the Goths' continental migration as much as for modern archaeology, which identifies the Wielbark culture, situated between the Oder and the Vistula, with the Gothic settlement.[18] Jordanes is then much more precise in saying that the place where the Goths landed on the coast is still today called *Gothiscandza*. This has been interpreted as a Gothic formation (**Gutisk andja* 'Gothic end, Gothic coast'), in which case Jordanes conserves good native tradition.[19] He next mentions a tribe already dwelling on the coast with whom the Goths had to struggle for territory, the *Ulmerugi*, again a vernacular name for 'island Rugii' with the characteristic Go. -*u*- in the first part and with parallels in ON *Holmrygir* and OE *Holmrygas*.[20] The next tribe which the Goths had to subdue in establishing themselves was the *Vandals* who together with Burgundians and Rugii are regarded by archaeologists as the main bearers of the so-called Przeworsk culture of western Poland.[21]

---

[14] Schwarz (1953a), 21, 22; Wagner (1967), 223ff.   [15] Wagner (1967), 226.

[16] Heather (1991), 19ff., 34ff., 61ff.

[17] Northern Poland: Schwarz (1951), 14; (1953a), 13. Pontic area: Vernadsky (1951), 351, 353; Schwarz (1956), 88; Bierbrauer (1994), 106.

[18] Bierbrauer (1994), 53ff.; Heather (1996), 18ff.

[19] Schwarz (1956), 85; Wagner (1967), 209; Much (1967), 487.

[20] Schwarz (1956), 80; *Widsith* 21.

[21] Schwarz (1956), 64; Wolfram (1988), 40; Struve (1991), 15, 16.; Heather (1996), 35ff.

After this initial focus on the lower and middle Vistula Jordanes skips, with too much of a jump for our purposes, to the Goths' arrival in *Scythia* which he says was called *Oium* in their language and was blessed by great (agricultural) wealth. For this reason, but also because he says that the furthest part of Scythia lies by the *Pontus* or Black Sea, the region now reached by the Goths is identified with the Ukraine. The agricultural wealth of this area is still true today, but is also borne out by the vernacular name *Oium* which, as a dative plural used as a place-name, agrees with a word **aujō-* or **auwō-*, widespread in Germanic and ranging in meaning from 'island' to 'well watered meadow'.[22] (The same word recurs later when Jordanes refers, *Getica* 96, to the Gepids occupying an island surrounded by the shallows of the lower Vistula and quotes the name they give it: *Gepedoios* 'island or fertile meadows of the Gepids'.)[23] After mentioning Scythia and the Pontus Jordanes lists in quick succession three rivers (*Ister*, the classical name for the lower Danube, *Danaster* 'Dniestr' and *Danaper* 'Dniepr') with all of which other classical sources and modern archaeological finds associate the Goths at this period of their migration. These are followed by references to the *Taurus* (a mountain-range in the Crimea), to lake *Maeotis* (the sea of Azov), to the *Caucasus* and to *Persis* (Persia), but also, further to the north and east, to peoples now identified as Slavs (*Venethi, Sclaveni, Antes*), to the river *Tanais* 'Don' and beyond that to the *Huns*. Also mentioned are *Thrace* and *Dacia*, where contact was made by the Goths with the Roman Empire.

Between the Polish coastline and the Roman Danubian frontier the Goths passed through a wide expanse which was a veritable ethnic melting-pot. During this first stage of their migration they therefore came into contact with a variety of peoples and languages: Balts, Finns and Slavs, but also with Thracians and Dacians and, after 375, with the Huns. Of particular importance was their encounter in southern Russia with a number of Iranian peoples who in succession had entered and settled in this region: the Scythians (to whose linguistic influence such river-names as the Danube, the Dniestr, the Dniepr and the Don are attributed), the Sarmatians and the Alans.[24] These peoples incorporated a completely different culture, largely adapted to the geographical conditions of the steppes, so that the entry of the Goths into this region

---

[22] Schwarz (1956), 87.   [23] Wolfram (1988), 23, 38.

[24] Scythians: Kretschmer (1935), 1ff.; Phillips (1965), 54ff. Sarmatians: Vernadsky (1951), 340ff.; Phillips (1965), 92ff.; Gimbutas (1971), 63ff. Alans: Altheim (1959), 57ff., 293ff.; Wenskus (1973a), 122ff.

and their new contacts brought about a process of acculturation before the even more overwhelming encounter with the Greco-Roman world.

Confirmatory evidence is provided by archaeology. The reliability of Jordanes is after all not so much above question that there is no need to buttress it from different angles, especially since the archaeological evidence suggests the equation of a particular culture in northern Poland with the Goths and its gradual movement south-eastwards to the Ukraine and Rumania.[25]

This Pontic settlement area of the Goths has been well investigated by archaeologists, who refer to it as the Sîntana de Mureş/Černjahov culture (the first part named after finds in Transylvania, the second after a site near Kiev).[26] This culture is dated to the later third and the fourth century, a period when literary sources attest the dominance of the Goths in this region adjoining the Roman Empire, lasting until the Hunnic invasions from 375. This chronology, together with the Germanic nature of the finds and their similarity to the Wielbark culture, suggests that this culture was predominantly Gothic, however many other factors may have been present in a highly polyethnic region. The identification of this culture is based on geographical as well as chronological considerations, for its extent (from the lower Danube north-eastwards across the rivers Prut and Dniestr, beyond the Dniepr out into the steppes) coincides with what Ammianus Marcellinus says of their sway, spreading from the Danube even as far as the Tanais (Don), since the Alans who are their neighbours there are called *Tanaites* 'people of the Don'.[27]

If archaeology can throw light on Jordanes in this way can the same be expected of linguistic evidence in view of the notorious inability of philology to offer precise datings and given the severe difficulties of coping with the range of languages involved? In dealing with this problem we shall consider two classes of evidence: names (of places and people) and appellative words.[28]

Difficulties arise with a place-name in the area of the lower Vistula: *Graudenz*, Pol. *Grudziądz*.[29] This name has been connected with *Greutungi*,

[25] Birnbaum (1984), 235ff.; Struve (1991), 9ff.; Bierbrauer (1994), 51ff.; Heather (1996), 18ff.

[26] Heather (1991), 84ff.; Heather and Matthews (1991), 51ff.; Heather (1996), 19ff.

[27] Heather (1991), 84.

[28] Two place-names which are too uncertain for discussion are *Danzig*, Pol. *Gdańsk* (held to be connected with Jordanes's *Gothiscandza*) and *Gdingen*, Pol. *Gdynia*. See Hermann (1941), 246ff.; Schwarz (1951), 31ff.; Wenskus (1961), 203ff.; Brauer (1981), 71ff.; Birnbaum (1984), 240f.

[29] Hermann (1941), 252ff.; Schwarz (1951), 33f.

the name given to one branch of the Goths by contrast with the *Tervingi*, which opens up the question when and where the Goths were regarded as made up of two branches with these particular names. For those who derive Graudenz from *Greutungi* the answer is clear: this branch of the Goths was termed thus already in northern Poland, but the attempt to take this nomenclature back to Scandinavia is not merely highly uncertain philologically, it also rests on the by no means uncontested assumption that the Goths came from Scandinavia.[30] The opposing view is that *Greutungi* arose as a term in the Pontic area (and therefore cannot explain Graudenz in the north), although this southern theory has been proposed on differing grounds. For some the twofold division of the Goths was the result of different responses to a specific historical event in the south, the Hunnic onslaught of 375,[31] but for others it arises from more general geographical features of the Pontic region which the Goths now occupied. A number of different languages suggest that the features of the south Russian terrain more than once called forth a twofold naming of those who inhabited its two types of ground: the cattle-raising nomads of the open steppe and the sedentary agriculturalists of the woodland steppe.[32] The Gothic distinction (*Greutungi* deriving from a Germanic root for 'sand, sandy soil' of the steppe and *Tervingi* from a root for 'tree') would thus be echoed in Slavonic for this region (*poljane* 'field-dwellers' and *drevljane* 'wood-dwellers'), but also similarly in Hunnic and Turkish. The genesis of this distinction of the Goths as late as their settlement in southern Russia would be borne out by the fact that the name *Greutungi* is attested only from the fourth century.[33] These factors, together with the phonological difficulty of -d- in Graudenz, make it uncertain that this place-name is a trace of earlier Gothic settlement.

Other place-names provide rather more certainty about Gothic traces. The OE poem *Widsith* mentions Goths and Huns in close association (v. 57), but also says that the Goths fought the Huns ('the people of Attila') for their homeland by the Vistula wood (v. 121: *ymb Wistla wudu*). Since historically no such battle is known to have taken place in the vicinity of the Vistula[34] it is more likely that this represents a conflation of repeated conflicts between the two peoples, placed near the Vistula because in retrospect this could be regarded as the Goths' homeland, if

---

[30] Wagner (1967), 171ff.; Hachmann (1970).   [31] Heather (1991), 17f.

[32] Specht (1939), 224ff.; Altheim (1956), 81ff., 241ff.; Rosenfeld (1956b), 195ff.; (1957), 36ff.; Wagner (1967), 235ff.; Wolfram (1988), 387, n. 58.   [33] Heather (1991), 8.

[34] Chambers (1912), 163; Hill (1994), 85.

not their earliest. This placing is confirmed by the Goths' being named in this poem as *Hrēðgotan* (v. 57, 120), a term also attested for them in ON and etymologically suggesting 'nest Goths', i.e. those who did not join the trek to the south-east.[35] In this connection we are reminded of the Gepids, seen by Jordanes as belonging to the Goths even if they were the last to settle in northern Poland (*Getica* 94f.), for they remained for some time in that region, east of the Vistula, after the main body of the Goths had moved on, certainly as late as the fourth century.[36] However distorted, the details given in *Widsith* are not entirely irreconcilable with linguistic and archaeological surmises.

References which can also be located geographically in more detail are given in another literary source, the ON *Battle of the Goths and Huns*. It is one of the oldest Germanic heroic lays, a genre which originated amongst the Goths in the south-east (as is suggested by its focus on such figures as Ermanaric, Attila and Theoderic). As regards an original location in the south-east this particular heroic lay includes linguistic fossils which would have meant little in the north, but which point to the region of Gothic settlement at the time of the Huns' invasion. The holy graves of the Goths (a reference to royal burial mounds?)[37] are said to lie on the banks of the Dniepr (7,6: *á stöðum Danpar*) and the battle is located on the plain of the Don (23,2: *á Dúnheiði*).[38] In this context reference is also made to mountains called the *Iassarfjöll* (23,4), where the first element can be identified with the Alans, also known as the *Assi*, whose language possessed an epenthetic *j*- which would explain the form in the lay.[39] *Iassarfjöll* therefore corresponds to what Ptolemy called the *Alanà órē* 'the Alan mountains' and the Alans, settled in this period between the Don and the Caucasus, were in close contact with the Goths and the first to suffer the onslaught of the Huns.[40] Although it has been suggested that *Dún*- may refer to the Danube instead of the Don,[41] the other names speak in favour of a location further to the east.[42]

Better prospects of information, but greater difficulties of interpretation are opened up when we pass from names to words which suggest contacts between the Goths and other peoples encountered on their

[35] Malone (1935), 168f.; Hill (1994), 73.   [36] Bierbrauer (1994), 90, 96, 98, 105.
[37] Attributed by some to the Goths (cf. Baetke (1942), 130), by others to the Scythians (Altheim (1959), 355).   [38] De Vries (1941), 37; Altheim (1943), 114; (1959), 354ff.
[39] Altheim (1956), 244; (1959), 358.   [40] Altheim (1959), 359; Wenskus (1973a), 122ff.
[41] Rosenfeld (1956b), 201ff.
[42] On the Gothic implications of the name of the Hunnic leader Attila see Vernadsky (1951), 375f.; Wagner (1967), 8f.; (1979), 11ff.; Beck (1973a), 470; Wenskus (1973b), 468; Schramm (1975), 71ff.; Kazanski (1992b), 205f.

trek. These contacts will be considered with regard to Gothic loanwords in the Baltic languages, in Slavonic and in the Finnic group.

The name given to the Balts by Tacitus and Jordanes is *Aestii* and they were situated in the first century AD along the Baltic coastline east of the Vistula, engaged in the amber trade.[43] Since the area of their first contact with the Germanic tribes was the lower Vistula any loanwords from Germanic at this time must first have been taken over by the Prussians, the westernmost of the Baltic tribes. The subsequent death of Old Prussian, however, has left us with few linguistic sources, whilst any Germanic loanwords which it may have passed on to other Baltic languages are difficult to retrieve.[44] Another difficulty concerns the precise Germanic language from which the Baltic languages may have drawn their loanwords. It is uncertain whether Prussian *sarwis* 'weapons' came from Go. *sarwa* 'weapons' or from Germanic at large (if the latter, may this not be 'pre-Gothic', a stage earlier than Wulfila?).[45] Similarly, we cannot tell whether Lith. *muĩtas* 'customs duty' derived from Go. *mōta* or OHG **mûta* (or could these words have entered Baltic *via* Slavonic?).[46] We also have to consider the possibility that the origin of a loanword may have been WG at large, as with Lith. *kùnigas* 'king' (a corresponding form is not known to have been present in Gothic).[47] Related to all these difficulties is the question whether a Gothic loanword entered Baltic directly or *via* Slavonic.

This last consideration suggests that it might after all be possible to propose some Gothic loans into the Baltic group. This could be the case with Go. *hláifs* 'loaf' and Lith. *kliẽpas*, with Go. *hilms* 'helmet' and Prussian *ilmis*, with Go. *katils* 'cauldron' and Prussian *catils*, with Go. *stikls* 'goblet' and Prussian *sticlo* 'glass'.[48] Two main cultural categories stand out from the range of correspondences. The first is military, although it is by no means clear that this could be tied down specifically to the institution of the war-band.[49] Examples under this heading include Prussian *brunyos* 'armour', Lith. *šálmas* 'helmet' (if we can accept this as a 'pre-Gothic' loan, earlier than Prussian *ilmis*) and Prussian *sarwis* 'weapons'.[50] The second category is made up of trading terms, two of which can be traced back ultimately to Latin, so that we are dealing with a linguistic trade-route from Latin into Germanic, thence into Baltic: Prussian *asilis* 'ass' (ultimately from Lat. *asinus/asellus*) and Prussian *catils*

---

[43] Tacitus, *Germania* 45; Jordanes, *Getica* 120; Schmid (1973), 116f.　　[44] Schwarz (1951), 44, 45.
[45] Otrębski (1966), 57.　　[46] *Ibid.*, pp. 50, 61f.　　[47] *Ibid.*, pp. 63f. See also above, pp. 130, 135.
[48] Otrębski (1966), 52f., 56f., 58, 61.　　[49] Suggested by Wenskus (1961), 373f.
[50] Otrębski (1966), 56, 56f., 57.

'cauldron' (going back finally to Lat. *catinus/catillus*).[51] Another trading term possibly indicates a shorter linguistic route, from Germanic into Baltic: Lith. *muĩtas* 'customs duty'.[52] This linguistic trade-route would even have to be lengthened by one additional stage if we were to regard Slavonic as transmitting these words to Baltic. That two categories such as warfare and trade should stand out should not surprise us, since these are historically two sides of the same coin.[53]

These cultural loans into the Baltic languages could therefore have been effected directly by the Goths or through the Slavs as intermediaries. Direct contact was established in the earliest period of Gothic settlement in northern Poland as the Wielbark culture expanded eastwards from the Vistula where the Aestii were settled and where, amongst the Goths, the Gepids in particular were to be found.[54] We may assume contact between Goths and the Prussians who in this period represent the point of entry for these loanwords into the Baltic languages.[55] This area east of the lower Vistula is not the only possibility of direct contact, however, for work on Baltic language hydronymy has made it likely that the boundaries of this linguistic group earlier reached much further south into White Russia and the northern Ukraine, an area which the Goths passed through on their gradual trek south-eastwards.[56] The other possibility (indirect influence *via* the Slavs) is suggested by archaeological evidence on trade-routes extending northwards from the Černjahov culture through Slav territory and as far as the Dniepr–Dvina culture associated with the Balts.[57] The purpose behind this radiation was not political expansion over such improbable distances, but military control and exploitation of trade with the north. This might explain the two categories of warfare and trade implied by the linguistic evidence.

The possible linguistic mediation of Slavs between Goths and Balts brings us to the question of Gothic influence on Slavonic. Jordanes, looking northwards from the Pontic region and just before saying that Ermanaric's influence reached as far as the Balts, mentions the Slavs (*Getica* 119) and associates them more closely than the Balts with the centre of Gothic power. He gives them three tribal names: *Venethi* (still surviving in German *Wenden* as a term for the Slavs), *Antes* (located by Jordanes between the Dniestr and the Dniepr, *Getica* 35, and attacked by the Goth Vinitharius, *Getica* 247) and *Sclaveni* (at home between the upper Dniestr and the Vistula). This location of the early Slavs partly at least

[51] *Ibid.*, pp. 50, 58. On the Latin forms see below, pp. 204, 205, 229f.   [52] *Ibid.*, pp. 61f.
[53] See below, p. 219.   [54] Bierbrauer (1994), 96ff.   [55] *Ibid.*, pp. 64, 67, 70, 74.
[56] Struve (1991), 9.   [57] Wolfram (1988), 87f.; Kazanski (1992a), 75ff., especially 84f.

in the region covered by the Černjahov culture, together with their contacts (warlike or not) with the Goths under Ermanaric and almost certainly before, explains their openness to Gothic loanword influence. That this must have begun early, before the expansion of the Slavs from their primeval habitat, is implied by the presence of individual loanwords in a wide range of Slavonic languages.[58]

Light is thrown on these contacts between Goths and Slavs by dividing the loanwords into cultural categories (in listing examples I give only the presumed Gothic starting-point and stress that scholars are not all agreed on the derivation of all these examples from Gothic).[59] Foremost in these categories is trade, with examples such as *káupōn* 'to trade', *mōta* 'customs duty', *katils* 'cauldron', *sakkus* 'sack', *stikls* 'goblet',[60] *akeit* 'vinegar',[61] *wein* 'wine', *asilus* 'ass', but also including two coins: *skilliggs* 'shilling' and *kintus* 'penny'. Political authority is represented by *gards* 'house' (cf. *þiudangardi* 'kingdom') and *dōms* 'judgment', perhaps also by **gastfaþs* 'lord'. Agriculture is covered by *haírda* 'herd' and *aúrtigards* 'garden' (perhaps also by the product *hláifs* 'loaf'); warfare by *brunjo* 'breastplate', *wargs* 'enemy' and *mēki* 'sword';[62] skills by *lēkeis* 'doctor' and *bōka* 'letter' (plural *bōkōs* 'book'). It is clear that Gothic loanwords into Slavonic are much more frequent than into Baltic and cover a more varied range.

The chronology of these loans extends over three stages.[63] An early stage (PG or 'pre-Gothic') is represented by an example from the category of warfare: Sl. **šelmъ* 'helmet', presumably from the Goths in the upper Vistula area while they still retained *-e-* as distinct from Wulfila's *hilms*.[64] By contrast, the bulk of the loanwords come later, when the Černjahov culture saw the Goths in close and protracted relationship with the Slavs. Examples from this stage include *biuþs* 'table' (producing Slavonic forms meaning 'eating-board') and *hansa* 'cohort' (leading significantly to Slavonic words to do with booty and theft). Finally, some loans from Gothic into Slavonic may be even later, when the Goths had penetrated into the Balkans and when the expansion of the Slavs had brought their southern branch into contact with them in this region. Examples include **ausahriggs* 'ear-ring' (the fate of Go. *-h-* in Slavonic shows that this loan was later than that of *hláifs*) and *weinagards* 'vineyard'

---

[58] Schwarz (1953a), 25.

[59] A division into categories is attempted by Kluge (1913), 41f., but not by Kiparsky (1934), to whose index attention is drawn for fuller discussion of the examples listed here.

[60] Included here against Knobloch (1965), 211ff.   [61] See also Szemerényi (1979), 117f.

[62] *Ibid.*, pp. 110ff.   [63] Kiparsky (1934), 168ff., 192ff., 214ff.   [64] Ritter (1993), 174f.

(unlike the mobile trade-word *wein* 'wine' the word for vineyard was taken over only in a wine-growing district further south).[65]

The richest category in this loanword traffic is represented by trade-words, but it is possible to extend the course they followed backwards and forwards. Backwards in that, as with Gothic loanwords into Baltic, some of those into Slavonic are ultimately Latin in origin (*káupōn, katils, sakkus, akeit, wein, asilus, kintus*). From this it has been surmised that such words can have been transmitted to the Slavs only after the Latin originals had been adopted into Gothic, i.e. from the third century, after the Goths' arrival in the orbit of the Empire. This ignores the fact that a number of Latin trade-words entered Germania earlier, reaching the Goths at a time when they were still in the north – and the seven words just listed are all candidates for inclusion in this early group.[66] However, it is also possible that the loanword traffic from Gothic to Slavonic went even further, into the Baltic languages. Although we cannot always tell whether a Gothic word entered the Baltic group directly or thanks to Slavonic mediation, some of the trade words are common to both loan-processes (*káupōn, mōta, katils, stikls, asilus*) and two military terms (*brunjo, hilms*) may conceivably have accompanied the objects as trading goods. Such loanwords would therefore point to a linguistic trade-route from Latin to Gothic to Slavonic and thence perhaps to Baltic.

To account for these loans more than one geographical point of contact needs to be taken into account. The earliest was provided by the Goths' trek towards the region of the Černjahov culture, for this brought them into territory inhabited by Slavs (Antes and Sclaveni?) still at a stage of common Slavonic.[67] At a slightly later stage the northern boundary of the Černjahov culture adjoined the area of Slav ethnogenesis where contacts, in trade and in warfare, are attested especially for the fourth century. This is the period of Ermanaric, whose war against the Venethi was presumably waged in southern Russia, but whose domination of sources of trade in the north brought the Goths into close touch with the Slavs not merely in a north-westerly direction, but also north-eastwards towards the Slavs of the upper Dniepr–Volga region.[68] Here, too, loanword traffic has to be seen against a background of trade and warfare.

The background to possibly Gothic influence on Finnish seemed reasonably clear a few decades ago, but recent work has suggested new

---

[65] **Ausahriggs*: Steinhauser (1928), 149; *Weinagards*: Pudić (1964), 867.
[66] Kluge (1913), 40. See below, pp. 207ff.   [67] Struve (1991), 15, 25.
[68] *Ibid.*, p. 14; Kazanski (1992a), 84, 94.

prospects which leave us more uncertain than before. This influence has been explained by postulating contiguity of Goths and Finns along the coastline of the south-eastern Baltic, but there is no evidence that the Finns extended as far as the Prussians and it is highly improbable that Baltic, with only a few loanwords from Gothic, transmitted the much larger number of Germanic loanwords to be found in Finnish.[69] However, this lack of geographical contiguity does not render contact between the Goths at the mouth of the Vistula and Finnic speakers in south-western Finland and Estonia impossible, for water connected as much as it separated, especially where trade was concerned.[70] The involvement of the Goths on the Vistula in this was made likely (in 1958!) by a phonological examination of early Germanic loanwords in Finnish, showing that the earliest date for this traffic was about the birth of Christ, when the Goths settled in the region of the lower Vistula. This in itself did not establish that the Germanic words came from Gothic, but this was suggested on non-linguistic grounds by archaeological evidence for Gothic settlements in south-western Finland and Estonia, particularly in the form of trading centres.[71]

In dividing the Finnish material into cultural categories I give only a brief selection in which, because of doubts about the precise point of origin within Germania, the words in question are best given in their Finnish form.[72] Political authority is exemplified by *kuningas* 'king' (hardly of Gothic origin), *ruhtinas* 'lord' (unattested by Wulfila, but probably known to Gothic),[73] *valta* 'power', *tuomita* 'to judge'. Warfare is represented by *keihäs* 'spear' and *miekka* 'sword'; agriculture by *lammas* 'sheep', *kaura* 'oats', *ruis* 'rye', *pelto* 'field'; the household by *lattia* 'floor', *patja* 'cushion', *laipio/laupio* 'ceiling'; minerals by *kulta* 'gold', *rauta* 'iron'; trade by *kauppa* 'trade'. The range of terms for political authority and agriculture suggests that we may be dealing here with more than trading centres: with long-term settlements from which political control was exercised.

Contact between the Goths and the Finnic peoples was possible by routes other than the maritime one from the mouth of the Vistula. Ermanaric's trade-routes northwards to the Dniepr–Volga area also reached as far as the Volga–Oka Finnic peoples with whom the names given by Jordanes (*Getica* 116: *Merens, Mordens, Imniscaris*) have been associated.[74] Even though linguistic traces have been claimed for this route, too,

[69] Senn (1925); Kylstra (1961), 161f. Also: Schwarz (1951), 46f.   [70] Fromm (1958), 83, 100.
[71] *Ibid.*, pp. 306ff., 310ff.; Kylstra (1961), 164, 166f., 171.
[72] Cf. the categories suggested by Kluge (1913), 42ff., Karsten (1928), 178f., Koivulehto (1995), 84f.
[73] See above, p. 110 and below, pp. 361f.   [74] Schramm (1974), 1ff.; Kazanski (1992a), 75ff.

our difficulty lies in the fact that by this time linguistic contact between these eastern Finnic peoples and those settled round the Baltic Sea had been lost, so that any Gothic loanwords could not have reached the latter from this direction.[75] However, Ermanaric's trade-routes also ran north-westwards, where they possibly reached the Baltic tribes, so that we may ask whether the loanwords they carried also conceivably penetrated to the neighbouring Finns. If they did, this was unlikely to have been *via* the Balts, so that transmission may have been through the Slavs. Amongst the Gothic loanwords into Slavonic which could be regarded as trading terms several are also attested in Finnish (and/or Baltic),[76] but we remain uncertain whether these were borrowed separately from Gothic into each of the three recipient languages or whether there was a consecutive loan-process running by stages from south to north.

The problem of Germanic loans into Finnish has been revolutionised by suggestions which transfer their beginning back to the Bronze Age, thus dating them at least a thousand years earlier.[77] It remains unclear how far this rethinking affects the Goths in particular, since it concerns the *earliest* loans, so that the duration of linguistic influence need not exclude later loans,[78] in a period such as that traditionally proposed when the Goths could be involved. With such a radical redating, affecting the internal chronology of PG as much as the relationship between Germanic and Finnish, the last word has not yet been spoken. We still need clarification on the dating of later loanwords (could they have come from the Vistula Goths?) and on the cultural categories into which they fit.[79]

Up to this point we have dealt with the Goths' contacts with peoples who, according to the line drawn by Tacitus between the Germani and those dwelling beyond them (*Germania* 46), lived in a state of abject barbarism. Even if we take possible exaggeration into account this could be true, for this attitude may have been shared by the Germani themselves if we accept the etymological derivation of 'Finn' (a people placed by Tacitus on the bottom rung of civilisation) from Germanic *finþan 'to find', denoting their status as mere hunter-gatherers.[80] On these bound-

---

[75] Altheim (1959), 315.   [76] Cf. Ritter (1993), 176ff.
[77] Koivulehto (1981), 167ff., 333ff.; (1995), 84ff.; Kylstra (1984), 1ff.
[78] Koivulehto (1981), 364; (1995), 84; Ritter (1993), 31f.
[79] The south-easternmost point reached by the Goths can be illustrated from Crimean Gothic. On this see Schwarz (1951), 162ff.; (1953b), 156ff.; Stearns (1978), *passim*; (1989), 175ff. Cf. Bierbrauer (1994), 136.   [80] Wenskus (1961), 162; Koivulehto (1995), 82.

aries of the civilised world Germanic possessed prestige amongst these other peoples so that the loanword traffic we have discussed ran in one way (with one exception only: Go. *plinsjan* 'to dance' from Slavonic, presumably because it denoted a particular form of dancing).[81] From now on the position changes: the Goths are now the recipients of cultural loanwords, first in their contacts with the Iranian nomadic horse-peoples of the steppes and then in the even more fundamental changes introduced by their encounter with the Greco-Roman world on the Danubian frontier.

Not merely the Goths, but all the Germanic tribes in the extreme south-east confronted new conditions in the open steppes to which they adjusted by learning from the nomadic peoples there, above all by adapting to the use of the horse to overcome the problem of distance.[82] In the treeless steppes, as distinct from the woodland of the north, the wild horse had been domesticated and stronger or faster varieties bred.[83] The horse was central to the military tactics of the nomads of the steppes. Our earliest evidence for this concerns the Bastarnae, followed by the Goths and other EG tribes whose model was provided by the Sarmatians and the Alans.[84] In addition to this adjustment to mounted warfare other features such as the short sword or a form of armour as body-protection were taken over.[85]

This acculturation of the Goths and others to the world of the steppes raises the question whether it left any reflection in language. In considering this our examples can be divided into two groups: words which were borrowed from the south-east so early that they reached the Goths (amongst others) while still in the north and words which were adopted only in the new surroundings of the south-east.

We have seen that the word for 'hemp' was probably an early loan from the south-east, passed from the Thracians to the Bastarnae before the First Sound Shift, then spreading through Germania before the Goths penetrated this far. Another early loan is possibly connected with it: Go. *páida* 'jerkin, short coat' (also in other Germanic languages).[86] It is cognate with Gr. *baítē* 'leather coat' (of Illyrian or Thracian origin), but the change of *b-* to *p-* implies a loan before the First Sound Shift.

[81] Ritter (1993), 57. *Plinsjan*: Lehmann (1986), 273.
[82] Altheim (1943), 92f., 106f., 108; Vernadsky (1951), 367f.; Wenskus (1961), 442; Wiesner (1968), 112f.
[83] Keegan (1994), 155ff., 177ff.
[84] Vernadsky (1951), 366, 368f.; Altheim (1959), 320f.; Wenskus (1961), 469; Wolfram (1988), 115.
[85] Wiesner (1968), 79, 110.
[86] Kluge (1913), 45; Karsten (1928), 98, 195; Frings (1955), 221ff.; Wenskus (1961), 206.

This renders unlikely any direct contact with Greek so early and suggests, as with 'hemp', contact between Thracians and Bastarnae. The reason for this loan is suggested by Wulfila's use of the verb *gapáidōn* derived from this noun (Eph. 6.14 *gapáidōdai brunjon garaíhteins* 'clad in the breastplate of righteousness') as well as by the use of the same noun in OE *herepād* 'coat of mail', suggesting therefore that this loanword denoted a form of protective clothing. This context provides a further link with 'hemp', since this piece of clothing was made of wool, linen or hemp,[87] the latter being a stout fabric used for protection as long as metal armour was rare in Germania. These considerations suggest that *páida* and 'hemp' could have been loaned together at an early stage.

An early loan has also been proposed for Go. *mēki* 'sword', with parallels in other Germanic languages, but also in Slavonic and Finnish.[88] This word is regarded as an itinerant word, not inherited by Germanic and Slavonic from IE, but borrowed from one of the Iranian languages where it originally denoted something attached to the waist-belt.[89] The word's presence in Gothic could account for its occurrence elsewhere in Germanic, but also possibly for its entry into Slavonic and Finnish. Yet if we make the tempting assumption that the Goths acquired their word from one of the Iranian peoples in southern Russia this places us chronologically in a tight corner, since the earliest NG example is from a runic inscription from Vimose, dated around AD 250.[90] This allows an improbably short time for the Goths to adopt the word in the south, pass it back to the north, and for NG to adopt it in turn. In view of this it is possible that the word reached the Goths (as a trade word?) while they were still in the Vistula area, from where transmission to NG by 250 is much more credible. This early loan would be confirmed if we can identify the *gladii breves*, mentioned by Tacitus (*Germania* 43) as characteristic, amongst others, of the EG tribes (as they also were of Iranian mounted nomads) with the *mēki* – the sword found at Vimose is also a short one.[91] Although the borrowing into Slavonic is phonologically later (fifth century)[92] this does not contradict an early spread into Gothic and elsewhere in Germania.

There are also words which were possibly adopted by the Goths only in the new conditions of southern Russia. Their need to adapt to the mode of life of mounted warriors explains why one example is the word

[87] Frings (1955), 227.
[88] Kiparsky (1934), 138ff.; Vernadsky (1951), 368; Schwarz (1953a), 25f.; Szemerényi (1979), 110ff.
[89] Szemerényi (1979), 111f.   [90] Schwarz (1953a), 26; Szemerényi (1979), 112; Euler (1985), 12.
[91] Much (1967), 491. Iranian nomads: Wiesner (1968), 40, 79.   [92] Szemerényi (1979), 113f.

for 'horse', even if it is not attested in the restricted lexis of Wulfila's bible, but rather in OHG *(h)ross*, OE *hors*, ON *hors/hross*.[93] As a new import this word competed with a native word (OE *eoh*, ON *jór*, cognate with Lat. *equus*) because it denoted a new breed of horse for fighting on horseback. The loanword has parallels in Finnic, in the western and eastern branches, which in view of their later separation suggests an early loan into common Finnic for which Gothic cannot come into question. The origin of both the Germanic and Finnic forms has been traced to Sarmatian (attested in Ossetian and some Caucasian languages which borrowed the word from the Alans). The Goths cannot have felt the need for such a loanword before they were forced to adapt to the empty expanses of the south-east. In this respect this word differs from trade words like 'hemp' and *páida* (and from another word for 'horse', OHG *marah-*, which found its way northwards earlier).

Our next example refers to living conditions of horsed nomads and was also probably taken over in the steppes. Cognates of English 'sour' occur in WG and NG with that meaning, but also in Slavonic ('raw', but also as a noun meaning 'cheese') and Lithuanian ('salted').[94] These forms have been linked with Iranian words from which they were probably borrowed, meaning 'fermented drink, beer' or 'koumis, mare's milk'. A word with such a meaning and in regular use with nomadic peoples spread from them to Germanic and Slavonic tribes in eastern Europe (also reaching the Baltic languages as well as Finnic) in much the same way as modern 'yoghurt' (of Turkish origin). Just how characteristic of the Iranian peoples the use of mare's milk as a standard food was can be seen from the description of the Scythians in the *Iliad* (13,4f.) as 'milk eaters'.[95]

The routes followed by these nomads on horseback are suggested by another word: English 'path', with parallels in WG, NG and Finnish.[96] Germanic words with *p-* are rare and generally loanwords, but parallels like Gr. *póntos* 'sea' and Lat. *pons* 'bridge' are semantically too remote. Only in Iranian **paθ-* 'path' do we find a unique combination of semantic, phonological and morphological agreements which explain the northern words.[97] If we accept Iranian origin the initial contact must have been with EG, after completion of the First Sound Shift (*p-* remains *p-*) but, since the word is common WG, before the Anglo-Saxon invasion of England. This leaves an uncomfortably long

---

[93] Brøndal (1928), 5, 15f., 24f.; Altheim (1959), 311ff.   [94] Brøndal (1928), 6f., 17, 24f.
[95] Wiesner (1968), 55, 110.   [96] Bailey and Ross (1961), 107ff.; Mayrhofer (1970), 224ff.
[97] Bailey and Ross (1961), 129ff.; Mayrhofer (1970), 226.

timespan (300 BC–AD 300). There is no indication that the word was adopted into Gothic, rather than EG at large, but equally no pointer to an early spread northwards, as with 'hemp' and *páida*. Instead, it was possibly taken over in the region through which the Sarmatian or Alan nomads' paths passed over the steppes (already with Aeschylus we find a reference to the 'Scythian path')[98] to which the Germani, too, had now penetrated.

By contrast, a loan from Iranian into Gothic in particular has been established for the second element in a group of Gothic compound nouns: *brūþfaþs* 'bridegroom', *hundafaþs* 'centurion', *þūsundifaþs* 'chil-iarch' and *swnagogafaþs* 'ruler of a synagogue'.[99] Gothic is the only Germanic language still to have this IE word for 'master' (cf. Lat. *potis* 'powerful', Gr. *pósis* 'husband'), which might suggest special factors at work.[100] The first of the Gothic examples stands apart as an archaism: *brūþfaþs* differs from all other Germanic languages (which employ another second element, e.g. OHG *brûtigomo*) and it belongs to the same household context as other IE compounds with the same element (e.g. Gr. *despótēs* 'master of a slave'). The remaining Gothic words refer either to a military formation or to a social group, where the last (*swnagogafaþs*) stands apart as a late (Christian) formation to render Gr. *archisynágōgos*.

Our problem is therefore reduced to accounting for the two words denoting leaders of a military formation of a hundred and thousand men respectively. For these forms Wulfila derived impetus neither from Lat. *tribunus, centurio* (derivatives, not compounds) nor from Greek compounds with *archi-* or *-archēs/-archos*, because his regular renderings of these Greek models follow a quite different pattern.[101] Where the impetus in Gothic came from is suggested by the fact that the Greek forms Wulfila translated (*hekatontárchēs, chiliarchos*) are themselves based on Persian models.[102] Their earliest occurrences in Greek refer to the organisation of the Persian army and administration, based on a decimal grouping. The Persian terms for those in charge of these decimal groups were compounds of the relevant number with *-pati*, which is the Iranian equivalent of Go. *-faþs*. Greek may have followed the Persians in coining terms for their military formations, but the Goths were instead dependent on Iranians of the Pontic region. (Gothic dependence on the decimal model of the Iranians may have gone even further: two Iranian loanwords in Crimean Gothic are words for 'hundred' and

---

[98] Mayrhofer (1970), 226, fn. 19.
[99] Vernadsky (1951), 369f.; Wenskus (1961), 443f.; Benveniste (1963), 41ff.
[100] Benveniste (1963), 41.   [101] *Ibid.*, pp. 47f.   [102] *Ibid.*, pp. 49ff.

'thousand'.)[103] A parallel with Gothic is found in another language which followed the Persian model: Armenian employs -*pet* (its equivalent of -*pati*) in its military titles, likewise decimal, but also in a Christian context in a term for 'ruler of a synagogue', as in Gothic.[104]

A last step in following the Goths on their trek to the point where they impinge upon the Roman frontier of the lower Danubian area is their encounter with the Latin speakers of the Sîntana de Mureş region, i.e. the possible presence of Gothic (or Gepid) loanwords in Rumanian.[105]

With the arrival of the Goths in the border-zone of the Roman Empire and their first direct contact with Latin speakers and the cultural influences to which they were now subjected we break off the sketch of their migration from the Baltic to the Black Sea. Up to this point their trek took them in a south-easterly direction, but after their period in the Balkans their direction was westwards (Italy, Gaul, Spain). The point where we break off is of pivotal importance in more than just a geographical sense, for now the Goths, whose earlier acculturation had been to the conditions of life on the steppes, came under influences which are pronouncedly western:[106] Roman civilisation (going far beyond what had earlier reached them by trade routes to the north), writing in a script of Mediterranean origin, Christianity. Wulfila was the focal point of all these influences; with him the Goths entered the realm of recorded history and left behind the period of prehistory.

---

[103] Kluge (1913), 46; Schwarz (1951), 172; Stearns (1989), 187, fn. 54.   [104] *Ibid.*, pp. 54f.
[105] Latin speakers: Bierbrauer (1994), 130. Rumanian: Diculescu (1921), 420ff.; (1929), 385ff.; Skok (1923), 187ff.; (1930), 257ff.; Gamillscheg (1934), 121; (1935), 245, 249ff.; Pudić (1964), 865.
[106] Altheim (1943), 116.

CHAPTER 10

Germanic loanwords in Latin

So far we have only briefly touched upon one isolated encounter between a Germanic tribe and the Romans: the arrival of the Goths in the Black Sea area in the first part of the third century brought them into contact with the Empire on the lower Danube. This was by no means the first contact made by the Germani, for already at the close of the second century BC the Cimbri and Teutons had penetrated, briefly and with no permanent success, as far as Gaul and northern Italy.[1] For more lasting contact we have to look further north.[2] In the year 72 BC Ariovistus crossed the Rhine and occupied the Palatinate and Alsace, so that Germani were now immediate neighbours of the Romans in the west. The Romans, after conquering the whole of Gaul under Caesar in 51 BC, finally established the Rhine as the imperial frontier and incorporated Germanic tribes on the western side into their administrative structure, *Germania superior* (Mainz) and *inferior* (Cologne). The Roman frontier continued in southern Germany along the Danube, with the *Limes* established as a link between the two river defence-systems in the first century AD. The increasing danger from Germanic tribes east of the Rhine, together with Roman plans (ultimately abandoned) to expand as far as the Elbe, meant that the Rhineland was a focus of Roman political and military activity in which Trier as a Roman city could rival Rome itself and that Romanisation of this frontier area was a policy deliberately pursued by the Romans. Despite gains by the Alemanni and Franks in the course of the third century, resulting in the abandonment of Roman centres east of the Rhine, the left bank remained in Roman hands until the beginning of the fifth century, so that this region of Germany was thoroughly Romanised for some centuries, perhaps (in view of the Romans' concentration on this part of the frontier) even more so than the Gallic hinterland through which their lines of communication ran.

[1] Schwarz (1956), 54ff.   [2] Gamillscheg (1970), 3f.; Petrikovits (1978a), 294f.

Under such conditions language could not remain unaffected, but the linguistic encounter was a two-way process, if not an equal one.[3] On the Roman side we have to reckon with Roman soldiers and office-holders in their civil administration, but also with merchants in large numbers and finally with the Latin-speaking Celtic population. On the Germanic side we are dealing primarily with those tribes which, although still independent, were now neighbours of the Romans, coming increasingly into military conflict with them, but also attracted by what a superior civilisation could offer in the way of booty or trading goods. We must also take into account those Germanic groups which had lost their independence and lived within the Roman Empire as mercenaries in the army, as slaves (captured as prisoners of war) and as *inquilini* or *laeti*,[4] i.e. Germanic peasants incorporated into the Empire, but generally settled away from the frontier district. (These last gave rise to French place-names such as *Allemanche/Allamant, Frisons* or *Marmaigne*, denoting centres where barbarian groups were settled far away from where most Alemanni, Frisians or Marcomanni were to be found.)[5]

Although this linguistic traffic ran in two ways the dominance of the Romans for some centuries and the superiority of their civilisation meant that the influence of Latin on Germanic was decisive and considerable, whilst that of Germanic on Latin was slight.[6] This disparity repeats what was the case with the contact of the Germani with the Celts, where the latter exercised a greater cultural, hence linguistic influence than the former. It also dictates the course of our argument in the rest of this part: Germanic loanwords in Latin are the subject of this chapter, but loan-traffic in the opposite direction demands fully four chapters.

This chapter covers two periods with AD 400 as the approximate dividing line.[7] At about this time the Germanic invasions and occupations of different areas of the Empire began in earnest, putting an end to the relative political and linguistic unity which had existed hitherto. In other words, we have to enquire whether a Germanic term was taken into Latin before this turning-point and like loanwords from other sources and external influences of all kinds could be spread throughout the Empire while its unchallenged unity and control from the centre at Rome still made this possible. The alternative is to ask whether a Germanic loanword entered a no longer unified Latin after about 400,

---

[3] Brüch (1913), 90.   [4] Much (1967), 329.   [5] Gamillscheg (1970), 200, 202f., 227, fn. 1, 234.
[6] *Ibid.*, p. 22.   [7] Brüch (1913), 4; (1926a), 38f.

so that a Frankish term could find its way into what later became French or a Langobardic one into Italian, without traces in other Romance languages. The disruption (and eventual destruction) of Roman traffic throughout the Empire caused by the Germanic invasions is therefore reflected in a change in the nature of the loanword traffic we have to consider.

Germanic loanwords before 400 can be established by two methods: a direct one (the words in question are attested in written Latin sources of the period) and an indirect one (based on the criterion, difficult to put into practice, that if a Germanic term is widespread amongst the Romance languages it was probably adopted and spread throughout the Empire while this was still possible).[8] The direct method is clearly the more reliable, but it produces only a very meagre yield of about a dozen examples at the most, mainly confined to the spheres of trade and warfare.[9] This suggests that Latin authors may have kept their style free from such barbarisms, introducing them only as technical terms because there was no precise Latin equivalent or because they provided an exotic local flavour.

One example comes not from Latin authors, but from inscriptions. Lat. *brūtis*, denoting the Latin-speaking bride of a Germanic soldier, is attested for the eastern part of the Roman Empire and for Raetia-Noricum by four inscriptions: from Bulgaria, Serbia, Aquileia and Noricum.[10] The dating of these inscriptions (third and fourth centuries) is enough to place them in the earlier period, as is the word's spread westwards (cf. OFr. *bru(t)*), even though it may not be attested in Italy itself. The focus of the Latin word in the Balkans (cf. also modern Gr. *broútis*) suggests a loan from EG, possibly from the Goths themselves, present there from the third century on the Roman frontier. That we should reckon with a geographically unremarkable loan from EG into Balkan Latin is also suggested on phonological grounds, for the Latin form with *-t-* is more readily explained as an adaptation (phonetic substitution) from a form such as Go. *brūps* than from WG forms with *-d-* (OS *brûd*, OE *brŷd*; OHG *brût* developed *-t* only later as a result of the Second Sound Shift). This word can therefore be added in retrospect to the conclusion of Chapter 9 as a solitary clear example of Gothic influence on Balkan Latin.[11] The possibility of such intermarriages anywhere in

---

[8] Brüch (1913), 14ff., 19ff.   [9] Gamillscheg (1970), 22f.
[10] Brüch (1913), 15, 48, 111f.; (1926a), 95; *FEW* 15, 1, 303f.; Altheim (1959), 303; Pudić (1964), 864.
[11] See above, p. 181.

the Empire and its border zone is a fact of human nature, but is also borne out for the area we have been considering by Rum. *mire* 'bridegroom', deriving from Lat. *miles* 'soldier'.

Examples of loanwords attested by Roman authors can be divided into the two major lexical groups for this period, warfare and trade (three examples for each). Ammianus Marcellinus uses the word *carrago* 'barricade of waggons or carts', made up of Lat. *carrus* 'waggon' together with Gmc. **hag-* (cf. OHG *hag* 'enfencement').[12] That the inclusion of a Germanic loanword in this Latin compound points back to Germanic military practice is suggested by a number of considerations. First, the passage in which the Latin historian uses the word refers to the conduct of Goths in a battle and, when quoting the word, he says that this is how the Goths themselves term their barricade. (Does this imply that we must reckon with a Germanic term for 'waggon', independent of Lat. *carrus*, rather than a Germanic-Latin compound?) Secondly, the practice of grouping waggons as a protection for women and children during a battle is attested elsewhere for the Germani.[13] Thirdly, the second element in Ammianus's compound occurs in a defensive function in OE *bordhaga* 'shield-wall', as in the wedge-formation on the battlefield. Despite the uncertainty of the first element there is every reason to accept the Germanic origin of the compound used by Ammianus, as he expressly says.

Germanic origin is also likely for *drungus*, attested by Vegetius in the sense 'band of warriors' (cf. also Gr. *droũngos* 'regiment').[14] Although the word looks as if it could well be Germanic it has been attributed to Celtic (cf. Gaulish *drungos*, Ir. *drong*), but this is unlikely if the Celtic forms are conversely held to derive from Latin. On the Germanic side this Latin term has been associated with words such as OE *þringan* 'to press forward, force a way' and *þrang* 'throng, crowd' (in a military sense), but Gmc. *þ* should have produced Lat. *t* (as with *brūþs: brūtis*). Because of this it has been suggested that *drungus* probably results from a conflation of Gmc. **þrung-* with **druht-*,[15] both with a comparable function.

Rather more information is available concerning a third military term, *framea*, used by Tacitus and other Latin writers in the sense 'spear', but in Christian Latin with the meaning 'sword'.[16] It is on the earliest usage by Tacitus that we have to concentrate, especially since, like

[12] Ammianus Marcellinus, *Rerum gestarum libri XXXI* 31, 7, 7; Walde (1906), 101; Brüch (1913), 16.
[13] Kuhn (1951c), 107; Much (1967), 163, 165.
[14] Walde (1906), 185; Brüch (1913), 16f.; Kuhn (1972), 44.   [15] See above, pp. 110f.
[16] Brüch (1913), 16; Krause (1936), 585ff.; Krahe (1966), 50ff.; Meineke (1995b), 366ff.

Ammianus Marcellinus on *carrago*, he employs it (*Germania* 6) when talking about the Germanic warriors' equipment in battle and says that this is their native word for this weapon. It is generally accepted that this Germanic word is cognate with other terms such as Go. *fram* 'further', ON *fram* 'forwards', OE *fram* 'thrusting forwards, bold', and a causative verb **framjan* meaning 'to advance, bring forward, accomplish'. What the force of these cognates of a term meaning 'spear' may be is best seen from words inscribed in runes on a number of Germanic spear-blades from around the third century and taken to be designations (magical or not) of the weapons: *tilarids* 'attacker' (Kowel), *ranja* 'charger' (Dahmsdorf) and *raunijaz* 'tester' (Øvre Stabu). The wide geographical spread of these runic finds suggests a CG practice of naming spears with an aggressive *nomen agentis* of this type, and Lat. *framea*, Gmc. **framja* is every bit as much a *nomen agentis* as *ranja* from Dahmsdorf. Morphologically the final -*a* is characteristic of weak masculine -*n*- stems in Gothic, but also in the earliest ON, OE, OFri. and OS,[17] so that there is no reason to assume that this word, like *brūtis*, necessarily entered Latin from Gothic. If the Latin word is feminine, whilst the Germanic was masculine, this is likely to be because a word ending in -*a* was easily regarded as feminine in Latin, possibly under the influence of a semantically close word like *hasta*.

The first of our three examples of trading loanwords is Lat. *ganta* 'wild goose', used first by Pliny and finding its way into OPr. *ganta*, OFr. *jante*.[18] Pliny is particularly informative, saying that the wild geese of the Germanic provinces were valued in the Roman market for their soft feathers (in making cushions), which suggests a trading context for the adoption of this technical term into Latin just as, with a reciprocity typical of trading transactions, Lat. *pluma* was also borrowed into Germanic (OHG *phlûmfedera*, OE *plûmfeðera* 'down').[19] Although the word *ganta* may not be attested as such in Germanic we need not hesitate to attach it to an IE root from which a family of words was created by different stem-forming additions: of -*s* (as in OHG *gans*, OE *gōs* 'goose'), of -*r* (as in OE *gandra* 'gander', with -*d*- inserted as a glide) and of -*t* (as in OE *ganet* 'gannet', OHG *ganazzo* 'gander').[20] The productivity of this root in Germanic confirms the express remark by Pliny that *ganta* was the word given by the Germani to the wild goose.

Two other trading words borrowed by the Romans create linguistic

---

[17] Krahe (1966), 51.   [18] Pliny, *Naturalis historia* 10, 54; Brüch (1913), 16, 95; *FEW* 16, 12f.
[19] See below, p. 227.   [20] Brüch (1913), 176.

difficulties, but not such as to call their Germanic origin into question. The first is *glaesum/glesum*, used by Pliny and Tacitus to denote 'amber', both of whom report on its abundance on the northern coastline of Germania and testify that this was the native term for it.[21] Pliny is of course aware of the nature of amber (a fossil resin, coming from the sap of certain trees, which was used for translucent ornaments and, when rubbed, becomes electric).[22] The normal Latin terms were therefore *sucinum* (< *sucus* 'sap') and *electrum*, but Pliny and Tacitus use the foreign term because they are talking about amber imported into Italy from this Germanic source. Together they make it clear that Roman traders drew their supplies both from the Baltic coastline (already under Nero a Roman knight had travelled to Samland and brought back samples and reports of what was to be found there) and from the North Sea coastline and islands.[23] Although Tacitus contemptuously claimed that the northern barbarians had no idea how this substance which they collected on the seashore was produced, there is no reason to think that they were any more ignorant than is implied for Latin (*sucus: sucinum*) or for Hungarian (*gyantár* 'amber': *gyánta* 'resin').

This is suggested by what can be reconstructed of the form of the Germanic word borrowed into Latin. Taking into account varying accentuation (therefore subject to Verner's Law) and ablaut alternatives we may postulate two forms. First, PG **glêzá-*, as reflected in Lat. *glesum* 'amber', but also OE *glǣr* '*sucinum, electrum*' (if the *æ* is in fact long), MLG *glâr* 'rubber', OS and OE *gler* 'rubber'. Secondly, PG **glazá-*, attested by OE *glær* (if the *æ* is short), MLG *glar* (if the *a* is short) and ON *gler* 'glass'. The semantic range of this evidence is reconcilable with the qualities of amber: its inclusion of 'rubber' (likewise the sap of a tree) suggests that Germanic speakers were as aware of its source in resin as were Latin speakers, and of 'glass' rests on the transparency of both substances. So far, ON *gler* 'glass', stands alone in this range and we have not yet encountered a change in accent, but this occurs in two related variants.[24] First, PG **glésa-*, reflected in OHG *glâs* '*electrum*', but also PG **glása-*, attested in OHG *glas* '*vitrum, electrum*' and OE *glæs* '*vitrum*'. The connection between amber and glass is therefore not restricted to ON and is best explained by the competition between native amber ornaments (beads) and Roman products made of glass. The transfer of the old term

---

[21] Pliny, *Naturalis historia* 37, 42; Tacitus, *Germania* 45; Walde (1906), 268; Much (1967), 512f.; Meineke (1984), 45ff. (who questions whether the Germanic word denoted amber).
[22] Meineke (1984), 45f.   [23] Much (1967), 512f.; Meineke (1984), 45ff.
[24] Meineke (1984), 59ff.

to the new product (cheaper and more common) created a lexical gap for 'amber' which was filled by the late term *brennstain*.[25]

Our last trade-word example, the word 'soap', would tie up with the argument for 'amber' if we could still accept what has now been questioned, namely that OE *sāp* also denoted 'resin, amber'.[26] Otherwise, the Germanic evidence points to 'soap' alone: OHG *seifa*, Al. *seipfa*, MLG *sêpe*, OE *sāpe*.[27] This form is connected with Lat. *sāpo*, first used by Pliny to denote a substance for dyeing the hair red: the new, imported product on the Roman fashion market was fit to be designated by a foreign term. Although Pliny attributes this invention to the Gauls they are now taken to be no more than middlemen, for Pliny adds that the practice of dyeing their hair was also widespread amongst Germanic men and Martial supplies detailed evidence on where this hair-dye or hair-wash came from in Germania. Together, Pliny and Martial imply two types of substance, liquid and solid, but Martial refers more specifically to *spuma Batava* and *Chattica spuma* on the one hand and to *pilae Mattiacae* on the other. His use of tribal names therefore locates the origins of the substance in question in Batavia (the area of Utrecht), Hessen and Wiesbaden respectively.

The difficulty with this word, as yet unresolved, is a phonological one: since the Germanic word was borrowed in the first century AD at the latest, how do we connect PG *ai* with Lat. *ā*? We cannot have recourse to OE *sāpe* because this characteristic sound-change of OE took place much later. Nor do changes in Gaulish or VL provide any help, whilst the parallel suggested by Brüch (Gmc. **wrainjo* is attested with -*a*- in place of the diphthong) is too isolated to carry conviction.[28] Despite this unsolved phonological equation the conclusion must be that the Romans imported a hair-dye or hair-wash from Germania and perhaps also the native word to designate it.

The direct method, illustrated here by seven examples, yields a total crop of only about a dozen, most of which are restricted to the army and trade. As such they did not belong to any higher social speech level, they were terms used by merchants and mercenaries,[29] which may explain why they did not find their way into literary Latin and why Roman

---

[25] *Ibid.*, pp. 59, 69.   [26] Schabram (1987), 120ff.

[27] Pliny, *Naturalis historia* 28, 191; Martial, *Epigrams* 8, 33, 20; 14, 26; 14, 27; Walde (1906), 545; Brüch (1913), 96f., 116; *FEW* 17, 3ff.; Much (1967), 306; Birkhan (1970), 248ff. See also Ploss (1956), 1ff.; (1959), 409ff.

[28] Brüch (1913), 127. Cf. also Gamillscheg (1970), 358f. (early, but how early?).

[29] Gamillscheg (1970), 29.

authors, when they did use them, often took care to add expressly that they were employing a barbarian word for a foreign feature.

The indirect method, to which we now turn, presents more problems and is not so reliable, but at least it puts up rather more examples of a loan from Germanic into Latin for discussion (over eighty according to Brüch). In adopting the criterion of the extent to which a loanword is attested in various Romance languages as an indication that it was taken into Latin before 400 we face a number of difficulties.

First, a word may be present in all the Romance languages, but conceivably as the result of separate, independent loans from one or other of the Germanic languages. Here the geographical extent of the Goths' migrations is a telling example, for theoretically they could be the source of a loanword at different stages of their wanderings (into Rumanian, but also into Italian, Provençal and French, Spanish and Portuguese), all the latter after 400. Although it is unlikely that one Germanic word proved so attractive that it was repeatedly borrowed into different Romance languages, we need a further check, e.g. the presence of a Germanic loanword in eastern Romance (Rumanian) in a characteristically WG form (thereby excluding Gothic as the source of the Rumanian word). An example has been suggested in a Germanic verb for 'to mar, annoy, grieve' (OHG *merren*, Go. *marzjan*), for this has reflections in a number of Romance languages, e.g. OFr./OPr. *marrir* 'to disturb, make sad', but also *marrit* 'downcast', OSp. *amarrido* (same meaning) and It. *smarrire* 'to disturb'.[30] To confirm the proposal that this was an early loan into the language of the Roman army (indicating that 'being browned off' is an unchanging feature of military life) Rum. *amărît* 'grieving' has also been adduced, showing no trace of the characteristic Go. -*z*-. This might be acceptable if only we could be sure that the Rumanian word did not derive from Lat. *amarus* 'bitter' and mean simply 'embittered'.

Secondly, this leads us to ask what must be the position with a Germanic word attested in all the languages of western Romance, but not in Rumanian. This need not necessarily point to a loan after 400, since the Roman provinces of Dacia, Moesia and Dalmatia appear to have been linguistically somewhat isolated from the west even before 400, as is suggested by the fact that Celtic loanwords in all the western Romance languages (e.g. *cambiare* 'to change', *caminus* 'way') must have

---

[30] Brüch (1913), 27, 165f.; *FEW* 16, 534ff.; Gamillscheg (1970), 25.

spread early throughout the western Empire, but do not occur in Rumanian.[31] In the light of this a Germanic loanword, even if not attested in Rumanian, could still have entered Latin before 400: *brūtis*, loaned in the Balkans before this date, has left no trace in Rumanian.

Thirdly, a Germanic loanword may be present in all the western Romance languages and yet have been adopted after 400, generally because of internal loanword traffic in western Romania, especially as the result of radiation from Francia in connection with the expansion of feudalism and the political authority of the Frankish empire. A leading example of this would be OFr. *fieu*, MLat. *feudum* 'fief, feudal benefice', deriving from Gmc. *fehu* 'cattle' or *fehu* + *ôd* 'wealth in the form of cattle'.[32]

Fourthly, a Germanic loanword may conversely be attested in only western Romance and still be an early loan before 400. Here Spanish and Portuguese in particular come into question, but only if the form of the word is such that it could not be derived from Gothic (and therefore be as late as the Visigothic occupation of the peninsula). One example concerns an item of wear which western Europe may have regarded as characteristic of the Germani, but which they had probably adopted from the horse-peoples of the steppes. Just as a Germanic word for trousers (Engl. 'breeches') was passed to Celtic (and thence to Latin as *brāca*), so too is another term for 'trousers, anklets' (Gmc. *hosa*) present as a loanword, first with Isidore of Seville (*osa*), but then in OFr. *huese*, It. *uosa*, OSp. *huesa*, OPort. *osa*.[33] None of these forms can be attributed to Gothic (which would be geographically conceivable), because they presuppose a Gmc. short *-o-*, rather than the short *-u-* characteristic of Gothic. The word was possibly brought across by Germanic mercenaries in the Roman army and spread as a result of their ubiquitousness. The same explanation probably underlies another loan, that of Gmc. *helm* 'helmet', attested in OFr. *helme*, OPr. *elm*, Sp. *yelmo*.[34] These Romance forms presuppose a Germanic form with a short *-e-* (as opposed to Go. *hilms*), but if a Spanish variant *elmo* (also Portuguese) presupposes a Gmc. short *-i-* this is likely to be the result of later Visigothic influence competing with an earlier, more widespread loan from WG.

If a Germanic word could thus be borrowed into VL before 400, but still not survive in all the Romance languages, this raises the question how many different Romance attestations are called for to constitute evi-

---

[31] Brüch (1913), 23f.; Straka (1956), 253, fn. 2.   [32] *FEW* 15, 2, 117ff; Gamillscheg (1970), 254, 276.
[33] Brüch (1913), 27; *FEW* 16, 228f.; Gamillscheg (1970), 318.
[34] Brüch (1913), 27; *FEW* 16, 192f.; Gamillscheg (1970), 286.

dence for an early loan and what particular combinations of Romance languages are the most persuasive.[35] That we are justified in asking this kind of question is clear if we look at even an extreme case, for we have already come across such cases where a word may be used by only a few Latin authors whose date makes it nonetheless clear that this is an early loan, e.g. *carrago* with Ammianus Marcellinus, *drungus* with Vegetius or *ganta* with Pliny. Even with this proviso, however, the more widespread a Germanic word is in Romance (we have seen why Rumanian can in effect be ignored) the more likely it is that it was taken across as an early loan.

The most convincing group is where as many as four different Romance languages (French, Provençal, Italian, Spanish) attest the word in question. Of the many examples which are found in this group I choose only two. The first is the Germanic verb represented by English 'to warn', for which two variants must be postulated: **warnjan* and **warnôn*, covering a range of meanings such as 'to warn, ward off, protect', but also 'to equip' in the sense of actively warning, making ready for the act of protection.[36] These forms are well represented in Romance (extending also to Catalan and Portuguese) with a spread of meanings reconcilable with the Germanic evidence. The Romance examples can therefore mean 'to warn' (OFr. *garnir*, OPr. *guarnir*), 'to protect' (OFr. *garnir*), but also 'to equip' (OFr. *garnir* 'to arm someone, to fortify a stronghold', cf. also the nouns *garnison* and *garniture*, both meaning 'provisions', and *garnement* 'defence, protection, equipment'). These last meanings are most widely attested in Romance, as is also at first the military context of their use, before their 'civilian' employment ('to provide someone with something'). The word may well have been in use by Germanic mercenaries.

This seems also to have been the case with our second example. Gmc. **wardôn* 'to direct one's gaze' is attested in all the Germanic languages: OHG *wartên* 'to look out, expect, wait for', OS *wardon* 'to guard, watch over', OE *weardian* 'to guard, defend', ON *varða* 'to guard, defend, ward off'.[37] The verb is not attested in Gothic, which has however *daúrawards* 'doorkeeper' and the *nomen agentis wardja* 'guard, watchman'. These forms have parallels in all the Romance languages (except Rumanian), falling into two semantic groups. First, 'to look at' (OFr. *garder/warder*, cf. also *regarder*, OPr. *g(u)ardar*), secondly 'to keep guard or watch' (OFr.

---

[35] Brüch (1913), 48f. [36] *Ibid.*, pp. 61f.; *FEW* 17, 529ff.; Gamillscheg (1970), 337.
[37] *FEW* 17, 510ff.; Gamillscheg (1970), 279.

guarder, OPr. *gardar*, cf. also OFr. *garde* 'guard' as a singular or collective noun). The wide spread in Romance suggests an early loan before 400: an originally military term taken into the Latin of the imperial age. Significantly, Go. *wardja* is reflected only in those parts of Romania where the Goths later settled, where preservation of *-dj-* points to a relatively late reception: with a Romance suffix (It. *guardiano*, Sp. *guardián*, Port. *guardião*) or without (It., Sp., Port. *guardia*).

Less widespread in Romance, but still likely to be an early loan from Germanic, is OFr., OPr. *bastir*, It. *bastire* 'to build'.[38] This is derived from the Germanic word for 'bast' (OHG *bast*, together with the verb *besten* < **bastjan* 'to plait (with bast)'). The fact that in Romance this word has the specialised meaning of building is explained by the Germanic practice of tying the posts of a house together with bast in construction or (if we can assume a generalised meaning in Germanic 'to plait, intertwine', not necessarily with bast) of building with wattle and daub. The suggestion that Romance usage points earliest to the construction of fortifications rather than buildings for living in need cause no difficulty in view of the Germanic practice of protecting by means of a fence-like stockade, made firm by plaiting.[39]

Even if we lacked the written testimony of Palladius from the fourth century an early loan could reasonably be argued for Gmc. **wanga* 'spade' (originally a tool with a bend or curve in it), with reflections in OFr. *wange* 'a gardener's tool', OPr. *fanga* 'spade' and Italian derivatives meaning 'hoe'.[40] Much later, in the *Visio Tnugdali* this rare word (*wangia*) is listed amongst agricultural tools and its conjunction with *fossoriis* suggests that it was a digging tool (which could occasionally be used as a weapon).

If we add all the Germanic words which this indirect method suggests entered Latin before 400 to those obtained by the direct method we arrive at a total of about one hundred for this earliest period. It is certainly possible, however, that there were more but that, as barbarian words of everyday speech, they never found their way into written texts. This need not stop us asking why or amongst what groups of speakers these loans took place.[41] Three such groups stand out. *Inquilini* or Germanic peasants settled within the Empire could well account for an agricultural term such as *vanga* or, if they lived anywhere near the frontier district, for the incorporation of *marka* 'frontier area' into VL (just

---

[38] Brüch (1913), 59f., 169f.; *FEW* 15, 1, 74ff; von Wartburg (1968), 639ff.
[39] Kellermann (1966), 114ff.; von Wartburg (1968), 646f.
[40] Walde (1906), 648; Brüch (1913), 54; *FEW* 17, 504.   [41] Brüch (1913), 89ff.

as, much later, Sl. *granica* in turn ousted the Germanic word from German in favour of 'Grenze').[42] Fortification work, as with **bastjan*, may also belong to this group. A second group is represented by merchants responsible for introducing Germanic specialities such as *ganta* and *sāpo*, but also, given the importance of fresh foodstuffs, a Germanic word such as *frisk*.[43]

Much more important (or frequent) than either of these groups, as far as our fragmentary evidence permits a conclusion, is the military sphere in which Roman soldiers could have adopted Germanic clothing habits to meet the needs of a northern climate (*hosa*) or in which Germanic mercenaries in Roman service continued to use the equipment to which they were accustomed (*helm*, *brand* 'sword', *sporo* 'spur')[44] or the technical military terms of their own language (*warnôn*, *wardôn*). Two such military terms deserve to be looked at separately.

The first of these is represented by OHG *herebergôn* 'to encamp' (< *hereberga* 'encampment'), where the first element, meaning 'army', places its military origin beyond doubt ('shelter/accommodation for an army').[45] The Germanic words find their way into Romance with two variants in the vowel of the first element of the compound: with -*a*- (e.g. OFr. *arberger/aberger*, OPr. *arbergar* for the verb and OFr. *auberge*, OPr. *albergue* for the noun), but also with -*e*- (e.g. OFr. *herberger/heberger* and OFr. *herberge/heberge*). These variants indicate that underlying them were two Germanic forms with *hari*- and *heri*-, an alternation which illustrates how difficult it can sometimes be to distinguish the geographical and chronological aspects of loanword traffic. The alternation between the Germanic forms has been interpreted to mean that the Romance words with -*a*- derived from *hari*- in either Gothic or Burgundian (which knew no umlaut of *a* to *e* before *i*), whilst those with -*e*- came from Frankish after this umlaut had taken place. Although the second part of this statement may well be true, it does not follow that the first part must also hold, since the forms with *hari*- could conceivably also have entered Romance from WG before the operation of umlaut. Indeed, this assumption would account for OFr. forms with *har*-/*ar*- outside the areas where we might expect the influence of Gothic or Burgundian in Gaul. This implies that this Germanic word may have entered VL on two separate occasions (before and after the operation of umlaut in Frankish), the

---

[42] *Ibid.*, pp. 98f., against Gamillscheg (1970), 260.
[43] Brüch (1913), 97f.; *FEW* 15, 2, 173ff.; Gamillscheg (1970), 340.
[44] Brüch (1913), 100; *FEW* 15, 1, 242ff.; 17, 185ff.; Gamillscheg (1970), 281, 287.
[45] Brüch (1913), 142; *FEW* 16, 158ff.; Gamillscheg (1934), 367; (1970), 378.

earlier of which could well point to the vocabulary of barbarian mercenaries in the Roman army.

Our last military example is of quite a different kind, for it represents not a loanword into Latin as hitherto, but a loan-translation. Lat. *companio* is attested in all the western Romance languages (originally in the sense of 'comrade' in the language of the army).[46] Its formation (collective prefix *cum* + stem meaning 'loaf' + personal ending) suggests a meaning 'someone with whom one shares a loaf', which corresponds to Germanic terms with the same meaning and a comparable formation (collective prefix *ga-* + stem meaning 'loaf' + personal ending), as in Go. *gahláiba* and OHG *gileibo*. If we accept a causal connection between these closely similar Latin and Germanic forms it is possible that the impetus came from Germanic. Latin may have other personal compounds with *con-* (*coniux, consors*), but they are not *-n-* stems, as *companio* is, whilst on the Germanic side Gothic alone has five such examples (e.g. *gadáila* 'participant').[47] This still makes it difficult, in view of the wide spread of the Romance examples of *companio*, to decide whether the word was borrowed from Germanic in the imperial period or only later in the context of the Frankish army. What might settle the issue in favour of the former is the presence of a Latin formation with *con-* which *is* an *-n-* stem, namely *concibo* in a similar sense 'someone with whom food is shared' and likewise a term of soldier's Latin (it is found on a Roman soldier's gravestone from North Africa). Like *companio*, it also has a parallel in Germanic from which it was probably derived: WG **gimato*, OHG *gimazzo* 'table-companion', cf. English 'mate' (all formed with the word for 'meat, food'). These two Latin nouns were probably introduced into imperial Latin as technical terms of an army now based on growing numbers of Germanic mercenaries.

This selective survey of examples of the indirect method confirms what we saw of the more restricted range covered by the direct method: the two spheres of trade and warfare play an undeniable part, even though the larger number of Germanic loanwords is from the latter sphere. It will be further confirmed when we look at the evidence for Latin loanwords in Germanic.[48]

Although Romance philologists employing the indirect method differ over whether a Germanic loanword was borrowed before or after about

---

[46] Brüch (1913), 81f.; *FEW* 2, 2, 965ff.; Gamillscheg (1970), 408; Kuhn (1972), 45f.
[47] Brüch (1913), 82; Kuhn (1972), 45.   [48] See below, pp. 219ff.

400 there is little doubt about the crucial importance of this dividing line. Before this the unity of the Roman Empire made it feasible that a loanword could spread throughout the Latin-speaking world, especially in the ubiquitous contexts of trade and army, but after that date the collapse of imperial unity resulting from the barbarian invasions rendered that impossible, so that linguistic contacts remained more isolated at separate points. On either side of the approximate turning-point of the year 400 this disruption of former unity is visible at various points on what had hitherto been the imperial frontier. At the lower Danubian end the Goths crossed the river-frontier as early as 376, in 378 the battle of Adrianople was fought and there followed Balkan campaigns until the end of the century, with the Gothic invasion of Italy itself in 401.[49] At the other extremity of the Roman frontier similar symptoms of collapse were visible in Britain: towards the end of the fourth century Saxon raiders harried the coastline, the *litus Saxonicum*, more and more, in 407 Constantine III was forced to withdraw the bulk of his army from Britain to Gaul to deal with a crisis there and in 410 the cities of Britain were informed that they were henceforth responsible for their own defence, so that Roman rule in Britain was effectively at an end.[50] Between these two end-points the position was not markedly different in Germany. Already between the years 234 and 260 the Romans had abandoned their bases east of the Rhine and pressure from the advancing Alemanni put a strain on communication between the Rhine and the Danube. In 403 Stilicho pulled back the Roman army of the Rhine to meet the threat to Italy, whilst in 406 the Vandals, Suevi and Alans crossed the Rhine and descended on Gaul, which amounted to the collapse of the Roman province of *Germania inferior*.[51] Under these conditions of disintegration we can no longer expect a unified loanword process from Germanic into a fragmented Empire,[52] but must perforce narrow our focus.

In choosing to concentrate now on the Franks and their linguistic influence on VL and the emergent language of French we deliberately abandon the Goths whose linguistic encounters we followed in the last chapter. This is partly because of the difficulty of recovering Gothic loanwords, say, in the Balkans (only *brūtis* has proved a candidate for serious consideration), but partly for the sake of a wider coverage of the encounter between Germanic and Latin. It also has the advantage that,

[49] Wolfram (1988), 117ff., 139ff., 150ff.   [50] Campbell (1991), 8ff.
[51] Gamillscheg (1970), 4, 38f.   [52] Brüch (1913), 4; von Wartburg (1950), *passim*.

by not dwelling any longer on the Goths in what now became their Mediterranean context (Balkans, Italy, southern France, Iberia) and by turning to the Franks in northern Gaul we are following the historic switch of the centre of gravity from the Mediterranean in antiquity to north of the Alps in the transition to the Middle Ages.[53] We are also dealing with a much more important encounter, both linguistically (about 600 Frankish terms found their way into the Gallo-Roman vocabulary, not all permanently, but far more Germanic loanwords than in any other Romance language)[54] and historically, given the Franks' rapid rise to ascendancy. This ascendancy was both external (the role played by this tribe within Europe at large) and internal (within Gaul). This last feature is illustrated by the designation of the territory they occupied no longer as *Gallia*, but as *Francia*, and of the form of Romance which evolved there as *lingua francisca*, so that French is the only Romance language to be named after a Germanic tribe.[55] It is also illustrated by the nature of Frankish loanwords adopted by Gallo-Roman, betraying the Franks' dominant position as rulers over their territory, in marked contrast to the speech-level of loanwords before 400, largely confined to merchants and mercenaries.

Because the loanwords which now concern us are numbered in the hundreds only a drastic selection is feasible, but one which, by concentrating on the vocabulary of the Frankish nobility and the terminology of their state for which Latin could provide no ready equivalents, illustrates once more the higher speech level with which we are now concerned.

Fittingly, we start with terms for various offices at the Frankish court, technical terms and therefore not to be ousted by Latin.[56] From the originally humble term for 'horse-groom' (OHG *marahscalc*), taken into Frankish Latin as *mariscalcus* (already in the *Lex Salica*), there derived OFr. *mareschal*, at times still in the same context (cf. modern Fr. *maréchal ferrant* 'farrier'). With the development of a mounted army, however, this word acquired a much more elevated function, denoting one charged with looking after the horses and stables of a ruler's household or even in command of a (mounted) army. In this function the word spread elsewhere in western Romance under Frankish influence. The senior office at court, held by the major domo, was expressed by a Frankish term meaning 'eldest servant' *sinaskalk* (cf. the Go. superlative *sinista* 'eldest'),

---

[53] Brown (1993), 68, 112; (1996), 103, 166.　　[54] Gamillscheg (1970), 405.　　[55] Brüch (1926a), 66.
[56] *Mareschal*: FEW 16, 517ff.; Gamillscheg (1970), 255. *Seneschal*: FEW 17, 69f.; Gamillscheg (1970), 255. *Eschanson*: FEW 17, 94; Gamillscheg (1970), 255f.

likewise occurring as a loanword early in Latin as *siniscalcus / senescalcus* and in OFr. *seneschal*, but also with duties going beyond looking after the king's household, as in the further loan to OPr. *senescalc*, designating a justiciary. The office of cup-bearer was expressed by Frk. **skankjo* (cf. OHG *skenco, skenkio*, literally 'someone who pours drink'), which found its way early into Latin as *scancio* in the *Lex Salica* (also as *scantio*) and into OFr. as *eschanson*, with the same meaning.

The presence of some of these words in the *Lex Salica* is an indication that Frankish law was another channel for Germanic words to enter Gallo-Roman.[57] We have already seen that a term such as OHG *mahal* 'place where justice is administered' could find its way into Frankish Latin as *mallum* (again in the *Lex Salica*), but also into OFr. *mal public*, furthermore as part of a compound place-name, in France as in Germany.[58] OHG *mundboro* 'guardian, legal protector' suggests that a cognate Frankish term lies behind OFr. *mainbourg* 'guardian, executor', even though false associations account for the final *-g* and the legal importance of ritual gestures explains the confusion between Germanic *mund-* 'protection' and Lat. *manus* 'hand'. The abstract from this word (OHG *muntburt*) is attested in Merovingian Latin formulas as *munburdum*. The word for a legal security, Frk. **waddi* (cf. OHG *wetti*, OS *weddi*, Go. *wadi*) entered Latin before umlaut took place, producing Merovingian examples such as *wadium* and *uuadius*, but also OFr. *wage* and *gage*. (In some dialects it is used in the context of marriage, cf. Engl. 'to wed', showing a survival of the Germanic practice of bride price.)

That a range of Frankish loanwords belongs to the field of warfare should not surprise us with a tribe which had occupied new territory by military conquest and whose army, even in the mixed society of Francia, was made up of Frankish warriors.[59] Examples of this vocabulary include Frk. **hariban* 'summons to military service' (cf. OHG *heriban*), to be found in Frankish Latin as *haribannum* and *harebannus*, but also in OFr. in the forms *arban / erban*, later subjected to popular etymology (hence *arrière-ban*) and applied to forced labour in the context of feudalism. The term for 'guard, sentry' may also be quoted here: the word *wahta* (as in OHG) was Latinised as *wacta* and is attested in Romance both as a noun (e.g. OFr. *waite, guaite, gueite*) and as a verb (*waiter, guaitier*), where it is uncertain whether the latter is a French formation from the former or from a Germanic verb, as in OHG *wahtên*. (Engl. 'to wait' is derived from

---

[57] *Mal (public)*: see above, p. 30, fn. 2, and *FEW* 16, 500. [58] Gamillscheg (1970), 134.
[59] *Arban*: *FEW* 16, 158; Gamillscheg (1970), 278. *Guaite*: *FEW* 17, 451ff.; Gamillscheg (1970), 279. *Brunie*: *FEW* 15, 1, 310; Gamillscheg (1970), 285.

French.) In French the meaning 'to keep watch' has largely been replaced by *garder* as a result of a functional distinction between the two verbs: *guetter* for keeping watch by night and in concealment (as in 'to lie in wait'), *garder* for more open watchkeeping. With the term for 'breast-plate' we come once more to a word originally loaned from Celtic into Germanic,[60] whence (rather than directly from Celtic) it was borrowed into OFr. and OPr. Frk. **brunnia* (cf. OHG *brunna*, Go. *brunjo*) is thus attested in the Reichenau glosses as *brunia*, in OFr. as *brunie, broigne* 'leather jerkin with iron plates sewn on, providing a primitive protection' and in OPr. as *bronha*.

The rise of feudalism as a new form of social organisation in Francia, from where it spread to the rest of western Europe, accounts for a number of terms of Germanic origin belonging to this sphere, of which two may serve as examples.[61] It is uncertain whether OFr. *fieu, fief*, Lat. *feudum* derive from Frk. **feh(u)* 'cattle' or **feh-ôd* 'property in the form of cattle', for the difficulty lies in reconciling the French with the Latin form. Either **feh(u)* was Latinised as *feum/fevum* or, as a new legal term, it was assimilated to the semantically close *allodium* (< **alôd* 'landed property'), thus producing *feudum*. Despite this uncertainty the Germanic or more specifically Frankish origin seems clear. Phonological difficulties also arise with the relationship between Frk. **frônjan* (cf. OHG *frônen* 'to perform (or claim) feudal (or public) service' and modern German *frönen*) and OFr., OPr. *fornir* 'to provide, deliver'. The problem here lies with the presence of two forms in Romance: with *-n-*, but also with *-m-* in OPr. (*formir, fromir*). This latter suggests a quite separate loan from a Gmc. verb **frumjan* (cf. OHG *frummen* 'to perform, accomplish', but also 'to be of service'?), which lies sufficiently close semantically to account for the confusion. Since the forms with *-m-* are attested only in the south, not in the Frankish north, the connection between a stem originally meaning 'belonging to the lords or lord' (*frôno*)[62] and a verb meaning 'to perform service for one's lord' or 'to furnish him with a tribute or something in lieu of service' seems to be close enough.

The terminology of hunting, which reveals a strong Frankish influence, may be included here, above all because of the distinction made between a wood in which no legal restriction was placed on cutting wood or hunting and one in which these rights, especially the latter, were the

---

[60] See above, pp. 155f.
[61] *Fieu: FEW* 15, 2, 117ff.; Gamillscheg (1970), 276. *Fornir: FEW* 3, 829ff.; Gamillscheg (1970), 337.
[62] See above, pp. 105f.

privilege of the Frankish lords.[63] Although Gallo-Roman retained Lat. *venari* 'to hunt' in its vocabulary, it employed a loanword for the typically Germanic mode of hunting with trained hawks. Frk. **gabaiti* 'hawking' (cf. OHG *beizen* 'to hawk', MHG *gebeize* 'hawking') thus lies behind OFr. *gebiez, gibiez* (cf. modern Fr. *gibier* 'game', suggesting an extension from hunting *with* birds to hunting *for* them). The two different vowels found in the OFr. forms suggest, not for the first time, a double loan-process, since the Gmc. prefix **ga-* would account for the French forms with *ge-* (found in Flanders, Normandy and Burgundy), whilst the variant prefix **gi-* yielded the forms with *gi-*. The retention of *-b-* in French points to a relatively late loan in either case. For the particular type of sparrow-hawk used in hunting in this way the Gmc. term is attested in OHG *sparwâri* (modern German *Sperber*), which entered Gallo-Roman as a hunting term, already in the *Lex Salica* (*speruarius*) and then in OFr. *espervier*, OPr. *esparvier*. Whether the Latin and Romance term for the wood in which hunting was forbidden to all but the Frankish nobility (*forestis, foresta*) is of Germanic or Latin origin is still open to discussion,[64] but about the other type of wood there is no such doubt. Frk. **wald* (cf. OHG *wald*) occurs in Latinised form as *waldus* (in the *Lex Salica* it denotes a wood in which any freeman may gather wood and hunt) and in OFr. *gaut*.

Finally, the Frankish household and its furnishings provide a recognisable group of loanwords.[65] From Frk. **laubja* 'arbour, arcade, roof-cover' (cf. OHG *louba*, OS *lôvia*) is derived OFr. *loge* 'foliage shelter' (often in the military context of a covering for warriors). It is attested also in Frankish Latin from the sixth century and was loaned from Francia to Italy (*loggia*) and to Spain (*loja*). For the fenced-off ground belonging to a house (OFr. *jart* 'orchard' and *jardin* 'garden') two Germanic equivalents are attested: OHG *gart* (strong) and *garto* (weak), with parallels elsewhere. The strong noun accounts for OFr. *jart*, whilst *jardin* presupposes Latin transmission in the form **gardinus*, possibly on the model of late Latin *hortinus* 'belonging to the garden', so that the starting-point was **hortus gardinus* 'a garden with a fence'. Moving inside the house for our last example we may note the Frankish origin of one item of furniture: the OFr. compound *faldestuel*, modern Fr. *fauteuil*, comes from Frk. **faldistôl* (cf. OHG *faltstuol*).

---

[63] *Gebiez: FEW* 16, 1f.; Gamillscheg (1970), 290. *Espervier: FEW* 17, 171f.; Gamillscheg (1970), 290. *Gaut: FEW* 17, 486; Gamillscheg (1970), 323f.

[64] *FEW* 3, 708ff.; Schützeichel (1957), 105ff.; Gamillscheg (1970), 324; Pfister (1972), 187; Meineke (1995b), 345ff.

[65] *Loge: FEW* 16, 446ff.; Gamillscheg (1970), 297. *Jardin: FEW* 16, 18ff.; Gamillscheg (1970), 300. *Faldestuel: FEW* 15, 2, 103f.; Gamillscheg (1970), 312.

From the beginning these forms denoted not simply a 'folding seat', but more specifically one which was richly decorated and meant especially for the higher clergy (a bishop's throne) or for secular rulers (as with the throne of Dagobert)[66] – a final reminder of the social elevation which these Frankish loanwords after 400 exemplify.

[66] Reproduced in Fossier (1989), 528.

CHAPTER II

Latin loanwords in Germanic

This chapter falls into three parts: the influence of Latin on Gothic, on OHG and on OE. (ON can safely be left out of account, since almost all its loanwords from Latin reached it later or indirectly through England or Germany.)

Although the types of cultural contact which this loanword traffic reveals cover a wide range, the lion's share falls to warfare and trade, so that these merit separate treatment in the next chapter. Only with Gothic can these two classes of loanwords be included in the present chapter, since, apart from Christian vocabulary, the influence of Latin on Gothic was confined almost entirely to these two spheres.

Contacts between two peoples in a frontier zone, in times of peace as well as war, involve linguistic interaction and with the Roman as with the British Empire this meant that those who came into contact with the imperial power had to learn something of the others' language. There is evidence to suggest knowledge of Latin on the part of individual Germani from an early date.[1] The presence of Germanic mercenaries in the Roman army, even of Germanic leaders in positions of high command, presupposes an acquaintance with Latin. The attractions of a higher civilisation encouraged trade far into the Germanic interior, with Roman terms accompanying these novel goods. How far this cultural and linguistic influence went can be seen numerically, with whatever reservations, since about 350 early Latin loanwords have been established for Germanic at large and about 50 for Gothic (with some degree of overlap).[2] In this chapter we shall be concerned only with secular loanwords, leaving the Christian vocabulary of Latin to Part III.

It has been argued that the greater number of Germanic languages in which a particular Latin loanword is recorded suggests that this word entered Germanic at an early stage before linguistic differentiation had

---

[1] Kluge (1913), 9f.   [2] Wollmann (1990b), 373; Corazza (1969), 3.

proceeded too far.[3] However, there are qualifications which need to be borne in mind, not least the possibility of polygenesis, the fact that one word could have been adopted by different languages at different points in time. Instead of simply assuming early monogenesis we must also take account of phonological considerations, both in Latin and in Germanic.[4] By correlating two systems of phonological chronology it is sometimes possible to show that a Latin word, although attested in a wide range of Germanic languages, did not cross into Germania on one single (early) occasion, but was borrowed at different times into different languages.[5]

In turning first to the Goths in the area of the lower Danube we revert to the point where we left them on their migrations, to their arrival in the Pontic region and first direct contact with the Romans.[6] Apart from earlier military encounters which may have provided the opportunity for loanword exchange the decisive date is the year 257, when the emperor Aurelian ceded the Roman province of Dacia to the Goths, who now occupied an area which had been thoroughly Latinised and from which they were in a position to engage in trade with the Empire. The acquisition of novel goods from the Romans led to the adoption of their Latin terms for these objects, but in addition mercenary service in the ranks of the Roman army exposed Gothic to the influence of Latin not merely in military terminology, but also in those aspects of Roman life encountered in the camp, not exclusively on the battlefield. In what follows we shall consider a selection of Latin loanwords in Gothic, dividing them first into various walks of life, then turning to the problem of dating.

The first category is military.[7] Go. *militōn* 'to do military service' is derived from Lat. *militare* with the same meaning (with a shortening of the long *i* in the first syllable of the Latin word, possibly because of its unaccented position at first).[8] As opposed to the suggestion that such a word was taken over as soon as the Goths came into conflict with the Romans in the third century it can be argued that the loan more probably arose from service by numbers of Goths in the Roman army. Although there is no linguistic pointer, it is possible that *militōn* at first denoted military service in this context as distinct from the native word

---

[3] Wollmann (1990c), 508f., quoting Pogatscher and Bartoli.
[4] Wollmann (1990b), 387; (1993), 22f.
[5] Examples are Lat. *uncia* 'a twelfth part' (Corazza (1969), 46; Wollmann (1990b), 389, fn. 42; (1990c), 515ff.) and *acētum* 'vinegar' (Corazza (1969), 13f.; Wollmann (1990a), 531ff.).
[6] Gamillscheg (1934), 300.   [7] Thompson (1966), 30f.
[8] Jellinek (1926), 180; Corazza (1969), 49f.; Kuhn (1972), 14.

draúhtinōn, denoting military service (in the Gothic army). The background of the Roman army is suggested even more forcibly by another loanword: Go. *anno* 'soldier's pay', derived from Lat. *annōna* 'wages, provisions'.[9] (The Latin word denoted an annual provision made by the state for public bodies, including the army, so that the Gothic meaning developed from the military function which concerned Gothic mercenaries.) The Gothic form is an abbreviation of the Latin, either because Germanic initial word-accent led to a reduction of the now unaccented *-o-* or because of the loss of the final *-a* and consequent association of the word with Gothic feminine *ō*-stems. In either case this loanword, like *militōn*, suggests Gothic service in the Roman army as mercenaries or *foederati* in receipt of pay or subsidies. Go. *spaíkulatur* 'guard' was borrowed from Lat. *speculator* 'scout, spy', but the fact that the Goths possessed a native word with the same meaning (*wardja*) suggests that, as with *militōn*, they adopted the loanword as a technical term of their service in the Roman ranks.[10] Another aspect of army life, subjection to Roman discipline, is touched on in Go. *karkara* 'prison', from Lat. *carcer*.[11] The transformation of a Latin masculine into a Gothic feminine is explained by VL *carcara*, a collective plural taken as a feminine singular (cf. *folium/folia*: Fr. *feuille*), and Go. *-a-* in place of *-e-* in the second syllable likewise echoes VL as opposed to the classical language (cf. the loanword into Greek, *kárkaron*, but also OHG *karkâri*, OS *karkari*, OIr. *carcar*).

Other examples may not be specifically military, but can still be associated with service in the Roman army as a point of origin. If Gothic has the verb *kapillōn* from Lat. **capillare* 'to cut one's hair' alongside the native verb *skaban*, used in the same sense, this is likely to be, as with *militōn* and *draúhtinōn*, because the Latin loanword was initially used in a Roman context.[12] That this context was the Roman army, suggesting that short haircuts are a feature of military life over the centuries, is borne out by the contrast between Germanic leaders wearing their hair long and in a knot and the short hair-style of the Romans.[13] Service in the Roman ranks also confronted the Goths with the custom of reclining when eating, as in the verb *anakumbjan*, partly Gothicised from Lat. *accumbere/recumbere*, and the noun *kubitus* 'group of people at a meal', derived from Lat. *cubitus* 'reclining (at a meal)'.[14] Both these words

---

[9] Jellinek (1926), 179, 182; Corazza (1969), 50ff.; Kuhn (1972), 14; Wolfram (1975), 310.
[10] Jellinek (1926), 181, 184; Corazza (1969), 55f. [11] Jellinek (1926), 180, 182; Corazza (1969), 56f.
[12] Jellinek (1926), 180; Corazza (1969), 29.
[13] Fischer (1912), 183ff.; Much (1967), 427f.; Wolfram (1975), 308; (1988), 103.
[14] Jellinek (1926), 180; Corazza (1969), 24ff.

probably entered Gothic in the same context and presuppose visual experience of this novel Roman practice.

The second category of loanwords has to do with trade.[15] We shall consider the verb *káupōn* 'to trade' later and restrict ourselves now to more specific examples. If we start with Go. *Saúr* 'Syrian' (from Lat. *Syrus/Surus*) this is because of the ubiquity of Syrian merchants in the Mediterranean world at large and in Dacia in particular.[16] Go. *asilus* 'donkey' may seem equally out of place here until we recall that this beast of burden was introduced to northern Europe by the Romans and, together with the mule (cf. OHG *mûl* from Lat. *mulus*), was used as a means of transporting their goods overland by Roman merchants.[17] For Go. *asilus* and its cognates in other Germanic languages a Latin diminutive *asellus* has been entertained, but *asinus* (from which all Romance languages derive their forms) is more likely, together with substitution of the more common Gmc. suffix *-il-* for *-in-*.[18]

A number of Gothic words testify to the goods circulated by Roman trade. To Go. *wein* 'wine' (from Lat. *vinum*), attested throughout Germania, we shall return later.[19] Indicating a luxury object imported from the Romans was the word for 'lamp', Go. *lukarn* from Lat. *lucerna*.[20] As with *karkara* Gothic shows *-a-* in place of Lat. *-e-*, which here, too, is probably a reflection of VL (cf. OIr. *locharn*, We. *lugarn*). The use of a lamp lit by the expensive import of oil[21] was very limited, which may explain why Go. *lukarn* remains so isolated within Germania (with a parallel only from Gotland: *lukarr* 'small fire').

Amongst the goods imported from the Romans a special group is formed by cloth materials, which is not surprising since the goods exported by the Romans to the Visigoths in the way of subsidies included luxury goods in high demand, amongst them various types of cloth.[22] As a reflection of this Wulfila employed a number of such loanwords. Among them we find *aúrāli* 'towel, napkin', from Lat. *ōrārium* 'face-cloth' (even though on the one occasion where the Gothic form is attested both the Greek and Latin versions use Lat. *sudarium* 'sweatcloth').[23] The changes between Latin and Gothic need cause no difficulty: VL shortening of *ō-*

[15] Thompson (1966), 33, 34ff.
[16] Jellinek (1926), 181; Corazza (1969), 53f. Cf. also Schulze (1907), 167, fn. 4; Thompson (1966), 37.
[17] See below, pp. 229f.   [18] Jellinek (1926), 179; Brüch (1926b), 11; Corazza (1969), 19ff.
[19] See below, pp. 227ff.
[20] Jellinek (1926), 180, 182; Schwarz (1951), 27; Corazza (1969), 15ff.; Polomé (1985), 310f.
[21] On Go. *alēw* 'oil', possibly brought to the Goths by Celtic merchants, cf. Untermann (1954), 390ff.; Polomé (1985), 309ff.   [22] Thompson (1966), 38f.
[23] Jellinek (1926), 179, 183; Corazza (1969), 62f.

before a stressed syllable and dissimilation of the second -*r*- to -*l*-. Go. *faskja* 'bandage' derives from Lat. *fascia* 'strip of cloth, bandage' and may therefore also have been loaned in the military context.[24] The word *saban* 'fine linen' comes from Lat. *sabanum*, originally a cloth from Saban, near Baghdad.[25] Since the word is also attested in Greek, the Goths could have taken their word theoretically from either Greek or Latin, but if it forms part of the secular vocabulary of trade the latter is more probable. The same conclusion is even more likely in the case of Go. *paúrpura/paúrpaúra* 'purple garment': although it is attested in Lat. *purpura* and Gr. *porphýra*, the former is closer to the Gothic form.[26] (The change of *u* to *aú* before *r* is regular in Gothic, not merely with loanwords.) The word *sakkus* was used by Wulfila in the penitential context of 'sackcloth and ashes' and is ultimately of Semitic origin, meaning 'coarse cloth' and attested in Greek and Latin, as well as the other Germanic languages.[27] The fact that in the two biblical passages where Wulfila uses this word the Greek version has *sákkos*, but the Latin has *cilicium* 'hairshirt' does not mean that the Gothic language acquired this word from Greek. Latin possessed the word in the double sense 'coarse material' and 'container made of such material'. The Latin origin of other trading terms for cloth materials, together with the regular incorporation of Latin nouns in -*us* into the Gothic declension -*us*, suggests that this cloth, too, was named after the term used by Roman traders. What Wulfila owed to Greek is therefore not the word itself, but its Christian adaptation to penitential usage.

The double usage of Lat. *saccus* (material and container) provides a bridge to another group of trade loanwords, denoting various types of container in which merchants transported their wares. Wulfila twice uses *arka* 'box (for holding money)', from Lat. *arca* 'box';[28] his word *katils* (or *katilus*) 'kettle, cauldron', with cognates in OHG, OS and OE, comes from Lat. *catillus* or, more probably, *catinus* (with a change of suffix, as with *asinus*).[29] Trading also presupposes the ability to measure accurately, especially money. Wulfila therefore employs several Latin terms for coins of different value: *assarjus* 'coin of small value',[30] *drakma* (whose final vowel suggests a loan from Lat. *drachma* rather than Gr. *drachmē*)[31] and *kintus* 'penny', a contraction from Lat. *centenionalis*.[32]

---

[24] Jellinek (1926), 180, 182, 183; Corazza (1969), 22f.   [25] Jellinek (1926), 181; Corazza (1969), 60f.
[26] Jellinek (1926), 180; Corazza (1969), 30f.   [27] Jellinek (1926), 181; Corazza (1969), 21f.
[28] Jellinek (1926), 179, 182; Corazza (1969), 46ff.
[29] Jellinek (1926), 180, 182; Corazza (1969), 18f. Less convincing is the explanation by Brüch (1926b), 6ff.   [30] Jellinek (1926), 179, 182; Corazza (1969), 43f.
[31] Jellinek (1926), 180, 182; Corazza (1969), 44ff.
[32] Schröder (1925), 8off.; Jellinek (1926), 209; Corazza (1969), 63f.

After this selective survey we turn to the question when and where this linguistic encounter took place. The most obvious answer is the period when the Goths arrived in south-eastern Europe in the third century, settled in Dacia and were in regular contact with the Empire. However, there are pointers to indirect contact with the Roman world long before this, while the Goths were still in northern Poland and were reached by Roman trade. We shall later consider these trade-routes in more detail,[33] but for the moment must content ourselves with the linguistic evidence for such early interchange. Here we must consider what phonological changes may tell us about its dating. These changes operate on both sides of the linguistic frontier, so that the correlation of changes between classical Latin and VL with changes between PG and the individual Germanic languages may narrow the timespan in question.

For Gothic the following sound-changes and their possible dating come into question. On the Latin side changes in pronunciation are attested in the first century AD (or even earlier). They include that of the ending *-um* to *-o* at the latest by the first century AD, but also the change of Classical Latin *v* from a semi-vowel to a bilabial voiced fricative and of the diphthong *ae* to the long vowel *ē*, both in the first century.[34] To these may be added the palatalisation of *c* before *i* or *e* from the fourth century on.[35] On the Germanic side we are concerned with what conclusions can be drawn about the *Auslautsgesetze* in Gothic, the reduction (or loss) of flectional endings in Germanic. With the exception of *u* in a final unaccented syllable (the Gothic flectional ending *-us* remained intact, thus permitting assimilation of Latin nouns in *-us* to the corresponding Gothic declension) vowels in this position have been lost by the time of Wulfila's Gothic (from about 340).[36] For sound changes of this type to become generally valid at least one generation must be assumed, so that they were completed in Gothic by about 300 at the latest, which would be confirmed by runic *tilarids* on the spear-blade of Kowel (with *-s* reduced from PG *-az*, as regularly in Gothic), if we can accept the dating about the middle of the third century.[37] With this approximate chronological framework we can consider some of the early Latin loan-words into Gothic, so early that they may have been adopted before the Goths made direct contact in south-eastern Europe.

[33]   See below, pp. 226f. Cf. Corazza (1969), 74f.
[34]   On *-um* > *-o* cf. Bonioli (1962), 101ff.; Väänänen (1967), 69f. On *v* see Bourciez (1946), 47; Bonioli (1962), 46ff. On *ae* > *ē* see Bonioli (1962), 30ff.; Wollmann (1990c), 510.
[35]   Bonioli (1962), 76; Wollmann (1990a), 534f.; (1990b), 389, fn. 42; (1990c), 513.
[36]   Jellinek (1926), 90ff.   [37]   Euler (1985), 9.

Go. *wein* (with cognates in OHG, OS and OE) is regarded as an early loan on the basis of the loss of final *-o* < *-um* in Lat. *vinum*, but also because Gothic (like the other Gmc. forms) presupposes Lat. *v* pronounced still as a semi-vowel (contrast this with *Naúbaímbaír* in the Gothic Calendar, where the first *b* presupposes now a fricative pronunciation in Latin).[38] We shall see later that there are archaeological grounds for thinking that Roman wine reached the Goths by trade while they were still in the north. Like *wein*, both Go. *saban* (with cognates in OHG and OE) and *akeit* (< Lat. *acētum* 'vinegar') presuppose early loss of Lat. *-m* and then of the final vowel in Germanic.[39] Loss of a final vowel is also to be registered with Go. *pund* (as with its cognates in OHG, OS and OE) and *lukarn*.[40] This last word has Celtic parallels and only one isolated cognate in Sweden. The presence of *k* cannot be used for dating if the following *a* was already VL, but the loss of the final vowel is enough to suggest an early loan. Finally, Go. *-us* is retained intact in *asilus* and *sakkus*, both of which are also paralleled in OHG, OS and OE and have been judged as early trading loanwords.[41] The same would hold of *katilus* (cognates in OHG, OE and ON), especially if its unattested nominative form were instead *katils* (*a*-stem, rather than *u*-stem).[42]

This group of Latin loanwords which passed into Germanic early enough to reach the Goths before their migrations from the Vistula region suggests that Roman wares were exported this far north in this early period, so that our linguistic conclusions independently confirm what archaeology suggests about this Roman trade.[43] These conclusions must also be seen in connection with Germanic, possibly Gothic, linguistic influence, especially in the context of trade, on other peoples in northern and eastern Europe, where the Latin words we have considered in Gothic are taken even further.[44] These peoples include the Slavs

---

[38] Jellinek (1926), 183, 184, 185; Schwarz (1951), 39; Corazza (1969), 10f.
[39] Jellinek (1926), 181, 183, 185; Schwarz (1951), 39, 40; Corazza (1969), 13f., 60; Wollmann (1990a), 540f.
[40] Jellinek (1926), 183, 185; Schwarz (1951), 39; Corazza (1969), 16; Polomé (1985), 310.
[41] Jellinek (1926), 185; Schwarz (1951), 38. An early loan of Go. *asilus* and its Germanic parallels would be suggested by their retention of short *a* if, with Wollmann (1990c), 523, fn. 49), we accept Straka's dating of the lengthening of Latin short vowels in open syllables already in the second century.
[42] Jellinek (1926), 185; Brüch (1926b), 9 (in agreement with Kluge at least over the dating); Corazza (1969), 19.
[43] It is necessary to differentiate between two different periods in trade between Romans and Goths: an early one reaching the latter in northern Poland and a later one on the Danubian frontier. We cannot argue, as is frequently done by Scardigli (1964, 100 *et passim*), that because a loanword is a trading term it may have reached the Goths in the north.
[44] See above, pp. 171f., 174.

(whose trading loanwords include *akeit, asilus, katilus, káupōn, pund, sakkus, wein*), the Finns (*katilus, káupōn, pund, wein*) and the Balts (*asilus, katilus, káupōn*), even though these last two may have received these words not directly, but through Slavonic mediation. What archaeology has established for trading connections can be confirmed by these linguistic trade-routes.

Nonetheless, the main exchange between Goths and Romans took place directly, once contact had been made on the Danubian frontier.[45] Roman eating habits, represented by *anakumbjan* and *kubitus*, were witnessed only in this region. Even though archaeological evidence suggests that Germani in the north drank wine with Roman wine-sets, the complete isolation of these two Gothic words within Germanic suggests that reclining to eat was a Roman practice observed by the Goths only much later. Military terms like *militōn* and *anno* presuppose service in the Roman army and again are unique within Germanic (OHG *miliza* and OE *milite* are nouns, not verbs, and likely to be independent loans). *Kapillōn* also is isolated within Germanic and suggests direct experience in the ranks of the imperial army.

These considerations can to some extent be confirmed linguistically. Whereas early loans underwent the loss of unaccented vowels in final syllables in Gothic, completed by the close of the third century, later loans were no longer affected by this change. Thus, *arka* and *drakma* differ from *lukarn* in retaining *-a*. The same is true of *karkara*, which derives its feminine gender from the use of its VL base as a neuter plural and thereby belongs to a different loan-process from OHG, OS *karkâri* and OE *cearcern* – and a late loan-process, because of the retention of *-a*.[46] Different loan-processes were also implied in the case of Go. *militōn*, OHG *miliza* and OE *milite* (the two WG nouns might belong together, but should be kept separate from the Gothic verb). Go. *aúrāli* (< *ōrārium*) cannot be an early loan, if we can accept that the second syllable in Gothic shows a long *ā*, re-created in Germanic at a later stage (after the change of *a* + nasal + χ to *ā* + χ).[47] For the rest, where there is no explicit phonological pointer to an early loan we have no reason to assume the adoption of a Latin word into Gothic before the third century.

To two Latin words in Gothic an even later borrowing, into Ostrogothic in Italy in the fifth or sixth century, can be attributed. *Kawtsjo*

[45] Jellinek (1926), 184f.; Schwarz (1951), 42; Corazza (1969), 77f.
[46] *Arka*: Jellinek (1926), 183, 185; Corazza (1969), 47f. *Drakma*: Jellinek (1926), 183, 209; Corazza (1969), 46. *Karkara*: Jellinek (1926), 185; Corazza (1969), 57 (with many qualifications).
[47] Jellinek (1926), 182f.

'bond, guarantee' (from Lat. *cautio*) occurs in the sixth-century deed of Naples and testifies to the VL assibilation of *t* (before semi-vowel *i*) to *ts*, recognised as a feature by grammarians in the fourth century and common practice by the fifth.[48] However, alongside this word we also have *laíktjo* '(section for) reading' in Codex B, placed repeatedly in the margin as a pointer to the lector.[49] We should expect assibilation here, too (cf. OHG *lekza*), but its absence may be due to no more than scribal conservatism. In any case, this word belongs to the manuscript transmission of Wulfila's text in Ostrogothic Italy.

The evidence of OHG covers a far wider range of cultural categories, so much so that we shall now defer the two most important ones (warfare and trade) until the next chapter.

The first category concerns Roman administration and law.[50] OHG *zol(n)* and OS *toln* 'tax, duty' are derived from Lat. *teloneum*, a word which, to judge by OFr. *tolneu*, presumably existed in Gallo-Roman as *toloneum*, from which the Gmc. forms were taken. A similar meaning is shown by OHG *zins* 'tax, tribute', taken over from Lat. *census*, although it is uncertain whether the OS form *tins* is a hypercorrect LG variation of OHG *zins* or (more probably?) a reflection of the Gallo-Roman pronunciation of *c* before *e* as a fricative *t'*.[51] MHG *phahte* 'rent, tribute' is not attested in OHG, but this word must have been borrowed from Lat. *pacta* (neuter collective plural of *pactum* 'legal agreement') early enough to undergo the Second Sound Shift. A specifically legal meaning is shown by OHG *kôsa* 'legal case' (as in *Muspilli* 40), coming from Lat. *causa* with a similar function, and by OHG *sihhura* 'legal excuse' (cf. OE *sicor* 'free from guilt or punishment'), based on Lat. *securus*.

Some terms may reflect Roman civil or military law and punishment (in the latter case they belong to the following chapter).[52] One example is OHG *carcar, charchâri* 'prison', borrowed early if we derive it from Lat. *carcer* (while *c* before *e* was still pronounced as a velar), but not if we postulate a VL variant *carcar*, as we saw with Go. *karkara*. Lat. *claustrum*, which later entered OHG as *klôster* in the Christian sense of a closed monastic community,[53] was also borrowed at an earlier stage. For this early loan we must postulate VL *clôstrum* 'lock, bolt', from which were

---

[48] Jellinek (1926), 199f.; Corazza (1969), 68.   [49] Jellinek (1926), 199f.; Corazza (1969), 69.
[50] *Teloneum*: Kluge and Seebold (1989), 816. *Census*: GR 2, 177. *Pacta*: GR 2, 239f. On *Caesar* cf. Kahl (1960), 162, fn. 20.   [51] GR 2, 177; Jud (1914), 6.
[52] *Carcer*: GR 2, 162ff. *Clôstrum*: GR 2, 188f.; Foerste (1967), 194f.; Ilkow (1968), 239f. *Catena*: GR 2, 170f.; Foerste (1967), 198f.   [53] See below, p. 339.

derived such NWG terms as OE *clūstor* and OS *klûstar* in the same sense (*ū* instead of *ō* points to closed pronunciation in Latin). To Roman penal practice belongs finally Lat. *catena* 'chain'. The need to borrow a term for a metal chain with which to tie up a prisoner is clear from linguistic evidence: Lat. *catena* can be glossed by OHG *stricki* 'rope, cord', OHG *kunawid* shows by its second element that the Germani fastened their prisoners with twisted cane or switch, whilst Wulfila had to add the word for 'iron' to express the novel idea of a metal bond.[54] The forms taken by the Latin word when borrowed into Gmc. suggest a double loan-process: LG forms with *-t-* point to VL **catīna* as their origin, whilst OHG *ketina* (where *-t-* results from the Second Sound Shift) points to a later Romance form *cadīna*, with intervocalic sonorisation.

A second category concerns the practice of building more permanently in stone, as opposed to the use of wood in Germania.[55] The Germani must have begun to imitate this method between the first and fourth centuries AD, if we accept the force of the distinction between Tacitus (*Germania* 16: they use neither stone nor tiles) and the reference by Ammianus Marcellinus to buildings constructed in the Roman manner.[56] Numerous loanwords testify to this adoption of Roman practice. Two words point to the use of stone or cement in laying the floor of a building: OHG *astrîh/estrîh* from Lat. *astracum/astricum*, and OHG *solâri* from *solarium*. *Chellâri* suggests a more ambitious kind of structure but, if it was used for the storage of wine, it also belongs under the heading of viticulture. A stone structure is also implied by the loan of Lat. *puteus* 'well, cistern', yielding OE *pytt* and OHG *puzzi/phuzzi*. The need for such a loan is clear, since the native Gmc. word, OHG *brunno*, denoted a naturally flowing spring, as distinct from the artificially constructed Roman *puteus*, equipped with shaft and well-house. How distinct these two sources of water were felt to be is brought out by Wulfila's use of *brunna* to refer to a woman's issue of blood (Mc. 5.29) and by the relative strangeness of the loanword in OHG in Otfrid's time, forcing him to employ both *brunno* and *puzzi* to make himself clear (II 14,8).

Even smaller details of the Romans' building methods called for the adoption of their technical terms.[57] Building with stone brought with it the use of lime or limestone, so that Lat. *calx/calcem* yielded OHG

---

[54] Helm (1909), 312ff.; Sieg (1960), 365ff.

[55] *Astracum: GR* 2, 101ff.; Frings (1928), 423ff. *Solarium: GR* 2, 463ff.; Frings (1928), 423ff. *Cellarium:* Alanne (1950), 76. *Puteus: GR* 2, 431ff.; Frings (1928), 437; Beck (1981b), 1ff.

[56] *Rerum gestarum libri XXXI* 15, 11, 1; Much (1967), 253f. Much later Bede still refers to stone buildings as constructed 'in the Roman manner': Campbell (1991), 75; Richter (1994), 104.

[57] *Calx: GR* 2, 141ff. *Murus:* Kluge and Seebold (1989), 467. *Tegula: GR* 2, 481f. *Regula: GR* 2, 441f.

calc/chalc/calh, a relatively early loan, since it presupposes that *c* before *e* was still pronounced as a velar. OHG *mûra* 'wall' derives from VL *mura*, and presupposes a method of construction different from that with wattle and daub implied by OHG *want* (cf. *wintan* 'to twist, plait'). With the Roman technique of roof construction came the word for 'tile', based on Latin forms with a short or long stem vowel: OHG *ziagal* with its diphthong thus goes back to *tēgula*, whilst OE *tigele* presupposes a short *e*. Lat. *regula* 'straight-edge' also developed the meaning 'a straight bar' and in northern France yielded a term denoting a 'bar for closing a door'. Like *tegula* it was adopted with both a short and a long stem vowel: from the former OHG *rigil* 'bolt' was derived, with the same restricted meaning as in northern France.

Our third category covers such closely related fields as horticulture, agriculture and viticulture.[58] To the first two belong such loanwords as OHG *kôl* 'cabbage' from Lat. *caulis* and *râtih* 'radish' from Lat. *rādix/rādicem* 'root', *phlanza* 'plant' from Lat. *planta*, *phersich* 'peach' (attested only in MHG) from *persicum (malum)*, literally 'Persian apple', and *phrûma/phlûma* 'plum' from Lat. *prūnum*.

Especially well attested is the terminology of viticulture, reflecting the Romans' introduction of wine-growing into Alsace in the first century and into the Rhenish Palatinate and the Mosel valley from about the second century.[59] It also reflects the predilection of the Germani for the Romans' wine, attested already by Caesar (*De bello Gallico* II 15, IV 2) and then by Tacitus (*Germania* 23). With this vocabulary we have to distinguish 'itinerant' terms such as 'wine' and 'vinegar' (products which could have been transported anywhere by traders) from 'static' terms such as 'to pick grapes' or 'winepress' which remained tied to the regions where viticulture was practised. Only these latter concern us at present.[60] The first example is the verb for 'to pick', MHG *phlücken* (not attested in OHG) and OE *pluccian*, derived from VL **piluccare*, reconstructed from Romance forms such as OFr. *peluchier* 'to pick', It. *piluccare* 'to pluck berries or grapes'. The Latin form originally denoted the act of plucking the hair (*pilus*) or feathers of a bird, then picking grapes from the vine, whilst the Gmc. derivatives, centred on NWG and unknown at first in south Germany, appear to have entered Germany in the Trier

---

[58] *Caulis*: Kluge and Seebold (1989), 388. *Rādix*: ibid., p. 597. *Planta*: ibid., p. 540. *Persicum*: GR 2, 381ff. *Prūnum*: GR 2, 416ff. Cf. also *furca*: GR 2, 258ff., *horreum*: GR 2, 464, fn. 1, *paganus*: GR 2, 351f.

[59] Alanne (1950), 20.

[60] **Piluccare*: GR 2, 387f.; Brüch (1938), 331ff.; Alanne (1950), 51. *Mustum*: Alanne (1950), 77. *Calcatura/calcatorium*: GR 2, 136ff.; Alanne (1950), 45f. *Traiectorium*: GR 2, 487f.; Alanne (1950), 48f.

region, where viticulture was early practised. Lat. *(vinum) mustum* 'a young wine' lies behind OHG *most* and OE *must* 'a new wine, not fully fermented', while the word for the winepress, *calcatura/calcatorium* (from *calcare* 'to tread') yielded OHG forms such as *calcture*, *calter* and *kelter*. The Latin word for the 'funnel' used in wine-making, *traiectorium*, produced OHG *trachter*, *trechtere* and in late OHG a form with *-i-*, *trihtaere*.

Contact with Roman civilisation revolutionised eating habits in Germania not merely by the introduction of southern fruits, novel vegetables and an immediately popular drink, but also by Roman culinary practice itself.[61] The words for the 'cook', 'to cook' and 'kitchen' are thus of Latin origin. OHG *koch/choh* was taken over before the Sound Shift from VL *cocus* with a short *o* (from Classical Latin *coquus*), whilst the long vowel of OE *cōc* points to a later loan, after lengthening of *-o-* in an open syllable. The verb *kochôn/chohhôn* could be a native OHG formation from the noun or a direct borrowing from Lat. *coquere*, although one should normally expect it to go back to a Lat. **coquare*. For the kitchen Latin used *coquina*, but also a VL form *cocina* which yields WG forms such as OE *cycene* and OHG *chuhhina*, the latter form, like its related terms, borrowed before the Sound Shift. Other loanwords connected with the culinary sphere include OHG *phistur* 'baker' from Lat. *pistor*, *simula* 'fine wheat flour' from *simila* (the meaning of the modern German *Semmel* is attested only in MHG), *oli* 'oil' from *oleum* (Go. *alēw* was borrowed quite independently)[62] and *kâsi/châsi* 'cheese' from *caseus* (a solid rennet cheese as distinct from the native liquid type made from sour milk).

Our further task with this Latin loanword material in OHG is to locate its entry in time and space. Dating these Latin words (a first instalment before the massive penetration of Latin vocabulary which later accompanied the Christianisation of Germany) can be approached in two ways: from the Germanic evidence and then from the Latin.

On the Germanic side the essential criterion is whether the results of the Second Sound Shift are present, as in *phlanza* < *planta* or *ziagal* < *tegula*. If a Latin loanword (in a dialect affected by the Shift) shows traces of this Shift, we may reasonably assume that it was borrowed before the sixth century. This uncomfortably long timespan is not relieved by taking into account the operation of the *Auslautgesetze*.[63] Whereas it was possible to date these changes in Gothic within the first three centuries AD because of Wulfila's fourth-century text, the position is uncertain in

---

[61] *Coquus*: Kluge and Seebold (1989), 387. *Coquere*: ibid. *Coquina*: ibid., p. 416. *Pistor*: GR 2, 395ff. *Simila*: GR 2, 461ff. *Oleum*: GR 2, 346ff. *Caseus*: Toth (1995), 565.　　　[62] Untermann (1954), 390ff.
[63] Kluge (1913), 27ff., 132f.

OHG because of its much later written tradition. Although it is conceivable, even likely, that the *Auslautsgesetze* began to operate in WG at about the same time as in Gothic, they cannot be used reliably to date Latin loanwords in OHG as they could in some cases in Gothic.

However, if some of these words entered OHG before the sixth century there are also grounds for assuming that many were adopted considerably earlier than this. A first indication is provided by Latin loanwords common to OHG and to Gothic, especially those which reached Gothic in the first two centuries AD. These constitute trading terms (*káupōn, asilus, katilus, pund, saban, sakkus, wein, akeit* and *lukarn*).[64] Apart from the last example all these loanwords are also found in OHG. Roman trade routes to Germania started in Gaul, passing across the Rhine or along the North Sea coastline to the Germanic interior, so that the tribes nearest the Rhine frontier were the first to receive trading goods and loanwords which eventually reached the Goths before their trek began towards the end of the second century. The loanwords which reached the Goths so early were also known in Germany by this time so that the OHG counterparts of the Gothic examples just listed belong to the earliest Latin loanwords in German.

For the rest we are dependent on the Latin evidence. As regards vowels the most important criterion is whether the Latin loanword betrays the quality and quantity of Classical Latin as opposed to VL. An example of vowel quantity (a short vowel in an open syllable in Classical Latin is lengthened in VL from the second century)[65] is provided by OHG *esil* 'donkey' from Lat. *ăsinus*, which confirms the last paragraph. Where the OHG word shows a long vowel in such a case, this points to a later borrowing from VL, as with OHG *krûzi* 'cross' as distinct from Classical Latin *crux/crucem* with a short *u* (the Christian nature of this word is another indication of a late loan).

The evidence of Latin consonants covers a wider chronological span. The change of Lat. *v* from a semi-vowel to a fricative, attested as early as the first century AD, suggests that OHG *wal* in *erdewal* 'earthwork' was an early loan from Lat. *vallum*, like *wîn* from *vinum* (which confirms the parallel with Go. *wein* as an early trading term). Where Lat. *v* is represented in OHG by *v* (or by *f* in final position) we may assume a later loan, as in OHG *briaf* 'letter, document' from *brevis* (where the OHG diphthong arises from a long *e*, which in turn presupposes VL lengthening of

---

[64] See above, pp. 204f. On *káupōn* see below, pp. 224ff.
[65] Wollmann (1990c), 523, fn. 49, based on Straka (1956), 249ff.

a short *e* in an open syllable). If the assibilation of Lat. -*ti*- to -*ts*- is attested from the second century on, then a loan such as Lat. *puteus* to OE *pytt*, LFr. *putte* and OHG *puzzi* (where -*zz*- presupposes -*ti*-) must have taken place before this (by contrast with Ostrogothic *kawtsjo*). The VL palatalisation of *c* before *e* or *i* from the fourth century likewise suggests an earlier loan of such words as *kellâri*/*chellâri* from *cellarium*, *kista* 'chest, box' from *cista*, and *wicka* 'vetch, sweet pea' from *vicia*, by contrast with later loans such as *krûzi* from *crux*/*crucem*. Finally, a deadline in the fifth century (from which point most western Romance languages show inter-vocalic sonorisation of -*t*- to -*d*-)[66] is suggested by OS *strâta* and OHG *strâz(z)a*, both of which derive from *strāta (via)* 'paved way', as distinct from the form underlying It. *strada*.

In locating the loanword traffic into Germania we have to bear in mind that in the fourth century the imperial capital was in fact Trier rather than Rome, that the main lines of communication to Germania ran eastwards from Gaul and that the Rhineland was even more heavily Romanised than Gaul. The middle and lower Rhine are therefore the principal areas of linguistic contact, so that on the basis of modern dialect geography it has been shown that many loanwords entered Germania in this region, without leaving any trace in southern Germany.[67] Likewise, a loanword such as *Saturni dies* ('Saturday', *Zaterdag*), confined to NWG (England, Holland, Westfalia), indicates lin-guistic contact in the lower Rhine area before the Anglo-Saxons left the continent.[68] This geographical focus also accounts for Latin loanwords which are attested only in OE (e.g. *cleofa* 'cell, cubicle' from *clibanus* 'oven') or in OE and Dutch (as with feminine *nomina agentis* in -*ster*, where a loanword such as OE *miltestre* 'prostitute' from Lat. *meretrix* throws light on the nature of Roman camp life in the lower Rhine area).[69] By con-trast with this linguistic concentration on the lower and middle Rhine the number of early loanwords restricted to UG is sparse indeed (they include OHG *phistur*, *segina* and *nâwe*). This disparity indicates a very weak accession of loanwords from the south (over the Alps) by contrast with Gaul as the main reservoir.

Different criteria underline the importance of Gaul as the direct source of most Latin loanwords in German in this period. They include a phonology peculiar to northern Gaul, the presence of a Latin word at home in this region in particular, a semantic development characteristic

---

[66] Straka (1951), 268f.; Bonioli (1962), 88; Wollmann (1990a), 437ff.; (1990c), 521.
[67] E.g. Du. *polder* from *pullarium* 'chicken coop' (*GR* 2, 425f.). Cf. Kluge (1913), 21.
[68] See below, p. 252.   [69] *Clibanus*: *GR* 2, 190. *Meretrix*: *GR* 1, 81; 2, 288f.

of Gallo-Roman, and also Latin words which, attested in Insular Celtic as well as Gmc., suggest a radiation centre in northern Gaul.[70] For a variety of reasons, therefore, Gaul emerges as the great reservoir out of which most Latin loanwords found their way into Germania. This conclusion is the counterpart to what has been claimed for the converse linguistic process: that Gaul was also the principal entry for Gmc. loanwords into Latin before 400.[71]

Why this should have been so is due to reasons which go beyond the fact that the danger constituted by the Germani drew the Empire's attention more to the north, so that Trier could outflank Rome as a political centre. To safeguard their position on the lower and middle Rhine the Romans developed the hinterland of northern Gaul economically, commercially and administratively, ensuring a prolonged boost for this region (including the Rhineland) which went far beyond what was to be found in south Germany along the Danubian frontier.[72] It is this switch of military, economic and political attention to the Rhine frontier and to the lines of communication and supply which ran to it through Gaul which explains why most of these Latin loanwords entered Germania across the Rhine.

Latin loanwords in OE can be dealt with more briefly, since the cultural categories into which they fall largely agree with OHG. We may therefore concentrate on the question: when and where can this influence on OE be placed?

Two chronological layers in this loanword traffic have often been distinguished: an older and a more recent period or a continental and an insular one.[73] Underlying this distinction is the fact that a considerable proportion of Latin loanwords in OE can be shown (on the basis of sound changes effected before their occupation of England)[74] to be early borrowings, brought by the Anglo-Saxons from the continent. By contrast, other loanwords are held to have been acquired only in Britain, taken over either from the native Celtic population, Romanised in part after four centuries of Roman occupation, or as specifically Christian terms. If we ignore this last possibility, this leaves us with two periods for these two layers: before about 450 (when the Anglo-Saxons began to settle in Britain in force) and between this date and about 600 (when their Christianisation from Rome began). In their turn, each of these

---

[70] Jud (1914), 38ff.   [71] Brüch (1913), 118.   [72] Aubin (1929), 11f.; *GR* I, 104f.; Kuhn (1951a), 57ff.
[73] Pogatscher (1888), 4f.; Wollmann (1993), 3; Toth (1995), 564f.
[74] On the dating of Latin loanwords in OE see Pogatscher (1888), *passim*; Campbell (1959), 199ff.

two periods of Latin influence has been divided into two: the continental period into an earlier stage when the Anglo-Saxons were still in Schleswig-Holstein and on the North Sea coastline as far as the mouth of the Ems and a later stage when they had penetrated along the continental coast as far as the *litus Saxonicum* (Flanders and Normandy).[75] The insular period has likewise been seen in two stages, represented by loanwords from the native Celts and then from the continental Franks as part of their influence across the Channel, especially on Kent.[76]

While the Anglo-Saxons were still in Schleswig-Holstein there was little possibility of direct contact with the Romans who, although their fleets occasionally sailed inland up the Ems, Weser and Elbe, had to abandon their plan to advance the imperial frontier as far as the Elbe.[77] An exception to this was Roman trade (its products have been found in Schleswig-Holstein, Denmark and Sweden) and here, too, we may assume that new trading goods were accompanied by the terms for them.[78] The loanwords which reached the Anglo-Saxons in their earliest homeland cannot have been very many, but neither was the number very great which, by an extension of this northern trade-route, also reached the Goths in the same period. More important than this, however, is the fact that (with the exception of Lat. *lucerna*) all the Latin loanwords attested for Gothic at this early stage, and also for OHG, are likewise to be found in OE, often with phonological indications that they are early loans. They are essentially trading terms (denoting Roman wares, containers, the beast of burden used by the merchant). If such terms, like the trade-routes themselves, crossed the lower Rhine and penetrated as far as the Goths they would also have reached the Anglo-Saxons.

There was a limit, however, to the type of word which could penetrate so far, as we see with other OE examples for which a continental origin has been suggested.[79] Words which, like their OHG counterparts, refer to Roman methods of building houses or streets and to aspects of their agriculture presuppose something quite different.[80] Whereas a word like 'wine' could be taken by merchants far into the Germanic interior, static details of Roman life like 'street' or 'tile' had to await the arrival of the Anglo-Saxons in the area where they could be seen *in situ*; they presuppose penetration into former imperial territory in the area of the

[75] Hoops (1905), 566ff.   [76] Wollmann (1993), 3f.; Toth (1995), 565.
[77] Hoops (1905), 567f.; Timpe (1989), 351ff.
[78] Hoops (1905), 569; Gneuss (1992), 116; Wollmann (1990b), 376; Toth (1995), 564. On Roman trade-routes to Germania see below, pp. 226f.   [79] Hoops (1905), 569.   [80] *Ibid.*, pp. 571ff.

Rhine estuary and westwards. On this migration of the Saxons along the North Sea coastline and their provisional settlement on the Channel coast of Gaul before crossing to southern Britain we are reasonably well informed.[81] They began as raids at the end of the third century, making Roman countermeasures necessary, the defences of the *litus Saxonicum* on the continent (as well as in Britain). This last continental staging-post for the Saxons on their migration from north Germany to Britain represented their first opportunity, on what had been Roman soil, to become acquainted with details of Roman life which could not have reached them by trading contacts over a long distance.[82] The fact that the Anglo-Saxons, moving westwards along the continental coastline, reached imperial territory around the mouth of the Rhine accounts for a stock of Latin loanwords common to England as well as to Germany (e.g. *tigele* and *ziagal*, *pytt* and *phuzzi*, *strēt* and *strâz(z)a*). This focus of loanword traffic in OE and OHG on the region of the lower Rhine has been placed in a wider context by Frings, who has established a common sphere of Latin influence which embraced not merely the lower Rhine area as far as Trier and Cologne, but also Holland, Gaul and Britain.[83] In this area, particularly between the mouth of the Rhine and northern Gaul, OE acquired most of its early Latin loanwords which fell outside the trading context of those which had been transmitted even earlier by merchants.

This last point casts a doubt on the first stage of the insular phase of Latin loanword traffic (from Britons to Anglo-Saxons): on the extent of this influence and on our ability to identify it.[84] We do not know to what extent and for how long Latin continued to be spoken by Romanised Britons after the departure of the Romans, and if some words were provided by the early British Church (e.g. *lǣden* < *Latinus*) this raises the question whether we can postulate any connection at all between this Church and the pagan barbarian invaders. Even such a word as OE *ceaster* 'town' < *castra*, frequently cited as an insular loan, is questionable because there is no attested Celtic counterpart and also because of parallels from the lower Rhine and Holland suggesting that a continental loan is more likely.[85] At this point the far-reaching sphere of Latin influence established by Frings creates the greatest difficulty for judging this first stage of insular loanwords. If it included both Britain on the one hand and Gaul and the lower Rhine on the other, this makes it uncertain how we

---

[81] *Ibid.*, pp. 578ff.; Wollmann (1990b), 377; Campbell (1991), 31, 37.
[82] Hoops (1905), 586.
[83] *GR* 1 and 2, *passim*; Wollmann (1990b), 390; Gneuss (1992), 117f.
[84] Wollmann (1990b), 392.
[85] *Ibid.*, pp. 382, 383, fn. 29; *GR* 2, 167ff.

are to isolate an insular loan as distinct from a continental one.[86] The difficulty of identifying such insular loans from the Britons to the Anglo-Saxons also exists at the other end of the timespan (around 600). Two ecclesiastical terms, OE *cirice* 'church' and *bisceop* 'bishop', also sometimes attributed to British mediation, may instead have been taken over towards 600 in the context of the first Christianisation of Kent from Francia.[87]

The second stage of the insular phase, the transmission of words of Latin origin by the Franks across the Channel, presupposes continuous contact between the Anglo-Saxons and the continent after the conquest of Britain, for which there is a range of pointers: e.g. Childebert I had power in *Brittania transmarina* and for obvious geographical reasons Kent was closely involved with the Franks in northern Gaul.[88] Linguistically, this is confirmed by continental place-names in OE forms which presuppose late phonological changes in VL, such as *Profentse* 'Provence' or *Sīgen* 'Seine'.[89] If in this Frankish context words such as *cirice* and *bisceop* were introduced into OE on the very threshold of Christianisation, this provides a bridge between the secular Latin influence of this chapter and the role of Church Latin which will preoccupy us in Part III.

---

[86] Pogatscher (1888), 4f.; Wollmann (1990b), 395; Gneuss (1992), 114.

[87] Pogatscher, (1888), 11f.; Wollmann (1990b), 392; cf. Gneuss (1992), 114f. See also below, pp. 300f., 304f.   [88] Campbell (1991), 38, 64; Wood (1994a), 235ff.

[89] Wollmann (1990b), 389, fn. 42, and 395.

CHAPTER 12

Trade and warfare with the Romans

Caesar makes it clear that for the Romans trade and warfare supported one another when he sent a legion to safeguard a route across the Alps which Roman traders travelled only at great risk and cost in tolls exacted.[1] Similarly, the Goths are unlikely to have begun their trek south-eastwards without advance reconnoitring, basing their military expansion along the course of an established trade-route on what they had learned from traders.[2] Moreover, the Goths' migration was not merely accomplished by force of arms, it was also accompanied by trading activity, as with their establishment of trading centres in Finland and Estonia or later with Ermanaric's domination of the trade-routes from southern Russia to the north.[3] Factors such as these justify the treatment of these two categories in the same chapter.

Since trade rests on an exchange of goods between two parties we may start by considering what the Romans and the Germani had to offer each other commercially. Caesar comments that the Germani allowed merchants into their territory more because they wanted to sell them their war-booty than to buy from them, but by the time of Tacitus the position was different: whilst the tribes in the interior still practised barter those near the imperial frontier made use of Roman coins in order to buy wine.[4] The use of Roman coins points to the first transition from a coinless barter society to a monetary one under Roman influence.

That Roman trade went far beyond the wine explicitly mentioned by Tacitus is clear from other evidence. He himself refers to silver vessels as gifts to Germanic chieftains and we should not underestimate the rôle of gift-giving in primitive societies and the Romans' ability to adapt it to

---

[1] *De bello Gallico* III 1. Cf. in more general terms Timpe (1989), 309.
[2] Wagner (1967), 225f.
[3] See above, pp. 174 and 175f. The Vikings, too, can be seen as traders and raiders, cf. James (1992), 99, 104; Roesdahl (1992), 109.   [4] Caesar, *De bello Gallico* IV 2; Tacitus, *Germania* 5.

their own political ends.[5] Archaeological pointers include coins, silver vessels and wine sets of Roman origin used in imitation in Germania,[6] but also vessels in bronze, glass and terra sigillata, brooches and ornaments, even weapons and statuettes.[7] Such objects are attested far into the interior, through Germany to Scandinavia, Pomerania and northern Poland. This archaeological evidence shows that the Roman example must have drastically heightened the demand for luxuries on the part of Germanic chieftains from whose graves these finds have been largely recovered.[8] They could afford to distinguish themselves from their followers by acquiring Roman imports, just as they also set themselves apart by the use of helmet and sword.[9] To a large extent the acquisition of Roman goods served as the status symbol of an élite, they could be used as gifts to strengthen ties between kindreds, as objects for further exchange with more distant tribes, or simply to provide raw material.[10]

On the other side of this trading relationship the range of what the Germani could offer in exchange was very restricted. Three of these goods we have come across in connection with Gmc. loanwords in Latin. Amber, *glēsum/glaesum* in Latin, was fashionable amongst the Romans in the early imperial period, much of it derived from Samland on the Baltic coast. The main Roman emporium for receiving and fashioning this amber from the north for the Roman market was Aquileia.[11] Two other Gmc. exports to Rome are summed up in the loanwords *ganta* and *sapo*, 'goose' and 'hair-dye', both equally prized in the Italian luxury market.[12] The evidence for the second of these Latin terms suggested imports from the lower Rhine area. Items other than these three were also available for trade or exchange across the frontier. Ox-hides were paid as a tribute by the Frisians (*Annales* IV 72) and it can be assumed that cattle was also used to pay for Roman goods.[13] More important and widespread than either of these was the trade in slaves, the more so since Germanic society itself knew the practice of owning and selling slaves (Tacitus, *Germania* 24).[14] It has been suggested that the vast increase in Roman goods which found their way into Germania by the time of Tacitus was met by a greater frequency of warfare in barbarian society (here again trade and warfare belong closely together). These wars could

---

[5] Cf. Heather (1991), 114, 164.   [6] Eggers (1951), 73f.
[7] Brogan (1936), 207ff.; Eggers (1951), 74.   [8] Thompson (1965), 20.
[9] *Ibid.*, p. 28. See also above, p. 71.   [10] Lund Hansen (1987), 194, 196, 249.
[11] Pliny, *Naturalis historia* 37, 45; Brogan (1936), 220; Eggers (1951), 74; Much (1967), 515.
[12] See above, pp. 186, 188.   [13] Brogan (1936), 221.
[14] *Ibid.*, p. 219; Eggers (1951), 74; Thompson (1966), 40f.; Much (1967), 324.

have taken the form of cattle-raids or slave-raids to provide the means of obtaining Roman goods, but in any case they led to the militarisation of Germanic society and the growth of the war-band. Seen in this light, the arrival of the Romans on the borders of Germania with attractive goods to offer for sale may have had results in Germanic society similar to the slave-trading which increased in West Africa after the arrival of Europeans with their own goods to offer.[15]

Comparing Roman goods exported to Germania with those which the barbarians sold to the Romans brings out a discrepancy between the level of craftsmanship and industrial organisation present in the Roman wares and the fact that the Germani had little to offer other than raw materials with a scarcity value in the Mediterranean world.[16] Given this imbalance between the two trading parties we may ask how the Germani managed to pay for their imports from the Roman world.

In the first place, war-booty may have constituted an acceptable means of exchange, as with Caesar's comment on the Suebi that they admitted traders to their territory more for the hope of selling their booty to them than for any need of imports.[17] Of the Germanic warriors who served as mercenaries in the Roman ranks many returned to Germania after their term of service was concluded – the pay they had received from Rome (cf. Go. *anno* < Lat. *annona*) was available for purchase and must to some extent account for the spread of Roman coins throughout Germania brought to light by archaeology.[18] We know, too, that the Romans, operating on the divide-and-rule principle, were ready to 'buy off' a tribe by paying a form of bribe or protection-money (suitably disguised as a tribute) to the chieftain.[19] The wealth of some chieftains of central Germania, as shown in their richly equipped graves, may well originate in Roman support of this kind.[20] None of this is meant to diminish the rôle played by slave-trade, the evidence for which in classical sources suggests that its main purpose in Germania was to round up victims in the hinterland for sale to the imperial power on the frontier, so much so that slaves may well have been the principal export from the barbarian world to Rome.[21] Finally, we should not dismiss the importance of what even the Romans would have recognised as genuine trade, although under Roman influence.[22] Tacitus (*Germania* 5) admits this in the case of those tribes nearest the imperial frontier (they value precious

[15] Thompson (1965), 24f.   [16] Aubin (1925), 33.   [17] See above, fn. 4.   [18] Eggers (1951), 73.
[19] *Ibid.*; Lund Hansen (1987), 168, 171.
[20] Wagner (1975), 179ff., discusses the same policy with regard to Roman (Byzantine) payments to the Huns.   [21] Thompson (1965), 16.   [22] Eggers (1951), 72f.

metals for their use in trade and prefer certain types of Roman coins), but distinguishes them from those in the interior who still traditionally rely on barter. This distinction need not exclude trade further inland, however, for Tacitus (*Annales* II 62) also refers to Roman traders and provisioners amongst the followers of Maroboduus, attracted to Bohemia by a trade agreement.

This last example demonstrates that trade between Romans and Germani was not confined to the frontier area, but that Roman traders could also penetrate to the hinterland of Germania. Where weight and quantity of goods to be transported were concerned the Romans relied on water transport rather than overland journeys,[23] which meant that their trading bases for Germania were difficult of access over the Alps to the Danube, but easier to the Rhine through the waterways of Gaul. Supplies and goods also came by sea round the Atlantic coast of Gaul to the lower Rhine, from where in the first century AD Roman fleets explored along the North Sea coast, opening up the hinterland of Germania from this direction.[24] Along this maritime route Roman provincial trade ventured inland by river, up the Ems, Weser and Elbe, establishing supply depots at the mouths of these rivers, also attaining the Jutland peninsula and even reaching as far as the eastern extremities of the Baltic. It remains unclear how far Roman traders themselves penetrated up these various rivers or whether this was done by native traders, but by either way Roman goods were conveyed far into the Germanic interior.[25]

Even by the more difficult overland route a wide expanse of Germania beyond the Rhine frontier was opened up for a time at least by the Roman army.[26] The campaigns of Drusus (12–9 BC) brought the Roman army as far as the rivers Elbe and Saale, and Tiberius likewise halted at the Elbe in the face of an army of Suebi on the other bank. These advance forces of the Roman army of the Rhine needed to be supplied and semi-permanent bases had to be set up which could also be supplied locally, so that a flow of Roman coins and goods followed in their wake. This was true of Roman influence, primarily commercial but based on military success, from another direction, for the Romans' occupation of the bend in the Danube by Carnuntum in the age of Augustus provided a firm base for the trade-route running northwards from the Danube through Moravia to the Oder and Vistula and along their courses to the Baltic.[27]

[23] Aubin (1925), 12, 16, 18f., 22.   [24] *Ibid.*, pp. 12, 30; Timpe (1989), 358, 368ff.
[25] Aubin (1925), 30.   [26] Timpe (1989), 357f., 359.   [27] *Ibid*, pp. 372ff.

This combination of military operations and trading ventures, each assisting the other, opened up the Germanic world for the Romans far more drastically than had hitherto been possible from local contacts on the imperial frontier, where only a vague idea of what lay beyond was possible. The information now made available about various tribes settled far to the north and remote from the frontier is echoed at various points in the *Germania* of Tacitus whose informants (of different types) may have included merchants or others who had penetrated to scattered parts of Germania.[28] By different routes and with different aims in mind the Romans therefore made increasing contacts with the Germanic world far beyond the imperial frontier. These contacts included trade, so that Roman influence was far from being restricted to the regions immediately adjoining the Rhine and the Danube.

To talk of trade in Roman goods does not necessarily mean that all the traders were Romans. We cannot ignore the possibility of Celtic traders including Roman goods in their commercial relations with the Germani.[29] Caesar knew of professional traders amongst the Gauls who had often had dealings with the Germani (and could therefore supply Caesar with information about them). Their trade with the Germani conveyed Italian as well as Celtic products from the first century BC and they also introduced them to minted money. As an example of a trade term of Latin origin which reached the Goths probably through Celtic trade the word *alēw* 'oil' has been suggested.[30] If this oil was also used to light lamps it might be possible to associate this word with Lat. *lucerna* 'lamp' as another trade word transmitted along the same route, especially in view of its presence as a loanword in Celtic and, within Germanic, in Gothic alone.[31]

Roman traders themselves are well attested. Roman trade over long distances was highly organised, with merchants operating overland (with oxen, asses and mules), by sea (*navicularii*) and by river (*nautae*), and with specialists for the transport of wine (*utricularii*).[32] Caesar may not specify who the traders are when saying that the Suebi admit merchants in order to sell their booty to them or that many merchants frequent the land of the Ubii.[33] However, Tacitus is more explicit: instead of simply saying *mercatores* he refers to traders and provisioners 'from our provinces' to be found in Bohemia or explicitly to Roman traders.[34] How

---

[28] Timpe (1992), 463, 465, 467, 473f.
[29] Schröder (1918), 246f.; Eggers (1951), 75 (Caesar, *De bello Gallico* I 39); Thompson (1965), 20.
[30] Untermann (1954), 390ff. [31] See above, p. 204. [32] Lund Hansen (1987), 216.
[33] *De bello Gallico* IV 2 and 3. [34] *Annales* II 62; *Historiae* IV 15.

far this long-distance trade could take the Roman merchant we have seen in the case of the Roman knight on the Baltic coast, but in other cases over such distances depots were built up where goods were unloaded and taken further by others.[35]

This use of others by Roman traders could also include Germani themselves, as interpreters and guides through unknown territories or in more general terms.[36] Further, there were native traders active in Germania who quickly saw the advantage of working in conjunction with their Roman counterparts.[37] To these may have belonged those who gathered amber for sale to the Romans in Pannonia, but also the Hermunduri who traded with the Romans in Raetia.[38] If the Roman traders along the northern coasts set up trading depots at the mouth of a river, it is likely that these served as centres where goods could be reloaded from water to land transport, the latter in the hands of Germanic traders through what was potentially dangerous territory for Romans.[39]

Two loanwords from Latin may throw light on how the Germani could have regarded this trade and on what a primitive level it operated at first. The first is a word attested in such forms as OE *mangian* 'to trade', *mangere* 'trader, dealer' (cf. 'ironmonger'), OS *mangon* 'to trade' and OHG *mangâri* with the same meaning as its OE counterpart.[40] Amongst the Latin terms which the OHG word glosses is to be found Lat. *mango*, but this denoted not simply a 'deceitful huckster', but more specifically a 'slave-trader'. For the Germani Roman trade must have been largely synonymous with this particular form of trade. Traces of the Latin forms are found in Spain and southern France, but also in old dialectal forms in French, stretching from Lille and Liège down to the Vosges.[41] From this area which was formerly north-eastern Gaul the Gmc. forms in OE, OS and OHG could have been taken across the language boundary together with the trade they denoted.

With the second example we move on the same level of unambitious trade, but the word in question succeeded in finding a much firmer niche for itself in Gmc. vocabulary. Lat. *caupo* had a general meaning 'huckster, haggler', but also the more specialised sense of 'publican, wineseller'.[42] This latter meaning gives a good indication of what importance the Germani attached to the Roman wine-trade, equating it with trade

[35] Lund Hansen (1987), 216; Heather (1996), 46 (map).   [36] Timpe (1989), 358.
[37] Eggers (1951), 75; Kunow (1980), 10.   [38] Pliny, *Naturalis historia* 37, 3; Tacitus, *Germania* 41.
[39] Kunow (1980), 17.   [40] *GR* 2, 314ff.   [41] Brüch (1952), 96.
[42] Alanne (1950), 19, 42f. Cf. also Aubin (1925), 31.

at large, since the Latin word, taken across into Gmc., is attested with the meaning 'trader', as in OHG *choufo/koufo* (from north-west Germany came ON *kaupi*) and OE (West Saxon) *cēpa/cȳpa*.[43] As long as it was held that these vernacular forms were of native Germanic origin, it was argued that their derivation from Latin was unlikely in view of the fact that the words for 'trader' in the Romance languages involved in loan-word traffic to western Germania were based on *mercans/mercantem* (cf. It. *mercante*) or on **mercātans/mercātantem* (cf. Fr. *marchand*).[44] Little force is now attached to this objection, since many Latin words crossed into Germania (or into Celtic) early enough to find a permanent home there before they were replaced in their Romance homeland by newer terms.[45] Although Lat. *mango* still survives in Spain and southern France, it would be difficult to argue its presence in north-eastern France, where influence on Germania could be entertained, were it not for isolated medieval dialectal traces. Even more telling is the Latin trade word *pondo* 'pound', present in Germanic and Celtic, but subsequently replaced in Romance by *libra*.[46] For *caupo* there is equally no reason to doubt transmission from Gaul to Germania before its replacement by a later term which survives in French.

The Gmc. noun for the trader which arose in this way could also have a suffix added to make its function as a *nomen agentis* quite clear: OHG *koufman*, OE *cēapmon* (cf. 'chapman') and also ON *kaupmaðr*.[47] It also provided the base for the OHG verb *chouffōn*, used without an object to mean 'to do trade', but with an object meaning 'to acquire by trading, to buy' (cf. also OE *cēapian*, OS *kôpon*, ON *kaupa*). The formation of these Gmc. verbs on the basis of what was now a native noun is much more likely than a derivation from the Latin verb *cauponari*, if only because this verb was at home in southern Italy, the western part of North Africa and Spain, but not apparently in Gaul.[48] The last step in the lexical spread of this word is the rise of the noun, as in OHG *chouf* 'trade', but also 'purchase', by back-formation from the verb. The origin of this lexical group lies therefore in Lat. *caupo*, taken over in the earliest period of contacts between Romans and Germani on the lower or middle Rhine frontier, early enough for trading contacts to take the verb as far as the Goths in northern Poland (*káupōn*), since it is quite unlikely that the Goths would have hit upon the same Latin word for this purpose on reaching the Danubian frontier. It is doubtful, however, whether we can be precise

---

[43] *GR* 2, 175f.   [44] Cf. Brüch (1952), 94f.   [45] Jud (1914), 29ff.   [46] *Ibid.*, p. 29; *FEW* 5, 306ff.
[47] Brüch (1952), 98ff.   [48] *Ibid.*, pp. 100f.

enough to say that the word was transmitted to the Goths by the Suebi or Marcomanni, however much they may have been involved in trade.[49] We must remain content with saying that the trade-routes which carried Roman goods and loanwords from the Rhine as far as the southern coast of the Baltic could also have conveyed the verb which summed up this trading activity.

This has brought us back to the question of the routes followed by Roman trade. Fundamental to the importance of a trade-route was the difference between transporting goods overland or by water.[50] Wherever possible, the latter was preferable, since large tracts of Germania were covered by woods and swamps, with no network of road-communications as in the Empire, and therefore difficult for passage by animal-drawn carts. Transport of goods was therefore cheaper by sea or river than by land, so that priority would be given to long-distance trade which could make use of this natural advantage. Water transport had the further advantage that it could convey larger loads, heavier material, but also more fragile goods such as glass or ceramics in greater safety.

If we ignore frontier trade (classical sources make it clear that Roman markets were available for Germani at certain points, albeit subject to tax and customs control),[51] four major trade-routes were used from the imperial frontier into the Germanic interior.[52] Two were noticeably less important than the others: from *Vetera* (modern Xanten), running up the course of the Lippe along a military road protected by *castella* as far as the middle Weser, and from *Moguntiacum* (Mainz) through the Wetterau to Thuringia and central Germany.

From *Carnuntum* (on the Danube, east of Vienna) there ran a route which served as a military road, following a line of *castella*, to Bohemia at the time of the Marcomannic wars.[53] This was the main gateway for large numbers of Roman imports to Bohemia and also formed part of a much more extensive line of communication, the amber road running from Aquileia *via* Carnuntum, Moravia, the Vistula to the Baltic, especially the region of Samland. Scattered finds on this trade-route between Carnuntum and the mouth of the Vistula show that Roman coins circulated in the first century AD and that Roman wares were imported from the south. (The direction of this route, starting so far to the east on the Danubian frontier, means that it had little bearing on trade goods and accompanying loanwords in southern Germany,[54] which again

---

[49] *Ibid.*, p. 101.   [50] Lund Hansen (1987), 217; Janssen (1994), 160f.   [51] Eggers (1951), 75f.
[52] *Ibid.*, pp. 66ff.   [53] Ekholm (1935), 50; Brogan (1936), 200; Eggers (1951), 76.
[54] Aubin (1929), 17.

explains why this region, more difficult of access over the Alps than the Rhineland open to water transport through Gaul, was largely inactive in Latin loanword traffic to Germany.) If the Gmc. word for 'amber' reached Latin as *glēsum* along the amber road, it is possible that, through Celtic traders, a word of Latin origin such as Go. *alēw* 'oil' (perhaps accompanied by *lukarn*) found part of its way northwards along this route.[55]

Much more important, because it could take full advantage of water transport and, by outflanking many of the Germanic tribes immediately facing the Romans on the Rhine, could penetrate deep into the hinterland, was the trade-route which started at *Fectio* (Vechten) at the mouth of the Rhine and transported Roman wares by sea along the North Sea coast (with incursions inland up rivers) as far as southern Scandinavia and the Baltic.[56] This last destination is rendered probable by the excavation of Roman goods in great quantities in Denmark and across the base of the Jutland peninsula, suggesting that some may have been reloaded for land transport at this point. Latin trade words which are attested in OHG, but also reached the Anglo-Saxons while still in Schleswig-Holstein and the Goths in the Baltic region, were almost certainly conveyed along this route, which provides the common factor for these three languages in this early period.

It is possible to divide trade words in OHG of Latin origin into a number of different categories. In the first place, they largely suggest the import into Germania of luxury goods.[57] As the converse of the Romans' interest in the fine down of geese from Germania (*ganta*) we find Latin loanwords denoting the use made of these geese by the Romans. In this context the primary value of these geese lay in their down, hence the borrowing of Lat. *pluma* 'feather', leading to OHG *phlûmfedera*, OE *plūmfeðera* 'down'.[58] The use to which this down was put is suggested by another loanword from Latin: *pulvinus* 'cushion' produced OHG *phulwî(n)/phulwo* (cf. modern German *Pfühl*) and OE *pyle*, both meaning 'pillow'.[59] If we recall that the Latin verb *piluccare*, from which 'to pluck' is derived, originally meant 'to pluck hairs' and then 'to pick grapes', it is possible that the verb was taken over into German in two different contexts, one of geese and down, the other in connection with viticulture.[60]

From this it is a short step to one particular luxury good of the

[55] Untermann (1954), 395ff.; Polomé (1985), 309ff.
[56] Brogan (1936), 196; Lund Hansen (1987), 177f.   [57] Aubin (1929), 15.   [58] *GR* 2, 399ff.
[59] *Ibid.*, pp. 427ff.   [60] See above, p. 211.

Romans: wine. Although the Germani, in addition to beer and mead, drank a fermented drink made from berries and fruit (OHG *līd*), they were introduced to the grape (and with it to the word *vinum*) by the Romans, already by the first century BC.[61] The Romans made use of a wine set when drinking wine (including a sieve built into a scoop as a way of decanting it and a vessel for mixing a heavy southern wine with water) and the quantity of such sets which have been found in Germania shows that with the wine went not merely the Roman word for it, but also the Roman practice in drinking it.[62] The important part played by these sets in trade suggests that Roman wine was imported far into Germania. Even though the containers used for transporting it (amphoras, barrels, skins) may not have been retrievable archaeologically, the presence of wine sets throughout Germania, including EG territory in northern Poland, is evidence of the extent of the popularity of wine.[63]

This evidence has not been regarded as sufficient by some, for whom the absence of Roman amphoras in the north suggests that the drinking sets found there were used not for drinking and mixing wine, but (on the basis of chemical analysis of these vessels) for drinking a native beverage comparable to shandy or *Radler*.[64] In other words, so it is suggested, objects produced for such special employment need not have been used by the Germani in the same manner as by the Romans. There are grounds for doubting the force of this argument. Out of the large number of finds only two have been subjected to chemical analysis, so that there is no reason to assume that the use to which these sets were put was true of all. Moreover, the practice of using Roman metal wine sets is attested archaeologically in the graves of Germanic chieftains for Denmark, Mecklenburg and the area of the mouth of the Vistula for as long as Roman wine exports could reach these areas. With the closure of this supply as a result of Germanic invasions the export of wine as well as drinking sets to the Baltic came to an end.[65] It may be as a result of this that the remaining Roman drinking sets were adapted *faute de mieux* to new purposes, now that wine was no longer available. That the Roman practice of mixing wine with water was known to the Germani and followed by them (by means of Roman wine sets) is finally suggested by the loan of Lat. *miscere* 'to mix', yielding OHG *misken* and OE *miscian*,

---

[61] Alanne (1950), 17ff.; Ilkow (1968), 415.
[62] Brogan (1936), 218; Klindt-Jensen (1949), 27ff.; Werner (1950), 168ff.
[63] Cf. Kunow (1980), 8.   [64] Klindt-Jensen (1949), 28f.; Jankuhn (1966), 418.
[65] Werner (1950), 172ff. See also Much (1967), 313ff. for a discussion of the problem.

for the Latin word was also employed in the context of wine.[66] The adoption of a Latin term, where alternatives such as *mengan* or *blandan* existed in Germanic, suggests that *misken* was at first restricted to a Roman context (mixing wine) and that, as long as the supply of wine lasted, Germanic chieftains who possessed wine sets used them in the same way as the Romans. Archaeological evidence of this kind, together with what we have seen of Roman trade-routes to the north, confirm the linguistic conclusion reached earlier that the Goths acquired the loan-word *wein* while still in the north.

Other categories of Roman trade words can be dealt with more briefly.[67] The containers necessary for the transport of goods include in OHG words which we have already considered in Gothic, such as OHG *arka/archa* from Lat. *arca* 'box', *kezzil* from *catillus* 'small bowl' and *sac/sakk* from *saccus* 'sack' (insofar as this is regarded as a container as well as the material from which it was made). To these can be added OHG *kista* from *cista* 'chest, box', not attested in Gothic. The amphoras which have been found in Germania close to the imperial frontier are reflected in another loan in NWG. The Latin word *amp(h)ora* is itself a loanword from Greek meaning a two-handled jug with a narrow neck. The transition of the jug with two handles to a type with only one lies behind the reinterpretation of the Latin loanword by popular etymology in Germanic (**aina* 'one' + *beran* 'to carry'), producing OHG *eimbar* (eventually modern German *Eimer*, 'bucket'), OS *êmbar/emmar*, OE *amber* 'pail, cask'. The accurate measurements called for in trade gave rise to loans such as OHG *phunt*, OE *pund* from Lat. *pondo* 'pound (in weight)' (as in Gothic) and OHG *unza*, OE *yntse* from *uncia* 'ounce' (whereas Go. *unkja* denotes measurement of a different kind, outside the context of trade).

A last category, concerning the Roman trader's transport of his wares overland, is represented by the loan of Lat. *asinus* 'ass, donkey' into all the Germanic languages (only ON *asni* is derived from OFr., rather than Latin), then from these into Slavonic and Baltic.[68] This animal, used by the Romans as a beast of burden both in the army and by their merchants, was introduced by them to Europe north of the Alps, where it

---

[66] *GR* 2, 324ff.; Jud (1914), 16; Alanne (1950), 43f. To this context belongs also the loan of Lat. *acetum*: see Alanne (1950), 75.

[67] *Arka*: *GR* 2, 98ff.; *kezzil*: *GR* 2, 171ff.; Brüch (1926b), 6ff.; *sakk*: see above, p. 205 and Kluge and Seebold (1989), p. 612; *kista*: *GR* 2, 185f.; *eimbar*: Beck (1986b), 582f.; *phunt*: *GR* 2, 402f.; *unza*: *GR* 2, 495.

[68] Olck (1907), 640f.; Kunow (1980), 19. On Slavonic and Baltic see above, pp. 171 and 173.

had previously been unknown. Since the horse collar was invented only in the Middle Ages, the horse was little used by the Romans for drawing loads, a task performed instead by the ox, the ass and the mule (OHG *mûl* is also derived from Lat. *mulus*). Although the Germani could theoretically have become acquainted with this animal and its Latin name in connection with the Roman army, its spread to Gothic and to non-Germanic languages in their region suggests that it was carried this far in connection with trade, first Roman and then Germanic.[69]

Reciprocity underlies the encounter between the Romans and the Germani in warfare – to the presence of Gmc. loanwords from this field in Latin (*carrago, drungus, framea*, but also perhaps *companio*) there corresponds a (greater) number of Latin words which left their trace in Gmc.

The explanation for this presence of Latin military terms must be sought in the Romans' technical superiority in this field, not merely by comparison with the Germani.[70] Wherever the various barbarian peoples of northern Europe, in Gaul, Britain or Germania, encountered the Roman army they were initially at a loss, even demoralised, in face of the invaders' equipment and technical skill. We have already discussed the technical inferiority of the Germani in the context of warfare with regard to both offensive weapons and defensive equipment. In connection with the former we may add that the fact that Roman weapons were often seized in a raid may be seen as a tribute to their higher quality, whilst the contrast between the light shield of the Germani and the metal helmet, breastplate and shield of the Romans meant that personal bravery on the part of the barbarians availed them little in hand-to-hand fighting and that their best hope lay in overwhelming the Romans in a wild rush.[71] Another difficulty encountered by the barbarians lay in their need to adjust to a particular form of warfare where their lack of technical skill put them at a further disadvantage. Although the Germanic armies had previously encountered the fortified *oppida* of the Celts their attacks on the urban civilisation of the Romans confronted them with the problems of siege warfare on quite a different scale.[72]

Lying deeper than these technical drawbacks was the disparity

---

[69] The transition from a barter to a monetary economy is reflected in terms for coins, for commercial as well as decorative purposes. These can be terms taken from Latin, e.g. OHG *silihha* < *siliqua* (Schröder (1918), 247, 249, 261, 267) or vernacular ones, e.g. the words 'shilling' (*ibid.*, pp. 254ff.) or 'penny' (*ibid.*, pp. 241ff.; Birkhan (1971b), 59ff.).   [70] Thompson (1965), 109f.
[71] *Ibid.*, pp. 120, 114.   [72] *Ibid.*, pp. 131ff.

between Roman discipline on the battlefield and the importance attached to individual bravery by the Germani, summed up in the wild headlong rush with which they sought to overpower the Romans. Even outside the context of warfare (but no doubt reinforced by experience on the battlefield) the view of the Romans was that the Germani lacked discipline and self-control in all walks of life. Their kings could therefore exercise no absolute authority (Tacitus, *Germania* 7) and dilatory attendance at tribal assemblies is put down to a 'defect of their freedom' (*Germania* 12), where *libertas* is regarded from the Roman point of view as a lack of firm leadership.[73] Using another term in a derogatory sense Tacitus also claims that the Germani do not accept orders or authority, but act as each thinks fit (*Historiae* IV 76: *ex libidine*). On the rare occasions when rational forethought and judgment are attributed to the barbarians this concession can be qualified by an addition like 'as measured by the standard of the Germani' (*Germania* 30: *ut inter Germanos*) or 'more than is customary with the barbarians' (*Historiae* IV 13: *ultra quam barbaris solitum*).[74]

It need not surprise us, therefore, to see the same lack of discipline attributed to the Germani on the battlefield. Even their leaders stand out more by their example than by authority (*Germania* 7), especially when they are in the van of the fight, from where little tactical control of their forces could be expected. Arminius may stand for many other Germanic leaders when it is said of him in an attack that he broke through a Roman column 'at the head of a picked force' (*Annales* I 65).[75] Of such a style of fighting, which the Germani expected of a commander who was also leader of a war-band, it could be said by their disciplined opponents that it was brave, but headstrong, emphasising the force of personal example at the cost of the leader's overall control of the battle. Speaking of the Germani at large, not just of their leaders, Seneca could therefore stress the need for reason and discipline by contrast with the lack of control shown by the Germani in their conduct of war.[76]

Nonetheless, there were exceptions to this, making it probable that some Germani learned from their opponents. This is particularly clear in the case of the Chatti, whose powers of judgment, setting them apart from others, led them to pick leaders whom they then obeyed, to keep their ranks and delay an attack and, in this resembling Roman discipline, to place reliance on the commands rather than individual fighting

---

[73] Much (1967), 157, 208. [74] *Ibid.*, p. 381. [75] *Ibid.*, pp. 157f. [76] *De ira* I, 11, 3f.

(*Germania* 30).[77] Such advantageous control of the fighting was a technique which had been copied from the opponents' *disciplina*. As Tacitus
himself makes clear elsewhere, however, the Chatti were not unique in
adjusting their ways. In connection with the armies of Arminius and
Maroboduus he says that the traditional ways (unruly order of battle and
chaotic charges) were now a thing of the past and that their wars with
the Romans had taught them their methods, to obey commands and to
keep troops in reserve (*Annales* II 45).[78] However ingrained their traditional method may have been, the practical experience of repeated
encounters with an army which was superior in its discipline as well as
its technical equipment was capable of bringing about a change of attitude on the part of the Germani, amongst three tribes expressly named
and no doubt with others, too. The example of the Goths' trek to the
south-east has already shown us their success in adapting to the new
conditions of the steppes, abandoning the methods which had been adequate to small-scale skirmishing at the mouth of the Vistula in favour of
new ones learned from mounted nomads and called for over the greater
distances of the Pontus.[79] The Goths' ability to learn from the steppe-
dwellers was matched by the readiness of WG tribes to learn from the
Romans.

Against this background of military inferiority in many respects,
together with the need to adapt and learn, we have to place the question
of loanword traffic in the military sphere from Latin into Germanic.
Obvious carriers of these loanwords were those Germani who served in
the Roman army, *either* in barbarian units into which, although Latin
may not have been spoken, the military terminology of the Romans
must have penetrated, *or* as *foederati* with the obligation to perform military service *or* as individuals who could attain officer's rank in the imperial army.[80] For these categories the barbarisation of the Roman army
must have meant, to a varying extent, a linguistic Latinisation. What
non-linguistic criteria there are suggest the late imperial period (from
about AD 300) for this linguistic influence, the period in which the
number of Germani serving in the Roman ranks increased significantly
and was drawn no longer mainly from tribes dwelling on imperial territory.[81] As a rough rule it can be assumed that only those Latin words
were adopted which had a specialist function within the army language
of the Romans and which had no obvious counterpart in Germanic.

---

[77] Much (1967), 381f.   [78] *Ibid.*, pp. 152, 384.
[79] See above, pp. 177ff. and Thompson (1965), 127f.   [80] Kuhn (1972), 13.   [81] *Ibid.*, pp. 19f, 42.

The conditions of service in the Roman army, quite different from those in barbarian formations, are suggested by a first category of loanwords. The verb for such service is attested in Go. *militōn* (from Lat. *militare*). Even though this verb is found only in Gothic (and was probably borrowed by the Goths on the Danubian frontier), the presence of two WG nouns, OHG *miliz* and OE *milite*, both to render *miles/militem*, suggests that in the west, too, such service was the occasion of their adoption (early enough to reach the Anglo-Saxons while still on the continent?).[82] The pay which was a feature of Roman service as *foederati* explains Go. *anno*, where the vernacular meaning 'army pay' derives from Lat. *annona* 'annual provision of crops' as a means of provisioning the army which could be commuted to a monetary payment.[83] The military context of Go. *kapillōn*, indicating not just an army hair-cut, but one which normally distinguished Romans from Germani, we have already considered. To these examples may also be added the adoption of Lat. *carcer* 'prison', *catena* 'chain' and *claustrum* 'bolt, lock', if we can assume that they could be used in the military context, applied to prisoners of war and those subjected to military punishment.[84]

Under the heading 'lines of communication' we may include a word such as Lat. *strata* (short for *via strata* 'paved way'), with its reflection in OHG *strâzza*, OS *strâta*, OE *strēt*.[85] The shortened Latin form, attested from the fourth century, indicated above all a military line of communication, as is suggested by explanatory compounds such as OHG *heristrâzza* and OE *herestrēt* 'military road'. Many German and English place-names which contain this element (e.g. *Strassburg*) owe their origin to a Roman road which passed through them.[86] It is possible that OHG *mîla* 'mile' (from Lat. *milia passuum* 'thousand paces') belongs to the same context, especially in view of the location of Roman bases at regular distances along the military roads.[87]

Tactical control of a battle formation can be illustrated by two loanwords from Latin which may be regarded as the linguistic equivalent of the observation by Tacitus that the Chatti, amongst other tribes, had learnt the lesson of discipline in battle from the Romans. In Latin the word *signum* was used in a technical sense to denote a military standard or ensign as a rallying point or command post in battle. We have to distinguish the (later) borrowing of this word into OHG *segan* in the Christian context (perhaps from *signum* or as a back-formation from the

---

[82] *Ibid.*, pp. 14, 15. See above, pp. 202, 208 and *GR* 2, 323f.   [83] Kuhn (1972), 14 and above, p. 203.
[84] See above, pp. 203, 209f.   [85] Kuhn (1972), 15f.   [86] Kaspers (1950), 293.
[87] Kuhn (1972), 16.

verb *signare*, in either case denoting the sign of the cross, then the 'blessing' which it accompanied) from OE *segn*, meaning 'battle standard'.[88] If the Latin word was adopted into OE in this specifically military sense this raises the question why such a loan was necessary, especially since Tacitus makes it clear that the Germani carried their own (holy) emblems into battle with them.[89] In view of Germanic terms with this meaning borrowed into Latin or Romance (*bandum*, *tufa* and **gundfano*) it seems probable that the Latin term was borrowed because it denoted a radically different ensign or one which served a different purpose, such as exercising a rational control over the course of a battle.[90] It is also possible that Lat. *draco* 'dragon' was loaned into Germanic (OHG *trahho*, OE *draca*) in the same context, for the dragon was used on Roman battle standards from the second century AD.[91] Although the word was later used in Christian texts, it must have been borrowed earlier than this into OHG (before the Second Sound Shift), but whether in the context of the Roman army must remain a hypothesis.

A further category is made up of terms for military ranks or classes of warrior for which a Latin origin has been claimed. To these belong OHG *kempho* and OE *cempa* 'fighter, warrior', derived from Lat. *campio*, used above all in the context of gladiatorial single combats.[92] Accordingly, Isidore of Seville reports that gladiators were known as *campiones*, an OE gloss translates *gladiator* by *cempa* and the characteristic attire with a belt (the *Lex Baiuvariorum* refers to a *campio cinctus*) is reflected in OE *gyrded cempa* (*Beowulf* 2078). The Latin word is derived from *campus* in the sense of a field or piece of ground staked out for training and combat, which explains how the loanwords OHG *kamph* and OE *camp* could acquire the more restricted sense of 'combat, contest'.

Considerably greater difficulties, linguistic as well as institutional, attach to another word, OHG *herizogo* (also attested in OS, OE and ON), for we are still undecided whether it is a native Gmc. formation or based on a foreign model, either Greek or Latin.[93] The traditional view was that it derived from PG **harjatuga* 'army leader' as the vernacular equivalent of the *duces* described by Tacitus (*Germania* 7), appointed for the specific function of leadership in war. This thesis was challenged by

---

[88] *Ibid.*, pp. 16, 43. See also *GR* 2, 460f.   [89] See above, pp. 77f.

[90] Chaney (1970), 140ff.; Kuhn (1972), 16.

[91] Chaney (1970), 127ff.; Kuhn (1972), 18f. Cf. also Helm (1953), 71.

[92] Kuhn (1956), 68ff.; (1971a), 521ff.; (1972), 16, 34.

[93] Schröder (1924a), 1ff.; (1932), 182ff.; Much (1925), 1ff., 406f.; (1933), 105ff.; Ilkow (1968), 198ff.; Kuhn (1972), 26ff.

Schröder who questioned the Gmc. ancestry of the word (its occurrence in OE and ON is relatively late) and also the assumption that the PG verb **teuhan*, unlike Lat. *ducere*, ever meant 'to lead' (as opposed to 'pull, bring' or 'bring up'). Instead, Schröder regarded the Gmc. word as a calque on Gr. *stratēgós* with the meaning 'army leader'.

This view was in turn challenged by Much whom we may largely follow in questioning Schröder's Greek theory. This theory rests on a shaky basis in postulating a Greek model which entered Germanic *via* Gothic, for the vernacular word present in WG and NG (however late in some cases) is nowhere attested in EG. Nor is it likely that Gothic acquired a specifically military term from Greek, for military loans in Gothic, as in OHG, came instead from Latin. Phonologically, too, it is difficult to reconcile the form **harjatuga* with Gothic, for this language abolished grammatical change in favour of *h* alone (as in the principal parts of the Gothic verb *tiuhan*), as opposed to WG, with its regular alternation between *h* and *g*. Finally, the verb *tiuhan* was used by Wulfila to translate forms which mean both 'to bring' and 'to lead', while ON *hertogi* could be expressly defined as one who 'leads an army into battle' and the parallel OE compound *folctoga* means 'chieftain, leader'.[94]

However, to argue against Schröder is not the same thing as accepting Much's traditional view of a native Gmc. origin, for the points made in the last paragraph tell against a derivation of the word from Greek *via* Gothic, not necessarily against outside influence as such, in this case from Latin. It has been suggested that, whilst the Gmc. verb originally meant 'to bring', the acquisition of the further meaning 'to lead' may have been under the influence of Latin, where *ducere* regularly had both meanings, so that *herizogo* derived its function 'army leader' from the model *dux*, with the addition of the explanatory first element *heri-* as in the case of *heristrâzza* and *strata*.[95] Later than this hypothetical development would be the shift of the word's function from 'military leader' to 'duke', probably under the influence of early Merovingian Latin *dux*, but still requiring further historical investigation.[96] Linguistically, however, it is significant that this semantic change from military to political leadership parallels what we have seen in the case of the noun *heri* itself, which early denoted both 'army' and 'people'.[97]

---

[94] *Tiuhan*: Ilkow (1968), 200 and fn. 80; Lehmann (1986), 346. *Hertogi*: Ilkow (1968), 201f. *Folctoga*: Bosworth and Toller (1954), 299.　　[95] Kuhn (1972), 26.　　[96] Cf. Zeiss (1932), 145ff.
[97] See above, pp. 84ff.

CHAPTER 13

Names of days of the week

The Germanic tribes reckoned the passing of time by nights, basing themselves on the state of the moon, as is made clear by Tacitus (*Germania* 11) and by linguistic survivals such as English 'fortnight' and German *Weihnachten*.[1] By contrast, the Romans reckoned by days and it was largely from them that the Germani adopted the method of counting by days, the idea of a seven-day week and the Latin names for days of the week. This adoption was probably occasioned by early legal, military and above all trading contacts with the Romans: payment or delivery had to be made by a certain day, fines or taxes were to be met by a fixed time-limit. Whereas the WG languages derived their terms for days of the week from Latin in such a secular context (Christianity played a part in the choice of these terms only later), Gothic seems to have been exposed early to the influence of the Greek Church in its terminology (insofar as this is preserved in Wulfila's translation or can be reconstructed from Gothic influence on Bavarian names for days of the week).

The seven-day week is first attested with the Hebrews from the fifth century BC.[2] Only the Jews developed the week as a unit of time constantly repeating itself without interruption and cutting across other units such as the month and the year.[3] The turning-point in the Jewish week was the Sabbath as the day of rest, so much so that the word could designate not merely this particular day, but also the whole week itself.[4] Around this day the other days of the week were grouped systematically: Friday was designated by the word for 'evening' (the eve of the Sabbath), whilst the others were counted by numbers. Sunday was therefore literally 'one in the week', Monday 'two in the week', and so on through to Thursday. The features about the Jewish week which are significant for

---

[1] Much (1967), 208. [2] Nöldeke (1901), 161ff.; Schürer (1905), 1ff.; von Wartburg (1956), 46.
[3] Jensen (1901), 150ff. [4] Nöldeke (1901), 162.

its adoption by an ultimately Christian Europe are the importance attached to one day of worship and the complete avoidance (effected by numbering or by a relative reference like 'eve') of polytheistic terms such as we find in the Roman week.

The week is first attested in Greek amongst Greek-speaking Jews (e.g. in the Septuagint). The first name for a day of the week to pass beyond the Jewish people (already in the first century AD) was the word for the Sabbath, most probably in connection with the spread of Christianity, for whose followers the word now denoted simply the last day of the week.[5] In Greek the Hebrew word appears either as *sábbata* (neuter plural) or as *sábbaton*, a distinction which accounts for Latin forms like *sabbata* and *sabbatum*. In addition to these forms with -*bb*- we must also reckon with variants with -*mb*-, attested for example in Syrian *šambat*, even if not in Greek itself, but to be assumed for this language, too, in the light of such derivatives as Rum. *sâmbătă*, OSl. *sąbota* and Hungarian *szombat*. The Greek-speaking Christians also devised two forms to designate the day which preceded it (corresponding to 'eve of the Sabbath' in Hebrew).[6] Friday is therefore rendered by *paraskeué* '(day of) preparation (for the Sabbath)', already in the New Testament, where on one occasion (Mc. 15.42) it can be explained as 'the preparation, that is the day before the Sabbath', where *prosábbaton* serves as an alternative rendering for this day of the week and is attested amongst non-Jews from the second century. So far, the Greek words we have considered have a clearly Jewish background,[7] but a specifically Christian term is found, also from the second century, to designate 'Sunday'. This day was rendered by *kyriakḗ hēméra*, literally 'the Lord's day', frequently shortened to *kyriakḗ*, with the adjective serving now as a substantive.

Only three consecutive days of the week (Friday, Saturday, Sunday) were designated in Greek by specific names. For the rest the method used by the Hebrews was adopted: these days were numbered through, beginning with Sunday as the first day (it could thus be called *prṓtē sabbátou* 'first of the week' or *mía sabbátōn* 'one of the week') and going through to Thursday as the fifth (*pémptē tou sabbátou* or *hēméra pémptē*).[8] These Greek forms also betray a further agreement with Hebrew practice, showing that *sábbaton* designated not merely the Sabbath, but also the week of which it was the focus. Apart from 'the Lord's day' for Sunday, therefore, Greek terminology was based on the Hebrew model: in borrowing the

[5] Thumb (1901), 166; von Wartburg (1956), 46f., 53f.; *FEW* 11, 3f.
[6] Thumb (1901), 166f.; von Wartburg (1956), 47.   [7] Schürer (1905), 8.
[8] Thumb (1901), 168; Schürer (1905), 9ff.; von Wartburg (1956), 47.

word 'Sabbath', in using it to denote this particular day, but also a week, in finding it necessary to coin terms for the day preceding the Sabbath, and in using a numerical system. Christian Greek, like Hebrew, disposed of a terminology adequate to the demands of monotheism.

However, from the second century there is evidence of the episodic use in Greek, as more frequently in Latin, of planetary names for days of the week.[9] By this method an entirely different nomenclature was devised, pagan insofar as the planets were associated with gods of antiquity. The Greek sequence for the week refers therefore to the day of *Krónos* for Saturday, the day of *Hélios* for Sunday, of *Selénē* for Monday, of *Árēs* for Tuesday, of *Hermēs* for Wednesday, of *Zeús* for Thursday, and of *Áphroditē* for Friday. The difference between this astrological or pagan terminology and that devised by Greek Christians on the Hebrew model could not be more striking, but there is plentiful evidence to suggest that some Christians continued to use the pagan terms, even though these never found their way into official usage. Even where the pagan terms remained in use in Greek, however, a significant distinction can be made: they were mainly used by Greek-speakers in the west (southern Italy and Sicily), rarely in Egypt or in Greece itself.[10] This does not mean that they were *never* used in Greece (we shall see that what is thought to be the Gothic term for 'Tuesday' was derived from *hēméra Áreōs* 'the day of Ares'),[11] but rather that, despite this pagan exception, the Christian terminology adopted by the Greeks from Hebrew was successful.

This can be confirmed by turning to a region exposed to Greek influence. In Slavonic the terms for days of the week show no trace of the planetary gods.[12] This is hardly surprising, given the influence of Greek Christianity in eastern Europe, but it is also borne out by a linguistic detail. Just as Greek (following Hebrew) used *sábbaton* to denote both a particular day and the week which hinged upon it, so does Slavonic, with a transfer from the holy day of the Jews to that of the Christians, employ the same word to denote 'Sunday' and 'week' (*nedelja*).

In establishing its Christian terminology for days of the week Slavonic used methods employed in Greek. First, it made use of terms which were expressly Christian, such as *sąbota* for 'Saturday' and *nedelja* for 'Sunday' (meaning a day of no work, a day of rest, thereby transferring to the Christian Sunday what had been true of the Jewish Sabbath).[13] Secondly, a day could be designated by its position within the week, such

---

[9] Thumb (1901), 168ff.; Schürer (1905), 13ff.; von Wartburg (1956), 47.   [10] Schürer (1905), 20ff.
[11] *Ibid.*, pp. 24f.; von Wartburg (1956), 55, n. 4.   [12] Skok (1925), 14.   [13] *Ibid.*, p. 16.

as *ponedeljĭnikŭ* for 'Monday' (meaning the day following Sunday) and *sreda* for 'Wednesday' (the middle of the week).[14] Finally, a numerical method was employed for the remaining days: *vŭtorĭnikŭ*, literally second, for 'Tuesday', *četvrŭtŭkŭ*, fourth, for 'Thursday', and *pętŭkŭ*, fifth, for 'Friday'.[15] (These forms presuppose that the days were counted beginning with Monday, not Sunday.) Not merely do these methods derive from the Greek precedent, they also go beyond it in their degree of Christianisation. First, they show no trace of the planetary gods which, with whatever restrictions, could still occur in the Greek names. Secondly, they conform more to Christian views in regarding Sunday, rather than the Hebrew Sabbath as the day of rest. Thirdly, they confirm this last point in numbering the days from Monday as the beginning, so that Sunday is the turning-point, no longer Saturday.[16] (This suggests that denoting Wednesday, rather than Thursday, as the middle of a week might go back to a time when the days of the Slavonic week, like those of the Greek, were counted from Sunday.)

From Slavonic the practice of naming days in this way was passed on to other languages in eastern Europe. Lithuanian makes use of loan-words from Slavonic, arranged in the same numerical sequence from *panedêlis* 'Monday' to *nedêlia*. Alongside this, however, Lithuanian, like Latvian, knows a purely numerical system, beginning with *pirmadienis*, first day, for 'Monday' and finishing with *sekmadienis*, seventh day, for 'Sunday'.[17] Hungarian follows the same method of counting by calling Monday *hétfö* 'head of the week' and Tuesday *kedd* 'two' and adopting Slavonic forms for Wednesday, Thursday, Friday and Saturday.[18] These languages reveal their dependence on Slavonic and thus, ultimately, on the Greek system. It is this system which governs eastern Europe (with the exception of Rumanian, deriving from Latin names of the days). To this system Gothic also belongs, attested directly or through Bavarian.[19] It uses the same three methods in constructing a Christian terminology: expressly Christian words (*sabbato* 'Saturday', *paraskeuḗ* 'Friday'), a numeral (*pémptē* 'Thursday') and a relative designation (*afarsabbato*, referring to 'Sunday', Mc. 16.2).

This expansion of the Greek system through eastern Europe throws light on the position within Greek. Although Greek shows traces of planetary names of days of the week these were largely confined to areas where Roman terminology used such names in their Latin form (Italy

---

[14] *Ibid.*, p. 17. [15] *Ibid.*, p. 16. [16] *Ibid.*, p. 18. [17] Rohlfs (1952), 45, fn. 13.
[18] Skok (1925), 21. [19] See below, pp. 310ff.

and Sicily). In Greece itself these planetary terms are only weakly attested, whilst in the languages influenced by Greek (with the sole exception of the Gothic word for 'Tuesday') they are altogether absent.

The same cannot be said of the Roman system, where the conflict between pagan and Christian terminology is much more marked.[20] The early Roman week consisted of eight days and was called *nundinum*; the other days were not specified, either by name or by number. This eight-day system remained in use well into the imperial period, but the seven-day week was introduced by Augustus, with support from the Jewish population, but also influenced by Chaldaean astrology which had gained a firm foothold in the Empire. This astrology associated the seven days with the seven planets and, in turn, with the gods attributed to these planets. Certain days were regarded as favourable for certain enterprises (or not) because of the particular attributes of the gods governing them.[21] As a result, the days of the week were named after these gods, so that, as in the Greek pattern, they were named after *Saturnus* (*Saturni dies* 'Saturday'), then *Sol, Luna, Mars, Mercurius, Iupiter* and finishing with *Venus*. About this sequence and the fact that it began with Saturday there can be little doubt because of depictions of the planetary gods on Roman monuments, attesting both this order and the popularity of the cult of these deities.[22] These depictions date from the first century AD and last through to the fourth century, with a noticeable frequency in eastern Gaul and the Rhineland.[23] This centre of gravity, testifying to the worship of gods associated with planets and days of the week, accounts for the spread of the Roman names for these days both to the Celts and to the Germani. Although the earliest evidence of this type shows the Roman week beginning regularly with *Saturnus*, from the fourth century the change was made to Sunday, presumably under the influence of Christians who wished to distinguish their holy day from the Jews' Sabbath.[24] Another factor may well have been the popularity of the pagan cult of the *Sol Invictus* at this time and the Christians' wish to appropriate this day for themselves,[25] leading Ambrose, for example, to argue that on the *Solis dies* Christ arose like the rising sun, bringing light to the world.

For Christians to avoid polytheistic terms was a doctrine of perfection, for many of the inscriptions with planetary names are found in a

[20] Gundermann (1901), 175ff.; Schürer (1905), 25ff.
[21] Gundermann (1901), 175f., 177, 179f.; Schürer (1905), 41, 48.   [22] Gundermann (1901), 178ff.
[23] Schürer (1905), 33.   [24] Gundermann (1901), 180f.; Avedisian (1963), 236.
[25] See also below, p. 353.

Christian context,[26] but at least the attempt was made to draw Roman practice into line with what was done in Greece. The re-naming of a planetary name of a day is confined to the two cases, Saturday and Sunday, which lie at the heart of the Jewish and Christian religions.[27] *Sabbatum*, perhaps because of its special religious importance for the Jews, found its way into Roman use alongside the planetary names for other days already with Horace as a designation for the Jewish holy day. Only in Christian texts (e.g. Tertullian, the Rule of St Benedict) was it employed instead of *Saturni dies*. A replacement for *Solis dies* as a Christian holy day was based on the Greek model. Corresponding to Gr. *kyriakḗ hēméra* 'the Lord's day' we find Lat. *(dies) dominicus / dominica* as a loan-translation, but only in Christian texts, such as Tertullian. Apart from these two cases, the hinge of the Christian week, the remaining days are indicated by numbering, again only with Christian authors.[28] Sometimes the Hebrew model for this practice was followed directly (*sexta sabbati* was used by Cassian for 'Friday'), sometimes Lat. *feria* (*feria secunda* for 'Monday' in the Rule of St Benedict). Only in modern Portuguese (*segunda feira*, etc.) has this method, combined with *sabado* and *domingo*, produced a nomenclature for the whole week in western Europe which, like the Slavonic system, is fully Christian.[29] Apart from this, Latin nomenclature differs from Greek in never completely resolving the contradiction between the planetary pagan week and the Christian week. Transposing this contrast between Latin and Greek into Germania, we shall see that it also accounts for differences between WG names for days of the week, based on Latin, and Gothic ones, based on Greek.

From Latin we move on to the Romance languages which show the same unresolved discrepancy between planetary and Christian terminology (with the exception of Portuguese), between *Lunae (dies)*, *Martis*, *Mercurii*, *Iovis*, *Veneris* on the one hand and *dominicus*, *sabbatum* on the other. Although the two Christian terms succeeded in driving out *Solis dies* and *Saturni dies* throughout Romania (they survive only in the neighbouring Celtic and WG languages to which they had been earlier loaned from Latin), the rest of the week remained irredeemably pagan.[30] For *sabbatum* the variants assumed for Greek (with *-bb-* or *-mb-*) are also attested in Romance: the first underlies forms in Italy, Iberia and Provence, whilst the second is found in northern Gaul (cf. OFr. *samedi*). By the addition

[26] Gundermann (1901), 181ff.; Schürer (1905), 35ff.
[27] Gundermann (1901), 184; *FEW* 5, 452 and 11, 3.   [28] Gundermann (1901), 185f.
[29] Meyer-Lübke (1901), 193.   [30] Von Wartburg (1956), 48, 49, 54; *FEW* 5, 452 and 11, 3f.

of *dies* to *sabbatum* in this form (superfluous since *sabbatum* was itself a substantive) the word for Saturday was formally incorporated into the sequence *lundi* to *vendredi*, thus distinguishing the weekdays from Sunday.[31] Although Sunday had originally been expressed by *dies dominicus*, the noun was dropped in the greater part of Romania and the adjective treated as a substantive. In the case of Sunday, therefore, the conjunction of *dominicus* with *dies*, originally necessary because the former was an adjective, has been abandoned, whilst in the case of Saturday, where *sabbatum* as a substantive did not call for *dies*, the latter has been added in Gaul. The result, a formal isolation of the word for 'Sunday' within the week, could only be welcome to the Church.

Apart from these two days the only attempt at re-naming as a means of avoiding a pagan god concerns Wednesday, a day of mid-week fasting in the ecclesiastical organisation of the week and therefore fit to be protected from pagan profanation.[32] Even so, this attempt is restricted to a very circumscribed area, to scattered dialects in northern Italy and the Engadin, where Lat. *media hebdomas*, literally 'mid-week', survives in forms like *mezzedima, missédma, mezemna*. These are reminiscent of Slavonic, where *sreda* 'middle' likewise designated 'Wednesday', but whereas the Slavonic word was out of place in a week which began only on Monday, the Romance words make sense in a week which began on Sunday. For the rest, the traditional method of keeping the Christian week free from contagion by counting the days is hardly employed at all in the Latin west: linguistically it found a home in Portuguese, but otherwise it is attested only with groups conscious of their Christianity.[33] Apart from these, pagan terminology continued in use, even amongst Christians.

It is hardly surprising that the neighbouring language-groups Celtic and WG should likewise reflect, in one way or another, the position in Latin, especially since these languages took over the Roman week before serious attempts were made from the beginning of the fifth century to deal with its pagan implications. The Roman cult of the planetary deities of the week, exemplified on votive stones and inscriptions, was particularly popular in eastern Gaul and the Rhineland, an area which acted as a linguistic reservoir for Roman influence on the Celts of Britain and on Germania, in this case also for the days of the week.

In the British dialects of Celtic the names of days of the week go back

---

[31] Von Wartburg (1956), 49f.   [32] Meyer-Lübke (1901), 192f.; Rohlfs (1952), 43f.
[33] Rohlfs (1952), 42.

to the Latin planetary names.[34] In Irish, however, there is evidence both of the planetary week and of Christian modifications.[35] This twofold grouping in Irish suggests a double loan-process, one pre-Christian (as with the British dialects) and the other in connection with the Christian mission to Ireland in the fifth century.

From this point we turn to the position in Germanic, applying the question which has been present throughout: the antithesis between paganism and Christianity in the days of the week. That there was a critical hostility of the Church to the planetary week is clear from early evidence, suggesting a rejection of the astrological fatalism which the cult of planetary gods involved, but also a rejection of names of these pagan gods.[36] In about the year 380 Philastrius called it a heresy to refer to the days of the week by their pagan names (he refers to *nomina dierum Solis* through to *Saturni*) and recommends instead the system of counting them (*primus* through to *septimus*). For Augustine it is characteristic of pagans and men of this world (*saeculares*) to refer to Monday as *Lunae dies* instead of using the innocuous method of counting (*secunda sabbati* or *secunda feria*). Maximus of Turin refers to Sunday as *dominica* but, even though he is aware that the name *Solis dies* can be justified by regarding Christ as the *sol iustitiae*, still sees it as characteristic of men of this world (*homines saeculi*) to use this term from the planetary week. At the beginning of the fifth century Caesarius of Arles warns his clergy against the sacrilege of using the *sordidissima nomina* of the pagan gods preserved in the Roman week and recommends them to set a good example by turning to the numerical system. Isidore of Seville is aware that the Hebrews referred to the first day of the week (known to Christians as *dies dominicus*) by the numerical phrase *una sabbati*, whereas the pagans and the *saeculares* dedicated that day to the sun. In such passages clerical opposition to what is regarded as pagan or worldly practice is clear beyond doubt, but equally clear is the fact that, for the days from Monday to Friday, their polemics were almost entirely fruitless in Romania, where the *sordidissima nomina* remained in force, finding their way into Celtic and Germanic, and surviving later into the various Romance languages. What Augustine says in his criticism of this practice may be taken as characteristic, for the planetary names were used by many Christians, a fact which remained true long after his day.

---

[34] Thurneysen (1901), 186ff.   [35] *Ibid.*, pp. 189ff.
[36] Gundermann (1901), 184, 185f.; Schürer (1905), 52f.; Rohlfs (1952), 42; *FEW* 5, 452.

Despite the Hebrew model and the successful example of Greek, despite the urging of clerics in the Latin Church the success of Christianity in this was very limited. If this was so even in the Latin-speaking world, the presence of pagan names in the Germanic world should not surprise us.

Different factors account for the ability of pagan names still to be preserved in various Germanic languages. One reason is that classical names, fully capable of ringing the alarm bells we have just considered in the Latin-speaking world, were rendered largely innocuous whenever they crossed the linguistic frontier into Germania by not being understood. When *Saturni dies* occurs in OE in the form *sæterndæg*, this word may have been transparent to clerics educated in Latin (as in the gloss *Sæternesdæg of Saturnus Iovis fæder*),[37] but remained unintelligible, and therefore innocuous, to an Anglo-Saxon layman unacquainted with this Roman god. The same is true of the Bavarian word for 'Tuesday', *ertag*, derived from one of the infrequent Greek planetary names, *Áreōs hēméra* 'day of Ares', *via* Gothic transmission. The word is unusual in presupposing a Greek original which is non-Christian, but that does not mean that it was consciously used by the Goths in a pagan sense. That would imply that they knew of the Greek (or Thracian) god Ares, but Wolfram goes further, assuming that they even worshipped this foreign god.[38] For this he produces no evidence, whereas to regard Go. **arjausdags* as an innocuous term, because devoid of religious implications for the Goths, as was Saturn for the Anglo-Saxons, fits in much better with the avoidance of pagan implications in the other Gothic terms.

A second reason why the classical pagan names could remain preserved in Germanic, and also in Insular Celtic, is the marginal position occupied by these languages on the fringe of the Latin-speaking world. This position made them accessible to Roman trade and its vocabulary, and also to the Roman names for days of the week insofar as these performed a trading function, but it also ensured, with the withdrawal of the Roman presence from the frontier region and the disruption caused by Germanic invasions, that later changes in Latin vocabulary no longer penetrated beyond the frontier.[39] Where Christian Latin managed to substitute *sabbatum* for *Saturni dies* and *dominicus* for *Solis dies*, Celtic and Germanic were not affected by these changes. This is no more than the Christian counterpart to what we have seen before: Lat. *pondo*, for example, is preserved in Germanic and Celtic, whilst in Gaul it was later ousted by *libra*.

---

[37] Kluge (1885), 321, l.17.   [38] Wolfram (1976), 247f.   [39] *GR* I, 45. Cf. Jud (1914), 33f.

A further reason is the fact that, in the cases of Sunday and Monday, there were no active pagan Germanic cults of the sun and the moon to make these names dangerous.[40] In Germania the position regarding the worship of the sun was quite different from that in the Roman world, where the imperial promotion of the cult of a sun god had occasioned attempts to appropriate it for Christian ends and to drive out *Solis dies* by *dominicus*. In Germania rock-carvings and the Trundholm find may point to a cult of the sun in the Bronze Age, but Caesar's statement that the Germani worship only what they can see (including the sun and the moon) conflicts with what Tacitus later says and is better regarded as a generalised topos of barbarian worship applied willy-nilly to this particular case.[41] This means that when the Roman days of the week were introduced into Germania *Solis dies* and *Lunae dies* no longer had implications which could become dangerous for Christianity. By this time, in western as in eastern Germania, this cult had been driven back in favour of the worship of personal, named gods and it was with these that the Church faced its real conflict.

The WG nomenclature for the days of the week thus remained impregnated with paganism. This is obviously true of those days in which Roman pagan deities are replaced by Germanic ones, as with English Tuesday (Tiu in place of Mars), Wednesday (Wodan in place of Mercurius), Thursday (þunor in place of Jupiter) and Friday (Friga in place of Venus), where the Germanic names still meant as much in religious terms to the Germani as did the Latin ones to the Romans. Saturday may have conveyed no idea of the pagan god Saturn to most Germani, but its employment in England and north-western Germany meant that these areas had no term corresponding to *sabbatum*, in use elsewhere throughout the Christian world. Finally, even if Sunday and Monday no longer had pagan implications in Germania, the most that could be said for them is that they were innocuous, whereas on the debit side Germanic possessed no term like *dominicus* or *kyriakḗ*, singling out this one day as the Lord's day. The names of the WG week remained as stubbornly pagan as they had been in Latin (before Christianity made its first inroads) or in Insular Celtic (even more so, since the pagan names meant something to Germanic-speakers, whereas Latin loans did not to Celts). In this pagan legacy the languages of western Europe (Germanic, Celtic, Romance with the exception of Portuguese) are in striking contrast with

---

[40] Helm (1937), 31f.; de Vries (1956a), 355ff.; Lange (1958), 236ff.; Polomé (1986), 277f.; (1992), 407.
[41] Caesar, *De bello Gallico* VI 21. Cf. Timpe (1992), 455.

the Christianisation of the week in the east (Greek, Gothic, Slavonic). To focus on the situation within Germania: this distinction means that there is a marked contrast between WG and Gothic.

At this point we pass to the particular ways in which the Roman week was adopted in western Germania. As regards the dating of this adoption the agreement between the Germanic and Roman systems means that the model was imitated only after the introduction of the seven-day week by Augustus and its spread within the Empire in the first centuries AD. This is precisely the period when contacts between Rome and Germania became closer, when votive stones and sculptural representations of the gods of the Roman week are to be dated in Gaul and (from about AD 200) in Roman Germania. This is also the period in which trading contacts between the two worlds grew more active, prompting the need to regulate punctual supply and payment by means of a more detailed time-scheme than the state of the moon. The presence of names of the Germanic gods in the WG week means that it was adopted while the WG tribes were still pagan and also, because of the reflection of *Saturni dies* and *Solis dies*, before Christianity had begun to exercise any influence on the Roman system. The adoption of this system in Insular Celtic is best explained as taking place before the Romans' abandonment of Britain, just as the detailed parallels between OE and north-western Germany in these names suggest an adoption of this system by the Anglo-Saxons while they were still on the continent. By taking these considerations together it has been suggested that the fourth century is the likely date for this loan-process.[42]

Where no loanword was used by the Germani, a loan-translation was called for. This was easy with Sunday and Monday, but how was the problem solved in the other cases? Here we have to consider two methods of interpretation used in the contact between Roman and Germanic paganism, known as *interpretatio Romana* and *interpretatio Germana*.

The first method was a typical device used by Greeks and Romans in reporting on barbarian practices: whenever they observed a point of similarity between a foreign practice and their own, the former could be designated by a term or name already in use in the classical world, even at the cost of ignoring vital differences.[43] This practice was so well established in the Roman world (Tacitus used what he expressly called an *inter-*

---

[42] E.g. *GR* 2, 318.   [43] See above, p. 11.

pretatio Romana in *Germania* 43) that even individual Germani, living on Roman territory, could make use of it, referring to a Germanic god to whom they dedicated a votive inscription by the corresponding Roman name.[44] The Germanic gods most frequently referred to in these inscriptions bear the names Mercurius, Hercules and Mars.[45] These are also the names listed by Tacitus (*Germania* 9) as the gods mainly worshipped by the Germani. Although he does not use the term, Tacitus here employs the *interpretatio Romana* to which he later refers.

Mercurius could be associated with Wodan because of common features: the former (like Hermes) conducted souls to the nether world and the latter led the army of the dead; both were characterised by a floppy hat (*petasus*) and spear-staff (*caduceus*).[46] Inscriptions to Mercurius in the Main/Neckar region have been associated with worship of Wodan by the Cimbri and Teutons.[47] Much later the *Vita Columbani* refers to sacrifices to Wodan 'whom others call Mercurius' and Paulus Diaconus mentions Wodan, 'called Mercurius amongst the Romans'.[48] Hercules can be equated with Donar on the basis of comparable attributes (exploits against giants or demons) and Donar's hammer resembles Hercules's club.[49] Votive inscriptions to a Gmc. Hercules, associated with the Batavians, are interpreted as dedicated to Donar.[50] Finally, Mars is equated with Tiu as the god of war (before he was ousted by Wodan).[51] This does not conflict with dedications to a Gmc. *Mars Thingsus* by Frisians stationed at Housesteads: *Thingsus* is an attribute of Mars/Tiu, presiding over battle, but also over the tribal assembly.[52]

The evidence for the equation of these three Germanic gods with their Roman counterparts is concentrated in north-western Germany. For Wodan the attestations came from the Main/Neckar region, for Donar from Batavia and Utrecht in particular, for Tiu from the Twente region in Holland (where the Frisian cohort was raised). This suggests a region where contacts between Germani and Romans were active, making it possible for the Romans to learn enough from informants about the Germanic gods and the features which made it possible to find Roman equivalents.

Confirmation can be gained by looking at the way in which, by an

---

[44] Gutenbrunner (1936), 23.   [45] *Ibid.*
[46] Mogk (1909), 630f.; Helm (1953), 259, 260, 265, 266; Much (1967), 171f.; Timpe (1992), 456.
[47] Gutenbrunner (1936), 52ff.; Helm (1953), 251.   [48] Much (1967), 172.
[49] *Ibid.*, p. 175; Helm (1953), 245; Derolez (1963), 113, 117, 122.
[50] Gutenbrunner (1936), 58ff.; Helm (1953), 244f.; Derolez (1963), 114.
[51] Helm (1953), 236; Much (1967), 176; Derolez (1963), 133, 134, 136.
[52] Gutenbrunner (1936), 24ff. See also above, pp. 34f.

interpretatio Germana, native equivalents were found for the gods named in the Roman week. *Mercurii dies* was therefore rendered by OE *wōdnesdæg*, MDu. *wôdensdach*, MLG *gudensdach*, whilst ON *óðinsdagr* is a loan from either England or Germany.[53] By the same method *Martis dies* produced OE *tiwesdæg*, MHG *zîstag* (ON *týsdagr* is again a later loan).[54] Both these days therefore confirm the way in which the Romans rendered the corresponding Germanic names into Latin.

The position is more complex when we come to the third day, for in the translation of *Iovis dies* by OE *þunresdæg*, OHG *donrestag* we no longer encounter the equation of Donar with Hercules, but instead with Jupiter. Attempts have been made to explain this discrepancy by suggesting that, in the period between Tacitus and the time when the Roman week was adopted into Germania, the position of Donar must have changed, so that he came to be seen less as a hero of many exploits (like Hercules) and more as a supreme god (like Jupiter).[55] This argument suffers from being geared to the particular need to explain this one point, for there is no indication that Donar's position in the pantheon was radically changed in this way (other than the possibility of equating him as the god of thunder with *Iupiter tonans*). Instead, it seems better to explain this discrepancy between Jupiter and Hercules by the different nature of the translation problems to which they provided a solution. In one case it was a question of a Roman finding an equivalent for a Germanic god Donar who fought giants and demons and could therefore be readily seen as Hercules. In the other case, however, Germani had to find a native equivalent for a Roman god Jupiter who demonstrated his power in thunder and lightning and could hence be identified with Donar.

To these three cases we may add a last one, even though it is not matched in the opposite direction: Lat. *Veneris dies* was rendered by OE *frigedæg*, OHG *frîjatag*, MDu. *vridach* (ON *frjádagr* shows by its form that it is a loan from WG).[56] This name belongs etymologically with the group of words connected with the adjective *frî*, including *frijōn* 'to love' and also embracing courtship and marriage, so that OE *frēo* and OS *frî* also meant 'woman, wife'.[57] A goddess with such a name lent herself to being regarded as the equivalent of Venus.

For Sunday the Latin term *Solis dies* was translated literally, as in OHG *sunnûntag*, OE *sunnendæg* (and later ON *sunnudagr*). Since the Anglo-Saxons share this word, they are likely to have brought it with them from

[53] Helm (1953), 255; Much (1967), 172.   [54] Much (1967), 176.
[55] Derolez (1963), 113f.; Beck (1986c), 5f.   [56] Helm (1953), 268f.
[57] See above, p. 56 and Scheller (1950), 101ff.

the continent, which implies a loan from Latin before about AD 400. This is confirmed by another consideration: as a pagan term for the holy day of the Christian week *Solis dies* was early replaced by the more acceptable *dies dominicus*, a loan-translation of Gr. *kyriakḗ*. The official nature of this new word helped it to oust the older one throughout Romania, but this change no longer crossed the language frontier to reach those languages (Celtic and Gmc.) which had already taken over the earlier term. From what we have seen of Latin loanword traffic which found its way into German, but also into OE and Celtic, its centre of radiation is likely to have been northern Gaul, with the lower Rhine as the probable point of contact with Germania.[58] By contrast, an imitation of Lat. *dies dominicus* is found only late in OHG and with one author only, when Notker uses *frôntag*. This must be regarded as a learned translation, made possible once the stereotyped genitive plural of *frô* 'lord', *frôno*, had acquired adjectival force as a rendering for Lat. *dominicus*.[59]

Lat. *Lunae dies* 'Monday' was taken over as a loanword into Celtic and as a loan-translation into WG, as in OHG *mânetag*, OE *mōnandæg* (and later ON *mánadagr*). As with Sunday, this suggests a centre of gravity in northern Gaul and on the lower Rhine, as well as a loan before 400. Indeed, this is a likely conclusion for all the WG terms which derive from the Roman planetary week, if only because it is barely conceivable that some days were taken over, but not others. An isolated learned imitation of the Christian Latin numerical system occurs in OHG *anderes tages*.[60]

Tuesday presents a greater range of WG alternatives. The rendering which most closely resembles the Latin model uses the Germanic god Tiu as the equivalent of Mars. This is reflected in OE *tiwesdæg*, OFri. *tisdei*, MHG *zîstag*, confined to south-western Germany (and later ON *týsdagr*). Amongst the German tribes only the Alemanni are attested in connection with this Germanic god: not merely does *zîstag* survive down to this day only in this region, but an OHG gloss contains the entry *Ziuwari suapa* 'people of Ziu, Swabians' and renders *civitas Augustensis* or Augsburg by *Ciesburg*.[61] Apart from this, worship of this god is attested in southern Germania only for the Frisians and the Anglo-Saxons (as in the evidence of place-names such as Tuesley < *Tiweslēah* 'holy grove dedicated to Tiu'). In view of this agreement between Frisians and Anglo-Saxons it is probable that this god was known on the continent at least in the area through which the Anglo-Saxons passed on their migration

---

[58] See above, pp. 214f.   [59] See above, p. 106.
[60] *Benediktinerregel* 59 (p. 40), translating *secunda feria* literally.   [61] Rosenfeld (1955), 306ff.

to Britain. This restriction of evidence to north-western and south-western Germany does not mean that this god was not known elsewhere in Germania. Jordanes, for example, says that the Goths worshipped Mars and the Salzburg–Vienna runic manuscript gives the name *tyz* to the rune *t*, as do other runic manuscripts.[62] The Goths may not have employed the name of this god in their terminology for the week because, under the influence of Greek, they followed a different (Christian) system. Even if the Bavarian evidence suggests that the Goths may have used the name of the Greek god of war for this day, the position is quite different: whereas Tiu would have been recognisable to the Goths as one of their pagan gods, the same was not true of a Greek deity.

Another rendering of Tuesday, *Dingstag*, occurs in the central German dialects and in LG (cf. MLG *dingesdag*).[63] Luther still used *Dinstag*, from which the modern form *Dienstag* arose by association with *Dienst*. Even these forms lead back to Ziu if we recall the full form of one of the inscriptions from Housesteads: *Deo Marti Thingso*.[64] The word *deus* and the fact that other days of the week were named after gods suggest that *dingesdag* did not signify the day on which the *þing* or assembly was held, but rather a day named after a god *Mars Thingsus* or **Tiu þings*. The Germanic mercenaries on Hadrian's Wall are referred to as *cives Tuihanti*, i.e. from modern Twente, so that this particular rendering of *Martis dies* possibly arose in this frontier region between the Empire and Germania, spreading to other parts later.

The forms *ertag, eritag, ergetag* for Tuesday are confined to Bavarian and derive from Gr. *Áreōs hēméra*, through Gothic transmission.[65] If a reference to the Greek god, unlike one to a Germanic god, was innocuous, because unintelligible to Gothic-speakers, the same is even more true of Bavarians, further removed from any awareness of what Ares stood for.

More deliberate was the step taken, in a region between Bavaria and the south-western region where Ziu was known, to avoid this god's name by terming Tuesday *Aftermontag*.[66] The artificial nature of this word, together with the fact that, in indicating this day's position in the week, it follows one of the methods used from the beginning to escape profanation of the Christian week, suggests that behind this word there lay avoidance of another word for Tuesday. Bavarian *ertag* is unlikely to have caused offence, but where the danger lay can be seen in the fact that

---

[62] Helm (1937), 38f.   [63] Helm (1953), 241ff.   [64] Gutenbrunner (1936), 24ff., 48f.
[65] See below, pp. 311f.   [66] Kranzmayer (1929), 39; Rosenfeld (1955), 309ff.

Aftermontag is largely confined to the diocese of Augsburg, to that part of Germany where we have testimony for the worship of the god Ziu who was still commemorated in the name of the day *zîstag*. The area around Augsburg therefore had a pressing reason to avoid any reference to this god. Another innocuous name for this day is even more isolated within Germania: it is designated by *drittin tages* in the OHG *Benediktinerregel*, translating *tertia feria*.[67]

For Wednesday Lat. *Mercurii dies* was translated with reference to Wodan in OE, MDu., MLG (and also ON), but as far as Germany is concerned this word is confined to the north-west, to the ecclesiastical province of Cologne, whilst beyond these boundaries *mittawecha*, literally 'midweek', took root.[68] This agreement between OE and north-western Germany suggests that this loan-translation was effected in the region of the lower Rhine. It has been suggested that this form may not have found acceptance in south Germany because the god Wodan was not known there. This is quite uncertain because, given the poverty of our evidence, we cannot deduce ignorance of a god from the absence of any reference to him.[69] Precisely the opposite could in theory be maintained. As with *Aftermontag* in the area around Augsburg, the absence of a god's name could suggest that he had been worshipped there and that the continued existence of his name in the day of a week could not be tolerated.

The UG form *mittawecha* has a parallel in Lat. *media hebdomas*, of which it is probably a loan-translation. The Latin form was common in northern Italy and in Raetia, so that the UG word could be a rare example of loanword traffic from Italy across the Alps to south Germany. The contrast between OE *wôdnesdæg* and UG *mittawecha* cannot be claimed as a distinction within Germanic heathendom between those who worshipped Wodan and those who did not, but rather as a difference in the vocabulary of the Latin-speaking world between *Germania inferior* and *Germania superior*. That *mittawecha* was so successful in spreading northwards, reaching early as far as Trier, is probably because its innocuous character made it especially acceptable to the Church. In this it resembles the choice of *sreda* in Slavonic, but whether there is any causal connection between the two is uncertain.[70]

In Germany two different forms are attested for Thursday. We have already mentioned the translation of *Iovis dies* by *donrestag* (with parallels in OE and OFri.) and why Donar should have been regarded as the

---

[67] *Benediktinerregel* 59 (p. 40).   [68] Frings and Niessen (1927), 293ff.; *GR* 2, 318ff.
[69] Derolez (1963), 90.   [70] Cf. Skok (1925), 14f.

counterpart of Jupiter. Only in Bavaria is another name attested for this day, *phinztag*, derived from Gr. *pémptē hēméra* 'fifth day' through Gothic transmission.[71]

With Friday Germany again has two forms. The first, rendering *Veneris dies* by OHG *frijatag*, has its counterparts in OE and OFri. The name of a goddess with this etymology was particularly fitted to render Lat. *Venus*, but it remains surprising that, although so many Germanic goddesses are mentioned by name on votive stones in the Roman period, Frija is not amongst them. Bavarian alone has *pherintag*, probably of Greek origin (*paraskeuḗ*) by Gothic transmission.[72] Like the Bavarian term for Thursday, it goes back to a Greek source which is pointedly Christian.

Saturday is represented by three different words. Its importance in the Christian week is shown by the fact that, with one exception, specifically Christian terms were successful by contrast with the retention of names from the planetary week for every other day. The exception, the reflection of *Saturni dies* in England, Holland and parts of north-western Germany, but also in Insular Celtic, again betrays a distribution suggestive of an early loan from northern Gaul and the lower Rhine.[73] No traces of this Latin original survive in Gaul, because it was replaced by the Christian term *sambatum*, as in OFr. *samedi*, which also gained a firm foothold in parts of Germany where *Saturni dies* has left no trace.[74] Like OFr., with its combination of *sambatum* with *dies*, the OHG form was *sambaztag* which, by assimilation (*-mb-* > *-mm-*), yielded MHG *sam(e)ztag*. How far this Gallic explanation for this German word needs to be combined with a Gothic explanation of the same form in Bavarian is quite uncertain, if only because a derivation from eastern Europe is not the only way of accounting for *sambatum* instead of *sabbatum* as a base.[75] (Gothic remains true to its terminology of Greek origin in this case, too: *sabbato* means both 'Sabbath' and 'week',[76] for which there are no parallels in the western vernaculars.)

Although England and north-western Germany borrowed *Saturni dies*, they also share a term which, by contrast, is specifically clerical in origin: OE *sunnanǣfen*, MHG *sun(nen)âbent*.[77] This corresponds to Lat. *dominica vespera* and, in meaning the evening before Sunday, is a Christian equivalent of the Jewish use of the word for 'evening' to mean 'Friday', the

---

[71] See below, p. 310.   [72] See below, pp. 310f.

[73] Frings and Niessen (1927), 292f., 301f.; *GR* 2, 444ff.; Avedisian (1963), 246f.

[74] Frings and Niessen (1927), 292f.; *GR* 2, 444ff.; *FEW* 2, 3f.; Avedisian (1963), 232ff.

[75] See below, pp. 312f.   [76] Once only: Lc. 18.12.

[77] Kretschmer (1918), 460ff.; Avedisian (1963), 242ff.; *GR* 2, 445f.

eve of the Sabbath. The word was not originally used as a substitute either for *sæterndæg* or for *sambaztag*. It denoted the last part (following vespers) of the day before Sunday, not the whole of the last working day: in this sense *sunnûn âband* is used by Otfrid (v 4,9). In this restricted meaning the word could be employed in areas where either of the two terms for 'Saturday' was known. Where these terms were not in use, however, *sunnenâbent* came to stand for the whole day preceding Sunday, first when the Sunday in question was a feastday (so that mass was celebrated in the morning of the preceding day), then applied to any Saturday. The origin of this last term for Saturday, in which Germany may well have followed the English impetus, is thus clearly Christian.

However varied the range of linguistic possibilities for naming days of the week may have been in Germany, a distinctive pattern has begun to emerge. In the first place, many of these names suggest a borrowing from northern Gaul and the area of the lower Rhine (Sunday, Tuesday, Wednesday, Thursday, Saturday). As distinct from this, another grouping is discernible in south-eastern Germany or in the south at large. What the examples of this group all have in common is that, by one method or another, they avoid any reference to the pagan gods whose names occurred in the group from the north-west.[78]

[78] On the implications of this contrast see below, pp. 359f., 368f.

CHAPTER 14

The vocabulary of writing

In this chapter the three constituent factors of the Middle Ages which provide the framework for this book come together. In their adaptation to the needs of a barbarian society the runes can be regarded as a typically Germanic form of writing, but in the acquisition of literacy by Germania they have to be seen in connection with two other factors: with Rome (whose use of writing made a further contribution to European literacy) and with Christianity (whose status as a religion of the book brought it into collision with the background of pagan magic to runic practice). Writing was therefore introduced to Germania from three different sources (all of Mediterranean origin)[1] and it is the interplay between these three, as reflected in the linguistic evidence, which will now engage us.

When precisely the runes, a mode of writing derived from a northern Italic script, were first adopted is uncertain: some have argued for a date around 100 BC, others have suggested AD 100.[2] In either case, they were taken over at about the time when classical sources begin to provide us with our first detailed information about the Germani. This does not mean that Germania, in anything other than a technical sense, can be regarded as a literate society when we begin to learn more about it, for runic practice is not to be seen on a par with writing as practised in the Mediterranean world. The runes were not used for purposes of every-day communication as was the alphabetic script by the Romans, for they were employed in magic and divination, and were therefore tied up with the Germanic religion, they were largely confined to short, terse inscriptions and knowledge of them was restricted to a small, closed circle of rune-masters.[3]

---

[1] Green (1994), 35.   [2] Rosenfeld (1952), 194; Klingenberg (1973), 56.
[3] Klingenberg (1973), 56, 96ff., 111ff.; Ebenbauer (1981a), 36; Nielsen (1985), 75ff.; Düwel (1988), 70ff.; Müller (1988), 111ff. Even Page (1995a), 105ff., despite his scepticism about Anglo-Saxon runes and magic, has to admit some cases.

It is difficult to determine what words were early used of runic writing in Germania, but the best approach is to begin with terms used in runic inscriptions themselves, supplementing them with what other (non-runic) sources may tell us.[4] The widest range of such terms comes to us from Scandinavia, where the persistence of paganism and the large number of runic monuments amply account for this. However, despite the disparity between Scandinavia and the rest of Germania, it is safer to regard as common Germanic only those runic terms used both in Scandinavia and elsewhere in the Germanic world. With this restriction we are faced with an unquestioned basic list of four words, for each of which a general, non-technical usage needs to be distinguished from a specialised runic function.

The first word, **rûna*,[5] has a general meaning attested throughout Germania with the following range: Go. *rūna* '(closed) consultation, decision', ON *rín* 'mystery, secret wisdom', OE *rūn* 'deliberation, mystery', OS *rūna* 'council, discussion' and *girûni* 'secret', OHG *rûnôn* 'to whisper'. In its specialist usage the word occurs in ON, OE and OHG, meaning a 'rune' or 'runic writing'. Outside Gmc. the word was borrowed into Finnish, where it denoted first a 'magic song, incantation', then a poem of any kind, whilst Celtic cognates (We. and OIr.) mean either 'secret' at large or, more specifically, a secret which in its written form is not access-ible to all.[6] The attestation of the Gmc. word in its technical usage, applied to runic writing, outside Scandinavia in two WG languages sug-gests a CG ancestry for runic use. As a term belonging to the vocabulary of writing it was only used of the runic script, never of the Roman alphabet. Outside this context, however, the word could later be used safely by the Church in a general sense: Go. *rūna* rendered 'mystery' (of the kingdom of God) in Mc. 4.11, while OHG *girûni* translated *sacra-mentum*.[7] Semantically this word seems therefore to have developed from 'low-voiced, secretive speech' (cf. modern German *raunen*) to 'secret, secret knowledge, magic' and finally to a 'mysterious sign, character' used in magic practice.

The second word, PG **staƀ-*,[8] occurs in the earliest written texts in ON, OE and OHG with the general meaning 'staff', but in the special-ised sense 'stave, runic sign (carved on a stave)' only in ON (already about 620 in a runic inscription from Gummarp). This restriction of the technical usage to Scandinavia only apparently argues against a CG

---

[4] Kuhn (1938), 55. [5] *Ibid.*, pp. 55, 58, 67; Arntz (1944), 294f.; Ebel (1963), 82ff.
[6] Ebel (1963), 82f. [7] Starck and Wells (1990), 218.
[8] Kuhn (1938), 55, 58; Arntz (1944), 282; Ebel (1963), 86ff.

employment of the word for runes, however. The word *stæf* is applied in
OE to the letters of a Mediterranean script (Greek or Latin, designating
book learning at large),[9] which suggests that before the introduction of
the Roman script to Anglo-Saxon England this word had been in use, as
in Scandinavia, for the earlier system of writing. Even more telling is the
distinction made in OE between the compounds *rūnstæf* 'runic sign' and
bōcstæf 'letter of the Roman alphabet'.[10] This distinction became necessary only after the Latin script was introduced alongside the runic one,
but presupposes the earlier use of the word *stæf* meaning a 'sign used in
writing'. This OE distinction is also found in OHG *rûnstab* and *buohstab*
which, given the absence of the simplex in Germany to denote a 'letter'
(by contrast with England), suggests imitation of the OE precedent in
the context of the Anglo-Saxons' mission to Germany and the influence
of their scriptoria on the continent.[11] A comparable distinction, also
based on the OE model, is found in Scandinavia, once writing in Roman
letters was introduced there in connection with the Anglo-Saxon mission
to the north. Here the variants *bókstafr* and *latínustafr* point to a contrast
between writing in Latin in Roman letters (for ecclesiastical purposes)
and writing in the vernacular in runic characters (*rúnastafr*). (The forms
bōcstæf, buohstab, bókstafr have no counterpart in Gothic, presumably
because they were coined late, after the transition of the first element of
the compound from meaning 'writing tablet' to 'parchment codex'.)[12]
With the abandonment of writing in the runic script OHG *buohstab*
came to designate *littera* at large, it stood now for the only written character in use and replaced the simplex *stab* from which it had derived.

  Although Gothic shows no counterpart to *buohstab*, it is dubious
whether we can assume the meaning *littera* for Go. *stafs*, used to render
Gr. *stoicheîon*, Lat. *elementum*.[13] It has been suggested that the Greek word
sometimes indicated the element of a sentence, hence a 'letter', so that
Wulfila's translation by *stafs* would show that this word must have been
a Gothic term for a written character, originally a rune. Against this it
can be argued that *stoicheîon* denoted a simple sound of the voice, the first
element of speech, rather than necessarily a letter as an element of
writing. Furthermore, another meaning of *stoicheîon* was a 'small upright
pole', close enough to the general (non-runic) meaning of the Gmc.
word for Wulfila to be able to imitate Greek by a loan-meaning. It is also

---

 [9] Bosworth and Toller (1954), 907.
 [10] Kuhn (1938), 60f.; Ilkow (1968), 67f.; Hoops (1913b), 349f.; Ebenbauer (1981b), 87f.
 [11] See below, pp. 341ff. [12] See below, pp. 260f.
 [13] Kuhn (1938), 56; Ebel (1963), 89; Ebenbauer (1981b), 88.

revealing that he nowhere translates *grámma* 'letter' by *stafs*, but uses *bōka* instead. None of this suggests that *stafs* in Gothic designated a written character.

Our third term for consideration, **wrîtan*,[14] is used with the general meaning 'to tear, cut, scratch' in OE, OS and OHG (with the cognate *rísta* attested in ON), but with the specialised meaning 'to cut, incise runes' in runic inscriptions in ON and OHG. In addition, it occurs as an overall term for 'to write' in OE, both in the runic script and also, overwhelmingly, with letters of the Roman alphabet. This term is the second one used in its technical runic sense outside Scandinavia, where it was employed in runic inscriptions of the sixth and seventh centuries, even though it was later ousted by *rísta*. In OHG the word is used in the runic inscription on the fibula of Freilaubersheim (second half of the sixth century), but outside that context the verb or a derivative noun occurs only rarely in the sense of writing, e.g. to gloss *characteres litterarum* or *notae* meaning 'written characters'.[15] Otfrid employs the verb twice (III 17,36: *in erdu tho mit themo fingare reiz* = Joh. 8.6; III 17,42 = Joh. 8.8) in the context of Christ writing with His fingers on the ground. From this restricted use we may conclude that the idea of writing by scratching or making an indentation (as at first with runes carved on wood, bone or metal) may still have attached to the word.[16] In Gothic the noun *writs* occurs (Lc. 16.17), but only in the restricted metaphorical sense 'tittle, iota' (deriving from the meaning 'dash, point'). The word thus clearly existed in Gothic, but was not used by Wulfila as a specialised term of writing. To sum up: only in OE did the term *wrîtan*, formerly used of runes incised into a material, come to be used at all regularly of writing at large, including the use of the Latin script on parchment. In thus expanding the application of this term the Anglo-Saxons repeat what they did with *stæf* and what is also the case with the next term.

This fourth term, PG **rêðan*,[17] is attested in its general sense in all the Gmc. languages with a range of meanings from 'to determine, order, take care of' through 'to advise' (modern German *raten*) to 'to interpret' (modern German *erraten*). In its technical runic sense the word occurs only in Scandinavia, where ON *ráða* means not merely 'to interpret', but 'to read' runes: *ráða rúnar*, no doubt assisted by alliteration, occurs on a number of rune-stones.[18] Outside Scandinavia, however, the position is similar to what we saw with **wrîtan*. Although there is no evidence for

---

[14] Kuhn (1938), 55, 58, 71ff.; Arntz (1944), 284; Ebel (1963), 14ff.
[15] Arntz (1944), 284, fn. 5; Starck and Wells (1990), 489.   [16] Schröder (1924b), 58.
[17] Kuhn (1938), 56, 58, 68; Arntz (1944), 294; Ebel (1963), 73ff.   [18] Ebel (1963), 74f.

the use of OE *rǣdan* in connection with the runic script, the fact that it is regularly employed of reading the Roman script implies that it had earlier been used for reading runes by the Anglo-Saxons. Even without further evidence from other Gmc. languages it is probable that this was another technical runic term, earlier in use beyond the north.

The conclusions to be drawn from these four technical terms are clear. To start with, the position of OE is worthy of attention, since it is the only Gmc. language to apply three of these runic terms regularly to using the Roman alphabet (*stæf, wrītan, rǣdan*). On the other hand, OHG uses *rízan* very rarely and *stab* only in two compounds which it adopted from OE, so that it largely, if not entirely, failed to adapt runic terms to Latin texts, as OE had done. In this OHG is eventually followed by ON.[19] At the opposite extreme to OE Gothic stands alone, for none of these terms is attested for Gothic runic inscriptions (which may be because of their rarity), but none was used by Wulfila for other forms of writing, including that devised by him for the needs of Gothic, where an opportunity did present itself.[20]

We come now to what may be called the post-runic vocabulary of reading and writing in Germania. This can be divided into two separate parts, one antedating the coming of Christianity to northern Europe and the other closely connected with the new religion.

Only one pre-Christian example has been seriously entertained, but one central to the rise of literacy. Although it has been claimed that the word 'book' is yet another example of a runic term adapted to a new writing practice, the general consensus now sees it rather in connection with the Romans' use of writing, brought with them to Germania either by their army or by merchants. The Roman army was dependent on a regular flow of written information and on the transmission of orders over long distances, there is evidence for a correlation between rank and literacy in the army, with certain offices in the legions requiring educated, i.e. literate soldiers.[21] For Roman merchants literacy and written records became necessary with the growing complexity of trade, especially extending over more than just local transactions. In such circumstances writing could take various forms: names or other details scratched on an amphora, the use of a writing tablet for short messages or even longer communications.[22] It was the simple and

[19] Kuhn (1938), 64.   [20] *Ibid.*, pp. 64f.
[21] Rosenfeld (1952), 201ff.; (1956a), 262, fn. 3; Harris (1989), 166f., 253ff., 293f.
[22] Rosenfeld (1952), 201, 205; Harris (1989), 18, 202, 286.

adaptable writing tablet which influenced the vocabulary of writing in Germania.

The word *bōka*, employed at first usually in the plural, has the meaning 'book' or 'written text' in all the Gmc. languages, which of itself points to the early use of this word in the context of writing.[23] In Gothic alone, however, the word is also used to denote one single letter in a written text (II Cor. 3.6 and Rom. 7.6). It is generally agreed that there is a connection between this word and the related Gmc. term for 'beech' (ON *bók*, OE *bōc*, OHG *buocha*), so that the name of the particular wood used served to denote an object employed as a surface for writing. This has its parallels elsewhere in Gmc. (OE *æsc* 'ash tree' and 'spear', *lind* 'lime tree' and 'shield'),[24] but also, in connection with writing, in the classical languages (Gr. *bíblos* 'inner bark of the papyrus' and 'book', with the same two meanings attested for Lat. *liber*).[25] Our problem with Gmc. *bōka* is to decide what kind of object made of beech-wood was meant. Some have argued that this word, when used as a term for writing, originally denoted a beech-stave with a rune carved on it for casting lots (as described by Tacitus, *Germania* 10), then the runic sign itself.[26] Others see the word as denoting a flat board carved from this wood and used as the writing tablet employed by Roman officers or merchants.[27] Accepting the first explanation means adding *bōka* to the runic vocabulary we have been considering, whilst according to the second explanation the word would be of post-runic, but still pre-Christian, origin.

In deciding between these two possibilities a difficulty has always lain in the anomaly of Wulfila's use, unique within Gmc., of the singular *bōka* meaning a single written character (Gr. *grámma*, Lat. *littera*), a usage which is confirmed by the similar function of Sl. *buky*, thought to be loaned from Gothic.[28] The first explanation just referred to saw it as an obvious development for Wulfila then to use the plural *bōkōs* to mean a consecutive text (Gr. *grámmata*, Lat. *litterae*) or book. Conversely, so it was argued, if the plural *bōkōs* had meant 'writing tablets' or a 'book' or longer communication made up of several tablets, it would be difficult to explain how a singular word meaning 'writing tablet' (or 'beech tree') could be used for a single letter. From this the conclusion was drawn that Wulfila made use of a word originally denoting a beech-stave with a rune carved on it, then a runic sign, to translate in the singular *grámma* or

---

[23] Hoops (1913a), 338f.; Kuhn (1938), 59ff.; Rosenfeld (1952), 193ff.; Ebel (1963), 95f.; Ebenbauer (1981a), 35ff. [24] Hoops (1913a), 339; Ebenbauer (1981a), 35. See above, pp. 69f.
[25] Hoops (1913a), 337; Ebenbauer (1981a), 35. [26] Ebenbauer (1981a), 36.
[27] Rosenfeld (1952), 193ff. [28] Kuhn (1938), 59; Rosenfeld (1952), 196.

littera, but in the plural to denote a consecutive text or book, and that the word in this latter meaning was transmitted to WG as a term of the Gothic mission.[29] About this explanation doubts are justified. If Wulfila did make use of a native term from runic vocabulary in the context of a new script which he evolved from Mediterranean models for a Christian purpose, this would be the only example of a policy which Gothic, in sharp distinction from OE, otherwise shunned. In addition, we shall see that the influence of the Christian vocabulary of Gothic may have reached Bavarian (geographically nearest to the Christian Goths in the south-east), but other German dialects only rarely and OE not at all.[30] The wide spread of the word 'book' in WG thus presents a major difficulty for a theory of its Gothic origin.

By concentrating on Wulfila's use of the singular *bōka* to denote an individual letter this explanation ignores another singular use of the word which is even more widespread in Gmc. and hence provides a firmer starting-point. There is evidence to suggest that the object made from beech-wood, easily split into thin slices, which was termed *bōka* was not a rune-stave, but rather a writing tablet (Lat. *tabella* or *pugillaris*) covered in wax to provide a writing surface. The word denoting this common Roman implement conveyed in the singular the idea of a short message or 'document', in the plural it denoted a number of tablets bound together for a longer communication. With the introduction of Christian writing practice, using parchment pages and a bound codex, the word *bōka* was then used of the book or codex: consecutive pages replaced a group of tablets, and the bound covers of the book (still often of beech-wood) resembled the outer covers of two or more tablets put together for sending.

That the word *bōka* could have originated from a term to render a writing tablet is suggested at three different points in Germania. In the OS *Heliand* the word *bôk* (vv. 232, 235) is used in the scene where the Vulgate (Lc. 1.63) has Zachariah, struck dumb, write the name of his son John on a writing tablet (*pugillaris*). In OE the transition of this word's meaning from tablet to parchment is already registered when *bōc* (in addition to its meaning 'book') also denotes a shorter document or 'charter' (*bōcland* is therefore land held by written charter).[31] Finally, the Ostrogothic Deed of Arezzo contains the word *frabaúhtabōka* 'document of sale', where the word is used in a sense comparable to OE *bōc*.[32] The

---

[29] Gothic mission: Kuhn (1938), 65; Arntz (1944), 281.   [30] See below, pp. 308ff.
[31] Bosworth and Toller (1954), 113, 114.   [32] Streitberg (1919), 480.

spread of these examples through Germania suggests that *bōka* 'writing tablet', then 'short communication' (short enough for one tablet or, after the transition to a different material for writing, one parchment document) was CG. The Ostrogothic testimony heightens the possibility that Wulfila's use of the word for one individual letter (*grámma*, *littera*) was peculiar to his ecclesiastical vocabulary and cannot be taken as the starting-point for what is found elsewhere in Germania.

Two linguistic details lend support to this view.[33] First, the earlier practice with writing tablets is reflected in a common construction for reading or writing books. In the case of a bound codex we might expect either verb to be followed by the preposition 'in' ('to read in a book'), whereas a more common construction with 'on' refers back to consulting a tablet: ON *ríta á bókum*, OHG *lesan ana buohhum*, Go. *gakunnan ana bōkōm*. Secondly, the use of this word for 'book' in the plural, as these examples indicate (only later was the OHG neuter plural, *diu buoch*, replaced by a singular), reflects the fact that at an earlier stage in the history of literacy any lengthy communication in writing was transposed to a number of writing tablets (*bōkōs* in the plural) bound together. These two grammatical details therefore survived the technical change from one medium to another.

The use of the plural for 'book' also throws light on Wulfila's anomalous singular with a different meaning ('letter'). His plural employment of *bōkōs* agrees with the position elsewhere in Germania, but it also agrees with the use of the plural of the word for 'letter' applied to a lengthy written text in both the classical languages on which his Gothic bible was based: Gr. *grámmata*, *graphái*, Lat. *litterae*.[34] In other words, if the Gothic plural *bōkōs* corresponded to the Greek plural *grámmata*, then it is understandable that Wulfila used the singular *bōka* to render the Greek singular *grámma*, especially since the Goths now occupied territory beyond the limits in which the beech grew, so that any semantic confusion in using the singular was avoided.[35] Far from reflecting past practice with native runes, Wulfila's singular *bōka* instead illustrates his encounter with the terminology of writing in the classical world.

Germania therefore learned of Roman writing tablets and designated them with a word common to Gothic and to WG, but this raises the question how this word spread throughout Germania in this sense. If we fall back on polygenesis and assume that WG acquired knowledge of

---

[33] Hoops (1913a), 339f. [34] Ebenbauer (1981a), 36.
[35] Rosenfeld (1952), 196. See also Hoops (1913b), 342ff. (with map); Behre (1981), 58f.

Roman writing practice across the Rhine frontier, while the Goths made their contact across the lower Danube, we confront the remarkable, indeed incredible coincidence that at both geographical extremities of the imperial frontier the same vernacular word (not even a loanword) was independently chosen to designate this novelty.[36] However, if we postulate monogenesis (the Gmc. word was coined at only one point of contact and then spread to both WG and EG), we must dismiss, as we saw, the possibility of a spread from Gothic to WG. The converse possibility, from WG to Gothic, is only feasible while the Goths were still in northern Poland, which would tie up with other terms, including Latin loanwords into Gmc., where the same assumption must be made, especially in the sphere of trade.[37] To explain the adaptation of a native word like *bōka* to new ends, however, it is not enough to refer simply to Roman trade with northern Europe in the first centuries AD, which of itself could explain at the most Latin loanwords adopted in Gmc. Instead, we need to assume Germanic-speakers, already making use of *bōka*, accompanying Roman traders as interpreters and guides or acting as trading middlemen themselves.

Wulfila's acquisition of a meaning for the singular *bōka* which was anomalous within Germania (it resulted from his contact with two classical languages and the need to render *grámma* or *littera* in the bible) may serve as a bridge to the second aspect of post-runic vocabulary. Under this heading we deal with technical terms in ecclesiastical literature, applied either to the Gothic script devised by Wulfila or to the Roman script employed elsewhere in Germania. Some of these terms are loanwords from Greek or Latin, others are loan-translations, so that we are now concerned, as was the case with *bōka*, with terminology evolved after the Germanic tribes had made closer acquaintance with Mediterranean writing practice, but now in a Christian context.

We may start with the two complementary essentials of any literate culture, writing and reading. In Gothic Wulfila needed to find a vernacular term for the new technology of writing (with pen, ink and parchment in contrast to runes carved on wood, bone or metal).[38] This need can only partly account for his avoidance of runic *wrîtan*, for this was applied in OE to the new technology with no difficulty. Wulfila's choice of word for reading, where no novel technology was involved, also avoided a runic term such as OE *rēdan*, so that we may suspect that, in

---

[36] Kuhn (1938), 60; Rosenfeld (1952), 195.   [37] See above, pp. 206ff.   [38] Rosenfeld (1952), 207.

addition to finding terms for a new technology, Wulfila may also have wished to avoid runic vocabulary.

For writing Wulfila employed the verb *mēljan* for Gr. *gráphein* and the plural noun *mēla* for *grámmata* and *graphḗ*.[39] Only in Gothic are these words used in the context of writing, their cognates in OHG are *mâlên* 'to mark, stain, paint' and *mâl* 'a mark, stain, point', with further developments in OE and ON. It is conceivable that Wulfila used words with the general meaning 'mark' and 'to make a mark' which had not previously been applied to writing in order to designate the novel type of writing found in the Mediterranean world. This is confirmed by etymological cognates of the Gothic stem: its counterparts in Gaulish and Latvian mean 'black', in Lithuanian 'dark blue dye', while Lat. *mulleus* means 'dark red' and Gr. *mélas* 'black'.[40] These cognates suggest that Go. *mēljan* denoted writing with a dark ink on parchment, as opposed to incising runes on other materials or scratching on the wax of a writing tablet. Why Wulfila chose a word meaning 'to make a black or dark mark' is explained by his word for 'ink', which like his Mediterranean models suggests the colour black: Go. *swartizl*, Gr. *mélan*, Lat. *atramentum*. (It is even possible that the Greek model suggested the phonetically similar Gothic stem *mēl-*, differing only in the length of the vowel.)

A Greek model also lies behind the Gothic word for 'to read', likewise unique within Germania: *gakunnan* renders *anagignṓskein*, two words which correspond closely in their formation.[41] The Greek verb derives from one meaning 'to know' and conveys the idea 'to get to know, to recognise', therefore 'to recognise the meaning, to read'. Similarly, Go. *gakunnan* is a perfective formation from *kunnan* 'to know' and was used to mean both 'to recognise' and 'to read'. This parallel, as well as the unique position of the Gothic word within Germania, makes it likely that Wulfila followed the Greek model, which is suggested even more forcibly when the Gothic prefix *ga-* is replaced by another which is the same as in Greek: *anakunnan* as a variant rendering of *anagignṓskein*.

For the same two literate activities OHG similarly based its choice on the precedent of classical literacy, turning to Latin rather than to Greek. For writing WG uses a word, as in OHG *skrîban*, which was loaned from Lat. *scribere*.[42] Within WG there is a semantic differentiation: in OHG the verb means 'to write', but in OE it means 'to impose penance (after

---

[39] Kuhn (1938), 61f.; Arntz (1944), 288; Rosenfeld (1952), 207f.   [40] Lehmann (1986), 250f.
[41] Kuhn (1938), 62. Cf. Ebel (1963), 76f.   [42] Zimmer (1892), 145ff.; Kuhn (1938), 63.

confession), to shrive'. OS and OFri. seem to have agreed first with OE, but then been influenced by OHG. In ON *skrífa* means 'to write', but *skript* 'confession, penance, shrift'. This double function (OE knows nothing of 'to write', OHG knows only this) suggests a twofold loan-process from Lat. *scribere* in England and in Germany, independently of each other. This implies a late loan (no longer common WG), borne out by the Christian usage of the OE term in penitential practice. In this field the Anglo-Saxons influenced the continent in developing a closely organised system of confession and penance, based on *interrogationes* and *canones*, drawn up in Latin texts (*scripta*, cf. OE *scriftbōc* 'penitential').[43] The Latin term therefore found its way into OE in this specialised context, then from OE into those Gmc. languages on the continent most closely exposed to the Anglo-Saxon mission (OFri., OS, then ON).[44]

That the adoption of *scribere* in Germany (OS and OHG) was also relatively late can be seen from two points. When in the *Heliand* (231ff.) Zachariah writes on a writing tablet (*bôk*) his activity is summed up in two words: *wrîtan*, in agreement with OE, and *giskrîban*, in agreement with OHG.[45] This could suggest that there was a period on the continent when both words for writing, one runic in origin and the other introduced with Roman writing practice, were in use. How they could be differentiated is shown in OHG by Otfrid, who uses the new verb *skrîban* (of Latin and Christian texts) with reference to classical authors, the evangelists and his own activity as an author, but the other verb *rîzan* in describing Christ writing with His fingers on the ground.[46] Implied by this is a reluctance to see the new word as applicable to anything but parchment, whereas the runic term could be used of making a meaningful incision in wood, metal or earth. (The physical similarity between incising a rune and using a stilus on a wax tablet may also justify the use of *wrîtan* in the passage on Zachariah in the *Heliand*, as also when Notker uses it of writing Latin letters with a stilus on a tablet.)[47] If *skrîban* in Germany was closely connected with writing on parchment and was introduced with it, it was as much an ecclesiastical term as its OE counterpart, even though not used in penitential discipline.

For the act of reading OHG employs the verb *lesan*, probably passing it on in this sense to OS and ON, as was the case with *skrîban*.[48] OHG *lesan* is also used in the sense 'to gather, collect', as is likewise the case in OS and ON, whilst the meaning 'to gather' is the only one attested for

---

[43] Zimmer (1892), 146ff.   [44] *Ibid.*, p. 148.   [45] Schröder (1924b), 57.   [46] *Ibid.*, pp. 57f.

[47] Notker, *Boethius, De Consolatione* 223, 31; 372, 15.

[48] Kuhn (1938), 62f.; Arntz (1944), 293; Ebel (1963), 78.

Gothic and OE, where the semantic gap for 'to read' was filled from elsewhere (*gakunnan, rēdan*). In the case of *lesan*, too, a runic origin has been suggested, combining the ideas of 'reading' with 'gathering' on the basis of the description of the casting of lots given by Tacitus (*Germania* 10): the priest picks up a wooden stave with a rune carved on it in order to read its meaning. However, this suggestion operates with a meaning for *lesan* 'to choose, pick out – by picking up' which is not attested. Just how distinct this verb originally meaning 'to gather' (cf. *Heliand* 2568f., where *lesan* is used in conjunction with *tesamne* 'together') must be kept from the idea of selection is shown in a passage from Wulfila. When rendering Mc. 13.27 (Christ gathers together His elect) he makes a clear distinction between *galisan* 'to gather' and *gawaljan* 'to choose'.[49] If the verb *arlesan* occurs very occasionally in OHG in the sense 'to choose' (and also very seldom in the case of OE *ālesan*, OS *alesan*), this meaning was probably loaned from Lat. *eligere*.[50] It is in fact Latin which explains how OHG developed the meaning 'to read' from a verb meaning 'to gather'. Not merely was this secondary OHG meaning unique within Germania, it must also be set against the fact that Lat. *legere* meant 'to read' as well as 'to gather'.[51] OHG *lesan* is therefore as much a loan-meaning from Latin as Go. *gakunnan* was a loan-translation from Greek. The Gothic and OHG words for 'to read' are both unique within Germania because each is a copy of a non-Germanic model.

The exposure of OHG to the Latin vocabulary of literacy in the context of Christianity went much further than a loanword for 'to write' and a model for 'to read'. To illustrate this we may start by turning back to the vernacular word, OHG *buoh*, for the Roman writing tablet, *tabella*. The later development of this German word, under the impact of literacy in the hands of Christian clerics, first to 'document' and then to 'book', gave rise to a lexical gap for the original meaning, which still needed to be expressed, since the writing-tablet remained in use through the Middle Ages.[52] Although Lat. *tabula/tabella* had been taken over in German as a loanword (OHG *zabal*), this is attested only in the meaning 'gaming board',[53] as still in MHG *schâchzabel* 'chessboard', so that the lexical gap still persisted. It was filled by borrowing the same Latin word a second time, producing now OHG *tavala*, meaning primarily 'writing tablet' alongside occasional 'gaming board'.[54] From the phonological difference between *zabal* and *tavala*, it is clear that the second form was

---

[49] Kuhn (1938), 63. [50] *Ibid.* [51] This against Arntz (1944), 293. [52] Bischoff (1979), 26ff.
[53] Starck and Wells (1990), 752. [54] *Ibid.*, p. 623.

borrowed later: it shows VL -*v*- in place of Classical Latin -*b*- and it must have been loaned after the completion of the Second Sound Shift.

Other words belonging to the vocabulary of writing in OHG point to the same conclusion: they are all loanwords from Latin which must have been taken over late. We may divide them into various aspects of writing practice, the first of which, as with *tabula/tabella*, concerns the object or material on which writing was done. The Roman writing tablet, as we have seen, was important enough to call forth various attempts to name it in Gmc.: *bōka* as a counterpart formed from native linguistic material, then *zabal* as an early loanword (but outside the context of writing) and finally *tavala*. Although the Roman object could be made ambitiously from ivory, the more frequent form was of wood, which accounts for its wide spread and persistence as a cheap and practical writing instrument. For more pretentious writing purposes papyrus, largely an Egyptian monopoly, was used in classical antiquity in the form of scrolls and then by Christians from the second century in the shape of folios folded into a codex.[55] It continued to be used well into the Middle Ages, so that documents from the Merovingian royal chancery, for example, still used papyrus towards the end of the seventh century. The Latin word is attested in OHG, even if once only, in the form *papîr*.[56] The Latin word *charta*, used of a sheet for writing made from papyrus, has found an equally faint reflection in OHG *karta* (one example only).[57] The disadvantage of papyrus (its durability in the European climate is questionable) may be one of the reasons why writing in late antiquity made the transition not merely from scroll to codex, but also from papyrus to parchment. The new material, made out of sheepskin, was more durable, even if more expensive because of the careful preparation required (the Codex Amiatinus, produced in Northumbria, demanded as many as 500 sheepskins).[58] The Latin word for this new material, *pergamenum*, was in origin the adjective from the place-name Pergamon, in Asia Minor. It was borrowed into OHG, where it is attested reasonably frequently in the forms *pergamîn/pergamente*.[59]

The different surfaces used for writing demanded different instruments for inscribing the letters. The wax surface of the writing tablet had to have shallow incisions made on it, which could then subsequently be erased so that the tablet could be used again. The instrument for performing both operations was the stilus, with one end sharp for incisions and the other

---

[55] Bischoff (1979), 19ff. [56] *GR* 2, 358. [57] Starck and Wells (1990), 323.
[58] Bischoff (1979), 21ff. [59] Starck and Wells (1990), 458.

blunt for erasures (it could also be used for faint entries on parchment).[60] In the biblical passage (Lc. 1.63) where Zachariah wrote on a writing tablet (*pugillaris*, rendered as *bôk* in the *Heliand*) the *Tatian* translators refer not to this, but to the writing instrument he used: *scrîbsahs* (4,12), literally 'writing knife'.[61] Elsewhere, the word more commonly used for this tool was *griffil*, probably derived from another Latin word of Greek origin, *graphium* (cf. OHG *graf* in this sense), with assimilation to *grîfan* 'to grip' by popular etymology and the addition of the suffix *-il*, used for tools.[62] Although the stilus could also be used on parchment, the result was too faint to be easily legible for practical purposes, so that the use of ink demanded another form of writing instrument. Although classical antiquity had used the *calamus* or reed pen (which continued to be used in the Mediterranean world in the early Middle Ages), the more widespread instrument for conveying ink on to parchment in the Middle Ages was the quill pen, made from a bird's feather. The word for this was Lat. *penna* (or *pinna?*),[63] meaning originally no more than 'feather', but then 'pen', which found its way into Germania not as a loanword (Engl. 'pen' is a later borrowing from OFr.), but as a loan-translation: OE *feðer*, OHG *federa*.[64]

As regards the use of ink, although Wulfila devised a native word for it on the model of Greek and Latin, preference is given to loanwords from Latin elsewhere in Germania. Each of the three most common Latin terms, reflecting different ways of making ink, is attested in Germany. *Atramentum*, conveying the idea of a black liquid which we saw in Go. *swartizl*, was loaned into OHG as *atrament* and, showing a closer assimilation to OHG phonology, *atraminza*.[65] Another word, deriving from Lat. *encaustum* (originally the purple ink used by the Roman emperor for his signature), occupies a more restricted area in northern WG, as in MDu. *inket, inkt, ink* and Rhenish *enk, ink*. This word also found its way into OFr. as *enque* (cf. modern Fr. *encre*).[66] Both these forms were unable always to hold their own against a third form: Lat. *(aqua) tincta* 'coloured liquid', attested in OHG as *tincta / tinte / timpte* and glossing both *atramentum* and *encaustum*.[67] Another word, restricted in its scope on the continent, points to the possibility of OE influence, this time by means of a loan-translation. Just as Wulfila coined *swartizl* for the new technology, so was *atramentum* copied in OE by *blæc*, an adjective used as a noun to mean 'black ink'. This form has counterparts on the continent in OS

---

[60] Bischoff (1979), 32.   [61] Cf. also Starck and Wells (1990), 548.

[62] *Ibid.*, p. 239; Kluge and Seebold (1989), 278.   [63] *FEW* 8, 526ff.

[64] Bosworth and Toller (1954), 285; Starck and Wells (1990), 143.   [65] *GR* 2, 103ff.

[66] *Ibid.*; *FEW* 3, 224f.   [67] *GR* 2, 105f.

blac, MDu. *black*, EFri. *blak* (with scattered outriders in Franconian and UG, not always understood).[68] That we are justified in seeing these continental forms as under the influence of OE is suggested by palaeographic evidence: Irish and Anglo-Saxon scriptoria used a characteristic dark brown ink, the employment of which can be traced on the continent in those areas which, as with the word for ink, were particularly exposed to the influence of the Anglo-Saxon mission and scriptoria.[69] It looks therefore as if the OE word for 'ink' accompanied the particular type of ink the Anglo-Saxons used.

A practical advantage with the writing tablet was the possibility, after using it once, of wiping the wax smooth and clean in order to use it again. This was not possible when using the stilus on parchment, but it was feasible (and desirable in view of the expense of parchment) if pen and ink had been used: the surface was washed or scraped clean of the ink already used for the first text, and then used again for a new one, a 'palimpsest'.[70] The word used in Latin for this procedure was the verb *delere*, meaning originally 'to destroy', but also acquiring a technical meaning in the context of writing: 'to delete' in order to use the surface again. With or without the addition of a prefix the word is found in OE *(ā)dilegian* (with -*g*- functioning as a glide), above all in clerical translations, especially of the Psalms, where it renders Lat. *delere* both in the general sense 'to destroy' and with the specialist meaning 'to delete, erase'.[71] Whereas in OE the loanword remains tied to ecclesiastical usage, it passes beyond this in Germany. Here it can also be used in the context of the Psalms both with OS *fardiligon* and OHG *firdiligôn/firtiligôn* (*nomen delere* 'to delete a name from the Book of Life'), but also with a much wider range ('to abolish, consume, exterminate'), especially with Notker.[72] If we accept the suggestion that the Latin word was first borrowed into OE in clerical scriptoria and then taken to the continent by the Anglo-Saxon mission,[73] then the path of this word southwards in Germany would be marked by the variation in OHG between -*d*- and -*t*-, where the latter represents an attempt to give an UG form to a word from the north. In this connection it may be suggestive, but certainly not conclusive, that Lat. *pumex* 'pumice', used in scraping parchment clean, was borrowed into OE (*pumic*) and OHG (*pumez*).[74] However, the frequency of this practice in scriptoria could well mean that the word was loaned into the two languages independently.

---

[68] *Ibid.*, pp. 104f.   [69] Rosenfeld (1952), 208; Bischoff (1979), 30.   [70] Bischoff (1979), 23ff.
[71] Schröder (1923), 246ff.   [72] *GR* 2, 226ff.   [73] Schröder (1923), 248.
[74] Bosworth and Toller (1954), 779; Starck and Wells (1990), 465.

For the finished product of this scribal activity, the actual written communication, Latin used *libellus brevis*, which could then be abbreviated to *libellus* or to *brevis*. The first, a diminutive of *liber* 'book', is attested in OHG in the forms *libel/livol*, where the latter, so far from denoting only a short book, as the Latin diminutive might suggest, is even applied to one of the longest works in OHG literature, Otfrid's *Evangelienbuch*.[75] This form differs from *libel* (which points to a learned borrowing direct from written Latin *libellus*) in presupposing an origin in VL *livellus*. *Brevis*, on the other hand, is reflected in OHG *briaf* 'letter, document, sheet' and may thus be said to have retained the force of a shorter communication (cf. also *brieftabula* 'writing tablet').[76] In the OS *Heliand* 230ff. *brêf* is used of a short communication (one name only) and is varied by *bôk* 'writing tablet'. The OHG diphthong presupposes an earlier long *e*, as in VL in this position in an open syllable by contrast with the short *e* in Classical Latin. A stage later than Classical Latin is also implied by the final *-f* in OHG, indicating that in its Latin model *-v-* was no longer pronounced as a semi-vowel, but as a fricative.

This last word has brought us to the question of dating these loan-words by phonological means, where we are helped by the evidence from German sound changes. By chance many of the words acquired from Latin in this lexical field contain consonants which would have been subject to the Second Sound Shift, but it cannot be fortuitous that none of them shows its effects: *tavala* (as opposed to *zabal*, not used in the context of writing), *papîr, karta, pergamîn/pergamente, griffil, atrament, firdiligôn*. Two exceptions are more likely to be only apparent, representing assimilations to UG phonology: *firtiligôn* alongside *firdiligôn* (cf. for a later stage in German, OFr. *danser* > MDu. *dansen* > MHG *tanzen*) and *pergaminza* alongside *pergamente* (cf. Lat. *pigmentum* > OHG *pîminta*, but also *pîminza*).[77] (OHG *paffûr* as a rendering for *papyrus*, with one *p* shifted and the other unshifted, remains a problem.)[78] If none of these words was therefore borrowed early enough to be affected by the Sound Shift and if they are attested once a written tradition in OHG began this suggests a probable loan in the seventh and eighth centuries (in some cases even later).[79] They represent a stage in the introduction of writing to Germany considerably later than the runic script or the Romans' use of the writing tablet, as is confirmed by the technical fact that the wide use of papyrus, parchment and ink, together with all the other appurtenances of a

---

[75] Starck and Wells (1990), 372; Otfrid: III 1, 1 (cf. also Kelle (1881), 369).
[76] Starck and Wells (1990), 77.   [77] *GR* 1, 191; 2, 386f.   [78] *GR* 2, 358.
[79] Hüpper (1986b), 112.

growing literacy, were brought to northern Europe by the Church. Whether we have to locate this writing activity of the Church in the monasteries, whose schools and scriptoria were focal points of literacy, or in the Merovingian chanceries is immaterial besides the fact that in either case this activity and the employment of such technical terms as these were in the hands of clerics.[80]

In quite different ways this chapter and the preceding one have had to some extent to take account of Christian influence. With the days of the week what might be called a Christian censorship of pagan planetary names played a more successful rôle in eastern Europe (including Gothic) than in the west, but was not completely absent here, especially with names which were regarded as holy within the Christian week. With the vocabulary of writing the wish to avoid any association with pagan runic magic combined with the rôle of Christianity as a religion of the book to make this vocabulary a growing concern of the Church. To the religious implications of these points we shall have to return later. Taken together, these last two chapters prepare the way for Part III, in which we consider the impact of Christianity on Germania.

---

[80] Monasteries: Bischoff (1979), 58; Ebenbauer (1981a), 36; Hüpper (1986b), 112, 122. Chanceries: Schröder (1924b), 58.

PART III

Contact with Christianity

Introduction to Part III

In Part II we were mainly concerned with the growing contact of the Germanic tribes with the Roman Empire, above all in the case of the Franks on the lower Rhine and the Goths on the lower Danube. By the fourth century, however, Christianity had become an important part of the Empire and of classical civilisation, but had not developed any policy of a planned, systematic mission. It was therefore not the case that the new religion was brought to Germanic barbarians by missionaries, but rather that the migrations of these Germani, in taking them to the frontier zone of the Empire, and then across it, also brought them into contact with Christianity.[1] As long as they remained beyond the imperial frontiers these tribes were pagan, but they were converted to Christianity, in one form or another, within a generation or so of arriving in the Empire.[2] If not in the sense in which he meant it, the apologia made by Orosius can be said to be correct: God is to be praised because the barbarians were granted entry on to Roman territory so that the churches of Christ in east and west should be filled with believers, Huns, Suevi, Vandals and Burgundians.[3] Contact with Rome was therefore tantamount to contact with Christianity.

The theme of Part III is therefore a particular aspect of the subject of Part II, but one of such historical importance that it has to be treated separately. Moreover, the Church, having assimilated many Roman traditions itself, was the primary means by which these traditions were conveyed to medieval society: in episcopal organisation, administration, literacy and learning. It was the crucial factor which assisted in the amalgamation of classical and barbarian traditions, in bringing about the threefold conjunction which is the subject of this book.

In looking at the contact of Germania with Christianity we shall have to narrow our focus somewhat by concentrating principally on the

---

[1] Schmidt (1954), 155.   [2] Thompson (1966), 127f.   [3] Schäferdiek (1978a), 508.

evidence from OHG. This is forced upon us for the practical reason that the enormous scope of this theme, chronologically as well as geographically, makes selectivity imperative. Even so, to focus on OHG still allows a reasonably wide treatment, both because of the variety of external Christian influences on Germany (Gothic, Merovingian Frankish, Anglo-Saxon) and ultimately because of OHG influence beyond its own boundaries (on OS and indirectly on ON).

CHAPTER 15

Problems of Christianisation

In the earliest period Christian communities lived very much as small groups turned inwards and anxious, especially in the age of persecutions, to give no offence to the pagan society in which they lived and not concerned to convert pagans at all costs.[1] The gaining of new believers was an act of individual conversion, confined at the most to contact between small groups and far removed from political concerns of state. Proselytising arose from chance encounters with non-Christians who may have shown interest, often with women and slaves, the underprivileged of antiquity especially open to the revolutionary prospects of the new religion. Although Christianity had its apostles and evangelists the early Church dispensed with public missionary preaching, if only to avoid the attention of a hostile pagan state. Instead, whoever showed interest in the new religion (and the impetus had to come from that direction) was allowed to attend the service of a local parish, where the sermon to the congregation also served as a missionary sermon to the unconverted interested enough to attend. If the early Christians were forced by circumstances largely to dispense with verbal propaganda, they were able to make this good by a propaganda of the deed. Pagan outsiders were therefore drawn to the new religion (as in the case of Tertullian) by observing the Christians' readiness for self-sacrifice and their high moral standards, their care for the poor and the weak in society (it may be no accident that one of the earliest Christian terms to find its way into Germanic concerned such activity: *Almosen* 'alms').[2] In this sense every Christian who attracted favourable attention by living up to such ethical demands was his own missionary. The same was even more true of the Christian ready to embrace martyrdom.

The lack of an active missionary policy, together with the fact that the impetus to conversion had to come from those outsiders who were

---

[1] Frend (1974), 32ff.; Holl (1974), 3ff.; Kahl (1978), 45ff., 60ff.   [2] See below, p. 306.

interested, meant that particular importance was attached to the institution of the catechumenate, the instruction of the candidate for conversion in the tenets and demands of the new religion as a precondition of baptism. For the Church to impose this requirement, however, means that it gave pride of place to the would-be convert's individual freedom of choice, to his informed awareness of what he was about to undertake. This emphasis ties up with the rejection of force as a means of conversion (even Augustine, despite his attitude to the Donatist heretics, seems not to have contemplated the use of force against non-Christians) – quite apart from the fact that in the earliest centuries the Church was more the victim than the wielder of compulsion. The small-scale nature of the earliest spread of Christianity, from individual to individual or at the most from group to group, and its divorce from the rôle of the state meant that the widest limits which the early Church could conceive for itself were those of the Roman Empire. If Christianity was taken beyond these boundaries in the earliest centuries (to Armenia or to the Goths while they were still outside the Empire) these were not the outcome of a consciously adopted universal mission.

In almost all these respects the early medieval Church, as it arose after Constantine, Chlodwig and Gregory the Great, adopted a different attitude towards the spread of its religion. From Constantine's victory and conversion there date the great increase of Christians within the Empire and new types of missionary activity, including missions organised by the emperor himself (in which religious and political factors are intertwined) or by bishops to restore peace to their dioceses (so that an element of compulsion is involved), but also isolated proselytising by individuals amongst the barbarians beyond the imperial frontiers.[3]

The connection of conversion with the state and politics has a twofold explanation. On the one hand, this would be a natural consideration for possible converts in Germania, where the pagan tribal religion was intimately associated with the social and political life of the tribe. On the other hand, the missionary entering pagan territory under the protection of a neighbouring Christian ruler would be regarded above all as the political emissary of an expansive power. Nor could the missionary, setting foot on pagan soil beyond the Roman frontier, dispense with such protection (as with the Frankish support given to Columbanus or Boniface), even if that meant entering a ruler's service.[4] Concomitant with this political dimension and with princely support was the phenomenon of mass conversions, of whole peoples following the example of their ruler, perhaps the most pronounced difference from the early Church.[5] The conversion of a ruler generally meant the adhesion to Christianity of many of his followers, however superficial the process may have been, so that the real task of religious education remained to be accomplished afterwards. This is a feature recurrent in the Christianisation of the Germanic tribes and is especially well attested for Anglo-Saxon England. Religious education taken in hand only after a mass baptism testifies to a drastic reduction of the rôle of the catechumenate which had been an indispensable preliminary to baptism in the early Church.[6] Whereas hitherto Christ's twofold command to the disciples (Mt. 28.19: 'Teach all nations, baptising them') had been followed in that sequence, now it was reversed. If baptism represents the ritual borderline between paganism and Christianity it was often crossed at what we can only regard as an astonishingly early point in a missionary process in which the emphasis fell primarily on the power of the Christian God and the need to acknowledge this by renouncing the tribal gods, thus leaving the main task of dogmatic instruction to subsequent pastoral supervision.

Although Gregory the Great remained opposed to forcible conversion he accepted the principle that it might be necessary to prepare the way for preaching the gospel to pagans outside the Empire by first subjugating them militarily and thus providing a protective framework for peaceful preaching.[7] He was sanguine enough to see this use of military force as proceeding not from a wish for bloodshed, but from a desire to bring the gospel to the subjugated peoples (*per subditas gentes*). Indirectly Gregory therefore advocated the possibility of missionary warfare, a policy later carried to extremes by Charles the Great against the continental Saxons, calling forth the criticism of Alcuin. If the use of military force was made necessary by the wish to spread the gospel beyond the frontiers, this points to a final difference from the position in the early Church which had not regarded it as its task to be active outside the Empire. The historic change in policy is represented again by Pope Gregory whose pontificate was marked from the beginning by a concern with the conversion of pagans (Langobards, Sardinians, Anglo-Saxons) and whose mission to Kent was a decisive step in inaugurating an organised universal mission to northern Europe.[8]

[5] Baetke (1944a), 123; Levison (1946), 47f.
[6] Baetke (1942), 221f.; Kahl (1978), 47ff.; Schneider (1978), 242.
[7] Kahl (1978), 63f., 68; Schneider (1978), 244.   [8] Frend (1974), 41ff.

The different attitudes shown by the Church to the need to convert pagans in the periods before and after the victory of Constantine and the institution of Christianity as the religion of the Roman state are therefore considerable, so much so that they make it difficult to employ a number of key-terms in a way which does justice to such widely differing conditions.

With regard to 'mission' we need to be more cautious than those philologists who have attributed Christian terms in OHG to the influence of a variety of mission movements bringing them to Germany. This makes no distinction between the occasional, interpersonal proselytising of the early Church and the more organised form of universal mission which later developed.[9] How relevant this distinction is to Germania can be seen in the traces of the vocabulary of the provincial Roman Christians of the Rhineland or in the conversion of the earliest Gothic Christians by Cappadocian prisoners of war. In neither case was any organised mission responsible for the formation of an early Christian vocabulary, as was later the case with the Gregorian mission to England or with the Anglo-Saxons in Germany. Instead, these terms result from the personal contact of Germanic pagans with Christian communities still surviving in the Rhineland, they need not even indicate that the Franks who first used the word for 'church' to designate the buildings they saw were themselves Christian.[10] To associate a group of Christian terms in OHG with a fully fledged mission to Germany begs the question in another way if we recall that to the probable presence of some German terms of Gothic origin there corresponds no known Gothic mission to Germany, whilst conversely the historically attested presence of Irish missionaries (even if their rôle has been exaggerated) has yielded no reliable examples of their linguistic influence on German. Doubts about the term 'mission' are also called for by the attempt of the Church in sixth- and seventh-century Francia to regain ground lost as a result of the barbarian invasions. This may well have involved the conversion of individual pagans, but from the point of view of the Church it was more an ecclesiastical restoration or a *Reconquista*, still operating well within the boundaries of the Empire. Given such reservations it is best to avoid using 'mission' as a blanket term altogether, certainly in the linguistic context, and to speak instead more generally of the creation of a Christian vocabulary in German from various sources.

Even the term 'conversion' has its pitfalls. Strictly speaking, it involves

---

[9] Fritze (1969), 78ff.   [10] See below, pp. 299, 300.

conversion from sinfulness by means of repentance (Acts 2.38: 'Repent and be baptised every one of you in the name of Jesus Christ for the remission of sins'), but the difficulty in Germania lay in conveying the religious dimension of repentance and sin, for pagans may well have regretted some of their actions or even regarded them as a *níðingsverk*, but not in the context of their religious practices. Until they understood this religious dimension their renunciation of the old religion could only fall short of what the Church meant by conversion. This shortfall is heightened by the contrast between individual conversion and a mass process involving a whole tribe. There may be no cause to doubt the genuineness of the conversion of individual Visigoths, won over by the example set by Christian prisoners they had taken and ready to accept martyrdom in repeated persecutions, but can it be meaningfully said that a whole tribe was converted together in the same sense?[11] Even if religious motives (alongside political ones) may have informed the individual conversion of Constantine or Chlodwig, can it be said that their followers, who accepted baptism with their leaders, were likewise prompted? In what sense can the term 'conversion' be applied to the Saxons, forced to baptism by Charles the Great? What is involved here is at the most a change of cult or of religious observances far removed from the religious sense of *metánoia*, a superficial change of ritual allegiance to which a neutral term such as 'adhesion' to the new religion or even 'Christianisation' is better suited than the more loaded 'conversion'.

How far short of the Christian sense of conversion the change of many Germanic tribes actually fell is suggested by the need to describe their newly found Christianity as syncretistic, combining the old with the new. One cause of this syncretism was the encounter between a tribal religion (whose gods guaranteed fertility and victory, therewith the survival of the tribe) and a universal God who was claimed to have the power to intervene in any tribe's life, for the common reaction of a tribal religion to such a situation is to incorporate the new divinity into its existing pantheon. Widukind therefore reported of the Danes that, although nominally Christian, they also worshipped their ancestral gods and even held them to be superior to Christ.[12] The religious psychology behind this is understandable, for it must have been difficult for worshippers in a polytheistic religion to accept that the new God was the only one and that all their tribal gods were false, an argument which has been used in

---

[11] Baetke (1944a), 84, 123.   [12] Kahl (1978), 34f., 51, fn. 89.

the case of Constantine himself.[13] Nor need the Church always reject such mixed beliefs, for they provided opportunities to missionaries willing to adopt a policy of accommodation by working with these half-beliefs in external form, but hoping to outplay them.[14]

Apart from such cases of a short-term policy of accommodation for the sake of long-term advantages these syncretistic beliefs could only be opposed by the Church, but their very presence testifies to the superficial conversion of those nominal Christians to whom they are attributed.[15] Long after their nominal conversion the Franks are supposed to have performed human sacrifices on the Italian campaign of Theudebert I, whilst from Iceland it is reported that Helgi the Lean had a mixed belief: he believed in Christ, but in difficult undertakings he appealed to the god Thor. Examples like these are many and run the gamut from a subsidiary role granted to the new religion to its grudgingly tactful toleration of traces of the old.[16] They are an indication of how drastically novel the idea of one universal, 'supertribal' God must have been and suggest that this new God must have been regarded for some time by many as a *primus inter pares*.

The interaction between a tribal and a universal religion also underlies the idea that the Church had a universal mission to all pagans. A tribal religion does not proselytise, since its adherents all belong to the tribe, just as the benefits conferred by the gods are confined to that tribe, even though there may be other gods for other peoples.[17] Acceptance of the Christian God could only take place when His power to intervene in tribal affairs was shown, but for this the new God had to be brought to the Germanic tribes, i.e. the Church had to develop a missionary policy going beyond the Empire. The idea that Christianity as a universal religion automatically developed a universal mission is historically by no means self-evident,[18] for the early Church relied for proselytising on personal encounters, on chance contacts, rather than planned ones, it dispensed with missionaries and developed no mission programme. For Pope Leo the Great the universality of the Empire, embracing so many peoples, argued against the need for a mission beyond its frontiers.[19] However, the fall of the Empire and its invasion by pagan tribes destroyed the basis of this argument and granted renewed relevance to Christ's command to the disciples to go and teach all peoples (Mt. 28.19: *Ite, docete omnes gentes*). Whereas the early Church had understood *gentes*,

---

13 Lane Fox (1988), 330, 619f.   14 Flint (1991), 305f.
15 Schäferdiek (1978a), 526, 538; Baetke (1944b), 165f. (3 and 4).   16 Kuhn (1978), 316f.
17 Thompson (1966), 62; Kahl (1978), 30ff.   18 Fritze (1969), 123.   19 *Ibid.*, pp. 124f.

in imitation of Hebrew *goyim*, to refer to all Gentiles or pagans, seeing them as individuals to be proselytised, the barbarian invasions granted urgency to the ethnic sense of *gentes*, now conceived as the pagan tribes in and beyond the Empire.[20]

The decisive step in this development of a universal mission was the mission of Augustine, sent by Pope Gregory to convert the Anglo-Saxons.[21] Where the disciples had been enjoined to preach the gospel to every creature (Mc. 16.15: *omnis creatura*), Gregory interpreted this in ethnic terms (*omnis natio gentium*), a widening of scope from earlier individual proselytising to pagan peoples at large, especially those outside Rome's frontiers.[22] Later the compliment was to be returned when the christianised Anglo-Saxons themselves sent missionaries abroad, to some Germanic tribes with whom they felt a degree of kinship (Frisians, Saxons), but also, if we can trust the list given by Bede, to such distant peoples as the Slavs and Avars.[23] Geography may have made the latter goal unreachable, but their intention, together with what they did achieve, shows that Gregory's universal mission had borne fruit and was now continued by those whose Christianisation he had himself inaugurated.

The problems of christianising pagans were accompanied by the linguistic problems posed by Christianity. Words had to be devised every time a language boundary was crossed to express features of the new religion, so that each language had to be 'baptised' as much as its speakers.[24] The universalism of Christianity gave rise to linguistic problems from the start, for with the gift of tongues bestowed upon the apostles (Acts 2.1ff.) a range of languages from the eastern Mediterranean and beyond is listed so that 'every man heard them speak in his own language'.[25] This linguistic problem has two aspects. The first is how far the early Church was ready to make use of various languages in translating the bible and in the liturgy, whilst the second concerns the ways in which terms of the new religion were rendered in the various languages.[26]

The first of these aspects soon presented itself as a problem with various languages within the sphere of influence of the classical oecumene (e.g. Syriac in Asia Minor, Coptic in Egypt). Speakers of these languages, coming into contact with Christianity, each time faced the problem of devising a vocabulary for its novel message. After the first

---

[20] *Ibid.*, pp. 88f, 127f.   [21] Schäferdiek (1978a), 534; Fritze (1969), 106ff.   [22] Fritze (1969), 110.
[23] *Ibid.*, pp. 78ff.   [24] Bartelink (1974), 397ff.   [25] Mohrmann (1957), 11f.   [26] *Ibid.*, pp. 12ff.

transposition (from Aramaic into Greek) the Greek language rapidly became the standard language of Christianity, both in the west and the east, but in Italy and Gaul Latin came to the fore as well, so that Christendom was divided into two linguistic areas, characterised by two different linguistic policies.[27] In the Greek east there was never a centralising factor like Rome in the west: the philological tradition of translation at Alexandria, which had earlier brought foreign literature into Greek, now returned the compliment by translating Christian ideas from Greek into other languages of the east (e.g. Syriac, Coptic, Armenian). First the bible (or parts of it), then liturgical prayers, but also lives of saints and martyrs now found their way into a number of vernaculars within the orbit of the Greek Church.[28] These include Gothic, so that Wulfila's translation of the bible is a result of the linguistic decentralisation of the Greek Church. In this respect the position was different in the west, where Rome represented a centralising force by which vernacular languages in Gaul and Iberia succumbed to Latin as the language of Empire, a process paralleled by the complete Latinisation of the western Church.[29] This dominance of Latin as the language of the Church was not confined to those regions of the west whose vernaculars had given way to Latin, for it was also used as an instrument in extending Christianity to regions where native languages still survived (Celtic and Germanic). Here, too, Latin retained its monopoly as the language of the bible and the liturgy, in contrast to the east with Gothic, Slavonic, Armenian and Georgian.

With the second aspect of the linguistic problems raised by the spread of Christianity we touch on a number of points where the difficulties and solutions found in German recur in other Germanic languages and can be observed at earlier stages in the development of a Christian vocabulary for Greek and Latin. The Christian conviction of 'newness' led to a rejection in Christian Greek of terms which had earlier belonged to the religious sphere and might therefore have lent themselves to Christianisation. Instead, words were chosen which lay outside the religious sphere of paganism altogether or completely new words were coined: by either means the danger of contamination could be avoided.[30] In the early Christian period Latin showed a similar attitude. This is reflected in the large number of Christian Greek loanwords present in Latin, not just from the time when Greek was the language of

---

[27] *Ibid.*, p. 15.   [28] *Ibid.*, pp. 16ff.; Herrin (1989), 92.   [29] Mohrmann (1957), 16f.
[30] *Ibid.*, pp. 20, 23f.

the oecumene, but a conscious choice of loanwords from without (already hallowed by their Christian function) as a way of avoiding suspect association with religious ideas of pre-Christian Latin.[31] After the Edict of Toleration, Latin revealed a change of attitude, a greater willingness to adapt pre-Christian terms to Christian ends. Terms which had previously been rejected because of their pagan associations were accepted as Christianity became more established and less threatened by paganism.[32]

Behind these two linguistic attitudes of rejection or adoption of pre-Christian religious vocabulary there lay two different options available for the expansion of Christianity. The Church could proceed *either* polemically, presenting its doctrine in all its shocking newness, making no concessions to the pagan world around it and therefore ready to accept only slow gains in proselytising, *or* it could adopt a more eirenic stance, prepared to accommodate itself to the beliefs of pagans whom it could thereby hope to win over more easily, even if this at first jeopardised the authenticity of the Christian message and opened the way for a religious syncretism which could only be remedied subsequently by long-term pastoral instruction.[33]

Bearing in mind these two options (polemic and eirenic) and their effects on the choice of Christian terms in any language which is to be opened up to missionary activity, we may now consider the various classes of linguistic loan traffic involved in the transmission of Christian terms from Greek to Latin and then to OHG. Although we are dealing with three such classes (the third of which falls into two subcategories), their basic division is twofold, corresponding to the two options available to missionary expansion.[34]

The first class, *loanwords*, illustrates the historical continuity of Christianity. Greek therefore made use of loanwords from Hebrew (e.g. *pascha*), just as Latin in turn borrowed from Greek (e.g. *heremita, ecclesia*). Continuity was preserved into OHG when this language borrowed from Latin either a term which ultimately went back to Greek (e.g. *evangelio, alamuosan*, 'alms') or one of Latin origin (e.g. *signum* 'sign of the cross' > *segan* 'blessing', *cantico* 'hymn'). The advantage of this method is clear: it is an easy linguistic process, making for an international terminology fit for a universal religion and offering quick linguistic returns. Its disadvantage

---

[31] *Ibid.*, pp. 23, 28, 29f.   [32] *Ibid.*, pp. 33f.; Bartelink (1974), 400, 416f.
[33] Flint (1991), 71, 77. The so-called 'Germanisation of Christianity' has been criticised by Rathofer (1962), 51ff. and Schäferdiek (1984a), 521ff., but unconvincingly proposed again by Russell (1994).
[34] Betz (1974), 135ff.; Kahl (1956), 94.

is equally clear, however. This method was only effective in the case of material objects and persons, where the meaning of the strange word was conveyed by what could be heard (*cantico*) or seen (*evangelio* in the form of a gospel-book, *segan* as the sign of the cross). In the case of other concepts (e.g. *angelus* > *engil*), however, a loanword remained largely foreign to those who were to be converted, so that the price of a nominal, uncomprehending Christianisation had to be paid for the easy creation of a vocabulary by this means.

The second class, *loan-translations*, consists of cases where a new word was created in the recipient (hitherto pagan) language by a part-for-part translation of the giving (Christian) language. Greek *dikaíōsis* yielded Latin *iustificatio*, or Latin *evangelium* produced OHG *cuatchundida* (whether by someone who understood the meaning of the Greek original or was acquainted with Isidore of Seville's explanation: *bona adnuntiatio*).[35] The advantage of this method is that the use of native word-material was less artificial than a preference for loanwords and held out some promise that the new Christian term would be effectively understood (e.g. *cuatchundida* by contrast with *evangelio*). The drawback is that this linguistic process was still to some extent artificial, since the result of this part-for-part translation was a word which had never existed before and must therefore have had a flavour of novelty. Moreover, although these coinages were often readily understandable, this was by no means always the case, as with *gewizzenî* as a strictly derivative rendering for *conscientia*.

The third class, *loan-meanings* (a word in the recipient language acquired a wider (Christian) semantic range under the influence of a word in the giving language), falls into two subcategories, religious and secular. To the words in this class we can apply what has been said of the conversion of Greek *eirḗnē* 'peace' to Christian ends under the influence of Hebrew *shalom*: that it is a Greek ship laden with a strange cargo.[36] Since the need was for a religious vocabulary the temptation was to appropriate established religious terms for new, Christian purposes. This had already happened in Latin (*dominus* was christianised under the influence of Greek *kýrios*, *salus* followed the precedent of *sōtēría*),[37] and a similar pattern was repeated in OHG (*heil* fell under the influence of *salus*, *sêla* under that of *anima*).[38] The advantage of this method is that it shows the least degree of artificiality, producing a term which was readily understood and making the transition to Christianity largely

---

[35] See below, p. 331.   [36] Mohrmann (1957), 24.
[37] Heiler (1959), 549f.; Bartelink (1974), 413f.
[38] On *sêla* see Weisweiler (1940), 25ff.; Eggers (1957), 1ff.; La Farge (1991).

painless. However, this success was achieved at the cost of deleting the essential difference between paganism and Christianity, so that the initial gain concealed the fact of a deferred payment. One solution to this difficulty was held out by secular loan-meanings adapted to a Christian function, for these avoided associations with the pagan religion by rejecting religious terms altogether. Examples of this method in Christian Latin are found in *redemptio* (originally 'buying back' or 'ransoming from captivity') and *gentes* (earlier used of other peoples or barbarians, as opposed to the *populus Romanus*, and therefore capable of transferring its negative connotation to gentiles or pagans, as distinct from the *populus Dei*).[39] In these cases the novelty lay not in the word itself, but in its religious function acquired only from the new religion. The same is true in OHG of such words as *huldi*, used to render *gratia*, or *truhtin* as a translation of *dominus*.[40] But these secular loan-meanings avoid the drawback of their religious counterparts only by opening the way to other disadvantages. If the words had previously had only a non-religious function it would take some time to bring home to native speakers precisely what Christianity had done to them. More importantly, the non-religious terms chosen could often introduce secular associations which threatened to distort the picture of Christianity, as with OHG *huldi* and *truhtin* as terms at home in the war-band which could involve a reinterpretation of Christianity not as intended by the translator, but as misunderstood by those whom he addressed.

Each of these methods traditionally used in creating a Christian vocabulary in the language of a freshly converted people had therefore advantages and disadvantages. A decision in favour of one advantage almost inevitably entailed a corresponding loss of effectiveness or distortion of the Christian meaning. When we find one Germanic language repeatedly choosing or giving priority to one method, whereas another language adopts another, this contrast implies not just a different linguistic choice, but a different attitude to Christianity and a different policy of Christianisation.

Another problem posed by linguistic loan traffic is whether we are dealing with primary or secondary loans. In Gothic, for example, although the majority of Christian loanwords were taken as primary loans from Greek, this does not exclude the possible influence of Christian Latin (*armahaírtiþa* may be connected with *misericordia*), even in the case of words which Latin had itself acquired from Greek.

[39] Bartelink (1974), 399.   [40] Green (1965), 140ff., 322ff.

Candidates for such secondary loans (Greek > Latin > Gothic) have been seen in *aiwaggelista* and *aíkklesjo*, but even more strikingly in *Iesus Xristus*.[41] In such cases Greek words enter Gothic as secondary loans *via* Latin, alongside the more commonly attested direct route. Secondary loans like these, reflecting the expansion of the new religion, occur frequently elsewhere.[42]

The mobility suggested by these examples makes it imperative to inquire into the dynamics of such loanword traffic, to ask what historical forces carry specific words so far. How necessary this is, even if an answer is not always possible, can be shown by a negative example. The proposal that Gothic Christian terms could have reached OE through the Frankish interpreters taken by Augustine on his mission to Kent has been rejected on the grounds that the OE attestations occur in isolation in a few glosses of the tenth century which cannot have miraculously preserved traces of these interpreters' linguistic practice centuries earlier.[43]

How it is sometimes possible to answer this kind of question can be illustrated from Gothic, this time with regard to classical loanwords in Wulfila's text. As far as Greek is concerned the evidence consists of biblical place-names (and matching ethnic names) which fall into two classes: on the one hand names which have adopted Gothic flectional endings and phonology (e.g. *e* > *i*; *ia* > *ja*) and have been 'Gothicised', and on the other hand names which have retained their Greek inflection and phonology (e.g. *e* = *ai*), thus representing Hellenised forms.[44] Behind this linguistic distinction a wider difference is detectable. Whereas the second group is largely made up of names from the Holy Land with which the Goths became acquainted only with the coming of Christianity (e.g. *Galeilaia, Iudaia, Israeleites*), the first group includes names of the Empire known to the Goths in the Pontic area, Asia Minor and the Balkans from their earliest raids in this region before any missionary activity amongst them (e.g. *Galatja, Makidonja, Makidoneis*).[45] Whereas Wulfila's Hellenising Gothic and his linguistic loyalty to the bible meant that the one group retained Greek features, the other group was Gothicised by having been adopted into the language of the barbarian raiders before they heard of the Holy Land from Christianity.

---

[41] Jellinek (1923), 443ff.; Corazza (1969), 92.
[42] E.g. Greek > Gothic > OHG (*phaffo*), Greek > Latin > OHG (*alamuosan*), Latin > OE > OHG (*gotspel*), even Greek > Latin > Irish > OE > OHG (*einchoran*).   [43] Gneuss (1992), 122f.
[44] Schulze (1907), 165ff.; Gaebeler (1911), 1ff.
[45] Rappaport (1899); Thompson (1966), index; Wolfram (1988), 52ff.; Schwarcz (1992), 47ff.

Not all the classical loanwords of Christian content in Gothic came from Greek, however, for a few stemmed from Latin. If these suggest Latin- as well as Greek-speaking Christians amongst the Goths before the days of Wulfila, they can best be sought in Dacia, where archaeological finds of a Christian nature from the first half of the fourth century, confined to what was then the Latin-speaking area, imply Christians amongst these Latin-speakers. Even later, in Wulfila's day, this Latin presence was still important: he enjoyed imperial backing, the emperors in question (Constantius II, Valens) were Latin-speaking and had Latin-speaking clerics in their households.[46] For these Latin terms as for the Greek ones in Wulfila's Christian vocabulary it is not sufficient to base our argument on language alone when the historical evidence can so strengthen our case.

The expansion of Christianity into new language-areas thus presented a number of linguistic difficulties, both for those who had to devise a vocabulary from scratch in a barbarian vernacular and for the new converts. These difficulties come to a head in the choice between two methods of translation which the Church inherited from classical antiquity.[47] Translation could be either literal (word for word) or loose (sense for sense). As far as the bible is concerned, the first method rests on the conviction that in a sacred text every word had its meaning and that, as Jerome maintained, even the word-order concealed a meaning. It is a method which was followed by Wulfila, who tried to remain as true to the Greek text as with his Hellenised place-names, but which produced a Gothic text which must have been to a considerable extent unintelligible to Goths without Greek.[48] The second (freer) method follows the meaning rather than the word and is best represented in OHG by Notker's translation of the psalms where, by contrast to the Windberg and Trier renderings with their regular equations of *spiritus* with *geist*, the St. Gallen author used a variety of additional vernacular terms for *spiritus*, dictated by context and ease of understanding.[49]

Both in theory and in practice the newness of Christianity produced problems in the creation of a religious vocabulary: for Greek, for Latin and for the barbarian vernaculars. These difficulties are also reflected in the problems facing modern philology in interpreting these early

[46] Jellinek (1923), 446f.; Thompson (1966), 82; Gschwantler (1976), 176; Schäferdiek (1978a), 498.
[47] Beck (1981a), 579; Copeland (1991), 9ff.
[48] Kahl (1956), 95. Similarly, Gregory the Great lamented the difficulties caused by a literal translation. Cf. Copeland (1991), 51.   [49] Betz (1957), 51f.

endeavours, which can be illustrated by an example central to the Christian message: the choice of a verb for 'to believe'.

The pagan religions of antiquity have been described as essentially concerned with cult acts: pagans performed rites, but held no creed or doctrine.[50] This attitude dictated the way in which the pagan Roman state dealt with Christians in its midst: they were required to perform a nominal act of worship to the gods without attention to what their beliefs might be. The pagan religion therefore had no fear of heresy, no need to impose orthodoxy as long as the required ritual acts were performed. What was true of the Roman religion was also applicable to the Germanic one. The Gothic Christian Saba was expelled from his community not because of the unacceptability of his Christian opinions as such, but because he offended against the tribal gods by not taking part in a ritual meal.[51] In ON the verb *trúa* 'to believe' (in the gods) could be seen in terms of *blóta* 'to sacrifice', whilst the epithet *goðlauss* was used of someone no longer willing to sacrifice to the gods.[52] Perhaps because of this association of paganism with ritual cults the Germanic word **blótan* 'to sacrifice' was not christianised in WG and NG (it was applied only to pagan practices). The Christian use of the same verb in Gothic, however, is only an apparent exception, for its meaning was generalised to 'to serve, worship' and it was used of fasting, prayer and good works, whilst the meaning 'to sacrifice' (by pagans or Jews) was transferred instead to *hunsljan*.[53]

By contrast with this ritual nature of paganism the concept of belief is central to Christianity both in the sense of trust in God, entrusting oneself to Him, and in the sense of holding tenets of the new religion to be true.[54] This concept created the need to find a word which could be christianised, a need which was met by the same term in Gothic (*galáub-jan*) and WG (OHG *gilouben*, OS *gilôbian*, OE *gelýfan*), whilst NG chose a different solution. The verb *galáubjan*, together with its modern German cognates *erlauben*, *loben*, *lieb*, suggests a word-field whose central semantic function embraced such ideas as love (cf. Go. *liufs*), praise (cf. OHG *lobôn*) and trust or hope (cf. Go. *lubáins*). *Galáubjan* therefore meant something like 'trust' before it was adopted for Christian purposes, whilst *usláubjan* meant 'to entrust (oneself)'. It is probable that the earliest construction was *galáubjan* + dative (commonly attested with Wulfila), implying trust or belief in someone. Other constructions were probably influenced by

[50] Lane Fox (1988), 31, 253; Bartelink (1974), 406.   [51] Thompson (1966), 68.
[52] Ström (1951), 23; Ljungberg (1947), 171.   [53] Kuhn (1978), 313.
[54] *Ibid.*, pp. 310f.; Meid (1992), 505ff.

Christian Greek or Latin. Following the model of Greek with the preposition *eis* Wulfila also used *du* and rarely *in*, whilst the Latin construction *credere in* is echoed by OHG *in*, OS *an*, OE *on* (these last two also using *te* and *tō*). The difference between these alternative constructions (with a simple dative or with a preposition) is still detectable in the contrast between 'to believe someone' and 'to believe in God'.

As far as their gods were concerned the question of believing in their truth was irrelevant to Germanic pagans, just as they had little cause to doubt the existence of the Christian God. What counted was their trust in the gods' power to assist the tribe, so that the missionaries' task was to call this into question and to awaken trust in the superior power of the Christian God.[55] Initially, therefore, *galáubjan* remained close to the concept of trust: Wulfila used it to render a verb like *pisteúein* (but not a verb meaning 'to think, be of the opinion'), just as the OHG *Tatian* regularly translated *credere* by *gilouben*, but *putare* and *arbitrari* by *wânen*. How *gilouben* could come to imply belief in the truth of something as well as trust in someone can be illustrated in OHG versions of the Creed, where a formula like *Ich kelouben an got* may well concern trust in the power of the new God (*alemáctigen*), while the subsequent construction (*Hich kelouben . . . daz thie drî genenneda ein got ist*) refers to acceptance of the truth of an article of religious belief.[56]

A comparable semantic extension can be demonstrated with another verb meaning 'trust, confide' which also lent itself to Christianisation and thus also came to mean 'believe': OE *(ge)truwian*, OS *(gi)trûên*. How this extension could come about we can see in the OS *Heliand*. On one occasion Christ's miracles and the help He brings are summed up in their effect on beholders (2350: *that sie gitrûodin thiu bet*), which could amount to their trust in His superior power. This half-line is then varied by another (2351: *gilôbdin an is lêra*) which equates *gitrûên* with *gilôbian*, but also, by referring to Christ's teaching, suggests belief in the truth of what He says. Taken together, these two half-lines move from trust in Christ to holding His sayings to be true, in much the same way as in the Creed formulas. On another occasion, even without the equation with *gilôbian*, a similar extension is shown: Christ's miracles may again awaken trust in Him (3114: *that sie gitrûodin thiu bet*), but the introduction of the following line with the conjunction 'that' (3115: *that he selbo uuas sunu drohtines*) shows that this trust is subsumed under belief in the dogmatic truth that Christ is the Son of God.

[55] Kuhn (1978), pp. 312, 314; Ljungberg (1947), 170.   [56] Kuhn (1978), 312f.; Steinmeyer (1916), 341.

The use of *(ge)truwian* and *(gi)trûên* as Christian variants of *gelȳfan* and *gilôƀian* in OE and OS explains the religious employment of the cognate *trúa* in ON,[57] where the satisfactory use of a verb corresponding to *galáubjan* was excluded by the regular reduction of prefixes. In ON *trúa* could therefore be used with the dative to mean 'to trust' in a non-religious context, but also in a pagan religious context (with reference to Oðin), possibly under Christian influence. Finally, the construction *trúa + á* (where the preposition corresponds to WG *an* or *on*) occurs in a religious context with Christian poets. Like the religious use of *galáubjan* in Gothic and WG, the similar use of *trúa* in ON appears to be the outcome of Christian influence, where the model for Scandinavia was OE or OS (from both regions missionaries were active in Scandinavia), more probably OS.[58]

Several problems remain unresolved with *galáubjan*. The suggestion that the WG forms are the result of a Gothic mission[59] runs up against doubts about this theory and also the difficulty of explaining how it may have reached far enough to account for OS and OE. If the choice of this verb was an obvious one in Germanic and if the prepositional constructions were based on Greek and Latin models, the influence of these languages could have independently produced similar results in different Germanic languages. This possibility of polygenesis is likely for the OE and OHG forms (there is no evidence that Anglo-Saxon missionaries were responsible for introducing their word to Germany), whereas it is quite conceivable that the OS form was influenced by either OE or OHG.

---

[57] Ljungberg (1947), 151ff.   [58] *Ibid.*, p. 168.   [59] Kuhn (1978), 310.

CHAPTER 16

The influence of provincial Roman Christianity

The earliest contacts of the Germani with the Romans, and therewith with Christians among them, took place along the Rhine and Danube frontiers of the Empire from the second century, but cannot have been very extensive before Constantine's conversion in 312 and the declaration of Christianity as the state religion. Christian communities on the Roman frontier must have kept a low profile during the pagan period and were hardly obtrusive enough to attract the attention of Germanic outsiders. Even extending the period to be surveyed down to the conversion of Chlodwig and his followers does not result in a large number of terms taken over into German from provincial Roman Christianity because widespread Christianisation set in only after the fifth century.[1]

The historical evidence for early Christianity in the frontier region of the Empire in what is now Germany presents a picture markedly different in the south (with the Alemanni and the Bavarians) and in the Rhineland (concerning the Franks). In south Germany centres of Roman Christianity are known above all in towns: in the area later occupied by the Alemanni in Basel, Konstanz, Chur and Augsburg, in what was known later as Bavaria in Lorch, Salzburg, Passau and possibly Regensburg.[2] This situation in the south, permitting even an early episcopal organisation, was drastically changed with the Alemannic penetration to the foothills of the Alps and with Bavarian ethnogenesis in the first half of the sixth century. The disturbances which these barbarian invasions brought to the incipient Christian communities are reflected in the evidence for episcopal seats being pulled back from threatened areas in the sixth century. Despite the large-scale disruption which this suggests there is evidence for the survival of scattered pockets

---

[1] Eggers (1978), 473f.
[2] Büttner (1951), 8ff.; Milojčić (1966), 231ff.; Schäferdiek (1976), 181; Ewig and Schäferdiek (1978), 117f.; Prinz (1985), 329.

of (Romance-speaking) Christian groups in these regions now under Germanic occupation.

The position in the Rhineland was different in two respects. First, although the extreme north-west presents a picture of episcopal retreat similar to the south, the sector of the Middle Rhine and Mosel showed greater continuity and thus presented more opportunities for the Germani to make their first acquaintance with Christianity, however external.[3] Secondly, the Rhineland was more important for the Romans than south Germany for a number of reasons, which means that Latin loanword traffic (and therewith the possibility of Christian terms) is better attested from Gaul to Germany than over the Alps.[4] It was through Gaul that the Romans' most important line of communication ran: up the Rhône to Lyon, thence to Trier and the Rhine frontier with such bases as Xanten, Cologne, Bonn and Mainz. The geographical importance of Trier on this route was heightened by the presence of the emperor's court there in the fourth century. All this brought trade, administration, agriculture and a greater military presence in its train, amounting to a more thorough Romanisation of this area than in south Germany, reflected in Latin loanwords which entered Germany from Gaul.

Christianity penetrated Germany from the same direction, radiating from Gaul to the Roman provinces Germania I and II which belonged politically to Gaul. Particularly important was Lyon with its earliest organised Christian community in Gaul (attested from a persecution in 177) linked to a Greek colony from Asia Minor, especially amongst the merchants.[5] Of the martyrs of the persecution whose names are known a good half were Greeks. Above all in the frontier region the officials of the pagan Roman state had every reason to proceed as ruthlessly against what they regarded as a disloyal religion as in the hinterland of Lyon. The towns in which Christianity first gained a foothold in the Empire were also fewer in the Rhineland than in Gaul and in any case under the watchful eye of Roman civil and military administration. There is therefore no evidence, written or archaeological, for a Christian presence in these provinces before the second half of the third century. Indeed, Germania I and II and Belgica I, together with Raetia and Noricum in the south, underwent sparse Christian influence before the conversion

---

[3] Büttner (1951), 9f.; Schäferdiek (1976), 181; Ewig and Schäferdiek (1978), 116f.; Prinz (1985), 329.
[4] Kuhn (1951a), 57f., 60; Hatt (1963), 63ff.
[5] Hegel (1962), 94; Demougeot (1963), 23ff; Petrikovits (1978a), 252; (1978b), 576f.; Schäferdiek (1987), 150f.

of Constantine. What evidence there is suggests that Trier was influenced by Lyon and in turn passed on some Christianity, however sporadic, to the Rhineland.[6] We are dealing up to the end of the third century with a small number of Christians whose sparse communities were not organised under episcopal leadership. A further factor making for a reduced presence of Christianity was the persecutions before the Edict of Toleration in 313. It produced its crop of Christian martyrs whose memory, albeit with pious accretions, is preserved with what is presumed to be a historical nucleus in legends of martyrs (e.g. the Theban legion, St Ursula) or of bishoprics (e.g. concerning Maternus, Helena). The legend of the Theban legion suggests the possibility that some of these early martyrs may have come from the ranks of the Roman army after their conversion had brought them into conflict with the authorities.[7]

The fourth century presents a totally different picture: the victory of Christianity. After the Edict of Toleration it was possible to practise the new cult in public and Christianity could develop freely in the Rhineland with some measure of organisation. Not merely did the number of Christians increase significantly, they also made their victorious presence more obvious, even ostentatiously, as with the programme of Constantinian church building, reaching Trier (cathedral and the Liebfrauenkirche) and Cologne (St. Gereon). Christian symbolism also appeared on coins struck by Constantine, as did the Christian labarum on the battle-standards of his troops.[8] How different the position now was from the earlier martyrdom of Roman soldiers because of their Christian allegiance is illustrated by a complex of five military gravestones of the last third of the fourth century from Cologne. Their inscriptions commemorate soldiers from the imperial retinue: two of them were certainly Christian, one probably.[9]

An indication of the more thoroughgoing organisation of the Church is the creation of bishoprics in the Rhineland by the middle of the fourth century.[10] In this an early lead was given by Trier, where the bishopric was founded in the middle of the third century with responsibility for both Germanic provinces before they received their own bishops. In these provinces Cologne provided the best conditions for the rise of a large Christian community, yet the first bishop known there, Maternus, was active only from the beginning of the fourth century. He seems to

---

[6] Schäferdiek (1987), 151; Demougeot (1963), 39ff.
[7] Hegel (1962), 93ff.; Petrikovits (1978b), 582ff.   [8] Schäferdiek (1987), 152.
[9] Petrikovits (1978a), 255.   [10] Hegel (1962), 96ff.; Petrikovits (1978a), 253ff.; (1978b), 593ff.

have been responsible for creating the bishopric of Tongeren by 342, when Servatius is attested as a bishop attending a council of the Church. The evidence for Mainz follows, whose first named bishop, Martinus, took part in another council in 346, where bishops are also named for the first time for Worms, Speyer and Strassburg. In addition to this incipient episcopal organisation of the Rhineland the ecclesiastical hierarchy is attested by occasional references to other clerical ranks: a deacon accompanied Maternus of Cologne to a synod at Arles, we hear of a subdeacon from Trier, a lector is known from what is probably Koblenz, and a presbyter is attested for Bingen.[11] These scraps of evidence conform to the general picture of early Christianity in all referring to clerics in towns. The presence of Christianity in the countryside was certainly much weaker.

The early Christian communities in Trier and Cologne resembled what was true of the community at Lyon from which they had received their religion: they all show traces of an eastern, specifically Hellenistic presence.[12] Artistically this is true of sarcophagi found at Trier and of glassware at Cologne, tombstones at Trier had inscriptions in Greek or bore Greek names, just as the name of the Trier bishop Eucharius suggests a Greek. The same is true at Cologne with bishop Euphrates.

However decisive the victory of Christianity in the fourth century may have been, the timespan available for the Christianisation and ecclesiastical organisation of the Rhineland after the Edict of Toleration should not be exaggerated, since already by the fifth century this area witnessed a repaganisation.[13] The reasons for this include the persistence of pagan Roman cults: even after the conversion of Constantine there was at first no official policy of destroying pagan sanctuaries, least of all in the countryside where Christianity had scarcely made headway. Pagan practices continued even in the neighbourhood of Christian centres, as with a temple of Isis outside the townwalls of Cologne (on the site of the later church St. Gereon) or with two Mithras temples. Such pagan sanctuaries were still frequented by worshippers as late as the middle of the fourth century or even until its close, so that Christianity faced considerable opposition from Roman and oriental pagan religions even in the period of its victory.

The balance was decisively tipped against the progress made hitherto by Christianity with the Franks' onslaughts on the Roman frontier dis-

---

[11] Petrikovits (1978a), 257; (1978b), 603f.
[12] Hegel (1962), 98; Demougeot (1963), 43; Frend (1964), 125ff.
[13] Petrikovits (1960), 140; (1978a), 260; (1978b), 610.

trict which began early in the fifth century. In 420 they took temporary possession of Trier, by about 440 Cologne was occupied by Franks and Mainz largely destroyed, while other sectors of the Rhine frontier were subjected to attacks by other tribes (Alans, Vandals, Burgundians, Huns), so that by the middle of the century the whole of the west bank was in Germanic hands. This meant a considerable setback for the Church, the more so since its recent gains had been confined to towns destroyed or seized by the barbarians. The gravity of this setback is effectively suggested by the episcopal lists recorded for the Rhineland.[14] Whereas Reims and Trier, further removed from the zone of greatest danger, record no interruptions in episcopal succession from the third century, the lists for Cologne, Tongeren, Mainz and Worms show significant gaps in the approximate period 460 to 550. In this period the Church must have suffered considerable disorganisation as a result of the invasions, not merely as the victim of active pagan hostility, but simply because economic dislocation and impoverishment made it financially impossible for the native population to build (or rebuild) churches and sustain an ambitious ecclesiastical organisation.[15] It is not surprising that pagan cults persisted in this period: those connected with the Germanic religion introduced by the invaders, but also those surviving from the Roman and pre-Roman period, especially among the rural population. The long-term result was that when a missionary movement began work in this area (in the sixth, but mainly in the seventh century) it had to face two types of paganism. In this it was to some extent able to build on scattered Christian communities which had managed to weather the storms of the invasions.

One last detail concerns that aspect of Christianity which presented itself most obviously to the incoming Germani: its church buildings, especially in the demonstrative form encouraged by Constantine as an outward token of the victory of Christianity. For obvious reasons there is no evidence for such buildings in the age of persecutions, but after this an approximate dating has been suggested for various centres.[16] At Trier a place of worship was present towards the end of the third century, but the twin building (cathedral and Liebfrauenkirche) was begun in 326 and was constructed on a striking scale. At Cologne St. Severin was begun towards 320, St. Gereon was possibly influenced or encouraged by Constantine, whilst St. Ursula was standing by 355, when it was

---

[14] *Ibid.* (1978a), 292; (1978b), 623. [15] *Ibid.* (1978b), 623f.
[16] Hegel (1962), 101f.; Demougeot (1963), 41ff.; Gaudemet (1963), 8; Hatt (1963), 58, 63.

destroyed by the Franks. A cathedral at Bonn was built in the fourth century. There is no comparable evidence for the building of churches in the period of disruption brought about by the barbarian invasions. A new beginning was made possible only after the conversion of Chlodwig and the mission of the sixth and seventh centuries.[17]

The linguistic aspect of our survey is confined to four Christian loan-words which probably entered German from Gaul in this period. The first, the word for 'church', ties up with what we have seen of church buildings in the Rhineland and with the presence of Greek speakers along this western route. In the earliest days of Christianity the private houses of individual believers served as places for meeting and worship, so that there was at first no technical term for the place of worship: its unobtrusiveness was adequate to what were still small groups of Christians and was in any case advisable in the age of persecutions. This began to change in the third century with the spread of the new religion and with the measure of toleration with which it came to be regarded by the Roman state, so that only now do we encounter technical terms for the Christian church building.[18]

The terms designating this building in most European languages go back to three Greek words from the third century: *ekklēsía, kyriakón* and *basilikḗ*.[19] The first was taken *via* Latin into all the western Romance languages and Celtic, the second was loaned into Germanic (thence also into Slavonic), whilst the third survives in eastern Romance (but also in isolated pockets in the west). The questions which this distribution poses are: how was it that Germanic did not take over the *ecclesia* of the western Church, when and where did it make contact with the second of these Greek terms?

Originally, Greek *ekklēsía* had a political function before Christianity, meaning 'summons', then 'assembly of citizens', but from the third century it is attested in a Christian context meaning 'congregation'. This meaning of the word was extended to the building where the assembly was held (*oíkos ekklēsías*). The word established itself quickly as a technical Christian term in Greek and was borrowed in the third century into Church Latin with both the meanings now present in Greek: 'Christian community' and 'church building'. From Latin it passed into western Romance (e.g. OFr. *glise*, OPr. *gleize*) and Celtic (OIr. *eclís*, We. *eglwys*).[20]

[17] Petrikovits (1978a), 292, 297.   [18] Kretschmer (1906), 539f.; Mohrmann (1977), 211, 212.

[19] Kretschmer (1906), 539ff.; Dölger (1950), 161ff.; Mohrmann (1977), 211ff.; Masser (1966), 17ff.

[20] Kretschmer (1906), 540f.; Mohrmann (1977), 215f.; *FEW* 3, 203.

Barely later than *ekklēsía* the second term, *kyriakón*, occurs for the first time in the third century. Its formation ('that which belongs to the Lord, the house of the Lord') made it more acceptable in this sense than *ekklēsía*, for there are suggestions that this word's extension to 'building' was felt to be incorrect. Nonetheless, although *kyriakón* was in use throughout the fourth century, it eventually succumbed in Greek to *ekklēsía* and died out by the fifth century, so that it must have made contact with Germanic during the century dominated by Constantine.[21] Although this Greek word was not adopted as a loanword into Latin, it left its mark indirectly in a loan-translation, *dominicum*, which shadows it also chronologically: attested first in the third century, it was in use in the fourth and died out in the fifth century. *Dominicum* appears not to have been a native Latin formation, but dependent on its Greek model, whose eclipse it accompanied.[22]

Basilikḗ was taken into Latin as a secular word denoting a large public hall used for trade or meetings, but acquired a Christian function mainly as a result of Constantine's programme of church-building, particularly the *Basilica Constantini* at Jerusalem (the Holy Sepulchre). Only in this period were churches first erected of a size imposing enough to merit such a term (originally 'royal'). That this word's Christian adaptation was later than with *dominicum* is suggested by a passage in the fourth-century *Itinerarium Burdigalense*, where the word *basilica* is employed, but has to be explained by the better known *dominicum*. Like *dominicum*, *basilica* differed from *ecclesia* in denoting only the church-building.[23] Apart from its survival in eastern Romance (e.g. Rum. *biserica*) the word survived only peripherally in Gaul, where OFr. *basoche* was applied to the basilica of St Martin at Tours and occurs as a place-name in western, northern and eastern France.[24]

From the distribution of these three terms *kyriakón* emerges, especially as regards the Latin west, as a foreign element in the competition between *ecclesia* and *basilica*. Early intensive Christianisation established *ecclesia* in Italy and southern Gaul, whereas *basilica* was brought as a newer term in the fourth century to areas evangelised only later. Given the conflict between these two words, we have to ask how *kyriakón* fits into this picture and how it found its way into Germanic.

If the Greek word was used mainly in the fourth century, but hardly later, then it must have crossed the linguistic frontier during this short

---

[21] Kretschmer (1906), 541; Mohrmann (1977), 222; Masser (1966), 19.

[22] Kretschmer (1906), 543; Dölger (1950), 175ff., 189; Mohrmann (1977), 223.

[23] Kretschmer (1906), 543; Dölger (1950), 172ff.; Mohrmann (1977), 228.   [24] *FEW* I, 270.

timespan, but how and where? That there is a connection between *kyri-akón* and a Germanic word which on WG evidence must have been originally **kirika* there can be no doubt, even apart from minor discrepancies. The least troubling is the abandonment of accentuation of the final syllable in Greek in favour of regular initial accentuation in Germanic. The loss of Greek medial *-a-* in the Germanic form has parallels in Vulgar Gr. *kyrikós* alongside *kyriakós*.[25] The change of gender to Germanic feminine is best explained by the way in which this word is inserted into the conflict between *ecclesia* and *basilica*, from which it takes over their gender.[26] Finally, the change in the stem vowel from *y* (= *ü*) to *i* can be accounted for either from Greek (assimilation of *y* to following *i*) or from Latin (replacement of Greek *y* by *i*, criticised already in the third/fourth-century *Appendix Probi*).[27] With these qualifications we can explain how the Greek word issued in a Germanic form **kirika*, attested in OHG, OS, OFri. and OE (already from the late seventh century) and later carried to ON. In Germanic the word became so firmly established that it remained unaffected by the subsequent victory of *ecclesia* in western Romania, just as other Latin loanwords crossed the linguistic frontier into German before they were replaced by newer terms in Romance alone.[28] At first OHG *kirihha*, denoting the place of worship, did not correspond fully to *ecclesia*, denoting also the Christian community, as is clear from the *Abrogans*, where *ecclesia* in the first sense is rendered by *chirihha*, but the abstract meanings by *ladunga* 'summons' and *samanunga* 'assembly'. In the course of time *kirihha* came to be so much the regular equivalent of *ecclesia* that its meaning was extended under the influence of the latter.[29]

The earliest suggestion (going back to Walahfrid Strabo) for the route by which this word found its way into German invoked transmission by the Goths, an explanation which seemed persuasive with a Christian term of Greek origin, present as a loanword in Germanic, but not in Latin, especially if we take into account the conversion of the Goths in the fourth century and the undoubted influence of Greek on Gothic Christian vocabulary at large.[30] This earlier view still survives unquestioned with some non-Germanists,[31] although it has been decisively questioned on linguistic grounds. In the first place, a word corresponding to WG **kirika* is nowhere attested in Gothic. Wulfila had no call for

[25] Kretschmer (1906), 542; Masser (1966), 19f.   [26] *GR* 2, 118.
[27] Keil (1864), 4, 147 (*gyrus non girus*). Cf. *Benediktinerregel* (54), p. 37 (*kirieleison*).
[28] See above, p. 244.   [29] Masser (1966), 28f.   [30] Kluge (1909), 125f.
[31] Dölger (1950), 194f.; Mohrmann (1977), 222.

a word 'church' in his bible translation, but he used *aíkklēsjo* in the sense of 'assembly, congregation', whilst the Gothic Calendar used it meaning 'house of God'.[32] Both meanings of Greco-Latin *ecclesia* are therefore attested in Gothic, but with no suggestion of a loanword from *kyriakón*, so that it is risky to base the spread of a word through Germania on an unattested starting-point. Nor is the assumption that the Slavonic term points to a Gothic one from which it was borrowed any more reliable as long as Slavonic could equally well have acquired its term from German.[33] In addition, whereas Gothic Christian terms which found their way into German from the south-east reveal an understandable centre of gravity in Bavaria, only rarely spreading beyond this, there is no suggestion of this with *kirihha*. Instead, the earliest attestations of the word, occurring in place-names from the beginning of the eighth century, but pointing to an earlier period when a place could be characterised by the by no means self-evident presence of a church, show no such concentration. In the eighth century some of these place-names may be from Bavaria, but others are in Alsace, Francia and Frisia: an early distribution in the west which we should not expect with a word transmitted by the Goths.[34] Finally, doubts are called for by another western weighting of the evidence, the OE form *cirice*, for we have grown more sceptical about the ability of Gothic words to travel 'up the Danube and down the Rhine' to reach the Anglo-Saxons so early, without any evidence of a mission to carry them.

Attention has turned instead to the possibility of a western transmission of the Greek word into WG. In principle, it is unsafe to assume that a Greek word must have entered Germania from the east, for this ignores the presence of Greek trading communities, including Christians, in the west: their main base was Marseilles, from where a trade route ran to Lyon and onwards to Trier and the Rhineland.[35] Christianity as well as trade may have been carried along this route, but this tells us nothing about this specific word. Nor is it enough, although it is certainly significant, that Constantine's programme of ostentatious church-building in the fourth century throughout the Empire also left its traces in Trier and Cologne.[36] These were buildings of a size and importance to attract attention, even on the part of pagan Frankish mercenaries in the Roman army who did not have to be Christians themselves to feel the need of a word with which to designate such buildings.

---

[32] Masser (1966), 23f. [33] *Ibid.*, pp. 24f. [34] *Ibid.*, pp. 32ff. [35] *Ibid.*, pp. 21ff.
[36] *GR* 2, 116ff; Krautheimer (1965), 18f., Herrin (1989), 114.

This raises the question whether Gr. *kyriakón* was in fact taken over in this context, whether its presence can be assumed in the west. The first indication is too specific to bear much weight, but it is suggestive that Athanasius of Alexandria, in exile at Trier during the fourth century, used the Greek word in his Christian writing, for with that the question whether the word found its way to Germania in the short span of its life is answered, on however narrow a basis.[37] Secondly, the presence of the Greek word is suggested on a wider footing by its adoption as a loan-translation in Lat. *dominicum*, especially in Gaul, where it is attested with Hilarius of Poitiers, in the *Itinerarium Burdigalense*, and in the loan of the word into Irish *domhnach*, used as an element in place-names.[38] The use of a neuter adjective as a substantive to denote a place of worship, common to the Greek and Latin forms, is not so obvious as to exclude the dependence of the Latin word on the Greek model, which it further matches in its brief chronological span.[39] Thirdly, WG *kirika* as a loan-word from Greek shows that even in the west *kyriakón* was not completely ousted by *dominicum* and that it survived long enough to cross the linguistic frontier.

We must assume that this loan into Frankish took place in the fourth century, while the Greek model was still in active use, presumably in Trier, hence passing to Germanic mercenaries serving there. That would be far too narrow a basis to explain the word's expansion, for while these mercenaries may have needed a word to describe what they saw around them they had no occasion to pass the word further into the Germanic hinterland where there was no call for the word. This need must have grown in the fifth century, however, with the Frankish occupation of Cologne and Trier, so that we must distinguish between the first encounter with the word (fourth century, Germanic mercenaries) and its wider adoption (fifth century, Frankish occupation). Neither of these stages presupposes christianised Franks, merely speakers requiring a word for this aspect of Roman life. By contrast, Christianity lies behind the later spread of the new vernacular word to other German dialects, part of the subsequent expansion of Frankish power east of the Rhine.[40]

In connection with this expansion of the word from its point of entry in the lower Rhine/Mosel area a problem presents itself: how did it find its way to OE? Pagan Franks had no interest in passing on such a term beyond the area where it was relevant, any occasional Frankish converts

---

[37] Dölger (1950), 193; Petrikovits (1978a), 258.
[38] Dölger (1950), 172, 181, 187; Mohrmann (1977), 223; Schäferdiek (1984b), 50, fn. 17.
[39] Schäferdiek (1984b), 48.   [40] *Ibid.*, p. 50.

on Roman soil were not active as missionaries in Germania, whilst Latin loanwords which may have reached the Anglo-Saxons while still in Schleswig-Holstein were trading words, i.e. the word accompanied the thing, precisely what could not happen with a word for a church building.[41] The first opportunity the Anglo-Saxons had of adopting 'static' loanwords from Latin as opposed to the mobile ones of trade was when, moving along the North Sea coastline towards northern France, they settled (temporarily) on former imperial territory where they encountered such novelties and, like the Franks, felt the need to name them. Yet precisely this part of Roman territory had been rarely touched by Christianity and had few church buildings of any size or number, so that there is little chance that the word reached the Anglo-Saxons in this area.[42] Instead, it is more likely that the word entered OE once they had reached Britain, as a loan from Frankish. The occasion could have been the marriage of the Frankish princess Bertha to Æthelberht of Kent, for in the last third of the sixth century she worshipped at a church just outside Canterbury, dedicated to St Martin of Tours.[43] Or the loan took place slightly later with Augustine's mission to Kent ca. 600 (in which he made use of Frankish interpreters), for he converted pagan temples into churches, re-used Romano-British churches and founded a monastery at Canterbury.[44] Either occasion called forth the need for an OE word for 'church' and Frankish affiliations in either case explain how the Frankish term reached England, just as it was spread further in Germany.

In some respects the position is very similar with the second example, the word 'bishop'. Its origin was likewise Greek: *epískopos* 'overseer', applied at first to someone in charge of a Christian community, but already in the second century to one in authority over *presbýteroi* 'priests'.[45] The word was adopted in Church Latin and is also found in Germanic (Gothic, OHG, OS, OFri., OE and later in ON). Within Germany the word was present before 800 over the whole of the Upper and Middle German area. Like *epískopos*, the Germanic derivatives meant 'bishop', even if they can sometimes be equated in OHG and OE with 'priest'.[46]

The Goths have been invoked here, too, as intermediaries between Greek and WG, although the case for this is even weaker.[47] In the first

---

[41] See above, pp. 216f.   [42] Schäferdiek (1978a), 535; Ewig and Schäferdiek (1978), 116.
[43] Schäferdiek (1978c), 152; Richter (1982), 132; Prinz (1984), 315ff.
[44] Schäferdiek (1978c), 154, 156, 158; Masser (1966), 22, fn. 30.   [45] Waag (1932), 20f.
[46] *Ibid.*, pp. 23ff.; Rotsaert (1977), 198, 201.
[47] Kluge (1909), 135f. On this see Waag (1932), 29 and Rotsaert (1977), 184f.

place, Wulfila used *aípiskaúpus*, a learned ecclesiastical form which differs markedly from WG **biskop*. One of the most telling facts that suggested Gothic transmission of *kyriakón* to WG (the absence of this Greek word from Church Latin) does not apply to 'bishop', where Latin has *episcopus*, so that there is less compulsion to look for an eastern transmission. It is an oversimplification to assume that a Christian term of Greek origin (even when there is no Latin parallel) could only enter Germania in the east and that the Goths must therefore have been involved. Lastly, what constituted a difficulty for 'church' is also a problem for 'bishop': how to explain the presence in OE of a Christian term supposedly transmitted by a Gothic mission which, even if it existed, barely penetrated Germany beyond Bavaria.

If the case for Gothic intermediaries is a shaky one, it can be weakened still further by an argument directed against the further suggestion that the WG forms derived directly from Greek or from Latin. Whereas Greek, Latin and Gothic all share the recognisable form *epískopos*, the WG equivalent **biskop* has two features (voicing of intervocalic *-p-* to *-b-*, then loss of unaccented *e-*) which show that it could not derive directly from Greek or Church Latin, but must have come *via* Vulgar Latin.[48] We encounter difficulties, however, when we turn to the VL evidence for this word in western Romania, for the different vernaculars point to a variety of alternative forms as their starting-points. Thus, forms in northern France and the Grisons derive from **episcu* (cf. OFr. *(e)vesque*), in southern France and Iberia from **epispu* (cf. OPr. *bisbe*, Sp. *obispo*), in southern Italy from **viscopu*, in northern Italy from **viscovu*, and in Sardinia from **piscopu*.[49] Although this last VL form most closely resembles the WG basis, this must be reckoned as chance, unless we assume that Sardinia happened to retain a variant which was originally more widespread.

Our problem lies therefore with the relationship not between WG and Gothic, but rather between WG and Latin, between **biskop* and *episcopus*. The main phonological problem lies in the twofold presence of an intervocalic *-p-* in the Latin word, the first of which has undergone VL voicing, whereas the second seems not to have. In addition, difficulties were created by OE *bisceop* as long as it was assumed that its agreement with continental WG indicated an early loan into WG, before the Anglo-Saxons came to Britain in about the middle of the fifth century. Other possibilities exist, however: Germany and England could have acquired the word from the same source independently and

---

[48] Rotsaert (1977), 186.   [49] Waag (1932), 30; *GR* 2, 236.

at different times *or* the continental form could have been taken to England at a later date.[50]

The phonological difficulty can be divided into various stages. First must come the voicing of intervocalic *-p-* (more particularly of the first *-p-* in *episcopus*), for this is a regular feature of VL in western Romania, which for that reason must be regarded as the source of the WG forms. Only after this voicing could the loss of the initial *e-* have taken place in the VL form. This was assisted by the threat to this unaccented syllable, coming immediately before the word-stress on *-i-* (cf. *ecclesia* and OFr. *glise*, OPr. *gleiza*, whereas modern French *église* results from subsequent assimilation to Church Latin).[51] In addition, we may reckon with a faulty division of the construction definite article + substantive (**illebescobo*) producing a substantive in which the initial vowel has now been lost (cf. It. *l'ospedale* > *lo spedale*).[52] This still leaves unexplained the apparent discrepancy between the voicing in what has now become the initial *b-* of the Germanic word and the retention of the second *-p-* of the Latin word (changed to *-f* only in OHG by the Second Sound Shift). The most convincing explanation of this discrepancy sees in it an example of phonetic substitution, to which loans from one language into another are especially prone.[53] As regards voiced labial consonants WG possessed the stop *b-* in the initial position, but not in some dialects medially, which knew only the fricative *-ƀ-*. With the loss of *e-* in what had become VL **ebiscobus* the initial *b-* therefore remained unaffected in WG, whereas there was no equivalent available in some dialects for the medial *-b-*. In the intervocalic position of this *-b-* these WG dialects could therefore employ only *-ƀ-* or *-p-*, where the latter, although voiceless, had the advantage of corresponding more closely as a stop to the VL model.

This explanation has been used to throw light on the date and area where the VL word found its way into Germanic. Dating this loan is assisted by the fact that Romance introduces a further change into the development of intervocalic labial consonants: after *-p-* had been shifted to *-b-* this was later changed to the fricative *-ƀ-*. From this it is clear that the word was transmitted to Germanic after the first change in Romance, but before the second (even though *some* of the forms attested in OHG may have been adopted after the second change was completed).[54] It would be helpful if Romance philologists were more in

---

[50] Waag (1932), 29. [51] Knapp (1973), 189; *FEW* 3, 231f.
[52] Rotsaert (1977), 190, 195; Knapp (1973), 186.
[53] Pogatscher (1888), 195; Gysseling (1961), 24; Rotsaert (1977), 188f. [54] Knapp (1973), 180ff.

agreement about the chronology of these changes, but whereas there is consensus about the voicing of *-p-* to *-b-* in the fifth century, the subsequent change (*-b-* to *-ƀ-*) is dated either soon afterwards in that same century or as late as the seventh century. This suggests the fifth or sixth century as a time for the loan into Germanic, possibly already in the fifth century if we are to allow enough time for the word's spread and use in a place-name like *Bischheim*, attested for Alsace as early as about 530.[55] As regards the location of this loan we receive complementary assistance from the phonology of WG, for the absence of a medial *-b-* and hence the need to replace it by *-p-* are characteristic of OE, Low Franconian and Middle Franconian. We are therefore probably dealing with radiation of the word from Gallo-Roman to the area of Trier and Cologne.[56]

Still to be accounted for is the early presence of the word in OE where, as with 'church', the loan was probably from Frankish rather than Gallo-Roman. A loan of this word into continental WG in the fifth century (let alone in the sixth) leaves hardly enough time for internal traffic within Germania to carry it as far as the Anglo-Saxons while still on the continent, even assuming that any Germanic mediator or recipient was interested in a Christian bishop. The continental *litus Saxonicum* was moreover weakly christianised, so that if the Anglo-Saxons were struck by no churches there before crossing to Britain they are hardly likely to have encountered a bishop or paid much attention to him. Amongst the earliest Christian loanwords in OE there are some which go back to the beginning of Christianisation or even slightly before, and 'bishop', like 'church', probably belongs to them.[57] Before any official evangelisation of Kent the Frankish princess Bertha was allowed to practise her Christian religion and to that end had taken a bishop, Liudhard, with her from Francia, so that in a narrow circle in still pagan Canterbury there was call for a term to denote his office. If that is too isolated a basis to account for the word's history in English, the field is widened shortly afterwards with the coming of the papal mission: Augustine was entrusted with the organisation of bishoprics for the English Church, had the pallium conferred on him by the pope, and brought with him Frankish interpreters and therewith their Christian terminology. Whereas the terms for 'bishop' and 'church' entered WG in the context of provincial

[55] Rotsaert (1977), 189f.; Wollmann (1993), 24; Waag (1932), 22.
[56] Gysseling (1961), 24, fn. 7; Rotsaert (1977), 210.   [57] Wollmann (1993), 3f.

Roman Christianity, the same words were later brought to England under Frankish auspices.[58]

Our third example, OHG *offrôn*, derives from Latin *offerre*, used in the religious sense 'to sacrifice', and stands in contrast to another verb, OHG *opharôn*, from Latin *operari*.[59] This contrast is primarily geographic: whereas the second German form was at home in the south (SRhFr., Alemannic, Bavarian) the first was concentrated in the northwest (OS, Low Franconian, Middle Franconian, *Isidor*). This northwestern centre of gravity for *offrôn* is confirmed by the presence of *offrian* in OE which, in conjunction with Celtic examples (e.g. *offerendum*: OIr. *oiffrend*), points to radiation of this word from northern Gaul, reaching as far as Trier and northwards. From the geographical spread of another word in Germany it is assumed that *operari* also entered this same region from northern Gaul, not in the religious sense which underlies *opharôn* in Upper German, but in the secular sense 'to work' (cf. OFr. *ovrer* and such north-west German dialect forms as *oppermann* 'workman, handyman').[60] Whereas this north-western form was brought to Germany by the Romans (as part of their building programme?), the southern import was reinterpreted as an ecclesiastical term ('work, service' > 'religious service'). Because this word retained its original secular meaning in the north-west, the way remained open for *offrôn* as a Christian term.[61]

Whereas *operari* came to the Lower Rhine as an early Roman loanword, there is no reason to assume that *offerre* reached this area so early as a Christian term. In dating this latter word's entry into the Christian vocabulary of German we best proceed from the fact that the Latin word acquired popularity as a Christian term meaning 'to offer, dedicate, sacrifice to God' especially in the fourth and fifth century.[62] This is also the time when early attempts at evangelising Celtic Britain were undertaken from Gaul, which would account for the presence of the word in Insular Celtic. If *offerre* was therefore established as a Christian term in northern Gaul in the fourth century and in that usage in Rhenish Franconian (*Isidor*) by the end of the eighth century, we are left with a wide margin in which to date the loan. However, this is likely to have taken place towards the early part of this timespan, if only because northern Gaul, the reservoir from which so many Latin loanwords were drawn, was capable of active radiation to north-western

---

[58] Schäferdiek (1978c), 152, 157.　　[59] Müller (1966), 152ff.; *GR* 2, 340ff.; *FEW* 7, 333.
[60] *GR* 1, 106f.　　[61] *GR* 1, 107; Wesche (1937), 70.　　[62] *FEW* 7, 333.

Germany only as long as the Empire provided the wider political and military framework within which even isolated Christian terms could be transmitted. It is even possible that *offrôn* entered German at about the same time and in the same context as *kirihha* and *biscof*. OE *offrian*, for the same reasons as with *cirice* and *bisceop*, can hardly have been taken by the still pagan Anglo-Saxons from the continent to Britain. Once again, Augustine's mission is a more convincing candidate, introducing to Kent either the Latin term itself or, through his interpreters, its Frankish form. In all these cases the linguistic agreement between OE and continental WG should not blind us to the chronological difference in the entry of a loanword into these language groups.

Our last example concerns Christian almsgiving. The Greek word *eleēmosýnē* 'mercy, compassion' was also used in the Christian sense of 'alms' and as such was borrowed into Latin as *eleemosyna*. From Latin the word was taken into Germanic (OHG, OS, OFri., MDu. and OE) and within German it is found in Franconian, Alemannic and Bavarian (from the eighth century).[63] Although German shows occasional forms like *elimosina* or *elimyosa*, best regarded as learned, bookish forms under the influence of Church Latin, more commonly a form such as *alamuosan* occurs, whose initial *a-*, in place of *e-*, is also found in the other Germanic dialects. This points to radiation from Gaul, where the same initial *a-* is also found (OFr. *almosne*, OPr. *almosna*), in contrast to the rest of Romania (It. *limosina*, Sp. *limosna*, Port. *esmola*).[64] Since Insular Celtic also shows the same loanword (e.g. OIr. *almsan*) with the same feature, radiation from northern Gaul seems to be assured, as with *offrôn* (and at the same time?).

Here too a special position is taken by OE, whose term *ælmesse* has been derived on phonological grounds either from a Latin form **alimosina* or from a Frankish **alamôsina* (itself a conflation, such as we also find in OHG, between *alamôsan* and *elemosina*). On the basis of the complex sound changes to which this loanword was subjected in OE (unaccented *-sin-* > *-sn-* > *-ss-*, but before this *ō* (before *i*) > *ē*, then shortened before *ss* to *e*) it has been concluded, with specific reference to the umlaut, that this word could not have been taken into OE much before 600.[65] In other words, OE acquired this word from the continent, in Latin or in Frankish form, at about the same time as the other words we have considered.

---

[63] *GR* 2, 88ff.   [64] *GR* 1, 48; *FEW* 3, 212.   [65] Pogatscher (1888), 137; Wollmann (1993), 3f.

From this early group of four Christian loanwords from Gaul into Germany it is clear that they all indicate only elementary externals of Church life and practice which even the pagan outsider could not fail to notice: the church building, the bishop, the liturgical act of sacrifice, almsgiving. None of these terms necessarily suggests that the loan of the word was tantamount to adoption of Christianity, rather than first superficial contacts with it.

CHAPTER 17

The influence of Gothic

The first beginnings of Christianity amongst the Goths can be traced back to the third century.[1] Captives made in the Black Sea area on raids to Asia Minor included some Christians (among them Wulfila's maternal grandparents) and a linguistic reflection of this earliest Gothic Christianity is seen in Christian loanwords in Gothic which antedate Wulfila's bible translation of the fourth century. This translation, probably accompanied by a vernacular liturgy, provided the linguistic basis for the spread of the new religion to other EG tribes, for which Gothic served as a *lingua franca*.[2] The missionary activity of the Visigoths in spreading their Arian Christianity was known to Jordanes ('they invited all people of their speech everywhere to attach themselves to this sect') and is borne out by historical testimony.[3] They converted the Burgundians and Vandals by the end of the fourth century, and the Ostrogoths, Sciri, Gepids, Rugii and Langobards during the course of the fifth century. From the fourth to the sixth century the Goths therefore carried their new religion to a variety of Germanic tribes settled, like themselves, on the frontiers of the Roman Empire and within it, but we have no evidence of their likewise being active as missionaries among the tribes further west (Franks, Alemanni, Bavarians). Can the words of Jordanes be applied to Germanic-speakers in what is now Germany and not simply to EG tribes?

The first detailed attempt to fill this gap in historical evidence by linguistic means was made by Kluge,[4] who postulated a Danubian point of entry in south-eastern Germany (Bavaria) and Gothic missionary activity as a vehicle. With rare exceptions this thesis is still accepted in general principle, even though some words have been subtracted from his list, but others added to it. Because of disagreements which Kluge's thesis

[1] Schäferdiek (1978a), 497ff.   [2] Gschwantler (1976), 175ff.; Schäferdiek (1978a), 498, 500.
[3] Jordanes, *Getica* 133; Gschwantler (1976), 177ff.; Schäferdiek (1978b), 79ff.
[4] Kluge (1909), 124ff. Cf. already von Raumer (1848), 401ff.

has called forth we can best approach the problem he raised by discussing some of his examples which have withstood the test of time, then some which have since been withdrawn from his list, and finally some of the newest suggestions for adding to it.

The word about whose transmission from Gothic the greatest consensus exists is OHG *phaffo* 'priest', even though alternative derivations have to be excluded before we can consider the Gothic explanation.[5] This word, about whose derivation from Gr. *papās* there can be no doubt, is attested in OHG texts only from the tenth century, but must be considerably earlier than this because of place-name evidence dating from 739 (e.g. *Pfaffenhofen*) and because it shows the effects of the Second Sound Shift. Both the textual and the place-name evidence show a common distribution, with the earliest and most frequent examples occurring in Bavarian, then in Alemannic, followed by SRhFr. and the other Franconian dialects, together with OS. Such a distribution in time and space suggests a south-eastern origin for the word's career in OHG: it spread first in Bavaria as a sub-literary term (to judge by its absence from written texts for so long), was used at first in place-names, then in texts. Once adopted into the ecclesiastical language it spread northwards and westwards.

A direct loan from Greek is out of the question (how was contact possible between Greek and Bavarian and how do we explain *phaffo*, instead of **phaffes*?). Although the Greek word found its way into Latin, the form *pāpa* is equally excluded because of its long *ā* (whereas OHG presupposes a short vowel) and because the Latin word meant not 'cleric' (as in Greek and OHG), but 'supreme cleric, pope'. By the same token VL cannot come into question: it had the same meaning 'pope', but also underwent voicing of the intervocalic *-p-*, which then became a fricative (cf. in both respects OS *pâvos*, which must have come from Romance). Finally, a loan from OIr. *popa* is just as improbable: it meant not 'cleric', but 'pope, monk, ascetic', there are doubts about the linguistic traces of the Irish mission to Germany, which in any case would have barely left enough time for the Second Sound Shift.

The Gothic theory faces the difficulty that Wulfila regularly used *gudja* 'priest'. However, *papa* occurs in the Gothic Calendar (ca. 400) and in a Gothic document from Naples (with the same meaning as in OHG), so that its absence from Wulfila's bible and occurrence soon after suggests

---

[5] Kluge (1909), 126ff.; Waag (1932), 5ff.; Schäferdiek (1982), 242ff.

that the Gothic word, like the OHG, was at first sub-literary. This is also confirmed for Greek, where the earliest evidence for Christian *papãs* is a little later than the Gothic Calendar. The Goths must therefore have acquired this word from the spoken vocabulary of Greek Christians and used it first in writing a little earlier than its official recognition in Greek. Gr. *papãs* should have produced Go. *papas* (cf. Gr. *Satanãs*: Go. *Satanas*), but since in this latter equation the Gothic word passed over into the weak declension in inflected cases this allowed the back-formation of a weak nominative *Satana*. Similarly with Go. *papa*, and hence OHG *phaffo*. The peculiarities of the German word can therefore be explained by Greek ('priest'), but only if we postulate Gothic transmission (sub-literary function at first, Second Sound Shift, weak declension, initial focus in Bavaria).

We come next to three Bavarian names for days of the week: *ertag* (with variants) 'Tuesday', *phinztag* 'Thursday' and *pherintag* 'Friday'.[6] These words occur only in Bavarian and presuppose a Greek background, visible in the first part of each compound even though an originally Greek word has been phonologically Gothicised or Bavarianised. The restriction of these words to south-eastern Germany suggests entry from the east (hence Gothic transmission).

Although *phinztag* occurs for the first time in the twelfth century (the names for days of the week occur very rarely in the whole OHG corpus) the double effect of the Second Sound Shift shows that it must be of considerable antiquity.[7] Before this *phinz-* must have been **pint-*, a regular Germanic adaptation of Gr. *pémptē* (*hēméra*) 'fifth day, Thursday'. Wulfila may not attest Go. **pintēdags*, but neither did he use *papa*, and if *phinztag* had not occurred in MHG we should have had to deny it for OHG, too. The south-eastern centre of gravity suggested by the sequence Greek–Gothic–Bavarian is confirmed by parallels from eastern Europe (Sl. *pętŭkŭ*, Hung. *péntek* 'Friday' because Monday, not Sunday, was regarded as the first day of the week) and by their absence from the west. The case for Gothic transmission is a strong one.

All the evidence for *pherintag* is confined to Bavaria and although it occurs in glosses of the eighth and ninth centuries the effect of the Second Sound Shift shows, as with *phinztag*, that it must be older still.[8] In the glosses *pherintag* renders Lat. *parasceue*, itself a loan from Greek, where the word meant 'preparation, preparation for the sabbath, therefore

---

[6] Kranzmayer (1929), 70ff.; Stutz (1980), 214ff.
[7] Kluge (1909), 138f.; Stutz (1980), 214f.; Wiesinger (1985), 159.
[8] Kluge (1909), 139f.; Stutz (1980), 214f.; Wiesinger (1985), 160.

Friday'. This Greek word was also loaned into Gothic, where Wulfila used *paraskaíwē* in the sense '(day of) preparation'. The OHG word reveals in its first element a contraction of the original word to **parē* (to which *-tag* has been added by analogy with other days), which could have taken place either in Gothic or in Bavarian, but in any case is paralleled by other abbreviations, especially where foreign words were assimilated (cf. for OHG *sarcophagus > sarc, discipulus > disco*). In this case we have therefore a juxtaposition of a learned, ecclesiastical term (*paraskaíwē*) with a word from popular speech (**parē*), such as we found with *papa* and will meet again with *sabbato*.

To this derivation from Greek *via* Gothic a rival suggestion has been opposed, seeing in *pherintag* a loan from Lat. *perindie* 'second day before a fixed date', therefore 'Friday' (by reference to Sunday).[9] Acceptance of this learned monastic coinage from Latin into Bavarian would make the sequence Greek–Gothic–Bavarian irrelevant, but doubts are in order. It is significant that the OHG examples gloss Lat. *parasceue*, not *perindie*, so that some awareness of their association was still felt. The Latin theory also suffers the disadvantage of not being able to account for the restriction of this loan to Bavarian. Thirdly, the relevance of the Second Sound Shift means that the Bavarian word must have been coined at the latest early in the seventh century, at a time when there were no monasteries in Bavaria where such a learned adoption was conceivable. We may conclude that although the group *phinztag, pherintag* and (as we shall see) *sambaztag*, all suggesting Gothic transmission from Greek to Bavarian, may not of itself be compelling, it is highly suggestive.

With *ertag* we come again to a Bavarian word which is attested only much later in MHG.[10] Although the Sound Shift provides no help for an early dating, this word agrees with the others in permitting a regular phonological derivation from a Greek word for 'Tuesday'. Gr. *Áreōs hēméra*, corresponding to Lat. *Martis dies* and likewise including the name of the pagan god of war, is attested in Greek sources of the third and fourth centuries.[11] Even though there is no reflection of it in Wulfila's Gothic the intermediate position of Gothic is suggested by the regular phonological development which can be reliably reconstructed: from *Areōs hēméra* to Go. **arjaus dags*, then to OHG **ariôtag* (cf. Go. *friþus/-aus*: OHG *fridu/-ô*), and finally to MHG *ergetag* (cf. OHG *fario*: MHG *ferge*), one of the variant forms of this word. We need not be disturbed by the

---

[9] Knobloch (1960), 430ff. [10] Kluge (1909), 140ff.; Stutz (1980), 214f.; Wiesinger (1985), 158f.
[11] Thumb (1901), 171.

pre-Christian origin of this Greek name (incorporating the name of a planetary deity of pagan antiquity) as opposed to the Christian nature of other names for days of the week passed on from Greek to Gothic, for the double origin of this nomenclature is reflected elsewhere in Germania (cf. _mittawecha_ and _Woensdag_). Even if this Bavarian term differs from the others in deriving from a pre-Christian Greek form this does not mean that it had a pagan overtone for the Goths (let alone the Bavarians): for them it was simply a phonetic loan, otherwise meaningless in the new linguistic context, and it cannot be taken as an indication that they knew of Ares as the god of war or used his name in place of a Germanic deity.[12] Nor can the suggestion that the Goths accepted this word because it reminded them of Arius, the supposed founder of their Christian sect, be seriously maintained any longer.[13] We are left therefore with a Greek and a German term whose connection with each other can be explained by Gothic mediation.

This is no longer entirely the case with another name for a day of the week: OHG _sambaztag_ 'Saturday'.[14] The word is attested from the ninth century (Otfrid, the _Tatian_ translation, Notker), but this wider geographical spread, making it a word characteristic of southern Germany at large, is something new in the days we have considered and prompts the question whether this now tells against a possible Gothic influence. The Christian origin of this word ('sabbath') is clear, but why should it have come to Germany from Greek rather than Latin, which also took over the word from Greek? That the source of the OHG word with its characteristic -_m_- is to be sought in the east is clear from a distinction running through Romania between western forms without -_m_- (It. _sabbato_, Provençal _sabde_, Sp., Port. _sabado_) and eastern forms with -_m_- (e.g. Rum. _sâmbătă_), supported by other eastern, but non-Romance languages (e.g. OSl. _sǫbota_, Hung. _szombat_). Although ecclesiastical Greek as well as Wulfila's Gothic know only forms without -_m_-, these east European forms allow us to reconstruct a VG variant *_sámbaton_ and hence *_sambato_ for popular speech in Gothic, too. With that reconstruction we have a distinction between ecclesiastical and popular speech, such as we saw with _papa_ and *_parē_, but also the means of explaining OHG _sambaztag_, the end-result of a line of influence from Greek _via_ Gothic.

That is only part of the picture, however, for there is another explanation for German forms with -_m_- in southern Germany at large and in

---

[12] Kluge (1909), 144; Wiesinger (1985), 159.   [13] Schäferdiek (1982), 241, fn. 11.
[14] Kluge (1909), 137f.; Meyer (1894), 326ff.; Avedisian (1963), 231ff.; Stutz (1980), 215f.

the west, namely the possibility that these forms entered from the west, as is suggested by French forms with -*m*- (*samedi* in the whole of northern France). As an explanation of these French forms various suggestions have been made: Greek Christian communities along the Rhône valley and in Lyon (as with *kyriakón*), Visigoths in south-western France at a later stage of their migrations, or VL speakers (under the influence of VG).[15] These two centres of gravity, suggesting two points of entry for *sambaztag* into Germany, one in the east and one in the west, would account for its wider spread than with the other terms.[16] Or should we place greater weight on the absence of Bavarian examples from OHG and reckon with influence from the west alone, as with *kirihha*? In that case this word would belong to the next stage in our argument (subtractions from Kluge's list).

Those who question Gothic influence on OHG accept it in some cases (*ertag*, *phinztag*), but rescue their thesis by seeing these names for days of the week in the context of trading contacts, which devalues them as examples of Gothic religious vocabulary.[17] This argument operates with a distinction between secular and religious which is much too disjunctive, and it conflicts with a striking feature of classical loanwords in Gothic. Whereas those in the sphere of trade and warfare derived from Latin,[18] those for Christianity came overwhelmingly from Greek (even if sometimes *via* Latin), so that the Greek source for these names suggests a Christian context for their adoption in Gothic. Nor does the attempt to reinforce this trading argument by reference to **mûta* 'customs' (regarded as a loanword from Gothic to Bavarian in the context of trade) carry much weight: given the absence of any effect of the Second Sound Shift, this loan must belong to a later period.[19]

If we base ourselves on the examples so far considered the following criteria suggest themselves for Gothic influence on OHG.[20] First, a peculiarity about the German word which suggests an origin in southeastern Europe and therewith Gothic transmission (for the most part a word of Greek origin with no counterpart in the Latin of the western Church). Secondly, a parallel, semantic or phonological, between the German word and its Gothic counterpart. Thirdly, a suggestion that the German word had its centre of gravity in the south-east (Bavarian) or in the south (Bavarian and Alemannic), even though this need not exclude

---

[15] Meyer-Lübke (1923), 9; von Wartburg (1953), 296ff.; *GR* 2, 444f.; Avedisian (1963), 232f.
[16] Stutz (1980), 216; Wiesinger (1985), 190.   [17] Knobloch (1960), 430.
[18] See above, pp. 202ff.   [19] Schäferdiek (1982), 242. Against this Wiesinger (1985), 193ff.
[20] Cf. also Stutz (1980), 219.

its later spread elsewhere by internal German loanword traffic (as with *phaffo*). Fourthly, a dating in the sixth century or earlier (here the relevance of the Second Sound Shift is decisive). Not all these criteria are present in every case, so that room for doubt remains, and some criteria are not always applicable (a Greek word could enter German sometimes from the west, so that Gothic transmission was not necessarily involved).

So far, all the examples discussed from Kluge's list have come ultimately from Greek, which has been of assistance in recognising them as loanwords and in establishing Gothic transmission. However, the influence claimed for Gothic is not confined to Greek terms unknown to Latin Christianity, although the borrowing of native Gothic words into OHG is more difficult to establish than with obviously non-Germanic ones. For this purpose we need further criteria. First, a parallel between the German word and the Gothic one (either the same Germanic word or different words, but with the same function). Secondly, the word must be used as a Christian, not just secular term in German and in Gothic. Thirdly, we need to ask whether the OHG word, of south-eastern origin, was in opposition to other Christian terms in Germany, deriving from elsewhere. These additional criteria increase our philological difficulties, so that there is more room for doubt. These uncertainties explain why subtractions from Kluge's list have been made as well as additions to it.

With regard to a number of OHG words to which Kluge attributed a Gothic origin the present consensus places them in a different context. *Kirihha* and *biscof*, far from entering Germany in the east, probably derived from the provincial Roman vocabulary of Christian Gaul. We shall later argue that *pharra* 'parish' was probably an import of the Frankish mission, just as *heilag* and *ôstarun* acquired their Christian function under the influence of the Anglo-Saxon mission. These terms therefore now have to be dropped from Kluge's Gothic list. Apart from them we may now turn to an example for which Kluge claimed a Greek model.

With this example (Go. *dáupjan*, OHG *toufen* 'to baptise')[21] Kluge proceeded from the assumption that it was unlikely that this Christian concept was conveyed by the same word twice in Germanic independently, especially in view of the range of alternatives found in Germania, and concluded that the Gothic choice had influenced

---

[21] Kluge (1909), 131f.; Knobloch (1960), 435f.; Loi (1969), 67ff.; Stutz (1980), 212f.; Schäferdiek (1982), 244f.

German. Go. *dáupjan* resembles Gr. *baptízein* in several respects. The Greek word is a causative verb, derived from the adjective *baptós* 'dipped, dyed' and therefore meaning 'to dip, wash', just as the Gothic is a causative verb, derived from the adjective *diups* 'deep' and hence meaning 'to dip, immerse'. Just as Greek retained this general meaning of its verb after its Christian specialisation of meaning, so did Wulfila use his Gothic verb in the sense 'to dip, wash' alongside the meaning 'to baptise'. From this agreement it was concluded that the Gothic word had been christianised in imitation of Greek and in full understanding of the linguistic composition of the Greek verb, hardly surprising in view of the exposure of the Goths, and of Wulfila especially, to the Greek language. It was also concluded that such knowledge of Greek was impossible in early Germany (where Christian Latin *baptizare* would not suggest *toufen*, as its Greek model had for the Goths), so that the Christian use of *toufen* derived from Gothic. Although we are dealing with a vernacular term, the linguistic route followed (Greek–Gothic–OHG) was the same as in the previous cases.

This argument rests, however, on the assumption that knowledge of Greek was not possible in Germany at this time, and about this, on however elementary a level, doubts may be entertained.[22] What has been said of Anglo-Saxon England in this connection is equally applicable to Germany: understanding of a considerable number of Greek words was available from a variety of sources, from Greek–Latin glossaries, Isidore's *Etymologiae* and patristic writings. For the OHG *Benediktinerregel* an acquaintance with Greek terms which bypasses their Latin equivalents has been suggested (it renders *kirieleison* directly by *truhtin kinade uns*) and knowledge of central terms of Greek Christianity was occasionally passed on in glosses (e.g. *soter grece salvator latine heilant*). Even apart from this it is still possible to account for OHG *toufen* by a Latin model, thereby avoiding any need to involve the Goths. The Latin verb *(in)tingere* originally meant 'to dip' (and 'to dye by dipping'), but was then used in application to Christian baptism, especially by Tertullian about 200. If it seems a far cry from Tertullian's Africa to Germany we may recall that the verb was also used in this sense by such writers as Augustine, Gregory the Great, Isidore and Bede. Where *tingere* was used alongside *baptizare* in Christian Latin the former denoted the ritual act of immersion, the latter the sacramental act of baptism.[23] Of particular

---

[22] Gneuss (1992), 119; Ibach (1960), 403ff.; *Benediktinerregel* (54), p. 37; Steinmeyer and Sievers (1879ff.), III 182, 12.   [23] Loi (1969), 73, 81f.

interest is the evidence from Isidore (*Baptisma graece, latine tinctio inter-pretatur*), for his use in clerical schooling ensured that a Latin word meaning 'to dip' could be imitated in a Germanic vernacular to denote baptism without any dependence on Greek.

We can go a step further, for even without any knowledge of the Greek or Latin term the practice of baptism by immersion, known from the bible with Christ's baptism in the Jordan and in use by the western Church, could lead to the adoption of a Germanic verb meaning liter-ally 'to dip' as a term to describe a ritual act visible to pagans and new converts alike.[24] Only if baptism by immersion had been unknown in the west would we be driven to assume that *toufen* was borrowed from Gothic. Instead, if we regard the derivation of Go. *dáupjan* from Greek as unconnected with the dependence of OHG *toufen* on Latin (or on visual observation of baptismal practice) we face once more the proba-bility of polygenesis. Even though OS *dôpian* may conceivably be a loan-word from OHG (as part of the Frankish conversion of the Saxons), the argument for polygenesis must still be used for OE *dēpan/dyppan*. These verbs occur in England rarely as Christian terms in tenth-century glosses which cannot be adduced as witnesses to continental WG (or even Gothic) usage centuries earlier.[25] They probably owed their chance formation as much as their OHG parallels to knowledge such as that conveyed by Isidore or to contemporary Church practice. The case for a Gothic background to OHG *toufen* must therefore be regarded now as extremely weak.[26]

We turn now to additions which have been made to Kluge's list. They are examples of vernacular origin, the first of which suggests the possibility of Greek influence *via* Gothic in yet another way.

The semantic field of OHG *(ir)fullen* 'to fill, fulfil'[27] covers three usages: physical (a space is filled), metaphorical (a person is filled with joy or time is fulfilled) and abstract (a prophecy or commandment is ful-filled). Of these the second and third represent biblical usage so that the question arises, if they are Christian extensions of the first usage, where this adaptation may have taken place. The linguistic reflection of this question is seen in Otfrid (or even more so in Notker), who prefers *(gi)fullen* for the physical usage, but *irfullen* for the biblical, thus making a

[24] *Ibid.*, p. 77; Schäferdiek (1982), 244.   [25] Gneuss (1992), 122.
[26] Another suggestion by Kluge to be included here is Go. *armahaírts*, OHG *armherz*, OE *earmheort* 'merciful'. On this see Kluge (1909), 148f.; Wahmann (1937), 134ff.; Betz (1949), 73; Beck (1979), 109ff.; Gneuss (1992), 122f.   [27] Hinderling (1971), 1ff.

distinction by means of the prefix *ir-*. The variant *irfullen* is attested early (eighth century), especially in UG. By contrast, further north *Tatian* uses *(gi)fullen* and the *Heliand (gi)fullian* in both the physical and biblical sense, with no differentiation. In this northern Germany agrees with OE *(ge)fyllan*. In UG the examples of *irfullen* come chiefly from religious texts and the verb is used predominantly in the biblical context of prophecies, commandments or time being fulfilled, so that it is a standing theological term.

This OHG differentiation between *(gi)fullen* and *irfullen* could not have been prompted by Latin, which used a range of variants (*replere, implere, adimplere, complere*) without any semantic distinction or correspondence to the German pair. We do better to turn to Gothic for a parallel with OHG, since Wulfila used *fulljan/fullnan* predominantly in the physical sense, but *usfulljan/usfullnan* (whose prefix corresponds to OHG *ir-*) sometimes in the physical or metaphorical sense, but much more frequently in the abstract (of a prophecy or commandment).[28] Although Wulfila based his Gothic translation on the Latin as well as the Greek model, Latin can have given him no lead in this. By contrast, the Greek bible did differentiate between the physical meaning (for which it used a variety of verbs: *pimplánai, gémein, gemízein*) and the metaphorical or abstract (*plēroũn*). Wulfila's text may lack the variety of physical verbs, but more important is the point that, following the Greek model, he differentiated at all. The fact that UG usage with its verbal distinction had no parallel further north (*Tatian*, OS, OE), but agreed with Gothic practice (behind which lies Greek biblical usage) suggests, as was more obviously the case with *phaffo*, Gothic influence.

No such Greek background can be detected for the equation of OHG *abgot* with Go. *afguþs*.[29] The formation of the German word for 'idol' (with its derogatory prefix expressing scorn for the pagan gods) must be Christian, since for Germanic paganism there was no antithesis between gods and false gods. This relatively late birth of *abgot* is confirmed by its distribution within Germanic, confined to continental WG (OHG, OS, OFri.), for whenever a similar distinction had to be made in OE and ON the pagan gods were designated in another way.[30] Gothic, too, went its own way as regards the substantive by using *galiugaguþ* ('false god'), but Wulfila also employed an adjective *afguþs* to render *asebḗs* 'impious'. There are, however, difficulties in using the similarity between Gothic

---

[28] In each of these Gothic pairs the second verb is an inchoative, doing duty for the passive.
[29] Karg-Gasterstädt (1945), 420ff.   [30] Cahen (1921), 73 and 49ff.

and continental WG to suggest a common origin in Germanic: one form
is an adjective and the others are substantives, one form describes man's
relationship to God while the others denote the pagan god himself, and
it is difficult to imagine an early, Germanic origin for a specifically
Christian concept.

A useful pointer is provided by word-formation, where the Gothic
adjective constitutes no problem, whilst *abgot* stands alone among noun
compounds with *ab-* and is clearly anomalous. This prefix occurs in
verbal abstracts (e.g. *ablâz: ablâzan*), but also in forming compound adjectives (e.g. *abtrunni*, also Go. *afguþs*) or adjectival abstracts (e.g. *abtrunnigî*).
This shows up OHG *abgot* as exceptional, whereas Go. *afguþs* belongs to
an established category, so that we may suspect the possibility of a loan
accounting for the German anomaly. The Gothic adjective occurs twice:
once to denote the impious, those who do not acknowledge God by their
behaviour, and once with reference to heretics, meaning therefore not
'godless', but having a false conception of God. If we can apply a
context like this to OHG, this would suggest that *abgot* belonged to the
missionary period when Christianity was struggling with the old religion. The transfer of the word from one language to another would
explain how the Gothic adjective came to be an OHG substantive
(probably also under the influence of *got*), in other words how the
anomaly in word-formation came about. The flectional variants in
Bavarian and Alemannic, in particular, suggest that the loan from
Gothic to OHG is likely to have taken place in southern Germany.[31]

A Bavarian centre of gravity and the possible influence of Gothic are
also found with OHG *stuatago* 'judgment day'.[32] The first element of this
compound belongs etymologically to an UG group of verbs with several
variants: *stouwon* (Bavarian, 'to complain, criticise, accuse'), *stouwôn*
(Bavarian, Alemannic, SRhFr., 'to complain, criticise'), *stuowen*
(Bavarian, 'to criticise'), *stuowôn* (Bavarian, Alemannic, 'to quarrel'),
stuoen (Bavarian, Alemannic, 'to make amends, suffer punishment'). The
last of these variants, emphatically Bavarian, was dying out already at
the beginning of the written tradition and is connected with forms more
actively represented in Gothic: *staua* fem. 'trial', *staua* masc. 'judge', *stojan*
'to pass judgment', *stauastôls* 'tribunal'. Both in OHG and in Gothic
these are legal terms, but view the process from different angles: the
accused 'suffers punishment' (OHG), but the judge 'passes judgment'

---

[31] Karg-Gasterstädt (1945), 433.
[32] Freudenthal (1949), 89; Müller (1957), 308ff.; Mastrelli (1975), 75ff.

(Gothic). In view of this contrast there are no grounds for assuming Gothic influence on this German verb. The position is different, however, with *stuatago*, attested once only, in Bavarian (*Muspilli* v. 55). From OHG usage of the verb this should mean 'day of punishment', but in treating the 'day of judgment' *Muspilli* presupposes the Gothic meaning. The relationship between the two forms suggests a loan from Gothic to Bavarian, for whereas the Gothic words are semantically coherent, *stuatago* is anomalous in two respects: it occurs only in Bavarian and in a meaning isolated within German.[33]

One final example is Gothic in origin, but in a different way. OHG *kûski* 'virtuous, pure' as a specifically Christian term shows a wide range of word-formations: the adjective *kûski*, the substantives *kûski* and *kûskida* (all three in positive and negative forms) and the negative verb *biunkûsken*.[34] The range of this word within WG points to an origin within OHG: in contrast to the frequency and range of formations in OHG the word occurs only twice in OS (once in the *Heliand*, once in the *Genesis*), which suggests a loan from the south, whilst the one attestation in OE (in the *Genesis*, translated from OS) points to onward transmission from OS to OE. If the WG evidence implies radiation from OHG the range of evidence within OHG is similarly informative: the word's centre of gravity from the eighth to tenth century was markedly UG, especially Alemannic or more specifically the monastery of Reichenau. By contrast, it was relatively unproductive in Bavarian and came to Franconian only later. Such a specific point of radiation (Reichenau) within OHG and then within WG suggests a specific cause and argues against the word being a common Germanic inheritance. It is in fact a loanword from Latin *conscius* 'conscious, aware', capable of indicating ethical awareness (especially of guilt) in pre-Christian Latin and hence eminently adaptable to Christian ends, as in *conscientia*.

Apart from OPr. and OC *cusc* (with a later spread to OFr.) Lat. *conscius* has left no traces in Romance. Even these isolated forms cannot have come directly from Latin, for whilst *o* + *n* before *s* could have produced *ō* (cf. It. *Costantino*) this cannot account for *u*, and there is the further irregularity that *c* before *i* has not been palatalised. These irregularities can be accounted for, however, if we assume that the Latin word entered

---

[33] Other suggestions under this heading include Go. *weihs*, OHG *wîh* 'holy' (Baetke (1942), 85ff., 165ff.; Stutz (1980), 210, fn. 15), Go. *ansts*, OHG *anst* 'grace' (Wahmann (1937), 121ff.; Green (1965), 239ff.; Stutz (1980), 210) and Go. *dulþs* 'festival', Bavarian *tuld* 'fair' (Wesche (1937), 94ff.; Bohnenberger (1948), 468ff.).

[34] Sperber (1915), 55ff.; *FEW* 16, 430; Frings and Müller (1951), 109ff.

OPr. and OC not directly, but *via* Gothic (even though the word is not found in this language). Already as attested by Wulfila, Latin *ō* could become *ū* in Gothic (e.g. *Rumoneis*) and *c* before *i* could be represented by *k* (e.g. *fascia* > *faskja*). What is irregular as a direct development from Latin to Romance can therefore be accounted for by Gothic transmission, a fact rendered more significant by the way in which Catalan and Provençal together match the area of the Visigothic kingdom. An isolated form within Romania and a specific point of radiation within Germania suggest a definite point of contact, transmission of the Gothic form (or its Romance derivative) from the south-west, and learned, monastic rather than missionary contact. OHG *kûski* exemplifies Gothic linguistic influence, but not a Gothic mission.[35]

Kluge avoided the question of the historical context for Gothic loanwords in OHG, leaving it to historians to answer,[36] but he still talked of Gothic words coming up the Danube to Germany, in which he has been followed by others who extend the range of this traffic to England and Scandinavia. Dissatisfaction with this and the lack of evidence for a Gothic mission to Germany have led at times to a rejection of Gothic influence on the Christian vocabulary of Germany at all.[37] Such dissatisfaction on the part of historians is likely to be increased by three suggestions made by philologists as to how Gothic influence entered Germany (from the east, the south and the west), for this could be symptomatic of philological uncertainty. On the other hand, this diversity could be merely the result of the changing locations of the Goths on their migrations (Black Sea, Moesia, Pannonia, northern Italy, southern France, northern Spain). We must now consider these three possibilities, bearing in mind that different geographical stages in the Goths' migrations imply different datings of a possible linguistic influence,[38] that Gothic words could be transmitted indirectly, not necessarily by the Goths themselves, and not as part of any missionary activity.

Entry of Gothic words from the east (the Danubian theory) would imply Balkan radiation of the Arian Christianity of the *Gothi minores* while still settled north of the Danube in Gothia or on imperial territory south of the river and in the period between Wulfila and the Avars' invasion of Pannonia, i.e. in the fifth century.[39] To explain the adoption of

---

[35] Betz (1949), 49ff., has pointed to Go. *(ga)timreins* and OHG (Reichenau) *zimbar* 'religious edification' in a similar monastic context.   [36] Kluge (1909), 160.

[37] E.g. Schäferdiek (1982), 239ff.   [38] Stutz (1980), 221; Wiesinger (1985), 183f.

[39] Stutz (1980), 220; Schäferdiek (1982), 248f.

these words in south-eastern Germany we have to take into account the ethnogenesis of the Bavarians in the first half of the sixth century in Raetia Secunda (now Bavaria) and western Noricum Ripense (Upper Austria, south of the Danube).[40] This newly formed tribe incorporated various EG tribal groups (Sciri, perhaps the Rugii, Heruli) and could have entered its new territory from Bohemia, Pannonia or Raetia-Noricum. The Ostrogoths had been Arians while still in Pannonia, the Rugii had an Arian royal house while in Lower Austria (and the Sciri, too?), and the Langobards were Arians during their period in Lower Austria and Pannonia. In short, in the course of their ethnogenesis the Bavarians were surrounded by Arian tribes to the south and east, they included within their own formation elements which had broken loose from these tribes, already nominally converted to Christianity. Knowledge of Christianity brought to the Bavarians in this way in the course of their tribal formation was bound to be confined to scattered groups and to be external and rudimentary, hence the later need for a more thoroughgoing Christianisation of the Bavarians in the seventh and eighth centuries.[41]

This route from the east was probable when behind the parallel between Gothic and OHG there stood a Greek model not adopted by Latin and possibly with reflections in eastern Europe (Rumanian, Slavonic, Hungarian). It was also probable when a Gothic term was attested only in Bavarian or at the most in UG.[42] The rudimentary acquaintance with Christianity which this route provided is confirmed by the nature of Gothic loanwords initially or entirely confined to Bavarian (*phaffo*, names for certain days of the week), for these suggest no more than an external contact with Christianity, not necessarily conversion, let alone a Christian mission to the Bavarians. This amounts to a modified version of the Danubian theory as put forward by Kluge. Gothic linguistic influence still remains, but transmitted indirectly by scattered groups from EG tribes converted by the Goths, and then involved in the ethnogenesis of the Bavarians. Any missionary activity was therefore conducted earlier among these EG tribes, not with the newly formed Bavarians. Although we are dealing directly neither with Goths nor with a mission, this does not preclude Christian terms of Gothic origin in Bavarian.

The transmission of Gothic terms from the south (the Alpine theory)

---

[40] Wiesinger (1985), 185ff.; Schäferdiek (1982), 249. [41] Wiesinger (1985), 189, 190.
[42] Stutz (1980), 219.

embraces two possibilities, with slightly different dating: they came either from the Ostrogoths in northern Italy (in the period 489–553) or from the Langobards, their successors in that region (in the late sixth or early seventh century).[43] The obvious route for this traffic would have been over the Brenner or from Aquileia to Juvavum, while the transmitters involved were either the Ostrogoths under Theoderic or the Langobards, converted to Arianism by the Goths before becoming Catholic. The indications of heretical Christianity and syncretism to be found in Bavaria from the second half of the sixth century could tie up with Arian influence from the Goths and still from the Langobards.[44]

For each of these possibilities a wider framework has been suggested. For the Ostrogoths it is above all Theoderic's political alliance with the Thuringians against the combined threat from the Franks and Byzantium, leading the Gothic ruler to extend his authority to southern Germany as far as the Danube, the frontier with the Thuringians.[45] For more than a generation southern Germany was therefore under Ostrogothic influence. It has been questioned whether this was long enough for Gothic religious influence to make itself felt in Germany in the face of Frankish penetration, but precisely this policy of Theoderic has been seen as the context for the transmission of Gothic loanwords to German.[46] Admittedly, there is no evidence that Theoderic's policy of alliances had a religious dimension, but given the political-religious nature of his relationship with Chlodwig this is by no means unlikely. Alternatively, for the Langobards a strong cultural influence has been argued across the Alps on Bavaria before the Franks, so that religious terminology, ultimately of Gothic origin, could have been carried by them.[47]

It has not proved easy to suggest specific words which may be attributed to this route, although *tuld* is a possible candidate. Its presence in Bavarian, but also in Alemannic suggests two possible entries: *either* from fifth-century Pannonia to the 'pre-Bavarians' and then to the Alemanni *or* from sixth-century Italy across the Alps to Bavaria or independently to the Alemanni (a later entry still reconcilable with the operation of the Second Sound Shift).[48] Either explanation would involve only indirect Gothic influence: other EG tribes by the eastern route, Langobards by the southern.[49]

[43] *Ibid.*, pp. 220f.; Wiesinger (1985), 184.   [44] Wiesinger (1985), 192.   [45] Beyerle (1955), 65ff.
[46] Schäferdiek (1982), 250; Beyerle (1955), 81.
[47] Baesecke (1930), 148ff., 158; Kranzmayer (1960), 30ff.   [48] Bohnenberger (1948), 476.
[49] Cf. Eggers (1954), 136, fn. 4.

Penetration of Gothic terms from the west (the Aquitanian theory) is connected with the Visigoths and their kingdom of Toulouse or in northern Spain.[50] In the former case the period in question would be 418–507, although this might have to be extended to the seventh century if we postulate Gothic influence on Romance (as in OPr. *cusc*) and then transmission to Germany by the strong Aquitanian component in the Frankish mission east of the Rhine. In the latter case the period would be from 484 to the end of the sixth century, when the Visigoths in Spain were eventually Romanised linguistically.

The argument for a western entry for Gothic terms has lately been conducted as part of a wider thesis suggesting a Frankish mission eastwards, mainly to the Alemanni and Bavarians, in the sixth century.[51] Knobloch assumes that Gothic elements entered the Frankish ecclesiastical vocabulary as a result of the Frankish conquest of the Visigothic kingdom (507–11), but regards 596, the date of the mission to the Anglo-Saxons, as a *terminus ante quem* because he believes that some of the Gothic terms were carried to England by this mission. His examples are not argued in detail and some remain very uncertain (e.g. *Welt, glauben*). Moreover, by restricting this influence to the sixth century in order to accommodate what are regarded as Gothic terms in OE this thesis runs into a dangerously tight chronology.[52] The Spanish Visigoths were converted to Catholicism in 589 and the mission to England began in 596, so that in the space of merely seven years Christian terms of a hitherto heretical confession had to be adopted officially by the Frankish Church and taken by Frankish interpreters to England. Frankish Christian terms may have reached OE in this way, but we have no evidence that Gothic ones were amongst them. If we abandon this hypothesis of Gothic words in OE this has the result of providing a longer period for the Catholicised Goths to be linguistically active in the Frankish Church, a period extending now to the seventh century, when the more active Frankish mission to Germany could have taken words with it which were ultimately of Gothic origin.

However uncertain the historical context suggested for the Aquitanian theory may be, we are left with the western associations of OHG *kûski* and with Gothic connections with Reichenau, as in the case of *zimbar*. The latter example suggests an individual monastic contact, possibly in the context of Aquitanian recruits to the Frankish ecclesiastical

---

[50] Stutz (1980), 221, fn. 64; Wiesinger (1985), 184; Schäferdiek (1982), 256; Thompson (1969), 314.
[51] Knobloch (1960), 427ff.; (1966), 221f.; (1967), 300ff. Cf. also Stutz (1980), 211ff.
[52] Schäferdiek (1982), 255ff.

penetration of the area east of the Rhine. In this connection Pirmin, the founder of the monastery at Reichenau, has been suggested as the point of contact, together with monks in Reichenau confraternity lists whose names are Gothic. This would be more persuasive if we were certain that Pirmin was in fact a Goth and that the monks' names were Gothic.[53] Again, we remain with the fact of Gothic linguistic influence on OHG, but with no trace of a Gothic mission.

It is this mission which, as a historian, Schäferdiek has rightly rejected on the grounds that there is no historical evidence to support it. From this he proceeds, equally rightly, to reject the suggestion that there were linguistic effects of such a mission in southern Germany. From this point, however, he argues incorrectly that there are no loanwords of Gothic origin in OHG. This last step ignores two points. It pays no attention to the possibility that these loanwords could be transmitted indirectly, not by Goths themselves. It also fails to consider that the loanwords need not have been spread in the context of missionary activity. The case for Gothic loanwords in the Christian vocabulary of German does not stand or fall with that for a Gothic mission.

---

[53] Betz (1949), 51f., 101f.; Schäferdiek (1982), 256, fn. 94.

CHAPTER 18

The influence of the Merovingian Franks

Under this heading we have to consider two topics: what has been regarded as an Irish mission in Francia and in southern Germany (where effects on OHG vocabulary have been proposed) and a Frankish mission east of the Rhine. The former is to be questioned and stress will be placed instead on the latter.

These topics have to be seen against the background of the loss of Christian territory resulting from the barbarian invasions.[1] In the *Reconquista* the conversion of Chlodwig was a vital first step, but no more, since between his death (511) and the arrival of Columbanus (590) Christianity made little headway, apart from at the Merovingian court itself.[2] Although there was a first hesitant phase of Christianisation in the sixth century (e.g. the episcopal lists start again in the Rhineland, first with Gallo-Roman, then with Germanic names), this was confined to the Franks, built on still surviving Christian pockets, and aimed at no more than the *status quo ante*. Only in the seventh century did this change with a thoroughgoing re-Christianisation of the former frontier area, but also with a missionary advance into areas east of the Rhine. Behind this advance lay the alliance between the monastic movement of the Irishman Columbanus (mainly centred on his foundation at Luxeuil) and Merovingian kings and nobles expanding Frankish power amongst the Alemanni and Bavarians.[3]

Early in the seventh century attempts were made to extend the authority of the Church to north-eastern Gaul by figures such as Amandus and Eligius, with connections with Frankish royalty and with Luxeuil, aiming at areas still largely pagan. Luxeuil also stood behind another missionary impetus: to the Alemannic area, opened up to Christianisation initially by Columbanus himself, sent there by

[1] Büttner (1951), 9; Schäferdiek and Schäferdiek (1976), 180f.; Ewig and Schäferdiek (1978), 116ff.
[2] Ewig (1970), 30f.; Schäferdiek (1976), 181f.; (1978a), 537.
[3] Schäferdiek (1978a), 541; Hillgarth (1987), 323.

Theudebert II after his expulsion from Luxeuil, then by others with similar affiliations. The influence of the Vosges monastery reached as far as Bavaria, where Eustasius, successor of Columbanus at his foundation, and other monks from Luxeuil made up a systematic mission over some period of time for which a connection with Dagobert's authority over the eastern territories seems likely. An eastward extension of Christianity in conjunction with Frankish political expansion can also be assumed for the sector east of the Middle Rhine in this century.[4]

The turn from the sixth to the seventh century thus saw the beginning of missionary activity on a broad front carried into new territory. The impetus lay with Frankish rulers, but also with the Irish monastic ideal of Columbanus, who sought assistance and protection from rulers in founding monasteries in Francia and whose form of Christianity helped to legitimise their expansive authority. By the end of the seventh century the Anglo-Saxon mission largely took over, so that any Irish linguistic influence will have to be sought in this century. Its location will have to be attempted in areas where we have evidence for Irish activity in Germany, i.e. mainly amongst the Alemanni, but also the eastern Franks and Bavarians. However, Irish traces are not the same thing as Irishmen, let alone their influence on the German language. In historical research a reaction has set in against an earlier equation of seventh-century Christianisation simply with an 'Irish mission'.[5] Instead, the Irish are now seen as providing the impetus to a much wider movement, both Gallo-Roman (e.g. the combination of the rules of Columbanus and Benedict) and also Frankish (e.g. the Frank Waldebert, the second successor of Columbanus as abbot at Luxeuil). From the Irish impetus there arose a joint movement which Prinz has defined as 'Hiberno-Frankish'. At least three historical factors justify this greater stress on the Frankish contribution.

In the first place, the Irish impetus would have achieved little without Frankish leadership and support.[6] On the frontiers of Christendom a mission could only thrive under the protection of a local king or nobleman, so that Columbanus, on arriving in Francia, turned to the royal court, thereby linking his monastic and missionary efforts with the power of the Merovingian state. A second qualification of Irish influence is called for by Prinz's distinction between Irishmen active in Germany

---

[4] Büttner (1951), 13ff.; Schäferdiek (1976), 181ff.; Prinz (1978), 133, 458; (1981), 81.

[5] Büttner (1951), 12f.; Prinz (1982), 202.

[6] Ewig (1970), 48f.; Ewig and Schäferdiek (1978), 126; Prinz (1978), 447f., 452f.; (1981), 77f., 80; (1982), 208ff.; Hillgarth (1987), 314.

(Columbanus himself or Kilian, Colmán and Totnán, martyred in Würzburg in 689) and missionaries under Irish influence, but of Frankish, Franco-Burgundian or Gallo-Roman origin.[7] This distinction makes it clear, for example, that no Irish foundation can be placed in Bavaria, by contrast to Francia, and that the number of known Irish missionaries in Germany is extremely small. Thirdly, the indirect nature of Irish influence can be shown in another way.[8] Apart from the short spell of Columbanus in the Lake Constance area and a few of his compatriots known to have been in Germany, the influence of Luxeuil was only indirectly Irish: continental monks won for Irish monasticism, but as missionaries incapable of transmitting Irish terms to the nascent Christian vocabulary of German. Taken together, these three considerations qualify the extent to which we can talk of a purely Irish mission in Germany and justify the alternative term 'Hiberno-Frankish'.

Only one Irish loanword into German has been suggested: OHG *glocka* 'bell', but even here there are difficulties.[9] The use of a bell in a church service is attested from the fourth century with Lat. *signum* for northern Gaul and from the sixth with *campana* for southern Gaul and Italy. However, in the seventh century *clocca* was used in place of *signum* in northern France (cf. Fr. *cloche*) and spread over part of the *campana* area in northern Italy. This new word also gained entry into WG and ultimately NG. In Germany two variants occur: *clocka* in the Low and Middle German dialects, *glocka* in the south. For these variants two different entries into Germany have been suggested, behind each of which an Irish word has been thought to stand: *clocka* thus reached northern Germany *via* the lower Rhine and northern France (where the Irish are said to have brought the word), whereas *glocka* is held to be an import to southern Germany from Italy (the Irish foundation Bobbio has been suggested as a point of origin).

For the Irish origin of the word the evidence is no more than circumstantial. A vernacular form is attested in Middle Irish (tenth century), but before this the earliest evidence is Hiberno-Latin *clocca* in the late seventh century (in Adomnán's *Vita Columbae*) and then in Anglo-Saxon circles on the continent with Irish connections. Much more hypothetical is the

---

[7] Prinz (1965), 347, 351; (1981), 81; (1982), 210; Schäferdiek (1976), 186f. Franks: Ewig (1970), 32f., 37; Prinz (1978), 459. Franco-Burgundians: Prinz (1978), 453, 455; (1981), 78. Gallo-Romans: Ewig (1970), 30ff., 44; Ewig and Schäferdiek (1978), 128.   [8] Cf. Weisgerber (1952), 14f., 32.

[9] Förster (1921), 37; Weisgerber (1952), 22; Eggers (1978), 492; Strasser (1982), 402ff.; Herren (1984), 201f.; *FEW* 2, 149ff., 790ff.; *GR* 1, 131; 2, 190ff.

suggestion of an Irish origin simply because of the word's geographical spread on the continent (northern France, Germany, northern Italy) in areas where Irish missionary activity is attested, for Lat. _clocca_ is so widely distributed that it need not be tied down to Irish transmission. Even less convincing is the proposal that the word was felt to be Irish because of a reference to what 'in Irish is called the excommunication bell (_clog_) of Blaithmac', for this evidence is late and attests the word in Irish, but not as specifically Irish. An Irish origin would be quite excluded if we were to accept the suggestion of a Latin or Romance derivation (from a verb 'to strike' to a noun meaning 'the stroke of a bell' or denoting the instrument itself, 'bell').[10] This proposal is based on the argument that an Irish origin would be too late to explain the palatalisation found in Italian and Iberian dialect forms. Our evidence suggests that the Latin word was the source of the continental forms, but the fact that the first attestation was Hiberno-Latin is not enough to establish an Irish origin for the Latin word.

Even if we were to accept an Irish origin for this word, that is not the same as accepting its transmission to Germany by Irish missionaries. That is particularly clear with the north German _clocka_: although the Irish could conceivably be associated with the beginning of the word's route (France and even the lower Rhine), none was active in northern Germany, so that other forces must have brought it this far. Nor can we fall back in this case on a transmission of the word first from Irish into OE and only then to OS (as part of the Anglo-Saxon mission to Germany). The OE form of this word is _clugge_, so that if the Anglo-Saxons brought the word at all it cannot have been in this form, but as a Latin term in use in the circle around Boniface.[11] The south German form _glocka_ also presents difficulties for the Irish theory. We know of no Irish mission from Bobbio to Germany, so that Irish impetus is as uncertain in this case as with its north German counterpart. Whereas an importation of _glocka_ from Italy cannot explain initial _g-_ in place of _c-_ (the north Italian dialect forms suggest only the latter), this could be regarded as a native UG change attested from the tenth/eleventh century.[12] If that is accepted, there is no need to postulate a loan from Italy or to bring in Bobbio or an Irish impetus at all. This could imply a common entry for both the north and south German forms, opening up the possibility of an Irish influence in the south which was excluded for the north. But this is no more than a possibility for which we lack proof.

---

[10] Meier (1975), 283ff. [11] Haubrichs (1987), 402, fn. 53. [12] Strasser (1982), 405ff.

Irish influence on German of another type has been proposed for Lat. loanwords which, it is claimed, entered German *via* Irish. For this we need specific pointers which for different reasons are lacking.

German terms for 'psalm, psalter' (OHG *salm, salteri* alongside occasional *psalm, psalteri*) have been attributed to the influence of Ir. *salm, saltair*.[13] This is highly improbable, not merely because the consonant group *ps-* was unusual in German and could therefore have been simplified to *s-*. The same is true in OE (*sealm*) and already in VL (all the Romance derivatives likewise drop the *p-* and only restore it later, as occasionally in OHG, under the influence of Church Latin). Given the wide range of languages where this simplification of an unusual sound group occurred we need a positive reason for assuming Irish influence in the case of German. Another proposal concerns Lat. *versus* 'verse', OHG *fers* (alongside *vers*) and Ir. *fers*.[14] Two arguments tell against Irish influence on German here. Although Lat. *v-* can become *f-* in Ir. (e.g. *verbum : ferb*), this substitution can also occur elsewhere. The alternation between *v* and *f* is also an internal OHG feature: the *Ludwigslied* has *fand* alongside *uolgon* (where *u* stands orthographically for *v*) and Otfrid uses our word in both forms (*fers* and *vers*). With this alternation within German it is difficult to argue that *fers* must betray external influence from Irish. Secondly, the form *fers* also occurs in OE where it may well be the result of Irish influence on England (cf. also *Firgilius*). This English evidence now radically changes the position for OHG *fers*, for if we were to attribute this after all to external influence it is more likely to have come from the Anglo-Saxons (whose linguistic loans to Germany are well attested) than from the Irish (where these still have to be established).

The remaining suggestions for Latin–Irish–German loanword traffic may be taken together: they all contain a Latin long *ē*.[15] This regularly produced a diphthong in direct Latin loans into German (e.g. *spēculum: spiagal*), but a long *ī* in Latin loans into Irish (e.g. *census*, VL *cēsus: cís*), so that Irish transmission has been put forward for some German forms with *i*. Among these, however, we find *sēta: sîda* 'silk' and *crēta: krîda* 'chalk', trade words unlikely to be connected with an Irish mission and, with their intervocalic *-d-*, suggesting Romance transmission. Another consideration implies that a long *ī* need not point to the Irish.[16] At the time of its earliest contacts with Romania Germanic possessed the long vowels *ō* and *ē* which were open, not closed, so that Latin words with

[13] Weisgerber (1952), 25; Eggers (1978), 492f.; *FEW* 9, 500; *GR* 2, 421ff.
[14] Jellinek (1925), 111ff.; Weisgerber (1952), 23 (and fn. 60); Strasser (1982), 402.
[15] Weisgerber (1952), 23ff.; Eggers (1978), 492.   [16] Frings (1939), 107.

closed long vowels were taken over as long $\bar{u}$ and $\bar{\imath}$ instead. Both these vowels were affected and not just in German alone, which argues against restricting the German examples with long $\bar{\imath}$ to a specifically Irish influence.

Other factors bear this out for the words in question. As a term of monastic discipline Lat. *poena* > *pēna* 'punishment' was loaned into German as *pîna*, with Ir. *pén* (long and closed) as a suggested intermediary.[17] Quite apart from the argument of the last paragraph, the Latin word was also loaned into OE (*pīnian*) so that, whether or not the OE form was under Irish influence, there is no certainty that the German derived from Irish rather than English. With *clēricus: clîrih* it is uncertain whether the vowel was long or short in Latin and in Germanic, but apart from that the word is also attested in Ir. *clérech* and OE *cliroc*.[18] The fact that in German as in English these forms are isolated *hapax legomena* constitutes a classic case for loan-traffic and weakens further the suggestion of direct influence from Irish to German. This is weakened even more radically in the remaining cases. Whereas there is no reason to doubt the loan of Lat. *dēlere* as a term of the scriptorium into OE *(ā)dilgian* and OHG *diligôn / tiligôn* 'erase, destroy' it is by no means certain that We. *dileu* and Ir. *dílegaid* (only from Middle Irish) are loanwords rather than native formations.[19] Even if they were to go back to Latin, the OE testimony and the importance of Anglo-Saxon book culture on the continent mean that we lack evidence for *direct* Irish influence on German. This is excluded for the last two cases suggested as examples of Irish transmission: Lat. *feria*: OHG *fîr(r)a* 'ecclesiastical feastday, church service' and *expensa* > *expēsa / spēsa: spîsa* 'monastic provisions, food'.[20] In neither case is the word attested in Irish or Celtic at all (OIr. has only *feróil* < *feriālis*), so that the argument for the Irish mission rests on pure surmise. Nor could these words have come to OHG from OE, where they are likewise unattested. Instead, since the meaning 'expenditure' for *spēsa* is best attested in Italy this word could have reached Germany from the south at a time when, as with *sēta* and *crēta*, German *î* was an obvious replacement for a closed long *ē*.

With that we have come to the end of the loanwords into OHG for which an Irish origin or transmission has been proposed. They amount

---

[17] Weisgerber (1952), 23f.; Frings (1939), 106ff.; *GR* 2, 401f.

[18] Weisgerber (1952), 24f.; Betz (1949), 43; *GR* 1, 194; 2, 189.

[19] Weisgerber (1952), 24, fn. 64; Schröder (1923), 246ff.; *GR* 2, 226f.

[20] *Feria*: Weisgerber (1952), 23f.; *FEW* 3, 462ff.; *GR* 1, 34; 2, 251. *Expensa*: Weisgerber (1952), 23f.; *GR* 2, 242f.

to a meagre crop, numerically and as regards their persuasive force: one Irish word where no certainty has been reached and seven Latin words whose route through Irish was quite unlikely. This suggests that traces left by the Irish mission were not strong enough to make a mark on the German language.[21]

Suggested Irish influence on the basis of loan-translation is no more convincing. Why should OHG *foresiht/forescauwunga* go back to Ir. *remdéic-siu* or *remcaisiu* rather than Lat. *providentia*?[22] Or OHG *cuatchundida/kuot ârende* to Ir. *soscélae* instead of Lat. *evangelium* (especially since Isidore interprets this as *bona adnuntiatio*)?[23] The search grows even less persuasive when the rendering of Lat. *gratia* by OHG *ginâda* is attributed to the Irish mission on the lame ground that any other mission is out of question.[24] Just as arbitrary and based on an argument by exclusion is the equation of a 'south German ecclesiastical language' with Irish influence.[25]

To return to our starting-point. The inquiry into the possible influence of Irish on the Christian vocabulary of OHG proceeded from the discrepancy between what was taken as historical evidence for an Irish mission in Germany and the lack of any linguistic confirmation. Subsequent work concentrated on the attempt to devise more refined philological methods for recognising Irish influence. This has not proved convincing, so that we are forced to consider the possibility that any Irish influence was not strong enough to leave its mark linguistically. In short, we have to accept what was once regarded as too revolutionary to be acceptable,[26] but in doing so we are liberated from the discrepancy which earlier worried philologists. We have reached a position of agreement between historians (who now attach much less importance to a specifically Irish mission in Germany) and philologists (for whom there is no reliable trace of its linguistic influence).

In place of an 'Irish mission' Prinz introduced the term 'Hiberno-Frankish', implying that although the Irish may have supplied the spiritual impetus they were not especially active in the mission itself. In view of the philological questioning of an Irish element in the earliest Christian vocabulary of OHG this prompts the question whether we

---

[21] Cf. Weisgerber (1952), 11f., 21.
[22] Weisweiler and Betz (1974), 94; Eggers (1978), 493. Cf. Betz (1949), 119.
[23] Weisweiler and Betz (1974), 94; Eggers (1978), 493; Weisgerber (1952), 41. Isidore of Seville, *Etymologiae* VI vi 43.
[24] Wahmann (1937), 121ff.; Weisgerber (1952), 18, 26; Strasser (1982), 414f.
[25] Weisgerber (1952), 19ff.; Eggers (1978), 494ff.; Strasser (1982), 408ff. Cf. also Schmidt (1948), 111f.; Brinkmann (1948), 124ff.   [26] Schmidt (1948), 106.

might not go one step further and shift the emphasis from 'Hiberno-Frankish' to Frankish missionary activity in Germany and determine its linguistic reflections. This is meant not in the mechanical sense of replacing 'Irish' by 'Frankish', but as a means of drawing attention to a Frankish contribution which, because in the shadow of the Irish mission, has been largely neglected.[27]

In the non-religious sphere Frankish political expansion east of the Rhine, especially in the Alemannic and Bavarian areas, brought linguistic changes in its train concerning legal and social innovations introduced by them.[28] In the legal sphere *urteil* 'judgment' and *urkundo* 'witness' result from Frankish influence, as do *hêrro* 'lord' and *man* 'vassal' in the social sphere. Even so central a term as the German word for 'German' (*thiudisk*) may have spread from Francia, where it denoted the Germanic vernacular still spoken by the settlers as opposed to Romance. There is in principle no reason why such innovations in political vocabulary should not have been accompanied by changes in religious terminology, since Frankish rulers drew legitimacy from their divinely sanctioned status and saw to it that the Church, one of the pillars of their power, accompanied the expansion of their authority.[29] This possibility is suggested by what has been proposed as Frankish hegemony in Anglo-Saxon England, illustrated in the marriage of the Frankish princess Bertha to Æthelberht of Kent.[30] Although the Franks may have failed to exploit religion to enhance secular power in the late sixth century, a fusion of religion with politics informs their support of Gregory the Great's mission to England, amounting to a deliberate policy. In this instance Frankish political and religious influence beyond the borders of Francia was accompanied by an influence on the nascent Christian vocabulary of OE: key-terms like 'church' and 'bishop' were brought to Kent under Frankish auspices.[31] This justifies our asking the same question of another area subject to their hegemony: did the spread of Frankish political and religious authority likewise take any Christian terms with it east of the Rhine? Our answer to this question will be concerned with three aspects of Church organisation: the vocabulary of baptism, of the clergy, and of monasticism.

---

[27] Cf. however Eggers (1964), 8of., but especially Knobloch (1959), 27ff.; (1960), 427ff.; (1966), 221f.; (1967), 300ff.

[28] See above, pp. 46ff., 112ff., 116, fn. 61, but also Freudenthal (1949), 27ff., 100ff.; Weisgerber (1949), 67ff., 81ff.   [29] Cf. Ewig (1963), 7ff.

[30] Wood (1994a), 235ff. Cf. also Geake (1994), 91; Stevenson (1994), 178f.

[31] See above, pp. 300f., 304f.

Coining a vocabulary of baptism is essential for any Church, especially one, as in Francia in the seventh century, engaged in a *Reconquista* in north-eastern Gaul and in the conversion of pagan tribes east of the Rhine. The three words chosen as examples all show a geographical grouping in north-western Germany, together with a radiation to England. None is attested in Irish.

Although *christian(iz)are* is not attested in early Christian Latin for the act of baptising, it is from such a form that a number of vernacular words derive: OFr. *chrestiener*, MDu. and MLG *kerstenen* and OE *cristnian*.[32] Alternatives to these words are based in Romance on *baptizare* and are represented in Germanic by Go. *dáupjan*, OE *fulwian*, ON *skíra*. The vernacular words derived from *christian(iz)are* are thus concentrated in the north-west (OFr., OE, MDu., MLG), a geographical grouping suggesting radiation from northern Gaul. Although there are no phonological pointers to the dating of this radiation it was probably a Christian loanword of the Merovingian period. It is unlikely to be earlier, for the collapse of Church organisation in north-eastern Gaul with the Frankish invasion would have prevented such radiation. Moreover, the Anglo-Saxons who made the crossing to England as pagans from the continental *litus Saxonicum* are unlikely to have felt the need for Christian loanwords. Nor can the word have been taken into OE from Christian Britons, because there is no reflection of the Latin term in any Celtic language and, what is more, Bede tells us that the Christian Britons were hostile to converting the Anglo-Saxons. Instead, this word was probably brought from Francia to England, whether in connection with Augustine's mission to Kent (the Frankish interpreters he took with him?) or as part of a more general Frankish evangelisation among the Anglo-Saxons.

A physical requirement for the ritual of baptism is the font.[33] Lat. *fons* 'spring' acquired the Christian meaning 'font', attested in ecclesiastical Latin from the fourth century and reflected in the western Romance languages. Only in northern Gaul did it mean 'font' alone; elsewhere in Romania it also retained its pre-Christian meaning. From northern Gaul the word was taken into Germanic, but confined to the north-western area which also acquired *christianizare*: OE *font*, Dutch *vont*, OFri. *font*, Lower Rhenish *fünt* (with one outrider in south Germany: *funtdifillol* 'baptizand', literally 'font-godchild'). Apart from this anomaly, the

---

[32] Eggers (1978), 489, fn. 92; *GR* 1, 30; 2, 181.
[33] Eggers (1978), 502; *FEW* 3, 695f.; *GR* 1, 53, fn. 1; 2, 258.

restriction of evidence to the north-west suggests radiation from a common source in northern Gaul. Here too there is no reason why this word should have spread before the missionary expansion of the Frankish Church, but every reason to assume that it reached England as part of this process, possibly in close connection with *cristnian* (especially since OE *font* could not have come from Insular Celtic, since We. *ffons* is a learned loanword from the fourteenth century).

The personal accompaniment to baptism is the presence of godparents, attested from towards 200 (Tertullian). Three Latin terms concern us: *pater* (standing for *pater in Deo*), *patrinus* (one who holds the child over the font) and *compater* (the name given by the parents to the *patrinus* of one of their children).[34] Each of these terms is reflected in Gallo-Roman and also in continental WG, the last also in OE. Derived from *pater* are MDu. *pete(r)* and MLG *pade*, from *patrinus* came such forms as *peterin, pheterin, petter, phetter*. *Compater* produced loan-translations such as OHG *gifatero* and MLG *gevadder*, but also OE *gefædera* (alongside the loanword *cumpæder*). Even with their weaker reflection in OE these words reveal a similar geographical grouping to 'baptise' and 'font': attestations in Gallo-Roman, but not in Insular Celtic, and within Germania a focus in Dutch, Low German and Middle Franconian (reflections in Upper German are not regarded as autochthonous). Because of this focus these words are seen as spreading from Francia into these other Germanic dialects and, for the same reasons as with *kerstenen* and *font*, during the Merovingian period.

The development of a vocabulary for various offices and spheres of duty of the clergy presupposes a degree of ecclesiastical organisation. Although this may also have been true of the earliest provincial Roman Christian communities in the Rhineland we cannot assume that such early organisational terms (especially before Constantine) were taken over by Germanic pagans in the frontier area or spread by them in the Germanic hinterland before the Anglo-Saxons made the crossing to Britain. This suggests that the words in this group were later loans in a period when the Frankish Church was establishing itself and were then taken eastwards with Frankish expansion. Where OE parallels are also present they are probably loans from Francia, as with the vocabulary of baptism.

Our first example is the word for 'priest': Lat. *presbyter*, a loanword from the Greek for 'elder', coined for Christian use in imitation of

---

[34] Eggers (1978), 502; *FEW* 2, 2, 973f.; 8, 22f.; *GR* 1, 130; 2, 368ff.

Hebrew.[35] As a Christian term it was already known to Greek by the year 100 and was borrowed into Latin in the sense 'priest' by 200 (Tertullian). The term originally denoted an experienced member of a Christian community who acted as official adviser to the *episcopus*, but with the third century this office could be held only by one ordained by the bishop to whom, with the strengthening of the episcopate, the priest was subordinate. As long as Christianity was largely confined to cities mass and baptism were performed in the episcopal church, but with its spread to the countryside rural centres with a *presbyter* became indispensable.

The Romance languages distinguish between **prebyter* in the east (It., Rum.) and *presbyter* in the west (Gaul, Iberian peninsula). The latter form produced two variants, both attested in Romance dialects and as loanwords into Germanic. The first lacks the second *r*: *preste*, attested in Iberia and in French dialects of the north-east. In Germania it occurs in OE *prēost* and in isolated south German forms like *prest(lih)* and *priast* from the eighth and ninth centuries. The second variant retains the second *r* (OFr. *prestre*) and is attested for Gaul, from where it spread into OFri., OS, Alemannic and Bavarian, appearing earliest in south Germany only in texts connected with the Franks. In the south it competed with the earlier form derived from *preste*, but also with another term (*phaffo*) from Gothic. Whether we can be more precise about the point of entry of this second variant into Germany (Trier has been suggested, in connection with Frankish monastery foundations from the seventh century) is uncertain.[36] What does seem uncontested is that the *preste* form was carried both to England and to Germany and the *prestre* form to Germany, both from a common source in Francia.

The appointment of priests in a north European countryside slowly won from paganism necessitated the organisation of this new terrain into smaller units: Lat. *parochia*, OHG *pharra*.[37] The Latin word goes back to a Gr. verb *paroikéō* 'I am a stranger or guest' which was applied to the Christian's mode of life ('to be a stranger in this world'), so that the noun *pároikos* extended its meaning from 'stranger' to 'follower of Christ' and the collective *paroikía* denoted Christians living in one place under the leadership of a bishop. This meaning 'diocese' is attested in Greek from the second century and in Latin (*paroecia, parochia*) in the fourth. With the spread of Christianity from cities to countryside and the difficulty of running the whole diocese from one episcopal centre the diocese was

---

[35] Waag (1932), 43ff.; Eggers (1978), 502; *FEW* 9, 357ff.; *GR* 1, 42, 48; 2, 414f.   [36] *GR* 2, 415.
[37] Knobloch (1960), 435; Masser (1966), 87ff.; *FEW* 7, 658ff.; *GR* 1, 33; 2, 360f.

subdivided into smaller administrative units. Both the larger and the smaller unit could be termed *dioecesis* or *parochia*, but with a tendency to apply the former to the bishop and the latter to the priest. This development, especially in Francia in the sixth and seventh centuries, called forth the need for a vernacular term, the basis of which was *parochia* in Gaul, as distinct from Italy (*plebs*). The word is attested in France and from there in OIr. and in Germany (English *parish* is a later loan from French). The OHG form *pharra* has been drastically simplified by shortening, but that is also the case with other foreign loanwords (e.g. *phropho* < *propago*). If the German forms regularly show *-rr-*, that is frequently also the case in Merovingian Latin (*parrochia*) and is reflected in OFr. *parroche*, particularly in the north and east. Even though in this case England was not involved there is no objection to deriving *pharra* from *parrochia* and no reason to doubt that the force behind the spread of this word was the organisation of the Frankish Church into smaller units from the sixth century.

Another reflection of Frankish Church organisation within Germany has been seen in OHG *betabûr*, used as a place-name, but also to denote a smaller place of worship such as a chapel or oratory (*sacellum, martyrium, titulus*).[38] Apart from one example of a possibly mechanical translation all the cases where the German word is used concern an *ecclesia minor* in which regular services could be held, but without the right to perform baptism or burial. It can be assumed that *betabûr* designated such a church as distinct from a *matrix ecclesia* with fuller rights. If we add to this the fact that *betabûr* as a place-name is found in those parts of Germany reached by the Frankish mission it is likely that we have here another linguistic reflection of the ecclesiastical organisation taken in hand by the western Franks.

A further term for an ecclesiastical office derived from Lat. *custos* (gen. *custodis*) 'custodian', which in Late Latin had the variant *custor* (gen. *custoris*) and was then used of an ecclesiastical office ('sacristan').[39] In this meaning the late form survived in northern France (OFr. *costre*) and in the Grisons. This geographic restriction of form and meaning in Romania suggests that German reflections of the word (English has no parallels) are loans from northern France as part of Frankish ecclesiastical vocabulary. East of the Rhine the forms are OFri. *kostere*, OS *costarari* with an uncertain additional suffix, and OHG *custor* (even though the earliest examples come from the south, particularly from Bavaria). Most

---

[38] Masser (1966), 100ff.   [39] *FEW* 2, 1595f.; *GR* 1, 48; 2, 222f.

telling about this connection between northern France and Germany is the fact that it is in these areas that the word has the specialised ecclesiastical meaning 'sacristan'.

The last example under this heading is a word for 'cathedral', confined in the Middle Ages to the German language area: OFri. *dom*, OLFr. *duom*, OHG *tuom* (England and Scandinavia acquired the word later).[40] The connection of this word with Lat. *domus* is undoubted, but difficulties arise in deciding what kind of *domus* produced a vernacular word with this meaning. The obvious suggestion (*domus Dei*) is unsatisfactory because, whilst every church may be a house of God, not every church is a cathedral. Another derivation proposed was from *domus ecclesiae* in the sense 'parish house with a dwelling for the clergy', especially in use for collegiate churches where a number of clerics were employed and, in connection with a cathedral, suggesting that its hallmark was the presence more of a *collegium*, a cathedral chapter, than of a bishop. This proposal, too, is not without its difficulties. If the *collegium* accommodated in the *domus ecclesiae* was the decisive feature of a cathedral, why was every collegiate church not called a cathedral or why were there towns which boasted of two or more collegiate churches, but only one cathedral? Moreover, the need for a *domus ecclesiae* as an abode for clergy was not confined to larger churches (let alone cathedrals), but was true of any church, however small, where accommodation had to be provided for a priest.

Greater promise is held out by *domus episcopalis*. With *domus Dei* as an equivalent to *ecclesia* the addition of the place where the church was situated necessitated the formula *domus Dei* (or *ecclesia*) *in loco X*, but when the saint to whom the church was dedicated was mentioned we find *domus* (or *ecclesia*) *sancti Georgii in loco X*. As a result of dropping *Dei* in this longer formula *domus* by itself conveyed the meaning 'church'. With the gradual development of the parish system it became necessary to distinguish between different types of church: *ecclesia parochialis/filialis/baptismalis* as distinct from *ecclesia cathedralis/episcopalis*. Only in the last case was *ecclesia* replaced by *domus* (*domus episcopalis*, attested frequently). From this phrase, standing for *domus Dei episcopalis* or *domus sancti X episcopalis*, OHG *tuom* acquired its meaning 'cathedral'. It is attested in this function from the ninth century (in a gloss to *matrix (ecclesia)* in the sense of the bishop's church), but it is not certain that we must date the loan before the Second Sound Shift (*d-* > *t-*, by early in the seventh century), since this could be

---

[40] Kretschmer (1906), 595ff.; Masser (1966), 53ff.

a case of sound substitution. Regarding the area where the loan took place we are in a somewhat better position. Of central importance was the ecclesiastical organisation in Francia (above all in the north and east, where the earlier diocesan pattern had been most disrupted by the barbarian invasions),[41] but also, as a consequence of the spread of Christianity to the countryside, the greater variety of churches, larger and smaller, and the need to distinguish linguistically between them and the episcopal church. From Francia, under conditions which also brought forth the vernacular term for 'parish', the Frankish word for 'cathedral' was carried east of the Rhine.

A third lexical group is formed by the vocabulary of monasticism. Despite the importance of Gallo-Roman monasticism (Lérins) Frankish monasticism was of decisive importance in Christian expansion: monasteries were founded in the rural areas of north-eastern Gaul from which the conversion of pagans was taken in hand as well as the spread of Christianity east of the Rhine.[42] Monasticism reached Germany only from the beginning of the seventh century,[43] so that the terms which concern us date from then (even if the vocabulary of monasticism may have been created in Francia before this we are dealing only with its subsequent penetration to Germany).

A key-term is of course the word *monasterium*.[44] In Greek it designated a hermitage and in this sense it was borrowed in the fourth century into Latin, where it soon stood for *coenobium* 'monastery'. With this meaning it was used in Gallo-Roman (cf. OFr. *moustier*) and in this area, as attested in Merovingian Latin, *-a-* could be replaced by *-e-* or *-i-* (*monestirio, monistirio*). The form with *-i-* is reflected in OHG *munist(i)ri* and OE *mynster*, perhaps also in OIr. *monister, mainister* (although the *-i-* could here be a parasitic vowel to deal with the unfamiliar group *-nst-*). A parallel between Merovingian Latin on the one hand and OHG and OE on the other is also present in the semantic range of this word. In Merovingian Latin it was applied to a monastery, but also to a collegiate foundation because at this stage the boundary between the two was still fluid, but in addition *monasterium* could also designate a church (especially in northern Gaul), possibly because the church-building was the most obvious physical feature of a monastic or collegiate community. These three meanings are also to be found in OHG and (in part) in OE. The meaning 'monastery' occurs in OHG, above all in the *Benediktinerregel*

---

[41] Masser (1966), 60; Wood (1994b), 71.   [42] Prinz (1981), 76.
[43] Cf. Schäferdiek (1982), 243, fn. 19.
[44] Betz (1949), 56f.; Masser (1966), 70ff.; Eggers (1978), 486; *FEW* 6, 3, 72f.

about 800, but also in place-names (e.g. *Kremsmünster* from the eighth century), as well as in OE. Despite these early examples the German word was later ousted in this sense by *klôster*. The meaning 'collegiate foundation' is also found in OHG, but more rarely and only in place-names. More common in OHG as in OE and corresponding to Lat. *monasterium* is the application of the word to the church of a monastic or collegiate foundation. On one occasion in OHG it designates a church at large: *domus Dei* is glossed *za munistiure*. Although the loan into OE has been placed in the sixth century, there is no reason for going back earlier than the seventh century for OHG. Various considerations thus speak for an origin in Francia: phonological (the presence of *-i-*), semantic (the range of three meanings) and institutional (the introduction of Frankish monasticism into Germany in the seventh century).

Another term in this group is *monachus*.[45] It is attested in Greek with the meaning 'hermit' from the second half of the fourth century and its later shift to 'monk' parallels what we saw with *monasterium*. Early Christian Latin inscriptions from Gaul show two forms: *monachus* and *monicus*. From the first derived OFr. *munie*, *moigne* and OPr. *monegue*, as well as *manach* in Irish. The second form (showing *-a-* > *-i-*, as in *monasterium* > *monistirium*, and *-ch-* > *-c-* as in It. *monaco*) is the basis of such Germanic words as OFri. and OS *munik*, OE *munuc*, OHG *munih*. This last form (with its final voiceless fricative) is not to be seen as somehow having bypassed the Latin change *-ch-* > *-c-* or as having entered OHG early enough to undergo the Second Sound Shift. Instead, it parallels learned loanwords partly adapted to High German sound structure (e.g. *grammatica* > *grammatih*, *canonicus* > *knünich*) for which an early loan is out of the question.[46] This word thus probably entered Germany in the same context and at the same time as *munist(i)ri*.

We conclude with one word for an office within the monastic hierarchy: *propositus*.[47] The origin of this in classical Latin was *praepositus* 'a superior in charge', used since Tacitus in the military sphere and since Tertullian in the organisation of the Church (*praepositus ecclesiae* 'bishop'). Augustine used it in the context of a monastic community, for Gregory of Tours it denoted the prior of a monastery. With this range of secular and ecclesiastical meanings it survived in OFr. *prevost*, OPr. *prebost*. Late Latin or early Romance brought a change of prefix to *propositus*, particularly in Gaul (*provost*, *probost*). This latter variant found its way into languages within the radiation area of northern France: MIr. *propost*, OE

---

[45] Eggers (1978), 486; *FEW* 6, 3, 64ff.   [46] *GR* 1, 194.   [47] *FEW* 9, 302ff.; *GR* 1, 42, 48; 2, 412f.

prōfost (which also has *prāfost* < *praepositus*), OFri. *provest*, OHG *probost* (already from the eighth century). There is every likelihood that this word entered Germany from Francia as part of monastic expansion, but no reason to assume that OE may have assisted its entry into German.[48] Instead, the loans into OE and OHG are probably independent of each other, sharing only a common source in Francia.[49]

Two conclusions emerge from this chapter. First, the change in nomenclature employed, moving from 'Irish mission' to 'Hiberno-Frankish' and then to 'Frankish', reflects the course of our argument. As a historian, Prinz introduced the second term because, despite the fact of an Irish impetus, he saw the mission more under Frankish auspices, whilst for the philologist, seeking linguistic traces, the omission of any reference to the Irish is even more justified. He cannot deny their historical presence, but can question their part in the creation of a Christian vocabulary in German. Secondly, the extension of Frankish Christian vocabulary to Germany can be seen as part of the Franks' political expansion eastwards, but alongside this we have to set the extension of their terms northwards to Anglo-Saxon England, not in every one of the cases considered, but strikingly often.

[48] *GR* 1, 48.
[49] OHG *jungiro* has been suggested as a loan-meaning from Merovingian Latin *iunior* (Kauffmann (1900), 25ff.; Eggers (1964), 62ff.; Green (1965), 431ff.; *FEW* 5, 74). As the counterpart of *hêrro* < *senior*, likewise of Frankish origin, *jungiro* denoted a secular subordinate rank, but also a clerical one. It could also be applied to the monastic hierarchy. Cf. Eggers (1964), 69.

CHAPTER 19

The influence of the Anglo-Saxons

The pilgrimage on behalf of Christ adopted by Irish monks took them to the continent, but also to the Picts and then the Anglo-Saxons who were thus introduced to this form of Christian asceticism. As a result Anglo-Saxons who followed their example likewise forsook their homeland (voluntarily embracing exile either in Ireland or on the continent) and could also be described as exiles or as pilgrims on behalf of Christ. Even more explicit is the fact that the earliest Anglo-Saxon missionaries on the continent had Irish connections.[1] There is every reason for thinking that the Anglo-Saxon mission to the continent was inspired by the Irish model and that any possible transmission of Irish loanwords to the continent could just as well be due to Anglo-Saxon mediation as to the Irish themselves.

Other factors also played a part in initiating the Anglo-Saxon mission. Chronologically, this move to the continent followed on immediately after the conclusion of the conversion of the last remaining Germanic pagans in England (Sussex and the Isle of Wight), so that only when this was accomplished was it feasible for Anglo-Saxons to combine missionary activity with pilgrimage abroad and to switch their attention from insular to continental Saxons.[2] That in doing so they were impelled by a wish to ensure the salvation of their continental kinsfolk is suggested by a number of pointers.[3] When dealing with Ecgbert Bede referred expressly to pagan tribes in Germania from which the Angles and Saxons had sprung. Boniface claimed in connection with his plans for converting the continental Saxons that they were of the same blood and bone and referred to his native Wessex as *transmarina Saxonia*, whilst a bishop of Leicester described the continental Saxons as 'our people'. The Anglo-Saxons who went to Germany were also motivated by a

---

[1] Richter (1982), 120ff.   [2] *Ibid.*, pp. 122f., 131.
[3] *Ibid.*, p. 125; Löwe (1978), 201; Levison (1946), 77, 92.

sense of the universal mission inaugurated by Gregory the Great in his plan for the conversion of England.[4] According to Bede the Anglo-Saxons' missionary programme embraced Frisians and Saxons, but also Danes and Avars, whilst the Avars as well as the Slavs were still envisaged by Boniface in his programme. Unrealised these wider hopes may have been, but they still attest the strength of the impetus which took the Anglo-Saxons to the continent, far beyond the relatively confined scope of an exile in Ireland.

Despite earlier attempts at Christianisation the religious position in Germany was certainly such as to provide work enough for the Anglo-Saxons.[5] In those regions which were only loosely attached to the Frankish empire or had only recently been incorporated in it paganism still managed to maintain itself to varying degrees. This religious picture is reflected in the geographical distribution of the main centres of Anglo-Saxon missionary activity in Germany: Würzburg (the episcopal see of an Anglo-Saxon pupil of Boniface), Fulda (where the monastery was founded by Boniface), Mainz (the seat of Boniface) and Echternach (the monastery was founded by Willibrord).[6] Behind these centres there lie different mission-fields where the Anglo-Saxons were active (Frisia, Saxony, Hessen, Thuringia) and provided priests for many of the parishes. Their presence is attested even further south, in areas long since christianised (e.g. Boniface was charged in 739 with the organisation of the Bavarian Church).

The chronology of Anglo-Saxon missionary activity in Germany is reasonably well established, running from the late seventh to the early ninth century, from Wilfrid's arrival in Frisia in 678 to Willehad, the first bishop of Bremen and the last Anglo-Saxon missionary known to us by name. No traces of Anglo-Saxon linguistic influence are known from the ninth century on.[7] Collating the geographical and chronological evidence we may place the Anglo-Saxon mission roughly in the eighth century, starting about a hundred years after the arrival of Columbanus in Francia and Gregory the Great's mission to England. Its centre of gravity was where the need was greatest, in northern and central Germany, but with some outriders in the south.

However late in the historical sequence of the various attempts to christianise Germany the Anglo-Saxon mission may have come, its importance is beyond doubt. By his organisation of the Church in

---

[4] Fritze (1963), 316ff.; (1965), 231ff.; (1967), 358ff.; (1969), 113ff., 121ff.   [5] Löwe (1978), 193.
[6] Braune (1918), 381; Haubrichs (1987), 412.
[7] Levison (1946), 53ff., 70ff.; Richter (1982), 123ff.; Haubrichs (1987), 405.

Germany, above all in Franconia, Hessen and Thuringia, Boniface, who until 739 had been an archbishop without bishops, but afterwards disposed of eight suffragans and was accepted as leader by other bishops, created the basis on which Charles the Great was later to carry through his Saxon mission. Thanks to this, the new Saxon dioceses were incorporated into the ecclesiastical provinces of Cologne and Mainz.[8] Secondly, by acting under papal orders in Germany Boniface (he termed himself a legate of the Holy See to Germany) placed this newly organised Church expressly under the authority of Rome.[9] The Anglo-Saxons, attached to St Peter and Rome since the days of the Gregorian mission to England,[10] put these views into practice in their organisation of the German Church, in marked contrast to an earlier period when the influence of the Pope on the Church of the Merovingians had been negligible.

In our survey we exclude (with one exception) the eighth-century OHG gloss MSS which betray Anglo-Saxon influence.[11] The Anglo-Saxon character of this influence emerges from the centres largely involved (Würzburg, Fulda, Mainz, Echternach), even though some were also in Bavaria (Freising, Regensburg). These centres constitute what can be called an Anglo-Saxon cultural province without providing direct evidence of missionary activity. Of special interest are four MSS which include both OHG and OE glosses: one of these shows connections with the circle around Willibrord in Echternach between 702 and 731, and another two with Fulda, one of them with the group around Boniface himself.

The fourth MS with OHG and OE glosses is a MS written in an Anglo-Saxon hand of the second half of the eighth century, of pocket size and showing signs of wear and tear.[12] It contains a variety of texts, or fragments of them, including the so-called *Vocabularius Sancti Galli*, the earliest German glossary. References to or connections with England are unmistakable in this MS. It contains fragments of an alphabetic glossary connected with the OE Corpus glosses, as well as glosses to a poem by Aldhelm of Malmesbury. The glosses refer at times to the fact that a particular animal is not to be found in Britain and quote on one occasion a certain Adrianus who, in view of the rarity of the name and the insular context of the whole, has been equated with Hadrian, a pupil of Theodore, archbishop of Canterbury. These details by no means

---

[8] Levison (1946), 81, 95f.; Löwe (1978), 215.   [9] Levison (1946), 89.   [10] Zwölfer (1929), 20ff.
[11] Haubrichs (1987), 390f.; (1988), 229f.   [12] Haubrichs (1987), 391f.; (1988), 230f.

exhaust the Anglo-Saxon affiliations of this MS. The *Vocabularius Sancti Galli* itself, a Latin–OHG glossary of 450 words, falls into three parts which go back to insular sources. The MS also concludes with a number of OE glosses to the names of animals and birds together with German translations. Unlike Latin–OHG glosses (for school use, for the purpose of learning Latin), the presence of OE–OHG glosses served the aim of understanding German and presupposes a non-German, Anglo-Saxon user. Combined with the practical use for which the MS was meant (the words glossed in the *Vocabularius* belong to everyday speech, the wear and tear and marks of use which it shows, its pocket size), this suggests that it was meant as the vademecum of an Anglo-Saxon missionary, for practical use in the mission-field in Germany. If that is so, it constitutes the type of concrete evidence for the Anglo-Saxon mission to Germany which was so signally lacking in the case of the Irish.

Something similar is true of another MS (Cod. Vat. Pal. Iat. 577),[13] written in a German–Anglo-Saxon minuscule towards the end of the eighth century, possibly in Hersfeld, Fulda or Mainz, but in any case within the area exposed to Anglo-Saxon influence. It has been described as a collection of texts relevant to the missionary and visitational needs of a Church including pagans (or recent converts) in its territory. This is especially true of a self-contained part (*libellus*) with texts or excerpts from patristic literature, from the context of the mission to the Anglo-Saxons in England and from Boniface's reform synods of the eighth century. They deal with questions such as the position of priests, parish churches, mission practice, the combat with superstition and the doctrinal instruction of believers. From this thematic variety two major concerns stand out. One is connections with the Anglo-Saxons: the ecclesiastical reform urged by Boniface, a quotation from Pope Gregory's responsions to Augustine of Canterbury, an allusion to bishop Lull of Mainz (an Anglo-Saxon) and two sermons from the circle of Augustine of Canterbury. The other concern is a repeated preoccupation with pagan (or specifically Germanic) practices or superstitions: a rejection of marriage between close relatives (as was practised in the Germanic world), the adaptation of the *Indiculus superstitionum et paganiarum* to specifically Germanic practices (where the inclusion of occasional Saxon terms suggests that it was aimed at them) and the kinship theme of one of the Augustinian sermons (of obvious importance to a Germanic society formed around kinship groupings). The conjunction

---

[13] Haubrichs (1987), 392ff.; (1988), 285f.

of Anglo-Saxon references with allusions to Saxon paganism suggests a missionary context in northern Germany, where the texts taken from the context of the conversion of the insular Saxons by Augustine were applied to the analogous conversion of the continental Saxons.

The missionary context to which this *libellus* probably belonged is made quite explicit by two further details. One is the inclusion of Jerome's commentary on St Matthew, specifically the apostolic command to teach and baptise all peoples which underlay the conviction of a universal mission informing both the papal mission to the Anglo-Saxons and their own mission to Germany.[14] The other detail concerns a vernacular text which comes shortly after this and immediately before the *Indiculus*, the OS baptismal formula (*Altsächsisches Taufgelöbnis*).[15] Unlike other baptismal formulas from the Carolingian period, this one stands out by not simply renouncing the Devil and the anonymous pagan gods, for it names the latter specifically (*Thunaer ende Uuoden ende Saxnote*), where the third is a tribal god of the Saxons, known also in England. This suggests a close link between this formula and the conversion of the Saxons towards the end of the eighth century, whilst its unusual explicitness could well reflect the worry voiced by Boniface (understandable in view of the conversion policy of mass baptisms ordered from above) that many were baptised without fully understanding what they were renouncing. The language of this formula reveals a number of interferences between OE and OS (e.g. in the gods' names *-aer* instead of *-ar*, *-en* instead of *-an*, *-x-* instead of *-hs-*, but also OE masc. plur. *-as* instead of *-os*, the prefix *ge-* instead of *gi-*, *ā* instead of *ē*). These uncertainties suggest an Anglo-Saxon imperfectly acquainted with OS adapting a presumably OE text as best he could for OS addressees. The *libellus*, together with this baptismal formula, therefore reflects missionary opposition to the still pagan practices of Saxons in the late eighth century (or to the syncretistic beliefs of those imperfectly converted). Like the MS containing the *Vocabularius Sancti Galli* it affords a valuable glimpse into the day-to-day difficulties of an Anglo-Saxon missionary in Germany.

Not all the terms common to OE and continental WG, even when they are specifically Christian, can simply be attributed to the Anglo-Saxon mission (e.g. 'Saturday' and 'Wednesday' reached both the Anglo-Saxons and the later ecclesiastical province of Cologne in late antiquity across the lower Rhine frontier, whilst OE *cirice* is probably the result of

---

[14] Haubrichs (1987), 394; Fritze (1969), 88ff. [15] Haubrichs (1987), 396ff.; (1988), 285f.

Frankish influence on England).[16] Not even all the terms shared by OE and the OHG *Tatian* translation (at Fulda) can be ascribed to the Anglo-Saxon mission, since the vocabulary of *Tatian* is pronouncedly conservative, retaining, like OE, terms which had died out in southern Germany. For the same reason, lexical innovations of the south German ecclesiastical language were resisted by the *Tatian* translators (and are not present in OE): this negative consideration may account for terms common to OE and *Tatian*, but cannot be converted into a positive argument for the influence of OE on *Tatian*.[17] Moreover, the fact that some words common to OE and *Tatian* (especially those which cannot be regarded as missionary words) are also shared by OS and OLFr. (or their descendants) suggests that we are dealing here with a shared stock of WG vocabulary, not with loans from OE.

These restrictions reflect the difficulty for the OE vocabulary to gain more than a foothold on German soil. To take account of this we may divide the linguistic examples into three groups. First, Christian terms where OE influence was geographically very restricted and where the OE term was soon abandoned altogether. Secondly, cases where terms of OE origin (at least in their Christian use) were more widely accepted, spreading over more than one text or dialect and enjoying a longer lease of life. Thirdly, examples where an OE term carried all before it, gained acceptance even in the south and could survive, as a recognised Christian word, even down to the present. Although this third group contains some important Christian terms, it remains a very small category, easily outclassed by the others.

The first example of restricted OE influence is the term for 'gospel': OE *godspell*, OHG *gotspel*.[18] Lat. *evangelium* was translated correctly into OE as *gōdspell* 'good tidings' (not necessarily under the influence of Irish): that the meaning of the original was understood in this translation, as was the case with Isidore of Seville, is made clear when OE *gōdspell* glosses *evangelium, id est, bonum nuntium*.[19] By a regular shortening of a long vowel before two or more consonants the vernacular term became OE *godspell*, understood by popular etymology as 'God's message' instead of 'good tidings'. However, such a development cannot be native to Germany and explain OHG *gotspel*, since the German distinction between *got* and *guot* could not have occasioned the popular etymology

[16] See above, pp. 251, 252 and 300f. Cf. Haubrichs (1987), 401f.
[17] See still Gutmacher (1914), 1ff.; Braune (1918), 362ff.; Brinkmann (1965), 109ff.
[18] Braune (1918), 393; Betz (1949), 60; Ilkow (1968), 150f.   [19] Bosworth and Toller (1954), 484.

possible in England. The suspicion that the OHG term here follows the OE model is strengthened by the word's distribution, associated with a centre of Anglo-Saxon influence like Fulda, as with *Tatian* (*gotspel*, but also the verb *gotspellôn*, corresponding to OE *godspellian*) and the *Heliand* (*godspell*), as well as the *Monseer Fragmente* and the *St. Pauler Lucasglossen* (where the verb *cuatspellon* may well be a new formation from Latin).[20] How close the *Heliand* author stood to understanding this term as 'God's message', as in England, is seen in his coinage of the synonym *ârundi godes*. In other words, acceptance of this term on German soil points to Anglo-Saxon influence (*Tatian*, *Heliand*), as is also the case with ON *guðspjall*, likewise a result of Anglo-Saxon missionary activity. In addition to this geographically restricted range, however, both the noun and the verb enjoyed only a short life in Germany: Otfrid, despite his associations with Fulda, used only *evangelio*, whilst even the *Heliand* author employed *evangelium* alongside *godspell*.

A similar case can be made for deriving the term for hermit (OS *ênkora*, OHG *einchoran*) from OE *āncora*,[21] even though these vernacular forms go back to Lat. *anachoreta* and ultimately to Gr. *anachōrētēs* (meaning originally someone who withdrew from the affairs of the state or of the world). With the rise of this form of religious practice in the Church of the Near East in the third century the Greek term, like many other Christian words, was adopted by the western Church. Nor is it surprising that Irish Christianity, with its marked predisposition for the solitary religious life, should also have taken over this term. What does demand further explanation is the suggestion that the OS and OHG forms do not derive directly from Latin, but from OE (together with the further view that the OE form was not taken over from Latin, but from Irish).

The equation of MIr. *anchara* (gen. *ancharat*) with Lat. *anachoreta* shows that *-eta* was treated as a *-t* suffix, so that like dental stems it lost its *-t* in the nominative. In other words, the Lat. word produced Ir. *ancharat* in the oblique, but *anchara* in the nominative case. This assimilation of a foreign word to native dental stems was assisted by the popular etymology to which it was subjected: *an-* as a negative prefix + nominative *cara* 'friend', so that the hermit was understood as being 'friendless' in his solitary life. A comparable assimilation to the nature of the receiving language, also based on popular etymology, can be detected in OE *āncora*, where the loss of the final syllable of the Lat. form is best explained by transmission *via* Irish, understandable in view of the prevalence of the solitary

---

life in the Irish church and its missionary influence on England. The OE evidence suggests that the word was first borrowed with a short *a*-,[22] as in Irish, but that this was then lengthened on the basis of popular etymology (OE *ān* 'one, alone', cf. *ānād* 'solitude'), whilst the second element was associated with the verb *ceōsan* 'to choose' (past part. *coren*). The result of this was that OE *āncora* could be understood as 'someone who has chosen solitude'.

This OE adaptation of the word must lie behind OS *ênkora* and OHG *einchoran*. Their first element likewise meant 'one, alone', but phonologically only OE could associate the first element of this loanword with a Gmc. term suggesting solitude. As in OE, this association may have been assisted in Germany by the presence of such words as *ênôdi* and *einôti* 'solitude'. Again as in OE, the second element may have been connected with the verb 'to choose', but it could have called forth associations with the OHG verb *korôn* 'to test, tempt',[23] implying that the hermit, like Christ in the wilderness, was tempted in his solitude. The Anglo-Saxon origin of the two forms in Germany is also suggested by attestation only in the *Heliand* and in the *Benediktinerregel*, a work whose linguistic affiliations with OE ecclesiastical vocabulary are borne out by other examples.[24] The fact that only two works betray the influence of OE *āncora* in Germany is a clear pointer that the spread of this OE term did not reach very far.

The same is even more true of the parallel between OE *rōd* and OS *ruoda*, used as terms for 'cross'.[25] The most frequent OHG equivalent to Lat. *crux* is *krûzi*, well established in southern Germany, but also the term regularly used in *Tatian* and in the *Heliand*, where we might most readily expect OE influence. We can ignore another term used in the context of the crucifixion, OE *gealga* 'gallows', since this is an obvious transposition of the cross or the *patibulum*, the Roman method of capital punishment, to its regular counterpart in Germanic law, death by hanging. So obvious was this transposition that the same word could be used in this context in various Germanic languages (Go., OHG, OS, OE) independently, without any need to postulate a causal connection between them. The position is different, however, with OE *rōd*, since only in England was this word used regularly to mean 'pole, rod', but also 'cross' in the Christian context, in poetic and also in everyday speech (cf. 'roodloft'). In Germany the word *ruota* had only the first meaning, so that the regular

---

[22] Förster (1922), 209.   [23] Freudenthal (1959), 86ff.   [24] Betz (1949), 99ff.
[25] Schröder (1900), 231; Braune (1918), 390f.

usage was either the loanword *krûzi* or the native equivalent *galgo*. In OS, however, the *Heliand* offers one occasion where *ruoda* occurs in the context of the crucifixion, a passage where the theme demanded stylistic highlighting.[26] This the author achieved in the manner best known to Germanic alliterative poetry, by the use of variation, so that he employed here *krûci, galgo* (twice) and *ruoda* in the space of only eight lines. It is the formal requirements of alliterative verse which explain this solitary example. It shows that the Saxon author was acquainted with the Christian function of OE *rōd*, but not that the OS equivalent was regularly so employed. This OE Christian term therefore gained no more than one precarious foothold in Germany, and then only because of the formal requirements of poetry.[27]

We come now to the position where OE influence on the Christian vocabulary of Germany is rather more extensive. By this we may understand terms which occur in a number of different dialects or texts (certainly not confined to the *Heliand* or *Tatian* alone) or which are attested with noticeably more frequency or over a longer period of time.

The first example concerns the consolation provided by the Holy Ghost, expressed in OE by the noun *frōfor* and the verb *frēfran*, in OS by *frôbra* and *frôbrean*, in OHG by *fluobara* and *fluobiren*.[28] This example illustrates how a German term was baptised in imitation of an English model (the OHG examples, showing dissimilation of the first *-r-* to *-l-*, cannot be regarded as loanwords from OE, but as loan-meanings, acquiring their Christian function from this model) and initially spread over a wider extent in Germany. It was eventually driven back and defeated by an UG rival (*trôst, trôsten*).

OHG *fluobara* and *fluobiren* occur regularly in *Tatian*, but also on UG soil in the *Abrogans*. Elsewhere the regular Christian terms are *trôst* and *trôsten*, e.g. in the *Abrogans* (alongside the rival) and with Otfrid in SRhFr. Since *trôst* and *trôsten* do not occur as Christian terms in *Tatian*, the *Heliand* or OE, we have a clear division between northern Germany (with one outrider in *Abrogans*) going with England on the one hand and southern Germany on the other. This geographical distribution suggests that the Christian use of *trôst* to convey *consolatio* first arose in southern

---

[26] Vv. 5726ff.

[27] Almost as restricted to one German text alone is the agreement between *sibbisam* 'peaceful' in *Tatian* and OE *(ge)sibsum* (by contrast with *fridusam* elsewhere in OHG). The replacement of *fridu* by *sibba* 'peace' in the Fulda region accounts for the *Tatian* translators' adoption of the OE model. Cf. Braune (1918), 395; Hagenlocher (1992), 24f.   [28] Braune (1918), 383ff.

Germany, from where it spread northwards. By MLG it has ousted *frôbra*, possibly assisted by the fact that the *Heliand*, although it did not use *trôst* as a religious term, was at least acquainted with it in secular usage (*erlo gitrôst, helmgitrôsteon*).[29] Against this spread northwards even the Fulda region was unable to retain *fluobara*, which was subsequently lost for central as for northern Germany.

Whereas the etymology of *trôst* and *trôsten* (in addition to 'protection' and 'to protect') suggests 'trust, confidence' and 'to give trust, confidence', therefore 'to console', the pre-Christian meaning of *fluobara* can possibly be reconstructed as 'assistance, protection'. The UG choice of *trôst* to signify consolation by the Holy Ghost as paraclete was not available in England, however, where **trēast* had died out (modern English 'trust' is a later loanword from ON), so that recourse was had to *frōfor* instead. Understandably, Anglo-Saxon missionaries made use of a term cognate with their *frōfor* wherever they encountered it in Germany, which accounts for its use in Saxony and Fulda in the ninth century. This same term must also have spread in its Christian function to southern Germany, where it was able to offer some slight competition to the already established *trôst* (*Abrogans* uses *fluobiren* alongside *trôst*), but was eventually rejected. This rejection of *fluobara* in the south was the first step in the successful advance of *trôst* northwards.

This suggests that *fluobara* was already dying out in German and retreating slowly northwards. It was weakest in the south, but still strong enough in the north for Anglo-Saxon missionaries to use it successfully for a while. Fundamentally, therefore, *fluobara* was chosen as a Christian term in OHG and OS because it was the cognate of the regular OE term, but its career was cut short because these missionaries, in choosing a term related to their own, unwittingly chanced upon a word which was slowly dying out in Germany, even though this threat was initially more obvious in the south than elsewhere.

Another word of OE origin which extends beyond *Tatian* concerns the Christian concept humility.[30] The OE forms (adjective *ēaðmōd*, noun *ēaðmēde*, verb *geēaðmēdan*) are paralleled on the continent in OS (adjective and noun *ôdmôdi*), in *Tatian* (*ôdmuotîg, ôdmuotî, giôdmuotîgôn*), but also elsewhere. The adjective also appears in *Isidor, Abrogans* and Otfrid, thus extending over OS, the Franconian dialects and even penetrating into UG. The noun is found also in Otfrid and the *Lorscher Beichte*, thereby covering OS and Franconian, but not reaching UG. Finally, the verb also

---

[29] Green (1965), 365ff.   [30] Braune (1918), 395ff.

occurs in *Isidor* and *Abrogans*; in other words it is found in EFr. and UG, but not in OS or the remaining Franconian dialects.

By contrast, the UG equivalents for these terms are *diomuotî(g)*, *diomuotî*, *diomuoten*. These forms occur in all the UG dialects (but not in *Isidor*) and despite cases such as *Abrogans* and Otfrid (where these forms and the rival *ôdmuotîg* group are to be found) the forms belonging to *diomuotîg* are not attested in *Tatian*, OS and OE. We therefore have another distinction between northern Germany and England on the one hand (*ôdmuotî*) and southern Germany on the other (*diomuotî*), with only a few examples of the northern term found in the south. This distinction corresponds to what we saw with *fluobara* and *trôst*, even to the extent that the southern *diomuotîg* group also later penetrated northwards into Franconian, covering most of central Germany and even reaching MDu. The presence of *ôdmuotî* in Germany (possibly based originally on Fulda) is therefore best explained by the model of OE Christian vocabulary and the influence of Anglo-Saxon missionaries in those areas where the corresponding German word still persisted.

A last example in this second group is the term for 'Easter' (OE *ēaster*, OHG *ôstarun*).[31] In Germany the word occurs in *Tatian* and in the major early UG texts, including so early an example as *Abrogans*.[32] From what we have so far seen of OE influence on Germany it might seem surprising, however, that the spread of this word, although wide, should not include OS, where the word in use (in the *Heliand* and other texts, down to the modern LG dialects) was *pâscha*. This term has to be seen within a much wider context, for it obtains throughout Romania, but within Germania is also found in Go. *paska* and in ON *páskar* (probably a loan from LG). In this choice of term OS was influenced by Francia, for the form *pascha* lies behind OFr. *pasque* and corresponding forms in OFri., MDu. and MFr., thus constituting a continuous block stretching from northern France to Saxony. Placing the evidence for *ēaster/ôstarun* in this wider setting reveals that OE and OHG stand alone in their choice of a native word for this Christian festival in place of the term from ecclesiastical Latin, which has prompted the question whether there may not be a connection between England and Germany with regard to this word.

The most striking explanation of this choice of word was provided by Bede, who said that the *paschalis mensis* was called *Eosturmonath* by his

[31] *Ibid.*, pp. 409ff.; Frings and Niessen (1927), 276ff.; *GR* 1, 381f. and 2, 361ff.; Knobloch (1959), 27ff.; (1960), 433f. [32] Wesche (1937), 101.

people after a goddess *Eostrae* whose festival they celebrated at about the same time of year.[33] Whether or not we accept this as evidence for a pagan goddess, Bede's testimony can be extended to Germany on the assumption that at least a pre-Christian festival was known by this name in those parts where the OE word was adopted. Similarly, the ending of OHG *ôstarun* is less likely to be a gen. sing. ('the day of *ôstara*') than a plural suggesting a festival lasting several days (cf. *Weihnachten, saturnalia*).[34] Bede's explanation can also be supported by the etymology of the English and German words, for they derive from **austrō* and ultimately from **ausrō*, which in turn underlies Lat. *aurora* and Lith. *auszrà* 'dawn'.[35] The apparent discrepancy between different timespans (the start of a day and of summer) could be resolved by parallels in other IE cognates, e.g. Go. *dags* 'day' and OPru. *dagis* 'summer', where a similar variation in timespan is attested.[36] If there is a connection between the English and German words, however, the impetus is likely to have come from the former, not merely because of Bede's early evidence or because of other linguistic reflections of Anglo-Saxon influence on Germany, but primarily because of other evidence for the readiness of Anglo-Saxons to adapt native terms to Christian usage. The objection raised by Knobloch (OHG *ôstarun* is attested so early in south Germany that OE influence must be excluded) need not disturb us, since terms like *ôdmuotîg* and *fluobara* likewise occur as early as in *Abrogans*.[37]

A rival explanation has been made by Knobloch in more general terms.[38] He bases himself on the term *Albae paschales* (used for the Easter octave because of the white robes of baptisands) which as a result of confusion between *alba* 'white' and *alba* 'dawn' he claims was given a mistaken loan-meaning where *ôstarun* 'dawn' (as in other IE forms) acquired the meaning of white, as worn in the Easter period. It is, however, unsafe to base an explanation on what is admitted to be a misunderstanding of *alba* and it is even more unjustified to grant priority to this hypothetical explanation over against the early testimony of Bede. When Knobloch has to explain how OE and OHG came to share their term for Easter he proposes a common radiation from the Merovingian Franks.[39] In theory there would be no objection to this but for the fact that we already have such radiation from Francia for the same festival in the case of *pascha* (from northern France to Saxony). Since he nowhere

---

[33] Cf. Knobloch (1959), 36.　　[34] Wesche (1937), 101; Knobloch (1959), 37.
[35] Streitberg (1894), 306; Kluge (1902), 42; Braune (1918), 410. Against this cf. Knobloch (1959), 32ff.
[36] Feist (1923), 84; Lehmann (1986), 86.　　[37] Knobloch (1959), 45; (1960), 434.
[38] Knobloch (1959), 27ff.; (1960), 433f.　　[39] Knobloch (1959), 42ff.

accounts for what amounts to a twofold radiation for the same concept, Knobloch has simply replaced one problem (the unique position of OE and OHG) by another. Finally, his objection to the idea of a Christian festival being named after a pagan one[40] can be turned round by asking why Bede should have invented a pagan festival to account for a Christian one. His point also ignores parallel cases in the encounter between Christianity and the pagan world: the transfer of the celebration of the birth of Christ from 6 January to 25 December (in competition with the festival of the *Sol Invictus*), the use of the name of a pre-Christian midwinter festival to refer to Christmas as 'Yuletide' or the application of the name of the pagan festival *Hilaria* to Easter (falling at about the same time of year, as with Bede's explanation).[41] The parallel between OE *gēol* and ON *jól* (by contrast with *Weihnachten*) on the one hand and OE *ēaster* and OHG *ōstarun* (by contrast with *pascha*) on the other suggests a Christianisation of these festival terms in England and their transmission elsewhere by the Anglo-Saxon mission.[42]

With *ōstarun* we therefore encounter an OE word which is found in *Tatian*, but which also firmly established itself in south Germany (if not in the north). It serves as a transition to a third group of examples: words of OE origin (in their Christian function) which overcame the resistance of the UG Christian vocabulary and were accepted in the south.

Our first example (OE *hālig*, OHG *heilag*)[43] has to be seen in the wider context of two CG words for 'holy', represented by Go. *háilags* and *weihs*. The latter term belongs to Gothic influence on UG, but is absent from OE (apart from *wīg* 'idol', *fulwian* < **fulwīhjan* 'to baptise', *wēofod* < **wīhbēod* 'altar') and from OS (apart from odd traces such as *wīh* 'temple', *wīhdag* 'feastday'). The former term is absent from Christian Gothic, but is the regular word in OE. Both words are present in OHG, but with a preference for *wīh* in UG.

Under the influence of the OE Christianisation of the word priority was given to *heilag* in northern and central Germany. It enjoys a monopoly in OS and in *Tatian*, it occurs in the Franconian baptismal formula (Mainz) and in *Isidor*. Further south it occurs in the *Weißenburger*

[40] *Ibid.*, p. 38.
[41] Birth of Christ: Usener (1911), 348ff. Yuletide (Go. *jiuleis*, OE *gēol*, ON *jól*): Braune (1918), 412f.; Nilsson (1918), 137ff.; Helm (1953), 209. *Hilaria*: Bartelink (1974), 414f.
[42] Another example concerns the OE terms for 'mercy, compassion': adjective *mildheort*, noun *mildheortness*, verb *miltsian*. These agree with *Tatian* (*miltherzi*, *miltida*, *milten*) and the *Heliand* (adjective *mildi*) and contrast with UG *armherz*, *armherzida*, **bi-armen*. Cf. Braune (1918), 394; Weisweiler (1923), 352ff.   [43] Braune (1918), 398ff.; Baetke (1942), 160ff.

Katechismus and in Otfrid; other Franconian texts of the ninth century show no cases of *wîh*, whilst in UG some texts show the early arrival of *heilag* in isolated cases, completed by the second half of the ninth century. In short, the adaptation of *heilag* to Christian ends which linguistically was by no means a foregone conclusion in Germany and which it shares with England appears chronologically and geographically to have begun in Franconian (Mainz and Fulda) and have spread both to the north and to the south.

We cannot argue in this case (as with *ēaster*) that OE in particular was characterised by its readiness to baptise a pagan term, for both *heilag* and *wîh* had been pre-Christian words. Instead, we may account for the choice of OE *hālig* because of its specific pre-Christian function, not shared by *wîh*, in particular its close association with the *fortuna* or *heil* of Germanic kingship, involving especially victory in battle, a feature repeatedly illustrated in the course of the conversion of the Anglo-Saxons.[44] Why the German adjective should have proved victorious over *wîh* in the south is not at all clear. It is by no means certain, as has been suggested, that *wîh* was already moribund,[45] nor can it be claimed without qualifications that *heilag* received support from the propaganda formula *heilager geist*. It may however have profited from the religious usage of related terms like *heil* 'salvation' and *heilen*, as also from the fact that there are indications that *wîh* was semantically overloaded, so that an additional term was welcome.[46]

Closely connected with *heilag* was the term *geist* because of the recurrence of the Christian formula *spiritus sanctus*, so that conceivably the advance of one term may have assisted the other.[47] There was however no CG term for *spiritus*: Gothic used *ahma* (related to *aha* 'mind'), UG employed *âtum* as a loan-meaning from *spiritus* ('breath' > 'spirit'), whilst ON developed a comparable loan-meaning (*andi*). Over against these renderings OE *gāst* goes with OS *gêst* and OHG *geist*, so that once again we register a unique position within Germania for England and Germany (north and central). For Germany we have therefore a division between north (in the wider sense) and south, with *gêst/geist* employed exclusively in OS and all the Franconian dialects (except early SRhFr.). *Geist* spread to the south, however, earlier than *heilag* (e.g. *St. Galler Credo: wîhan keist*), reaching UG by 800 or even earlier in the case of *Abrogans*.

[44] Chaney (1970), 109ff., 156ff.   [45] Baetke (1942), 178f.

[46] *Ibid.*, p. 182. On the semantic spread of this word in the *Benediktinerregel*, involving such concepts as 'holy', 'Christ', 'blessing', 'hymn of praise' and 'relic', see Baetke (1942), 165ff. and Ibach (1956), 46f.   [47] Braune (1918), 404ff.; Betz (1957), 48ff.

It presents the same pattern of linguistic movement as in other cases where the impetus for baptising a pre-Christian term came from an OE model.

Behind the adaptation of OE *gāst* to Christian ends various earlier meanings have been suggested.[48] Some OE poetic kennings for the human body could imply a function for *gāst* close to that of ON *fylgja* 'attendant spirit', whilst the Go. cognates *usgeisnan* 'to take fright' and *usgáisiþs*, like the OE verb *gǣstan* 'to frighten', have been interpreted as pointing to an ecstatic state. Two conclusions as to the pre-Christian function of *gāst* have been drawn from these cognates, either suggesting a terrifying spectre or implying an ecstatic state, as with shamanism. In either case we are dealing with a pre-Christian usage adapted to new ends by the Anglo-Saxons, conceivably under the impression of the Whitsun descent of the Holy Ghost, terrifying in its impact and granting the apostles the ecstatic gift of tongues. The adoption and spread of this OE term in Germany may have been encouraged by the pre-Christian idea of the *fylgja* as a protective spirit (OE *frōforgāst* is thus paralleled by *fluobargeist* in *Tatian*), whilst no such positive implication was present in *ātum*, which was in any case, like *wîh*, semantically heavily overloaded.[49]

Only a handful of OE Christian terms (although central ones) were thus accepted in southern Germany, whilst the others remained further north and were ultimately ousted by southern rivals. This relative failure can be explained by a chronological consideration. As far as southern Germany is concerned the Anglo-Saxons represented the latest in a series of Christian linguistic influences, they came too late to have much effect on a Christian vocabulary already largely established. In addition, the religious position in Germany at the time was such that the Anglo-Saxons had work to do in the north (for which they needed bases in central Germany), but less in the south. Also relevant is a linguistic feature: the refashioning of continental WG vocabulary, largely completed by the time of the Anglo-Saxons' arrival, in which innovations in

[48] Braune (1918), 405f.; Betz (1957), 53ff.

[49] In addition to meaning 'breath' it had to cover (for example, in the *Benediktinerregel*) concepts like 'frame of mind', the third person of the Trinity, and 'spirit' as opposed to matter. Cf. Ibach (1956), 45, 46, 49f.

Also connected with *hālig/heilag* is the use of the originally pagan magic-religious stem in OE *hǣlend*, OS *hêliand*, OHG *heilant* for Lat. *salvator* 'saviour', by contrast with Go. *nasjands* 'rescuer' (with parallels in OS, OE). Cf. Baetke (1942), 75ff.; Eggers (1978), 498 in contrast to (1963), 167. See also Kieckhefer (1989), 33ff.; Flint (1991), 301ff.

the vocabulary of southern Germany had not penetrated northwards, meant that the Anglo-Saxons may have found German equivalents for their native terms still alive in the north, but no longer available for Christianisation in the south. What also needs to be stressed with regard to the next chapter is the fact that with the last four words (*ēaster, hālig, gāst, hǣlend*) the Anglo-Saxons, together with those who followed them in Germany, displayed a policy of accommodation in developing their Christian vocabulary, a readiness to baptise terms which had early been used in Germanic religious practice. In all these cases Gothic followed a different course.

CHAPTER 20

Contrasts in Christian vocabulary

In our survey of the four influences at work on the Christian vocabulary of German a recurrent pattern has emerged: the contrast between the north and the south. Thus, OE terms could gain acceptance in OS and Franconian, but much less easily in UG, whilst many Christian terms originally at home in the south only later spread northwards, largely defeating their northern rivals.

This contrast played out on German soil has been seen in terms of a wider, extra-German contrast between Gothic and OE.[1] Despite qualifications which had to be made UG contains a number of terms, used in a Christian context, which show connections, direct or indirect, with the Christian vocabulary of Gothic. Similarly, a connection between the Anglo-Saxon mission and the Christian vocabulary of north and central Germany is also justified. It has therefore been suggested that the contrast running through the Christian vocabulary of Germany is largely a reflection of the wider differences between Gothic and OE.

This view calls for a number of qualifications. In the first place, explanations of this contrast concern much more than just Gothic and OE, for we shall see that other considerations also play a decisive part: the date of the conversion of a Germanic tribe, the differences between the eastern and the western Church, the fact of an individual or collective conversion (of a whole tribe). Another qualification concerns several important linguistic choices made by Gothic and OE, for any contrast between them is lessened by the number of identical terms which they share in their respective Christian vocabularies, e.g. *fráuja* and *frēa* 'lord', *nasjands* and *nerigend* 'saviour'.

However, even this qualification needs to be qualified in its turn. Behind several of these lexical agreements there lurk different word-field patterns. Thus, although *fráuja* is Wulfila's only term for Gr. *kýrios*, the

---

[1] Baetke (1942), 220ff.; Kahl (1956), 93ff.

use of *frēa* as an OE counterpart of Lat. *dominus* is sporadic by comparison with the overwhelming predominance of *dryhten*. Since Wulfila
nowhere made use of Go. **draúhtins* there stands behind the obvious
agreement between *fráuja* and *frēa* the more suggestive difference
between *fráuja* and *dryhten*. Similarly, although Wulfila used only the verb
nasjan as a religious term for 'salvation' (with him *háiljan* is confined to
the context of medical healing), the Christian vocabulary of OE used
hǣlen much more frequently than *nerigen*.

The following discussion falls into two groups: first, cases where OE,
by contrast with Gothic, was prepared to make use of pagan religious
terms in a Christian context, and then cases where OE likewise differed
in applying terms from the Germanic vocabulary of warfare to
Christianity, a religion of peace.

To start with runes and the terminology of writing might seem at first
remote from pagan religious vocabulary and its possible adaptation to
Christian ends.[2] However, runic inscriptions frequently served a magico-
religious purpose, they conveyed a supernatural protective power (especially in warfare, hence their presence on helmets or swords), they
invoked the gods' wrath on enemies (ensuring their military defeat or a
disastrous harvest) and the runes themselves had been invented by
Wodan, who was also the god of magic and warfare.

The occasional readiness of Gothic and OE to revert to the odd runic
sign even in writing a Christian text[3] suggests an identical attitude, but
a contrast can still be detected in the terminology of reading and
writing.[4] The position of OE is remarkable, since it was the only
Germanic language regularly to apply three of the technical runic terms
(*stæf* 'letter', *wrītan* 'to write', *rǣdan* 'to read') to (Christian) writing in the
Latin alphabet. OHG may also use *rízan* in this technical sense, but only
extremely rarely, it did not use *stab* independently, but only in two compounds imitated from OE, whilst *râtan* was used only in the general sense,
not technically as in OE. At the opposite extreme to OE stands Gothic,
where none of the terms was used by Wulfila with regard to his Gothic
Christian script. OHG therefore stands between the two extremes of
OE and Gothic, using two of three runic terms of Christian writing as
in OE, but only very infrequently. In eventually abandoning these terms
OHG came to agree with Wulfila's practice.

---

[2] See above, p. 254.
[3] Arntz (1944), 117, 171ff.; Elliott (1959), 45f. Against this: Marchand (1959), 277ff.
[4] See above, p. 258.

Examples from the post-runic vocabulary for reading and writing show how Wulfila was able to avoid runic terms.[5] His words for writing (*mēljan* and *mēla*) were used for the new technique of writing with pen and ink, in place of carving on wood, stone or metal. Similarly, his word for reading (*gakunnan*) was coined as a loan-meaning from Greek, whilst the term for letter (*bōka*) was developed from the word used in Germanic originally to designate a (Roman) writing-tablet. Germany agreed with the spirit of Wulfila's choices by turning to classical vocabulary, thereby avoiding the pagan associations of runic terminology. For writing OHG made use of *skrîban*, an early loanword from Latin, and for reading the native term *lesan* acquired a loan-meaning on the model of Lat. *legere*. Gothic and OHG may use completely different words, but agree in using classical models, Greek or Latin, to escape the unwelcome implications of runic terminology. England remains content with baptising runic terms.

A second context in which pagan religious terminology could find its way into Christian usage concerns the names for the days of the week.[6] The WG loan of these names (in the lower Rhine area) must have taken place when the Germanic tribes concerned were still pagan: this is suggested by the technique of *interpretatio Germana*, presupposing that the Germanic recipients were not yet Christian. By contrast, the Gothic names (largely known to us through their reflection in Bavarian) were taken over from Greek in the lower Danube area at a time when the Goths may still have been largely pagan, but when the Greek terms were fully Christian (with the exception of Bavarian *ertag* < Go. **arjaus dags* < *Áreōs hēméra*).

What may have started as a secular loan-process acquired religious implications with the coming of Christianity, which wished to avoid constant reference to the pagan gods, which stressed the importance of the liturgical week and attributed a special Christian function to certain days. The new, Christian function of these names is best revealed in Greek, where in place of names referring to pagan gods we find innocuous numbering ('first day', etc.), a christianising procedure which, *via* Gothic transmission, is reflected in Bavarian *phinztag* 'fifth day'.[7]

As distinct from north-western Germany (the frontier area where the Latin names first entered WG) there is another grouping of names in southern Germany at large and Bavaria in particular. Peculiar to Bavarian are *ertag*, *phinztag* and *pherintag*; to the ecclesiastical province of

---

[5] See above, pp. 262f.   [6] See above, pp. 243ff.   [7] See above, pp. 237f.

Augsburg the form *Aftermontag*; to southern Germany at large *Mittwoch* and *Samstag*. All these six names (three of which betray the likelihood of Gothic influence) avoid any reference to pagan gods by using a specifically Christian term (*Samstag* < *sambaztag*), by employing a neutral, innocuous term (*Mittwoch*), by coining an artificial term (*Aftermontag*) and by borrowing words of Greek origin (*ertag, phinztag, pherintag*), where *ertag* could be regarded as harmless, because not understood in Germania.[8]

The names which entered Germania in the north-west present a different picture. Here we need not count OE *sæterndæg* because it is a clear counterpart to *ertag / *arjaus dags*, where the name of a classical deity could be safely retained, because not understood. For the rest, these north-western names retain, even after the conversion to Christianity, their allusions to the pagan gods of Germania, with no attempt to provide unobjectionable substitutes. This contrast suggests a greater tolerance towards using the names of pagan gods in OE and in north-western Germany, but an avoidance of any such pagan associations in Gothic, in Bavarian and in south Germany, together with a gradual acceptance of the linguistic choice of south Germany further north. This conclusion agrees largely with what was the case with the vocabulary of reading and writing.

In the context of Easter OE *ēaster* (followed by OHG *ôstarun*) betrays a readiness to employ the name of a pagan feast, whilst Gothic relied on the Christian loanword *paska*,[9] a contrast which echoes that between Bavarian *pherintag* < *Gr. paraskeuḗ* and OE *frigedæg*. Even though OE *ēaster* found no followers in northern and central Germany, the contrast between the aloofness of Gothic in falling back on a Christian loanword and the readiness of the Anglo-Saxons to baptise a pagan term is again striking.

In considering now terms where OE differs from Gothic in adapting Germanic military terminology to Christian ends we start with an example which had a religious function before Christianity, but which was also used in what early Christians could only regard as a non-religious sense, involving military victory. This word (OE *hālig*, OHG *heilag* by contrast with Go. *weihs*, UG *wîh*) may therefore serve as a bridge between our two groups.[10]

The contrast between these two choices could not be included in the first group, since both *hālig* and *weihs* had performed a religious function

---

[8] Against this Wolfram (1976), 247f., assumes that the Goths knew of a god of war whom they called with the Greek name *Ares*. [9] See above, pp. 351f. [10] See above pp. 319, fn. 33 and 353f.

before the conversion to Christianity. The problem no longer concerns why OE, as opposed to Gothic, was prepared to christianise a pagan religious term, but why each language felt that a different aspect of paganism was more easily reconcilable with its view of Christianity. To ask such a question presupposes that, if Gothic and OE made a different choice, each possessed both these words. For Gothic the answer is fortunately easy because, although Wulfila used only *weihs* in his bible translation, *háilags* is attested in the approximately contemporary Gothic runic inscription on the ring of Pietroassa, so that Wulfila had a choice to make. Conversely, although **wīh* does not occur in OE as an adjective its presence at one stage is suggested by other forms (e.g. *fulwian*), even though we do not know how long this adjective may have survived into OE.

This contrast between Gothic and OE (the one selects for the Christian concept precisely the term which the other avoids) suggests that different aspects of Germanic religion were adapted to the Christian concept 'holy'. PG **hailigaz* had denoted a gift of the gods conferred on their tribal worshippers and embodied in certain physical objects (e.g. helmets, amulets), but especially in persons acting as intermediaries between tribe and gods (e.g. priests, kings).[11] The most common application of the adjective was to divine protection against tribal foes, victory in battle, but also prosperity in crops and cattle. The function of the adjective was therefore twofold, both metaphysical (a gift of the gods, obtained by worship and sacrifice) and physical (concrete advantages in the here and now). A different aspect of the pagan gods was covered by PG **wîhaz*: their remoteness, power and numinous quality, arousing awe and fear.[12] This adjective was therefore commonly applied to objects or places regarded as sacrosanct or taboo. Wulfila may therefore have shunned **hailigaz* because of its combination of the metaphysical with the physical, with what he could only regard as the secular implications of the word. He may also have taken offence at a particular type of secular function commonly performed by **hailigaz* (concerning assistance in battle, victory),[13] refusing to suggest that Christ's blessings included the gift of victory and that, like the pagan gods, He presided over warfare.

Whereas WG used *frēa, frô* 'lord' occasionally as a Christian term, but much less frequently than OE *dryhten*, OS *drohtin*, OHG *truhtin* as a standing equivalent for *dominus*, Wulfila made exclusive use of one term, *fráuja*.

---

[11] See above, pp. 19f. and Baetke (1942), 207ff.   [12] Baetke (1942), 196ff.   [13] *Ibid.*, p. 208.

Yet Wulfila's choice of *fráuja* is only significant if we can be sure that he had a choice, that the word **draúhtins* existed in the Gothic of his day.[14] This is made probable by Wulfila's use of related terms like *draúhtinassus* and *draúhtinōn*. If **draúhtins* therefore existed in Gothic and Wulfila avoided it (so that Gothic here differs from the Christian vocabulary of the rest of Germania), it is conceivable that, as with *háilags*, this was because of some offence taken. What the nature of this offence may have been is suggested by the military sense of the word ('warrior lord', 'leader of a war-band').[15] This etymological suggestion is borne out by the evidence of OE heroic literature, where *dryhten* was used predominantly of the lord in his military function, whilst *frēa* denoted him more in the peaceful context of the household.[16] What Wulfila objected to was not the secular nature of **draúhtins* as such (*fráuja* also had a secular function), but rather its military function and the suggestion, if he had used it, that Christ could be regarded as a military leader. By contrast, *fráuja* had no such unwelcome overtones and even positive advantages.[17]

Behind the linguistic contrast between Go. *fráuja* and the WG terms cognate with OE *dryhten* we may therefore detect a pacific conception of Christianity with Wulfila, leading him to reject a military title for Christ, by contrast with a readiness in WG to make use of such a title. That the chronological priority within WG lay with OE is clear from the occurrence of *dryhten* as early as in *Caedmon's Hymn*, but the Christianisation of OHG *truhtin* need not therefore be due to OE influence. For that the word is too widespread in OHG, too much the standing term in all the German dialects.[18] This suggests a Christian adaptation of the word before the Anglo-Saxon mission, possibly by the Franks, who could have spread the word throughout Germany. This implies an independent choice by the Anglo-Saxons and by the Franks of the title for Christ which Wulfila had earlier rejected. In other words, we are dealing here with a contrast between Wulfila's Christianity and the attitude to the new religion not merely of the Anglo-Saxons, but of WG at large. Wulfila's rejection of the military term **draúhtins* suggests finally that he may also have avoided *háilags* because of its pre-Christian implication that the Germanic gods conferred victory on their worshippers.

Although Wulfila avoided **draúhtins* it was possible to establish the existence of this word in the Gothic of his day by reference to his use of

---

[14] Green (1965), 265f.   [15] See above, pp. 110ff.   [16] Green (1965), 276f.   [17] *Ibid.*, pp. 33ff.
[18] Schmidt-Wiegand (1974), 524ff.

related terms (*draúhtinassus, draúhtinōn, gadraúhts*). It could be objected that, although Wulfila avoided the military overtones of **draúhtins* by rejecting the word altogether, these unwelcome implications could still have crept into his translation *via* these other terms. However, Wulfila's employment of these terms was more careful than this objection suggests.[19] The noun *draúhtinassus* may be used in a Christian context, but in contrast with its secular counterpart (the Christian fights a spiritual battle for God, not with material weapons), so that it is the contrast with secular service which justifies the translator in using the secular term. The verb is used in a similar contrast between religious and secular service, but elsewhere, where no contrast is involved, *draúhtinōn* is used only of secular military service. Finally, *gadraúhts* occurs only in a secular, not in a religious context. In other words, when Wulfila did employ terms from the vocabulary of the Germanic war-band he restricted their function: by applying them to a secular military context or to cases where Christian duties are set apart from such a context. His reluctance to use these words as positive terms is as marked as his rejection of **draúhtins* in favour of *fráuja*.

A double contrast should now be clear. First: Gothic avoided using pagan religious terms in application to Christianity, whilst OE (together with OS and OHG to a greater or lesser extent) showed no such compunction. Secondly: Gothic refrained from adapting military terminology to Christian ends, whilst WG was prepared to baptise terms from the war-band. Is there any historical evidence to support this contrast?

An obvious chronological distinction presents itself. The main body of the Goths may have been converted from 382 on, but a Christian vocabulary had earlier been established in Gothic. Wulfila's translation of the bible must have been taken in hand long before this (no matter whether we place it before or after his expulsion from Gothia in 347/8), but his Christian vocabulary shows that there existed before him an established Christian terminology on which he could draw.[20] We also know of Christians amongst the Goths already in the third century, for whom a range of Christian terms must have been indispensable.[21] This means that the creation of a Christian vocabulary in Gothic was largely completed by about the middle of the fourth century. The position was quite different in western Germania, where the conversion of

---

[19] Green (1965), 282ff.
[20] Gaebeler (1911), 1ff. (especially pp. 88f.); Jellinek (1923), 434ff.; (1926), 188ff.
[21] Schäferdiek (1978a), 497ff.

the Anglo-Saxons was systematically begun by Gregory the Great only
at the beginning of the seventh century and that of the continental
Germanic tribes was seriously taken in hand at about the same time,
with a considerable time-lag after the adherence of Chlodwig to the new
religion.[22] The time-lag which concerns us now, however, is that between
the conversion of the Goths (and the establishment of a Christian vocabulary in their language) in the fourth century and that of the WG tribes
in the seventh. How far might this chronology imply historical reasons
for the linguistic contrast between Gothic and WG?

We may best start with a historical divide (before and after the conversion of Constantine and the proclamation of Christianity as the state
religion) which can be differentiated more precisely later. A number of
significant features distinguish the religious attitude of the early Church
from what obtained after Christianity became the state religion, in the
period from Constantine to Gregory the Great. In oversimplified terms
we may equate the period before Constantine with the Goths (more precisely: with the earliest creation of their Christian terminology) and
regard the period after Constantine as relevant to the subsequent
establishment of a Christian vocabulary in the WG languages.

Many features which characterised early Christianity also recur in the
initial acceptance of the new religion by the Goths. Individual persuasion, as opposed to mass conversion, was true of them from the beginning when captives made by the Goths on a raid on Cappadocia
(including some Christians) began to convert their captors by word and
example.[23] This first acceptance of Christianity was brought about by
individual persuasion amongst the lowest ranks of society, by captives
and victims of warfare appealing to the humblest in Gothia, without any
penetration among those who held power.[24] How despised by their
society and yet how personally persuaded of the truth of their new religion these earliest Gothic Christians must have been is illustrated by the
persecutions to which they were exposed.[25] Although the Gothic rulers
may have ordered the persecutions for political reasons (as an anti-
Roman measure and as a defence of the tribal religion) there is no reason
to doubt the personal conviction of those who suffered martyrdom or
sought to spread their new religion. Whether as prisoners of war or as

---

[22] Hillgarth (1987), 311.   [23] Baetke (1942), 225 ('Einzelmission'); (1944a), 84.
[24] Thompson (1966), 81, 96, 102; Gschwantler (1976), 175, 178; Kuhn (1978), 202, 206, 208;
Schäferdiek (1978a), 502.
[25] Thompson (1966), 96f., 100f.; Gschwantler (1976), 176; Schäferdiek (1978a), 501, 502.

victims of persecutions these earliest Christians in the Gothic world could only be regarded as outcasts to whom *heil* in the traditional sense of divine rewards bestowed in this life had no possible application.[26] (Nor is there any evidence that, as later with the WG tribes, attempts were made to convert Gothic society at large by first converting the rulers.)[27] From the pagan point of view these Christians were impoverished and unprotected, their God had conferred no gift of *heil* upon them, so that it is comprehensible that the Gothic Christians should stress the difference of their position by rejecting *háilags* as a secular, pagan concern. Because they stood for no tribal religion, but were persecuted by the upholders of a tribal religion, they could reject *háilags*. Because their Christianity rested on individual conversion, it was less concerned with opposing the communal aspects of pagan worship and could make use of *weihs*.[28] In all this, Christianity amongst the Goths, as with other centres of the new religion beyond the frontiers of the Empire, remained initially unaffected by the revolutionary changes instituted by Constantine.[29]

The Church which the Franks and Anglo-Saxons later joined occupied a different social position from that to which the earliest Gothic Christians had belonged. Bede's account of the conversion of Kent illustrates a normative pattern for northern Europe from the beginning of the seventh century: a ruler (in this case Æthelberht) was first won over, who then allowed missionaries to preach to his people and set up churches.[30] However different this pattern may be from the earliest position with the Goths ('from the top down' instead of 'from the bottom up'), there were precedents for it. In Roman tradition the ruler's responsibilities also included religion, and in Germanic practice the king acted as mediator between the tribe and their gods, he was the essential channel through which *heil* reached the tribe.[31] For the Germanic ruler this pattern held out certain advantages, for Christianity strengthened his position, endowing him with a God-given authority which set him above his subjects.[32] For the Church the gain was equally clear, since it could only make headway with the support of

---

[26] Cf. the attitude of a Gothic chieftain towards the Gothic martyr Saba: Thompson (1966), 53; Wolfram (1975), 309, fn. 92.   [27] Kuhn (1978), 220.   [28] Baetke (1942), 221, 225.

[29] Kuhn (1978), 205. Although a different picture emerges later when political considerations play a part in the Goths' conversion (Baetke (1944a), 84; Schäferdiek (1978b), 85; Heather (1986), 289ff.; (1991), 105, 127f.; cf. also Gschwantler (1976), 179), this came after the creation of a Christian vocabulary in Gothic by Wulfila and his predecessors.   [30] Stancliffe (1980), 59.

[31] *Ibid.*, pp. 6of., 65, 74.

[32] Ullmann (1961), 117ff.; Stancliffe (1980), 90; Wood (1987), 352; Hillgarth (1986), 89ff.

a local ruler or nobleman. (Boniface admitted that his missionary endeavours would have led nowhere without the protection of the Frankish rulers and he lost his life when he went beyond their effective scope.)[33] There were also dangers in relying too openly on the political support of a ruler. If his conversion brought with it that of his tribe, so could his apostasy mean their abandonment of the new religion, thus demonstrating just how skin-deep the first move had been, whilst a missionary's dependence on a ruler would not always assist him with other tribes in conflict with that ruler.[34] Whether positive or negative in its results, however, the policy in conversion (from Chlodwig or Æthelberht on, or earlier still from Constantine on) was now to work from the top down, in striking contrast to the position in early Christianity or with the first Gothic converts.

The politicisation of Christianity which this method involved brought with it an expectation of divine rewards in this life which had much in common with what Germanic worshippers had assumed from their gods. Coifi's argument for accepting the new religion in Northumbria is characteristic of this attitude (he hoped merely to replace the ineffectiveness of the old gods in rewarding him by the greater power of the Christians' God),[35] but his argument was not just that of a pagan judging from a traditional point of view. Avitus reassured Chlodwig that, after baptism, his heathen good fortune (*felicitas*) in battle would be surpassed by a Christian charism, effective in the same sphere.[36] The Anglo-Saxon Lebwin stressed to the Saxons that the Christian God would protect them and allow them to flourish in this world, and Daniel of Winchester advised Boniface to use a similar argument with the Saxons.[37] To stress the common factor of good fortune in this way (success, fertility, victory in battle), but to maintain that the Christian God was more effective in this than the tribal ones, granted an important Christian role to *heil/heilag*, so that the Anglo-Saxons and other WG tribes were able to accept terms in a Christian sense which Wulfila had rejected.[38]

In expanding within the pagan world of northern Europe and in having to make a number of adjustments Christianity now accepted certain features foreign to early Christianity. The Church was now prepared to point to common ground between pagan practice and

---

[33] Baker (1970), 99; Löwe (1978), 217, 219; Hillgarth (1987), 314; Russell (1994), 196.
[34] Löwe (1978), 218; Schäferdiek (1978c), 162; Stancliffe (1980), 73.   [35] Stancliffe (1980), 71.
[36] Wallace-Hadrill (1962), 171; Russell (1994), 152.   [37] Löwe (1978), 220; Russell (1994), 193f.
[38] Baetke (1942), 223f.

Christian belief in the hope of easing the passage from one to the other as an effective way of gaining converts. This policy of accommodation underlies a number of aspects of the Christian vocabulary of WG.

A first aspect concerns the readiness to adapt pagan terms to Christian ends, above all in OE. The policy behind this linguistic procedure is best illustrated in Bede's account of the letter sent by Gregory the Great to Mellitus, laying down the policy which Augustine was to follow in converting the Anglo-Saxons.[39] The Pope stressed that it was unrealistic to think that their beliefs could be eradicated at a stroke, rather than step by step, that the pagan temples in England were not to be pulled down, whereas the idols inside were to be destroyed and altars set up instead, so that the people would come to these places as before and gradually acknowledge the Christian God. The novelty of this policy of eirenic accommodation is clear not merely from the course of Gregory's own thoughts on the mission to England (he had previously urged Æthelberht of Kent to tear down pagan temples, yet now went back on this in his letter to Mellitus), but also from the fact that before Gregory Christians had generally been reluctant to transform a pagan temple into a Christian church.[40] The earliest date for transforming a temple into a church was about the middle of the fifth century and where in Gaul, for example, temples were consecrated for Christian purposes this has been expressly compared with the spirit animating Gregory in his instructions for Augustine.[41]

This can be compared with a wider range of parallels. The suggestion that a pagan temple could house a Christian altar can be compared with the employment of a classical pagan sarcophagus to contain the remains of a saint even though the external decoration was by no means Christian.[42] The revaluation of Greek words for Christian ends by changing their meaning, even by filling them with Hebrew content, has been described as Greek ships sailing with a strange cargo.[43] This description could also be applied to words which had a pagan function in the Germanic past undergoing a semantic Christianisation. In each case the outer shell (a building, a sarcophagus, the form of a word) was given a new content, so that Gregory's policy with a pagan building in England can be equated with the linguistic policy adopted in OE religious vocabulary. This equation is the more acceptable in view of Gregory's views on biblical language at large, which he regards as

[39] Kahl (1956), 190ff.; Markus (1970), 29ff.; Russell (1994), 185ff.
[40] Mâle (1950), 31ff.; Hanson (1985), 347ff. [41] Mâle (1950), 32. [42] *Ibid.*, p. 65.
[43] See above, p. 284.

expressing sacred themes by worldly or carnal means, condescending to its recipients so that, in the same image as in his letter to Mellitus, they may ascend 'step by step' to understanding.[44] In both respects Gregory represents a turning-point in the missionary strategy of the Church: the Pope who urged this policy of accommodation was also responsible for initiating a universal mission which ultimately reached beyond the frontiers of the former Empire into Germania.

The use of names of pagan gods for days of the week is another example of linguistic accommodation. The contrast between Gothic and WG terminology must be seen in terms of the difference between the eastern and western Churches.[45] Greek took over from Hebrew the practice of naming days of the week by simply numbering them, but added some of Hebrew or Greek origin.[46] By one means or other the result was a nomenclature which caused no offence to Christian scruples. The position was different in the west, where the planetary week, based on the astrological belief in the power of the gods equated with particular planets, was introduced by the first century BC and came to be accepted throughout the western Empire.[47] Inscriptions and monuments dedicated to planetary gods testify that this practice reached parts of Germany occupied by the Romans, especially the Rhineland (together with eastern Gaul), i.e. that area where these names are thought to have crossed the linguistic frontier by a process of *interpretatio Germana*. This distinction between eastern and western Europe, between names deriving from Hebrew practice and names based on the planetary deities, was reinforced by the fact that the planetary week made relatively little headway in the eastern half of the Empire.[48]

For the Church the position was clear: any reference to the pagan gods and any astrological belief in their power were to be avoided, so that in the earliest centuries recourse was had to following the Greek model. There may have been special reasons why the Church was prepared to tolerate *Solis dies*, but for the rest it vigorously attacked the planetary names as fit for use only by *pagani, ethnici, gentiles* and *barbari*, preferring the innocuous method of numbering the days.[49] In his rejection of the planetary names Augustine admitted, however, that they were used by many Christians and they continued to be employed outside official Church Latin, as the vernacular evidence of western Romance (apart from Portuguese), Celtic and Germanic attests. This problem did not

---

[44] Kahl (1956), 195.   [45] Schürer (1905), 1ff.   [46] See above, pp. 237f.
[47] Schürer (1905), 18f., 25ff.   [48] *Ibid.*, pp. 20ff.   [49] *Ibid.*, pp. 51ff.

exist for the eastern Church: just as the planetary week had gained little acceptance there, so was its use by Greek-speaking Christians fairly restricted.[50] It occurs in Egypt and in Greek communities in the west (Sicily, Italy), but rarely in Greece itself, which would account for its absence amongst the Goths and Slavs. In its combat with this particular survival of paganism the Church was therefore successful in the east, but not in the west. It is this difference within Christendom which explains the difference between Gothic and WG.

Another sphere in which linguistic accommodation with pre-Christian practice contrasts OE (together with some traces in Germany) with Gothic concerns the vocabulary of writing: acceptance of some runic terms even in Christian writing as opposed to their replacement by post-runic terms of Mediterranean origin. Beneath this contrast there lay the clash between the belief in the religious origin of the runes and their employment in pagan magic on the one hand and the importance of the book and the scriptures to Christianity on the other.

The adaptation of runic terms to the vocabulary of writing Christian texts, vernacular or Latin, is paralleled by the employment of the runes themselves in a Christian monument or manuscript, especially in England. A grave marker from Lindisfarne has incised on it a cross, but also the name *Osgyð*, in runes and in Anglo-Saxon capitals of the Latin alphabet, whilst a bilateral stone fragment from Falstone likewise contains a cross with two inscriptions, one in Latin and the other in runic characters, concluding with a request to pray for the dead man's soul.[51] To regard examples like these in syncretistic terms as taking out a double insurance policy (as may well be true of the York helmet) is much less convincing than to see them in the light of Gregory's advice to Augustine to mingle the old and the new.[52] By contrast, German examples of runic inscriptions in a Christian setting may be fewer and less varied but, as with the occasional German examples of runic terminology in Christian texts, they do exist.[53]

The contrast in Gothic is clear. Not merely was runic terminology replaced by innocuous post-runic innovations, we also know of no Christian runic inscriptions in Gothic. This may not count for much in view of the small number of Gothic runic inscriptions at large, but the

---

[50] *Ibid.*, pp. 36ff., 54; Avedisian (1963), 236.
[51] Webster and Backhouse (1991), 103f.; Elliott (1959), 71. Discussed in a wider context by Page (1995b), 315ff. Other examples include the OE *Solomon and Saturn* (Elliott (1959), 69), Cynewulf's *Juliana* (*ibid.*, p. 74) and the Ruthwell Cross (Dickins and Ross (1945), 1ff.; Swanton (1970), 9ff.).
[52] Elliott (1959), 41, 71.
[53] Klingenberg (1976), 185, fn. 32 (examples and bibliography); Düwel (1982), 78ff.

absence of Christian examples does suggest a possible parallel with the
terminology for writing and reading. What was possible in England and
to some extent in Germany is not attested at all with the Goths.

Our last example of linguistic accommodation has to do with military
terminology: how far may Wulfila's rejection of a word like *draúhtins* be
explained by the views of the Church of his day and how far may the
employment of the corresponding term in WG Christian texts reflect a
later change of attitude by the Church?

The Church of the earliest centuries remained true to the spirit of the
New Testament in opposing the use of military violence.[54] In this it followed the Sermon on the Mount, but was also guided by the consideration that, before Constantine, war was waged by a pagan and
persecuting state for which no religious justification was conceivable.
Hence the rejection of warfare in general by the early Church and its
use of the term *militia Christi* to denote spiritual warfare against evil as
opposed to secular military service, precisely the contrast for which
Wulfila had to find adequate expression in Gothic.[55] To this pacific view
of the early Christians the Old Testament with its wars of the chosen
people of God presented a considerable problem, which was dealt with
in several ways.[56] One drastic solution was to repudiate the Old
Testament, a path taken for example by the early heretic Marcion largely
because of its justification of such warfare. In this Marcion was not
speaking specifically as a heretic, but rather in conformity with ethical
principles also acknowledged by the orthodox.[57]

Another early heretic held similar views, for Philostorgius reported of
Wulfila that, in translating the bible, he left out the Books of the Kings
on the grounds that their warlike episodes would further inflame the
warlike spirit of the Goths, whereas it was rather necessary to quieten it.
The Romans could also hope that the spread of Christianity might
pacify these dangerous barbarians.[58] The biographical statement by
Philostorgius agrees with the linguistic evidence that Wulfila excluded
draúhtins from his Christian vocabulary and with the much later description of his followers, the *Gothi minores*, as an unwarlike people (*inbellis*).[59]
Wulfila's linguistic decision was no isolated act, but reflects the
characteristic attitude of early Christianity. It is true that a different position could later be adopted by Goths or other EG tribes converted by

---

[54] Erdmann (1935), 1ff.; Russell (1975), 8ff.   [55] Harnack (1905).   [56] Bainton (1946), 212.
[57] *Ibid.*, p. 210.
[58] Haendler (1961), 21ff.; Green (1965), 279f.; Wallace-Hadrill (1975), 22; Heather (1986), 316f.
[59] Jordanes, *Getica* 267; Haendler (1961), 22; Green (1965), 281.

them (the joint victory of Fritigern and Valens persuaded many Goths to turn to the Christian God who had granted this success, the Vandals quoted the bible as a form of battle-cry),[60] but these are later examples, coming after the creation of a Christian vocabulary in a very different spirit by Wulfila and even earlier Gothic Christians.

After Constantine the Church began to adopt a different attitude towards warfare, initiated by the fact that his adoption of Christianity rested on the conviction that the Christian God had granted him victory over Maxentius. Not merely did Christianity, as the new state religion, accept military service as unobjectionable, it also developed liturgical prayers for the military undertakings of the now Christian Empire and could even produce spokesmen for exterminating paganism by fire and sword.[61]

Already with Ambrose the Roman just war could be defended by an appeal to Old Testament warfare: he was prepared, in other words, to turn round the argument used by Marcion and (implicitly) by Wulfila.[62] Augustine provided a justification of war (*bellum iustum*) and upheld the use of force as a punishment for heretics and schismatics.[63] With the conversion of Chlodwig the Constantinian pattern recurs (whether in historical fact or in legendary interpretation): he faced defeat in the battle against the Alemanni and, convinced that his gods had deserted him, prayed to his wife's God for victory and was granted it.[64] The king's move was made feasible by the belief that the Christian God, like his pagan gods, bestowed victory on His followers, but was more willing or more capable than they to do this. The letter of bishop Avitus to Chlodwig argued on similar lines: he assured the Frankish king that he might now, as a Christian, expect more fortune or success than in the past and explicitly included warfare in this (*rigor armorum*).[65] A war waged by Chlodwig as a Catholic king (against the Arian Alaric) was also put forward as a model by Gregory of Tours: whereas the nominally Christian Merovingians of Gregory's day engaged in internecine strife Chlodwig's campaign met with his approval because his extension of Frankish power was reconcilable with a missionary goal.[66] Finally, Gregory the Great recommends warfare as an indirect missionary policy against pagans, involving military subjection as a first step towards

---

[60] Green (1965), 280; Baetke (1944a), 84; Schäferdiek (1978a), 507.
[61] Baetke (1944a), 112; Erdmann (1935), 3f. [62] Russell (1975), 14f.
[63] Erdmann (1935), 6f.; Russell (1975), 16ff.; Kahl (1978), 53f.; Markus (1983), 1ff.
[64] Wallace-Hadrill (1962), 169f.; Schäferdiek (1978c), 121; Hillgarth (1986), 72ff.
[65] See above, fn. 36. [66] Wallace-Hadrill (1975), 25.

evangelisation under state protection.[67] This policy, which on a higher ecclesiastical level resembles the praise of Chlodwig's warfare by Gregory of Tours, has been seen as harnessing, rather than rejecting, the Germanic war-ethos to the Church's own ends. What counts with regard to Gregory the Great's role in initiating a universal mission (starting with the Anglo-Saxons) is not that he reckoned with missionary wars of conquest in northern Europe (as with Charles the Great against the Saxons), but that his conditional approval of military means for the expansion of Christianity came halfway towards a readiness of the Germanic tribes to associate the outcome of battle with religious practice.[68]

Whereas the early Church had stressed the gulf between Christianity and warfare, even in the Old Testament (Marcion, Wulfila), the later Church set greater store by accommodation, seeking out common ground between what it now held to be a divine approval of warfare under certain conditions and the Germanic war-ethos (Avitus, Gregory of Tours, Gregory the Great). Under these changed historical conditions words like OE *dryhten* and OHG *truhtin* were now fit to be adopted into Christian vocabulary, whereas for Wulfila only *frauja* had come into question. Rather than explain such differences in vocabulary between Gothic and WG in terms of a dubious ethnopsychology we should recognise instead that it is the views of the Church itself which had changed since the earliest apostolic age.[69]

It is now possible to qualify the chronological divide (before and after Constantine) with which we began. Even if Wulfila worked after Constantine, a Christian vocabulary had been evolved in Gothic before to whose spirit he remained true and in any case we should take into account the slowness with which the effects of the emperor's revolution reached the Goths, settled at first outside and then only in the frontier districts of the Empire. Secondly, although others may have prepared the way for a qualified Christian approval of warfare, only with Gregory the Great was this view taken further by someone heavily engaged in organising missionary activity. He occupies a crucial position as regards our problem in several respects: he organised a universal mission to the Anglo-Saxons, the first official one to any Germanic barbarians; he adopted a policy of conversion from the top downwards, starting with the ruler (Æthelberht); he advocated a mission policy of accommodation; as part of this policy he was prepared to grant a positive role to

---

[67] Erdmann (1935), 8; Wallace-Hadrill (1975), 30; Kahl (1978), 55; Schäferdiek (1981), 509.
[68] Cf. Baetke (1944a), 112, 114 with Wallace-Hadrill (1975), 30.   [69] Wallace-Hadrill (1975), 30.

Christian warfare. He may have had forerunners in some of these features, but only with him did they all come together. The change in historical conditions which may account for the differences in Christian vocabulary throughout Germania should not be seen as a turning-point (Constantine or even Gregory the Great), but as a transitional period running from one to the other.

CHAPTER 21

The vocabulary of ethics and fate

The pagan religion of Germania was essentially a religion of the tribal cult, focused on the worship of the gods and the sacrifices due to them. It cannot be said that this religion imposed what we should recognise as ethical demands on Germanic worshippers.[1] Although the Germani acknowledged of course a code of moral behaviour it was not dictated to them by their gods. These gods (to judge them by mythological evidence which comes to us mainly from Scandinavia) were no moral exemplars, for they had the same deficiencies as humans and were capable of deeds which even their worshippers regarded as evil. Correspondingly, the deeds of men could expect no divine reward or punishment, whether in this life or the next. Even the mythological struggle between the Germanic gods and the giants or demons, in which men had most to hope for from the gods' victory, could not be seen in ethical terms, for here, too, the gods fought for themselves, not because they stood for what was right or upheld any moral order. The most that could be said for them was that their victory would also be advantageous to men.

In all this Christianity was essentially different. It, too, may have demanded ritual worship of the new God in the form of the liturgy, but it also insisted on moral precepts which this God imposed, and maintained that at the end of time He would judge men's deeds and motives, rewarding or punishing accordingly. For this religion the cosmic struggle between God and the Devil was one between the principles of good and evil. An ethical code of behaviour was therefore an integral part of the Christian religion, unlike pagan Germania, whose ethical values were derived from secular social institutions such as the kinship or the war-band. When a Germanic tribe suffered a setback the cause was sought in a failure in sacrificing to the gods, thus blocking the channel

---

[1] Schneider (1938), 161ff.; Kuhn (1951b), 177ff.; Derolez (1959), 255ff.

through which *heil* could flow to the tribe, but when a Christian people faced a similar situation, as in the OHG *Ludwigslied*, an explanation from the Old Testament was applied: God was punishing His sinful people or testing them in readiness for higher things.[2]

This contrast means that it was a vital necessity for Christianity to show Germanic converts that the new religion included this ethical dimension, that God was served by ritual service in church, but also by the moral behaviour of worshippers. Christianity therefore faced a double linguistic task in the conversion of Germania: first, to show that its terms for moral qualities expressed obligations towards the new God, and secondly to devise vernacular equivalents for qualities often unknown to Germani as moral imperatives (e.g. humility, forgiveness).

The difficulties facing the Church can best be illustrated by examples where it had to introduce an ethical concept, and therewith a word to express it, which was novel to Germania. Our first example is Lat. *obedientia*, OHG *hôrsamî*. Just how novel this concept was in Germanic eyes can be seen in the way in which the Romans were struck by the marked absence of military discipline and obedience among their barbarian foes.[3] In place of these qualities, which were learnt from Rome (first in the military, then in the political and religious sphere), it was the bond of reciprocal loyalty, above all in the kindred and the war-band, which promised the best hope of creating unity in Germanic society. Obedience and loyalty differ from one another in that the latter is potentially stronger by requiring service according to the spirit rather than the letter of an agreement, but can prove weaker in its stress on the subordinate's responsibility to consider and even criticise what a leader may require of him.[4]

This contrast was heightened with the coming of Christianity, which preached unilateral obedience as a virtue, as different from *triuwa* as had been the military discipline of the Roman army. The mission policy of concentrating first on the conversion of a Germanic ruler, from whom support could then be had in preaching to his tribe, may have been a practical necessity for the Church, but it held out to the ruler the advantage of buttressing his authority by divine sanctions which by their origin overrode any claims which his people might have on him.[5] The Frankish king could now claim obedience (no longer merely loyalty) from his

---

[2] Yeandle (1989), 70ff.   [3] See above, pp. 68f. Cf. Picard (1991), 98f.
[4] Herwegen (1912), 27f.; Mitteis (1933), 531ff.   [5] Ullmann (1961), 121ff.; Ewig (1963), 41ff.

subjects because he was the *vicarius Dei*, so that a rebellion against him amounted to a rebellion against God. Such an argument was put forward by Jonas of Orléans, who argued with biblical support that the subject owed obedience to royal power because it was divinely ordained and that resistance to its orders was tantamount to resisting God's commands.[6]

Obedience as a specifically Christian virtue can be illustrated from two ecclesiastical contexts: the obedience to his abbot which the Benedictine monk swore to observe and the similar promise of the priest to his bishop at his ordination.

The absence of anything corresponding to obedience in Germanic society meant that Christian obedience could often be misconceived initially as if it were loyalty and only later understood for what it was, as can be seen from early formulas in Francia for the vows taken by the monk.[7] Whereas Benedict had sought to remove any justification for a monk's failure to obey his abbot, some of these formulas were instead assimilated to the concept of loyalty with the monk pledging himself to his superior just as the Germanic follower swore loyalty to his lord. The Frankish monk might therefore swear *obedientia*, but then circumscribed this with qualifications, with escape clauses in the spirit of loyalty rather than unilateral obedience ('insofar as God grants me assistance', 'as far as I am able'), reservations which parallel the legal loopholes to be found in Carolingian capitularies (*in quantum ego scio et intelligo* or *quantum sciero et potuero*). Later formulas of Benedictine vows from Francia react against such concessions and in the spirit of Benedictine views of the importance of this virtue demand now unqualified obedience, with no escape clause (*omni excusatione postposita*).

We find a parallel to this tension between loyalty and obedience in the OHG *Priestereid*, a formula used in the ordination of a cleric, summing up his obligations towards his bishop.[8] The central ecclesiastical requirement of obedience occurs here in the bishop's question (*obediens et consentiens esse*) and in the ordinand's vernacular reply (*kahorich enti kahengig*), but this oath also has resemblances to contemporary secular oaths of loyalty. The opening phrase employs an adjective characterised more by reciprocal loyalty than by unilateral obedience (*daz ih dir hold pin*),[9] which is confirmed by a qualifying clause (*so mino chrephti enti mino chunsti sint*), a hedging reservation such as was found with secular oaths

---

[6] Green (1965), 228, 378 (and fn. 4).   [7] Herwegen (1912), 23ff.; Green (1965), 386ff.
[8] Steinmeyer (1916), 64; Ehrismann (1932), 356f.; Green (1965), 389f.
[9] On the reciprocity of this adjective see Green (1965), 140ff.

and early Benedictine vows on Frankish soil. Germanic loyalty and Christian obedience are still in uneasy juxtaposition here: only the unilateralisation of an originally reciprocal term like *hold* could allow full scope to the new concept of Christian obedience.[10]

The difficulty of introducing a new concept to Germania is therefore reflected in the linguistic problem this created: the imposition of a loan-meaning on *hold* by using it in the context of *obedientia* resulted at the best in an approximation, so that it is not surprising that other attempts were made, this time involving OS and OHG loan-translations of the Latin term. The Latin verb *ob(o)edire* (derived from *ob* + *audire* 'to hear, listen, pay attention') could therefore be rendered in OS and OHG by *(gi)hôrien*, which suffered the disadvantage that, unlike the Latin distinction between *audire* and *oboedire*, the same vernacular verb was used to mean both 'to hear' and 'to obey'.[11]

Another attempt, OHG *hôrsam*, was much more successful.[12] This adjective, a rendering in the *Benediktinerregel* of *obediens* as a monastic virtue, cannot be a native formation and presumably follows a foreign model. The suffix *-sam* was used in OHG to form adjectives denoting character, ability or inclination and was added to nominal stems, so that *hôrsam* is the only case where it was added to a verbal stem (because of the Latin model). Strict imitation of this model would have produced *hôrenti* or more accurately *kaganhôrenti* (the corresponding verb occurs once in the *Benediktinerregel*), but *hôrsam* is a more successful rendering, combining a feature of the Latin model (a verb of hearing) with a vernacular peculiarity (*-sam* as a suffix fit to render a virtuous disposition). Although the adjective *hôrsam* occurs elsewhere only in *Abrogans* and with Otfrid, the success of this formation is clear from its adaptability in the *Benediktinerregel*, where this adjective also produced its negative counterpart (*unhôrsam*), the positive and negative verbs *(un)hôrsamôn* as well as the corresponding abstract nouns *(un)hôrsamî*. *Hôrsam* and its derivatives could now supply terms for the adjective, the noun and the verb, whereas only the verb could be supplied by *(gi)hôrien*. In addition, the ambiguity of this verb ('to hear' or 'to obey') was resolved by the distinction between *hôrien* 'to hear' and *hôrsamôn* 'to obey', where the vernacular could now render the Latin contrast between *audire* and *obedire*.

The geographical distribution of *hôrsam* and its family points to the

---

[10] *Ibid.*, pp. 368ff.

[11] *Ibid.*, pp. 380f. Occasional attempts to distinguish these meanings (with an accusative object for 'to hear' and a dative for 'to obey') are stylistically awkward and suffer the disadvantage that they could be used of the verb, but not the adjective or noun.   [12] Betz (1949), 140ff.; (1974), 158f.

Benediktinerregel and (possibly) to Reichenau as the linguistic centre of gravity: in this text the word was used more frequently and produced more derivatives than elsewhere in OHG.[13] Although the translator of this text was not responsible for introducing this Christian term into OHG (he was preceded by the *Abrogans*), it was he who developed the word's potential. Even here, however, he did not stand alone. Apart from OHG the cognates of *hôrsam* are very restricted in the other Germanic languages and, as with OFri. *hârsum* and OS *ungihorsam*, are likely to be loans from German. An exception is made by OE, where the cognate word occurs early, but in a similarly wide range of derivatives: adjective *(un)hīersum*, verb *hīersumian* and noun *(un)hīersumness*. Since it is quite unlikely that a loan-translation of this kind (it is not a slavish rendering of the Latin model, but shows a measure of creative independence) should have been chanced upon independently in both OHG and OE, there is probably a causal connection between the two languages. Given the possibly early dating of the OE examples, this could be another case of OE linguistic influence on Reichenau although, since the context was monastic, it could not be included earlier under Anglo-Saxon missionary influence on Germany.

Another linguistic problem lay in devising a vernacular equivalent for the abstract ethical concept *virtus* 'virtue'. Although the Germanic languages possessed terms for certain individual virtues they lacked any overriding term for virtue as such. It is perhaps a sign of the difficulties facing the Church that only towards the close of the OHG period did the word *tuged* 'virtue' (modern German *Tugend*) occur as a rendering of Lat. *virtus* in the ethical sense.[14]

OHG *tuged* is derived from the verb *tugan* 'to be of use, of value' + suffix *-unþi* (with loss of *-n-*). Outside the religious or ethical context this word could be applied to objects, suggesting their particular quality or what makes them useful or valuable, but also to persons with a similar range. In this personal application the word could designate a man's strength or energy, but also a ruler's power, as in the *Ludwigslied*, where it is conferred on the ruler by God (5: *Gab her imo dugidi, fronisc githigini*). Since the ruler's power here is in apposition to the body of warriors (*githigini*) at his disposal, it is possible that this usage parallels OE *dugoð*, denoting a band of mature, experienced warriors, as opposed to *geogoð* (young warriors with less experience).[15]

The Latin word *virtus*, an abstract from *vir* 'man', denoted originally

---

[13] Betz (1949), 141.   [14] Aumann (1939), 143ff.   [15] *Ibid.*, p. 145.

the qualities that become a man, hence 'manliness, strength, bravery'.[16] Under the influence of Stoicism and Ciceronian ethics an attribute like *fortitudo* came to be regarded as moral fortitude, just as *virtus* was conceived as bravery of character. *Virtus* summed up a man's ability to be of use and service to the state in any respect, not merely on the field of battle. The Latin texts which were translated into OHG contain very few examples of *virtus* in the restricted military sense 'bravery' and where they occur they are regularly translated by *theganheit* or *knehtheit* with a corresponding military implication. Outside the religious or ethical sphere the contact between *virtus* and *tuged* was quite insignificant: what counted for the development of the German word as an ethical term was understandably its encounter with *virtus* as an ethical term, either under Stoic influence or in imitation of Grk. *areté*.

Difficulties were caused for translators in the OHG period by the Christian use of *virtus* in two senses, corresponding to two Greek terms earlier rendered into Latin. The most frequent use of *virtus* in the Vulgate was to render Gr. *dýnamis* 'power', a semantic equation suggested by the meaning of the Latin word: 'manliness' or 'strength'.[17] In this sense *dýnamis* and *virtus* repeatedly conveyed such ideas as the power of God or Christ, the heavenly hosts as incorporating God's power, the miraculous or healing power of Christ, a miracle as a manifestation of His power, but also the power of an angel, the Devil or man. Vernacular equivalents for *dýnamis* and *virtus* in this sense include *tuged* (where the meaning 'strength, power' provided a semantic bridge) and *kraft* (another obvious candidate).

Greater problems were created by the use of Lat. *virtus* also to render Gr. *areté* 'virtue', even though the ethical development of the Latin word assisted its equation with the Greek term.[18] Otfrid and the *Benediktinerregel* employed *kraft* as a translation of *virtus* in this ethical sense. In both cases the ethical function of the German word is quite clear: Otfrid is talking about *caritas* as the supreme Christian virtue, whilst in the *Benediktinerregel crefti* (*virtutes*) are contrasted on the ethical plane with *âchusti* (*vitia*) and *sunton* (*peccata*). Where an OHG dialect happened to lack the word *kraft* recourse was had instead to *megin*, similarly meaning 'strength, power', as a rendering of *virtus* in the ethical sense, e.g. with *Isidor*, where *via virtutis* was translated as *dhes meghines weghe*. These two vernacular terms meaning originally 'power, strength' were used in an attempt to convey the ethical concept 'virtue' because they

---

[16] *Ibid.*, pp. 146f.   [17] *Ibid.*, pp. 151ff.   [18] *Ibid.*, pp. 156f.

shared one meaning with *virtus* whose further, ethical function they took over as a loan-meaning. This attempt can have conveyed initially little of what Christianity understood by *virtus* as an ethical term, so that new converts are likely to have taken it crudely as implying little more than 'power, strength'.

The difficulty in finding an adequate vernacular term for the ethical concept 'virtue' lay in Christian Latin, in the employment of *virtus* in the Vulgate in the overwhelming sense of *dýnamis* 'power' alongside its later use in ecclesiastical Latin also as an equivalent for *areté* 'virtue'. Translators from Latin into OHG, slavishly content to follow the Latin precedent of conveying two meanings by the one word, made words like *tuged*, *kraft* and *megin*, inadequately and approximately, do duty for 'strength' and for 'virtue'. Whereas Stoicism, Ciceronian ethics and the Greek model *areté* ensured that the ethical employment of *virtus* would be distinct enough from the meaning 'power' for Latin-speakers, none of these aids to understanding was available in OHG.

The position changed only with Notker.[19] He was the first to realise, conceptually and also linguistically, that *virtus* had two distinct meanings and that two separate vernacular equivalents were desirable to capture this difference. In his works *virtus* as the counterpart to *dýnamis* was regularly translated by *kraft*: in this he followed other precedents such as the *Murbacher Hymnen*, *Heliand* and Otfrid. On the other hand, *virtus* as the equivalent of *areté* was translated regularly by him as *tuged*. The equation of *virtus* ('manliness, bravery, strength') with *tuged* ('strength', but also in its military usage close to 'bravery') need not occasion surprise, but what was not so self-evident was the perception that Christian Latin *virtus* had two meanings. By using *tuged* as a standing equivalent for *virtus* in the ethical sense of *areté* Notker now had the linguistic means to distinguish it from *kraft* as a rendering for *virtus* as the counterpart to *dýnamis*. Notker therefore employed *tuged* with a loan-meaning from *virtus* in its ethical sense and made this new function clear by the context, above all by what he contrasted it with. *Tuged* was frequently opposed to *âkust* (*vitium*) in his theological, but also in his philosophical works. It was further contrasted with *ubelî* (*improbitas*), *arg* (*nequitia*) and *unreht* (*iniquitas*): from the ethical import of these contrasting terms the new, ethical function of *tuged* was made clear, as also when the precise nature of the virtue was specified, generally in Latin (e.g. *temperantia, patientia, fides*). By such means Notker clarified the ethical function of *tuged* and established it as a moral term

---

[19] *Ibid.*, pp. 148f., 150f., 152.

of Christianity. Soon after him, with Williram, the word was firmly established as the Christian term for 'virtue'.[20]

The development of an ethical vocabulary by Christianity was over-shadowed by a much wider problem. The coming of Christianity, both in the classical world of the Mediterranean and in Germania, involved an encounter between Christ and the pagan gods, but also a clash between belief in Him and the pagan belief in fate.[21] Against the back-ground of this belief we have to understand St Paul's words (Gal. 4.3) about earlier being 'in bondage under the elements of the world', an allusion to the slavery imposed on the pagan by his blind belief in astro-logical deities (cf. also Gal. 4.10). The Church's opposition to the plane-tary names of days of the week was not merely because they preserved the names of pagan gods, but also because they perpetuated an astro-logical belief in fate which was widespread in the classical world at the birth of Christianity. When a day was named *Martis dies*, for example, this was objectionable to the new religion because it commemorated a pagan god, but also because of the belief that a particular day was under the control of a particular planet so that, as Origen complained in the case of many Christians, it was felt to be impossible for anything to happen other than as the planets laid down.[22]

The opposition of the Church to the pagan belief in fate, whether astrological or in connection with the *parcae* or the more abstract *fatum*, was based on two arguments. To believe in the power of the planetary divinities was demeaning to the omnipotence of the Christian God and it was a sacrilege to worship what He had created rather than the Creator himself. The astrological belief in the immutability of what the planets laid down was in flat contradiction to the Christian view of God's merciful omnipotence, watching over every aspect of human life. For Tatian the demons incorporated in the planets were real enough, but powerless by comparison with God, while Clemens of Alexandria held it madness to worship God's work of art in place of the deity Himself.[23] On the other hand, belief in the control of events on earth by the plan-etary gods was demeaning to man's freedom of action, as St Paul argued in proclaiming that Christ had freed man from bondage to the ele-ments.[24] Origen and Methodius likewise opposed fatalism out of a

[20] *Ibid.*, p. 160.
[21] Schürer (1905), 46ff.; Jente (1921), 196ff.; Kauffmann (1926), 361ff.; Philippson (1929), 228ff.; von Kienle (1933), 81ff.; Matthews (1993), 149f.   [22] Schürer (1905), 49.
[23] *Ibid.*, pp. 44f.; von Kienle (1933), 106.   [24] Schürer (1905), 45, 46, 50.

concern for man's freedom and responsibility for his own actions.
Augustine referred to a Christian (!) who maintained that he had not
committed adultery of his own free will, but under the compulsion of
Venus. At this point fatalism impinges upon ethics, for if the early
Church had been unable to overcome such belief in the overriding
power of fate there would have been no place for moral responsibility
and no point in its creation of an ethical vocabulary.

The battle waged by the Church against the belief in fate in the
Mediterranean world had to be fought out again when Christianity was
brought to Germania for, even if in different ways, these barbarians
shared similar views. A belief in fate lies behind their consultation of
oracles or casting of lots, a practice already attested by Caesar and also
much later, for the custom still attracted the censure of Christian missionaries.[25] The difficulties they faced in northern Europe can be illustrated from the *Hildebrandslied*, a heroic lay partly assimilated to
Christianity. At one point (49: *welaga nu, waltant got, wêwurt skihit*) an
address is made to the Christian God, correctly seen as governing the
world (*waltant got*) and as a personal deity who can be addressed. But
alongside this, and not reconciled with it, mention is made of the power
of fate (*wêwurt*), impersonal (cf. the verb *skihit* 'happens') and
unapproachable. The question which is the more powerful is left unan-
swered, but this example illustrates the nature of the problem for the
Church: to show that its God was more powerful than the pagans' gods,
but could also override fate, *wurt*.

The term *wurt* used in the *Hildebrandslied* is only one of many words
for fate attested in the Germanic languages.[26] Their frequency is testimony to the persistence of these beliefs, and the variety of these terms
provides us with the chance of reconstructing these beliefs and the ways
in which the Church coped with them. We can consider no more than
four examples, one from EG and three from WG.

Our EG example is Go. *stabeis*,[27] used in translating the passage where
St Paul celebrated man's liberation from bondage to the 'elements of the
world' (Gal. 4.3): where Wulfila used *stabeis*, the Vulgate had *elementa
(mundi)* and Greek used *stoicheîa (toû kósmou)*, both technical terms of
Roman and Hellenistic astrology, denoting the controlling forces of the
universe, the powers of fate that dictate man's life.

In Germanic the stem **stab-* was used not simply to denote 'staff, rod',

---

[25] Caesar, *De Bello Gallico* I 50; von Kienle (1933), 97f.; Helm (1953), 280.
[26] Discussed by von Kienle (1933), 81ff.   [27] Kauffmann (1926), 380, 386ff.

but also had the particular meaning 'stave with a rune carved on it', hence 'rune'.[28] Although Wulfila nowhere employed technical runic terms in a Christian context because of their pagan implications, there is no need to regard *stabeis* as a solitary exception. The Germanic word, originally because of the use of staves with runes carved on them for consulting the oracle, was also employed in the context of the oracle and learning what fate had to decree. There are linguistic traces of this in ON and OE, where *stafir* and *stafas* occur in compounds whose first element defines the nature of the fate decreed, e.g. OE *ārstafas* 'success, blessing', *endestafas* 'death'. Furthermore, OE doublets such as *inwitstafas* 'jealousy, anger' and *inwitrȳn* or *wyrdstafas* 'fate's decrees' and *wyrda gerȳnu* point to a connection between the ceremony of the oracle and runes. This suggests that, although runic practice might ultimately lie behind it, Wulfila used *stabeis* in the passage from St Paul not in any technical runic sense, but with the derivative function of denoting the powers of fate. This is confirmed by the context of this biblical passage, concerned with the pagan belief in fate and its enslaving effects on man.

If Wulfila was not prepared to employ the technical terms of runic practice with their pagan associations, why should he have been willing to use *stabeis* in the equally pagan sense of fate? Two considerations may have thrust the choice of this word upon him. The double function of Germanic **staƀ-* ('staff, pole', but also, because of the use of runes in consulting the oracle, 'workings of fate') had a parallel in the Greek word used by St Paul, for the plural *stoicheîa* meant 'controlling forces of the universe' (*elementa mundi*), while the singular form meant 'pole, stick, column'. The coincidence of a double semantic correspondence between *stabeis* and *stoicheîa* must have made the choice of *stabeis* irresistible. Secondly, even though *stabeis* was a pagan Germanic term for fate, this was now an advantage in a passage attacking the pagan belief in fate. By using this vernacular term Wulfila could oppose the superstitious belief in fate of the pagan Goths. Where St Paul had attacked the fatalism of Hellenistic society, Wulfila stressed the fatalism of the Goths, thereby giving St Paul a topical relevance. In using *stabeis* Wulfila therefore employed a pagan term of fatalism as a means of defeating that fatalism.

Our three WG examples we may list briefly before considering the ways in which the Church dealt with the problems which they presented. *Metod* is absent from OHG, but occurs in OS (*metod* 'fate', *metodogiskapu*

---

[28] See above, p. 255.

'decree of fate', *metodigiskaft* 'fate') and in OE (*metod* 'fate', *metodgesceaft* 'fate, death', *metodwang* 'battlefield' = 'death-field', *metten* 'goddess of fate'). The formation of the word is clear: it is a *nomen agentis* formed from the verb *metan*, meaning 'to measure out/apportion, to estimate, to judge'.[29] Underlying this word is therefore the idea of a power that measures, apportions and judges (cf. the connection between German *erteilen* and *urteilen*). That the judgments and decrees of a power of fate which disposes of men's lives could be seen negatively in terms of death is clear from two of the OE compounds, but also from ON *mjötuðr* 'death'.

OHG *wurt* occurs in both WG and NG in the sense of fate (in ON *Urðr* was personified as the name of one of three norns, spinning out man's fate). The noun derives straightforwardly from a verbal stem as in OHG *werdan* ('to become', but also 'to happen' in the sense of 'to be destined by fate'), itself cognate with Lat. *vertere* 'to turn'.[30] Placing the Germanic word in its IE setting has proved more contentious: either the active meaning 'to turn' came to mean 'to become' or the active meaning was retained in a more specified function, suggestive of spinning (cf. OHG *wirtel* 'spindle') and of a power, as with ON *Urðr*, spinning out fate. Whether conceived more personally (as a norn) or abstractly, this word expressed the idea of fate in OHG, OS, OE and ON.

The last case to be considered includes different forms of the same stem, as represented by OHG *schephenta* and *sceffarin*, OS *giskapu*.[31] The personal conception of fate which was uncertain with *wurt* is clear with the first two of these examples, for they are feminine *nomina agentis*, used to gloss Lat. *parca*. Whether they are *ad hoc* translations with no independent life in Germania is not at all clear, but at least there is no doubt that the stem with which all three words are formed did function as a term for fate. In ON, for example, the word *skapa* is used for the idea that the norns shape the life (*skapa aldr*) of a newly born child and the plural noun *sköp* means 'fate', whilst in OE *gesceapum* is employed adverbially to express what one is destined to do.[32] The first of these examples illustrates the original force of these terms: 'shaping' or 'creating' a life and its course.

The tension between the pre-Christian function of these words and the new use to which they had to be put gave rise to different possibil-

---

[29] Kauffmann (1926), 394; von Kienle (1933), 90f.; Ilkow (1968), 292f.
[30] Kauffmann (1926), 389f.; von Kienle (1933), 81f.; Ilkow (1968), 434ff.
[31] Kauffmann (1926), 403ff.; von Kienle (1933), 88f.; Ilkow (1968), 293ff.
[32] *Skapa aldr*: von Kienle (1933), 89; *sköp*: Ilkow (1968), 293; *gesceapum*: *Widsith* 135.

ities in accommodating them to Christian ideas. These possibilities may be grouped under four headings representing a progressive Christianisation of this vocabulary.

The starting-point, still pagan, is the view that fate is superior to the gods and exercises power over them.[33] In ON mythology the end of the world is also seen in terms of the death of the gods, *ragna rök* means not just the end of things, but more precisely the fate which overtakes the gods. If the gods, like men, cast lots in order to divine the future this implies that they, too, are subject to a higher power. This view, worked out in ON mythology, might be peculiar to Scandinavia, but against this may be set the testimony of Daniel of Winchester's advice to Boniface on the arguments most effective in the mission-field.[34] One argument rests on the fact, conceded by the pagans, that the gods had a beginning (and an end, as in ON mythology), just as fate dictated men's birth as well as death, for this raises the possibility of a pre-existent power, to be equated in Daniel's eyes with the eternal God of the Christians. One OE gnomic text admittedly knew nothing of this argument, for it transposed to the Christian God what had earlier been held of the pagan gods' subjection to fate, saying that Christ's power is great, but fate is strongest (*Wyrd byð swiðost*).[35] This view can best be interpreted as an unreflected survival from the pagan past into the Christian present.

This suggests the possibility of survivals of the Germanic conception of fate elsewhere or at least that no attempt was made to christianise them. Fate can therefore still be seen as controlling the course of man's life. In OE fate (*wyrd*) proceeds as ordained (*Beowulf* 455) and in OHG *wêwurt* goes its way just as inexorably (*Hildebrandslied* 49). The same view can be expressed with another of our terms: in ON no man is said to escape what is preordained for him (*sem honum er skapat*), just as in OE one is destined to do something (*gesceapum*).[36] Most common amongst these unresolved survivals is the negative view of fate, especially as involving death. This is expressed in OS when men's death is described by their being taken away by *wurd* (*Heliand* 3633), when *wurdgiscapu* approaches its victim (3354f.) or when *wurd* is at hand (4619f.) when Christ prophesies Judas's betrayal. Constructions like these occur also in OE, so that however formulaic they may be they testify that the view of fate bringing death was common WG.[37] Nor was it confined to the term *wurd*.

[33] Schneider (1938), 106ff., 110, 151, 156; Rathofer (1962), 139.
[34] Lange (1962), 112ff.; Baker (1970), 93f.; Hillgarth (1986), 172ff.
[35] Brandl (1936), 82ff.; Helm (1953), 284; Rathofer (1962), 136.
[36] Cf. von Kienle (1933), 89; *Widsith* 135.   [37] Kauffmann (1926), 390f.

Without any reference to God *metod* could be used in OE in a military context in the negative sense of death (*Beowulf* 2526f.) and in association with a likewise negatively conceived *wyrd*. When *wyrd* 'sweeps' men away it is to their *metodsceafte* (2814f.). That the corresponding compound could be used in the same context in OS is suggested by the widow's son being taken from her by *uurð*, but also by *metodogescapu* (*Heliand* 2189f.). In another negative sphere, destruction rather than death, *wurðegiskefti* can also be employed with reference to the downfall of Jerusalem (3692): in this prophecy Christ may know of the future destruction, but nowhere is any connection of fate with God's will expressed linguistically. By contrast with these negative examples fate is only rarely seen positively, as active at the outset of life. In the *Heliand*, for example, Elizabeth's expectation of a child is phrased as her waiting for *wurdigiskapu* (197), a passage which may reflect the belief that the norns assisted at the act of birth.[38]

A decisive step in the Christianisation of fate was the attempt to equate it with God, a process culminating in Notker's decision to translate *fatum* on one occasion by *gotes uuillen*.[39] Of the author of the *Heliand* it has been said that his view of fate did not determine his conception of God, but rather illustrated a (providential) aspect of that conception.[40]

In marked contrast to the OE gnomic text fate is no longer stronger than God, but can instead be equated with His power. This equation was obviously easier in a positive context, as with Elizabeth's expectation of a child in the *Heliand*, where the *wurdigiskapu* for which she is waiting is correlated with *thiu maht godes* (192). A similar correlation could also be made when death is involved, so long as this could be shown to be God's inscrutable will. When Christ criticises the disciples for falling asleep on the Mount of Olives, just before His capture, He expresses prophetic knowledge that *wurd is at handun*, but adds that this is how God the Father had ordained it in His power (*mahtig*, 4778ff.). A comparable method is employed on the occasion of Christ's actual death: *uurd* is described as approaching towards midday, but is then shown for what it is in a variation: *mâri maht godes* (5394f.).[41] That other terms for fate could be similarly reinterpreted is suggested by Gabriel's words to Zachariah, announcing that the birth of John the Baptist and the course of his life have been preordained by *uurdgiscapu* and by *metod*, both summed up as *maht godes* (127f.). Here all three of these WG terms for fate are presented

---

[38] Ilkow (1968), 437. [39] *Boethius, De consolatione philosophiae* I 3, 295, 6f. Cf. von Kienle (1933), 109.
[40] Hagenlocher (1975), 166 (cf. also pp. 99ff.). [41] Rathofer (1962), 159f.

as synonymous with God's might. From this it is but a short step to seeing fate as an aspect of God's will, as in the flight to Egypt, where *thiu berhton giscapu* is varied by *uualdandes uuillion* (778f.).

Drawing these various terms for fate into the sphere of God's providential power and intentions made possible their occasional semantic equation, especially in the case of *metod*, with God. Alongside the meaning 'fate' for *metod* in OE and OS must be set the meaning 'God' in the Christian context. Although also present in OS (by close association with *(wurd)giskapu* as an attribute of divine power), the Christianisation of *metod* is most clearly accomplished in OE. The author of *Beowulf*, talking of the pre-Christian past, says that at that time men did not know *Metod*, the judge of men's deeds (*dǣda Dēmend*), the Lord God (*Drihten God*, 180f.). Not merely has this term for fate been converted into an epithet for God here, it is also employed in an ethical context where God is shown judging men's deeds. Elsewhere thanks can be given to *Metod*, in apposition to the eternal Lord (*ēcean Dryhten*, 1778f.). How suitable this particular term was for Christian use is clear from its formation from a verb signifying judgment or decree, for this qualified it admirably as an epithet for God as a judge over men, meting out reward and punishment for their deeds,[42] as made clear in the passage from *Beowulf*.

An even more successful Christianisation can be shown not so much for the noun *giskapu*, but for its verbal form: Go. *gaskapjan*, OHG *schephen*, OS *skeppian*, OE *scyppen*, 'to create'.[43] From this verb the Christian vocabulary of OE developed a present participle for God as creator, *scyppend*, which is the new religion's counterpart to the OHG feminine *schephenta* (as a term for *parca* and perhaps for the Germanic norn). What reasons can be adduced for the more successful Christianisation of this word as a verb ('to create') than as a noun ('fate')? The Germanic verb already existed in the general sense 'to shape, to fashion', which was sufficiently close to the idea 'to create' and to the concept of God as *artifex*. In this general sense (as opposed to the restricted, technical sense of *giskapu* 'fate') Wulfila used the verb in the Christian context of creation, just as he used *rūna* in its general meaning 'mystery', but not in its technical runic function. Some examples of the OS usage of *giskapu* occur in the context of birth (the power of fate exercised at the outset of life) and demonstrate the possibility of linking the stem with the concept of creation (*Heliand* 336ff., 367ff. on the birth of Christ, 4064 in the

---

[42] Ilkow (1968), 293.   [43] Kauffmann (1926), 372, 404.

context of His raising of Lazarus to a new life). It was this same question (what creative force was there before the pagan gods came into existence?) that Daniel of Winchester had advised Boniface to bring up before potential converts. Finally, whilst *wurd* was generally seen in a destructive context and was therefore only partly christianised in OS (but not at all in OHG), the positive, creative implications of *schephen* made it fit for adoption as a Christian term throughout Germania.

A last step was to suggest, in opposition to the OE gnomic example, that God was superior to fate, which is hence demoted to being an attribute of providential omnipotence. This view was rendered into German by Notker in translating Boethius (*Wanda fatum chumet fone prouidentia*),[44] but is suggested less explicitly elsewhere. When a term for fate is combined with the Christian God in the genitive (e.g. OS *godes giskapu* or OE *gesceapu heofoncyninges*)[45] the implication is that God possesses or disposes of fate, that its decrees are really His. God's control over fate can also be expressed by the converse construction, where God is juxtaposed with a word for fate in the genitive, so that to the ruler of a people (e.g. *Engla waldend*) there corresponds God as ruler over fate (e.g. *wyrda waldend* or *mihtig metodes weard* or *se metoda drihten*).[46] In agreement with this a word for fate could be correlated with God in such a way that His power or will was stressed, so that fate, as Notker following Boethius had expressed it in philosophical terms, was an executor of *providentia Dei*. Finally, even in one case in the *Heliand* where *metodigiskaft* retains its negative function, making it unadaptable to Christian reinterpretation, this is only to show Christ as superior to fate, imposing His will upon it.[47] The passage concerns the healing of the widow's son, where Christ offers protection (2210: *mundoda uuiðer metodigiskeftie*). Here the compound for 'fate' incorporates the destructive power of the demons driven out by Christ.

In this adaptation of a pre-Christian terminology of fate to novel ends we find the same pattern as with the Christianisation of pagan vocabulary at large. The most strenuous attempts were made in OE, whilst Gothic and OHG made noticeably fewer moves in this direction, with OS in between. If Gothic or OHG accepted one of these terms into its Christian vocabulary this was only for a special reason: either because of the positive implications of the pre-Christian term, as with *gaskapjan*, or because of a chance linguistic convergence, as with *stabeis*. Where no

---

[44] *Boethius, De consolatione philosophiae* I 3, 298.15f, Cf. Kauffmann (1926), 366.
[45] *Heliand*, 336, 547; OE *Genesis* 842f.   [46] Kauffmann (1926), 368, 386, fn. 3.
[47] Rathofer (1962), 136.

such reason was present, the terminology of fatalism, in contrast to OE and OS, was not used.

So far we have considered only one of the two Christian objections to the belief in fate, the conviction that God was more powerful than fate. The other objection (what room did fatalism leave for man's freedom and ethical responsibility?) has only been glanced at, by implication when *metod*, implying judgment, was found acceptable to a religion stressing a Last Judgment. Accordingly, in his homilies Ælfric attacked the mistaken belief that there was any fate (*gewyrd*) other than the almighty creator (*scyppend*, so that a christianised term of fate here defeats a word which was not adapted).[48] However, Ælfric then added that God foresees the life of each man 'according to his merits' (*be his geearnungum*), so that the replacement of fate by providence was felt to leave sufficient scope for man's ethical freedom.

If Christianity criticised pagan fatalism for depriving man of such freedom, but then equated fate with God or even subordinated it to Him, this still left open the problem of the relationship between providence and man's free will. Or in the terms of Ælfric's criticism: if God foresees the life of each man what scope did this leave for men's freedom of action, for them to show merits or not? This problem found expression in the German language for the first time when Notker translated Boethius's *De consolatione philosophiae*, so that the attempt to establish freedom of will (as a concept and as a linguistic term) was something quite new in OHG. Notker was also the first vernacular author to use a word in the explicit sense of a moral virtue (*tuged*): with him freedom of will and the recognition of a general concept of virtue which it alone made possible belonged together.

Notker also commented on Boethius and it is in his commentary, especially when he differed from him, that we can see something of the German's attitude to this problem.[49] He quotes what Boethius had to say about the relationship, even contradiction, between divine foreknowledge and the freedom of the human will: 'For if God foresees everything and cannot be deceived in any way, then what providence foresaw as the future must of necessity come to pass.' Notker then accurately translated Boethius's Latin text into OHG, but also added his agreement with this stage of the argument: *Taz ist uuar.*[50] Following his usual practice Notker proceeded to the next stage of Boethius's thoughts in Latin: 'If He knows

---

[48] Kauffmann (1926), 367, fn. 4.   [49] Schröbler (1958), 76ff.
[50] *Boethius, De consolatione philosophiae*, I 3, 334, 2–7.

from all time not merely men's actions, but also their thoughts and intentions there will be no freedom of will.' This passage was likewise translated into OHG, but before doing so Notker added his comment in
Latin: *Hoc falsum est.*[51] This comment sums up Notker's disagreement
with Boethius's fatalistic attitude towards the relationship between providence and free will, made all the more obvious by its contrast with his
approval of the preceding (and following) stages of the argument. What
the German monk objected to was the view that God's prescience, the
passive aspect of providence, necessarily puts an end to the freedom of
man's will: *so ist selbuualtigi aba.*[52]

In order to conduct this argument in the vernacular Notker had to
have at his disposal German equivalents for key terms, as when he rendered *libertas arbitrii* by *selbuualtigi*. His terminology for freedom of the
will covered a wide range of different renderings, many attested with
him for the first time.[53] Even when a term used by him is attested earlier
Notker still demonstrates his novelty by being the first to apply it to the
context of moral freedom and responsibility. The noun *selbuualtigi* was
used already in glosses of the ninth and tenth centuries, but more in the
sense of freedom of political action (it glossed *emancipatio*).[54] Another
word used by Notker in the sense of 'free will', *selbuuala*, is also attested
(once) before him, this time in the external sense of a choice which one
makes for one's self, which is not made by someone else.[55] Of both these
words it can therefore be said that only Notker made them terms of an
ethical vocabulary by using them to render the *libertas arbitrii* of
Boethius.[56] Although it cannot be claimed that Notker, either in his own
argument or in his linguistic decisions, solved the problem of the relationship between freedom of will and God's providence, it was he who
posed the problem for the German language by granting a linguistic
existence to man's freedom of will and his moral responsibility.

In the last few pages the name of Notker has recurred on a number of
different occasions. It was he who was the first to devise a general vernacular term for virtue in the abstract sense and also to coin German
equivalents for the concept of free will. In his translation of Boethius he
also tackled the problem of fate and providence, conceptually and lin-

---

[51] *Ibid.,* 7–10.   [52] *Ibid.,* 12. Cf. also *ibid.,* 350, 1–7 (*Daz ist falsa conclusio*).
[53] Schröbler (1958), 102ff.
[54] *Ibid.,* pp. 104, 106. On *frîtuam* and *selptoom* as legal terms see above, pp. 41f.
[55] *Ibid.,* pp. 102, fn. 1, 106.
[56] For the novelty of Notker's linguistic position cf. Hagenlocher (1975), 158.

guistically. The importance of Notker's intensive encounter with classical culture is that his work began to break down the onesidedly clerical nature of OHG literature.[57] We have repeatedly had occasion to observe that the semantic value of OHG words was not always to be reliably deduced from the religious or theological context of most works because they were subject to the inevitable distortions of an *interpretatio christiana*. Notker's concern with classical as well as Christian texts began to undo this bias. He therefore represents a fitting conclusion to a book devoted to the linguistic conjunction of Germanic, classical and Christian traditions at the threshold to the Middle Ages.

[57] Schröder (1967), 83.

Bibliography

Alanne, E. (1950) 'Die deutsche Weinbauterminologie in althochdeutscher und mittelhochdeutscher Zeit', *Annales Academiae Scientiarum Fennicae*, B 65,1

Allen Brown, R. (1996) *The origins of modern Europe. The medieval heritage of western civilization*, Woodbridge

Altheim, F. (1943) *Die Krise der Alten Welt im 3. Jahrhundert n. Zw. und ihre Ursachen. I: Die außerrömische Welt*, Berlin

(1956) 'Greutungen', *BzN* 7, 81ff., 241ff.

(1959) *Geschichte der Hunnen. I: Von den Anfängen bis zum Einbruch in Europa*, Berlin

Althoff, G. (1995) 'Freund und Freundschaft. Historisches', *RLGA* 9, Berlin, pp. 577ff.

Ammianus Marcellinus, *Rerum gestarum libri XXXI*, ed. J. C. Rolfe, Cambridge, Mass., 1982ff.

Andersson, T. (1992) 'Orts- und Personennamen als Aussagequelle für die altgermanische Religion'. In: H. Beck, D. Ellmers, K. Schier (ed.), *Germanische Religionsgeschichte. Quellen und Quellenprobleme*, Berlin, pp. 508ff.

Arntz, H. (1944) *Handbuch der Runenkunde*, Halle

Atlamál, ed. G. Neckel, *Edda. Die Lieder des Codex Regius nebst verwandten Denkmälern*, Heidelberg 1914, pp. 242ff.

Aubin, H. (1925) 'Der Rheinhandel in römischer Zeit', *Bonner Jahrbücher* 130, 1ff.

(1929) 'Die wirtschaftliche Entwicklung des römischen Deutschlands', *HZ* 141, 1ff.

Aumann, E. (1939) '*Tugend* und *Laster* im Althochdeutschen', *PBB* 63, 143ff.

Avedisian, A. D. (1963) 'Zur Wortgeographie und Geschichte von *Samstag/Sonnabend*'. In: FS for W. Mitzka, ed. L. E. Schmitt, *Deutsche Wortforschung in europäischen Bezügen*, Giessen, II 231ff.

Bachrach, B. S. (1970) 'Charles Martel, mounted shock combat, the stirrup, and feudalism', *Studies in Medieval and Renaissance History* 7, 49ff.

Baesecke, G. (1930) *Der deutsche Abrogans und die Herkunft des deutschen Schrifttums*, Halle

Baetke, W. (1942) *Das Heilige im Germanischen*, Tübingen

(1944a) *Vom Geist und Erbe Thules. Aufsätze zur nordischen und deutschen Geistes- und Glaubensgeschichte*, Göttingen

(1944b) *Die Religion der Germanen in Quellenzeugnissen*, Frankfurt

(1948) '*Guð* in den altnordischen Eidesformeln', *PBB* 70, 351ff.

(1964) 'Yngvi und die Ynglinger. Eine quellenkritische Untersuchung über das nordische "Sakralkönigtum"', *Sitzungsberichte der sächsischen Akademie der Wissenschaften, Philologisch-historische Klasse* 109,3, Berlin

Bailey, H. W. and Ross, A. S. C. (1961) 'Path', *Transactions of the Philological Society*, pp. 107ff.

Bainton, R. H. (1946) 'The early Church and war', *Harvard Theological Review* 39, 189ff.

Baker, D. (1970) 'Sowing the seeds of faith. Theory and practice in the mission field'. In: D. Baker (ed.), *Miscellanea Historica Ecclesiastica III*, Louvain, pp. 92ff.

Bartelink, G. J. M. (1974) 'Umdeutung heidnischer Termini im christlichen Sprachgebrauch'. In: H. Frohnes (ed.), *Kirchengeschichte als Missionsgeschichte*. Vol. 1, ed. U. W. Knorr, *Die Alte Kirche*, Munich, pp. 397ff.

Battle of the Goths and the Huns, ed. A. Heusler and W. Ranisch, *Eddica Minora*, Dortmund 1903, pp. 1ff.

Beck, H. (1965) *Das Ebersignum im Germanischen. Ein Beitrag zur germanischen Tier-Symbolik*, Berlin

(1968a) 'Waffentanz und Waffenspiel'. In: FS for O. Höfler, Vienna, pp. 1ff.

(1968b) 'Die Stanzen von Torslunda und die literarische Überlieferung', *FMS* 2, 237ff.

(1970) 'Germanische Menschenopfer in der literarischen Überlieferung'. In: H. Jankuhn (ed.), *Vorgeschichtliche Heiligtümer und Opferplätze in Mittel- und Nordeuropa*, Abhandlungen der Akademie der Wissenschaften in Göttingen III 74, Göttingen

(1973a) 'Attila. Sprachliches', *RLGA* 1, Berlin, pp. 1ff.

(1973b) 'Bajuwaren. Philologisches', *RLGA* 1, Berlin, pp. 601ff.

(1974) 'Philologische Bemerkungen zu einigen Rechtswörtern des Mittelalters'. In: FS for H. Güntert, Innsbruck, pp. 47ff.

(1978) 'Blei. Sprachliches', *RLGA* 3, Berlin, pp. 72f.

(1979) 'Gotisch *armahaírts*, althochdeutsch *armherz* – Lehnübersetzung von lateinisch *misericors*?', *ZfdPh* 98 (Sonderheft, Festgabe H. Moser), pp. 109ff.

(1981a) 'Christentum der Bekehrungszeit. II. Gebrauch der Volkssprachen in der christlichen Bekehrung', *RLGA* 4, Berlin, pp. 577ff.

(1981b) 'Brunnen. Philologisches', *RLGA* 4, Berlin, pp. 1ff.

(1984) 'Ding. Philologisches', *RLGA* 5, Berlin, pp. 443f.

(1986a) 'Eid. Sprachliches', *RLGA* 6, Berlin, pp. 537ff.

(1986b) 'Eimer. Philologisches', *RLGA* 6, Berlin, pp. 582f.

(1986c) 'Donar – Þórr', *RLGA* 6, Berlin, pp. 1ff.

(1989) 'Eisen. Sprachliches', *RLGA* 7, Berlin, pp. 58ff.

Beck, H. and Buchholz, P. (1976) 'Bewaffnung. Sprachliches', *RLGA* 2, Berlin, pp. 473ff.

Bede, *Historia ecclesiastica gentis Anglorum*, ed. C. Plummer, Oxford 1896

Behre, K.-E. (1981) 'Buche. Archäologisches', *RLGA* 4, Berlin, pp. 58f.

Benediktinerregel, die althochdeutsche, ed. U. Daab, Tübingen 1959

Benveniste, E. (1963) 'Interférences lexicales entre le gotique et l'iranien', *Bulletin de la Société Linguistique de Paris* 58, 41ff.

Beowulf, ed. F. Klaeber, New York 1941

Betz, W. (1949) *Deutsch und Lateinisch. Die Lehnbildungen der althochdeutschen Benediktinerregel*, Bonn

(1957) 'Die frühdeutschen *Spiritus*-Übersetzungen und die Anfänge des Wortes "Geist"'. In: P. T. Bogler (ed.), *Schöpfergeist und Neuschöpfung*, Maria Laach, pp. 48ff.

(1974) 'Lehnwörter und Lehnprägungen im Vor- und Frühdeutschen'. In: F. Maurer and H. Rupp (ed.), *Deutsche Wortgeschichte* (third edition), Berlin 1 135ff.

Beyerle, F. (1955) 'Süddeutschland in der politischen Konzeption Theoderichs des Großen'. In: *Vorträge und Forschungen 1: Grundfragen der Alemannischen Geschichte*, pp. 65ff.

Bierbrauer, V. (1994) 'Archäologie und Geschichte der Goten vom 1. – 7. Jahrhundert. Versuch einer Bilanz', *FMS* 28, 51ff.

Birkhan, H. (1970) *Germanen und Kelten bis zum Ausgang der Römerzeit. Der Aussagewert von Wörtern und Sachen für die frühesten keltisch-germanischen Kulturbeziehungen*, Österreichische Akademie der Wissenschaften. Philosophisch-historische Klasse. *Sitzungsberichte*, Bd. 272, Vienna.

(1971a) 'Die "keltischen" Personennamen des boiischen Großsilbers', *Die Sprache* 17, 23ff.

(1971b) 'Pfennig', *Numismatische Zeitschrift* 86, 59ff.

(1978) 'Boier. Sprachliches', *RLGA* 3, Berlin, pp. 205f.

Birnbaum (1984) 'Indo-Europeans between the Baltic and the Black Sea', *JIES* 12, 235ff.

Bischoff, B. (1979) *Paläographie des römischen Altertums und des abendländischen Mittelalters*, Berlin

Bohnenberger, K. (1948) 'Alemannische Festtagsnamen', In: FS for P. Kluckhohn and H. Schneider, Tübingen, pp. 468ff.

Bonioli, M. (1962) *La pronuncia del latino nelle scuole dall'antichità al rinascimento*, Turin

Bosworth, J. and Toller, T. N. (1954) *An Anglo-Saxon dictionary*, Oxford

Boudriot, W. (1964) *Die altgermanische Religion in der amtlichen kirchlichen Literatur des Abendlandes vom 5. bis 11. Jahrhundert*, Darmstadt

Bourciez, E. (1946) *Eléments de linguistique romane* (fourth edition), Paris

Brandl, A. (1936) 'Zur Vorgeschichte der Weird Sisters im Macbeth'. In: *Forschungen und Charakteristiken von Alois Brandl*, Berlin, pp. 82ff.

Brauer, W. (1981) *Prussische Siedlungen westlich der Weichsel. Versuch einer Deutung heimatlicher Flurnamen*, Lübeck

Braune, W. (1918) 'Althochdeutsch und Angelsächsisch', *PBB* 43, 361ff.

Brinkmann, H. (1965) *Studien zur Geschichte der deutschen Sprache und Literatur. Bd. I: Sprache*, Düsseldorf

Brogan, O. (1936) 'Trade between the Roman Empire and the free Germans', *Journal of Roman Studies* 26, 195ff.

Brøndal, V. (1928) 'Mots "scythes" en nordique primitif', *Acta Philologica Scandinavica* 3, 1ff.

Brown, P. (1993) *The world of late antiquity, AD 150–750*, London
(1996) *The rise of western Christendom. Triumph and diversity, AD 200–1000*, Oxford

Brüch, J. (1913) *Der Einfluß der germanischen Sprachen auf das Vulgärlatein*, Heidelberg
(1926a) 'Die bisherige Forschung über die germanischen Einflüsse auf die romanischen Sprachen', *Revue de linguistique romane* 2, 25ff.
(1926b) 'Kessel'. In: FS for P. Kretschmer, Vienna, pp. 6ff.
(1938) 'Lat. **pilūcāre* und deutsch *pflücken*', *ZfrPh* 58, 331ff.
(1952) 'Die Herkunft des Wortes *kaufen*', *ZfdA* 83, 92ff.

Brunner, H. (1887) 'Der Reiterdienst und die Anfänge des Lehnwesens', *ZRG(GA)* 8, 1ff.

Büttner, H. (1951) 'Die Franken und die Ausbreitung des Christentums bis zu den Tagen von Bonifatius', *HJLg* 1, 8ff.

Caesar, *De bello Gallico*, ed. R. du Pontet, Oxford n.d. [1900]

Cahen, M. (1921) *Le mot 'dieu' en vieux-scandinave*, Paris

Callies, H. (1978) 'Boier. Historisches', *RLGA* 3, Berlin, pp. 206f.

Campbell, A. (1959) *Old English Grammar*, Oxford

Campbell, J. (1991) Ed., *The Anglo-Saxons*, Harmondsworth

Capelle, T. (1989) 'Eisenverhüttung', *RLGA* 7, Berlin, pp. 61ff.

Chambers, R. W. (1912) *Widsith. A study in Old English heroic legend*, Cambridge

Chaney, W. A. (1970) *The cult of kingship in Anglo-Saxon England. The transition from paganism to Christianity*, Manchester

Copeland, R. (1991) *Rhetoric, hermeneutics, and translation in the Middle Ages. Academic traditions and vernacular texts*, Cambridge

Corazza, V. (1969) 'Le parole latine in gotico', *Atti dell'Accademia Nazionale dei Lincei. Memorie, Classe di scienze morali, storiche e filologiche*, Serie VIII, vol. XIV, 1, Rome

Cramp, R. J. (1957) '*Beowulf* and archaeology', *Medieval Archaeology* 1, 57ff.

Critchley, J. S. (1978) *Feudalism*, London

Davies, N. (1996) *Europe. A history*, Oxford

Demougeot, E. (1963) 'Rome, Lyon et la christianisation des pays rhénans'. In: *Rome et le christianisme dans la région rhénane. Colloque du Centre de recherches d'histoire des religions de l'Université de Strasbourg (19–21 mai 1960)*, Paris, pp. 23ff.

Deor, ed. K. Malone, London 1949

Derolez, R. L. M. (1963) *Götter und Mythen der Germanen*, Einsiedeln

Dickins, B. and Ross, A. S. C. (1945) *The Dream of the Rood*, London

Diculescu, C. (1921) 'Altgermanische Bestandteile im Rumänischen', *ZfrPh* 41, 420ff.
(1929) 'Altgermanische Bestandteile im Rumänischen, Erwiderung und neue Forschung', *ZfrPh* 49, 385ff.

Dölger, F. J. (1950) ' "Kirche" als Name für den christlichen Kultbau. Sprach- und Kulturgeschichtliches zu den Bezeichnungen *kuriakón, oĩkos kuriakós, dominicum, basilica*', *Antike und Christentum* 6, 161ff.

Dopsch, A. (1961) *Wirtschaftliche und soziale Grundlagen der europäischen Kulturentwicklung aus der Zeit von Caesar bis auf Karl den Großen*, Aalen

Drögereit, R. (1952) 'Kaiseridee und Kaisertitel bei den Angelsachsen', *ZRG(GA)* 69, 24ff.

Dronke, U. (1969) *The poetic Edda. Vol. I: Heroic poems*, Oxford

    (1992) 'Eddic poetry as a source for the history of Germanic religion'. In: H. Beck, D. Ellmers, K. Schier (ed.), *Germanische Religionsgeschichte. Quellen und Quellenprobleme*. Berlin, pp. 656ff.

Düwel, K. (1970) 'Germanische Opfer und Opferriten im Spiegel altgermanischer Kultworte'. In: H. Jankuhn (ed.), *Vorgeschichtliche Heiligtümer und Opferplätze in Mittel- und Nordeuropa, Abhandlungen der Akademie der Wissenschaften in Göttingen* III 74, Göttingen, pp. 219ff.

    (1982) 'Runen und interpretatio christiana. Zur religionsgeschichtlichen Stellung der Bügelfibel von Nordendorf I'. In: J. Wollasch (ed.), *Tradition als historische Kraft*, Berlin, pp. 78ff.

    (1988) 'Buchstabenmagie und Alphabetzauber. Zu den Inschriften der Goldbrakteaten und ihre Funktion als Amulette', *FMS* 22, 70ff.

Ebel, E. (1963) *Die Terminologie der Runentechnik*, dissertation Göttingen

Ebenbauer, A. (1981a) 'Buch. Sprachliches', *RLGA* 4, Berlin, pp. 35ff.

    (1981b) 'Buchstabe', *RLGA* 4, Berlin, pp. 87f.

Edward's Death, ed. C. Plummer, *Two of the Saxon Chronicles parallel*, Oxford 1892, pp. 192ff.

Eggers, H. (1954) 'Gotisches in der Altbairischen Beichte', *ZfMf* 22, 129ff.

    (1957) 'Altgermanische Seelenvorstellungen im Lichte des Heliand', *NdJb* 80, 1ff.

    (1963) *Deutsche Sprachgeschichte I. Das Althochdeutsche*, Reinbek

    (1964) 'Althochdeutsch *iungiro*, altsächsisch *iungro, iungaro*'. In: FS for T. Starck, The Hague, pp. 62ff.

    (1978) 'Die Annahme des Christentums im Spiegel der deutschen Sprachgeschichte'. In: H. Frohnes (ed.), *Kirchengeschichte als Missionsgeschichte*. Vol. II 1, ed. K. Schäferdiek, *Die Kirche des früheren Mittelalters*, Munich, pp. 466ff.

Eggers, H. J. (1951) *Der römische Import im freien Germanien*, Hamburg

Ehrismann, G, (1906) 'Die Wörter für "Herr" im Althochdeutschen', *ZfdW* 7, 173ff.

    (1932) *Geschichte der deutschen Literatur bis zum Ausgang des Mittelalters. Erster Teil. Die althochdeutsche Literatur* (second edition), Munich

Ekblom, R. (1945) 'Germ. **kuningaz* "König" ', *Studia Neophilologica* 17, 1ff.

Ekholm, G. (1935) 'Zur Geschichte des römisch-germanischen Handels', *Acta Archaeologica* 6, 49ff.

Ellegård, A. (1986) 'The ancient Goths and the concept of tribe and migration'. In: FS for C. Weibull, Göteborg, pp. 32ff.

Elliott, R. W. V. (1959) *Runes. An introduction*, Manchester

Ellmers, D. (1992) 'Die archäologischen Quellen zur germanischen

Religionsgeschichte'. In: H. Beck, D. Ellmers, K. Schier (ed.), *Germanische Religionsgeschichte. Quellen und Quellenprobleme*, Berlin, pp. 95ff.

Erben, J. (1979) 'Die Herausforderung der *ur-hēttun* im althochdeutschen Hildebrandslied', *ZfdPh* 98 (Sonderheft, Festgabe H. Moser), pp. 4ff.

Erdmann, C. (1935) *Die Entstehung des Kreuzzugsgedankens*, Stuttgart
(1951) *Forschungen zur politischen Ideenwelt des Frühmittelalters*, Berlin

Eska, J. F. (1990) 'Another look at Gaul. *celicno-* and Goth. *kelikn*', *NOWELE* 16, 63ff.

Euler, W. (1985) 'Gab es ein ostgermanisches Sprachgebiet in Südskandinavien? (Zur Frage gotisch-ostgermanischer Runeninschriften in Südschweden und Dänemark', *NOWELE* 6, 3ff.

Evans, D. E. (1967) *Gaulish personal names. A study of some continental Celtic formations*, Oxford
(1980) 'Celts and Germans', *Bulletin of the Board of Celtic Studies* 29, 230ff.

Ewig, E. (1963) 'Zum christlichen Königsgedanken im Frühmittelalter'. In: *Das Königtum. Seine geistigen und rechtlichen Grundlagen. Mainauvorträge 1954 (Vorträge und Forschungen, 3)*, Darmstadt, pp. 7ff.
(1970) 'Die christliche Mission bei den Franken und im Merowingerreich', *Bibliothèque de la revue d'histoire ecclésiastique* 50. (D. Baker, ed., *Miscellanea historiae ecclesiasticae* III, Louvain 1970, pp. 24ff.)

Ewig, E. and Schäferdiek, K. (1978) 'Christliche Expansion im Merowingerreich'. In: H. Frohnes (ed.), *Kirchengeschichte als Missionsgeschichte*. Vol. II 1, ed. K. Schäferdiek, *Die Kirche des früheren Mittelalters*, Munich, pp. 116ff.

Fanning, S. (1991) 'Bede, *Imperium*, and the Bretwaldas', *Speculum* 66, 1ff.

Feist, S. (1923) *Etymologisches Wörterbuch der gotischen Sprache mit Einschluß des Krimgotischen und sonstiger gotischer Sprachreste*, Halle

Fischer, H. (1912) 'Der germanische Nodus und verwantes', *ZfdA* 53, 183ff.

Flint, V. I. J. (1991) *The rise of magic in early medieval Europe*, Oxford

Foerste, W. (1967) 'Der römische Einfluß auf die germanische Fesselungs-Terminologie', *FMS* 1, 186ff.

Förster, M. (1921) *Keltisches Wortgut im Englischen. Eine sprachliche Untersuchung*, Halle
(1922) 'Englisch-Keltisches. I. Ae. *ancora, ancra, ancor* "Einsiedler" ', *Englische Studien* 56, 204ff.

Fossier, R. (1989) Ed., *The Cambridge illustrated history of the Middle Ages. I: 350–950*, Cambridge

Frauenholz, E. von (1935) *Entwicklungsgeschichte des deutschen Heerwesens*, Munich

Frend, W. H. C. (1964) 'A note on the influence of Greek immigrants on the spread of Christianity in the West'. In: FS for T. Klauser, Münster, pp. 125ff.
(1974) 'Der Verlauf der Mission in der Alten Kirche bis zum 7. Jahrhundert'. In: H. Frohnes (ed.), *Kirchengeschichte als Missionsgeschichte*. Vol. 1, ed. U. W. Knorr, *Die Alte Kirche*, Munich, pp. 32ff.

Freudenthal, K. F. (1949) *Arnulfingisch-karolingische Rechtswörter. Eine Studie in der juristischen Terminologie der ältesten germanischen Dialekte*, Tübingen

(1959) *Gloria Temptatio Conversio. Studien zur ältesten deutschen Kirchensprache,* Göteborg

Friedrich, P. (1970) *Proto-Indo-European trees. The arboreal system of a prehistoric people,* Chicago

Frings, T. (1928) 'Estrich und Oler = Speicher', *PBB* 52, 423ff.

(1939) 'Germanisch *ō* und *ē̆*, *PBB* 63, 1ff.

(1955) *'Paida', PBB* 77, 221ff.

Frings, T. and Müller, G. (1951) 'Keusch'. In: FS for K. Helm, Tübingen, pp. 109ff.

Frings, T. and Niessen, J. (1927) 'Zur Geographie und Geschichte von "Ostern, Samstag, Mittwoch:" im Westgermanischen', *IF* 45, 276ff.

Fritze, W. (1954) 'Die fränkische Schwurfreundschaft der Merowingerzeit. Ihr Wesen und ihre politische Funktion', *ZRG(GA)* 71, 74ff.

Fritze, W. H. (1963) 'Slaven und Avaren im angelsächsischen Missionsprogramm I: Theologia naturalis und Slavenmission bei Bonifatius', *ZSlPh* 31, 316ff.

(1965) 'Slaven und Avaren im angelsächsischen Missionsprogramm II: Bedas Rugini und Willibrords Dänenmission', *ZSlPh* 32, 231ff.

(1967) 'Slaven und Avaren im angelsächsischen Missionsprogramm III: Bedas Hunni und die Entstehung der angelsächsischen Missionsvölkerliste von 703/04', *ZSlPh* 33, 358ff.

(1969) 'Universalis gentium confessio. Formeln, Träger und Wege universalmissionarischen Denkens im 7. Jahrhundert', *FMS* 3, 78ff.

Fromm, H. (1958) 'Die ältesten germanischen Lehnwörter im Finnischen', *ZfdA* 88, 81ff., 211ff., 299ff.

Gaebeler, K. (1911) 'Die griechischen Bestandteile der gotischen Bibel', *ZfdPh* 43, 1ff.

Gamillscheg, E. (1934) *Romania Germanica. Sprach- und Siedlungsgeschichte der Germanen auf dem Boden des alten Römerreiches. Bd. I: Zu den ältesten Berührungen zwischen Römern und Germanen. Die Franken. Die Westgoten.* First edition, Berlin

(1935) *Romania Germanica. Sprach- und Siedlungsgeschichte der Germanen auf dem Boden des alten Römerreiches. Bd. II: Die Ostgoten. Die Langobarden. Die altgermanischen Bestandteile des Ostromanischen. Altgermanisches im Alpenromanischen,* Berlin.

(1970) *Romania Germanica. Sprach- und Siedlungsgeschichte der Germanen auf dem Boden des alten Römerreiches. Bd. I: Zu den ältesten Berührungen zwischen Römern und Germanen. Die Franken.* Second edition, Berlin

Gaudemet, J. (1963) 'L'église d'occident et la rhénanie'. In: *Rome et le christianisme dans la région rhénane. Colloque du Centre de recherche d'histoire des religions de l'Université de Strasbourg (19–21 mai 1960),* Paris, pp. 5ff.

Geake, H. (1994) 'Burial practice in seventh- and eighth-century England'. In: M. O. H. Carver (ed.), *The Age of Sutton Hoo. The seventh century in north-western Europe,* Woodbridge, pp. 83ff.

Geary, P. J. (1988) *Before France and Germany. The creation and transformation of the Merovingian world,* New York

Genesis, Old English. The relevant parts are included in O. Behaghel, *Heliand und Genesis*, Halle 1933, pp. 211ff.

Genzmer, F. (1950) 'Die germanische Sippe als Rechtsgebilde', *ZRG(GA)* 67, 34ff.

(1951) 'Staat und Gesellschaft in vor- und frühgeschichtlicher Zeit'. In: H. Schneider (ed.), *Germanische Altertumskunde*, Munich, pp. 123ff.

Georgslied, ed. E. von Steinmeyer, *Die kleineren althochdeutschen Sprachdenkmäler*, Berlin 1916, pp. 94ff.

Gillespie, G. T. (1973) *A catalogue of personal names in German heroic literature (700–1600) including named animals and objects and ethnic names*, Oxford

Gimbutas, M. (1971) *The Slavs*, London

Gneuss, H. (1992) 'Anglicae linguae interpretatio: language contact, lexical borrowing and glossing in Anglo-Saxon England', *PBA* 82, 107ff.

Goetz, H.-W. and Welwei, K.-W. (1995) Ed., *Altes Germanien. Auszüge aus den antiken Quellen über die Germanen und ihre Beziehungen zum römischen Reich. Quellen der alten Geschichte bis zum Jahre 238 n. Chr. Erster Teil*, Darmstadt

Green, D. H. (1965) *The Carolingian lord. Semantic studies on four Old High German words: balder, frô, truhtin, hêrro*, Cambridge

(1994) *Medieval listening and reading. The primary reception of German literature 800–1300*, Cambridge

(1995) 'The rise of Germania in the light of linguistic evidence'. In: G. Ausenda (ed.), *After Empire. Towards an ethnology of Europe's barbarians*, Woodbridge, pp. 143ff.

(1997) 'From Germania to Europe. The evidence of language and history', *MLR* 92, xxixff.

Gregory of Tours, *Historiarum libri decem*, ed. R. Buchner, Darmstadt 1951

Grípisspá, ed. G. Neckel, *Edda. Die Lieder des Codex Regius nebst verwandten Denkmälern*, Heidelberg 1914, pp. 160ff.

Gschwantler, O. (1976) 'Bekehrung und Bekehrungsgeschichte. I. Ostgermanen', *RLGA* 2, Berlin, pp. 175ff.

Guðrúnarkviða I, ed. G. Neckel, *Edda. Die Lieder des Codex Regius nebst verwandten Denkmälern*, Heidelberg 1914, pp. 197ff.

Gundermann, G. (1901) 'Die Namen der Wochentage bei den Römern', *ZfdW* 1, 175ff.

Gutenbrunner, S. (1936) *Die germanischen Götternamen der antiken Inschriften*, Halle

Gutmacher, E. (1914) 'Der wortschatz des althochdeutschen Tatian in seinem verhältnis zum altsächsischen, angelsächsischen und altfriesischen', *PBB* 39, 1ff., 229ff.

Gysseling, M. (1961) 'Proeve van een oudnederlandse grammatica (eerste deel)', *Studia Germanica Gandensia* 3, 9ff.

(1976) 'De germaanse woorden in de Lex Salica', *Verslagen en Mededelingen van de Koninklijke Academie voor Nederlandse Taal- en Letterkunde*, Afd. 1, pp. 60ff.

Hachmann, R. (1970) *Die Goten und Skandinavien*, Berlin

(1971) *Die Germanen*, Munich

Haendler, G. (1961) *Wulfila und Ambrosius*, Stuttgart

Hagenlocher, A. (1975) *Schicksal im Heliand. Verwendung und Bedeutung der nominalen Bezeichnungen*, Cologne
  (1992) *Der guote vride. Idealer Friede in deutscher Literatur bis ins frühe 14. Jahrhundert*, Berlin
Hamðismál, ed. U. Dronke, *The poetic Edda. Vol. I: Heroic poems*, Oxford 1969, pp. 161ff.
Hanson, R. P. C. (1985) 'The transformation of pagan temples into churches in the early Christian centuries'. In: R. P. C. Hanson (ed.), *Studies in Christian antiquity*, Edinburgh, pp. 347ff.
Harnack, A. von (1905) *Militia Christi. Die christliche Religion und der Soldatenstand in den ersten drei Jahrhunderten*, Tübingen
Harris, W. V. (1989) *Ancient literacy*, Cambridge, Mass.
Hatt, J.-J. (1963) 'Les plus anciens témoignages du christianisme en Rhénanie d'après les fouilles et les découvertes archéologiques à Cologne, Bonn, Xanten et Trèves'. In: *Rome et le christianisme dans la région rhénane. Colloques du Centre de recherche d'histoire des religions de l'Université de Strasbourg (19–21 mai, 1960)*, Paris, pp. 55ff.
Haubrichs, W. (1987) 'Die Angelsachsen und die germanischen Stämme des Kontinents im frühen Mittelalter: sprachliche und literarische Beziehungen'. In: P. Ní Chatháin and M. Richter (ed.), *Irland und die Christenheit*, Stuttgart, pp. 387ff.
  (1988) *Die Anfänge. Versuche volkssprachiger Schriftlichkeit im frühen Mittelalter (ca. 700–1050/60)*. Vol. 1, part 1 of J. Heinzle (ed.), *Geschichte der deutschen Literatur von den Anfängen bis zum Beginn der Neuzeit*, Frankfurt
Haug, W. and Vollmann, B. K. (1991) *Frühe deutsche Literatur und lateinische Literatur in Deutschland 800–1150*, Frankfurt
Heather, P. J. (1986) 'The crossing of the Danube and the Gothic conversion', *GRBS* 27, 289ff.
  (1991) *Goths and Romans, 332–489*, Oxford
  (1996) *The Goths*, Oxford
Heather, P. and Matthews, J. (1991) *The Goths in the fourth century*, Liverpool
Hedeager, L. (1994) 'Kingdoms, ethnicity and material culture: Denmark in a European perspective'. In: M. O. H. Carver (ed.), *The Age of Sutton Hoo. The seventh century in north-western Europe*, Woodbridge, pp. 279ff.
Hegel, E. (1962) 'Die rheinische Kirche in römischer und frühfränkischer Zeit'. In: K. Böhmer et al. (ed.), *Das erste Jahrtausend. Kultur und Kunst im werdenden Abendland an Rhein und Ruhr*, Düsseldorf, pp. 93ff.
Heiler, F. (1959) 'Fortleben und Wandlungen des antiken Gottkönigtums im Christentum'. In: *La regalità sacra. Contributi al tema dell'VIII Congresso Internazionale di Storia delle Religioni (Roma, Aprile 1955)*, Leiden, pp. 543ff.
Helgakviða Hundingsbana I and II, ed. G. Neckel, *Edda. Die Lieder des Codex Regius nebst verwandten Denkmälern*, Heidelberg 1914, pp. 126ff. and 146ff.
Heliand, ed. O. Behaghel, Halle 1933
Helm, K. (1909) 'Zur Erklärung des ersten Merseburger Zauberspruches', *PBB* 35, 312ff.

(1937) *Altgermanische Religionsgeschichte. Bd. II: Die nachrömische Zeit. I: Die Ostgermanen*, Heidelberg

(1953) *Altgermanische Religionsgeschichte. Bd. II: Die nachrömische Zeit. II: Die Westgermanen*, Heidelberg

Hermann, E. (1918) 'Sachliches und Sprachliches zur indogermanischen Großfamilie', *Nachrichten der Göttinger Gesellschaft der Wissenschaften, Philologisch- historische Klasse 1918*, pp. 204ff.

(1941) 'Sind die Namen der Gudden und die Namen Danzig, Gdingen und Graudenz gotischen Ursprungs?', *Nachrichten der Göttinger Akademie der Wissenschaften, Philologisch- historische Klasse Bd. 3*, pp. 207ff.

Herold, G. (1941) *Der Volksbegriff im Sprachschatz des Althochdeutschen und Altniederdeutschen*, Halle

Herren, M. (1984) 'Old Irish lexical and semantic influence on Hiberno-Latin'. In: P. Ní Chatháin and M. Richter (ed.), *Irland und Europa*, Stuttgart, pp. 197ff.

Herrin, J. (1989) *The formation of Christendom*, London

Herwegen, I. (1912) *Geschichte der benediktinischen Profeßformel*, Münster

Hildebrandslied, ed. E. von Steinmeyer, *Die kleineren althochdeutschen Sprachdenkmäler*, Berlin 1916, pp. 1ff.

Hill, J. (1994) *Old English minor heroic poems*, Durham

Hillgarth, J. N. (1986) *Christianity and paganism, 300–750. The conversion of western Europe*, Philadelphia

(1987) 'Modes of evangelisation of western Europe in the seventh century'. In: P. Ní Chatháin and M. Richter (ed.), *Irland und Europa*, Stuttgart, pp. 311ff.

Hinderling, R. (1971) ' "Erfüllen" und die Frage des gotischen Spracheinflusses im Althochdeutschen', *ZfdS* 27, 1ff.

Höfler, O. (1952) *Der Runenstein von Rök und die germanische Individualweihe*, Tübingen and Münster

(1954) 'Über die Grenzen semasiologischer Personennamenforschung'. In: FS for D. Kralik, Horn, pp. 26ff.

(1963) 'Der Sakralcharakter des germanischen Königtums'. In: *Das Königtum. Seine geistigen und rechtlichen Grundlagen. Mainauvorträge 1954 (Vorträge und Forschungen 3)*, Darmstadt, pp. 75ff.

(1976) 'Berserker', *RLGA* 2, Berlin, pp. 298ff.

Hofmann, D. (1955) *Nordisch-englische Lehnbeziehungen der Wikingerzeit*, Copenhagen

Holl, K. (1974) 'Die Missionsmethode der alten und die der mittelalterlichen Kirche'. In: H. Frohnes (ed.), *Kirchengeschichte als Missionsgeschichte*. Vol. 1, ed. U. W. Knorr, *Die Alte Kirche*, Munich, pp. 3ff.

Hollyman, K. J. (1957) *Le développement du vocabulaire féodal en France pendant le haut moyen âge*, Geneva

Holmberg, B. (1992) 'Über sakrale Ortsnamen und Personennamen im Norden'. In: H. Beck, D. Ellmers, K. Schier (ed.), *Germanische Religionsgeschichte. Quellen und Quellenprobleme*, Berlin, pp. 541ff.

Homann, H. (1965) *Der Indiculus superstitionum et paganiarum und verwandte Denkmäler*, dissertation Göttingen

Hoops, J. (1905) *Waldbäume, Kulturpflanzen im germanischen Altertum*, Strassburg
(1913a) 'Buch', *RLGA* 1 (first edition), pp. 338ff.
(1913b) 'Buchstabe', *RLGA* 1 (first edition), pp. 349f.

Howlett, D. (1992) 'Inscriptions and design of the Ruthwell Cross'. In: B. Cassidy (ed.), *The Ruthwell Cross*, Princeton, pp. 71ff.

Hübinger, P. E. (1969) 'Spätantike und frühes Mittelalter. Ein Problem historischer Periodenbildung'. In: P.E. Hübinger (ed.), *Zur Frage der Periodengrenze zwischen Altertum und Mittelalter*, Darmstadt, pp. 145ff.

Hunter Blair, P. (1963) *Roman Britain and early England 55 BC–AD 871*, Edinburgh

Hüpper, D. (1986a) '*Sikihelm chaisurlih* und *chunichelm*. Althochdeutsche Glossen zu dem Helm als Herrschaftszeichen'. In: FS for R. Schmidt-Wiegand, Berlin, 1 284ff.

(1986b) '*Buoh* und *scrift*. Gattungen und Textsorten in frühmittelalterlichen volkssprachigen Schriftzeugnissen: Zur Ausbildung einer Begrifflichkeit', *FMS* 20, 93ff.

Hüpper-Dröge, D. (1981) 'Schutz- und Angriffswaffen nach den Leges und verwandten fränkischen Rechtsquellen'. In: R. Schmidt-Wiegand (ed.), *Wörter und Sachen im Lichte der Bezeichnungsforschung*, Berlin, pp. 107ff.

(1984a) 'Der gerichtliche Zweikampf im Spiegel der Bezeichnungen für "Kampf", "Kämpfer", "Waffen" ', *FMS* 18, 607ff.

(1984b) 'Pfeil'. In: *Handwörterbuch zur deutschen Rechtsgeschichte*, Berlin, 3, 1726ff.

Ibach, H. (1956) 'Zu Wortschatz und Begriffswelt der althochdeutschen Benediktinerregel, 1', *PBB* 78, 1ff.

(1960) 'Zu Wortschatz und Begriffswelt der althochdeutschen Benediktinerregel, 5', *PBB* 82, 371ff.

Ilkow, P. (1968) *Die Nominalkomposita der altsächsischen Bibeldichtung. Ein semantisch-kulturgeschichtliches Glossar*, Göttingen

Innocente, L. (1990) 'Per una definizione semantica del gotico *þeihs*', *Incontri Linguistici* 13, 39ff.

Isidor, der althochdeutsche, ed. H. Eggers, Tübingen 1964

Isidore of Seville, *Etymologiae*, ed. W. M. Lindsay, Oxford 1910

Jacoby, M. (1974) *Wargus, vargr 'Verbrecher' 'Wolf', eine sprach- und rechtsgeschichtliche Untersuchung*, Acta Universitatis Upsaliensis, Studia Germanistica 12, Uppsala

James, E. (1991) *The Franks*, Oxford
(1992) 'The northern world in the Dark Ages, 400–900'. In: G. Holmes (ed.), *The Oxford History of medieval Europe*, pp. 59ff.

Jankuhn, H. (1966) 'Archäologische Bemerkungen zur Glaubwürdigkeit des Tacitus in der Germania', *Nachrichten der Akademie der Wissenschaften in Göttingen*, pp. 411ff.

(1967) 'Archäologische Beobachtungen zu Tier- und Menschenopfern bei den Germanen in der römischen Kaiserzeit', *Nachrichten der Akademie der Wissenschaften in Göttingen*, pp. 117ff.

Janssen, W. (1994) 'Fahren und Reiten. Merowingerzeit. Verkehrswege', *RLGA* 8, Berlin, pp. 160ff.

Jellinek, M. H. (1923) 'Zur christlichen Terminologie im Gotischen', *PBB* 47, 434ff.

(1925) 'Ahd. *v = f*', *PBB* 49, 111ff.

(1926) *Geschichte der gotischen Sprache*, Berlin

Jensen, P. (1901) 'Die siebentägige Woche in Babylon und Nineveh', *ZfdW* 1, 150ff.

Jente, R. (1921) *Die mythologischen Ausdrücke im altenglischen Wortschatz*, Heidelberg

Jordanes, *Getica*. MGH AA 5, 53ff.

Jud, J. (1914) 'Probleme der altromanischen Wortgeographie', *ZfrPh* 38, 1ff.

Kahl, H.-D. (1956) 'Papst Gregor der Große und die christliche Terminologie der Angelsachsen', *ZfMR* 40, 93ff., 190ff.

(1960) 'Europäische Wortschatzbewegungen im Bereich der Verfassungsgeschichte. Ein Versuch am Beispiel germanischer und slavischer Herrschernamen. Mit Anhang: Zum Ursprung von germ. *König*', *ZRG(GA)* 77, 154ff.

(1978) 'Die ersten Jahrhunderte des missionsgeschichtlichen Mittelalters. Bausteine für eine Phänomenologie bis ca. 1050'. In: H. Frohnes (ed.), *Kirchengeschichte als Missionsgeschichte*. Vol. II 1, ed. K. Schäferdiek. *Die Kirche des früheren Mittelalters*, Munich, pp. 11ff.

Kalbow, W. (1913) *Die germanischen Personennamen des altfranzösischen Heldenepos und ihre lautliche Entwicklung*, Halle

Karg-Gasterstädt, E. (1945) '*got* und *abgot*', *PBB* 67, 420ff.

(1958) 'Althochdeutsch Thing – Neuhochdeutsch Ding. Die Geschichte eines Wortes', *Berichte über die Verhandlungen der sächsischen Akademie der Wissenschaften zu Leipzig. Philologisch-historische Klasse* 104,2

Karsten, T. E. (1915) 'Germanisch-finnische Lehnwortstudien. Ein Beitrag zu der ältesten Sprach- und Kulturgeschichte der Germanen', *Acta Societatis Scientiarum Fennicae* 45,2

(1928) *Die Germanen. Eine Einführung in die Geschichte ihrer Sprache und Kultur*, Berlin

Kaspers, W. (1950) 'Wort- und Namenstudien zur Lex Salica', *ZfdA* 82, 291ff.

Kauffmann, F. (1900) 'Die jünger, vornehmlich im Heliand', *ZfdPh* 32, 250ff.

(1913) 'Got. *gawairpi*', *IF* 31, 321f.

(1918) 'Aus dem Wortschatz der Rechtssprache', *ZfdPh* 47, 153ff.

(1923a) *Deutsche Altertumskunde*, Vol. II, Munich

(1923b) 'Der Stil der gotischen Bibel', *ZfdPh* 49, 11ff.

(1926) 'Über den Schicksalsglauben der Germanen', *ZfdPh* 50, 361ff.

Kazanski, M. (1992a) 'Les *arctoi gentes* et "l'empire" d'Hermanaric. Commentaire archéologique d'une source écrite', *Germania* 70, 75ff.

(1992b) 'Les Goths et les Huns. A propos des relations entre les barbares sédentaires et les nomades', *Archéologie Médiévale* 22, 191ff.

Keegan, J. (1994) *A history of warfare*, London

Keil, H. (1864) *Grammatici Latini*, Vol. IV, Leipzig

Kelle, J. (1881) *Glossar der Sprache Otfrids*, Regensburg

Kellermann, V. (1966) *Germanische Altertumskunde. Einführung in das Studium einer Kulturgeschichte der Vor- und Frühzeit*, Berlin

Kern, F. (1954) *Gottesgnadentum und Widerstandsrecht im früheren Mittelalter. Zur Entwicklungsgeschichte der Monarchie* (ed. R. Buchner), Darmstadt

Kieckhefer, R. (1989) *Magic in the Middle Ages*, Cambridge

Kienle, M. von (1933) 'Der Schicksalsbegriff im Altdeutschen', *WuS* 15, 81ff.

Kienle, R. von (1939) *Germanische Gemeinschaftsformen*, Berlin

Kiparsky, V. (1934) 'Die gemeinslavischen Lehnwörter aus dem Germanischen', *Annales Academiae Scientiarum Fennicae* B 32,2

Klindt-Jensen, O. (1949) 'Foreign influences in Denmark's early Iron Age', *Acta Archaeologica* 20, 1ff.

Klingenberg, H. (1973) *Runenschrift – Schriftdenken. Runeninschriften*, Heidelberg
    (1976) 'Die Drei-Götter-Fibel von Nordendorf bei Augsburg. Zum Typus der mythologischen, exemplarisch-aktuellen Runenschrift', *ZfdA* 105, 167ff.

Kluge, F. (1885) 'Angelsächsische Excerpte aus Byrhtferth's Handboc oder Enchiridion', *Anglia* 8, 298ff.
    (1902) '*Ôstarun*', *ZfdW* 2, 42f.
    (1909) 'Gotische Lehnworte im Althochdeutschen', *PBB* 35, 134ff.
    (1913) *Urgermanisch. Vorgeschichte der altgermanischen Dialekte*, Strassburg

Kluge, F. and Seebold, E. (1989) *Etymologisches Wörterbuch der deutschen Sprache*, 22nd edition, Berlin

Kmieciński, J. (1962) 'Problem of the so-called Gotho-Gepidian culture in the light of recent research', *Archaeologia Polona* 4, 270ff.

Knapp, F. P. (1973) 'Althochdeutsch *biscof* – altfranzösisch *(e)vesque* – altgalloitalienisch **vescof*', *Die Sprache* 19, 180ff.

Knobloch, J. (1959) 'Der Ursprung von nhd. Ostern, engl. Easter', *Die Sprache* 5, 27ff.
    (1960) 'Recherches sur le vocabulaire de la mission mérovingienne', *Orbis* 9, 427ff.
    (1965) 'Haben die Slaven ihre Bezeichnung für das Glas von den Goten übernommen?', *Abhandlungen der sächsischen Akademie der Wissenschaften* 57,2, pp. 211ff.
    (1966) 'Ein weiteres Wortzeugnis für die merowingische Mission in England und im oberdeutschen Raum'. In: FS for K. Pivec, Innsbruck, pp. 221f.
    (1967) 'Abendländische Kulturwörter aus merowingischer Zeit', *FuF* 41, 300ff.

Köbler, G. (1970) 'Richten–Richter–Gericht', *ZRG(GA)* 87, 57ff.

Koivulehto, J. (1981) 'Reflexe des germ. /ē'/ im Finnischen und die Datierung der germanisch-finnischen Lehnbeziehungen', *PBB* 103, 167ff., 333ff.
    (1995) 'Finnland. Sprachliches', *RLGA* 9, Berlin, pp. 77ff.

Kolb, H. (1962) '*dia weroltrehtwîson*', *ZfdW* 18, 88ff.
    (1964) '*Vora demo muspilli*. Versuch einer Interpretation', *ZfdPh* 83, 2ff.
    (1971) 'Himmlisches und irdisches Gericht in karolingischer Theologie und althochdeutscher Dichtung', *FMS* 5, 284ff.

Kousgård Sørensen, J. (1974) '*Odinkar* og andre navne på *-kar*', *NoB* 62, 108ff.

Krahe, H. (1954) *Sprache und Vorzeit*, Heidelberg
   (1966) 'Zu germ.-lat. *framea*', *IF* 70, 50ff.

Kranzmayer, E. (1929) *Die Namen der Wochentage in den Mundarten von Bayern und Österreich*, Vienna
   (1960) *Die bairischen Kennwörter und ihre Geschichte*, Vienna

Krause, W. (1936) 'framea'. In: FS for H. Hirt, Heidelberg, II 585ff.

Krautheimer, R. (1965) *Early Christian and Byzantine architecture*, Harmondsworth

Kretschmer, P. (1906) 'Wortgeschichtliche Miscellen. 1. Kirche, Dom, Münster', *ZVS* 39, 539ff.
   (1918) *Wortgeographie der hochdeutschen Umgangssprache*, Göttingen
   (1935) 'Zum Balkan-Skythischen', *Glotta* 24, 1ff.

Kristensen, A. K. G. (1983) 'Tacitus' germanische Gefolgschaft', *Det Kongelige Danske Videnskabernes Selskab, Historisk-filosofiske meddelelser* 50,5, Copenhagen

Kroeschell, K. (1960) 'Die Sippe im germanischen Recht', *ZRG(GA)* 77, 1ff.
   (1968) *Haus und Herrschaft im frühen deutschen Recht*, Göttingen

Kuhn, H. (1938) 'Das Zeugnis der Sprache über Alter und Ursprung der Runenschrift'. In: FS for G. Neckel, Leipzig, pp. 54ff.
   (1951a) Review of T. Frings, *Grundlegung einer Geschichte der deutschen Sprache*, *AfdA* 65, 53ff.
   (1951b) 'Sitte und Sittlichkeit'. In: H. Schneider (ed.), *Germanische Altertumskunde*, Munich, pp. 171ff.
   (1951c) 'Kriegswesen und Seefahrt'. In: H. Schneider (ed.), *Germanische Altertumskunde*, Munich, pp. 98ff.
   (1956) 'Die Grenzen der germanischen Gefolgschaft', *ZRG(GA)* 73, 1ff.
   (1971a) *Kleine Schriften*, Vol. II, Berlin
   (1971b) *Das alte Island*, Düsseldorf
   (1972) 'Das römische Kriegswesen im germanischen Wortschatz', *ZfdA* 101, 13ff.
   (1978) *Kleine Schriften*, Vol. IV, Berlin

Kunow, J. (1980) *Negotiator et Vectura. Händler und Transport im freien Germanien*, Marburg

Kylstra, A.D. (1961) *Geschichte der germanisch-finnischen Lehnwortforschung*, Assen
   (1984) 'Das älteste Germanisch im Lichte der germanisch-finnischen Lehnwortforschung', *ABäG* 21, 1ff.

La Baume, W. (1959) *Ostgermanische Frühzeit*, Kiel

La Farge, B. (1991) '*Leben*' und '*Seele*' in den altgermanischen Sprachen. Studien zum Einfluß christlich-lateinischer Vorstellungen auf die Volkssprachen, Heidelberg

Lane Fox, P. (1988) *Pagans and Christians*, Harmondsworth

Lange, W. (1958) *Studien zur christlichen Dichtung der Nordgermanen 1000–1200*, Göttingen
   (1962) *Texte zur germanischen Bekehrungsgeschichte*, Tübingen

Lehmann, W. P. (1986) *A Gothic etymological dictionary*, Leiden
   (1987) 'Linguistic and archaeological data for handbooks of proto-languages'. In: FS for M. Gimbutas, Washington DC, pp. 72ff.

Levison, W. (1946) *England and the continent in the eighth century*, Oxford

Ljungberg, H. (1947) 'Trúa. En ordhistorisk undersökning till den nordiska religionshistorien', *ANF* 62, 151ff.

Loi, V. (1969) 'Nota sulla terminologia battesimale latina'. In: FS for A. Pagliaro, Rome, III 67ff.

Löwe, H. (1978) 'Pirmin, Willibrord und Bonifatius. Ihre Bedeutung für die Missionsgeschichte ihrer Zeit'. In: H. Frohnes (ed.), *Kirchengeschichte als Missionsgeschichte*. Vol. II 1, ed. K. Schäferdiek, *Die Kirche des früheren Mittelalters*, Munich, pp. 192ff.

Loyn, H. R. (1962) *Anglo-Saxon England and the Norman Conquest*, London
(1974) 'Kinship in Anglo-Saxon England', *ASE* 3, 197ff.

Ludwigslied, ed. E. von Steinmeyer, *Die kleineren althochdeutschen Sprachdenkmäler*, Berlin 1916, pp. 85ff.

Lühr, R. (1982) *Studien zur Sprache des Hildebrandliedes*, Frankfurt

Lund Hansen, U. (1987) *Römischer Import im Norden*, Copenhagen

McCormick, M. (1990) *Eternal victory. Triumphal rulership in late antiquity, Byzantium and the early medieval West*, Cambridge

Magoun, F. P. (1933) 'Cynewulf, Cyneheard and Osric', *Anglia* 57, 361ff.

Mâle, E. (1950) *La fin du paganisme en Gaule et les plus anciennes basiliques chrétiennes*, Paris

Marchand, J. W. (1959) 'Les Gots ont-ils vraiment connu l'écriture runique?'. In: FS for F. Mossé, Paris, pp. 277ff.

Markus, R. A. (1970) 'Gregory the Great and a papal missionary strategy'. In: G. J. Cuming (ed.), *The mission of the Church and the propagation of the faith*, Cambridge, pp. 29ff.
(1983) 'Saint Augustine's views on the "just war" '. In: W. J. Sheils (ed.), *The Church and war*, Oxford, pp. 1ff.

Marold, E. (1992) 'Die Skaldendichtung als Quelle der Religionsgeschichte'. In: H. Beck,
D. Ellmers, K. Schier (ed.), *Germanische Religionsgeschichte. Quellen und Quellenprobleme*, Berlin, pp. 685ff.

Martial, *Epigrams*, ed. D. R. Shackleton Bailey, Cambridge, Mass., 1993

Maschke, E. (1926) 'Studien zu Waffennamen der althochdeutschen Glossen', *ZfdPh* 51, 137ff.

Masser, A. (1966) *Die Bezeichnungen für das christliche Gotteshaus in der deutschen Sprache des Mittelalters*, Berlin

Mastrelli, C. A. (1976) 'I verbi germanici del "giudicare" e un passo del Muspilli'. In: FS for V. Santoli, Rome, I 75ff.

Matthews, T. F. (1993) *The clash of gods. A reinterpretation of early Christian art*, Princeton

Mayrhofer, M. (1970) 'Germano-Iranica', *ZVS* 84, 224ff.

Meid, W. (1966) 'Die Königsbezeichnung in den germanischen Sprachen', *Die Sprache* 12, 182ff.
(1992) 'Die germanische Religion im Zeugnis der Sprache'. In: H. Beck, D.

Ellmers, K. Schier (ed.), *Germanische Religionsgeschichte. Quellen und Quellenprobleme*, Berlin, pp. 486ff.

Meier, H. (1975) 'La cloche, die Glocke'. In: H. Meier (ed.), *Neue Beiträge zur romanischen Etymologie*, Heidelberg, pp. 283ff.

Meineke, E. (1984) *Bernstein im Althochdeutschen. Mit Untersuchungen zum Glossar Rb*, Göttingen

  (1994) 'Fehde. Sprachliches', *RLGA* 8, Berlin, pp. 279ff.

  (1995a) 'Forst. Sprachliches', *RLGA* 9, Berlin, p. 345ff.

  (1995b) 'Framea. Sprachliches', *RLGA* 9, Berlin, pp. 366ff.

  (1995c) 'Freund und Freundschaft. Sprachliches', *RLGA* 9, Berlin, pp. 575ff.

Meissner, R. (1921) 'cuonio uuidi'. In: FS for F. von Bezold, Bonn, pp. 126ff.

Merseburger Zauberspruch, Erster, ed. E. von Steinmeyer, *Die kleineren althochdeutschen Sprachdenkmäler*, Berlin 1916, p. 365

Meyer, G. (1894) 'Zur Geschichte des Wortes *Samstag*', *IF* 4, 326ff.

Meyer-Lübke, W. (1901) 'Die Namen der Wochentage im Romanischen', *ZfdW* 1, 102f.

  (1923) 'Senyor "Herr" ', *WuS* 8, 1ff.

Mezger, F. (1956) 'Zur Frühgeschichte von Freiheit und Frieden'. In: FS for T. Frings, Berlin, pp. 12ff.

  (1957) 'Zur Frühgeschichte von "Urteil" '. In: FS for P. Kretschmer, Vienna, II 62ff.

  (1960) 'Oheim und Neffe', *ZVS* 76, 296ff.

  (1965a) 'Germ. Adjektiva auf -iska-', *ZVS* 79, 38ff.

  (1965b) 'Germ. *frijōnd-* "Verwandte"', *ZVS* 79, 32ff.

Milojčić V. (1966) 'Zur Frage des Christentums in Bayern zur Merowingerzeit', *JRGZM* 13, 231ff.

Mitchell, B. and Robinson, F. C. (1987) *A guide to Old English*. Fourth edition, Oxford

Mitteis, H. (1933) *Lehnrecht und Staatsgewalt*, Weimar

Mogk, E. (1909) 'Die Menschenopfer bei den Germanen', *Abhandlungen der sächsischen Akademie der Wissenschaften* 27, pp. 601ff.

Mohrmann, C. (1957) 'Linguistic problems in the early Christian Church', *Vigiliae Christianae* 11, 11ff.

  (1977) 'Les dénominations de l'église en tant qu'édifice en grec et en latin au cours des premiers siècles chrétiens'. In: C. Mohrmann, *Etude sur le latin des chrétiens*, Rome, IV 211ff.

Möller, H. (1903) 'Ahd. *frôno-* (nhd. *fron-*) als elliptischer Plural', *ZfdW* 4, 95ff.

Much, R. (1893) 'Die Südmark der Germanen', *PBB* 17, 1ff.

  (1925) ' "Herzog", ein altgermanischer Name des dux', *ZRG(GA)* 45, 1ff, 406f.

  (1932) 'Oheim', *ZfdA* 69, 46ff.

  (1933) 'Der Streit um das Wort Herzog', *Teuthonista* 9, 105ff.

  (1937) *Die Germania des Tacitus*. First edition, Heidelberg

  (1967) *Die Germania des Tacitus*. Third, revised edition by H. Jankuhn and W. Lange, Heidelberg

Müller, Gertraud (1957) 'Stuatago Musp. 55', *PBB* 79, 308ff.
  (1966) 'Aus der Werkstatt des althochdeutschen Wörterbuches. 28. Ahd. *opharôn–offrôn–offarôn*', *PBB* 82, 152ff.
Müller, Gunter (1967) 'Zum Namen *Wolfhetan* und seinen Verwandten', *FMS* 1, 200ff.
  (1968) 'Germanische Tiersymbolik und Namengebung', *FMS* 2, 202ff.
  (1970) *Studien zu den theriophoren Personennamen der Germanen*, Cologne
  (1988) 'Von der Buchstabenmagie zur Namenmagie in den Brakteaten-inschriften', *FMS* 22, 111ff.
Murray, A. C. (1983) *Germanic kinship structure. Studies in law and society in antiquity and the early Middle Ages*, Toronto
Muspilli, ed. E. von Steinmeyer, *Die kleineren althochdeutschen Sprachdenkmäler*, Berlin 1916, pp. 66ff.
Naumann, H.-P. (1986) 'dux. Sprachliches', *RLGA* 6, Berlin, pp. 296ff.
Neckel, G. (1936) *Edda. Die Lieder des Codex Regius nebst verwandten Denkmälern. II: Kommentierendes Glossar*, Heidelberg
Neumann, G. (1973) 'Baias', *RLGA* 1, Berlin, p. 600
Newton, S. (1994) *The origins of Beowulf and the pre-Viking kingdom of East Anglia*, Cambridge
Nibelungenlied, ed. H. de Boor, Wiesbaden 1961
Nielsen, K. M. (1985) 'Runen und Magie. Ein forschungsgeschichtlicher Überblick', *FMS* 19, 75ff.
Nilsson, M. P. (1918) 'Studien zur Vorgeschichte des Weihnachtsfestes', *AfR* 19, 50ff.
Nöldeke, T. (1901) 'Die Namen der Wochentage bei den Semiten', *ZfdW* 1, 161ff.
Nolte, T. (1990) 'Der Begriff und das Motiv des Freundes in der Geschichte der deutschen Sprache und älteren Literatur', *FMS* 24, 126ff.
Notker, *Boethius, De consolatione philosophiae*, ed. E. H. Sehrt and T. Starck, *Notkers des Deutschen Werke* 1 1–3, Halle 1933 and 1934
  Canticum Moysi, ed. E. H. Sehrt and T. Starck, *Notkers des Deutschen Werke. Dritter Band (Der Psalter). Dritter Teil*, Halle 1955, pp. 1070ff.
Oddrúnargrátr, ed. G. Neckel, *Edda. Die Lieder des Codex Regius nebst verwandten Denkmälern*, Heidelberg 1914, pp. 228ff.
Olberg, G. von (1983) *Freie, Nachbarn und Gefolgsleute. Volkssprachige Bezeichnungen aus dem sozialen Bereich in den frühmittelalterlichen Leges*, Frankfurt
  (1991) *Die Bezeichnungen für soziale Stände, Schichten und Gruppen in den Leges Barbarorum*, Berlin
Olck, F. (1907) 'Esel'. In: A. Pauly and G. Wissowa, *Real-Encyclopädie der classischen Altertumswissenschaft*, Stuttgart, VI 1, 626ff.
Otfrid von Weissenburg, *Evangelienbuch*, ed. O. Erdmann, Halle 1882
Otrębski, J. (1966) 'Die älteren germanischen Lehnwörter im Baltischen und Slavischen', *Die Sprache* 12, 50ff.
Page, R. L. (1995a) 'Anglo-Saxon runes and magic'. In: R. L. Page, *Runes and runic inscriptions. Collected essays on Anglo-Saxon and Viking runes*, Woodbridge, pp. 105ff.

(1995b) 'Roman and runic on St Cuthbert's coffin'. In: R. L. Page, *Runes and runic inscriptions. Collected essays on Anglo-Saxon and Viking runes*, Woodbridge, pp. 315ff.

Pappenheim, M. (1908) 'Über künstliche Verwandtschaft im germanischen Rechte', *ZRG(GA)* 29, 304ff.

Petrikovits, H. von (1960) *Das römische Rheinland. Archäologische Forschungen seit 1945*, Cologne

(1978a) 'Religion', 'Religion und geistiges Leben'. In: F. Petri and G. Droege (ed.), *Rheinische Geschichte*, Vol. II 1, Düsseldorf, pp. 252ff., 291ff.

(1978b) 'Germania (Romana)', *RLAC* 10, 548ff.

Pfister (1972) 'Die sprachlichen Berührungen zwischen Franken und Galloromanen', *ZfrPh* 88, 175ff.

Philippson, E. A. (1929) *Germanisches Heidentum bei den Angelsachsen*, Leipzig

Phillips, E. D. (1965) *The royal hordes. Nomad peoples of the steppes*, London

Picard, E. (1991) *Germanisches Sakralkönigtum? Quellenkritische Studien zur Germania des Tacitus und zur altnordischen Überlieferung*, Heidelberg

Pleiner, R. (1989) 'Eisen. Archäologisches', *RLGA* 7, Berlin, pp. 60f.

Pliny, *Naturalis historia*, ed. W. H. S. Jones, Cambridge, Mass., 1963

Ploss, E. (1956) 'Die Färberei in der germanischen Hauswirtschaft', *ZfdPh* 75, 1ff.

(1959) 'Haarfärben und -bleichen. (Zu Standeszeichen und Schwurritual der Germanen)', *GRM* 40, 409ff.

Pogatscher, A. (1888) *Zur Lautlehre der griechischen, lateinischen und romanischen Lehnworte im Altenglischen*, Strassburg

Polomé, E. (1954) 'Notes critiques sur les concordances Germano-Celtiques', *Ogam* 6, 145ff.

(1981) 'Lexical data and cultural contacts: a critique of the study of pre-historic isoglosses and borrowings'. In: FS for E. Coseriu, Berlin, III 505ff.

(1983) 'Celto-Germanic isoglosses (revisited)', *JIES* 11, 281ff.

(1985) 'Two etymological notes'. In: FS for J. Knobloch, Innsbruck, pp. 309ff.

(1986) 'Germanentum und religiöse Vorstellungen'. In: H. Beck (ed.), *Germanenprobleme in heutiger Sicht*, Berlin, pp. 207ff.

(1987) 'Who are the Germanic people?'. In: FS for M. Gimbutas, Washington DC, pp. 216ff.

(1992) 'Quellenkritische Bemerkungen zu antiken Nachrichten über die germanische Religion'. In: H. Beck, D. Ellmers, K. Schier (ed.), *Germanische Religionsgeschichte. Quellen und Quellenprobleme*, Berlin, pp. 399ff.

Powell, T. G. E. (1987) *The Celts*, London

Predigtsammlung A, ed. E. von Steinmeyer, *Die kleineren althochdeutschen Sprachdenkmäler*, Berlin 1916, pp. 156ff.

Prinz, F. (1965) *Frühes Mönchtum und das Frankenreich*, Munich

(1978) 'Peregrinatio, Mönchtum und Mission'. In: H. Frohnes (ed.), *Kirchengeschichte als Missionsgeschichte*, Vol. II 1, ed. K. Schäferdiek, *Die Kirche des früheren Mittelalters*, Munich, pp. 445ff.

(1981) 'Columbanus, the Frankish nobility and the territories east of the

Rhine'. In: H. B. Clarke and M. Brennan (ed.), *Columbanus and Merovingian monasticism*, BAR International Series 113, Oxford, pp. 73ff.

(1982) 'Die Rolle der Iren beim Aufbau der merowingischen Klosterkultur'. In: H. Löwe (ed.), *Die Iren und Europa im früheren Mittelalter*, Stuttgart, pp. 202ff.

(1984) 'Zum fränkischen und irischen Anteil an der Bekehrung der Angelsachsen', *ZKG* 95, 315ff.

(1985) *Grundlagen und Anfänge. Deutschland bis 1056*, Munich

Pudić, I. (1964) 'Die altgermanischen Elemente in den Balkansprachen und die Frage des sgn. Balkangermanischen'. In: *Proceedings of the ninth International Congress of Linguists, Cambridge, Mass. 1962*, The Hague, pp. 862ff.

Quedlinburger Chronik, MGH SS 3, 22ff.

Rappaport, B. (1899) *Die Einfälle der Goten in das Römische Reich bis auf Konstantin*, Leipzig

Rathofer, J. (1962) *Der Heliand. Theologischer Sinn als tektonische Form. Vorbereitung und Grundlegung der Interpretation*, Cologne

Raumer, R. von (1848) 'Über den geschichtlichen Zusammenhang des gothischen Christenthums mit dem Althochdeutschen', *ZfdA* 6, 401ff.

Reichert, H. (1994) 'Feldzeichen', *RLGA* 8, Berlin, pp. 307ff.

Rexrodt, F. (1995) 'Franken. Rechtsaufzeichnungen', *RLGA* 9, Berlin, pp. 454ff.

Richter, M. (1982) 'Der irische Hintergrund der angelsächsischen Mission'. In: H. Löwe (ed.), *Die Iren und Europa im früheren Mittelalter*, Stuttgart, pp. 120ff.

(1994) *The formation of the medieval West. Studies in the oral culture of the barbarians*, Dublin

Ris, R. (1971) *Das Adjektiv reich im mittelalterlichen Deutsch. Geschichte – semantische Struktur – Stilistik*, Berlin

Ritter, R.-P. (1993) *Studien zu den ältesten germanischen Entlehnungen im Ostseefinnischen*, Frankfurt

Roberts, J. (1994) 'Anglo-Saxon vocabulary as a reflection of material culture'. In: M. O. H. Carver (ed.), *The Age of Sutton Hoo. The seventh century in northwestern Europe*, Woodbridge, pp. 185ff.

Roeder, F. (1899) *Die Familie bei den Angelsachsen*, Halle

Roesdahl, E. (1992) *The Vikings*, Harmondsworth

Rohlfs, G. (1952) *An den Quellen der romanischen Sprachen*, Halle

Rosenfeld, H. (1952) 'Buch, Schrift und lateinische Sprachkenntnis bei den Germanen vor der christlichen Mission', *RhM* 95, 193ff.

(1955) 'Alamannischer Ziu-Kult und SS. Ulrich- und Afra-Verehrung in Augsburg', *AfK* 37, 306ff.

(1956a) 'Die Inschrift des Helms von Negau', *ZfdA* 87, 241ff.

(1956b) 'Goten und Greutungen', *BzN* 7, 195ff.

(1957) 'Goten und Greutungen (Schlußwort)', *BzN* 8, 36ff.

Ross, A. S. C. and Thomson, R. L. (1976) 'Gothic *reiks* and congeners', *IF* 81, 176ff.

Rotsaert, M.-L. (1977) 'Vieux-haut-allem. *biscof*/gallo-roman **(e)bescobo, *(e)bescobə*/lat. *episcopus*', *Sprachwissenschaft* 2, 181ff.

Russell, F. H. (1975) *The just war in the Middle Ages*, Cambridge
Russell, J. C. (1994) *The Germanization of early medieval Christianity. A sociohistorical approach to religious transformation*, New York
Scardigli, P. (1964) *Lingua e storia dei Goti*, Florence
  (1995) 'Fremde Einflüsse im Germanischen', *RLGA* 9, Berlin, pp. 552ff.
Schabram, H. (1987) 'Altenglisch *sāp*: ein altes germanisches Wort für "Bernstein"?' In: R. Bergmann, H. Tiefenbach, L. Votz (ed.), *Althochdeutsch*, Heidelberg, pp. 120ff.
Schäferdiek, K. (1976) 'Bekehrung und Bekehrungsgeschichte.II. Deutschland und Nachbarländer', *RLGA* 2, Berlin, pp. 180ff.
  (1978a) 'Germanenmission', *RLAC* 10, 492ff.
  (1978b) 'Die geschichtliche Stellung des sogenannten germanischen Arianismus'. In: H. Frohnes (ed.), *Kirchengeschichte als Missionsgeschichte*. Vol. II 1, ed. K. Schäferdiek, *Die Kirche des früheren Mittelalters*, Munich, pp. 79ff.
  (1978c) 'Die Grundlegung der angelsächsischen Kirche im Spannungsfeld insular-keltischen und kontinental-römischen Christentums'. In: H. Frohnes (ed.), *Kirchengeschichte als Missionsgeschichte*. Vol. II 1, ed. K. Schäferdiek, *Die Kirche des früheren Mittelalters*, Munich, pp. 149ff.
  (1981) 'Christentum der Bekehrungszeit', *RLGA* 4, Berlin, pp. 501ff.
  (1982) 'Gab es eine gotisch-arianische Mission im süddeutschen Raum?', *ZfbLg* 45, 239ff.
  (1984a) 'Germanisierung des Christentums', *Theologische Realenzyklopädie* 12, 521ff.
  (1984b) '*Kirihha – *čyrica – kuriakón*. Zum geschichtlichen Hintergrund einer Etymologie', *PBB* 106, 46ff.
  (1987) 'Zur Frage früher christlicher Einwirkungen auf den westgermanischen Raum', *ZKG* 98, 149ff.
Scheller, M. (1950) *Vedisch* priyá- *und die Wortsippe* frei, freien, Freund. *Eine bedeutungsgeschichtliche Studie*, Göttingen
Scherer, A. (1955) 'Die keltisch-germanischen Namengleichungen'. In: FS for F. Sommer, Wiesbaden, pp. 199ff.
Schirokauer, A. (1946) 'Wortgeschichte von *Herr*', *GRev.* 21, 55ff.
Schlesinger, W. (1963a) *Beiträge zur deutschen Verfassungsgeschichte des Mittelalters. Bd. I: Germanen, Franken, Deutsche*, Göttingen
  (1963b) 'Über germanisches Heerkönigtum'. In: *Das Königtum. Seine geistigen und rechtlichen Grundlagen. Mainauvorträge 1954 (Vorträge und Forschungen 3)*, Darmstadt, pp. 105ff.
Schmid. W. P. (1973) 'Aisten', *RLGA* 1, Berlin, pp. 116ff.
Schmidt, K. D. (1948) *Germanischer Glaube und Christentum. Einzeldarstellungen aus dem Umbruch der deutschen Frühgeschichte*, Göttingen
  (1954) *Grundriß der Kirchengeschichte*, Göttingen
Schmidt, K.H. (1984) 'Keltisch und Germanisch'. In: J. Untermann and B. Brogyanyi (ed.), *Das Germanische und die Rekonstruktion der indogermanischen Grundsprache*, Amsterdam, pp. 113ff.
  (1986) 'Keltisch-germanische Isoglossen und ihre sprachgeschichtlichen

Implikationen'. In: H. Beck (ed.), *Germanenprobleme in heutiger Sicht*, Berlin, pp. 231ff.

(1987) 'Handwerk und Handwerker im Keltischen und Germanischen. Beiträge zu einem historischen Vergleich'. In: W. Meid (ed.), *Studien zum indogermanischen Wortschatz*, Innsbruck, pp. 265ff.

(1991) 'The Celts and the ethnogenesis of the Germanic people', *Historische Sprachforschung* 104, 129ff.

Schmidt-Wiegand, R. (1967) 'Alach. Zur Bedeutung eines rechtstopographischen Begriffs der fränkischen Zeit', *BzN (N.F.)* 2, 21ff.

(1974) 'Fränkisch *druht* und *druhtin*. Zur historischen Terminologie im Bereich der Sozialgeschichte'. In: FS for W. Schlesinger, Cologne, pp. 524ff.

(1978) '*Wargus*. Eine Bezeichnung für den Unrechtstäter in ihrem wortgeschichtlichen Zusammenhang'. In: H. Jankuhn (ed.), 'Zum Grabfrevel', *Abhandlungen der Akademie der Wissenschaften* 113, Göttingen, pp. 188ff.

(1979) 'Die volkssprachlichen Wörter der Leges barbarorum'. In: FS for K. S. Bader, Zürich, pp. 419ff.

(1987) '*Reht* und *ewa*. Die Epoche des Althochdeutschen in ihrer Bedeutung für die Geschichte der deutschen Rechtssprache'. In: R. Bergmann, H. Tiefenbach, L. Votz (ed.), *Althochdeutsch*, Heidelberg, pp. 937ff.

(1994) 'Ewa', *RLGA* 8, Berlin, pp. 35ff.

Schneider, H. (1928) *Germanische Heldensage. I. Band. Einleitung: Ursprung und Wesen der Heldensage. I. Buch: Deutsche Heldensage*, Berlin

(1938) *Die Götter der Germanen*, Tübingen

Schneider, R. (1978) 'Karl der Große – politisches Sendungsbewußtsein und Mission'. In: H. Frohnes (ed.), *Kirchengeschichte als Missionsgeschichte*. Vol. II 1, ed. K. Schäferdiek, *Die Kirche des früheren Mittelalters*, Munich, pp. 227ff.

Schnetz, J. (1938) 'Unnamen beim Geographen von Ravenna', *ZNF* 14, 85ff.

(1951/2) '"Baias" und der Baiernname', *ZfbLg* 16, 1ff.

Schönfeld, M. (1911) *Wörterbuch der altgermanischen Personen- und Völkernamen*, Heidelberg

Schramm, G. (1957) *Namenschatz und Dichtersprache. Studien zu den zweigliedrigen Personennamen der Germanen*, Göttingen

(1974) 'Die nordöstlichen Eroberungen der Rußlandgoten (Merens, Mordens und andere Völkernamen bei Jordanes, Getica XXIII 116)', *FMS* 8, 1ff.

(1975) 'Hunnen, Pannonier, Germanen. Sprachliche Spuren von Völkerbeziehungen im 5. Jh. n. Chr.', *Zeitschrift für Balkanologie* 11,2, 71ff.

Schröbler, I. (1958) *Notker III von St. Gallen als Übersetzer und Kommentator von Boethius, De Consolatione Philosophiae*, Tübingen

Schröder, E. (1900) 'Zu Genesis und Heliand'. *ZfdA* 44, 223ff.

(1918) 'Studien zu den deutschen Münznamen', *ZVS* 48, 241ff.

(1923) 'Tilgen', *ZfdA* 60, 246ff.

(1924a) '"Herzog" und "Fürst": Über Aufkommen und Bedeutung zweier Rechtswörter', *ZRG(GA)* 44, 1ff.

(1924b) 'Bunte Lese II. 6. *Writan* und *skriban*', *ZfdA* 61, 57f.

(1925) 'Got. *kintus*', *ZVS* 53, 8off.

(1932) 'Herzog', *Nachrichten von der Gesellschaft der Wissenschaften zu Göttingen. Philologisch- historische Klasse*, pp. 182ff.

Schröder, W. (1967) Review of G. Becker, *Geist und Seele im Altsächsischen und im Althochdeutschen*, *AfdA* 78, 79ff.

Schultze, A. (1941) 'Das Eherecht in den älteren angelsächsischen Königs-rechten', *Berichte über die Verhandlungen der sächsischen Akademie der Wissen-schaften* 93, 5

(1943) 'Über westgotisch-spanisches Eherecht', *Berichte über die Verhandlungen der sächsischen Akademie der Wissenschaften* 95, 4

Schulze, W. (1907) 'Gotica', *ZVS* 41, 165ff.

Schürer, E. (1905) 'Die siebentägige Woche im Gebrauche der christlichen Kirche der ersten Jahrhunderte', *Zeitschrift für neutestamentliche Wissenschaft* 6, 1ff.

Schütte, G. (1902) Review of O. Bremer, *Ethnographie der germanischen Stämme*, *AfdA* 28, 4ff.

Schützeichel, R. (1957) 'Bezeichnungen für "Forst" und "Wald" im frühen Mittelalter', *ZfdA* 87, 105ff.

Schwab, U. (1972) *arbeo laosa. Philologische Studien zum Hildebrandslied*, Bern

Schwarcz, A. (1992) 'Die gotischen Seezüge des 3. Jahrhunderts'. In: R. Pillinger, A. Pütz, H. Vetters (ed.), *Die Schwarzmeerküste in der Spätantike und im frühen Mittelalter*, Vienna, pp. 47ff.

Schwarz, E. (1951) *Goten, Nordgermanen, Angelsachsen. Studien zur Ausgliederung der germanischen Sprachen*, Bern

(1953a) 'Die Urheimat der Goten und ihre Wanderungen ins Weichselland und nach Südrußland', *Saeculum* 4, 13ff.

(1953b) 'Die Krimgoten', *Saeculum* 4, 156ff.

(1956) *Germanische Stammeskunde*, Heidelberg

See, K. von (1964) *Altnordische Rechtswörter. Philologische Studien zur Rechtsauffassung und Rechtsgesinnung der Germanen*, Tübingen

(1972) *Kontinuitätstheorie und Sakraltheorie*, Frankfurt

(1981) 'Berserker', *ZfdW* 17, 129ff.

Sehrt, E. H. (1962) *Notker-Glossar. Ein althochdeutsch–lateinisch–neuhochdeutsches Wörterbuch zu Notkers des Deutschen Schriften*, Tübingen

(1966) *Vollständiges Wörterbuch zum Heliand und zur altsächsischen Genesis*, Göttingen

Seneca, *De ira*, ed. J. W. Basore, *Seneca. Moral essays*, Cambridge, Mass., 1994, pp. 106ff.

Senn, A. (1925) *Germanische Lehnwortstudien*, Heidelberg

Sieg, G. (1960) 'Zu den Merseburger Zaubersprüchen', *PBB* 82, 364ff.

Sigurðarkviða in skamma, ed. G. Neckel, *Edda. Die Lieder des Codex Regius nebst ver-wandten Denkmälern*, Heidelberg 1914, pp. 202ff.

Skok, P. (1923) 'Gibt es altgermanische Bestandteile im Rumänischen?', *ZfrPh* 43, 187ff.

(1925) 'La semaine slave', *Revue des Etudes Slaves* 5, 14ff.

(1930) 'Gibt es altgermanische Bestandteile im Rumänischen?', *ZfrPh* 50, 257ff.

Sonderegger. S. (1965) 'Die ältesten Schichten einer germanischen Rechtssprache'. In: FS for K.S. Bader, Zürich, pp. 419ff.

Specht, F. (1939) 'Greutungi – Graudenz?', *ZVS* 66, 224ff.

Sperber, H. (1915) 'Beiträge zur germanischen Wortkunde. D. *keusch*', *WuS* 6, 55ff.

Sprandel, R. (1978) *Verfassung und Gesellschaft im Mittelalter*, Paderborn

Stancliffe, C. E. (1980) 'Kings and conversion: some comparisons between the Roman mission to England and Patrick's to Ireland', *FMS* 14, 59ff.

Starck, T. and Wells, J. C. (1990) *Althochdeutsches Glossenwörterbuch (mit Stellennachweis zu sämtlichen gedruckten althochdeutschen und verwandten Glossen)*, Heidelberg

Stearns, M. (1978) *Crimean Gothic. Analysis and etymology of the corpus*, Saratoga, Calif.

(1989) 'Das Krimgotische'. In: H. Beck (ed.), *Germanische Rest- und Trümmersprachen*, Berlin, pp. 175ff.

Steinhauser, W. (1928) 'Eintritt der Stimmhaftigkeit bei den westgermanischen Reibelauten *f, þ, s, χ*,'. In: FS for M. H. Jellinek, Vienna, pp. 139ff.

Steinmeyer, E. von (1916) *Die kleineren althochdeutschen Sprachdenkmäler*, Berlin

Steinmeyer, E. von and Sievers, E. (1879ff.) *Die althochdeutschen Glossen*, Berlin

Steuer, H. (1994) 'Fahren und Reiten. 6: Karolinger- und Wikingerzeit', *RLGA* 8, Berlin, pp. 165ff.

Stevenson, J. (1994) 'Christianity in sixth- and seventh-century Southumbria'. In: M. O. H. Carver (ed.), *The Age of Sutton Hoo. The seventh century in north-western Europe*, Woodbridge, pp. 175ff.

Straka, G. (1951) 'Observations sur la chronologie et les dates de quelques modifications phonétiques en roman et en français prélittéraire', *Revue des langues romanes* 71, 247ff.

(1956) 'La dislocation linguistique de la Romania et la formation des langues romanes à la lumière de la chronologie relative des changements phonétiques', *Revue de linguistique romane* 20, 249ff.

Strassburger Eide, ed. E. von Steinmeyer, *Die kleineren althochdeutschen Sprachdenkmäler*, Berlin 1916, pp. 82ff.

Strasser, I. (1982) 'Irisches im Althochdeutschen?'. In: H. Löwe (ed.), *Die Iren und Europa im früheren Mittelalter*, Stuttgart, pp. 399ff.

Streitberg, W. (1894) 'Ost- Westgoten', *IF* 4, 300ff.

(1919) *Die gotische Bibel*, Heidelberg

Ström, F. (1951) 'Tro och blot. Två grundbegrepp i fornnordisk religion', *Arv* 7, 23ff.

Struve, K. W. (1991) 'Zur Ethnogenese der Slawen'. In: M. Müller-Wille (ed.), *Starigard/Oldenburg. Ein slawischer Herrschersitz des frühen Mittelalters in Ostholstein*, Neumünster, pp. 9ff.

Stutz, E. (1966) *Gotische Literaturdenkmäler*, Stuttgart

(1980) 'Die germanistische These vom "Donauweg" gotisch-arianischer

Missionare im 5. und 6. Jahrhundert', *Denkschriften der Österreichischen Akademie der Wissenschaften* 145, pp. 207ff.

Suerbaum, W. (1977) *Vom antiken zum frühmittelalterlichen Staatsbegriff. Über Verwendung und Bedeutung von Respublica, Regnum, Imperium und Status von Cicero bis Jordanes,* Münster

Swanton, M. (1970) *The Dream of the Rood,* Manchester

Swiggers, P. (1985) 'Gothic *siponeis*', *ZVS* 98, 109f.

Szemerényi, O. (1952) 'The development of the Indo-European mediae aspiratae in Latin and Italic', *Archivum Linguisticum* 4, 99ff.

(1960) 'Gothic *auhuma* and the so-called comparatives in *-uma*', *PBB* 82, 1ff.

(1979) 'Germanica I (1–5)', *ZVS* 95, 103ff.

Tacitus, *Agricola,* ed. M. Hutton, revised H. M. Ogilvie, Cambridge, Mass., 1970

Annales, ed. E. Koestermann, Leipzig 1952

Germania, ed. J. G. C. Anderson, Oxford 1938

Historiae, ed. E. Koestermann, Leipzig 1950

Tatian (Old High German), ed. E. Sievers, Paderborn 1872

Thompson, E. A. (1965) *The early Germans,* Oxford

(1966) *The Visigoths in the time of Ulfila,* Oxford

(1969) *The Goths in Spain,* Oxford

Thumb, A. (1901) 'Die Namen der Wochentage im Griechischen', *ZfdW* 1, 163ff.

Thurneysen, R. (1901) 'Die Namen der Wochentage in den keltischen Dialecten', *ZfdW* 1, 186ff.

Tiefenbach, H. (1995) 'Friede. Sprachliches', *RLGA* 9, Berlin, pp. 594ff.

Timpe, D. (1989) 'Entdeckungsgeschichte', *RLGA* 7, Berlin, pp. 307ff.

(1992) 'Tacitus' Germania als religionsgeschichtliche Quelle'. In: H. Beck, D. Ellmers, K. Schier (ed.), *Germanische Religionsgeschichte. Quellen und Quellenprobleme,* Berlin, pp. 434ff.

Todd, M. (1992) *The early Germans,* Oxford

Toth, K. (1995) 'Fremde Einflüsse im Germanischen. Das Beispiel des Altenglischen', *RLGA* 9, Berlin, pp. 563ff.

Ullmann, W. (1961) *Principles of government and politics in the Middle Ages,* London

Unruh, G. C. von (1957) '*Wargus*. Friedlosigkeit und magisch-kultische Vorstellungen bei den Germanen', *ZRG(GA)* 74, 1ff.

Untermann, J. (1954) 'Über die historischen Voraussetzungen für die Entlehnung von got. *alew*', *PBB* 76, 390ff.

Usener, H. (1911) *Das Weihnachtsfest,* Bonn. Second edition

Väänänen, V. (1967) *Introduction au latin vulgaire,* Paris

Vernadsky, G. (1951) 'Der sarmatische Hintergrund der germanischen Völkerwanderung', *Saeculum* 8, 340ff.

Völundarkviða, ed. G. Neckel, *Edda. Die Lieder des Codex Regius nebst verwandten Denkmälern,* Heidelberg 1914, pp. 112ff.

Vollmann-Profe, G. (1987) *Otfrid von Weißenburg, Evangelienbuch. Auswahl,* Stuttgart

Vries, J. de (1941) *Altnordische Literaturgeschichte* 1, Berlin

(1956a) *Altgermanische Religionsgeschichte* 1, Berlin

(1956b) 'Das Königtum bei den Germanen', *Saeculum* 7, 289ff.

(1960) *Kelten und Germanen*, Bern

Waag, A. (1932) 'Die Bezeichnungen des Geistlichen im Althoch- und Altniederdeutschen. Eine wortgeschichtliche und wortgeographische Untersuchung', *Teuthonista* 8, 1ff.

Wagner, N. (1967) *Getica. Untersuchungen zum Leben des Jordanes und zur frühen Geschichte der Goten*, Berlin

(1975) '*Cheisuringu gitan*. Zu v. 33–35a des Hildebrandsliedes', *ZfdA* 104, 179ff.

(1979) 'Ostgermanisch-alanisch-hunnische Beziehungen bei Personernamen'. In: R. Schützeichel (ed.), *Studien zur deutschen Literatur des Mittelalters*, Bonn, pp. 11ff.

Wahmann, P. (1937) *Gnade. Der althochdeutsche Wortschatz im Bereich der Gnade, Gunst und Liebe*, Berlin

Walde, A. (1906) *Lateinisches etymologisches Wörterbuch*, Heidelberg

Wallace-Hadrill, J. M. (1962) *The long-haired kings and other studies in Frankish history*, London

(1971) *Early Germanic kingship in England and on the continent*, Oxford

(1975) *Early medieval history*, Oxford

Wartburg, W. von (1950) *Die Ausgliederung der romanischen Sprachräume*, Bern

(1953) 'Sabbatum: Samstag'. In: FS for J. Orr, Manchester, pp. 296ff.

(1956) *Von Sprache und Mensch*, Bern

(1968) 'Ursprung und Geschichte des Wortes *bâtir*'. In: FS for E. Gamillscheg, Munich, pp. 639ff.

Webster, L. and Backhouse, J. (1991) Eds., *The making of England. Anglo-Saxon art and culture AD 600–900*, London

Webster, L. and Brown, M. (1997) Eds., *The transformation of the Roman world, AD 400–900*, London

Weisgerber, J. L. (1949) *Der Sinn des Wortes 'Deutsch'*, Göttingen

(1952) 'Die Spuren der irischen Mission in der Entwicklung der deutschen Sprache', *RhV* 17, 8ff.

(1953) *Deutsch als Volksname. Ursprung und Bedeutung*, Stuttgart

Weisweiler, J. (1923) 'Beiträge zur Bedeutungsentwicklung germanischer Wörter für sittliche Begriffe. Zweiter Teil', *IF* 41, 304ff.

(1929) 'Bedeutungsgeschichte, Linguistik und Philologie. Geschichte des ahd. Wortes *euua*'. In: FS for W. Streitberg, Heidelberg, pp. 419ff.

(1940) 'Seele und See. Ein etymologischer Versuch', *IF* 57, 25ff.

Weisweiler, J. and Betz, W. (1974) 'Deutsche Frühzeit'. In: F. Maurer and H. Rupp (ed.), *Deutsche Wortgeschichte*, Berlin, pp. 55ff.

Wenskus, R. (1961) *Stammesbildung und Verfassung. Das Werden der frühmittelalterlichen Gentes*, Cologne

(1973a) 'Alanen', *RLGA* 1, Berlin, pp. 122ff.

(1973b) 'Attila. Historisches', *RLGA* 1, Berlin, pp. 467ff.

(1978) 'Boihaemum', *RLGA* 3, Berlin, pp. 207f.

(1984) 'Ding. Historisches', *RLGA* 5, Berlin, pp. 444ff.

(1986a) 'druht', *RLGA* 6, Berlin, pp. 202f.

(1986b) 'dux. II. dux in altgerm. Zeit', *RLGA* 6, Berlin, pp. 301ff.

Werner, J. (1950) 'Römische Trinkgefäße in germanischen Gräbern der Kaiserzeit'. In: FS for E. Wahle, Heidelberg, pp. 168ff.

Wesche, H. (1932) *Das Heidentum in der althochdeutschen Sprache. I. Teil: die Kultstätte*, dissertation Göttingen

(1937) 'Beiträge zu einer Geschichte des deutschen Heidentums', *PBB* 61, 1ff.

White, L. T. (1962) *Medieval technology and social change*, Oxford

White, S. D. (1989) 'Kinship and lordship in early medieval England: the story of Sigeberht, Cynewulf, and Cyneheard', *Viator* 20, 1ff.

Whitelock, D. (1979) *English historical documents. c. 500–1042*, London

Widsith, ed. K. Malone, London 1935

Wiesinger, P. (1985) 'Gotische Lehnwörter im Bairischen. Ein Beitrag zur sprachlichen Frühgeschichte des Bairischen'. In: H. Beumann and W. Schröder (ed.), *Frühmittelalterliche Ethnogenese im Alpenraum*, Sigmaringen, pp. 153ff.

Wiesner, J. (1963) *Die Thraker*, Stuttgart

(1968) *Die Kulturen der frühen Reitervölker*, Frankfurt

Wissowa, G. (1918) 'Interpretatio Romana. Römische Götter im Barbarenlande', *Archiv für Religionswissenschaft* 19, 1ff.

Wolfram, H. (1968) 'Methodische Fragen zur Kritik am "sakralen" Königtum germanischer Stämme'. In: FS for O. Höfler, Vienna, pp. 473ff.

(1975) 'Gotische Studien I/II', *MIÖG* 83, 1ff., 289ff.

(1976) 'Gotische Studien III', *MIÖG* 84, 239ff.

(1988) *History of the Goths*, Berkeley

(1989) 'Ermanarich. Historisches', *RLGA* 7, Berlin, pp. 510ff.

(1991) 'L'itinéraire des Goths de la Scandinavie à la Crimée'. In: A. Rousseau (ed.), *Sur les traces de Busbecq et du gotique*, Lille, pp. 135ff.

Wollmann, A. (1990a) *Untersuchungen zu den frühen lateinischen Lehnwörtern im Altenglischen. Phonologie und Datierung*, Munich

(1990b) 'Lateinisch-Altenglische Lehnbeziehungen im 5.und 6. Jahrhundert'. In: A. Bammesberger and A. Wollmann (ed.), *Britain 400–600: language and history*, Heidelberg, pp. 373ff.

(1990c) 'Zu den frühesten lateinischen Lehnwörtern im Altfriesischen', *ABäG* 31/32, 506ff.

(1993) 'Early Latin loan-words in Old English' *ASE* 22, 1ff.

Wood, I. N. (1977) 'Kings, kingdoms and consent'. In: P. H. Sawyer and I. N. Wood (ed.), *Early medieval kingship*, Leeds, pp. 6ff.

(1987) 'Pagans and holy men, 600–800'. In: P. Ní Chatháin and M. Richter (ed.), *Irland und die Christenheit*, Stuttgart, pp. 347ff.

(1994a) 'Frankish hegemony in England'. In: M. O. H. Carver (ed.), *The Age of Sutton Hoo. The seventh century in north-western Europe*, Woodbridge, pp. 235ff.

(1994b) *The Merovingian kingdoms 450–751*, London

(1995) 'Pagan religions and superstitions east of the Rhine from the fifth to the ninth century'. In: G. Ausenda (ed.), *After Empire. Towards an ethnology of Europe's barbarians*, Woodbridge, pp. 253ff.

(1997) 'The transmission of ideas'. In: L. Webster and M. Brown (ed.), *The transformation of the Roman world AD 400–900*, London, pp. 111ff.

Wormald, P. (1991) 'The age of Bede and Aethelbald'. In: J. Campbell (ed.), *The Anglo-Saxons*, Harmondsworth, pp. 70ff.

Wulfila, *Die gotische Bibel*, ed. W. Streitberg, Heidelberg 1919

Würzburger Markbeschreibung, ed. E. von Steinmeyer, *Die kleineren althochdeutschen Sprachdenkmäler*, Berlin 1916, pp. 115ff.

Yeandle, D. N. (1989) 'The *Ludwigslied*: King, Church and Context'. In: J. L. Flood and D. N. Yeandle (ed.), *'Mit regulu bithuungan'. Neue Arbeiten zur althochdeutschen Poesie und Sprache*, Göppingen, pp. 18ff.

Yorke, B. A. E. (1981) 'The vocabulary of Anglo-Saxon overlordship'. In: D. Brown, J. Campbell, S. C. Hawkes (ed.), *Anglo-Saxon studies in archaeology and history* 2 (BAR British Series), Oxford, pp. 171ff.

Zeiss, H. (1932) 'Herzogsname und Herzogsamt', *Wiener Prähistorische Zeitschrift* 19, 145ff.

Zimmer, H. (1892) 'Aus der Bedeutungsgeschichte von *schreiben* und *schrift*', *ZfdA* 36, 145ff.

Zwölfer, T. (1929) *Sankt Peter. Apostelfürst und Himmelspförtner. Seine Verehrung bei den Angelsachsen und Franken*, Stuttgart

Index of words

Greek and Latin are included in this index as the languages of our earliest sources on Germanic society and as the languages providing concepts and models for adoption in the barbarian languages. No distinction is made between Classical and Vulgar Latin, and Latinised forms of Germanic terms are included under Latin.

Although the text of this book frequently quotes words from only one or other Germanic language, this index lists the cognate forms in the other languages to facilitate access from whatever particular language with which the reader may be concerned. Variant dialectal forms, especially in Old High German, are not listed.